PHANTASMAGORIA:
A SOCIOLOGY OF OPERA

For my parents, Trevor and Dorothy, who first took me *to the Gods*, and for Chris who later came with me.

Phantasmagoria: A Sociology of Opera

Edited by
DAVID T. EVANS

Ashgate
ARENA

Aldershot • Brookfield USA • Singapore • Sydney

Published by
Ashgate Publishing Limited
Gower House
Croft Road
Aldershot
Hants GU11 3HR
England

Ashgate Publishing Company
Old Post Road
Brookfield
Vermont 05036
USA

British Library Cataloguing in Publication Data
Evans, David T. (David Trevor), 1945-
  Phantasmagoria: A sociology of opera
  1.Opera - Social aspects
  I.Title
  306.4'84

Library of Congress Cataloging-in-Publication Data
Evans, David T.
    Phantasmagoria : a sociology of opera / David T. Evans.
      p.   cm.
    Includes bibliographical references.
    ISBN 1-85742-209-0 (paperback)
    1. Opera–Social aspects. I. Title.
  ML1700.E92   1998
  306.4'84–dc21   97-46174
                                                                     CIP

ISBN 1 85742 209 0

Printed in Great Britain by Galliards, Great Yarmouth

My grateful thanks to Bert Moorhouse for being brave enough to read and comment on early drafts, and for his deep interest and encouragement.

Contents

Preface

This is not a history of opera, nor an encyclopaedia, dictionary or even comprehensive sociology of opera. Rather it is intended as a sociological account of opera's current sociocultural standing, an account of contemporary representations of opera, a discourse on opera in all its aspects including those which I refer to throughout as 'opera', meaning opera's fragmented incorporation into mass or popular commercial culture. It is intended to be read by all interested in the sociology of popular culture, music, opera, theatre, whether or not they have any prior interest in, or knowledge of, opera. This poses the considerable problem for the writer of conveying to the reader the necessary basic information on opera and operas in a form which does not alienate and yet is sufficiently detailed. As elaborated in the text opera is a multilingual art form addressed by means of technical terms in as many languages. Opera is thus 'protected' by a series of barriers to understanding which any sociology has to try to break down or overcome. It is important to stress at the outset, therefore, that I have written this text with the expectation that readers will if necessary use alongside it, or as a complement to it, other sources of information. The following dictionaries, histories and opera synopses are thus recommended as among the best of their kind.

Dictionaries

- H. Rosenthal and J. Warrack (eds.) (1980), *The Concise Oxford Dictionary of Opera*, 2nd Edn., Oxford: Oxford University Press.
- As second choice try J. Anderson (1995), *Dictionary of Opera and Operetta* , Bloomsbury, London.

Histories

- L. Orrey (1986), *Opera: A Concise History of Opera*, with a Preface by Rodney Milnes, Thames and Hudson, London.
  More lavish with excellent more detailed essays is R. Parker (ed.) (1994), *The Oxford Illustrated History of Opera*, Oxford University Press, Oxford.

Opera Synopses

- Basic plot summaries can be found in dictionaries but for more comprehensive synopses with a few musical examples, despite many recent competitors, the most generally satisfactory remains: Lord Harewood (ed. and rev.) *Kobbé's Complete Opera Book*. Putnam, London and New York, the latest edition available.

General

- For the most comprehensive information on all aspects of opera see S. Sadie (ed.) (1992) *The New Grove Dictionary of Opera*, 4 vols, Macmillan, London.

Introduction

What is opera? For all that, or perhaps precisely because, it 'occupies a unique place in our traditional categorization of cultural objects into art and non-art, literature and non-literature, language and non-language' (Corse, 1987: 5), opera is by no means easy to define. Encyclopaedias and dictionaries designed for general readerships try to keep things simple. *The Metropolitan Opera Encyclopedia* states that opera is 'A staged drama for the most part sung, with instrumental accompaniment' (Hamilton, 1987: 260) while *The Concise Oxford Dictionary of Opera* tells us more elaborately that it is 'A drama meant to be sung with instrumental accompaniment by one or more singers in costume; recitative or spoken dialogue may separate set musical numbers' (Rosenthal and Warrack, 1980: 360). Apart from the bets hedged with phrases such as 'for the most part', 'meant' and 'may', neither clearly demarcates the generic boundaries between opera and other cognate art forms: masques, operetta, at times even ballets and oratorios but especially musicals — a situation compounded in some primer guides by indiscriminate or unqualified inclusion of musicals. Walsh (1995) for example, devotes more space in *Who's Afraid of Opera?* to Tim Rice's *Chess* than to Wagner's *Der Ring des Nibelungen*.[1] Some texts — again especially those aimed at more popular or introductory markets — don't even attempt a definition (Swanston 1978), while others, although differentiating between subgenres such as *opera seria, semiseria, opera buffa, opéra comique* and *opérette,* also leave a singular unifying definition to one side (Osborne 1983), sometimes explaining with exasperation why: 'It is impossible to write sensibly and analytically about "opera" ... There are simply too many kinds of opera, performed in too many different

1

ways' (Littlejohn 1993: 15). It would appear that so diverse and complex is opera in the plural that a resignedly simple and not especially useful definition of 'the union of music and drama' type (Brook, 1947: 11), is all that can embrace opera in the singular, except that, here too, the third key component — text or libretto — is left unspecified.

Dace (1989: 934) acknowledges that:

> Although there are many descriptions of opera, some ... quite clever, a convincing definition ... is hard to find. A definition should so limit what is being defined that it cannot be confused with anything else.

This is the problem: definitions of opera appear to create, rather than erase, such confusions. The reasons are broadly threefold or, more accurately, are triple-layered, concerned respectively with opera as unique artefact, elaborate institution and as sociopolitical ritual and commodity of distinction.

At base level are definitions concentrating on meticulous study-bound musicological analyses of precise relationships between music and libretti of usually a small select group of works in which both components bear such close scrutiny, especially the libretto since 'libretto-bashing has a distinguished tradition in the blood sport of opera' (Groos and Parker, 1986: 4). The dramatic component, and especially the theatrical context of its 'live' realisation, thereby tend to be subsumed under the well charted qualities of the 'dead' artefact. Articulated in technical prose, suggestive of keen objectivity and detachment, these accounts nevertheless frequently lapse into euphemisms that hint at an essence of opera somehow beyond rational discourse, as 'passion and artifice' (Lindenberger 1984: 18), where not understanding the text is crucial to the operatic experience, for 'incomprehension exalts and mystifies' (Conrad 1977: 5). For many musicologists study is therefore confined to 'masterpieces' precisely because these are works in which passion and artifice are most severely reined in. For them, when operas are good they are very good; when bad, they are passionately awful. The quest for a satisfactory definition of opera in the singular is thus already a flawed one:

> ... as anyone ought to know who buys an opera season ticket ... art

and *Kitsch* alternate night after night, with the same performers and the same audience, to the same applause, and with the same critical sanction (Kerman, 1956: 6).

Kerman in his well known *Opera as Drama* states that opera is '*properly* a musical form of drama, with its own individual *dignity* and *force*' (my italics) (ibid.: 3), his severe 'properly' leading him to a very small band of 'true' opera dramas including: *Orfeo* (Monteverdi), *Orfeo ed Euridice* (Gluck), *Le nozze de Figaro* (Mozart), *Fidelio* (Beethoven), *Tristan und Isolde* (Wagner), *Otello* and *Falstaff* (Verdi), *Pelléas et Mélisande* (Debussy), *Wozzeck* (Berg) and *The Rake's Progress* (Stravinsky), thereby circumnavigating the most exaggerated, passionate, artificial and popular works in the repertoire, especially those of Puccini and Strauss: 'Strauss's operas are more complex and advanced and intellectual than Puccini's; at the same time they are just as hollow' (ibid.: 259). At this level of analysis much conflict occurs around whether or which of opera's components — music, text, drama — has priority, the emphasis being on the first two. Kivy claims that opera is 'a musical form that has transmuted drama into music' (1988: 256) which he sets against Kerman's 'Opera is a type of drama whose integral existence is determined from point to point and in the whole by musical articulation' (1956: 13), contesting the latter's emphasis on opera as 'musical drama' with his own opera as 'dramatical music'. Heated mandarin debates of this kind beset the entire history of the genre through to mid-twentieth century works which dramatise them in operatic form — metaphorically in Schoenberg's *Moses und Aron* (1957) and explicitly in Richard Strauss' *Capriccio* (1942).[2]

At the second level the definitive focus shifts to opera in what one suspects many musicologists believe to be the inherently contaminated theatre, as drama in the institutional context of opera house, company and performance before paying audiences with preferences and tastes for works frequently dismissed or ignored in academic discourses. Langer (1953) reminds us that opera is not literature because the basic abstraction of literature is the word, while the basic abstraction of opera is dramatic poetry, the act. Conductor Mark Elder commenting on the wide reliance on gramophone recordings by audiences and analysts asserts 'it may be heretical but opera is primarily a visual art' (1980: 976). If so, no amount of study-bound analysis can equal the effectiveness or

3

experience of an opera's variable and transient presentations in the theatre, nor to what is received and understood by audiences divided in their opinions and tastes. Also what passes for opera in these establishments varies considerably between continents, nations and even within the same city. At the generic boundaries are, strictly speaking, non-operas which have been staged as such — *La Damnation de Faust* (described by Berlioz as '*légende dramatique*') and Bach's *St Matthew Passion* — whilst operas are frequently given in concert form and halls, shorn of their crucial dramatic and visual components. Under such circumstances do the former thereby 'become' and the latter 'cease' to be operas? Some dramas have elaborate 'incidental music' — *Peer Gynt* (Grieg), *Pelléas et Mélisande* (Debussy) and most famously *The Tragedy of Carmen* — in skeletal modified forms and in working 'spaces' which are the antithesis of the conventional opera house. Institutionally do these works still qualify as operas? Alternatively many opera companies include in their repertoires works which most opera texts do not recognise as operas or their composers as opera composers. Neither Hamilton (1987) nor Rosenthal and Warrack (1980), include entries on Stephen Sondheim's works, not even those such as *Sweeney Todd*, *Pacific Overtures* and *A Little Night Music* which are as likely to be encountered in the opera house as on Broadway or its equivalents. Sondheim argues that it is theatrical setting, culturally rather than structurally, which determines whether *A Little Night Music* is or is not an opera. In a Broadway theatre the audience brings to it expectations and assumptions as part of the 'entertainment' culture of the musical; at the New York City Opera, despite some possible audience overlap, the same work is judged as an 'art' by different operatic criteria, although perhaps with some uncertainty for it is highly unlikely that New York's Metropolitan Opera would ever stage this or any other Sondheim work. This piece can also be presented by national subsidised theatre companies, as currently at London's National Theatre, which compounds the work's status yet further.

For Sondheim, part of the cultural difference lies in processes of composition and preproduction. Musicals allowing for the much greater flexibility in last minute junking or creation of set numbers, which to an extent characterised opera in the early decades of the last century[3] (Levine 1988), but which is unheard of now except perhaps in rare studio presentations of small-scale new works. However, opera and musicals are **sensed** to be different in form as well. John Kander, composer of many musicals when asked 'do you write operas?' exclaimed:

> No, but I can't quite say why. You know it when you hear it. *Les Mis (Les Misèrables)* is not an opera. *Sweeney* comes closer, because the drama is forwarded through the music. *Porgy and Bess* is an opera (quoted in Rorem, 1991: 16).

Rorem argues that the sole difference between opera and musicals is that one uses conservatory trained, the other 'show-biz', voices: 'opera is merely musical comedy an octave higher' and rarely unamplified, the difference is practical not aesthetic, not a matter of art versus entertainment but of the kind of voice a composer has in mind (ibid.: 15). Faris made similar observations thirty years earlier in the British journal *Opera*, additionally remarking that the distinction between the two is artificial and does little service to the future and practice of either: 'whatever musical or dramatic value there is in a modern opera, it is not a live popular art form', for composers 'no longer write with the necessary compelling melodic directness' (1961: 296). In response, much to the consternation of its readers, 'where Grand Opera is concerned I am unashamedly a snob'; 'we don't want Opera adulterated'; 'corruption is a gradual process' and so on). *Opera* decided to review some musicals (those deemed loftier, that is). In the past 30 years opera productions have become much more informed by straight and musical theatre techniques, and musicals have increasingly taken up their place in operatic repertoires, Loppert (1990a) detecting what he called 'a cultural *glasnost*' in Britain in this respect.

These institutional definitions of opera rest as much on economics as on cultural norms and tastes. Musicals have to be profit-making (in intention at least) and therefore three-month or whatever 'sell-outs' are required to cover production costs; only later do they make money. By contrast, operas slot into a loss-making institution sustained artificially from various financial sources, for social and political as well as artistic reasons. Sondheim likens the opera audience to that of a rock concert, there to be affected 'by what they already know, by stars they already know' (Sondheim, BBC2 *Open University*, 5 April 1995), which inadvertently perhaps signals what is, for many 'experts', the greatest contamination of the institutional presentation of opera — much of the time it is not seriously concerned with opera as drama at all:

> In many ways opera audiences get short-changed. They think they're getting a better deal because they're getting the famous singers. Well, if they're only there for the songs, I suppose that's all right, but they are being short-changed in every other respect. There are houses ... which don't rate the drama as an important part of the work, but only as a series of pit-props for famous stars coming in and singing their songs: just charity shows. Gala charities. And that's the way many of the audiences see it: they're there to see very famous people with very, very delicious voices and they'll put up with what's happening on the stage as if it was incidental. The fact is that opera as an institution is deeply infected with a bourgeois vulgarity. This was something that entered at a fairly early stage in the nineteenth century and very few people have succeeded in cleaning the Aegean stables. It's a large, baggy, vulgar art form which you can sometimes straighten out and clean and rectify, but you are often thought to be pretentious and impudent for assuming that such a thing needs to be done (Miller, 1991: 20).

So, as dominant musicological discourses reify 'masterpieces' through in-study and library analysis, the 'serious' contemporary opera producer reifies 'serious' dramatic presentation. Both have a sense that beneath their earnest endeavours opera is essentially 'large, baggy and vulgar', on the brink of 'musical' values, and that audiences like it that way. It follows that, through audience demand, some opera houses will aesthetically as well as financially embrace Broadway especially where a local Broadway equivalent doesn't exist. In Germany and other middle-European companies as well as several in North America, *Fiddler on the Roof, My Fair Lady, Sweeney Todd* and other musicals share the opera stage as part of the normal season. Even more distracting definitional quandaries arise at the institutional periphery where, for many, 'opera' now consists of concerts, TV broadcasts or CD aria collections by The Three Tenors, Kiri Te Kanawa, Lesley Garrett and the like. Small wonder that Nicholas Payne wrote in the programme for Opera North's production of *Showboat:* 'a working definition of "opera" is horribly difficult to put together, even before one has ventured a distinction between "popular" and "serious", or "operetta" and "the musical"' (quoted in Loppert 1990a: 149).

Dace's definitional solution is to work from the classical inspiration for opera's disputed late sixteenth century 'invention' in Italy by the *Camerata*, and, none too successfully, impose the latter's values on today's 'large, baggy and vulgar' institution. Like Dace, Donington (1981) and Lindenberger (1984) also subscribe to the view that:

> ... unlike other arts whose evolution historians like to trace back to some mysterious often popular origin, opera was in fact invented by a group of learned theorists, the so-called *Camerata*, who provided it with a program before the first operas were composed around 1600 (Lindenberger 1984: 17).

Donington's account of *The Rise of Opera* tells us that, as a distinct cultural artefact, opera first appeared in Florence at the very end of the sixteenth century, it being 'staged drama unfolding integrally in words and music' (1988: 20). Rosselli (1992: 4) however exclaims: 'No one any longer sees it as the brainchild of a small group of Florentine intellectuals who thought they were recreating ancient Greek drama', for earlier operas have been recorded and uncovered. In 1908 Romain Rolland had drawn attention to Poliziano's verse-play *Orfeo* performed with some musical numbers, and both Sternfield (1994) and Pirrotta (1984) trace subsequent developments such as Tasso's pastoral *Aminta* and Guarini's *Pastor fido*, prior to the notorious deliberations of the *Camerata*, Sternfield focusing on specific musical elements such as the lament, finale, use of repetition and echo. In what is, in many respects, merely a dense 'game of nomenclatures',[4] Budden also derides as simplistic accounts which accept the *Camerata* 'myth' (Pirrotta 1982).

> True it was at the hands of the *Camerata*, which included the poet Rinuccini and the composers Peri and Caccini, that the genre first achieved its definition *a dramma con musica:* but it had a long and involved pre-history, an understanding of which is essential in order to account for many features that remained constant throughout the seventeenth and eighteenth centuries, even reaching forward to our own day (Budden 1994: 1129).

Kivy (1988) resists such reasoning however, drawing potent

7

comparisons with Panofsky's (1954) analysis of the cinema as an 'invented' art, arguing: 'what gives the theoretical underpinnings of the *Camerata* their power and originality is the sustained effort to portray a music of human speech as a consequence of philosophical presuppositions' (1988: 24). Dace follows a similar line of reasoning. 'Opera ... modelled on Greek dramatic poetry, is an imitation of a series of related actions, expressed by means of music, words and rhythmic movement, acted not narrated, arousing emotion in the spectator and achieving catharsis of such emotion into meaning' (Dace, 1980: 936).

But this is not any old meaning or any old catharsis:

Opera's object, identical to that of all other art forms, is the arousal of emotion in the spectator and the cathartic release of emotional tension by verbalizing or intellectualizing emotions felt, into meaning, knowledge etc., the nature of the emotion aroused (mirth as opposed to fear e.g.) being irrelevant ... The principal value of Aristotle's catharsis theory is that it enables us to separate art from entertainment. In the theatre a good performance of *My Fair Lady* is not so very different from one of *The Magic Flute.* ... But emotions aroused by the former die out as we leave the theatre, while those aroused by the opera transmute themselves into a special incommunicable kind of knowledge about the universal human desire to know. For this reason dramatic poetry may be regarded as an instrument of education, while entertainment ... merely arouses emotion for its own sake (Dace, 1989: 937).

Yet, as critics are constantly reminding or warning us, there are many operas which 'merely' do likewise — *Fedora* by Giordano for example — and that archetypal 'shabby little shocker', *Tosca* (Kerman 1956: 18-20).[5] Nor is it possible to draw such easy equations between artefacts aesthetically ranked and their effects on audiences who, it might as reasonably be argued, may very well perceive *The Magic Flute* as primarily entertainment and *Sweeney Todd* as anything but. No, this definitional solution merely leads to further confusion, not least because it hardly addresses the institutional inclusion of many works excluded by it — works such as *My Fair Lady*:

'Opera' as a word has always been a catchall for numerous kinds of musical theatrical experiences, some of which do not constitute 'opera' as purists define it. This broad definition is very healthy for the form since 'stretching the envelope' is a way of improving the breed (enough of these mixed metaphors!) (Smith 1995: 4).

Opera's **theatricality**, not limited to drama but as spectacle and diversion, is central to Smith's definition which, in addition to the 'catch-all' advocacy, suggests that all manifestations of 'lyric theatre' might help to break down opera as a somewhat fossilised institution, and one in which debates about its origins at the end of the sixteenth century are largely irrelevant, given that the great bulk of the international repertoire is of nineteenth century vintage as the detailed data in Appendix A clearly demonstrate. To seek a precise, exclusive but all-embracing definition of opera is therefore to mistakenly assume that it is an inert art form, to seek to straddle and ignore four or more centuries of operatic differences, development and change in rapidly but unevenly modernising societies. Ashbrook and Powers (1991) attempt to do so by referring to opera's 'Grand Tradition', which they claim effectively commenced not with the works of the *Camerata* but in the third quarter of the seventeenth century 'when patterns of production, in both the public and the musical senses, assumed their familiar forms' (p.6), in which travelling companies with their own (or hired) extremely minimal orchestral apparatus declined and were replaced by 'star' travelling soloists and when 'at the same time regularly operating theatres (with more or less stable orchestras) became established throughout Italy' (Bianconi and Walker 1984: 235). This was when the dramatic structure of operas became standardised as did the concerted aria (C1675) '... as the minimum significant entity ... on which the attention and interest of the spectator/listener are focused' (ibid.:253). Whilst they thereby set out certain common 'Grand Tradition' similarities, they cannot accommodate the equally important dissimilarities to be found in much of opera's development nor late twentieth century institutional practice. For today's operagoer, opera house and singer, opera, give or take some disputes at the boundaries, is an art form sandwiched between Mozart and Puccini, 1780—1926, in which there is little interest in or knowledge of this prehistory of 'several strands' (Rosselli 1992: 4). The authors of *The PAN Book of Opera* describe earlier use of singing in Greek

9

drama, medieval mystery plays, madrigal comedies and masques as precursors of what they are content to call 'opera as we know it' (Jacobs and Sadie, 1964: 13). For many, this opera 'as we know it' is a moribund and attenuated 'museum culture' (Conrad 1977; Lindenberger 1984) albeit of a particular kind:

> ... if the operas in the Grand Tradition are in one sense museum pieces, nonetheless they cannot be hung on walls; like other manifestations of the temporal arts, they must be produced ... Italian opera in the Great Tradition lives on in production — and in the affections of the opera-going public the tradition shows no signs of coming to an end (Ashbrook and Powers 1991: 4).

But this tradition is not the one limited by Kerman to qualities of 'dignity' and 'force', but one most frequently characterised through euphemistic and excitable references to the obverse qualities of exaggeration, 'passion and artifice' (Lindenberger 1984: 18). Even meticulous Dace deals in 'emotions' and hints that they are inexplicable: 'those aroused by opera transmute themselves into a special incommunicable kind of knowledge about the universal human desire to know' (1989: 937). Opera is regularly and often proudly described as the most complex and artificial of art forms because in the heat of the theatre it seemingly spins out of reach as 'staged drama', into transient passionate incoherence (though in the cold light of the library it combines sophisticated music and text, and in the hard world of the audit office is reduced to painstaking evidence of financial loss). This is no doubt partially due to opera breeding in its fans a siege mentality to fend off detractors who 'agree with Carlyle and Tolstoy, that opera is complete nonsense and a deplorable waste of time and money' (Dent 1965: 16), with the oft-quoted Dr Johnson that: 'opera is an exotic and irrational entertainment which has always been combated and has always prevailed', and concur that 'Opera is a bizarre mixture of poetry and music where the writer and the composer, equally embarrassed by each other, go to a lot of trouble to create an execrable work' (Charles de Saint-Evremond in 1677 quoted in Littlejohn 1993: 2). Despite the considerable age and irrelevance of these views, nothing has happened since to convince operaphobes that they no longer apply. In defence, therefore, for Littlejohn opera is *The Ultimate Art* (1993), for Christiansen *The Grand Obsession* (1988), for

10

Lindenberger *The Extravagant Art* (1984), which defies lucid description: '... in opera ... the promptings of irrational imagination are at their most uninhibited ... the restraints of naturalism. .. at their least intrusive' (Donington, 1990: 3), for it is the 'most hysterical and excessive of theatrical genres' (Christiansen, *The Observer* May 1993: 17).

> Opera is a mystery. This cumbrous, expensive relic of the past, so absurd in its conventional demand that people should sing when offering each other a whisky or lamenting that they have dropped their door key, refuses to fade away. Instead it acquires new converts ... and converts is what it demands for like a religion it changes the lives of those it wins over, transforming them into acolytes ... neophytes ... ushered into a secret and sensual knowledge, opera treats aspects of experience no other art has the boldness to address. It is the song of our irrationality, of instinctual savagery ... The characters of opera obey neither moral nor social law ... (Conrad 1977: 11).

Kerman would have none of this, nor this ...

> Opera is the greatest and most glorious artistic phenomenon which our civilisation possesses. It is a fusion of music, art and drama. Music alone can interest us, and it can produce different sensations and meanings for each listener: its acceptance is very personal. Pure art — painting, sculpture, cartoons — speaks with a silent voice. Sometimes we can feel what it is saying, sometimes it is beyond us. Actors at the play state their intentions clearly but we have to be in tune with their idiom. At the opera we are drawn into a story. The singers enact it for us in their special convention which we must accept. The music not only supports them as they talk or soliloquise but sometimes tells us things that they don't know or can't yet understand. This draws us in even closer until we are part of the drama, because opera depends that we give too. And by giving we get back so much (Jefferson 1976: 7).

Whatever else it is or is not, opera is certainly draining! Small wonder therefore that 'rational', 'sensible', singular definitions scarcely do justice to the phantasmagoric whole, which also embraces the third level of opera's meanings and knowledge and further source of definitional confusion. Both 'high' art analyses by musicologists of opera as a unique artefact and the organisation and experience of opera as elaborate institution are riddled with the implications of opera's particular privileged status within the stratified structures and cultures of developed societies, where opera exists in the cultural imagination and language not merely as some kind of 'union of music and drama' performed in specific venues but as an art form to which significant dominant cultural, sociopolitical and economic meanings and values are given and affirmed through the relatively inaccessible and highly ritualised circumstances in which it is normally presented. Opera is 'high' art, 'auratic' art,[6] 'élitist' ritual, expensive, and a symbol of nationhood, thereby justifiably financed by whatever means possible, despite its great costs. In one sense this is the most important level of opera knowledge because it does not necessarily depend on first hand direct experience of the manner and means of their theatrical presentations, but on generalised media-fed understandings of what the term means, which fuel strongly held values and readily expressed opinions. Most people will have a view on opera: in everyday interactions we take its definition as 'given', we talk about it with some certainty even though we regularly resort to the simplest of stereotypes in so doing, we express our views and attitudes, know whether we hate it or love it, whether we should pay for it through direct taxation or indirect Lottery funds, but the proportion of the population who have actually seen an opera in an opera house is very small:

> ... where differences of artistic appreciation are at issue, there is no greater chasm than that which divides those who like opera from those who don't. I have never heard anyone claim that he can take opera or leave it: there would seem to be no uncommitted middle-ground. If you don't like it, you can't stand it (Adair 1994: 10: 7).

This observation was stimulated by a gentleman repeatedly dozing off behind Adair at an English National Opera performance of *Der Rosenkavalier* ('scarcely a "difficult" work' he sniffed). Adair's snoring neighbour suspected to be an operaphobe unable to penetrate opera's inherent artifice (perhaps snores should be listened to more attentively!).

Even now opera tends to be perceived as 'apart'. Hovering over it is a pungent whiff of nineteenth century élitism (justified to a degree, one has to say, by exorbitant seat prices) and twentieth century philistinism (the still popular cliché of the opera house as a place of either dutiful or fashionable attendance, the cynical conviction that opera seats with 'restricted visibility' are those in which the spectators, not the performers, are visible). Then there is the tenacious prejudice of the opera singer as fat, virtually by definition, a prejudice reinforced by the extra-curricular activities of Pavarotti but statistically now untenable. To contend with finally, is the received notion that every opera of note has been saddled with a preposterous plot. Yet the most enduring works in the repertoire were scripted by librettists of genius, Da Ponte for Mozart, Wagner for Wagner and Hofmannsthal for Strauss (Adair 1994, 10: 8).

But the 'Grand Tradition' 'as we know it' originates with the nineteenth century construction of opera as bourgeois entertainment, as class-based ritual and commodity, the 'emotions' and 'passions' raised, not being those of spiritual uplift or even entertainment but of communion with status familiars in a conspicuous display of shared lifestyles and élite community (Tambling 1987: Small 1987-8). Although opera has been cast in the mould of one of the oldest of art-forms through analyses of the *Camerata* and its classical Greek inspiration as well as repetitive use of 'tradition' in so many of its discourses, it is one of the youngest, and one which has 'changed shape so often in its short history that an attempt to homogenise operas under the one genre-heading of "opera" may be deceptive' (Tambling 1987: 13). Opera is fetishised as 'traditional', 'quasi-aristocratic', and 'hierarchically organised' (on stage and in the auditorium), 'textually reverential', 'ritual' — in short 'a mode of cultural production aimed at the [capitalist] élite' (ibid.:13), who derive pleasure and social confirmation from it (Levine 1988: 89). Tambling's thesis on opera as a nineteenth century 'fake' traditional and 'auratic' 'high art' form, (though overly reductionist in its implications for *all* institutional aspects of opera, *all* operagoers and *all* works within, as well as at, the generic boundaries and thus excluding dynamic tensions and conflicts over and around this 'tradition'), and his emphatic contextualisation of opera within capitalist relations of production, consumption and reproduction has undeniable force. Rodney Milnes, editor of *Opera*, picks up on these inherent class meanings by suggesting that the term 'opera' be jettisoned altogether for: 'it harbours too many built in prejudices and begs too many questions; some such term as "lyric theatre" is perhaps to be preferred' (Milnes 1986a: 7).[7] Yet along with 'passion' 'artifice' and 'dignity', euphemisms of class, élitism and conspicuous ritual display are clearly fundamental characteristics of opera as dynamic social construct. By changing the name to one with no cultural associations misses the point in all sociological senses. Opera, whether we like it or not, is a morass of prejudice. No matter how welcome the spirit of his definition opera is:

> a branch of the theatre and deserves to be considered as such. Its essentials are dramatic confrontation and dialogue, intensified by music both on stage and in the orchestra. Like true drama, it transcends mere narrative [ibid.:71].

Milnes ignores the undoubted mandarin and common-sense discursive insistence that there is a distinctive 'opera' genre — a genre which is popularly and institutionally a 'grand opera' genre to which is attached layers of social, political and economic meaning. Opera is not a term used to describe inert cultural artefacts in a material or structural void, it is a term attached to whatever seems appropriate at a specific time and in a particular culture, given the genre's complexity as artefact, institution, symbol, ritual and commodity. Opera like all 'artistic' activities and objects may be anything that is collectively defined as such, thus accounting for the remarkable heterogeneity of art-works and the constantly changing definitions of what they are' (Martin 1995: 30). Yet also, like all artistic activities and objects, some of the discourses by which opera is defined are more powerful than others, and so powerful, that the majority have little power to resist.

Notes

1. Kornick's (1991) *Recent American Opera: A Production Guide* includes entries on *Flower Drum Song, My Fair Lady* and *The Sound of Music.* This guide is intended for amateur and college companies. In Britain the Guildhall School of Music and Drama has mounted a number of well received productions of musicals.

2. *Capriccio,* Strauss's last opera, is a dramatised conversation piece set in Paris at the time of Gluck's operatic reforms discussed briefly later in this text (Chapter 5) which debates whether words or music are more important in opera. The work takes its text (by conductor Clemens Krauss) from the old Italian saying: *Prima la musica e poi le parole* ('First the music, then the words'). At the end of the opera the matter is left unresolved. *Moses und Aron,* metaphorically reflects upon similar concerns also reflecting the struggle to find a future relevance for the operatic form once into the second third of this century. Aron sings through his worldly concerns, spiritual visionary Moses speaks/chants *(sprechgesang),* struggling to express himself. Act II ends with him sinking to the ground: 'O word, thou word, that I lack'. Hindemith's *Mathis der Maler* (1938) is another operatic exploration of communication in genre form as well as narrative content.

3. However, this was effected more by the inclusion of popular songs such as 'Home sweet home' and 'An old man would he a wooing go' than by the creation of new numbers (Levine 1988: 90).

4. This phrase is used by Arthur Jacobs and Andrew Porter in their discussion through the letter pages of *Opera* magazine over the identity and date of the first surviving British opera. The latter (May 1995: 606) named Blow's *Venus and Adonis* of 1683. Jacobs (July 1995: 767) accepts this if *all sung* is taken as a definitional requirement, but 'if spoken dialogue is admissible then prior claim falls to *Cupid and Death* (1659), the joint composition of Christopher Gibbons and Matthew Locke ... As staged in ... Bruges in 1983 it proved its operatic credentials — though, as with *Venus and Adonis,* the nominal designation is "masque"'. In the same edition, Porter replies that, at its first publication, the latter was named 'An Opera'.

5. ... we cannot exist solely on a rich diet of masterpieces, it is

15

salutary to be reminded that there are thoroughly bad operas as well, and that there may still be valid reasons for performing them occasionally. One reason is context: Giordano's *Fedora* (1896) certainly increases one's admiration for *Tosca* (1900). Both were based on vehicles for Bernhardt by Sardou. Puccini and his librettists transformed their slice of Sardoodledom into a taut moral drama, cutting the melodramatic plot down to bare essentials and clothing it in music that replaced action with character ... Giordano was modestly gifted, seemingly unable to develop a musical idea... This is a one-and-a-half-tune opera ... to call this a *"verismo"* opera is a misnomer: the characters are no more real than those in the novels of Elinor Glyn. Yet the Royal Opera is busy performing *Fedora*. Does the quality of the performance justify it? The answer by a whisker is 'yes'. Great stars (Mirella Freni, José Carreras) have always been part of the rich operatic experience (Milnes,*The Times*, 11 May: 37).

Critic Canning (1986a: 17) called *Fedora* 'this rubbishy opera', though Sir Jeremy Isaacs responded 'we sold every seat in the house' (1994: 18). The revival in 1995—96 with Maria Guleghina and Placido Domingo (top seat price £270) apparently did not sell as well.

6. Since the nineteenth century opera has been 'high' art with a 'low', that is, mass/popular underbelly: in other words, if it is accepted that 'art is of absolutely no use to the masses' (Debussy 1962: 66) and that 'if it is art it is not for all, and if it is for all, it is not art' (Schoenberg 1950: 51). Gans (1985: 24-37) argues that the dominance of 'high' art has now been overturned by the 'popular' and thus all the music theory arguments about the detailed technical demands of musical development are irrelevant. Popular culture has become more important and, within 'high' culture, commercial considerations have become paramount. There are increasing 'crossovers' of this divide, for composers and works, as well as 'performers'. Nigel Kennedy trying his hand at rock, Eric Clapton composes a *Concerto for Electric Blues Guitar and Orchestra*, the Kronos string quartet performs an arrangement of Jimi Hendrix's *Purple Haze*. Placido Domingo and Kiri Te Kanawa have ventured into the popular arena and José Carreras has hailed Andrew Lloyd

Webber as 'an amazing composer'.

Scott goes on to say that 'we can understand why a modern composer would wish to be disassociated from the market place. Penderecki's *Threnody for the Victims of Hiroshima* forces us to confront the problem head-on: how is it possible to write anything which might be perceived as making financial profit from such a horrific event? (1990: 386), and yet that is what has exactly happened with Gorecki's Symphony No. 3.

7. Similarly, Bawtree adopts 'singing theatre' as a more acceptable, all-encompassing label covering opera through to musical revue: 'At the heart of singing theatre, there is a performer who acts and sings a role, in a dramatic performance, with musical support, in a performance area, in front of an audience' (Bawtree 1990: 12).

1 Opera as music, text, drama and theatre

No better time to reassert the old truism that opera is drama than just after watching the relay from Pasadena of the *Three Tenors* doing their thing once more. Apart from the hype ... claims have again been made that this kind of event leads people to opera. It may lead them into opera houses, but it couldn't conceivably foster correct expectations of what they can, or should, find when they get there. The *raison d'être* of opera has always been that it is drama rendered through music. That was the principle upon which opera's first genius, Monteverdi, created his masterpieces; and it has been indignantly stressed in the great series of manifestos which have punctuated the history of an art-form which is always in danger of collapsing into decadence. Though great voices are never unwelcome, they are not a sufficient condition for great opera, its creation or its performance. The operas which survive thanks to one or two hit numbers which require singing by stars are a luxury which almost none of the world's opera houses can afford. Works such as *Adriana Lecouvreur* or *Fedora,* may deserve a recording or two in which prima donnas and their admirers can be indulged, but every time they are mounted they exclude the production of a masterwork, one of those contributions to the genre which provide food for the mind and spirit (Tanner 1994: 1).

Introduction

Opera discourses are full of implicit assumptions and explicit instructions on 'right' as opposed to 'wrong' kinds of knowledge, 'correct' expectations of what audiences **should** rather than **can** find in opera houses, the naming of 'masterworks' and 'genius' composers and warnings of 'decadence': diva worship, meretricious works, self-indulgence, 'entertainment'—all of which debase the 'true' and 'pure' meaning of opera as 'high culture', as 'auratic art'—ingestion of 'food for the mind and spirit', all this knowledge is suffused with normative and immanent power (Foucault 1981). However despite the overall consistency and authority of such pronouncements, deference from the instructed is not assured: incomprehension, 'ignorance', tensions, resistance, even conflicts can occur, largely for reasons which though not hard to identify (being derived from the peculiar hybridity of *form* and *function* which have made opera from its beginnings a cultural form 'in crisis') (Pleasants 1982),[1] are, by being so derived, accordingly difficult to fully describe and explain.

In terms of **form** the problems are those of stratified multilingual means of communication and their comprehension. That opera is the dramatised combination of text and music is basically agreed, but all three elements, separately and together, are 'expertly' analysed via armouries of technical terms which govern access to opera knowledge at even the lowest levels. As opera is Italian in origin and multicultural in development, these terminologies derive from many different tongues. In terms of voice types (for example, *coloratura, heldentenor, Falcon*[2]), opera types (for example, *dramma giocoso, zarzuela, opéra comique*[3]), opera titles (for example, *Così fan tutte, Die Frau ohne Schatten, Les Contes d'Hoffmann*[4]), aspects of musical structure (for example, *'Da Capo' aria, cabaletta, Leitmotiv*[5]), the languages of performance (most large international houses present all works in their original languages rather than those of the audience) and even the names of present and past singers (for example, Angela Gheorghiu, Nicolai Ghiaurov, Viorica Ursuleac), access to opera knowledge depends on the acquisition of a rich mixture of linguistic elements, the ability and confidence to use them 'correctly' for further 'study' and to pronounce them convincingly in interactions with others. Most discouraging of all is probably musical language, which in many mandarin discourses is credited with prior significance over text and drama, thus weighing heavily on opera's largely musically illiterate public, although in this age of 'produceritis' (Pleasants 1989) many amongst the latter may find 'live' discourses in the form of 'radical' stagings baffling.

Opera knowledge is thus stratified knowledge imbued with

differential power which accrues to those who possess or claim it. At the upper extreme are study-bound academic analyses, overlaid with the 'protective sheen of technical jargon and couched in inexpressive prose' (Abbate and Parker 1989: 2), of select 'masterworks'[7] treated as 'autonomous apolitical art' (Bokina 1993: 187), by 'genius' composers,[8] governed by 'abstract' musical principles (Schenker 1954; 1974), removed from the theatre wherein lurk the dangers of 'decadence'. At the lower extreme lie the 'in theatre' responses and box office demands of relatively 'untutored' audiences (Shepherd 1987: 60). Between these extremes exist many layers of knowledge and forms of instruction from meticulous analyses of 'the always tense marriage' (Corse 1987 after Conrad 1977[9]) between music and text, 'deconstructionist' and 'expressive' production techniques, the provenance of opera's 'great literary sources' (Schmidgall 1977) and close dissection of libretti (Smith 1971; Groos and Parker 1990).[10]

Middle-range materials consist of relatively specialised collections of plot summaries accompanied by basic musical quotations, such as classically found in Newman's *Wagner Nights* (1949) and Dent's *Mozart Operas* (1913) and yet more accessible compendium guides to the most popular repertoire works, such as, again classically, *Kobbé* (originally 1922 but frequently revised and currently edited by Lord Harewood).[11] Texts such as these, together with opera dictionaries, encyclopaedias and histories and the extensive essays which, these days, fill out most opera house programmes, typically provide 'serious' operagoers with their preparatory and post performance 'homework'. Specialised journals such as *Opera* and *Opera Now* in Britain and *Opera News* in the USA provide tutelage of varying degrees of difficulty,[12] whilst the lowest instruction is provided by critics' reviews in the arts pages of broadsheets. The higher the level of discourse, the greater the use of technical, especially musical, terminologies; the lower the level of discourse, the greater the emphasis on potentially 'decadent' elements—staging and design details, the indiscriminate treatments of operas regardless of their 'expertly' ascribed quality, reportage on audience behaviours especially at first nights and galas and preoccupation with the lives and loves of the 'stars', especially singers. Broadsheet reviews of opera in performance interconnect with other media representations on non-arts pages of 'opera' outside the opera-house, as technologically reproduced popular and commercial entertainment, most commonly in bite-sized aria fragmentary and 'star' gossip forms—'*Nessun dorma*' as TV World Cup theme, opera as cinema soundtrack, the Three Tenors doing their thing once again, aria extracts as advertising jingles, Big Lucy P's (Pavarotti's) diet, girth, marriage and customised cologne, Carreras' fight against leukaemia, Kiri's homes, gowns and Rolex, the latest Lesley Garrett recording and interview, National Lottery funds for Covent Garden and so on.

Opera may be 'high' art but it is also a public art—an 'industry' dependent on selling itself to audiences *in situ,* audiences also socialised into opera as *function,* as ritual and lifestyle, commodities conspicuously consumed in and outside opera houses as signs of differential wealth, taste and status. It is out of all these discourses, and the power relations which they reflect, that opera is socially and materially constructed. Mandarin discourses may depict opera as an artefact outside and above the sociocultural environment in which it exists—for example 'In opera various "systems" work together, each according to its own nature and laws, and the result of the combination is much greater than the sum of the individual forces' (Petrobelli 1981: 129)—but such depictions and the genre they describe are rooted in wider 'systems' of class, patronage, market and politics which ascribe to opera as an institution its particular social meanings and significance.

> Art as institution includes the art producing and art distributing apparatus as well as the dominant ideas about art in a certain epoch, which essentially determine the reception of works (Burger 1981: 29).

Accordingly opera is:

> ... nothing inherently: it is waiting to be used, as a series of signs, a series of rhetorical strategies that is ready to be taken up and used at any point, not only in the production of types of knowledge, but also in the formation of power relations ... What follows from the assumption that Mozart presents life-enhancing values? What but the creation of an élite who are in contact with those values, who alone can appreciate them? And what in terms of power flows from the creation of that élite, whose guarantee of rightness is the self-justifying one that they have access to this art and can appreciate it? (Tambling 1987: 20).

The following chapter will address opera as object of consumption and expression of taste; subsequent chapters will examine the significance of opera as audited 'industry', as 'museum' culture, within which singers, producers and audiences stake their claims. However, first it is necessary to address in more detail the social construction of opera as 'high' cultural artefact by 'expert' discourses on its key components—music, text and drama, their relative importance and their interdependence—commencing with those which ultimately contextualise opera within the paradigm of 'abstract' music and which lead 'Many of our most eminent leaders of music, both living and dead, to have taken the view that opera is a form of music which ought not to be encouraged' (Dent 1965: 14).[13]

'Abstract' music

Claims that music has autonomy from social practice, that it is 'hermetically sealed' (Burger 1986), that it must refuse to heed demands for practical utility and which account for its origins in non-social, natural or metaphysical terms, may be traced back at least as far as Pythagoras' 'discovery' of a 'correspondence between harmonious tones and numerical proportions' (James 1993: 20-40; McClary 1987: 15; Norton 1984: 80-104). This Pythagorean model reaches its zenith within the strict rationalised canon of aesthetic modernism, the so-called 'Beethoven legacy' (Scott 1990: 386), wherein 'abstract' music becomes 'transcendent and autonomous' (Wolff 1987: 1), governed by universal formal principles so that the '... essential hermeneutic problem about music is ... that it is all syntax and no semantics [it] lacks denotive or referential power' (Kramer 1990: 2). Stravinsky's *Poetics in Music* (1942) is amongst the most extreme modern statements of this formalist hegemony which seeks 'to expunge all traces of musical involvement with a world outside its own self-enclosed ontologically privileged domain' (Norris 1989: 7). Consequently, 'abstract' music ideology confirms as privileged those able to grasp and enact principles outside contingent historical interests, simultaneously offering a mystifying yet comforting sense to non-initiates

> ... who know well how music can influence their deepest feelings and convictions, but who don't want to think that such efforts can

be obtained through any kind of conscious or social manipulative grasp. [This aesthetic] ... polices the boundary between experience and knowledge, art for the consumer and art as a realm of specialised understanding inaccessible to all but the expert ... (Norris 1989: 9, 10).

This also reifies the idea of musical history as a kind of inevitable, unfolding destiny in sound—a process which involves the increasingly rational categorisation, use and exploitation of tonal resources believed implicit in the nature of all musical experiences, so that music only reaches its peak of achievement in the European 'high' cultural tradition which defines it, 'and then only in the works that manifest the kind of intensive thematic and tonal development that lends itself to precisely this approach' (Norris 1989: 11). From a sociological perspective wherein '... any particular kind of music can only be understood in terms of the group or society which makes and appreciates that music, which utilise an "objectively" conceived aesthetic' (Shepherd 1977: 1), the initial general problem is why the nineteenth century reification of this formalist aesthetic is regarded as the highest of 'high' culture. To, and for whom, did and does this ideology of music as an expression of 'the unspeakable' (Langer 1960: 235), speak?

In the present context, more specific questions arise: what is the relationship between this modernist musical aesthetic and the 'impure', because hybrid opera, which also reached its pinnacle in the nineteenth century, both as a genre with the highest of 'high' artistic pretensions and as entertainment with 'mass' appeal? As 'drama rendered through music' are 'abstract' critiques of opera valid? In opera, music has complex, often disputed, yet integral relationships with texts which, no matter how 'operatic' in the reputationally 'silly' sense, necessarily carry concrete narrative power within themselves and in some form into the music with which they are intended to be combined in staged lyric dramas, yet 'expert' discourses continue to defer to 'abstract' principles. Why should this be so?

Generally, Western music has been explicitly 'referential', more often than not using the human voice, 'discoursing explicitly about something' (Barzun 1980: 6); indeed, until the late eighteenth century, music with a verbal text was considered a higher form than that without. Only in the past two centuries has solely instrumental music assumed pre-eminence, '... critical enthusiasm for the pure and

24

absolute is the product of a very recent aestheticism. With ... the Beethovian watershed ... conceptless, instrumental music—precisely because of its lack of concepts—became elevated to a language above verbal language' (Dahlhaus and Zimmermann 1984: 179).[14] In the complex interaction of musical, literary and philosophical developments a 'topos of Unsayability' (Dahlhaus 1978: 14) emerged; all that cannot be articulated in verbal discourse *may* be addressed in the privileged sphere of '... musical rationalisation [which] means that the modern composer can achieve his or her aesthetic purposes only by adapting to the laws of musical technique' (Zabel 1989: 199).

This transcendence of 'abstract' music over the textual and vocal with the onset of modernity was contested. Hegel, for example, objected to abstract music precisely *because* of its lack of specific conceptual content, being thereby 'indeterminate and vague' (Hegel 1964: 181). Kant, too, defended the superiority of poetry which he credited with the higher values of culture, reflection and subjective autonomy, compared with music's indisputably lower order values— enjoyment, sensation, subjective contingency and so on, which reduced its communicability to 'the language of the emotions ... it does not leave any space for reflection [and is thus] ... more pleasure than culture' (1977: 267-8). It did not bear repeated listening, it was ephemeral '... rather like the smell produced by someone who takes out a perfumed handkerchief in company' (quoted in Bowie 1991: 73). Against such judgements it was beholden upon 'serious' musicians to demonstrate their transcendence of such easy virtues of 'emotion', 'enjoyment' and the 'theatre' by demonstrating the scientific principles of harmonic composition freed from textual constraints and diversions of spectacle, as epitomised in the Counter-Reformation's rationalisation of religious polyphony into harmony. The density of polyphonic sound in church services was deemed too

... richly layered. Horns, trumpets, pipes vie and sound along constantly with the voices. Amorous and lascivious melodies are heard such as elsewhere accompany courtesans and clowns. The people run into the churches as if they were theatres, for the sake of the sensuous charm of the ear (Erasmus quoted in Kivy 1988: 4).

Polyphony concealed the spirituality of text and ritual: hence the demand for a simpler music as intelligible '... accurate representations of human speech' (p.15; see Weber 1978: 95)

—subordinate and subordinating.

In post-Renaissance Western culture, visual and verbal languages were initially privileged as sources of rational knowledge and music, by comparison, seemed without knowledge other than of indeterminate, mysterious kinds. Yet these very traits also provided the abstract basis upon which it could become the highest of 'high' arts, the most elusive because the purest, in its natural state wholly beyond social, material and representational contamination, its 'abstract' laws only properly understood by its 'servant genius' composers and 'expert' theorists and practitioners, as the knowledge/property of the learned few 'chosen' to lead their congregations in the rituals of concert worship (McClary 1987). By the late eighteenth and early nineteenth centuries, the progressive harmonic rationalisation of music had left language and speech to one side, 'abstract' music being, for its proponents, the objective benchmark against which all musical history, before and after, could and should be judged, being: 'the precarious equilibrium between melody and development, between a new and richer thematic expression of subjective feeling and its objective working through in the form itself' (Jameson 1985: 40).

Conversely, the threshold between classicism and modernity marks the point:

> ... when words cease to intersect with representations and to provide a spontaneous grid for the knowledge of things. At the beginning of the nineteenth century they discovered their ancient enigmatic clarity (Foucault 1970: 304).

In this Romantic sense 'abstract' music is 'true' music, a 'true' language '... for its own sake ... an act of writing that designates nothing other than itself' (ibid.: 304), 'music liberated from ceremony, practical function and verbal connection' (Blumenfeld: 1984: 519). Only instrumental music can be 'abstract' or 'true' in this sense. Thus, at the very moment when the intersection of words and representations ceased, music became a privileged form of art when not accompanied by text (Bowie 1989), as well as privileged knowledge for those few equipped to use, articulate and reproduce it in its own and appropriately qualified terms so that they could explain it to the untutored and guide them through their 'moving' 'unaccountable', 'evocative', 'thrilling', 'powerful', 'meaningful', generalised 'emotional' appreciation. The emergence of 'abstract' music during the modern era is consistent with the rationalising tendencies of capitalist social relations and culture generally:[15] 'Western man does not change his nature when he turns to his arts. The same thematic tendencies apparent in other spheres of his life are apparent here' (Martindale and Riedel 1958: xxii). Yet because of the particular symbolic rhetoric of music, objections and its freezing into analytical and élitist notation (Wishart 1977: 128), the identification and interpretation of these 'thematic tendencies' is highly problematic. Against 'experts' claims that they can do both, untutored audiences invariably seek understanding by vague and generalised denotive means, believing that '... musical tones and rhythms ... "imitate" or "represent" the characters of men, ... their emotions, or the states of their souls' (Kivy 1988: 29).

> ... on the one hand, we have a priesthood of professionals who learn principles of musical order... and on the other a laity of listeners who respond strongly to music, but who have little conscious critical control over it. Because nonprofessional listeners usually do not know how to account intellectually for how music does what it does, they respond either by mystifying it (ascribing its power to extra-human sources—natural or implicitly supernatural) or by domesticating it (trivializing or marginalizing it, asserting that it really does not bear meaning). Neither priest nor consumer truly wants to break the spell: to reveal the social grounding of that magic. Thus the priesthood prattles in its jargon that adds a metaphysical component to the essence of music and abdicates responsibility for its power; and listeners react as though mystically not wanting to attribute to mere mortals the power to move them so ... Both ... collude in this mystification, both resist establishing connections between the outside social world and the mysterious inner world of music (McClary 1987: 16-17).

Rather than a priesthood, Shepherd conjures up the image of musicologists as bureaucrats and listeners as alienated dominated subjects rather than laity.

Notes stripped of much of their inherent sonic possibilities become a social code for the brand of individualism characteristic of industrial capitalist societies ... (but) the ideal of perfect intonation and mathematically precise rhythms that derives from analytic music notation ... is just as mythical as the ideal of a perfectly bureaucratic social system. 'Classical' music is, then, yet another justification of the ideology whereby people become objects and systems dominate individuals (Shepherd 1987: 159-161).

The inarticulate alienation and deference of the laity are dictated by its inability to comprehend reified aurally acquired knowledge. Visual and verbal knowledge are initially privileged within capitalism; both respond to the need to rationally structure and control the social world which they address. Vision stresses separation at a distance: '... and allows us to inject ourselves into the world, to operate on the world over time and space, rather than simply having the world come in on us circumambiently and simultaneously' (Shepherd 1987: 157). Touch, too, allows us to make rational sense of both our own physical entities and the distinction between us and other objects and persons. Through linguistic communications such rationalities may be verbalised with degrees of clarity. By contrast, music is less easily constrained and less clearly perceived by the layperson as rational. 'It is very difficult to speak about music... it is very difficult to link language, which is of the order of the general, and music, which is of the order of difference' (Barthès 1982: 247, 253). Music 'stresses the integrative and relational, it tells us that there is a world of depth surrounding us, approaching us simultaneously from all directions, totally fluid in its evanescence, a world which is active and continually prodding us for a reaction' (Shepherd 1987: 158). Music has *the potential* to touch and move us in ways that we are ill-prepared to understand or even control; it 'scripts' emotions and sensations and 'implicitly demands that individuals respond' (ibid.:158). Hence the rationalisation of musical form within capitalism is reflected by the routinisation of ways and conditions of listening wherein 'ambiguity of function is ultimately not permitted' (ibid.: 160). The 'experience' of music becomes institutionalised into specific social settings and appropriate rules of conduct so that all forms denigrated as irrational and potentially subversive, such as jazz and folk at particular past historical moments, (Attali 1977)—are incorporated into the rules of concert hall and opera house.

The inherent contradictions of 'abstract' music ideology and routinised listening should be clear. '"Pure" form in all the arts is meant to reinstate spirituality in the teeth of a vulgar materialism and practical life' (Barzun 1980: 6), but the pursuit, imposition and experience of artistic 'purity' depends on effective, rational capitalist social relations of production and, especially, consumption. Artistic 'purity' and 'abstract' ideology are myths—fetishes of a spirituality rooted in material interests and power relations. The nineteenth century triumph of 'abstract' music ideology was nineteenth century 'classical' music's rationalisation through commodification, contract law, copyright law, control by music publishers, impresario-led exploitation and marketing of performers, commercialisation of concerts, and the building of grand concert halls and palatial opera houses for organised stratified rituals and interaction. By the end of the century, for the purist composer, the only way was 'out'—out of audience demand, out of the market, out of the concert hall, out of tonality and into shocking new atonality, as rational in its precepts but uncompromising in its disavowal of the market. With the dodecaphonic revolution Schoenberg provided a

> rigorous immanent critique of how music might yet express truths of present-day existence, but express them in exactly that indigent, distorted form that would bring out the extent of our alienated condition (Norris 1989: 16-17).

Largely this has been a critique with but one logic:

> Instead of lamenting the no-doubt irreparable breach between avant-garde music and the public, composers like mathematicians should turn their backs on the public and demand their rightful place in the academy. Otherwise music will 'cease to evolve, and in that important sense will cease to live' (Babbitt 1963, quoted in Kerman 1985: 101).

Knowledge versus experience, church versus theatre, clergy versus 'courtesans and clowns', culture versus pleasure, spiritual uplift versus the 'sensuous charms of the ear', rational versus irrational, 'abstract' versus narrative power and principles: opera's form and development as a theatre-based performance art bridge all these oppositions, but with its weight heavily on the second of each. Unlike 'classical' music performed before audiences within the controlled conditions of the concert hall, recital room and sometimes actual churches, opera is theatre. Opera's congregation is frequently unruly, always likely to spontaneously erupt. Opera 'experts' may 'prattle in their jargon' but audiences may better trust their own ears and other senses. Anyway, opera's performing priesthood—producers, designers, conductors, singers—may not simultaneously prattle in identical jargon, let alone that of the original composer, librettist or even programme essay writer. An opera's music and text recorded on the page have arguably fixed and stable meanings but, realised through the inherently unstable dimensions of drama and theatrical diversion and spectacle in the form of diverse and transient productions, the fixity and stability of these meanings and of opera as an 'absolute' art form resting solely on 'natural' 'abstract' principles are practically subverted. Evidence suggests that opera, in the theatre where it belongs, is largely left flamboyantly waving the 'perfumed handkerchief', yet under certain special theatrical circumstances, festivals generally and most notably the pseudo-religious Bayreuth Wagner Festival with its proto-church-like, custom-built ascetic opera house and rituals, opera still aspires to convince that the conjunction of music, text and drama has a potential for achieving transcendent spiritual experience beyond that of all other art forms. In the immaterial formalist atmosphere of the dodecaphonic revolution, opera composers too sought to retain 'high' 'purity' of purpose and product—consider Berg's *Wozzeck* and *Lulu* (see Perle 1980: 1984); Schoenberg's *Moses und Aron* (see Babbitt 1963)—but as opera cannot retreat from theatres, it cannot exist without the audiences housed by them or the power they possess as consumers, their tastes. It is thus significant that these three works which, in their different ways, all discourse on the 'irreparable breach' between the operatic public and avant-garde opera composition (see Abbate and Parker 1989: 3), are also prominent as being amongst the last major acquisitions of current opera house 'museum' repertoire and culture. Overall then, the drama component, theatrical context and the 'culturally untutored' audience, which will insist on having its say, contaminate opera as 'high' art: hence 'expert' defence of its 'high' status rests mainly on meticulous analyses of music and text prior to, or removed from, the third component. Hence too the dynamic tensions and confrontations within opera discourses at and between all levels.

'The servant genius'

As proponents reify 'abstract' music principles, so too do they mystify the 'genius', or 'servant genius', composer:

> ... the idea that the work of art is the creation of an autocratic personality, that this personality transcends tradition, theory and rules, even the work itself' (Hauser 1962: 61), who is with other 'geniuses' 'the sole and privileged originator of the cultural world (Wolff 1987: 3).

Beethoven is the paradigmatic 'individual genius' of bourgeois criticism.[16] As Williams notes:

> ... the argument that an artist's precepts were ... the 'universals' (in Aristotle's terms) or 'permanent realities', is one that had been completed in the writings of the Renaissance ... the artist's business is to read the open secrets of the universe. The artist perceives and represents Essential Reality, and ... does so by virtue of his master faculty, Imagination ... doctrines of 'genius' (autonomous creative artist) and the 'superior reality of art' (penetration to a sphere of universal truth) were in Romantic thinking, two sides of the same coin ... (Williams 1961: 52: 56).

It is in this sense that the composer 'genius' has been rationalised as someone who through years of study and practice, succeeds in bringing usually *his* mind '... so into harmony with things, that things can express their laws through him' (Zuckerkandl 1956: 223). The composer 'genius' of modern musical aesthetics is not so because of the music he *creates* but because he becomes the medium through which 'abstract' music is channelled and, only in this sense, composed.

> The finer the medium the better tone, word, colour, form can express themselves. The greater the genius, the less it speaks itself ... In this sense music ... write(s) itself—neither more nor less ... than physics does (Zuckerkandl 1956: 222).

McClary recounts how, following her '... modest attempts at resituating Bach in his social, political, ideological context' (1987: 14),

31

she was told by prominent scholars that Bach, unlike 'second-rate composers such as Telemann (who unlike Bach, composed operas) had ... *nothing* to do with his time or place, that he was "divinely inspired", that his music works in accordance with perfect, universal order and truth' (ibid.: 14). It is in this sense that Stravinsky conferred on himself the status of genius: '... very little tradition lies behind *Le Sacré du Printemps* ... I am the vessel through which *Le Sacré* and Craft, passed' (Stravinsky 1950: 147-8).[17] Whilst opera may not qualify for 'abstract' musical status, the opera composer may yet well judge his or her mission as being that of a 'servant genius', but as opera is 'denotive', 'emotional' and 'theatrical', so too *its* 'genius' composers have great difficulty in elevating themselves above the 'referential' themes of their works, in the views of 'experts'. Customarily a text is referred back to its writer so that it becomes a matter of biography and 'the equation between "author" and "authority" is easily made' (Tambling 1987: 19).

> The *explanation* of a work is always sought in the person who produced it, as if it were always in the end, through the more or less transparent allegory of the fiction, the voice of a single person, the *author* "confiding" in us (Barthes 1977: 143).

An example here is one commentator's interpretation of *Die Meistersinger von Nürnberg* (1868):

> Translating the contest of song into the contest of life, we see the artist—namely Wagner—claiming for himself a privileged position in return for the blessings issuing from his divine calling, entitled by his divinity to ignore or violate the conventions and inhibitions imposed by society upon its mortal members- as Wagner did with respect to other men's money and other men's wives (Pleasants 1989: 85).

Given the 'Beethoven legacy' it is especially relevant that Wagner saw himself as Beethoven's only legitimate son, as '... symphonic opera composer born of the last great symphonist', who left 'a puzzling handful of autograph fragments for "symphonic themes" (Abbate and Parker 1989: 92) which critics (Voss 1971, 1977; Knopfinger 1975) have claimed could not have been more substantial because he could not abandon the Hegelian principles central to his

Oper und Musik (1874) claiming the inferiority of instrumental music and that composers of music directed by poetry take the greater risks. He was: 'struck compositionally silent by his own past philosophizing' (Abbate and Parker 1989: 93). The analysis of Wagner's operas as 'symphonic operas' has become 'a commonplace of Wagnerian lore' (ibid.: 93). 'Wagner recognised the essentially abstract nature of his music. He claimed he was not continuing the tradition of Gluck, Mozart or Carl Maria von Weber' (Peyser 1971: 5). 'The phrase [symphonic opera] passes judgement on the relationship of music to the poem and the drama with which the music must coexist, belittling both the poetic and the dramatic component' (Abbate and Parker 1989: 95). But Wagner's 'servant genius' was as 'opera as drama' composer as demonstrated in such writings as *Zukunftmusik* (1861) in which he acknowledged that his early opera texts (*Tannhaüser* and *Holländer*) had the usual failings of opera libretti—repeated words and lines to underpin operatic melody—a fault corrected by, and in, *Tristan und Isolde*.

Wagner wrote and produced his own libretti (as did Berg for *Wozzeck* and *Lulu*) and thus did not have to face his musical genius being undercut or thwarted by lesser librettists and producers. Within mandarin discourses the select few 'great' operas are invariably those for which the marriage between composer and librettist has been a marriage of 'geniuses'. Mozart with Da Ponte (*Le Nozze di Figaro, Don Giovanni, Così fan tutte*), Verdi with Boito (*Otello, Falstaff*), Richard Strauss with Hofmannsthal (*Elektra, Der Rosenkavalier, Ariadne auf Naxos, Die Frau ohne Schatten, Die Aegyptische Helena, Arabella*), are the most prominent with librettists, in many cases, drawing on original works by 'genius' dramatists such as Buchner, Shakespeare, Beaumarchais, Schiller, and Sophocles. The 'servant genius' ideology has other extensive implications for such an art form as opera. There are conductors of 'genius' and singers of 'genius', their status ascribed according to a wide range of qualities from technical proficiency to interpretative skill, vocal quality, acting ability, 'presence' and 'intensity'. The relative hierarchy of 'genius' interpreters of opera has altered during its development with perhaps the greatest contemporary 'geniuses' being producers, following earlier dominance by singers and later, during the inter-war years, conductors. Certainly opera culture is now replete with references to Visconti's *La traviata*, Chereau's *Ring*, Sellars' *Don Giovanni*, Zeffirelli's *Tosca* and so on. The dramatic realisation of opera also rests on orchestral 'genius' and now even choreographers of 'genius', all jostling for interpretive and technical control, and all, for musicologists, music theorists and not small proportions of audiences, potential contaminators of the original 'masterworks' of 'genius'!

Opera as music and text

From the early 1980s there has been, however, something of 'a crisis in music aesthetics, a collapse in modernist idealism and a questioning of the method by which music history is interpreted' (Scott 1990: 385)—a slow and haphazard paradigm shift towards analysing 'abstract' music as a complex social construct rather than universal and metaphysical 'truth'.[18] Music and opera have been increasingly recognised as '... media in which the unconscious historiography of society is recorded' (Horkheimer and Adorno 1969). In psychology, attention has moved from subjects' *perceptions* of music (passively perceiving its features as 'they really are') towards *cognition* (actively constructing them out of what the mind already knows—that is, has learnt and memorised [Serafine 1984: 218: see also Norton 1984; Mowitt 1987]), and to the distinction between psychological 'production' and 'reception' (Cook 1990). Cook's exploration of the latter, usefully employing Merleau-Ponty's metaphor of the tapestry, its decipherable surface towards the viewer and its knotted, almost indecipherable, reverse towards the maker, enables the distinction between 'just listening to music' and 'musicological listening'—both defensible reflections of music's sociocultural compositional origins, tastes, techniques, intentions, and so on—and the variable conditions and 'meanings' of its reception, from 'abstract' to concrete and 'denotive'. Elsewhere musicologists examine the factual, verifiable, documentary background of music, whilst ethnomusicologists driven by the constructionist truism 'between culture and language there cannot be *no* relations at all' (Levi-Strauss 1968: 79), continue to challenge universal principles and logic (Kerman 1985). Others, such as 'economist' Attali (1985), building on Benjamin and Adorno (to be discussed in Chapter 2) expose the political and commercial construction of 'abstract' music's 'high art' pretensions, and explore the subversive potential and subsequent incorporation of such forms as jazz, folk and rock. Recent 'expert' analyses of 'classical' music and opera—despite the resilience of the 'abstract' music hegemony—have, through their concentration on music and textual elements, sought to identify concrete meanings in music and pursued sociocultural origins and 'relations' to text. These analyses, however, are overwhelmingly couched in terms as inaccessible and mystifying to opera's public as those of the formalist paradigm, suggesting a new priesthood prattling a new jargon.

Kramer (1990), for example, has developed 'musical hermeneutics' based on four related claims. These are:

1. All works of music have discursive meanings.

2. Definite enough to support critical interpretations comparable in depth, exactness and density of connection to interpretations of literary texts and cultural practices.

3. Meanings are not 'extramusical' but lie within the formal processes and stylistic articulations of musical language.

4. These meanings are part of the general circulation of musical meanings—that is part of the continuous production and reproduction of culture.

Most of Kramer's test cases are not operatic but he observes: 'if my claims are tenable where music is furthest from language, they will *a fortiori* be tenable where music and language meet' (ibid.: 2).

Kramer's analysis provides much that is suggestive in demonstrating how music and speech patterns may be jointly interpreted in terms of their sociocultural contexts and components, and in so doing reflect generally on similar reasoning employed in symbolic interactionist perspectives on human behaviour within sociology (Plummer 1975; Gagnon and Simon 1986) and specifically on current opera production theory and practice. Kramer is guided by Austin's (1962) theory of speech acts which distinguishes between *constative* and *performative* utterances. The former make truth claims—what is referred to being either right or wrong—for example, 'It is raining heavily'; whilst the latter effect behavioural responses, for example, 'Put on a raincoat'. This, however, is an 'ideal' distinction for, in practice, even such a constative utterance as

'It is raining heavily' may have performative 'Put on a raincoat' effects, depending on intonation, emphasis, context, and so on. Thus, both are dimensions, rather than types, of utterance, and to illustrate this (though risking confusion) Austin changes his terminology by claiming that despite having no locutionary meaning in itself, that is, 'the claims or assertions that a speech act puts into play' (Kramer 1990: 7), a *constative* utterance can acquire *locutionary* meaning through intonation and so on, with the performative dimension manifesting itself in what he terms *illocutionary force.* This *illocutionary* force is variable, unpredictable, requiring improvisory interpretation by the actors involved, and by the social mechanisms which bring them together as 'listeners'. Meaning is never fixed; reading is always rereading (Holub 1984: Jauss 1982).

Intonation can transform the *locutionary* meaning of words into the complete opposite, furthermore, all acts of communication presuppose the possibility of their repetition and transformation in new contexts. In order to function all 'speech' must be *iterable,* that is, capable of functioning in situations other than those of its production, among persons other than those who initially produce and receive it. In their *iterability* 'speech acts' presuppose the possibility of difference, redirection and reinterpretation (Derrida 1982). Thus, they are implicated in the contexts within which they are deployed, they are always, in a sense, improvisations, and no cultural artefact exists in itself but only through reinterpretation or improvisation. Much of this discussion, like those on 'abstract' music, cannot but suggest through their abstraction that 'speech acts' too are divorced from the material contexts in which they occur. But if one places the discussion within the particular context of opera, opera reinterpretation through staging and opera knowledge possessed by all participating actors including audiences, then its concrete implications become apparent: producer's 'speech acts'—productions, may propose a considerable reinterpretation of a work to singers, conductors, audiences and the like. The reactions of audience members to this reinterpretation demonstrate the iterability of their speech acts as determined by various socially influential factors, such as levels and kinds of opera knowledge possessed but also wealth-determined location in the opera house, conformity to specifically relevant rules of conduct and so on. This also means that opera discourses at all levels—including those which proclaim on musical and textual qualities within an absolutist 'abstract' paradigm

36

and used by all levels of the priesthood to instruct 'publics' on the 'true' meanings of works—are open to refutation and negotiation. They tend not to be because of the authority of the priesthood, the inaccessibility of its knowledge and the technical terms by which it is expressed, and by pressures of conformity to the repetitive rules of ritual. Similar constraints of cultural order, reflecting inequalities of power, impose themselves on all speech acts. Kramer's analysis overstates the possibilities for speech act interpretation, but even the most routinised interactions can break down: those in the theatre, especially in the opera house, frequently do so—flowers or rotten fruit can be thrown, producers' 'concepts' or 'ideas' booed, singers cheered or catcalled.

It is one thing to argue against the formalist aesthetics treatment of music in terms of abstract, 'conceptless' principles by proposing that music *is* sociocultural in origin, composed to formulae related in some way to conventional musical norms, that it is a means of communication albeit of a rhetorically distracted kind, and that hence all music has the potential to acquire *locutionary* meanings and *illocutionary* power, but it is quite another to provide the evidence in terms accessible to the less than even highly specialised.

If we can ... concretize the *illocutionary* forces of music as we concretize its harmonic, rhythmic, linear and formal strategies, we can then go on to interpret musical meaning (Kramer 1990: 9).

Despite the fact that this can only be an élitist exercise, the ordinary listener becomes a key witness, albeit a reacting witness, not understanding but responding to the *illocutionary* power exerted by music over him or her and thereby demonstrating that music has the *illocutionary* force, which formalists previously derided as the typical response of the untutored. By implication Kramer's line of enquiry at this rarefied level brings music back to the public, to performances, the opera house and to audiences as interpreting actors, even if normally with limited power. In brief illustration, reference may be made to the several abnormal supportive echoes in the annals of opera. The effectiveness of Verdi's *Risorgimento* audience-rousing operas (*I Lombardi, Nabucco, Macbeth, Giovanna d'Arco*), with their choruses of slaves, exiles, their homelands dominated by foreign powers, were forged as much out of the *illocutionary force* of their distinctly 'town band' Italian musical sounds, techniques and vocal resonances,[19] as out of their dramatic narratives and textual sentiments. Similarly Auber's *La Muette de Portici*, the most famous of all revolution-inducing operas in 1830, 'the year of revolutions', exerted its influence through its musical *iterability* as by any other of its component means (Fulcher: 1987).

For Kramer, the meanings in all music may be glimpsed through three kinds of 'hermeneutic windows':

1. *Textual inclusions*. (For example, denotive titles: such as, the *Eroica, Manfred, Corialanus* Overtures, *A London Symphony, Pastoral Symphony, Symphonia Antarctica* and so on, epigrams, programmes, notes to the score, and expression markings or accompanying texts). Clearly indicating the complexities of the *illocutionary* power of opera he observes that, in dealing with these materials, it is crucial:

   ... to remember—especially with the texts of vocal pieces—that they do not establish (authorize, fix) a meaning that the music somehow reiterates, but only invite the interpreter to find meaning in the interplay of the expressive acts. The same cautions applies to the other two types (Kramer 1990: 9-10).

2. *Citational inclusions*. (These are a less explicit version of the first, titles that link the piece to, for example, a literary work or visual image, place etc.).

3. *Structural tropes*. (These are the most implicit and potentially the most powerful, defined in terms of their *illocutionary* force as 'units of doing rather than saying' [ibid.:10]), which cut across traditional distinctions between form and content, '... evolve from any aspect of communicative exchange: style, rhetoric, representation and so on' (ibid.:10). Here Kramer refers to Bourdieu's *habitus of the social sphere*—systems of durable, transposable dispositions, structures predisposed to principles of generation and recycling of practices and representations which can be objectively 'regulated' (Bourdieu 1977: 72, 78). In the case of opera this has fundamental relevance given that the repertoire is largely made up of nineteenth century works familiar to most of the audience, either complete or in 'famous' aria form, but it also has relevance in the latter sense through the use of aria or aria

38

'fragments' in commercialised 'opera', especially in commercials themselves.

Kramer's analysis involves dense musicological disputes which generally impinge upon opera's particular hybridity of form, function and 'museum' culture, emphasising how the overlay of text by music contains a considerable and complex range of relatively independent *illocutionary* possibilities, mediated by performers but especially by producers and designers and confronting audiences, who are largely regular visitors to the museum, with an assumed ready acquaintance with the 'original' work. Few in opera audiences can, or will, pursue Kramer-type exercises as preparation for performances but, for the more committed, the theatrical experience is more likely to be a tense dialectic between existing and newly acquired 'textual' and 'citational' inclusions—or, as colloquially described earlier, 'homework'—with the assistance (or distraction) of an understanding of the sung words, possibly with the help (or distraction!) of surtitles, and the producer who, not infrequently nowadays, stages a commentary on a work's *illocutionary power* rather than 'the work itself'.

Most important with regard to opera is Kramer's point that music does not 'reiterate' text, it can imply contrary meanings, take us back to past events, predict the future, can be suggestively ironic with the simultaneous expression of contrasting emotions which may turn into sound not only the differing opinions of the various characters, but also 'the accumulated tension in the air' (Herz 1975: 147).

Also on the page rather than in the theatre—though providing very detailed preparation for experiencing the works dealt with in the latter—Corse (1987) explores this complex relationship between words and music. The former, she argues after Barthès (1982), tend towards specific meanings—music tending towards the generalised. Opera requires that both languages be used in two ways, as communication—stable, economic, logical, developing, un-ambiguous, with precise meanings—and also as 'literature': aesthetic, indeterminate, rhetorical, metaphorical, ambiguous. Libretti include both forms but tend towards the former, being direct and simplified (characterisation is minimised, subplots removed, and so on) sometimes to the point of stereotypical absurdity. Music, however, adds aesthetic effects to the communicative experience of language:

... an (opera) composer reinvents in a different medium the ambiguity and multiple relationships of literary texts ... music like literary language tends towards indefiniteness and ambiguity and musical meanings may serve to restore openness and literariness to operas (Corse 1987: 15).

'The genius of opera lies in its potentiality for an enriching contradiction between its elements. Rather than a sedate marriage between text and music, it proposes a relationship of unremitting, invigorating tension' (Conrad 1977: 177), which enables this, above all other cultural forms, to explore what is complex, hidden, undefined or not openly addressed, or rather to give audiences greater freedom to variably explore all of these aspects and to reach different judgements.

Music is certainly an irrational means of expression, nevertheless it may communicate the gist of a dramatic action in a more exact and penetrating way than words are ever capable of' (Noske 1990: 91).

Ignoring the implications of all those wasted reams despoiled by musicologists and music theorists, Corse illustrates as much by reference to Kristeva's (1984: 24) distinction between semiotic and symbolic forms of human signifying functions. The former is effected by means of drives, rhythms, intonations, displacement, slippage, condensation and so on, the latter through the conscious production of meanings. Music is thus 'a *natural* semiotic system' (ibid.:24, my italics), Corse arguing that the aesthetic effects of music in opera inevitably work in dense and mysterious ways, made yet more illusive to definitive analysis by the addition of elemental theatrical and vocal qualities in performance. Corse remains desk-bound but demonstrates the value of such analyses for the minority of 'masterworks' which do work on the page as well as in the theatre, making observations which undoubtedly enhance the theatrical experience but which are not essential to it. For example, she claims via *Le Nozze di Figaro* that opera, because of the 'unique control that music with its structural indeterminate and "literary" elements exerts over the communicative function of language ... can be a dramatic form well suited to exploring deeply problematical issues in common in human life and society' (Corse 1987: 45). Music extends the context

40

and opens it out to 'suggest a separation from ordinary life' (ibid.:151) which is invariably individually, subjectively, experienced through subconscious referents.[20]

> Opera being more definite, more suggestive than music alone, and more indefinite and open than language alone, offers a unique combination of strategies by which to explore human motives and values (ibid.:151).

As an example she notes that Figaro's Act 1 *'Se vuol ballare'* begins as a minuet, a dance associated with the aristocracy, used ironically for it accompanies Figaro's description of how he will outwit Count Almaviva. The *presto* section uses an English dance as a model, again aptly, for Figaro is looking forward to the Count's predicted behaviour once he becomes Ambassador in London:

> .... the phrase *'Signor Contino'* is cleverly and triumphantly transformed through the simple device of transposing its last note up one octave as Figaro affirms how he will control the Count. This transformation, like the transformation of a minuet into an English dance, raises the music beyond the paralinguistic level: the musical structure becomes a means of revealing to the audience what is on Figaro's mind, such musical revelations going far beyond what his words tells us. Figaro is obsessed according to the words, with the Count's immediate efforts to cuckold him; according to the music however, he is concerned with the much more important threat that the Count's plans for life in England imply. The raised note *'suoneto si'* endows his character with more energy and strength than the words alone reveal—energy, strength that he will need in order to thwart Almaviva's plan (Corse 1987: 27).

This brief example demonstrates the strengths and limitations of such discourses: the clarity with which this 'dead' aria is dissected for the specialist reader with the required linguistic skills offset by its likely irrelevance to 'live' performances and reception by audiences largely without such sensitivity to textual and musical nuances, possibly not understanding Italian at all even if words are articulated clearly by the singer and possibly concentrating instead on the baritone's vocal beauty, technique and even looks and dash. What this passage also conveys, however, is the greater power of knowledge derived from, and exercised on, opera outside and away from the contaminations of opera house and the alternative and subversive 'knowledge' of its audiences unless, that is, Corse is embracing the latter within her 'unique combination of strategies by which to explore human motives and values', which seems unlikely.

For some analysts, especially those with a dominant interest in Wagner's works, the receiver's response and the *illocutionary force* of opera rests in the subconscious. Donington, for example, answers his own question: 'What ... is really happening when we find ourselves in the theatre enjoying an opera of which the libretto may strike us as improbable to the point of absurdity?' (1977: 10):

> ... in opera ... symbols both conscious and unconscious particularly abound. Almost as immediately as dreams and far more coherently, opera offers a royal road into the unconscious, drawing as it does on regions of the psyche where consciousness has little power to penetrate (Donington 1990: 3).

Opera presents 'the irrational imagination at its most uninhibited' and 'restraints of realism at their least intuitive ... music which inevitably somewhat obscures the words in opera, far more importantly enhances them by means of that singular directness of feeling and intuition which it can deduce and inflect' (ibid.:10).

Opera as theatre

For analysts such as Kramer, Noske, Corse and Donington, it is opera's particular hybridity of form which raises its communicative and spiritual potential above that of 'abstract' music but, and it is a big but, set against opera practice, only select chosen operas are used to demonstrate that this is so; music and text are still given prior significance over drama. Donington at least brings opera's 'masterworks' back into the theatre where they belong. What remains absent from his and these other musicological analyses is the recognition that the 'ordinary', 'regular, 'serious' opera lovers/fans/goers possess and exercise a range of different *theatrical* forms of knowledge which recognise that, in performance, critically derided or ignored operas can 'work' on audiences to thrilling effect.

Opera is not equal to mandarin analyses, it is both more and less. Poizat (1992) claims that opera devotees are able to experience a deeper and stronger experience than devotees of any other art form and, for reasons which have little to do with those among them who have read the latest treatise on hermeneutic windows. For audiences much depends upon the visceral effects of the human voice filling a huge theatre or the charisma of particular 'stars'. With Magda Olivero[21] in the title role, *Fedora* and *Adriana Lecouvreur*, singled out by Tanner at the opening of this chapter as especially impoverished, worked on audiences triumphantly. Such works of the generally maligned as 'popular' 'cheap' 'decadent' *verismo* school,[22] largely ignored in 'expert' accounts, demonstrate that audiences deploy theatrical values to access and understand opera rather than those of music, text and drama taught by the instructing priesthood. These values may be dismissed as distractions and ephemeral: star worship, vocal power and/or beauty, spectacle, 'thrilling', 'exciting', and 'moving', but in some respects it is these values which now dominate opera, for it is generally these values that are aroused or exploited by the new discursive élite who dominate most opera houses worldwide—the 'radical' and not so radical reinterpreting opera producers for whom theatrical communication takes precedence over 'dead' analysis. For example, what price the original text, and hence its links to music?

> A theatre is a place of communication, and language is a primary means of communication. It is therefore a very strange decision indeed to elect to address an audience in a language they do not understand. It is against the very nature of theatre' (Pountney 1992a: 404-8).

Of course, translations require compromises, especially of Italian because of the poetic forms employed: beauty of tone and length of line may be affected by English vowels, diphthongs and consonants, but if the prime purpose of text is to convey sense, how can it if the audience doesn't understand it? Singers often learn the original by rote. Texts should be enunciated clearly. 'Star' opera submerges 'sense' and 'balance' with 'tone' and 'volume'. Everything about a performance is vitalised by singers (and audiences) knowing in detail what they are singing.

As in contemporary critical theory, current critical stage practice asserts that no cultural artefact exists in itself—in its structural components—rather one text moves out of another: there is no directing 'presence' or absolute inherent meaning, or one way of reading, receiving and consuming. Instead how the text is reiterated, accented and nuanced depends on the controls placed on the production of meaning at any moment. Thus opera knowledge is not above or free from the constraints of each transient production (Derrida 1982); hence producers' power. There is no 'work in itself' or objective knowledge which arises out of the text; that knowledge has to be produced. There *is* a work of art and yet there isn't in the sense that art works can only be within the conventions of institutions by 'the authority of interpretive communities' (Fish 1980: vii). Whilst swayed by institutional norms, we may also at times challenge them, the 'we' being both key interpreters and the audiences to which they are interpreting, leading to all manner of additional tensions. Interpretive communities and traditions, especially those of so pronounced a 'museum culture' as opera, focus our attentions on certain features of art works and place a differential value on these parts, the value placed being reflective of power inequalities in the wider society. We bring to operas of all genres, normative interpretive values which were absent for their original listeners, but which have been dynamically imposed out of material and historical happenstance. We encounter the contemporary interpretations of art works from our participation in other social, political and intellectual institutions whose conventions and ideologies affect the judgements we make within the art world. The art world itself is enmeshed in other institutions and is never free of internal contradictions. To repeat Tambling:

> ... art is nothing inherently: it is waiting to be used, as a series of signs, a series of rhetorical strategies that is ready to be taken up and used at any point, not only in the production of types of knowledge, but also in the formation of power relations (1987: 20).

Analyses of opera as 'dead' artefacts, under the weight of 'abstract' ideology, not only shield opera from the contaminating environment of the opera house and its untutored audiences, they also remove it from the counterdiscursive challenge of producers who are frequently accused of offending against the 'original unity of the musical experience (original conception of composer, libretto, rhetoric of the music), the rhetorical structure of the piece... ' (Noske 1990: 91). 'Radical' producers view 'the "work" in itself' as diffuse rather than organically coherent and meaningful' (Neubauer 1993: 7), and hence feel inspired to change it in numerous ways—inserting arias from other works, cutting whole scenes and so on, to support their interpretations. Contemporary tensions which surround such producer-initiated restructuring of works in the face of the equally forceful contemporary lobby concerned with protecting their 'authenticity' focus on characteristics which are not altogether new. Cuts and insertions were once ubiquitous and few works were played complete.

> Puccini, who knew how to tailor his scores to an audience's attention span, probably has escaped with the fewest, while Wagner who wasn't in the least interested in the audience's attention span, was regularly docked. In fact it was not until the Met moved to the Lincoln Center in 1966 that it performed *Die Meistersinger* uncut (Smith 1995a: 4).

Two of the five consecutive arias in the last Act of *Le Nozze di Figaro* (those for Marcellina and Don Basilio) are normally omitted and up to 30 years ago all operas were cut to suit voices and time requirements. Only in the past 30 years have the 'purifying' reforms by Toscanini and others led to concerns for 'uncut' performances, difficult though it often is to be certain what 'uncut' means in the context of the 'original', given composers' first, second, and later thoughts. *Carmen, Boris Godunov, Don Carlos, La forza del destino, Madama Butterfly*, and *Les Contes d'Hoffmann* are merely some of the most obvious. *Bel canto*[23] works, frequently cobbled together from earlier 'failures', are now being reassembled as 'forgotten' and 'fabricated' 'masterworks'. For example, the Overture, now deemed entirely appropriate to Rossini's 'comedy', *Il barbiere di Siviglia* (1816) started life as Overture to the 'opera seria' *Aureliano in Palmira* (1813). The simultaneous development of the 'authenticity' movement and the 'radical' producer may appear contradictory, but both are concerned with capturing the 'original', in either its musical sound or 'spirit', while giving the fossilised operatic repertoire a semblance of 'newness' and 'live' art.

Directorial innovations became pronounced as the doors closed on opera as a museum. In his Opera Studio productions Stanislavski changed words—for example, those of Mimi's first aria in *La Bohème*—because he felt them to be 'too detailed for a singer to be able to project, supplying his own simplified version, enabling the singer to be more clearly understood by the audience' (Cannon 1983: 714). For Stanislavski too, the 'aesthetic' process did not rest in the work as originally written; librettists' instructions were extraneous and usually printed after early productions, not inherent parts of works, hence his insistence on pruning texts and music, changing period of settings and so on. The Opera Studio *Bohème* was updated to the year of production, 1927, the kind of interpretive 'vandalism' considered a very recent phenomenon. Wieland Wagner cut Gutrune's short scene at the end of *Götterdammerung* at post-war Bayreuth of all 'pure' places, because it didn't accord with his production concept. These were precursors of the new breed of producer for whom opera is 'total theatre', in a somewhat different sense than that originally proposed by Wagner, demanding 'psychologically truthful adherence to the plot' through 'a seamless unity' (Fuchs 1975: xi-xiii)—'a completely new method of perceiving human actions visually and aurally'. Opera turns into sound what lies below and beyond the external processes of life—the impulses of the will, the sentiments, the emotions (Herz 1975: 146), which it is the duty of the producer to reveal. But this philosophy too, like 'abstract' music ideology, is selective in works deemed worthy of such treatment:

> ... the repertory must be chosen very carefully among works that offer the qualities required. Works in which singing is *merely a tradition* and not a psychological necessity are of little or no use to the music theater producer (Fuchs 1975: xiv, my italics).

These works, once selected, have a 'weak identity for these producers, unlike the audiences they play to; they are 'open works of art' (Eco 1979), or 'scriptable texts' (Barthès 1970), open to inexhaustible interpretations by means of producers' 'deconstructionist' techniques which may mystify audiences whose sensibilities are arguably disdained by producers and musicologists alike (Shepherd 1987: 61, 60). Only those among the audience who are 'in contact with their values, who alone can appreciate them' (Tambling 1987: 20); this provokes amongst the non-comprehending majority 'the rage of the normal' (Horkheimer and Adorno 1969: 105).

'Homework'

Musicological analyses of opera music and text in their 'dead' on the page state may head the hierarchy of opera discourses, but 'interventionist' producers contest this dominance through their 'live' deconstructions played directly to the 'the social pyramid that makes the audience itself an ornament of the opera' (Clement 1989: 6). Academicians do not speak directly to audiences; their teachings and knowledge are mediated through critics and other 'lay' instructors. The 'radical' producer, by contrast, intervenes in or short-circuits this established hierarchy of knowledge by speaking to audiences directly. The result, not surprisingly, is much confusion and incomprehension as traditional teachings are subverted by apparently irreconcilable production practices. Whatever the sociopolitical distinctions of opera house audiences, distanced from the stage and behind the proscenium and orchestra pit, ranked in horseshoe-shaped boxes and tiers of the traditional opera house (see Rosselli 1992d: 431-37 and Appendix B), they possess differential knowledge to contextualise what they witness. Within opera houses, knowledge is popularly deemed to be distributed in inverse proportion to wealth and social status as indicated by seat location. Opera 'lovers', 'real opera lovers', 'genuine opera fans', 'serious opera lovers', 'regulars' are found, it is argued, in the gallery, amphitheatre and standing areas, not in the dress circle, royal box or stalls. Quite where this stereotype comes from and what it means will be discussed in the final chapter, but it is sufficient to note here that, as opera audiences are not unified by wealth, status and political power, so too they are differentiated by the levels of knowledge they possess. The more knowledge the greater the challenge to producers to deconstruct and reinterpret it. Where then does this knowledge come from?

For the regular operagoer it is accumulated out of experience and interactional exchange, as well as varieties of instructional materials but, for the 'occasional' operagoer too, it is a given that some 'homework' is necessary to enjoy opera although encouragement from existing 'opera lovers' might help.[24] There may be at one extreme corporate guests wholly unprepared for what they witness. Or, to use another currently familiar stereotype, at the other professional amateurs armed with the luminous insights of a Kramer or Corse. For the majority, however, opera culture is one in which it is the norm to prepare for the performance to varying degrees and, once over, appraise it through reference to programme essays too lengthy to read in intervals. Even the most basic of instructional texts employ some technical terms which may pose initial problems of understanding. Prior to the performance recordings of the work may be listened to, and the essays in recordings booklets read (although the size of print might be discouraging!). Some might brave the libretto—those for new or rare works often incorporated into programmes. Most commonly 'mugging up' will be done via opera guides of one type or another,[25] most classically and bulkily through Kobbé (1922 and revs), a compendium of most of the core repertoire, in which brief details of operas and composer backgrounds, of first and major early performances with casts, accompany succinct plot synopses with basic music examples, followed by a few fines of analytical judgements.

A commonsense definition of 'analysing opera' would impute no esoteric meaning to the phrase. For most people 'analyzing opera' would mean 'interpreting an opera' or 'explaining an opera' to contribute to a richer understanding of the work. Classical books such as Ernest Newman's *The Wagner Operas* or Edward J. Dent's *The Mozart Operas*, both highly literate commentaries on matters such as background, plot, and music, are analyses of opera in this sense. Both volumes tell the story in familiar and friendly words (Abbate and Parker 1989: 1).

'Familiar and friendly' words have a habit of becoming fusty and dry over time, nor do they speak to one readership. Also there is the implicit problem of how to deal with musical notation, the quoting of examples and key *motifs* and the like, so that even 'familiar and friendly' guides 'culturally segregate' readers by such knowledge and linguistic skills. Opera dictionaries come in all sizes and degrees of detail and have the added bonus of including biographical details of artists,[26] but unless they reach *Grove* (Sadie 1993) dimensions, are severely limited on how far they can delve 'behind the mere sonic surface of the work' (Abbate and Parker 1989: 2). There are specialist magazines or journals which often fulfil these functions. The US *Opera News*, the 'in-house' journal of the New York Metropolitan Opera Guild, prefaces the Texaco Saturday matinee radio broadcasts with a range of 'homework' materials on the works and their composers, producers, including much singer/artist gossip and interviews which constitute for many operagoers dominant forms of opera knowledge. In Britain *Opera* tends towards a more informed specialist readership mainly concerned with detailed reviews of performances worldwide, although even here it is rare for musical examples to be used 'in the way that poetry reviews cite verse, and art reviews regularly employ admittedly rough and ready reproductions of some of the works exhibited' (Kerman 1985: 17).27 *Opera Now* is much more glossy (though less so than when it first appeared as part of the 1980s' 'opera boom') and populist in intent, and concentrates on essays on operas, singers and major opera houses as part of lifestyles, where to stay, eat, and so on, plus information on opera house seasons and booking details. All such sources purvey knowledge and, in the normative sense, power, whatever the manner and content, even those tarred with the slur of 'journalism': 'Journalistic criticism has a very bad odour among the music profession' (Kerman 1985: 16). Press critics slither round the edges of this tar as key disseminators of 'high' professional knowledge in succinct, translated, more accessible forms to amateur audiences. They are the parish or lay priesthood, their function to instruct in basic language and practice—names of singers, producers, conductors, arbiters of taste, purveyors of opinion—but largely bereft of technical terminology; they instruct more by means of 'poetic fictions' than by 'dry technical designations' (Hanslick 1854: 34).

The supposed 'opera-boom' of the 1980s has seen a burgeoning of user-friendly publications to woo, and profit out of, the new rich younger population keen to translate their material capital into forms of cultural capital associated with 'high' taste and distinction. Few, however, have gone to the Forman (1994) extremes in attempting to dust away the Kobbé cobwebs, as illustrated by the following extracts as first Kobbé then Forman seeks to convey *Parsifal*, Act 1 Scene 2, where we first encounter the eponymous hero or if you prefer 'insufferable prick' (Forman 1994: 502).

A moment later a wounded swan, one of the sacred birds of the Grail brotherhood, flutters over the stage and falls dead near Gurnemanz. The knights follow in consternation. Two of them bring Parsifal, whom they have seized and accuse of murdering the sacred bird. As he appears the magnificent Parsifal Motive rings out on the horns ... full of the wild spirit and freedom of this child of nature [who] freely boasts of his marksmanship. Then follows Gurnemanz's noble reproof ... Even the animals are sacred in the region of the Grail ... Parsifal's gradual awakening to a sense of wrong is one of the most touching scenes of the music-drama. His childlike grief when he becomes conscious of the pain he has caused is so simple and pathetic that one cannot but be deeply affected. After Gurnemanz has ascertained that Parsifal knows nothing of the wrong he has committed he plies him with questions ... (Kobbé 1961: 298-9)

A dead swan falls from the flies and a squire shouts up to the flies Hey it isn't Swan Lake tonight that's on Thursday. Shut up you fool it's in the script says another. Who done this dastardly act? says a third. Some knights enter giving Parsifal the bum's rush. He done it they cry, this big loony with his bow and arrow. You done this? asks Gurnamanz. Yeh it was a great shot he was coming really high says Parsifal ... Gurnamanz ... goes on to give [Parsifal] a severe anti-blood sports lecture and ends by asking him how could you do such a thing? Dunno says Parsifal. Who's your father? ... dunno says Parsifal. Where are you from? Who do you work for? What school did you go to? University? What's your blood group? Dunno, dunno, dunno, dunno says Parsifal. What's your name then? Dunno. Lordy Lord we have a real thicky here says Gurnemanz, and maybe one for the men in white coats ... (Forman 1994: 487).[28]

On some stage recently Forman's interpretation has probably been reproduced. Forman highlights musical components such as those to 'look out for' and awards stars: three for the trio in *Der Rosenkavalier* Act III but only one for the Overture for although 'it is famous for starting the opera off with an orgasm ... honestly if nobody told you, you would never know' (ibid.: 645). Opera house programmes sometimes provide more than basic tutelage, as long as one gets to the theatre in time to read plot synopses and copious essays usually designed to explain, in case it isn't clear in performance, the work's 'meaning'.

The main task of the programme is to provide a context within which a production is seen. This context includes the basic information about who is performing what and when; the immediate details of the production (synopsis, previous performances etc); and more wide ranging material on the work and production (interpretative notes, source material, illustrations, design ... etc.) which is expected to be read after a performance (John McMurray Publications Editor, ROH letter *Opera* January 1989: 28).

In operagoing theory, as in playgoing practice, some will not care for textual guidance at all and 'Surely the performance should make sense in its own terms?' However some 'homework' is practically necessary if the works are being given in foreign language or incoherent translations. Singers may or may not be native speakers of the language in which the opera is being performed, may or may not understand the words they sing, thereby missing subtleties of expression and intonation (so much for *constative* and *performative* utterances!). Nor may they enunciate clearly or succeed in overcoming the blanketing effects of orchestral accompaniment. For some this matters little, merely confirming opera as a 'mysterious' irrational experience beyond analysis:

> ... the words in opera are seldom understood, either they are in another language, or they are made inaudible by the singing technique... one makes a pretence of not being interested in the plot, which is completely unimportant. So one is moved for no apparent reason... This gift is attributed to grace, to the prima donna, to leisure, to the miracle of opera (Clement 1989: 9).

Also, in a world in which operagoing for most must be sandwiched between work, meals, travel, possibly over long distances, the amount of 'homework' that can be done is limited. '

> With the best will in the world it is not possible to read a whole opera libretto before a performance and remember every detail of what is going on from moment to moment unless one knows the work exceptionally well' (Stephens 1990: 36).

Surtitles[29] have been hailed as making any such 'homework' unnecessary:

> With the introduction of surtitles ... no one can any longer complain that opera is impossible to follow. Once haughtily

indifferent to the utility of instant comprehension, now, like Garbo, it talks. It has, like theatre and film the capacity to lure us into its drama, to make us laugh or cry, to make us *believe*. There has ceased to be any excuse for cultural segregation (Adair 1994, 10: 7).

In contemporary opera, surtitles provide a major discursive tension between their claimed popularising purpose and effects and their counterclaimed devaluation of the works they accompany. Except at the New York Met where small screens have been inserted into the seat backs for the use of the row behind (MetTitles), surtitles are projected on to screens above or immediately below the proscenium. The text has to be large to be read by the whole theatre, timing is crucial for synchronisation with stage action, highly problematic if a standard translation is employed to accompany 'deconstructed', 'radical' productions. Audience attention is invariably (indeed intentionally) distracted from the stage action and singers. Most damagingly for their critics, surtitles cannot cope with the density of the more sophisticated libretti—the very libretti which qualify for consideration in 'expert' analyses. In a Covent Garden revival of *Der Rosenkavalier* 'The surtitles (were) unacceptable. Quite apart from the omission of key lines, the wit, colour and irony of Hofmannsthal's text are ironed out into bland anonymity, almost a case for action under the Trades Description Act' (Milnes, *The Times*, 7 February 1995: 32), leading the critic three days later to pose the anguished question 'Will people only go to the opera nowadays if they can "read" the performance rather than listen to it?' (Milnes, *The Times* 10 February 1995: 31). Given their widespread adoption, the answer would appear to be 'Yes'.

> Some music-lovers used to be put off opera by not understanding it. They liked the music, but had not the faintest idea what was going on. If I had to name one factor that has most contributed to the growing popularity of opera, I would choose surtitles. At the Royal Opera House we usually perform the operas we give in the original language. For almost all we translate the text on a screen above the stage (Sir Jeremy Isaacs in The Royal Opera House 1993b: 6-7).

Answering opposition by 'purists' to what they alternatively call 'celluloid messages for tourists', 'theatrical condoms' (Pountney 1992a) and 'sillytitles' (*Opera* January 1987: 14), Isaacs claimed that 'market research ... confirmed' that those who benefit from surtitles are 'in the great majority'. At first the ROH policy was surtitles at some performances only, but 'overwhelming research evidence' led the ROH to switch to all.[30]

This chapter has sought to represent the hierarchy of discourses which 'analyse' opera. As succeeding pages will hopefully show, these layers of knowledge are in constant tension and flux, pulled at opposite extremes towards 'high', 'abstract', spiritual, 'life-enhancing' principles, often out of the opera house and into the library and study, or 'emotional', 'escapist', 'entertainment' and commodification also out of the opera house but into 'opera' fragments at celebrity concerts, advertising jingles, soundtracks, or even background noise. DeNora asks 'How do people articulate with music? What do people *do* to music?' The answer is 'almost anything including listen... Things get done to music ... as it plays both in real time, and as it is played and replayed in memory and imagination (1995: 300). 'To enter into a piece of music is to enter a form of textual time' (Smith 1990: 74), and '... in providing non-verbal resources for activity, music also provides non-verbal resources for the clarification of perceived reality' (DeNora 1995: 301). At all levels of this discursive hierarchy summarised in the diagram below, there are tensions and conflicts within and between degrees and forms of 'knowledge', reflecting similar tensions and conflicts in the wider society.

> Any dominant ideology ... presents itself as the ideology of that society as a whole. Its work is to deny the legitimacy of alternative and oppositional ideologies and to construct out of its own contradictions a consensual ideology that will appear to be valid for all members of society. The operations of the ideology are therefore a ceaseless effort to mask or displace both its own contradictions and those contradictions to it that arise from alternative and oppositional ideologies. The latter always enter into the account with a popular or mass medium due to the fact that the medium must engage with audiences not themselves situated within the dominant groups of society. These operations are always in process, an effort to secure an 'hegemony' that is always under threat from within and without ... much ... interest

... [therefore] lies in this process of contradiction and its "management" and those moments when hegemony is not, or is only uneasily, secured (Dyer 1979: 3).

'ABSTRACT'/'PURE' MUSIC:
formal aesthetic principles

OPERA AS MUSIC (with text): understood through dense analyses of musical discourse, i.e. an academic, NOT a theatrical artefact. Elitist, because inaccessible through use of musical notation.

OPERA AS MUSIC AND TEXT: understood through close analyses of how the two combine, i.e. how the two languages come together. Again élitist but, because of the textual/narrative focus, possibly more accessible. Preparation possibly but not necessarily for ...

OPERA AS COMPLEX DRAMA: understood through elaborate 'homework', 'preparation', prior reading of libretti, synopses etc., 'deconstructionist' or 'postmodernist' interpretations which reflect upon a store of existing knowledge and often explicitly challenge it.

OPERA AS THEATRICAL ENTERTAINMENT: prepared for by some 'homework' and understood through generalised effects of singers and singing and to the performance as an affectional, emotional experience rather than through detailed knowledge of words, music or narrative and for which 'surtitles' are a basic textual help.

'OPERA': outside the opera house as 'favourite arias': 'bite-sized chunks', advertising jingles, celebrity concerts, CD highlight discs, etc.

POPULAR MUSIC/THE CULTURE INDUSTRY

Notes

1. Wilensky (1964) identifies 'high' culture by referring to two characteristics of the product: (1) it is created by, or under the supervision of, a cultural élite operating within some aesthetic, literary or scientific tradition, (2) critical standards independent of the consumer of the product are systematically applied to it. He identifies mass culture as cultural products manufactured solely for the mass market, and folk culture the traditional culture of the people predominant in rural society. (See Vulliamy 1977.)

2. Van der Merwe (1992) describes how in the days when entertainment was mainly home-based, knowledge of orchestral music was based on piano transcriptions or arrangements for other instruments. 'Recent studies suggest that it was by such means that an enthusiasm for opera was instilled amongst the Italian people largely outside the opera house, through workers chorale societies and amateur bands, even itinerant puppeteers' (Rosselli 1984: 163). Van der Merwe states: 'Some of these arrangements were of surprisingly bad taste ...' (1992: 19) citing a quadrille based by Chabrier on themes from *Tristan und Isolde* as one of the funniest. Popular music was undoubtedly vulgarised by the growth of commercial interests and the mass migration to the cities. Classical music, as it ceased to be the diversion of a small upper class, was acquiring its present overtones of culture and uplift. Composers, far from being mere skilled craftsmen, were beginning to see themselves as rather superior beings. He claims that by the end of the twentieth century there were three kinds of music, 'serious', 'good' or 'classical' music (of which opera was a part); 'parlour music' of which 'opera' is a part in extract aria form as it is now via the classical/pop CD orchestral or instruments arrangements of 'arias' as 'songs' and thirdly there was 'folk' music.

3. *Coloratura soprano* derived from the German *Koloratur* a soprano specialising in elaborate vocal ornamentation; *Heldentenor*, heroic tenor specialising in Wagner, Richard Strauss; *Falcon* after Marie Conelie Falcon (1812-97) a veiled mezzo-tinted dramatic soprano. Francoise Pollet (*1993 see Appendix F) '[s]earching for a comparison to Pollet's voice, the French critics looked to their own and—perhaps

55

maliciously—chose Marie Conelie Falcon, a soprano who has been dead for almost a century. "There are two camps. She is a *Falcon*, she's not a *Falcon*. Of course I'm not a *Falcon*, which usually means somebody with a brilliant top, a big bottom and nothing in between. Falcon sang only five years and so had many vocal problems".'

4. *Dramma giocoso* for example, Don Giovanni, a comic opera with serious undertones or inclusions; *zarzuela* popular Spanish opera mixing dialogue with music; *opèra comique*: despite literally meaning 'comic opera' this term refers to a changing body of French works in which dialogue alternates with music. Initially set against *opera seria* conventions it later applies to such tragedies as *Carmen*.

5. *Così fan tutte* ('Women are like that'); *Die Frau ohne Schatten* ('The woman without a shadow'); *Les Contes d'Hoffmann* ('The tales of Hoffmann').

6. *'Da Capo' aria* usually in three parts 'with the second in the relative major or minor key and the third a repeat of the first (to be ornamented by the singer)' (Rosenthal and Warrack 1980: 16); *cabaletta* which is a short aria or conclusion to an aria in which there is great embellishment often improvised by the singer; *leitmotiv* which is a short musical figure or theme associated with a particular character, object, place, event etc.

7. Musicologists proclaim few operas 'masterpieces' and then do so largely, it seems, because they apparently transcend the inherent contamination (theatrical, emotional, irrational) of the operatic form. The three Mozart-Da Ponte works—*Le nozze di Figaro*, *Don Giovanni*, and *Così fan tutte*—Wagner's *Tristan und Isolde*, *Die Meistersinger von Nürnberg*, and *Parsifal*, Verdi's *Otello* and *Falstaff* and (symbolically as well as musicologically central) Beethoven's *Fidelio*, are foremost amongst the uncontested few used to affirm opera's overall impoverishment. The *verismo* (realism) Italian school, immensely popular with audiences, is either ignored or dismissed, as for famous example, Kerman dismissed Puccini's *Tosca* based on a play by Sardou as 'a shabby little shocker' following George Bernard Shaw's disparagement of the whole school as 'Sardoodledum', cheap hokum, false emotionalism, phoney 'realism' and debased vocalism.

Corse (1987), discussed later in the chapter, provides convincing and instructive, though complex textual analyses of operas selected for their strong libretti as well as music. Her choice, *Die Zauberflöte*, *Le nozze di Figaro* and *Capriccio* (Strauss),*Otello*, *Falstaff*, and *Death in Venice* and *Owen Wingrave* (both by Britten). The critical nudging of questions of bad or poor taste frequently levelled at the works of Richard Strauss may be gleaned from the following review of Covent Garden's revival of *Der Rosenkavalier* of 1995 by Rodney Milnes in *The Times* (7 February: 32). 'If the court of posterity is still reserving judgement on Richard Strauss, as more austere music lovers would insist, then performances of *Der Rosenkavalier* as good as the Royal Opera's revival will be useful evidence for the defence.'

8. Tanner (1994) lists as 'genius' Verdi and Wagner which presumably means that the former's *I due Foscari* is as worthy as *Otello*, and that the latter's *Die Feen* is as skilled as *Parsifal*. Mozart, Beethoven, Verdi and Wagner are the unquestioned 'genius' composers of opera, although increasingly Rossini and Bellini have their champions (see, for example, Kendall: 1995) and even Puccini too is now receiving more serious musicological consideration (see Weaver and Puccini [1994] and Ashbrook and Powers [1991]) who regard *Turandot* as 'a significant historical symbol, an epitaph for an artistic epoch' (ibid.: ix).

By the 1980s, the 'abstract' aesthetic, 'genius' ideology was openly challenged by practitioners as well as theorists, conductor/composer Pierre Boulez, for example, quoting Rousseau on the unity of composer, performer and public within a sociocultural context:

> It is taste that enables a composer to grasp the ideas of the poet and a performer to grasp the ideas of the composer. It is taste which provides each with what he needs in order to decorate and bring out the full sense of these ideas, and taste that enables the listener to respond emotionally to all these accepted proprieties (Rousseau quoted in Boulez 1986a: 49).

For Boulez there is no such thing as 'absolute taste', taste is socially constructed and the meaning of 'genius' consists ... 'in a maximum awareness of the functions that bind the artist to society, after that it is of small importance whether in his later developments the artist finds himself 'in phase' with his age or not' (ibid.:51): 'geniuses' are those who have '... imbibed all the various "tastes" of their day and transcended them, in their own' (ibid.:52). Instead of reifying 'abstract' rules, the focus should be not on the fetishised imposition of personal meanings on works composed but, he claims, on the analysis of taste: identification of contemporary tastes; anticipation of future tastes, and the projection of contemporary tastes on the past.

9. Conrad actually states: 'The genius of opera lies in its potentiality for an enriching contradiction between its elements. Rather than a sedate marriage between text and music, it proposes a relationship of unremitting tension' (1977: 177).

10. There are now many detailed social histories of opera which, though more accessible to a wider but interested public, remain mandarin in their analytical perspectives and assumptions, being largely meaningless unless one has a prior working knowledge of opera, opera composers, titles and so on.

11. John Steane in his *Opera Now* review of *The Viking Opera Guide* (ed. A. Holden with N. Kenyon and S. Walsh 1994) states 'poor old Kobbé, he seems to have had his day'.

12. There are numerous other titles of course, *Opern Welt* and *Das Opernglas* in Germany; *Opera Monthly* in Canada; *Opera, La Musique de la Monde* in France; *L'Opera* in Italy.

13. According to 'abstract' principles, all opera is decadent and opera composers often cede as much. Franklin, for example, refers to Schreker's use of a string quartet in *Der Schatzgraber* (1920) was to enshrine 'the pure' (string quartet) music within the impure medium of the opera itself (1989).

14. 'All of this is musical and yet, in their aesthetic feel and social tone, these activities seem almost incommensurable. And it is precisely the social differences and the political distinctions they entail which we are least able to discuss, because the heritage of music criticism and analysis is largely a formalist one' (Hirschkop 1989: 283).

15. 'Tonal' music is also 'pure' music in another sense: that is as the triumphant reflection of Christianity's denial of the body (see Partch 1974).

16. A perverse version of the abstractness of genius music comes from Furtwangler's defence for staying in, and collaborating with, the Third Reich:

Men are always free when Wagner and Beethoven are being played. And if they are not free they will become so when they hear these works. Music will lead them into regions where the Gestapo will be powerless (quoted in Potts 1995: 25).

17. Stravinsky was an opera composer who, unlike Berg and Schoenberg, sought a future for opera in neoclassicism rather than dodecaphony but in spite of that his varied vocal-stage works betray a similar concern for the future of the operatic form. Of the following only the last provides a 'neoclassical' opera according to classical rules: *The Nightingale* (1914); *L'histoire du soldat* (1918); *Mavra* (1922); *Renard* (1922); *Les Noces* (1923); *Oedipus Rex* (1927) and *The Rake's Progress* (1951).

18. Silbermann, for example, had to observe 'how vague and confused are the notions which congregate around the term "music"' (1963: 67). He hardly refers to opera at all as a subject of sociological enquiry, being more at home with opera groups and their organisation than the works themselves or the form as a whole.

19. Witness also the music of the Triumphal scene in *Aida* and that of the *auto da fe* in *Don Carlos*.

20. For a similar analysis see McClary (1991, 1992) on *Carmen*, in which she argues that throughout the opera, music is made up of dance tunes for example, Habanera and Seguidilla. Musically and socially Carmen 'does things that "nice girls" shouldn't do' (De Nora 1995: 307). McClary argues that the infatuated Don José 'sets up a pitch-ceiling that constructs his melodic line (thus recreating in sound the experience of his frustration) which he penetrates in '*te revoir, o Carmen*'. Following this explosive moment, his energy gradually seems to subside almost to a kind of whimpering. But as he sings of submitting himself to her power masochistically ... he rises again—this time through an unaccompanied scale—and attains climax on b (flat), the highest most vulnerable pitch in the aria.'

21. Magda Olivero, Italian soprano. Date of birth varies from 1911-1914 depending on sources. Made her debut in 1933 and became associated with *verismo* works in particular, especially *Adriana Lecouvreur* by Cilea. Retired in 1941 on marriage but returned to the stage in 1950-51 at the behest of Cilea. Continued to sing

until well into the 1970s and 1980s. With not even a handful of studio recordings, being the possessor of a voice not easily captured by recording technologies and being overlooked by recording companies keen to promote Renata Tebaldi and Maria Callas, her great fame is based on 'pirate' recordings of 'live' performances in which her impact on audiences is all too clear.

22. All art is artifice—opera more so than probably all others bar ballet. *Verismo,* the realistic or naturalistic school of Italian opera which flourished in late nineteenth and early twentieth centuries, should not be taken literally, but rather as indicative of wider cultural concerns with representing reality or capturing it, and accordingly the casting of a 'representative' net to 'capture' all aspects of it including the impoverished, mundane and popular. Key composers were Puccini, Mascagni, Leoncavello, Alfano, Cilea, Giordano and so on. There will be more discussion of *verismo* in Chapter 4.

23. As an example of the variability in the use of technical terms Celletti (1991) uses *bel canto* to describe not, as is the custom, Italian works of the first three decades of the nineteenth century by such composers as Rossini, Donizetti and Bellini, but *baroque* opera, that is eighteenth-century opera of the pre-Gluck era.

24. What is the best way to learn to love opera? Get someone who already loves opera to explain it to you. This can be tricky. At worst—to paraphrase Wilde—one could end up with the unenthusiastic leading the uninformed in pursuit of the incomprehensible. In my experience, opera lovers fall into two categories. There are those who cling to opera's reputation as an élitist pleasure, believing its myriad joys are beyond the comprehension of the uninitiated. Ask these cognoscenti any questions about any opera, and your answer will be polite, brief accompanied by a cool smile, designed to keep further inquiries at bay. Feeling faintly foolish, you retire to your corner clutching the old copy of Milton Cross' *Opera Stories* you've had since junior high school, wistfully wondering how you'll learn what a *portamento* really is. There is a friendlier species of operaphile however, to whom a simple question represents the chance to win a friend for the grandest of the performing arts. These are the ladies and gentlemen who can be overheard at intermission explaining the next act of a labyrinthine Verdi libretto to a confused first time operagoer, or spotted in the

aisles of Tower Records patiently advising a complete stranger on the best available version of *La fanciulla del West*. They spend their hours away from the opera house proselytising tirelessly, creating opera fans wherever they see the opportunity. Eager though they may be, they know their mission is not easily accomplished. Preaching to the unconverted is as tricky in opera as in other regions: a badly planned education can lose a soul forever (Driscoll 1995: 47).

25. Plotkin (1995) summarises plots, provides a general history of opera, recommends top recordings and instructs readers on how to purchase tickets, what to wear to the opera in different cities, when and how to applaud and so on. Michael Walsh, (1995) wants his readers to 'develop their own philosophy of opera; what it is, what it's not, and what it can be', but cannot resist making highly opinionated judgements about singers, works, arias and so on, that one reviewer (Driscoll 1995: 47) considered the result probably to be the 'intimidation of the beginner into philosophical submission, and likens this chatty and irreverent text to barrelling through an art exhibition strapped to a speeding motorcycle: it's an interesting ride but you don't get to look at the pictures very closely'. Walsh describes *verismo* works with the usual sneers. *Adriana Lecouvreur* is 'a content-free singing contest'. As with Forman, Walsh's self-conscious outrageous vox pop style is allied to an array of references as élitist and patronising in intent and effect, in their own 'alternative' way, as anything to be found in the staid guides being challenged. For example his discography includes such esoteric works as *Satyagraha, Treemonisha, Saint François D'Assise, Nixon in China* and *Lady Macbeth of the Mtsensk District*.

There are now series of single opera study guides which provide much more detail such as: Hepokoski (1987) on *Otello*; Mitchell (1987) on *Death in Venice*; Rice (1991) on *La clemenza di Tito* in the series by Cambridge University Press. The English National Opera/Royal Opera House Covent Garden also jointly publish a similar series: for example John (ed.) Opera Guide No. 41: *Macbeth*. London Riverrun Press: John Calder (1986).

Several guides target young readers: DiGaetani (1991) 'is written for the potential operagoer who is favourably inclined but far from convinced that opera is his [sic] "scene"'.

There are numerous beginner's guides: for example Nicholas (1993) and Craker (1993). Both seek to bridge the discrepancy between those who will buy a Pavarotti CD and those who would sit through a whole *Turandot* without one of the three tenors. The first is a companion to a series on Channel 4 also part of the 80s opera-yuppie boom, *Harry Enfield's Guide to Opera*. Craker's was reviewed as 'shoddily ill written and patronising—relentlessly jaunty ... it could serve as a primer for lazy pin-striped buffoons as they pass through the Crush Bar at Covent Garden on the way up the corporate ladder' (Brunskill *Opera* August 1993: 1001), a judgement not remotely patronising in itself.

There is now a *Kobbé Illustrated* (Harewood 1989) for those who can't face the, by comparison, somewhat stark original. *How to be Tremendously Tuned in to Opera* Parrott (1990) consists of a group of authors providing 'explanations' in verse and prose of such thorny problems as exactly what has happened in *Il trovatore* before the curtain has gone up, and detailing such possible subtextual details as the theorised objections of '*La Gazzetta della Polizia*' Rome to Puccini's *Tosca* ('... has dealt one of the severest blows to the cause of community policing that has been felt in recent years'). Law (1990: 1511) praised some pieces: '... Fagg (on Mimi's obviously fraudulent claim to Supplementary Benefit) and Sharpless who dispatches Kipling for an evening at Glyndebourne ("They sits there gawpin' in the stalls, like they wos in a trance/while the bloke wot is conductin' seems to 'ave St Vitus Dance ...").'

The New York Metropolitan Opera Guild has produced *Sing me a Story* a collection of opera stories for young children by Rosenberg (1990) with an Introduction by Luciano Pavarotti. Holden (1990) in her review comments on the strange choice of the 15 works included (*Amahl* and *Night Visitors, L'Enfant et les Sortiléges, Carmen, Aida* and *La bohème),* the saccharine illustrations by the author 'safely reminiscent of Victorian nursery-rhyme books', and the less than simplistic text 'so it seems that the problems of presenting opera to children have not been considered carefully enough; surely they prefer blood and guts to being patronized?'. Some of the plot summaries are also taken on: for example '... how confusing that the Witch in *Hansel and Gretel* is repeatedly referred to as Rosina. Since that is the name she uses (once) to introduce herself, hasn't the author got the wrong end of the broomstick? ... (on the whole) this is U certificate book advertising PG works.'

In January 1990 *Opera* reviewed all the recent guides (Stephens 1990) in which, apart from many of the above, there is reference to the 'latest wheeze ... the Pagoda/ROH garish cartoon series, comic strip versions of the plots which would sell at 60p if published by Marvel comics for a mass market, but which in the rarefied world of opera, appear in hardback at £10', and observes that 'Even some programmes are so substantial as to be classed as guides' (ibid.: 35). Stephens asks 'Why do we need opera guides?' His answer? 'Opera is usually sung in a foreign language, so the audience needs assistance with dialogue: singers' enunciation is poor anyway ... it is possible to envisage a time when operas sung in English to an English speaking audience will have surtitles' (ibid.: 35). That time has arrived!

What should be in a good guide? The libretto? Plus translation? Opinions are divided—both are usually to be found in recordings, existing translations are poor, space should be used for essays about the work, detailed synopses suffice. Alternatively, Nicholas John (ENO Dramaturgue) argues that libretti are as brief as most synopses and tell the story most accurately.

The late Carl Dalhaus put his finger on the problem in a recently published article: 'There is no single opera guide in which the action of an opera is adequately recounted or the fact that there is a problem acknowledged'. Anyone who ventured on the task should begin with the musical form in which the events comprising the drama are presented rather than extracting a story from the libretto. The story underlying an opera does not exist independently of the music; and the story in the libretto as such is not the story of the opera as a musical drama (Stephens 1990: 36).

The CUP Opera Handbooks do not include libretti because the latter are now available in CD and cassette packaging, and the space can be put to better use. Also the choice of translation can be problematic. Instead of a libretto there is a detailed synopsis 'which aims to describe the musical and dramatic action and structure, not simply "tell the story" i.e. it is considerably more than a plot' (Penny Souster of CUP quoted in Stephens 199? p.36). The Calder series, however, does include libretti on the grounds that they provide the best way into an opera and audiences on the whole are not versed in musical language. Guides have to decide what and how to deal with musical quotations, structures and analysis, especially as the more detailed opera guides become they invariably take these latter elements the more seriously and assume a readership able to understand them. In this sense the hierarchy of opera knowledge is linked to the balance between text and narrative to an emphasis on musical language. To be more specific, the hierarchy of elements moves up from generalised responses to dramatic narrative, through closer textual examination of detail, thence to specific musical elements with ultimately analyses which concentrate on the most complex musical analyses, such as those of Berg's operas by Perle (1980, 1984).

Opera News advertises 'Talking About Opera' written and narrated by Peter Allen, a series of cassettes 'designed to bring the great operas of the Met's repertory into focus for adult audiences'. The series begins with 'Talking About the Ring'. Each cassette gives story, background information, musical analysis and examples: 'Together they provide a wonderful introduction to *The Ring* for those who do not know the work, as well as fascinating material for those who want to know more about these complex operas.' The four cassettes are available for $12.98 individually or as a set $45. (*Opera News* 18 March 1989: 38).

The important thing to remember here is that this flurry of publishing activity reflects the belief that the 80s 'opera boom' has been of a sufficient scale for the publishers to make a profit, and, as such, reflect opera's onward commodification—topics to be dealt with in later chapters.

26. See the Foreword for a brief list of recommended dictionaries and guides.
27. Even works like the two by Matheopoulos (1986, 1991a), which are pop-journalism collections of 'star' interviews, sometimes give a glossary of technical terms, although whether the newcomer can understand the definitions is another matter.

Hers include: *appoggiatura* '... a grace note inserted before a note but to be sung equal length, to support or emphasize a melodic or harmonic progression'; *da capo* a 'return to the beginning'; *cantabile* 'literally "songful" denotes *legato*, expressive singing'; *cavatina* 'technically a short aria but now used to describe widely differing "types" of song and therefore virtually meaningless'; *coloratura* 'elaborately embellished singing'; *covering* singing a note 'with a closed throat'; *fioriture* 'florid vocal embellishment'; *messa di voce* 'crescendo and diminuendo on a phrase or note'; *legato* 'to bind or tie notes together, the smooth passage from one note to another', as opposed to *'staccato'*; *passaggio* 'the notes E, F, G which lie between the head and chest registers; *portamento* 'to slide from one note to the next without a break'; *register* 'a certain vocal range or type, in German speaking countries referred to as *fach*; *rubato* 'a way of performing without strict adherence to musical time'; *verismo* 'realism'.

28. James Naughtie's review of Forman (*The Times* 8 October 1994) states that Forman 'has been driven to despair by the banal obfuscations of the traditional opera programme synopsis, which should take their place in the gallery of contemporary torments, along with hi-fi instructions translated from the Japanese vacuum packed junk mail and pins in new shirts.' Naughtie calls Forman's book a 'cry of pain'. Canning (*The Sunday Times* 23 October 1994: 7) was in pain when he read it. Canning believes the operatic bubble which could have justified this book, has burst: 'Elektra comes in looking pretty and calling out her father's name This is precisely the time they did for you in your bath dad she says and goes into the horrid details of what was clearly an unusually brutal crime.' In his Introduction Forman guides his presumably eager uninitiated readers to the world of Oprania 'peopled by fat sopranos and tenors shrieking at each other at full volume, ridiculous characters and ludicrous plots ... This inane and lamentable book!'

29. Alternatively called sopratitles or supertitles in their earliest manifestations, Pountney calls them theatrical condoms—'pieces of celluloid interposed between the audience and the performers' (1992a: 408). They were first used by the Canadian Opera Company, and in Britain by Glyndebourne Touring Company. 'For season 1995/96 MetTitles will be in place and

we'll start the season with a new marketing campaign. My hope is that we can build on our subscription base, which over the years has been lower than we'd like.' Volpe, Met General Manager, mentions that people or companies are much less likely to gift financial support for productions which will not be regularly revived, which means that, again, there is a pull towards the standard and popular repertory, which singers also want to sing. On MetTitles 'I resist anything that will be a distraction from the stage picture' (Smith 1994: 15). Therefore it would be wrong to use projected surtitles, nor could they be seen by large sections of the audience without considerable structural changes. So MetTitles are individual screens in the seat in front which audience members do not need to turn on if they don't want to. Volpe argues that, although they will distract to a degree, they lie below the pit lights' line of sight and that therefore the audience member not wanting to see them can cut them out. The titles will be done for each production by those involved. He didn't think there would be much impact on box office. However, Hugues Gall, when Intendant of Geneva Opera, claimed that surtitles are one means of claiming that opera has a broad appeal; he is opening up access to justify higher or maintained subsidies (Clark 1993: 145-6). Milnes (1991c: 1004) describes however how opera libretti have been sanitised through surtitles for fear of making audiences laugh: 'Opera is being reduced to its lowest common denominator to keep uncommitted flippant audiences quiet.' The MetTitles were tested at public rehearsals during 1994-95, and shown to the press. Reactions during season 1995-96 have been generally favourable although 'they must have cost a bomb!'

'Though everyone has got used to subtitles at the movies, you don't have to avert your eyes to read them, the film is a mechanical "frozen" medium anyway' (Pountney 1992a: 408).

Surtitles destroy theatre design, contradict composers and librettists, render useless comic timing, why not use them to instruct "This bit is in F major"? ... they strike directly at the integrity of people involved in opera production, the 'why bother?' syndrome, why bother sing in English especially ... The surtitle is a catastrophic gooseberry in the vital act of theatrical intercourse ... It is a device for a tourist who looks but does not participate ... The listening-seeing dichotomy and the non-attention problem are such that I cannot contemplate surtitles. The only reason for introducing them is a marketing one (Mathew Epstein quoted in Milnes 1992: 522).

The President of the Board of Directors of the Metropolitan Opera argued in 1993 that the value of 'titles' at the Met is not necessarily the generalised one of drawing in new audiences for all operas, but breaking down the barriers which surround unusual works for regular operagoers or light operagoers (he mentions *Khovanschina* and *The Makropoulos Case*) (1993: 66).

30. *Opera* (January 1987: 14-17; May 1988: 542-3) published letters both for and against. *Opera* was berated by some for its atavistic opposition to an 'unobtrusive' innovation, which takes but 'a moment to read', and which has 'vitalized' audiences, who are not all 'full-time students of opera' or 'as brilliant and well-informed as yourself'; 'if you don't find them helpful ... keep your eyes down'. Alternatively, surtitles were likened to 'being in a room with a television on, no matter how hard you try to avoid looking at it, you find your eyes creeping back to it'. 'They are banal intrusive and cheapen the spectacle on stage.' 'What research? ... No-one has ever canvassed my opinion.' 'I have experienced surtitles from most parts of the house and can say that they intrude, distract and spoil my concentration ... they are an insult.' It is being done for 'the growing army of tax-relieved super-rich'.

2 Opera as fetish and taste

Those divertimenti which
He wrote to play while bottles were uncorked
Milord chewed noisily, Milady talked (Auden 1968).

Introduction

The elaborate hierarchy of discourses discussed in Chapter 1, and the stratified priesthood which articulates, sanctifies and guards its 'secrets', does not exist in a material vacuum. Opera is the dramatisation of music and text, but dramatisations and the custom-built theatres in which they are mounted are expensive, their costs justified on national, political and social as well as aesthetic grounds, their audiences formally and spatially differentiated by wealth and status. Opera has social meaning as a form of art and entertainment of rare distinction, uniquely routinised in ritual and display at all levels of the theatre, but especially in the stalls, dress circle and boxes. As such, opera reflects, symbolises and serves the wealth, status and political interests of the dominant class, regardless of national and state differences. On a practical level, opera's materialism is a major preoccupation in terms of the large number and range of resources required; its sources of income from state subsidies and box office revenues to private and corporate gifts, all insufficient to prevent opera from being a loss-making institution, its finances are always in a parlous state. Where subsidies are provided, populations must be persuaded that their taxes should support such reputationally élitist entertainments; if ticket prices are high, audiences must be persuaded that their purchase is essential. Consumers at all levels are tempted to develop tastes for all manner of related 'opera' commodities—CDs, videos, books, films, laser discs, holidays and so on. As a largely 'museum' culture it has to be constantly *recycled*, *re*promoted, its discourses *re*written and *re*stated, but it is driven by underlying market pressures which repeatedly distance and conceal the 'original' creative act behind its constant *re*commodification.

The nineteenth-century triumph of 'abstract' music ideology was itself a product of the obfuscation of the artist as worker engaged in capitalist social relations of production, through the dissolution of the patron-artist bond and his/her movement into the market as a 'servant' of art—a 'pure' rather than economic being with an almost ironic sense of freedom and separation from materialism and external control:

> This literal freedom from constraint (of course also the cause for many other kinds of unfreedom and new constraints) completed the image of the artist as detached from society, as working in total independence from external pressures, and as expressing his or her own personality in the work of art. Essential to this development was the growth of numerous cultural institutions which effectively mediated between the free floating artist and potential patrons: dealers, critics, publishing houses, journals and so on ... Thus the actual situation of the artist ... from the mid-nineteenth century helped to produce the myth that art is an activity which transcends the social. In the twentieth century this myth has been sustained by the continued marginal existence of cultural producers, and by the persistence and proliferation of specialized arts institutions and personnel-publishers, agents, museum curators, arts editors, and even arts-funding bodies ... (Wolff 1987: 3).

Opera personnel, composers and conductors may also believe themselves to be 'detached from society' and, as we shall see, 'star' singers continue to claim that first and foremost they are but mere servants of their art, opera's nineteenth and twentieth century history is too littered with the ostentatious spread of palatial opera houses, impresario promotion of singers as 'stars' justifying higher

70

seat prices, the expanding role of music publishers in developing 'contract' and copyright law, of opera companies in various states of financial collapse, to conclude that opera can hardly play convincing host to 'abstract' immaterial notions. Manifestly, unlike non-theatre based cultural artefacts, from first realisation an opera speaks through the 'interpretations' or 'articulations' of those engaged in each act of *re*production, *re*promotion and *re*consumption but no: 'objects, artefacts and institutions ... have a single valency. It is the act of social engagement with a cultural item which activates and brings out particular meanings' (Willis 1978: 193), and theatrical acts of 'social engagement', especially those of the operatic kind, have elaborate meanings and cost!

In the late twentieth century, consumerist context opera has become limitless commodities: to witness one *Ring* cycle is to set this (expensive!) experience against existing 'bought' operatic knowledge, and to seek out comparisons with *Ring* cycles elsewhere. To hear one Brunnhilde is to contrast her with other 'live' and recorded Brunnhildes past. To possess on relatively poor quality CD's the 'pirated' performance of Magda Olivero in *Manon Lescaut* in Amsterdam 1964, is to compare it with other recorded performances by her of the same role, equally fuzzy in sound, from the Verona Arena of 1970 and Caracas in 1972.[1] To own a video of *Le Nozze di Figaro* is to have one technological reproduction, not *Figaro* itself, a version of which one will either eventually tire or judge wanting by comparison with alternatives. To be interested in opera one cannot help but be drawn into multiple acts of consumption in the fetishised pursuit of 'pure' knowledge. To go to the opera is to enter a marketplace in which the work on stage is but one component of a ritualised commercial experience framed by grant aid, sponsorship, advertising, dress codes, bar and travel costs etc. As for the work itself, it too, even when its presentation is justified by purist artistic claims of 'authentic' recovery of the 'original' artefact: as musically 'complete', pitch adjusted,[2] performed on period instruments with 'authentic' vocalism, or alternatively radically produced to bare the 'real spirit' of a piece,[3] cannot exist in decommodified form: none of these claims can avoid being in part marketing strategies. We have in short become witnesses to the commodified fetishism of opera as 'pure truths' although, thanks to inspiring producers and/or 'star' performers, the resultant experience need not always be merely: '... heart-breakingly decent, so

71

boring' (Nietzsche 1955: 296).

Wishart has noted that belief in the 'truth' or 'universality' of particular cultural artefacts 'can be traced to the ideological need of an economically isolated intelligentsia concerned to preserve its tradition, by reaffirming a tradition of cultural and political ascendancy' (1977b: 237), but this 'pure tradition' is myth. Opera is *the* 'public' cultural institution of the dominant class, and it is as much for this reason as its complex hybridity of form that it inspires awe and deference in populations, including, indeed especially in those largely excluded from it. This chapter considers the auratic qualities of opera and its commodification into hierarchies of taste and value within the consumer environment of the late twentieth century.

The technical production of sound

The legitimacy, reception, consumption and fate of 'high' musical culture, compared with music as 'background noise', 'wallpaper', 'jazz', 'pop', 'musak' and so on, has become a notable critical theme in the latter half of the twentieth century within debates which largely derive from the original 'blasphemies' of Adorno and Benjamin. Adorno's 1938 essay *On the Fetish Character in Music and Regression of Listening* (1991) outlined his musical-sociological paradigm through a critique of Benjamin's *The Work of Art in the Age of Mechanical Reproduction* (1969: 217-51). As these titles indicate Benjamin and Adorno were primarily concerned with visual and musical arts respectively, but shared a common interest in the changing and predicted production and consumption of artistic artefacts and tastes resulting from technological developments in their reproduction within inter-war and post-war capitalism.

In particular for Adorno, it was the singular sensory qualities of musical sound which, with burgeoning recordings, public address systems, and especially radio, signalled the routinisation and widespread politicisation of all music, including eventually the transformation of 'high' into 'mass listening' conditions, as parts of the expanding 'culture industry' which would effectively depoliticise the listening mass. We may comprehend and negotiate with written and verbal texts but we perceive only the most generalised of meanings in music. We may close our eyes and withhold our touch, but we cannot block our ears, we may try not to hear or, if practised, refuse to 'listen', 'to understand' what we hear, but nevertheless we remain at least conscious of 'noise' (Attali 1985). Mechanical reproduction has considerable and varied deleterious political, social and economic effects, claimed Adorno, including the seemingly unimportant consequence of reproduction technologies on the quality of what we thereafter expect to hear as 'live' sounds, instruments, voices, and so on. Adorno's thesis of repeated listening deadening the senses was, with early recording technologies, all too convincing. Schoenberg expressed this concern *vis-a-vis* radio reproduction, which:

> accustoms the ear to an unspeakably coarse tone, and to a body of sound constituted in a soupy, blurred way, which precludes all the finer differentiation. One fears, as perhaps the worse thing of all, that attitudes to such sounds will change; until now, one has taken them in, beautiful or otherwise, knowing them to represent the tone peculiar to one instrument, and knowing that other sounds also exist-the sounds that is of the instrument as it has existed until now. But as they become more and more familiar, one will adopt them as the criterion for beauty of sound, and find inferior the sound of instruments in art (Schoenberg 1950: 147-8).

Schoenberg's concerns have particular relevance to the possible disparities between the sounds of studio recorded and 'live' vocal instruments, especially in opera where the latter are normally experienced in large custom-built (i.e. in acoustical as well as social terms) opera houses, over-large orchestral forces without microphoned amplification,[4] sometimes for up to five or six hours of complete performance under conditions in which vocal blemishes and accidents are inevitable amongst even the most accomplished of artists, compared with studio recordings' meticulous multi and often short 'take'-based pursuit of technical perfection and (un)theatrical balance. 'Live' opera singing is a variable, and thus exciting, physically delivered experience. Recorded opera is a physically neutered or alienated experience, technically delivered. As we shall see in Chapter 5, as a result of many voices not recording well, being trained primarily for theatre use, greater sophistication in sound reproduction technologies has had a considerable impact on most aspects of opera singing and training in the last quarter of this century, but it is an impact to some extent complemented by the record industry's drive to recycle, usually on full-price CDs, a growing archive of poorly reproduced especially 'live' opera recordings from the 1930s onwards marketed as historical documents which to some degree 'precludes all the finer differentiation'. The 'auratic' tradition of opera is very much a recorded tradition. However, Schoenberg's concerns are further underlined by subsequent developments which he could hardly have foreseen, the coarsening of reproduced sound in a world technologically increasingly visual in emphasis, and opera is a visual as well as aural art:

> We live in a visually oriented world. At a basic level we watch television and movies, much more often than we listen actively to music or even play it ... our ears moreover have become lazy through disuse and through being pampered (or punished) by high decibel concerts or listening to music through earphones ... we no longer ... have the aural sensitivity our parents had ... opera audiences greater emphasis (by being decreasingly musically sophisticated) is on the visual (Smith 1990b: 3).

For Adorno it was the future technological perfection of recording combined with music's particular rhetorical qualities which made its reproduction so dangerous. To the technical dangers of 'flawless functioning' by 'metallically brilliant apparatus' in which 'all the cogwheels mesh so perfectly that not the slightest hole remains open for the meaning of the whole' (Adorno 1991: 39) were added those of musical form: 'The symbolism of language evokes external reality, however far-fetched the subjective imagery it uses to accomplish that end, while what is created by the symbolism of musical staff notation exists only in the world of ideas' (James 1995: 17). As noted in the first chapter, on the page or in concert hall these ideas may be idealised as '... the integrative and relational, (telling) us that there is a world of depth surrounding us, approaching us simultaneously from all directions, totally fluid in its evanescence, a world which is active and continually prodding us for a reaction' (Shepherd 1987: 158), but Adorno argued that the 'reaction' will not be actively inspired or imaginative if the music heard is repetitive, non-stop, background accompaniment to work, home life, shopping in department stores or, he *would* have agreed, 'emitted as part of the air conditioning ... [as] it seeps from other people's headphones' (DeNora 1995: 298). In all instances technologically reproduced musical transmissions bring a false sense of 'leisure' or 'play', make work appear non-work, the purchase of unnecessary goods necessary, both work and goods extensions of 'entertainment'. "Whilst in theory music has ...

> the *potential* to touch and move us in ways that we are ill prepared to understand let alone counter, ... insists on the feeling of emotions, sensations, implicitly demands that individuals respond ... reminds men of the fragile and atrophied nature of their control over the world ..." (Shepherd 1987: 158).

Adorno, unlike Benjamin, asserted that reproduction technologies would deny that potential and leave us passively colonised, exploited, manipulated, dispossessed of our musical imaginations. For example:

> If one seeks to find out who 'likes' a commercial piece, one cannot avoid the suspicion that liking and disliking are inappropriate to the situation, even if the person in question clothes his reactions in those words. The familiarity of the piece is a surrogate for the quality ascribed to it. To like it is almost the same thing as to recognize it (Adorno 1991: 26).

Adorno's dismissive tone underlines his assertion of the ultimate impossibility of 'delight' in familiar 'classical' music except by a few among the 'butterfly collectors. All music is banal, diversionary and fostering cultural goods' (ibid.:30).

Contemplation, distraction, regression and fetishism

Benjamin had distinguished between *contemplation* and *distraction,* the former being the affective state in which the subject receives 'high' or auratic art, art with the aura of tradition, given and unquestioned, and approached as though by means of a secular pilgrimage, awe inspired and from a distance. The subject's reception of the 'arts' ('culture' or Culture), is reduced to imbibing the acknowledged power that tradition holds over them and thus constituted for Benjamin, a 'fascist' experience. 'Aura' thereby is that which is eliminated when a work of art is reproduced: its vaunted uniqueness, its sense of having a mysterious wholeness. Aura appears rooted in absolute and universal standards but is, as opera ritual testifies all too clearly, a social construct:

> Certainly the palatial and plush opera houses that most spring to mind as centres for the live performances of opera belong to the last third of the nineteenth century ... and to the sense that a Western industrial society, with its bourgeois controls, needs the invention of tradition, this being so aptly provided for by the ritualising of opera in the quasi-aristocratic, stylised world of the opera house (Tambling 1987: 13).

For Benjamin, writing before the tense and still contested incorporation of film and photography into 'high' culture, the technological innovations of late nineteenth and twentieth century cinematography and photography provided conditions for the potential subversion, fragmentation and, insofar as it could survive, democratisation of 'auratic' art. The security and dominance of 'culture' would thereby be removed from its original 'high' context, become 'mass', 'realistic' and relatively cheaply reproduced and circulated, its construction fragmented as for example, 'frames' in the shooting of films, encouraging a more active role for subjects 'freed' from passive contemplation for '... the technique of reproduction detaches the reproduced object from the domain of tradition' (Benjamin 1969: 223).

By *distraction* Benjamin didn't mean to imply that subjects become so disoriented they cannot make sense of the fragments, rather their active interpretation of works demonstrated a democratisation of art: '... as a cultural apparatus, cinema embodied the adjustment of reality to the social presence of the masses. It was in other words, the technical realization of a political demand' (Mowitt 1987: 185).

For Adorno, Benjamin was misguided because he attempted 'to "redeem" all too undamaged the problematic of the industrial production of culture' (Adorno 1969: 117). To illustrate, Adorno focused on *fetishism* and *regression*, specifically as applied to music. The base materialism of capitalist rationalisation has, he claimed, progressively reduced the use values of musical communication, 'serious' and 'popular', to their exchange values. Adorno had claimed that the one needs the other for both to exist: 'Light art has been in the shadow of autonomous art. It is the social bad conscience of

76

serious art. The truth which the latter necessarily lacked because of its social premises, gives the other the semblance of legitimacy' (Adorno and Horkheimer 1972: 135 quoted in Burger 1968: 94). Since public opinion has become a commodity, and language the means for promoting that commodity, established linguistic and conceptual conventions cannot be trusted: '... there is no longer any available form of linguistic expression which has not tended towards accommodation to dominant currents of thought; and what a devalued language does not do automatically is proficiently executed by societal mechanisms' (Adorno and Horkheimer 1973: xi-xii). Culture is no longer the repository of reflective comprehension of the present in terms of a redeemed future, all becomes commodified, incorporated and controlled by the 'culture industry' (Adorno 1991: 85-92). 'Abstract' rational principles and practices are progressively subverted into 'commodity listening' by the rationalities of the market. Forms of music that did not have their origins strictly within the contemporary culture industry, such as opera and jazz, also become subject to its logic, are co-opted, standardised, and adapted for distribution on the commercial market. '"High" art is deprived of its seriousness because its effect is programmed; "low" art is put in chains and deprived of the unruly resistance in it when social control was not yet total' (Adorno 1991: 88).

Regression in listening is inevitable, the 'infantilization' of listening subjects who become subjects not in the 'liberated' distracted Benjamin sense, but distracted in the conventional, dislocated, passive sense. Regression in listening does not mean 'a relapse of an individual listener into an earlier phase of his own development', but that under conditions of *fetishism*, individual listeners lose 'the capacity for conscious perception of music ... they listen atomistically and dissociate what they hear ... they are not childlike ... but childish: their primitivism is not that of the undeveloped, but of the forcibly retarded' leading to their ready 'assent for hit songs and debased cultural goods' (ibid.: 40-41). Regressive listening is particularly pronounced in advertising:

> Just as every advertisement consists of the inconspicuous familiar and the unfamiliar conspicuous, so the hit song remains salutarily forgotten in the half-dusk of its familiarity, suddenly to become painfully over-clear through recollection, as if in the beam of the spotlight (ibid.:42).

All popular music betrays 'standardisation':

> into repeated and barely distinguishable melodies (the musical effect of the incursion of exchange value into composition), leads to comparable 'serious' music construction not ... as a function of a rigorously conceived musical structure ... but merely from a reproductive consideration: namely, the recognizability that allows the regressive listener to identify (with) the familiar but necessarily forgettable 'popular' song (Mowitt 1987: 95).

That Adorno's anticipation that these developments would engulf 'high' music, including opera, may be gleaned from his critique of the *leitmotiv* deployed by Wagner:

> Among the functions of the *leitmotiv* can be found, alongside the aesthetic one, a commodity function, rather like that of an advertisement: anticipating the universal practice of mass culture later on, the music is designed to be remembered, it is intended for the forgetful ... Wagner's music reckons with people who listen to it from a great distance, much as impressionist paintings require to be viewed from a greater distance than earlier painting. To listen from a great distance also means to listen less attentively ... The audience of these great works lasting many hours is thought of as unable to concentrate something not unconnected with the fatigue of the citizen in his leisure time. And while he allows himself to drift with the current, the music acting as its own impresario, thunders at him in endless repetitions to hammer its message home (Adorno: 1981: 31-33).

Wagner also drew Adorno's scorn for his concept of *Gesamtkunstwerk* (total work of art), within which the *leitmotiv* was a prominent feature. Referring to ancient Greek drama in which music, poetry and dance had been ideally unified, Wagner asserted that their subsequent development as separate genres had diminished the expressive force of each of them. Only through *Gesamtkunstwerk*, a reintegrated and unified operatic form, could this classical ideal be realised in the modern age, a form unified in all its components: theatre design, stage architecture, scenery, singing, acting and movement, 'democratic' and undistracting auditoria, in which the deferential dictates of realising the works' inherent intelligibility and beauty took precedence over empty rhetoric and ritual, hence the Bayreuth Festival with its custom built theatre for the performance of the 'servant genius' 'masterworks'. In his earlier theoretical essays of 1849-50 these *Gesamtkunstwerk* ambitions formed a distinctly socialist project:

> The new work of art would be brought into being not by a single creative artist but by a fellowship of artists, in response to a communal demand. The artist of the future was thus the *Volk*, and the *Gesamtkunstwerk* the product of necessity or historical inevitability ... (and) mirrored the socialist aim of restoring integrity to a fragmented, divided society (Millington 1992c: 397).

'Generally suspicious of opera' (Martin 1995: 107), Adorno's attack on *Gesamtkunstwerk*, particularly as realised in *Der Ring des Nibelungen*,[5] was generally on the grounds that it was anything but a work of communal fellowship, but rather served bourgeois self-glorification 'through a form of mob intoxication in which Nature and sensation are worshipped abjectly' (Blumenfeld 1991: 526). His assault on the *leitmotiv* as '... non-developmental and aridly repetitive', has to be understood in this context, being dismissively linked to its socioeconomic rather than 'pure' musical origins and purpose, being: 'a redundant set of gestures and signals designed to clarify its mystifications for a *nouveau riche* bourgeoisie', much as Strindberg had criticised the late nineteenth century dramatist as 'lay preacher, peddling the ideas of his time in popular form popular enough for the middle classes, mainstay of theatre audiences, to grasp the gist of the matter without troubling their brains too much' (quoted Brustein 1965: 9).[6] If the *leitmotiv* may be so debased what price Verdi or Puccini arias ripped from their contexts? Adorno did not specifically say, but we can imagine:

> The minuet from Mozart's E Major Symphony, played without the other movements, loses its symphonic cohesion and is turned by its performance into an artisan type genre piece that has more to do with 'Stephanie Gavotte' than with the sort of classicism it is supposed to advertise (Adorno 1991: 36).

Adorno berates 'colouristic arrangements' which make music more palatable. 'The tired businessman can clap arranged classics on the shoulder and fondle the progeny of their muse—giving a pretence of immediacy and intimacy' (ibid.:37).

> ... neither does the prize song from *Meistersinger* sound any more serious when played by a string orchestra alone. In monochrome it objectively loses the articulation which makes it viable in Wagner's score. But ... the listener can just listen to the melody. The practice of arrangement comes from salon music ... which borrows its pretensions from the *niveau* of cultural goods ... (ibid.:38).

Sensuality, superficiality and the cult of the personality

Whether in salon, opera house or factory, deconcentration results from the emphasis on surface style and 'the memorability of disconnected parts' (Adorno 1991: 36), which diverts interest from the whole. Music takes over as background, inhibiting speech, creating docility, through a repetitiveness barely concealed by an emphasis on *'sensuality' 'superficiality'* and the *'cult of the personality'* (1991: 32). 'All "light" and pleasant art has become illusory and mendacious ... The new phase of the musical consciousness of the masses is defined by pleasure in displeasure' (ibid.:29). Adorno's references to the beguiling trap of sensual pleasure in music, made more concrete by suggestive images of tired businessmen 'fondling the progeny of their muse', suggests interesting parallels between music and sexuality (though given their sometimes complex interrelationships 'parallels' is perhaps inapt) as efficient deceptive conduits for immanent power[7] and implies that his mass of listeners are comparable in their subject condition to that more recently described by Foucault in his analysis of sexuality (1981): deluded 'sovereign individuals', colonised by the seemingly harmless, inconsequential and repetitive, but normative power-laden knowledge of music and/or sexuality, acquired as they are constantly driven to 'find' and express their innermost 'unique' 'essential' spiritual/musical/sexual selves. Believing themselves 'free' and self-determining subjects, they become all the more easily subjected to the normative power lodged in the everyday and commonplace knowledge which fetishises 'individuality' and all that is not material as 'natural', 'universal', 'mysterious' existence, personal' experience, taste, opinion, feeling and choice. Critics confirm our delusion:

Of an evening at the opera, if the music was beautifully performed we say, 'It was sublime, a transcendent experience'. These words have become empty figures of speech, but they arise from the deep-seated human need to feel a connection with the Absolute, to transcend the phenomenal world (James 1995: 17-8).

... not recognising that one of the uses to which romantic music especially has been most clearly put 'is the privileging of (such) certain states of mind, certain heightened forms of awareness as natural' (Tambling 1987: 21). Thus as Foucault's subjects become subjects in the abject sense of being 'actively passive', so too Adorno's listeners, contrary to Benjamin's distraction thesis, are 'converted along (their) line of least resistance into the acquiescent purchaser, no longer do the partial moments serve as a critique of the whole' (Adorno 1991: 29). The parallel with contemporary expositions on sexuality continues:

Sexuality ... is not a domain of nature which power tries to subjugate, and which academic disciplines set out to explore. It is merely a name which one may give to a historical artefact—rather a ... hybrid mechanism which links together the stimulation of the body, the intensification of pleasures, incitement to discourse, the formation of knowledges, and reinforcements of controls and resistances to it (Hussain 1981: 178).

Though in a sense 'reproduction detaches the reproduced object from the domain of tradition' (Benjamin 1969: 223), it also 'frees' the reproduced object into an 'incitement to discourse' not least of a commodity kind and contrary to their apparent removal of music from the social, observations such as: 'Music contains in its essence a mystery: everyone agrees that it communicates but how?' (Jones 1995: 17), incite constructionist discourse. Music too is merely a name which may be given to historical artefacts, opera especially 'a hybrid mechanism which also links together the stimulation of the body, the intensification of pleasures, the formation of knowledges, and reinforcements of controls and resistances to it'. Adorno's use of *fetishism* in music is drawn directly from Marx as:

the veneration of the thing made by oneself which, as exchange-value, simultaneously alienates itself from producer to consumer-'human beings'. 'A commodity is therefore a mysterious thing, simply because in it the social character of men's labour appears to them as an objective character stamped upon the product of that labour; because the relation of the producers to the sum-total of their own labour is presented to them as a social relation, existing not between themselves, but between the products of their labour'. This is the real secret of success. It is the mere reflection of what one pays in the market for the product (Adorno 1991: 33).

The consumer is really worshipping the money he or she has paid for the exorbitantly priced ticket for, in Adorno's example, a Toscanini concert, or perhaps currently a Pavarotti appearance. The money spent expresses the exchange-value of 'stars' and affirms the star principle (which) has become totalitarian, especially in the CD age through the disinterment of past 'stars', their surfaces 'cleaned up':

... and this is of course how one attains ecstasy, while listening to the interpretation of a certain ... work by a performer who disappeared decades ago; but ecstasy will reach orgasmic heights when one can refer to a performance of 20 July 1947 or of 30 December 1938. One sees a pseudo culture of documentation taking shape, based on the exquisite hour and the fugitive moment which reminds us at once of the fragility and durability of the performer become immortal, rivalling even the immortality of the masterpiece (Boulez 1985-6).[8]

Regressive, fully documented, listening occurs through the recognisability of the singer as much as the song, and wider still this 'star' principle applies not only to people, but to theatres and works: all have the potential for higher 'star' exchange value. Boulez demonstrates as he remonstrates against one theatrical example:

In the provincial town of Paris the museum is very badly looked after. The Paris Opera is full of dust and crap, to put it plainly. The tourists still go there because you 'have to have seen' the Paris Opera. It's on the itinerary, just like the Follies Bergere or the Invalides ... These operatic tourists make me vomit (Boulez 1986a: 192).

Works too 'to take on the same role', these are not the musicologists chosen 'masterworks' though there may be some overlap, but '... a pantheon of best sellers builds up ... (concert) programmes shrink and the shrinking process not only removes the moderately good, but accepted classics undergo a selection that has nothing to do with quality', but is rather drawn into the 'fatal circle' in which 'the most familiar become the most successful and are thus revived all the more' (Adorno 1991: 32):

> in the first half of this century 'music lovers' found themselves listening at concerts and on the newly marketed long playing records to the same old music over and over again. The best loved Puccini operas and Mahler symphonies were (by the end of World War II) 50 years old ... [9] (Kerman 1985: 22).

Whatever the content of vocal music, the deployment of the voice itself establishes a human resonance which enhances accessibility to listeners and commodification potential ...

> .... the voice, which is the paradigm of sound for people, is fundamental to the particular form of communication, language, which facilitates and gives rise to that which is essentially human in people. The orality of *face-to-face* communication cannot help, in other words, but emphasize the social relatedness of individual and cultural existence (Shepherd 1987: 158).

Consequently of central significance to the implications of his analysis to the specific case of opera, Adorno observed that:

> At its most passionate, musical fetishism takes possession of the public valuation of singing voices. Their sensuous magic is traditional as is the close relation between success and the person endowed with 'material'.[10] But today it is forgotten that it is material. For musical vulgar materialists, it is synonymous to have a voice and to be a singer. In earlier epochs technical virtuosity at least was demanded of singing stars, the castrati and the prima donnas. Today, the material as such, destitute of any function, is celebrated ... Even mechanical control of the instrument is not even expected. To legitimate the fame of its

owner, a voice need only be especially very voluminous or very high ... Voices are holy properties like a national trademark (Adorno 1991: 32).

Adorno's strictures may not be descriptively accurate in every detail, but even so he graphically identifies the inevitability of pressures of commodification and regressive listening on even opera as 'high' cultural artefact. The holiest properties are those wherein the voice is immersed in the commodified 'star' personality. Repetitive listening is the acquisition of regressive knowledge, hence Adorno names the absurdity of 'star' hype as consumers/'fans' 'go into raptures' once informed that they are listening to the sound of a Stradivarius or Amati, which only the ear of a specialist can tell from that of any good modern violin, 'forgetting in the process to listen to the composition and the execution, from which there is still something to be had' (ibid.:33). Similarly '... the rule of the established conductor reminds one of the totalitarian Fuhrer' who provides the norm through his person. Orchestras could play as well without him, and few in an audience would know it was not him conducting if ill, and his replacement unannounced' (ibid.:39). 'Fans' pay for their rapture. In April 1995, £267 was the top seat price for a performance of Verdi's *Un ballo in maschera* at Covent Garden with Pavarotti. Regular seats in stalls and grand circle were £197.50, side stalls £187, a box for four could cost as much as £1068. Even in the amphitheatre the top price was £150, and not until the ninth listed price was there a seat for under £100. These were the highest ever prices in Britain for a non-charity event, and £7 higher at top price than for the 1994 Wembley appearances of Barbra Streisand. When Pavarotti cancelled a performance, though not until he had launched at Harrods his new range of men's aftershave and cologne *Pavarotti* (£21 and £40 respectively), the audience could claim a partial refund of £145.50 per £267 seat, the Pavarotti 'mark up'.[11] What was being sold, critics claimed was 'charisma (which) has no price' as fans confirmed in mystic prose: 'I know of no other singer (with) a voice that could penetrate my being' *(The Independent on Sunday* 14 April 1995: 2). Thus Pavarotti provides 'ersatz pleasure ... all it actually confirms is that ... the diner must be satisfied with the menu' (Adorno and Horkheimer 1973: 139) and the deadening effect of 'good taste' all too literally in this instance as: '... a branch of *haute couture*, a kind of special scents department' (Boulez 1986a: 45).[12]

So sensual pleasure in voices becomes detached from compositions, 'torn away from their function', work and voice fetishised in or as 'stars', 'immersed in their personality', the consumer reifying as objective, the phenomenal success of, in this instance Pavarotti, which s(he) has literally 'made', not by appreciating or even liking the opera or concert, but rather by simply buying the ticket.[13] Thus:

> The specific fetish character of music ... the feelings which go to the exchange value create the appearance of immediacy at the same time as the absence of a relation to the object belies it. It has its basis in the abstract character of exchange value. Every 'psychological' aspect, every ersatz satisfaction, depends on such social substitution (Adorno 1991: 34).

Exchange value, in progressively destroying use value, disguises itself as the object of enjoyment, has an integrative effect by fetishising consumption as an expression of 'individuality' shared with like others, which conceals the immersion of every feeling, response, pleasure, in exchange value rather than the music itself:

> ... in present day society, consumer conduct (consumer freedom geared to the consumer market) moves steadily into the position of simultaneously the cognitive and moral focus of life, integrative bond of society, and the focus of systematic management. In other words it moves into the self-same position which in the past ... was occupied by work in the form of wage labour. This means that in our time individuals are engaged (morally by society, functionally by the social system) first and foremost as consumers rather than producers. (Bauman 1988: 807).

The consumer with the money to buy is intoxicated with the act of buying (opera/concert tickets, CDs, opera videos, opera holidays, books, clothes etc..), acquiring knowledge about 'stars' (singers, conductors, works, theatres), referred to by first or nicknames: Kiri, Placido, Big Lucy, 'The Garden', suggestive of a bought familiarity, even intimacy. S(he), wears designer clothes, 'dresses up' according to norms and rituals of appropriate taste in, stalls, dress circle, amphitheatre or family circle (Adorno 1991: 30). The, by subcultural reputation, 'real' or 'true' (i.e. 'pure') opera lovers in 'the Gods'[14] who eschew the socially ritualised trappings of 'commodity listening' and 'commodity opera' engaged in by those below them, also avidly consume opera and imbibe its knowledge to extents relative to their means. When Adorno pours scorn on such knowledge and those who parade it, and in truth of course they inhabit all levels of 'commodity listening', he examples jazz in ways which are at times ambiguous, but whatever his exact meaning matters little for all forms of music become subjected to the same processes: 'the visitor to philharmonic concerts is confirmed in his status' (ibid.:34). Hence his dismissive: 'the expertise of the jazz enthusiast who legitimises himself by having knowledge about what in any case is inescapable' (ibid.:35), to become an expert or fan 'one must have much free time and little freedom (ibid.:48), applies to all expert enthusiasms in a fetishised world. Adorno thus conjures a material church and priesthood, all is mass produced, with the mere pretence of individuality: 'Before the theological caprices of commodities, the consumers become the temple slaves. Those who sacrifice themselves nowhere else can do so here, and here they are fully betrayed' (p.35).

> Connoisseurs of 'serious' music cannot help but listen in the distracted manner promoted by the consumer discourse of classical programming and by those musicological traditions that seek paradoxically to rescue music from the clutches of exchange by treating it as the gold standard (Mowitt: 1987: 95).

By 1995 one might be forgiven for believing that all Adorno's predictions had come true. In the mass media we are encouraged to address classical music and opera via album charts in which Gregorian Chant vies with selections by TV doctors in the 'stress busting' stakes, and glossily 'sensualised' 'stars' singing not necessarily operatic, songs and arias, constitute a substantial proportion of the listings.

Top 20 Classical Albums—April 1995

1	(1)	*The Choir*, Anthony Way, Decca.
2	(6)	*Canto Gregariano*, Monks Chorus, Silos EMI.
3	(4)	*The Ultimate Collection*, Jussi Bjorling, RCA Victor.
4	(2)	*100% Classics*, Various, Telstar.
5	(5)	*The Piano*, Michael Nyman, Virgin.

6		*The Greatest Pavarotti Album Ever!* Luciano Pavarotti Polygram TV.
7	(3)	*The Three Tenors in Concert 1994*, Carreras/Domingo/Pavarotti, Teldec.
8		*A Feather on the Breath of God*, Kirkby Gothic Voices, Hyperion.
9	(20)	*The Lesley Garrett Album*, Lesley Garrett, Telstar.
10	(13)	*Simple Gifts*, Lesley Garrett, Silva Classics.
11	(8)	*Classic Experience*, Various, EMI Classics.
12	(11)	*Tranquility*, Various, EMI Classics.
13	(7)	*Officium*, Jan Garbarek/Hilliard Ensemble, ECM.
14	(-)	*VE Day: Official British Legion*, Various, EMI Classics.
15	(4)	*The Ultimate Collection*, Mario Lanza, RCA Victor.
16	(9)	*Three Tenors in Concert*, Carreras/Domingo/Pavarotti, Decca.
17	(-)	*Diva*, Lesley Garrett, Silva Classics.
18	(14)	*Shostakovich/Jazz Album*, CGO/Chailly, Decca.
19	(17)	*Bingen/Canticles of Ecstasy*, DHM, Sequentia.
20	(10)	*Dr Hillary Jones Classic Relaxation*, Various, DGG.

(The previous month's placement is given in the second column).
(*The Sunday Times* 14 May 1995: 10: 19).

That the work of Benjamin and Adorno does not stand in necessary opposition is clear when applied to opera as it has developed through the age of advancing technical reproduction. As noted at this chapters beginning, with the closing of the museum's doors especially, reproduction becomes the essence of opera's survival in the opera house. Mechanical reproduction thus locks into what is at core a culture of *re*production and becomes a necessary part of opera's catalogued past and present knowledge, whilst its 'aria' form, equivalent to the cinematographer's 'frame', facilitates its fragmented transfer into technological forms accessible to wider 'mass' audiences, resulting in subverting and democratising *tendencies* at least, of which 'Pavarotti in the Park' and Three Tenor style events are typical examples, especially because despite 'mass' audiences being present, they exist for most as TV, CD and video artefacts.

Simultaneously in the opera house, opera as ritual has reaffirmed its aura through the exclusiveness of seat prices, the awe invoked by the latter inseparable from that inspired by the auratic qualities of opera's hybrid form. Each act of auratic 'contemplation' has a differential box office value, the highest valued commodity currently also being Pavarotti. The particular instance of the Pavarotti phenomenon or commodity is especially revealing as evidence of the incorporation of opera into 'the culture industry', through commodity fetishism and regressive listening. On the one hand he is the means by which, through 'repeated listening' or watching of 'Pavarotti in the Park', or as one of The Three Tenors, opera as 'opera' has become fully incorporated. On the other hand, through the ways in which Pavarotti's box office appeal translates in to high seat prices, he demonstrates how, in the opera house, opera too as an auratic art form is increasingly materialist, also colonised by 'culture industry' principles. Overall 'on both hands' considerable socio-political and economic tensions ensue not least within the context of the dominant opera discourses discussed in the Chapter 1. Whilst mass commercial processes constantly threaten, and to a degree invade, opera as performance art and ritual, the latter responds with new forms of social closure, many versed in terms of 'pure' aesthetic ideals, but mostly effected through the 'exclusivity' consequences of demand and supply mechanisms on seat price structures. The rituals of the conventional international opera house remain sites of auratic *contemplation*, but the cost of attendance places an exchange value on contemplation. 'Arena', video and film presentations undoubtedly broaden public access and appreciation of opera in potentially *distracted* terms, but even in such reproduced forms, secondary spirals of *contemplation* are set in place and marketed. It is marketing consensus that audiences of the latter type neither seek 'first-hand contemplation' nor take their *distraction* into the opera house to rattle the *contemplation* of the 'regular' inmates.15

Active listeners and consumer choice

Given the tone and content of his dread admonitions on the effect of fetishism and regressive listening on a single 'audience passively consuming the mass produced commodities of a "culture industry"' (Scott 1990: 385), it is hardly surprising that Adorno has had a baleful influence on the sociology of music. Disciples such as Burger followed his overreductionist reasoning which left little, if any, space for listeners' 'active' negotiations with what they hear: 'Art as institution' *(Institution Kunst)* includes 'the art producing and art distributing apparatus as well as the dominant ideas about art in a certain epoch ... which essentially determine the reception of works' (Burger 1981: 29). Opponents have accordingly often been stirred into over reaction. Studies of pop, rock and jazz have in the past twenty years claimed that the organisation and marketing of music is irrelevant to its use, all the creative possibilities being realised in its consumption as acts of democratic emancipation (see Hebdige 1979): 'popular culture is produced by the people out of the products of the cultural industries, consuming is an act of production not of reception' (Fiske 1992: 30). Culture, as demonstrated by particularly volatile[16] kinds of music, can have no stable or privileged sites of meaning, aesthetic or commercial.[17] For example, given his emphasis elsewhere on the late modern subject's passivity in the face of the immanent colonising power/knowledge onslaught, it is surprising as well as refreshing to find Foucault asserting active listening and plurality of musical styles, even though in a discussion of rock music which, as with jazz before it, has encouraged many otherwise rigorous intellectuals to relax their critical faculties and as 'cool cats' offer 'vague postscripts about the potential of rock as "people's music"'[18] (Negus 1995: 320):

Not only is rock music (much more than jazz used to be) an integral part of the life of many people ... it is a cultural *initiator:* To like rock, to like a certain kind of rock rather than another, is also a way of life, a manner of reacting; it is a whole set of tastes and attitudes ... it offers a relation which is intense, strong, alive, 'dramatic' (in that rock presents itself as a spectacle, listening to it is an event, it produces itself on stage) with a music that is itself impoverished, but through which the listener affirms himself ... [19] (Foucault 1985-6: 8—my italics).

Whatever the validity of such claims on behalf of the consumption of rock, it should by now be clear that the reception of opera is by contrast imposingly forged out of prior knowledge/power, not only about the artefact, but the ritual and display. It is though a cultural initiator in this sense, forged out of acts of consumption through which listeners affirm themselves.

Challenging such accounts verging on 'a celebration of

consumption' (Negus 1995: 322), other reception-oriented analyses assert that social practices may ill fit or abuse particular musical forms but that their consumption survives in patterned subcultural ways (Neubauer 1993: 6). Audiences may be formally scripted in manner and means of reception but there remains scope for various 'articulations': 'the "work" of drawing together cultural forms and social topics, music, movement and social identity' (Hall quoted in DeNora 1995: 299). Any one musical style or work may inspire diverse 'articulations'. Some, such as national anthems, are so entrenched in institutional practice it is hard to 'articulate' alternatives, perhaps in this case being no more than inspirational to some, oppressive to others (ibid.:308).[20] As noted in Chapter 1, particular musical resonances and textual affinities may inspire nationalist demonstrations as with Verdi's *Risorgimento* works. With technological reproduction 'articulations' are as likely to be commercial, music fragments locked into the products they *market*, *'Nessun dorma'* as World Cup theme, British Airways use (uncredited) of the duet from *Lakmé*[21] or the deployment of Rossini's Overture to *William Tell* as signature tune for the 1950s TV cowboy series which has passed into permanent 'repeat' popular culture: *The Lone Ranger*, though Ivry believes that 'nowadays youngsters would find The Lone Ranger as obscure as the Schiller play' (1989: 46), upon which the opera is based.

'Active' reception based studies have attended to tensions between 'creativity and commerce' (Negus 1995) though their focus again has been on the production and consumption of musical forms more volatile than opera. Chambers (1985) claims pop music of the '50s, '60s and '70s was marked by a 'continual series of fresh proposals', indicative of 'cultural struggles'. Others reject as clichéd this opposition arguing that it is impossible to disentangle the two: 'art categories have been dissolved by commerce, commercial categories have been resolved by art' (Frith and Horne 1987: 180): 'creativity, commentary and commerce have become indistinguishable' (ibid.:69). There is evidence that these strictures don't even apply to popular music let alone 'classical', Stratton (1982a: 1982b) and Cohen (1991) arguing that far from art categories being dissolved by those of commerce and commercial categories resolved by art, advocates on each side talk different languages, hard-edged reflections on market relations sitting uneasily with much mystifying rhetoric about artistic or aesthetic worth, and similar conclusions may be drawn *vis-a-vis* opera as will be evidenced in later chapters, though the ascendancy of the former in the past 15 years underlines the dynamics of these relationships. Now, opera company annual reports make great efforts to translate aesthetic rationales into financial accountability. Opera is too expensive to be commercial: subsidies, private gifts and/or sponsorship are essential to complement loss making box office revenues, but the source of income imposes differential constraints on creativity and pressures towards commercialism. Box office income reflects the overall preference for familiar works performed 'safely' by stars. Gifts and sponsorship bring publicity for donors who invariably wish to be associated with productions that will be 'popular' and frequently revived and again 'popular' largely means limited, familiar and conservative in repertoire and production style terms. Subsidies need not bring such controls, potentially enabling 'creative' broadening of the repertoire, the presentation of rare or commissioned new works for 'pure' or celebratory political rather than commercial reasons, but they also enhance state or city control of theatres and their artistic policies. In Britain where opera customarily has élitist connotations, pressure is on 'the people's' money being used to make it more accessible and popular if to be spent on opera at all, and again this can be done only through a re-emphasis on what is already a small core of repeatedly revived works. As these comments suggest, the 'creativity versus commercialism' continuum is overladen with the implicit and explicit assumptions about opera as 'high art' or 'low entertainment' discussed earlier.[22]

It is clear that market strategies to exploit and expand demand for opera as 'high' or 'mass' culture have made commercial inroads, but it is equally clear that tendencies towards fragmentation, fetishism and regression have been realised very much more effectively outside the opera house, in the various worlds of 'opera'. In opera itself they appear to be offset by dynamic reformulations of auratic closure in commodity form. In other words, opera's incorporation into the 'culture industry' has fetishised hierarchies of differential taste rather than obliterated distinctions into mass forms. Nor is this fetishisation imposed on passive populations, the latter's discursive knowledge of opera may be relatively extensive but it is also diverse and at times overtly contradictory (radical productions, new works, surtitles, seat costs, 'stars') so that associated actions are truly social, choices have to be made and decisions rationalised.

Classically, sociology is 'a science which attempts the interpretive understanding of social action in order thereby to arrive at a causal explanation of its cause and effects' (Weber 1947: 110). By 'action' is meant all human behaviour to which the actor attaches subjective meanings, action being social when 'by virtue of the subjective meanings attached to it by the acting individual (or individuals) it takes account of the behaviour of others and is thereby oriented in its course' (ibid.:110). Accordingly, the basic unit of sociological analysis is actor orientation, the anticipation of the reciprocal significance of action, which bestows upon them a social quality. Weber employed the term 'social relationship' to denote:

> the behaviour of a plurality of actors in so far as, in its meaningful content, the action of each takes account of that of others and is oriented in these terms.., Thus, as a defining criterion, it is essential that there should be at least a minimum of mutual orientation of the action of each to that of the others. Its content may be of the most varied nature: conflict, hostility, sexual attraction, friendship, loyalty or economic exchange[23] (Weber 1947: 118).

Opera then is not simply dramatised music with text, it is equal to all 'subjective meanings attached to it' and the social action which ensues. 'Active' listening to opera involves all such meanings. In Weberian accounts, as in Marxist, forged under circumstances of First World production-based economies, class was established as the prime determinant of opportunities for the acquisition of goods and income, under the conditions of the commodity and labour markets, but these opportunities are increasingly qualified in consumption led economies, by status identities and affiliations which reflect hierarchies of moral, social and material prestige and honour not inevitably consistent with those of class. Status 'communities' are constructed and expressed through the market, for 'status groups are stratified according to the principles of their consumption of goods as represented by special styles of life' (Weber 1947: 182). This stratification of status groups and their 'community' tastes implicates patterns of cultural consumption associated with material 'styles of life'. If 'Reality as the consumer experiences it is the pursuit of pleasure' as 'on display ... (we) move through the field of commodities' (Featherstone 1983: 19, 29), 'in search of personal and private satisfactions above all else' (Hobsbawm 1981: 2) the latter are in part expressed through musical tastes as both concrete and symbolic manifestations of the 'special styles of life' associated with status group membership. Opera is an object of consumption which draws together audiences in the loosest association of common interest rather than community. However, the various interrelated social meanings attached to opera by its audiences are indicative of wider 'styles of life' and distinctive tastes. If 'to like rock, to like a certain kind of rock rather than another, is ... a way of life' (Foucault 1985-6: 8), the same is true of opera despite, indeed because, of it's more formal trappings. The meaning of opera is not in itself but in the social uses to which it is variously put. Bourdieu illustrates by means of a telling simile:

> ... the apparent consistency of ... products conceals the diversity of (their) social uses ... What is there to be said about the collection of products brought together by the apparently neutral category 'cereals'—bread, rusks, rice, pasta, flour—and especially the class variations in the consumption of these products, when one knows that 'rice' alone includes 'rice pudding' and *riz au gras,* or rice cooked in broth (which tend to be 'working class') and 'curried rice' (more 'bourgeois' or precisely 'intellectual'), not to mention 'brown rice' (which suggests a whole lifestyle)? It is rarely possible to deduce the social use from the thing itself. Except for products specially designed for a particular use ... or tied to a class, by tradition ... or price, ... most products only derive their social value from the social use that is made of them ... Hence it is necessary to attend to *ways* of photographing and *ways* of cooking (Bourdieu 1984: 21).

Opera as status symbol and qualification

Opera, though reputationally 'tied to a class', also derives its social value from the uses to which it is put, its audiences containing various clusters of taste determined by the meanings given.[24] As any theatre audience is a loose association or collectivity one would not normally expect to find clearly distinguishable status groups in attendance but, as will become clear, large sections of opera audiences are through various informal and formal means (networks of 'regulars': ticket sales through subscription to regular series of performances, the operations of supportive clubs such as The Friends of Covent Garden, 'priority' booking for various cliques in all parts of the house etc.) more coherently organised than others, indeed so much so in certain theatres or parts of them, that the first, occasional or tourist visitor can feel as excluded by the apparent strength of exclusive informal subcultural ties as by the formal rules of conduct. These audiences attribute numerous meanings to opera which may be summarily identified as five which are not mutually exclusive: opera as ritual of high social value, opera as business, opera as 'high' art to be received auratically, opera as serious obsession and opera as entertainment. Others could be added such as 'opera as something to be got through', but these five at core predominate. Negotiations with these meanings occur in all parts of the house, whether they spill over between tiers etc., depends on spatial as well as social considerations. In Britain balcony and amphitheatre audiences are in the conventional theatrical space segregated from lower levels with separate entrances off side streets rather than through main foyers. Out of their negotiations opera audiences manifest various loose status groups. '*Status groups* are normally communities ... often of an amorphous kind' (Weber 1967: 186). For Weber a 'status situation' is one in which judgements and behavioural consequences depend upon positive or negative estimations of social *honour*, connected with any quality ascribed to or shared by a plurality, most obviously the class situation of the plurality. (ibid.:156-7).

Opera audiences are physically ranked in inverse proportion to their class distinctions, in inverse proportion to the prices paid for their seats: '... only the families coming under approximately the same tax class dance with one another' (ibid.:187), or sit next to each other at the opera. Opera as 'ritual of high social value' reflects opera's symbolic representation of Establishment interests: 'The social and economic order may not be identical, but possession of power of the latter kind of necessity requires binding expression through activities and expressions of the former' (ibid.:180) and emphatically reasserts status distinction within the theatre: 'In content, status honor is normally expressed by the fact that above all else a specific style of life can be expected from all those who wish to belong to the circle' (ibid.). Opera is the prime example of formal 'cultural performance' which also includes informal rituals such as prayers, readings and recitations, ceremonies and festivals: '... those things normally classified under religion and ritual rather than with the cultural and artistic, which encapsulate a culture and which may be repeatedly demonstrated and exhibited to visitors and ourselves' (Singer 1972). Opera as 'cultural performance' refers to its '... political and civil functions ... (which) once established as an institution that includes the possibility of impresarial initiative and subvention, functions as an *instrumentum regni*, a public demonstration and representation of authority' (Bianconi and Walker 1984: 259-60) demonstrated by restrictions on 'social intercourse' (Weber 1967: 187), and public display of the irrelevance of cost.

> From the contrariety between the status order and the purely economic order it follows that in most instances the notion of honor peculiar to status absolutely abhors that which is essential to the market: higgling. Honor abhors higgling among peers and occasionally it taboos higgling for the members of the status group in general. Therefore, everywhere some status groups, and usually the most influential, consider almost any kind of overt participation in economic acquisition as absolutely stigmatizing (ibid.:193).

Linked to this justification for opera is that of 'opera as business'. In an opera house's lower reaches are those who have direct financial involvement, corporate or fund-raising, with the company and possibly a presence or influence on the board and various committees:

> status honour ... always rests upon distance and exclusiveness, we find all sorts of material monopolies. Such honorific preferences may consist of the privilege of wearing special costumes, of eating special dishes taboo to others ... the right to pursue certain non-professional dilettante artistic practices, e.g. to play certain musical instruments ... With an increased inclosure of the status group, the conventional preferential opportunities for special employment grow into a legal monopoly of special offices for the members. Certain goods become objects for monopolization by status groups (ibid.:191).

This latter status group is riven with tensions between opera as traditional upper-class symbol and communal ritual and opera as commodity bought in order to ease entry into this exclusive core:

> If mere economic acquisition and naked economic power still bearing the stigma of its extra-status origin could bestow upon anyone who has won it the same honor as those who are interested in status by virtue of style of life claim for themselves, the status order would be threatened to the root ... all groups having interests in the status order react with special sharpness precisely against the pretensions of purely economic acquisition. In most cases they react the more vigorously the more they feel themselves threatened ... the 'parvenu' is never accepted, personally and without reservation, by the privileged status groups, no matter how completely his style of life has been adjusted to theirs (ibid.:192).

In the opera house two distinct patterns of status group formation, membership qualifications with conditions of closure at their margins may be discerned. The privileged status group in terms of wealth, class and political power and 'community' interests not only purchase the most expensive and best seats, they have in many theatres 'family' or 'corporate' boxes or seats, or priority seating set aside as reward for making the most generous (regular!) gifts. However negotiations with opera as 'high art' and 'serious obsession' provide the basis for an alternative form of status honour based on the demonstrated 'opera knowledge' of the 'true', 'real', 'regular' 'fan' which may cut across class lines: '... all sorts of circles set ... themselves apart by means of ... characteristics and badges ...' (ibid.:188), and 'community' practice. Opera house booking arrangements are generally labyrinthine in their complexity and variations enabling 'regulars' in all parts of the house, competing with the more amorphous 'general' public, to informally control seat purchase and distribution. The '... hindrance of the free development of the market occurs first for those goods which status groups directly withhold from free exchange by monopolization. This monopolization may be effected either legally or conventionally' (ibid.:192-3). Throughout the opera world there is the assumption that opera knowledge is distributed in inverse proportion to wealth, that the second of these two status group formations is physically as well as materially to be found in the upper reaches and in standing room where they make their presence and status as 'knowledgeable' felt through loud bar chat, cheers, boos, catcalls and flung flowers, fruit and vegetables. The manners of opera house audiences are also assumed to deteriorate with altitude but as Glyndebourne confirmed in 1994 with its Deborah Warner production of *Don Giovanni*, 'fat cats can boo too!' (Hillmore 1944).

Opera as cultural capital and taste

In addition to these two 'status communities' within the opera house, further reflections upon opera audiences may be gleaned from more general analyses of the consumption of specialist commodities of high prestige and cultural capital (Bourdieu 1984). Bourdieu's emphasis is on the interplay between forms of capital as sets 'of actually usable resources and power' (1984: 114; 1990: 117-18), taste being the result of the interplay between cultural and economic capitals. Cultural capital consists of knowledge and skills, including those certificated, which define the social value of activities, interests and the consumption of commodities within patterned hierarchies as life-styles. Economic capital is analysed in more or less classical Marxist terms of exploitation through dynamic relationships to the means of production; by extension the use of the composite phrase 'cultural capital' indicates the dynamic exploitative use and consequences of skills, qualities and qualifications, possessed. Cultural capital is accumulated over time, may be stored (in the 'habitus'), but is generally transmitted to others through socialisation, advertising and other forms of media by parents, teachers, 'experts', 'confessors' and instructors. People invest cultural capital to realise economic capital and vice versa, but only through the use of cultural capital to acquire organisational or economic power may others be directly exploited by it. It exists, however, to consistently demarcate the boundaries between hierarchies of social groups. Having economic capital enables the acquisition of cultural capital, as corporate sponsorship of the arts demonstrates, but cultural capital does not generally lead to the acquisition of economic capital; rather it is the means by which social groups define themselves and demarcate boundaries of social closure between themselves and identifiable others immediately above and below.

Studies of opera consumption as a form of cultural capital of distinction are based on attendance at performances where ritual elements are paramount, but the auratic qualities of opera appear to be resiliently attached to all things operatic including 'opera' in reproduced fragmented aria form, the acquisition of which for entertainment by popular audiences illustrates the complexities of the commodification process which 'trades-in' traditional auratic qualities into capital value. Benjamin claimed that 'It is significant that the existence of the work of art with reference to its aura is never entirely separated from its ritual function' (Benjamin 1969: 225) but, in an age with ever more efficient means of technological reproduction opera serves ritual functions additional to those of performance attendance. In their original form the 'aura' of the great works of Wagner and Verdi as the zenith of operatic creativity was inextricably tied to the palatial and plush theatres built to house them and the audiences to whom they spoke: 'a Western industrial society, with ... bourgeois controls, needs the invention of tradition' (Hobsbawm and Ranger 1983)' ... aptly provided for by the ritualising of opera in the quasi-aristocratic, stylised world of the opera house' (Tambling 1987: 13). But attendance at a Pavarotti concert or playing opera or compilation CDs in the home or car is as ritualised, their content inseparable from their cultural location and source as auratic works which convey degrees of culture power. Indeed, as international 'star' mezzo soprano Marilyn Horne argues, there is now a symbiotic relationship between opera and 'opera' in that the former is contextualised by mass communication in crucial ways:

> ... everything is done on such a scale that we can know about it immediately. There's no mystery left behind anything. Then there's that big tube to think about. What are the big productions on Broadway now? They're huge, spectacular things to see *visually* ... we live in a much more visual age in opera ... we have a few superstars who still pack a few pounds, but in a visual age (Horne 1990: 12; see Appendix F).

Varieties of reproduction suggest degrees of consumed 'aura' and displayed cultural capital the least distinguished perhaps being the ownership and playing of *The Greatest Pavarotti Album Ever*, but 'reproduction' may also be in the form of videoed, filmed, or audio recorded stagings, either studio or stage-based. Films and videos of opera house performances cannot but reaffirm opera's auratic qualities, excluding by implication the many viewers who have not experienced the ritual of attendance (Tambling 1987: 16), but one doubts the validity of Tambling's further claim that film is thereby the most powerful democratic agent, given that opera films with other 'art' films have developed their own performance rituals and 'auratic' pretensions. In all these ways Bourdieu's deployment of economic with cultural capital suggests the varieties of ways in which forms of the two interrelate with regard to any one particular composite of knowledge and associated activities. It is within these qualifying limitations that research evidence on opera as patterns of consumption providing status and lifestyle distinctions have to be judged. Bourdieu's French research-based arguments cannot be imported wholesale into the British context, where occupational and cultural landscapes are different, and, anyway, he says little specifically about opera. However, using the TGI (Target Research Index) of the British Market Research Bureau (BMRB) to identify key consumption patterns, opera's locus in British cultural standards may be quite accurately identified. There are inevitably problems with the BMRB Index of 'social class categories' which, like all other social class schemata to some degree, can only loosely approximate to coherent class/status class groupings, not least the incorporation of Britain's ruling class which, as Chapter 3 will demonstrate, so dominates Britain's opera industry empirically and symbolically into the 'upper middle class'. Even so broad opera consumption patterns or markets emerge. The scheme is as follows:

A   Upper middle class: higher managerial, administrative or professional.
B   Middle class: intermediate managerial, administrative or professional.
C1   Lower middle class: supervisors or clerical and junior managerial, administrative and professional.
C2   Skilled working class: semi-skilled manual workers.
D   Working class: semi and unskilled manual workers.
E   Those at lowest level of subsistence: state pensioners and widows, casual and lower-grade workers.

Selected items of consumption are hierarchically indexed for each population characteristic (age, level of education as well as 'social class').[25] Average participation is indexed at 100, scores above 100 indicate degree of above-average participation, those below 100 the opposite. Savage *et al.* (1993) exclude the 80 to 120 middle-ground rankings in order to more clearly identify extremes of taste. AB groups as a whole are the high spenders, who may spend on opera and comparable theatrical activities such as drama, ballet, classical concerts and contemporary dance but may not. C1s include those relatively high in certain forms of cultural capital including a knowledge of, and interest in, these activities, but who perhaps cannot afford to consume them as regularly or in the style which they might prefer. 'Middle-class' economic and cultural capital ownership did not correlate to these three class categories, however, for Savage *et al.* (1993) found three distinct patterns or clusters cutting across ABC1 boundaries: one associated with industrialists and senior managers, with high economic capital but less cultural capital: a second with those who in the 1980s were labelled 'yuppies' but termed the 'new petit bourgeoisie' by Bourdieu and Savage *et al.* in the then fast-growing service sector employments such as marketing, advertising, public relations, the media and the helping professions, and who are not only overall well endowed with cultural capital but also tend to be standard-bearers and taste setters for other groups including the first. Thirdly, there is a middle class professional group, typically high in cultural capital but relatively low in economic terms and comprising teachers, artistic producers and intellectuals (see Honneth 1986).

Whilst opera going is generally indicative of high cultural capital, it is not so across all three groups. Savage *et al.* (1993: 112) describe opera as representative of 'older' and 'high' forms of culture—auratic culture which the middle classes have long deferentially shared with the upper classes, including the landed aristocracy (Samuel 1983a). By income band, opera features at just under 200 (equal with ballet) for those earning £40,000 a year or more, after the consumption of French restaurant evening meals (at 419), 'by some margin the most élitist cultural practice in Britain' (ibid. p.108), champagne drinking (371), membership of tennis clubs (309), skiing holidays, consumption of mineral waters, membership of health clubs and the like, but as the highest theatre/concert-based 'live' activity. For lower income groups opera does not feature, although more generally theatre-based activities remain more pronounced for them, outside London at least. By occupational group, opera is by far the most important cultural activity for those whom Bourdieu labelled 'intellectuals'—teachers, medical workers, those employed in welfare services—at just under 250, compared with theatre attendance (under 150) and classical concerts (40). This occupational group attends opera, plays, ballet and concerts on a scale much greater than for ABs as a whole. By contrast opera features as very low (approximately 60) for managers and is not featured as exceptional for the 'new petit bourgeoisie'. For ABs as a whole, opera (with bridge playing) is the most important cultural activity (approximately 275), higher than ballet (245), classical music concerts (230) and visits to theatres and art galleries (180). For C1s opera is less popular than contemporary dance, classical concerts and ballet.

Opera's popularity increases the higher the age of education completion, being one of the highest for those completing at 24 years and over, sinking but still above 100 for those completing at 21-23, but disappearing from view for those completing education at a younger age.[26] These individual findings on the consumption of opera as commodity of rare but differential taste should not be divorced from the distribution of other listed items but seen with them as an empirical verification of distinct lifestyle patterns marked by consumption of other items such as foreign holidays, films, whisky, champagne and expensive food as advertising in opera programmes confirms. The 1993 Annual Report of The Royal Opera House Covent Garden thanked 43 companies for advertising through ROH promotional materials, including: art galleries (André Emmerich, New York; Phillips Fine Art Auctioneers and Valuers); cars (Ford Motor Company; BMW [GB Ltd]; Rolls Royce); hotels (Venice Simplon Orient-Express Hotels; The Regent-London); jewellers (De Beers; Patek Philippe, Geneva; The Burlington Jewellers); alcohol (Macdonald and Muir Ltd.; Glenmorangie; Campari [GB Ltd]); champagne (Taittinger); newspapers (*The Financial Times*; *The Times*); hi-fi equipment (Meridian Audio Ltd.; Bang and Olufsen; Pioneer High Fidelity Ltd.) and recording companies (Sony Classical; Polygram Classics; Warner Classics).

Remembering Bourdieu's strictures concerning the varied uses to which rice may be put, Savage *et al.* (1993) suggest that opera's consumption varies according to the patterned lifestyle groupings identified. For example, among 'intellectuals' opera consumption will be more likely to be stimulated by traditional 'high' precepts regarding its content rather than by ritualised social meanings or importance. Among managers (stereotypically the corporate guest,

Adorno's tired businessmen 'fondling the progeny of their muse'), have little 'natural' interest in opera. The new petit bourgeoisie 'yuppie' population may very well flirt with opera but in ways some commentators call 'pluralist, depthless and self-mocking' (Lash and Urry 1987), others 'vulgar'. This 'class', including the recording industry technicians and commercial managers referred to in studies of the popular music industry (Stratton 1982a; 1982b; Cohen 1991; Frith and Horne 1987), has a central role in defining 'high' and 'low' cultural forms, establishing new kinds of culture, determining dominant trends and breaking down distinctions between 'high' and 'low'. They are far less 'awestruck' with certain lifestyle and cultural forms than previous generations. They can easily engage in ballet, opera, rock music and 'Californian sports', treating none of these as *the* culture, each being an activity to be sampled in an apparently depthless, pastiche manner (Pfeil: 1988: Bagguley *et al.*: 1990). Lash (1985: 251) sees these occupational groups as working on symbols rather than things: 'they produce symbols which help realise the value of other symbols'. This results:

> ... from the steady penetration of commerce and the commodity form into the realm of art and culture. Previously well established cultural traditions are thus increasingly treated in a 'pastiche' way. Previously 'high' or 'unique' culture are mass-produced and treated as just one form of culture along with others. The distinction between 'high and low' culture ('taste' and 'tack') is steadily obliterated as forms of art and culture previously surrounded by a distinct aura stemming from their rarity become just another mass-produced commodity (Savage *et al.* 1993: 128).

Savage *et al.* (1993) identify this group as one which indulges in a wide range of disparate consumption practices. As a result, practices considered to have an auratic quality by previous generations become treated in a non-auratic way by the new (young and predominantly male) private sector, professional middle class. Opera, classical music, skiing holidays, foreign travel are all cases in point ... in the process the hackles of the old and traditionalist will be raised and 'high' art qualities defended, emphasising 'high' art principles set against the subversive and 'lower' principles of the new.

In Britain at least, the 'yuppie' 1980s were portrayed as boom years for opera and 'opera'—for the former as 'popular' art form, losing its traditional élitist connotations and attracting new audiences for 'opera' as mass event and commercial money-spinner. Now, in the mid-recession 1990s, evidence for the former portrayal appears less than convincing, yet so confidently was the 'boom/popular' trend predicted, opera's élitist reputation and practice has come under renewed and widely publicised scrutiny. The traditional élitist importance of opera as ritual and pastime appear unshaken behind the facade in which much noise is made about making this art form more accessible. Whilst mass concerts by celebrity 'stars' suggest advancing mass popularity and interest in 'opera', in the opera house such trends seem to have been offset by new forms of social and economic closure.

> Whilst opera is a 'broad church' it still belongs to the indispensably top social class. *The Observer* runs weekly profiles in the main newspaper part, not the social chat sections, dealing with the great and the good, and the last two I saw before writing this, of 16 March 1986 and 23 March, on Lord King and Jacques Chirac, both found it necessary to refer to their subjects in relation to their nights at the opera. Neither figure is to be instantly identified with operatic music in the public mind, of course, but they do go. So liking opera (not necessarily going to it regularly) is like voting for the Conservative Party: it demonstrates to yourself that you are able to buy into that way of life, that you wouldn't want to think of yourself as beyond it (Tambling 1987: 5).

Notes

1. 'Pirated' recordings are those illegally made either by audience members or from radio broadcasts, those of the former being of particularly unreliable quality, distanced singing, loud prompters, and even louder audience coughs, intakes of breath, seat creaks, comments and cheers. What they provide is the 'atmosphere' of the 'live' event, warts and all. They also provide a detailed record of particular performers and productions and, in some instances, of 'star' singers with few studio commercial recordings to their credit. Two in particular in the post-war period vie for the dubious title 'Pirate Queen': Leyla Gencer and Magda Olivero (referred to in the previous chapter). The former made studio recitals for the Italian company Cetra but not one complete opera studio recording. Her repertoire was very large but covered much of the *bel canto* school opened up by Maria Callas and Verdi roles associated with the latter's supposed (marketed) arch-rival, Renata Tebaldi during the 1950s. Decca (Tebaldi) and EMI (Callas) competed with each other during this period almost exclusively through these two 'divas', thus severely restricting the recording opportunities of others. Olivero's speciality was *verismo*, but she made just two complete studio recordings (30 years apart) of Liu in *Turandot* (Cetra) and *Fedora* (Decca) in place of an indisposed Tebaldi. Both Gencer and Olivero now have massive 'pirate' CD catalogues which largely confirm their reputations. In the case of Olivero the catalogue includes several versions of her major roles: *Manon Lescaut, Fedora, Adriana Lecouvreur* and Minnie in *La fanciulla del West.*
2. *Pitch* means 'exact height or depth of musical sound' according to the number of vibrations necessary to produce it. Standard A = 440 vibrations to the second, with all the other notes standing in relation to it' (Knapp 1984: 361). But over time and between countries there are variations in the pitch standard employed.
3. William Christie of Les Arts Florrisants in the booklet accompanying their 1995 recording on Erato (4509-96558-2) of *Médée* by Marc-Antoine Charpentier.
4. Amplification has hovered on the fringes of operatic discourses for at least a decade and possibly longer. One Japanese *Opera* correspondent (June 1988: 667) referred to developments in this

field and indeed their secret/insider use, and rumoured built-in amplification in certain European theatres

> ... the notion of amplified singing is totally incompatible with the accepted values of opera as an art form and makes a mockery of the conscientious efforts which I trust continue in the cause of the 'grand tradition'. It might be felt that the matter should be laughed off as so obviously ludicrous, but my source, an editorial member [of *Asahi Shinbun*], spoke so knowledgeably that I think a serious probing is in order. Surely what is at issue, if sustainable, is so momentous as to make those arguments over surtitles pale into insignificance.

Singers such as Marilyn Horne refer somewhat ambiguously to the practice, and rumours have circulated around sound amplification at the Met, New York. Several critics took the ENO to task for its 'unedifying' 'coarse amplification 'of Weill's *The Rise and Fall of the City of Mahagonny* in 1995 (Milnes in *The Times* 8 June and Porter *The Sunday Times* 11 June).

5. 'Of all the monuments of the century past, the *Ring*—revolutionary in its musical techniques and dramaturgic goals, all-embracing in scope and theme, and more than twenty-five years in the making—is at once the largest and most impressive in sheer scale' (Bowie 1989: 93).

6. An alternative, and more conventional view of *leitmotiv* construction is provided by Blumenfeld: 'its brilliant (and almost fortuitously apt) growth from the simple associative and expository in *Das Rheingold* to the status of ongoing subtextual enrichment in dramatically more complex phases of the cycle, particularly in the final acts of *Siegfried* and *Gotterdammerung*' (Blumenfeld 1984: 527). In short, as Blumenfeld demonstrates, Adorno neither adequately addresses the musical complexity of *leitmotiv* construction nor more relevantly, given the particularities of the operatic form, does he acknowledge the subtle, complex interrelationship between textual and musical discourses in these works and the later *Parsifal* and *Tristan und Isolde*. Adorno's emphasis was on the socioeconomic conditions of 'listening' or receiving' musical discourses, and as these criticisms of his lack of appreciation of Wagner's music dramas indicate, he was not inclined to treat opera's conjunction of text

and music by criteria other than musical ones.

7. Bourdieu has stated that with music and taste: '... the sociologist finds himself [sic] in the, area par excellence of the denial of the social' (Bourdieu 1984: 11). Similar arguments have been made about sexuality also mystified through a rhetoric of 'nature' 'emotion' 'feeling' 'drives' and so on.

8. '[T]he crucial thing ... now listeners could and did obtain great masses of music of all kinds and were able to browse through it on recordings, in something like the way they were used to browsing through literature of all kinds in books.' (Kerman 1985: 25). The Music Discount Centre sends out its *Classical Express*, with mini-reviews as well as lists including bargain CDs, once a month and the opera proportion is very high. September 1993 (Issue No. 47) was headed by Cecilia Bartoli 'Decca's rising star'. In this catalogue special adverts dealt with Decca's *Grandi Voce* series (Pavarotti, Kiri Te Kanawa, Leontyne Price, Giuseppe di Stefano, Joan Sutherland, Elena Souliotis, Giulietta Simionato, Mario del Monaco, Tebaldi and Dietrich Fischer-Dieskau), an 'EMI Opera Festival at MDC' and Teldec's 'Wagner-Bayreuth-Barenboim' first two issues in its new *Ring* recording. Buyers will probably not buy new studio recordings by mainstream companies via this catalogue, although they are reviewed and advertised, but rather the esoteric, 'old', 'pirated', legal but rare historical recordings which appear to be a speciality—'These recordings derive from acetate discs. Surface noise will be encountered. We advertise purchase be made only by those who are aware of the historical significance of these recordings' is a familiar warning—or imports of usually esoteric works. If Eklipse's release of a 'concert version of *Elektra* fulfilled the account given in the notes, it ought to carry a health warning. "Rose Pauly's breathtaking interpretation literally electrified her audience" we are told. I survived, but hers is an astonishing feat, especially with the acetate crackle and variable sound.' Another set of reviews is headed 'Bayreuth's Amazing Archives', yet others 'Wagner meets Marx', 'Figaro without laughs', 'Rossini restored', 'Bounteous Lehmann', 'Radiant Flagstad' and so on. So 'stars' are still 'stars' even though they are no longer singing or even alive.

9. ... it is a tribute to the Serious (sic) musician's skills, diligence and patience, that he is not a duller fellow than he (sic) is,

especially the orchestra musician, playing more or less the same notes in more or less the same way under the daily supervision of a variety of opinionated conductors, year in year out (Pleasants 1955: quoted in Small 1979: 14).

10. Steane (1995: 28), describes generally his interest in voices and singing but specifically in the voice and singing of tenor Franco Corelli, as a 'craving, a sensuality ... a thirst ... I once discussed it with a doctor. "Ah yes", he said, "it's a well known complaint. Several of my patients have it. In the profession we know it as corellidipsia".'

11. The subsidy at £8.8 million is perceived by some as a state subsidy of Pavarotti rather than of the Royal Opera House. 'It is denying the opportunity to far too many young people. It is becoming far too élitist' proclaimed Jeremy Eckstein, Arts Researcher for the Policy Studies Institute (*The Independent* 14 April 1995: 2). Covent Garden's response through Keith Cooper, Head of ROH Corporate Affairs, was: 'We are a business and this is the commercial end of our operation. We set a price we believe people will pay and they do. This helps to subsidise our ability to put on special performances of less familiar works.' As for Pavarotti's performance:

> A lot of rot has been written about Pavarotti's gifts as an actor. True after more than 35 years of experience, he has gathered a repertoire of facial expressions, including a winning, charm-the-pants-off-the-hardest-critic smile, a this-is-going-to-end-in-tragedy scowl, and after an Act III aria plagued by a frog-in-the-throat, a disarming, apologetic appeal to a sympathetic audience ... To the astonishment of even Pavarotti's uncritical admirers, he walked off stage during the love duet ... leaving his Amelia to express her love into thin air. Pavarotti's acting is essentially a solo communion with his audience, and the role he plays, that of the big, generous hearted tenor, is interchangeable ... He plays himself, the world's most popular tenor (Canning *The Sunday Times* 23 April 1995: 10, 16).

12. Boulez's prime concern was the fetishised conservatism of this routinised music—its 'meagre litany which drones on from century to century' (1986a: 33) and which resists innovation on the following grounds: (i) either too much science (no sensibility)

or too much art (no heart); (ii) the singular desire to be original, which is therefore artificial and exaggerated ('however much he exaggerates, an individual reflects the age in which he lives' ibid.: 34); (iii) loss of contact with the public owing to excessive individualism; (iv) refusal to accept history and historical perspective (which could be broadened into general cultural norms and values); and (v) lack of respect for natural order. For Boulez 'The only passion shown by the mediocre is their determination to defend ruins' (ibid.: 39), ruins ensconced in a false natural order: 'If this famous "natural order" really existed, it would be found in every civilization ... and this is far from the case. Each civilization has elaborated its own musical theories' (ibid.: 41).

13. To be sure exchange-value exerts its power in a special way in the realm of cultural goods. For in the world of commodities this realm appears to be exempted from the power of exchange, to be in an immediate relationship with the goods, and it is this appearance in turn which alone gives cultural goods their exchange value. But they nevertheless fall completely into the world of commodities, are produced for the market, and are aimed at the market. The appearance of immediacy is as strong as the compulsion of exchange value is inexorable ... (Adorno 1991: 33).

14. The cheap(er) seats at the 'top' or roof of the house.

15. In so arguing, Adorno's attack on the class basis of bourgeois aesthetics compromised itself with the raising of an alternative aesthetic marked by the similar 'abstract' qualities and commodity potential of high taste. Wishart demonstrates as much through reference to the following statement by Adorno:

> ... no *authentic* work of art and no *true* philosophy, according to their very meaning, has ever exhausted itself in itself alone, in its being—in itself. They have always stood in relation to the actual life-process of society from which they distinguished themselves (Adorno 1967: 23 quoted in Wishart 1977b: 234-5: my italics).

As Wishart indicates, the use of *authentic* and *true* here demonstrates 'an evaluative position for Adorno as critic which transcends the social position, a position which Adorno himself is in the process of demolishing' (ibid.: 235). In other words, the relationship between society and music is still held at arms length (Adorno, 1978c: 130). Whilst acknowledging that music is socially determined, or 'mirrors' society (Attali 1985), Adorno's resistance and solution to commodification retained a commitment to relative autonomy, which may be explained by, or explains, the relatively scant attention paid by him to opera, for only an 'inhuman concentration on matters of style and technique could express the full truth of this (alienated) predicament' (Norris 1989: 17).

Within the context of 'high' romantic early twentieth-century bourgeois culture, Schoenbergian dodecaphonic music understandably appeared 'true' in this sense—'pure' and uncorrupted by the fetishism affecting all other musical forms, including other radical challenges to the bourgeois institution. Adorno's proposed alternative to the commodifying regressive vortex he described doubly demonstrated the logic of his paradigm that there is no complete alternative. Schoenberg's revolutionary 'escape' into dodecaphony ('the only escape' [Adorno 1973: 1]), was into a musical language even more 'hermetically sealed, esoteric, dissonant, and inaccessible to all but the most learned' appearing '... to proscribe the transformation of culture in an emancipatory direction' (Bernstein 1991: 1). As Foucault was later to advocate equally nihilistically only a '"non-discursive language" can counteract and construct resistances against discourse' (quoted in Lash 1985: 4), so Adorno championed Schoenberg's 'rigorous immanent critique, [as] an account of how music might yet express truths of present-day existence, but express them in exactly that indigent, distorted form that would bring out the extent of our alienated condition' (Norris 1989: 16-17), and which therefore the great majority could not possibly be expected to understand.

But there is no such thing as a 'non-discursive language', only languages initially difficult to comprehend but which with repeated 'listening' establish themselves as having at least some exchange-value. Surtitles demonstrate the inroads made by 'the industry' into the opera house, but no amount of such technological assistance, not even the promise of Soho strippers, can ensure large audiences for such 'masterworks' as Schoenberg's *Moses und Aron*.

16. While corporations undoubtedly shape the way in which popular music is composed and communicated ... they cannot control and co-opt in such a straightforward fashion: partly due to the considerable uncertainty about what will be successful and partly due to the competing interests ... attempting to intervene in the commercial process (Negus 1995: 320).

17. Parallels with the 'abstract' aesthetic in classical music are clear:

Meaning is produced everywhere, like air or money it circulates everywhere ... the works, practices and activities for us the music—that we address as interpreters are not only products but also agencies of culture, not only members of the habitus but also makers of it (Kramer 1990: 17).

18. See, for example, Chapple and Garofalo (1977).
19. On musical pluralism Foucault states: 'Each is granted the "right" to existence, and this right is perceived as an equality of worth. Each is worth as much as the group which practices it or recognizes it' (Boulez 1985/6), which rouses Boulez to some ire: 'All those musics are good, all those musics are nice. Ah! Pluralism!' (Boulez 1985/6).
20. However arbitrary musical meanings and conventions and their relationship to their sociocultural origins are, once particular musical elements are put together in particular ways and acquire particular connotations, these can be hard to shift. 'It would be difficult for instance to move *The Marseillaise* out of the set of meaning sedimented around it ... which derive from the history of the revolutionary French bourgeoisie' (Middleton 1985: 9), unless it were to be used to sell a car, and for all I know in France it may.
21. Classical Album Charts in Britain and the US regularly list collections of opera or classical music as used in advertising. Chapter Seven will give more details.
22. By the last quarter of the nineteenth century, the distinction

between 'high' and 'low' or 'popular' culture, firmly grounded in class divisions had been clearly made (Wolff 1987: 5), a distinction which within music theory, musicology and opera analysis has gradually been subverted in the past twenty or so years under the pressures of technological advance and commercialisation. As late as the early 1980s commentators were still able to defend opera as unproblematically 'high' or 'auratic' culture. Lindenberger, for example, embarked on his *Opera: The Extravagant Art* (1984: 9) in search of opera as the 'lofty and extravagant form essentially distinct from other modes of artistic communication', although he recognised this as a prejudiced search for he acknowledged 'the peculiar status of opera as at once a popular and a high-minded medium', accepting that 'lofty' claims are contentious given 'the disparagement of opera in favor of "purer" forms such as spoken drama and instrumental music' (ibid.: 9).

Scott (1990: 385) argues that the distinguishing feature of the sociology of music during the 1980s, which marked a departure from previous socio-musicological discourse, was the erosion of the idea of mass culture, once the theoretical mainstay for élitists and Marxists who were concerned with distinguishing between mass culture and the Leninist proletarian 'second culture ... a single culture with universal musical values' (ibid.: 391). By mass culture was meant a mass audience passively consuming mass-produced commodities of the 'culture industry'. A linear paradigm excludes or marginalises certain types of music and musical figures and imposes 'false' rules of musical development as outside of culture and 'autonomous' in their development. Thus a belief in the historical necessity of atonality led to the neglect of many areas of twentieth century music. Scott notes: 'Jimi Hendrix is not in the *New Grove,* if you look for Charlie Parker in the *New Oxford History of Music,* you find Horatio Parker instead. Is the latter more 'important' than the former, of more significance musically to the twentieth century?' So the assumption is that mass production based on commercially viable formulae is opposed to, and cannot include, 'real' art, created without a view of the market and concerned with other non-profit-making goals and means. He notes that for a work to become 'high' or real art in this sort of context, each work of this type needs to be unique in terms of its problems and solutions

(Jones 1955). But operas by Puccini are, for example, more alike in their purpose and goals (musical, dramatic as well as commercial) and, while Adorno's injunction that the 'star' system preserves (or 'fetishises') the aura of uniqueness for products of the culture industry, it would be clearly wrong to exclude 'high' art such as Puccini from this industry,

> ... was not Karajan a superstar? Is not Pavarotti a superstar? The failure to see "art music" as involved in the marketplace has been a surprising omission even in the arguments of perceptive critics like Boulez (Scott 1990: 386).

Presumably the explanation is that 'high' art does not exist to make money, but can 'high' art be judged outwith the interests of publishers, recording companies, opera houses, star singers and other star participants in the business of opera? Scott (1990: 402) argues that a trawl through the major reference works indicates how 'low' culture or non-art music is excluded because 'mass'.

23. For Marx too, human activities might be constrained, limited and determined by aggregate forces and material conditions which lie beyond their individual wills, but still they are conscious activities:

> Man makes his life activity itself an object of his will and consciousness. He has a conscious life activity. Conscious life activity distinguishes man from the life activity of animals. Only for this reason is his activity free activity (Marx quoted in Frankl 1974: 22).

24. Opera's development in North America was rapid and somewhat chaotic. Di Maggio and Useem (1982) describes how, prior to their rationalisation and hierarchical institutionalisation, the arts in early nineteenth century Boston were a promiscuous mix of levels, genres and styles, which played to, and were enjoyed by, audiences from a wide range of social backgrounds.

> Museums were modelled on Barnum's ... fine art was interspersed among such curiosities as bearded women ... and popular entertainments were offered for the price of admission

to a clientele that included working people as well as the upper middle class (ibid.: 34).

25. The annual BMRB TGI surveys interview 24000 adults but there is an additional AB category survey of approximately 5500 adults. Savage *et al*. (1993) use combined data for two successive years 1986 and 1987.

26. With advancing age opera increases its visibility, being under 80 for those between 20-34 and between 35 and 44 but at 140 for those 45-54, and about the same level for those between 55 and 64, after which it disappears from the reckoning. For those aged 75 and over, nothing comes near to competing with the consumption of sherry!

As for region, ABs in London consume opera less than they do jazz, dance, ballet, rock concerts, classical concerts and plays, though it still measures 220. In the rest of the south-east outside London opera falls to 60 but, as with all of these theatre-based data, access and opportunity considering travel and cost are bound to play a major role. For example, in Wales and Scotland, with their own resident and touring opera companies opera surfaces to the top or near the top of consumption activities amongst ABs, although other sources for such regions assert that very small percentages of local audiences actually attend opera regularly (see Myerscough 1988).

3 The opera industry

A lettuce is not a wild rose, yet the public continues to be regarded as a primitive organism, a kind of untouched Nature, with which the fine arts ought constantly to commune (Rosenberg 1970: 62).

I have just returned from a performance of *The Rape of Lucretia* at Epsom by the London Opera Group ... (with) just 54 people in the stalls and some 350 empty seats ... It seems to me a big mistake to perform less popular operas in towns such as ... Epsom. Moreover the hall was not heated adequately, and there were no facilities for a drink of coffee, to warm one up at the interval. This is not the way to 'sell' opera to the public. It was quite apparent that a large proportion of the very small audience were not regular opera-goers. These people are unlikely to come again (Letter to *Opera* February 1970: 180).

Introduction

'Selling' opera has become a major preoccupation in Britain, as elsewhere, since this 'dreich' Epsom *Rape* of 25 years ago, but the scale and manner of this commerce and the form and content of the commodities marketed and consumed has, one suspects, surpassed this correspondent's wildest dreams or possibly worst nightmares.[1] Since 1946, when the Arts Council began to subsidise opera as part of nascent welfare state and 1944 Education Act thinking, a state-supported opera enterprise has been promoted as an integral part of 'culturism' out of 'the belief that a wider distribution of culture

115

through society is desirable and that it is to be secured by public expenditure' (Sinfield 1985: 164).[2] Amidst an atmosphere of buoyant optimism and idealism there was a steady growth of funding; these were the 'boom-years in the expansion of opera—not just one national company but four' (Till 1986: 122).[3] There was 'determination on **all** sides ... that opera along with the best in all art forms, should be available to everyone rather than just the privileged minority' (Milnes 1989a: 269). Culture was inherently good for people, whether they knew it or not, 'like orange juice and free medicine' (Till 1986: 122), a vision encapsulated in the work and person of Lilian Baylis, founder of Sadlers Wells Opera the forerunner of the English National Opera (ENO) '... who having given "her people" Shakespeare at the Old Vic, went on to give them opera. According to Tyrone Guthrie, her simple theory was that if you give people "the best" they will like it—not immediately, perhaps but eventually' (Platt 1990: 1169). 'Selling' opera meant proselytising, converting doubters and waverers to its very particular potential for spiritual enlightenment,[4] as this *Opera* correspondent's innocent concerns demonstrate. It would be mistaken to assume that 'culturist' ideals no longer remain, or that opera could survive in Britain without continuing substantial state support, but it would be even more innocent and naive now to believe that the evangelical 'selling' of opera as 'spiritual enlightenment' can be divorced from commerce: the converted are firstly consumers; 'spiritual enlightenment' is itself a commodity of 'opera as industry' (Royal Opera House, Covent Garden 1993a).

Opera companies have always been preoccupied with finance— pursuing survival rather than profits and more usually crying 'impending ruin', frequently as a result of political machinations as much as financial mismanagement.[5] For some critics, 'It is a measure of their health that they should be perceived to be so, for it is the perception of crisis which questions and challenges forms and structures, and which leads to renewal and reassertion' (Till 1986: 122) but, given that opera's 'renewal and reassertion' invariably manifest stalwart conservatism, one is tempted by an alternative conclusion:

> Opera involves singing, acting, an orchestra, usually a chorus, sometimes dancers, conductors, directors, designers and a correspondingly large music, technical and stage staff, a standing

116

invitation to megalomania and trivialisation (Platt 1990: 1169).

Not that the opera industry is everywhere the same, but whatever the variations between the particular sociopolitical, economic and historical contexts of nations' operatic institutions which are gradually succumbing to universalising pressures, certain key linked themes are common to them all—themes which rest fundamentally on opera being uneconomic.

Resource costs are simply too high to be recouped through free market forces. If seat prices were to be set at levels sufficient to so do, they would be priced out of the market. Opera is only financially sustained through additional 'unfree' market funding of broadly three types: government or federal state subsidies; gifts and donations from private, corporate and other sources; and private, association or corporate sponsorship for particular productions. Being 'unfree' in origin, each is likely, and certainly reputed, to impose other 'unfreedoms' on administrations, especially the constitution of governing boards, repertoire, planning, production styles and so on. Box office 'free' market income, reflecting public demand, reinforces popular nineteenth century 'museum' culture and repertoire, 'safe' production styles, 'stars' especially 'star' singers and so on. Private and corporate support invariably underwrite this conservatism given that donors have an interest in 'their' beneficence being prominently and repeatedly announced. Subsidies, however, being tax-dependent, require populations to be persuaded of not only their political, cultural as well as economic worth, but also their honest as opposed to corrupt and/or wasteful management, set against both the implications for 'artistic freedom' opportunities for experimentation and audited responsibility and efficiency in their use. The fact that opera is sustained at all under uneconomic circumstances raises the questions 'Should it be?' and 'If so, why?'. In Britain in the past 20 years more than a few politicians and journalists haven't got beyond a 'No' answer to the first, often on the grounds that 'the people's' taxes should not subsidise an élitist art form and the extravagant fees of Pavarotti, Domingo and other 'stars'. Answers to the second question range from: 'It is "high" art, "auratic" art and by definition important enough to be so defended' through to—at Covent Garden at least—'It is important as symbol of national well being and pride judged internationally', and the kind of 'culturist' justifications referred to earlier.

Invariably, however, such rationales carry a subtext tension concerning accessibility, or rather inaccessibility. If seat prices are so high for an art form of such complex hybridity of form and function, attended, reputationally as well as actually, by audiences unrepresentative of the wider population and in the most expensive seats by those very representative of the Establishment, then what price 'culturist' rhetoric?

Cross-cultural comparisons reveal all manner of ways in which such tensions are fought and/or resolved, but all may be related back to traditional and current funding practices along the state subsidy-to-private donation continuum. Traditions of government involvement in providing subsidies vary. In state socialist societies prior to the break-up of the Eastern bloc and Soviet Union, such support was almost a monopoly, seat prices being set at artificially low levels, justified according to all three criteria. The repertoire tended towards a strong nationalist flavour, productions being either old-fashioned or, in East Germany especially, marked by strong Marxist/socialist critiques. Following the break-up, subsidy crises, 'free market' readjustments at all levels from repertoire planning, singers' contract conditions and fees and so on, have wreaked a havoc that only the larger key houses in the East (for example, in ex-East Germany, Dresden and Leipzig) are beginning to resolve, although not without considerable competition between them, as in Berlin: 'Germany's days of producing opera in bulk may be numbered' (Midgette 1993a: 20).[6] Within ex-West Germany, France, Switzerland, Austria and Italy too, national, federal state or city subsidies have always been at levels substantially higher than in Britain. In Zurich, for example, high canton support and box office prices have been successfully defended by referenda, on grounds of attracting 'stars', allowing dramatic innovation and sizeable and adventurous repertoires. In Paris the Mitterand-inspired and lavishly government-funded Opéra Bastille was justified as a building of 'the people's opera': to present high-quality opera using the most advanced technology, as accessible as possible to as many as possible; to sever connections with the industrial relations problems of the Palais Garnier; to place Paris at the centre of the opera map; and to commemorate the bicentenniary of the Revolution (Clark 1989). However, since its opening it has been beleaguered by political interference on a scale possibly even greater than the level of subsidy provided: 'Clochemerle writ large, by 1994 19 directors/

administrators had been engaged and dismissed' (Couling 1994). In Italy not a season passes without fresh scandals surrounding the use and abuse (financial and artistic) of subsidies.[7] By marked contrast, in the US, subsidies provide an extremely small, barely significant, proportion of funding which rests instead on private and corporate fund-raising for opera presentations and culture at their most conservative.

As with so many aspects of contemporary opera, the British experience is somewhere between the two extremes, relying on income from a mixture of subsidies, private and corporate fund-raising and box office revenues, without the scandals of Italy, the high subsidies of Germany and France, or the brute North American reliance on fund-raising and box office in which 'opera as art' is crudely fused with the realities of the market: 'Opera relies on being able to show that the product is something a corporation or foundation wants to be associated with, that it improves the quality of life' (Mauney 1989: 12). The post-war British experience must thus be seen within this broader frame, commencing with 'culturist' commitments requiring increased subsidies, followed by a Thatcherite 'free market' emphasis on increased private and corporate support for newly efficient companies to enable and offset subsidy retreat. In the process the relative independence of the fund-distributing body, the Arts Council, which held government interference in arts policy at 'arm's length', has been dented by successive Conservative administrations and Arts (Heritage) Ministers' attempts to impose 'free market' reforms through direct influence. These monetarist policies drew predictable brickbats to '... the most Philistine Government since the end of World War II ...' (*Opera* March 1985: 267),[8] for its attacks on the 'welfare state mentality of those who work in the arts' (*Opera* August 1987: 859), its introduction of 'incentive funding' according to which public subsidies are dependent upon the raising of specified amounts of funding from other sources ('subsidy capping') giving rise to predictions of dire consequences for all aspects of administration, repertoire, production values and residual 'culturist' ambitions through faster than rate of inflation seat price rises. By March 1994 *Opera* claimed: 'Every possible administrative cut has been made: interminable "assessments" have consistently cleared opera companies of financial profligacy. Now the real cuts have started...' (ibid.: 267). These resulted in production cancellations, corporate pressures on 'safe' repertoire, last-minute borrowed or shared productions,[9] reduced rehearsal time and so on.

It could be argued that the Thatcher government was merely reverting to Britain's long history of anti-intellectualism (Savage *et al.* 1993: 112), post-war 'culturism' becoming the exception and 'Philistinism' the norm: 'The historical formation of cultural capital out of aristocratic cultural forms led to an identification of culture with leisured amateur pursuits that was antagonistic to any idea of "learning as a vocation ..."' (ibid.: 113),[10] and there is still in the Covent Garden stalls and grand circle culture at least, a sense of opera being an Establishment leisure pursuit, rather than a 'high' dramatisation of music and text. Post-war 'culturism' hardly supplanted this contempt for culture as 'highbrow', upper middle-class, amateur leisure but, like all 'welfarist' ideology, legitimised against this dubious background, a democratic cultural claim on opera as in itself serious, 'for all' given the opportunity, raising tensions hardly resolved with the development of a culture industry seeking to commodify and in market terms make acceptable all aspects of intellectualism. Consequently the relationship between intellectuals and 'the rest', in the British middle class especially, has become highly complex and ambiguous:

> While it can hardly be said that all the values of contemporary 'highbrows' are endorsed with alacrity by other middle class groups, there are some aspects of intellectuals' priorities (especially those which offer long-term economic benefits) which are indeed adopted by those with higher levels of economic capital. This we contend is linked to the growing salience of cultural assets in contemporary Britain (Savage *et al.* 1993: 113).

Thus, as a key commodity of distinction, the consumption of opera as cultural capital has had consequences in auditoria as well as boardrooms, orchestra pits and on stage. As noted in the last chapter, a large part of opera's regular audience consists of middle-class professionals, high in cultural but low in economic capitals, employed in education, health, welfare and so on, who in the past 15 years have also suffered relative economic decline and status deprivation, compared with their private sector, corporate, counterparts. A core challenge for opera administrators is to maximise and manage its diverse actual and potential audience and box office revenues against the reputation and presence of élitism. The major national and international companies, whatever their publicity materials imply to the contrary, remain primarily under the control of, supported by, and symbolic of, the traditional Establishment and their political, social and economic interests. To be financially viable they must build audiences amongst their new corporate paymasters and their employees, 'sell' opera to the 'new petit bourgeoisie' but also retain traditional middle-class professional support and the opera house as 'leisure' haven for the Establishment at play. Hence repertoire, production and marketing strategies veer from promoting opera as 'sexy', 'subversive' and contemporary entertainment, to staid guarantees of ritual and performance quality in the most conventional and safest terms. Hence also the tensions of the commercialism/creativity axis: 'radical productions' especially at élite establishments,[11] repertoire content, length of seasons, exchange of productions, surtitles, 'miking', maximum hiking up of seat prices for 'superstars', substantial use of National Lottery funds and so on.

State support for opera in Britain remains essential to opera's survival, but with subsidy conditions becoming more specific and stringent, corporate and private funding, though 'notoriously capricious' (*Opera* June 1990: 644)[12] more widespread and influential, the 'culturist' conscience has become incorporated into opera as business. On the financial and geographical continuum, post-1979 arts policy has been for 'mixed patronage' tending towards North American reliance on private funding and away from the East European level of subsidised support which is, on average, one third higher than in Britain. Away from the East which, some argue, has subsidised the 'freedom' to be creatively radical, towards the West where the arts are 'authentically Big Business ... the leaders of symphony orchestras, opera houses, museums ... [are] solid businessmen, not radicals or eggheads, anxious to throw away money in a great cultural boondoggle' (Schonberg 1950: 19 quoted in Martorella 1982: 77).[13] Funding policies trade in blow and counter-blow 'freedom claims: 'Mixed patronage' claimed Norman St John Stevas in 1980 meaning 'freedom for the arts' (see Blyth 1981: 115), but private funding, unlike state subsidies, is not guaranteed long-term and thus imposes even greater conservatism on planning repertoire (see Haitink, *Opera* April 1988: 405).

Because of these debates, opera companies have become much more cost and income accountable, 'good' financial practice being as important as good artistic practice, audit language in annual reports vying for discursive dominance with those of music, text and drama, as pages of figures accompanied by seemingly merely decorous select press praise not infrequently mismatch with accountants' views that good artistic and financial practice necessarily coincide.[14] As opera has been commodified, so too 'opera' outside the opera house has become increasingly deployed in popular commercial culture. Discussion of the material construction of opera in the 1990s cannot ignore such 'operatic' consequences with which there is much interaction and overlap: 'They're all Pava-potti!' screamed the *Daily Star*. This chapter concentrates on opera as funded theatrical institution, later chapters, especially Chapter 7, deal more widely with 'operatic' commodities—fragments consumed outside the opera house.

Aims and aspirations

Of the 40 worldwide companies approached for this study 28 responded to requests for information (see Appendix C). In all cases annual reports were provided for season 1992-93, some for the two prior seasons as well, plus in some instances promotional literature for season' 93-94,[15] a few providing financial accounts so minutely detailed that, as with those for the Deutsche Oper Berlin, they included budgeted allocations for such activities as *Schneebeseitigung* (snow removal).[16] Unfortunately, limited space prevents specific reference to all the cooperating companies, but general themes and common concerns have been exemplified through reference to as wide a range as possible. Inevitably most examples are British and, by the time this is read, actual figures will no doubt be outdated, but overall circumstances and the language deployed to describe and contest them will not.

Few companies have responded to quality audit requirements as energetically as the British institution which attracts the largest single amount of state subsidy, approximately 10 per cent of the UK arts budget, the Royal Opera House Covent Garden, as exemplified by its *Annual Report for the Financial Year 6 April 1992-4 April 1993: Opera as Industry* (ROH 1993a). Against the background of a continuing outstanding deficit of over £2 million,[17] was claimed evidence of keen financial management, artistic success, plus pleas for more Arts Council assistance. Chairman Sir Angus Stirling, praised the three companies under the ROH aegis—the Royal Opera, the Royal Ballet and the Birmingham Royal Ballet—all of which had 'performed with distinction'. 'A great opera house cannot, however, flourish today by the excellence of stage performance alone. It must also show that it is operating economically and with good business sense' (ibid.: 6). During the year the Board commissioned Price Waterhouse to review working practices, and they reported in August 1992 at more or less the same time as the Arts Council appraisal carried out by a team headed by Baroness Warnock (1992).[18] 'The recommendations of both reports have been implemented with vigour and determination (ROH 1993b): 'Thanks to these efforts a modest surplus of £349,000 on the operating account was earned ... in spite of the effects of recession and a volatile box-office.' Regretfully it was noted that a surplus unaccompanied by 'pain and sacrifice, including an overall pay freeze (there was a voluntary wage freeze by staff for 12 months from September 1992) and redundancies in some departments...' is nowadays impossible.[19] This 'positive' financial outcome: '... coupled with the first instalment of an exceptionally generous private benefaction of £2.5 million (spread over three years), has enabled us to reduce our outstanding deficit to £2.79 million by the end of the year' (1993a: 6).

Stirling paid 'tribute to our many private and corporate donors and sponsors' who through the ROH Trust made a total contribution of £6 million in 1992-93: 'Without this support the work of the ROH could not continue. We owe an incalculable debt of gratitude to all our patrons and supporters for their loyalty and generosity in these difficult times' (1993a: 6). Also praised were the Friends of Covent Garden for their invaluable financial support for eight new productions as sole or joint sponsor. Echoing sentiments to be found in all company documents concerning donors and fund-raisers, he added: 'The importance of the Friends is measured not only in terms of money, but also because we value each individual as a committed, interested and loyal member of our regular audience' (1993a: 6). On the same page was quoted a *Guardian* leader (June 1992) affirming artistic success:

The last few months have seen a remarkable renaissance at Covent Garden ... What has made the succession of new shows so generally impressive has been the consistently high quality of these performances and productions. It's easy to knock Covent Garden and it has often deserved to be knocked. But at the moment [it] deserves acclaim rather than abuse. Right now it's an opera house for Britain to be proud of,[20] doing a top quality job at a cripplingly difficult time for theatre box office on a subsidy far lower than its European peers.

The phrase 'an opera house for Britain to be proud of was reused in the guide to the following season (1993c), in which a set of quality assessment 'aims and aspirations' were listed:

1) - To present opera and ballet of high quality at the highest possible standard of performance.
   - To offer a wide range of repertory, including new and lesser known works as well as the established classics.
   - To encourage and promote creativity in composition, production, choreography and design.
   - To promote and provide performance opportunities for the development of British council orchestral musicians, singers and dancers.

In pursuing these aims, the Royal Opera House and its Companies seek to serve the following purposes.

2) - To provide the widest possible access to British audiences for opera and ballet;[21]
   - To extend public understanding and enjoyment of opera and ballet;
   - To act as cultural ambassadors for the nation through tours by the three Companies overseas;
   - To preserve and develop the art forms of opera and ballet for the audiences of today and tomorrow.

Among the objectives necessary to achieve these purposes, the Board of the Royal Opera House have set the following:

3) - To secure financial viability to eliminate income and expenditure deficits;
   - To realize equally at the Royal Opera House the full potential of both the Royal Opera and the Royal Ballet;

- To extend audiences, including those from ethnic minorities, through a programme of education and outreach work related to the strategic aims of the Royal Opera House;
- To provide a high level of customer service and value for money;
- To develop fully the key resource of staff and artists by improving productivity through the adoption of efficient working practices; providing a safe working environment for artists, technicians and administrative staff; and increasing staff development through a programme of training and the promotion of equal opportunities;
- To make the Royal Opera House as accessible as possible to people with disabilities;
- To exploit every opportunity to increase access to the work of the Companies by means of video, realm, television and radio broadcasts, recordings and sponsored performances at Covent Garden and elsewhere.

In the Royal Opera House the country has a beautiful historic and much-loved theatre but a great deal now needs to be done to bring its facilities up-to-date and equip it adequately to fulfil its functions into the 21st Century. The Board is committed to a staged development programme at Covent Garden which will provide:

4) - An increased number of performances and seats, thereby improving public access to the work of the Royal Opera House;
- Improved customer facilities including air conditioning, improved sightlines, more foyer space and more rooms for entertaining;
- A home for the Royal Ballet at Covent Garden;
- Up-to-date technical and stage facilities, and a working environment for artists and staff which satisfies contemporary requirements in the matter of health and safety and is cost-effective and efficient;
- Reduced seat prices, wherever possible through cost efficiencies, improved working practices and revenue returns (1993c: 3-4).

As with all such exercises, these aims and aspirations are largely anodyne and ambiguous. The commitment to 'present opera ... of high quality' implies a consensus between management, artists, critics and audiences on 'high quality' in the standard repertoire, and at least compromises the commitment '... to encourage and promote creativity in composition', the quality of which cannot be guaranteed in advance—not that there has been much evidence of encouragement or promotion of creativity in the main auditorium. Similarly, to aim for 'the highest possible standard of performance' is, as the major international opera houses and festivals dependent on 'star' singers are well aware, to go easy on '... creativity ... in production, choreography and design'. There may be little to question in aiming 'To promote and provide performance opportunities for the development of British council orchestral musicians, singers and dancers', but at Covent Garden opera is an international 'industry', dependent on 'stars'. Some of whom are British, should Covent Garden nurture them? There has been much tension and criticism over the years about Covent Garden's seeming predilection for foreign singers at all costs:

> ... there's not a policy that says we don't want British singers or one that excludes non-British singers; we just try to make the best casting as we think it should be' (Haitink, *Opera* April 1988: 405).

The fourth aim under 1) is in many ways the most fascinating for it highlights the continuance of opera world-wide, as a 'museum culture' made even more conservative by audit control, despite the latter's seemingly challenging language. 'To offer a *wide* range of repertory, including *new* and *lesser known* works as well as the established classics' (my italics), has to be seriously qualified if, in any reduced sense, its realisation, in *any* opera house—not only Covent Garden, is to be claimed. The purposes proposed under 2) are especially anodyne. 'The widest possible access to British audiences' hinges on the customary impossibility of 'possible'. The ROH 'remains the most inaccessible of all the national companies to the general public' (*Opera* June 1990: 644),[22] but Covent Garden claims that the fault is not theirs but the Arts Council's:

> ... what is happening at Covent Garden is a negation of one of the Arts Council's principal charter responsibilities: to improve access to the arts. Part of the difficulty is attributable to the increasingly invidious choice between regional and central arts funding that tight resources force the Arts Council to make. It is reasonable to question how much longer the nation's premier opera and ballet

companies must continue to be penalised in that unproductive equation (Stirling 1993 in ROH 1993c: 6).

The Royal Opera used to tour but, even in its home base, the narrowness of its British audience is beyond question. All four items under 2) are severely constrained not only financially but by the sociocultural inequalities of contemporary Britain which have survived post-war 'culturism'. Objectives under 3) are a peculiar mixture, ranging from politically correct 'noises off' about ethnic minorities and the disabled (although some wheelchair spaces are available for every performance) to hard-core financial management, plus the assumption that, through video and recordings, consumers are somehow gaining the same 'Covent Garden Experience' (*The Times* 12 July 1993) as audiences in the theatre.[23] Whilst:

> ... it is the arts that touch our spirits, lift us most excitingly out of ourselves, opera and ballet high among them ... We aim to give ... each visitor to the Theatre, at each and every performance, the thrill of great art done as well as it can be done... Opera is music theatre but it is also an art for the virtuoso. (Jeremy Isaacs, General Director, Royal Opera House Covent Garden 1993c: 6-7).

But this is clearly not enough. Following an attendance fall during 1992-93 from 88 per cent to 85 per cent of seat capacity, Covent Garden was reported to be working with Virgin Airlines on marketing techniques: TV advertising, telephone sales, discounted tickets and 'aria miles', rewarding regular operagoers by upgrading them for a night from, for example, amphitheatre to stalls, as from tourist to business class. Covent Garden's grand image is emphasised: 'high production standards, interval suppers, red carpets ... We need to sell the whole experience rather than just *La Bohème* ... We are trying to learn the way to have a brand image from Virgin—to say the ROH experience is more than just the performance' (Keith Cooper, Marketing Director, *The Times* 12 July 1993). Without upgrading for the majority the 'experience' is somewhat different.

The Covent Garden redevelopment programme, started in 1997, lies behind the items under 4), subsequently the basis for a successful £78.5 million claim (£58.5 million for rebuilding, £20 million to cover loss of earnings whilst the theatre is closed) from National Lottery funds, as controversial as the use of the said funds for the £12.5 million purchase of Sir Winston Churchill memorabilia from the Churchill family and further evidence for critics claiming that the National Lottery is a devious tax on the poor to pay for the lifestyles of the rich. With news that the ROH had been granted £80 million *The Sun*'s 'You the Jury' phone poll (3 July 1995: 9) asked, 'Where would you like your Lottery cash to go?', reported overwhelming disapproval setting this award against the lack of funds for health care, jurors' claiming: 'All these Arty types have to do is sit back and wait for the money to roll in'; 'It's a disgrace that ill people are less important than some fancy theatre where the rich waste their money': 'The sick get sicker and the rich get richer'. 'It's the Greedy Beggar's Opera' (*The Sun* 21 July 1995: 11). As Till (1986: 122) warned ten years earlier; 'the more cynical will pit kidney machines against opera'; 'The rich get their opera house done up because it looks good for the tourists'. There was a lone dissenter: 'Our national arts institutions have been neglected for years. It's time we repaid them'. 'Guarantees' of matching Lottery revenue with private and corporate donations merely reinforced Covent Garden's élitist status—'... it is nonsensical for the ROH to be given taxpayers' money to subsidise performances for the wealthy and privileged ...' (*Opera* letter August 1990: 903).

Despite these qualifications, overall these aims and aspirations reflect the current material 'facts of life' which face all opera companies, affecting administration, financial management, revenue raising, repertoire planning, structure and content, whatever their particular circumstances which are many and varied: house capacities; number of auditoria at their disposal; relationship with other house companies such as ballet;[24] length of season; number of productions, performances; season structure; whether *stagione* (two or three works during a given period with a stable cast rehearsed together as at Covent Garden) or *repertory* (a large number of works presented through the season with differing casts often not rehearsed together, as at The Vienna State Opera); split locations (Australian Opera is based in Sydney and Melbourne); touring commitments (Opera North, Scottish Opera and Welsh National Opera tour outside their base theatres); national variations in repertoire; the inclusion or exclusion of 'musicals'. Festival opera presents different conditions which are also highly variable and range from the grandest (financially and/or socially) *stagione* (Salzburg and Bayreuth) or *repertory* (Munich, where Festival productions are staged with the same casts as part of normal season's repertoire, but at inflated prices), and their pale pretentious imitators such as Garsington, to open-air amphitheatre-based more populist festivals such as Verona. Given such complex variations, this discussion of the opera industry will necessarily concentrate on common characteristics.

Industry facts (i) Income

The Royal Opera House Covent Garden owns three companies:[25] *Art as Industry* (1993a) records 496 performances (15 per cent up on 1991-92); 158 the Royal Ballet (24 on international tour); 179 the Royal Opera (13 on international tour); 152 the Birmingham Royal Ballet (63 in Birmingham, 27 on national tour), giving 'Greater productivity—on less subsidy—than any other comparable European opera house' (ibid.: 8). Paid attendance for the Royal Ballet was 87 per cent: for the Royal Opera, with much higher seat prices on average, 85 per cent (1988-89, 89 per cent: 1989-90, 92 per cent: 1990-91, 94 per cent: 1991-92, 88 per cent): and for the Birmingham Royal Ballet 74 per cent (ditto). Overall costs per performance had been reduced: 496 performances at a cost of £18.2million (£36,700 per performance, a reduction of 17 per cent on the previous year). The Royal Opera income and expenditure account for period 1992-93 (ibid.: 44) shows net box office receipts of £16,458,000 (£12,310,000 in '91-92). Artists' fees totalled £9,782,000, ROH orchestra: £2,950,000: production £4,210,000: stage and transport £4,144,000.

Arts Council funding to Covent Garden has decreased by 18.3 per cent over the past four years, but each seat is still subsidised by about £24. The PR dilemma for the company is clear: 'Many in the arts world and beyond will ask whether those who can afford to pay £100 a seat should expect a heavier subsidy'. By 1993 26.7 per cent of the Royal Opera's income was in the form of subsidy: 13.7 per cent private funding and 59.6 per cent box office (50 per cent: £14 million) and other. Private funding raised by the ROH Trust equalled £6.1 million in the financial year 1992/93. Income proportions were: 40 per cent public subsidy: 60 per cent self-generated: surplus achieved £349,000. At the ENO, with one theatre, one company, 1993 income was £7,963,000 (box office and other), £11,528,000 grants (£157,200 from the City of Westminster, the remainder Arts Council) and £1,678,000 from sponsorship and donations (ENO 1993: 7).

Between seasons 1988/89 and 1992/93 ROH income source contributions as proportion of the whole changed as follows: grants down from 41.5 per cent to 36.8 per cent: donations from 14.9 per cent to 12.8 per cent: house receipts up from 30.8 per cent to 37.4 per cent: touring receipts (ballet only) up from 3.1 per cent to 4.2 per cent: other income down from 9.7 per cent to 8.8 per cent. Staffing levels in the same period fell for the Royal Opera down from 122-114. The Orchestra of the ROH from 124 to 117: Production from 151 to 142: Stage 170 to 169: Front of House 217 to 213: Others 79 to 73.[26] These figures show box office income as necessarily the largest and most critical source of earned income. Because grant aid available is steadily declining in real terms, and sponsorship is at best static:

> we have no choice but to look to income from paid attendance to fill the gap ... It cannot be too strongly stated that the Board deplores the need to charge the current high seat prices ... We are well aware that they are a discouragement to the wide accessibility to ballet and opera ... To squeeze the public resources available to sustain this artistic excellence to the point where accessibility to the general public begins to be denied is a self-defeating policy. It does little service to the rest of the country's artistic life and it runs counter to present trends, which seek to encourage greater public participation in the arts (ROH 1993a: 8).

Towards the end of the 1980s the ROH clarified its financial problems by drawing comparisons with other major British and foreign houses, showing it to be more successful at obtaining sponsorship, more reliant on box office receipts and receiving lower subsidies. The 1988/89 annual report tabulated comparisons including, at one extreme of the income continuum, the New York Metropolitan Opera (Met) with 67 per cent of revenue coming from box office sales, 31 per cent from gifts and sponsorship (charitable donations tax deductible[27]) and 2 per cent only from public subsidy, and Rome at the other with figures of 4 per cent, 1 per cent and 92 per cent respectively. Remembering that this table compares the Royal Opera House with some institutions concerned solely with opera, the figures were as shown opposite.

Funding in international context: public subsidy-box office-sponsorship: relative % of contribution to total

	Met[28]	ROH	ENO	Köln	Mil	Hamb	Vien	Mün	Ven	Paris	Berl	Flor	Rome
Box office	67	39	38	26	21	25	23	22	4	17	17	9	4
Sponsorship	31	17	7	-	5	-	1	-	16	1	-	3	1
Public subsidy	2	44	55	74	74	75	76	78	80	82	83	88	92
Performance													
Opera	232	135	209	210	81	194	253	223	46	126	209	76	68
Ballet	-	312	-	35	44	88	54	69	19	118	61	90	50
Total:	232	447	209	245	125	282	307	292	65	244	270	166	118

1. ROH performances take place in two home base theatres and in two home base cities: London and Birmingham.
2. The figures are for financial year 1988/9 for the ROH and the closest equivalent for the other Houses.
3. Currency conversion rates on 31 March 1989.
4. Only opera and ballet performances are included, not concerts.
5. Annual Reports amidst the figures it is customary to present graphically broad breakdowns of income and outgoings as typically for one large company: The Metropolitan Opera, New York as given in Apendix D.
6. British regional companies receive funding from regional ACGBs and local government sources.
(Source: *Royal Opera House Covent Garden Annual Report*, 1988/9: 4).

Whatever the particular box-office, subsidy, gift breakdown, all companies face the general revenue raising problem of setting and achieving artistic aims and aspirations cost efficiently.[29] The 1992 annual report of the Australian Opera showing 73.7 per cent of income ($22.7 million) from box office, earned income and contributions, 26.3 per cent ($8.2 million) from subsidy, drew attention to one common problem: singers and other artists are contracted years in advance, preventing short term recession economies to counter income shortfall.[30] The aim of 'maintaining the highest possible artistic and production standards' also constrains responses to income crises. The Chairman reported: 'Our costs in 1992 exceeded budget levels by 1.7 per cent. Our income fell short of budget by 2.1 per cent. The combined effect of these two seemingly small variances was a loss for the year of $595,073', illustrating the narrow safety margins on which companies operate (Australian Opera Annual Report 1992: 3), hence the need for reserves but as the Company's communications administrator added 'like companies closer to your home, we also have found it impossible over the past years to build and maintain reasonable capital reserves' (ibid.: 5). Part of the justification given by the ROH claims on Lottery funds has been to establish such a reserve to stabilise seat prices.

British permanent regional companies such as Welsh National Opera (WNO), Scottish Opera (SO) and Opera North (ON), though at the time of writing SO has gone part-time, draw income from regional Arts Councils and local and regional authority sources (depending upon touring commitments,[31] small-scale as well as main company) and commercial sponsorship. In 1992/93 SO was supported by 7 Regional Councils and by 38 District Councils in Scotland:[32] 'the main task to get the company's finances in order without sacrificing artistic standards' (Managing Director of SO: *The Sunday Times* 5 September 1993). Arts Council funding specifies the work of Scottish Opera Go Round which gave 32 performances of Mozart's *Seraglio* in Northern Ireland, Wales and Scotland.[33] At this end of 'the opera industry' commercialism has of necessity to play second best: 'Could anyone who has crammed into a tiny village hall, heard singing mingled with seagull cries, and Mozart waft amongst the woodsmoke, go home and annotate their evening's experience on a balance sheet?' (Millar 1993: 11). SO, WNO and all three Royal Opera House companies operate 'schools' programmes.[34]

Industry facts (ii) Sponsorship and donations

As the British move towards greater emphasis within 'mixed patronage' on private funding, Euro distrust of sponsorship has become more outspoken, Yves Fremion French Green MEP *rapporteur* to the European Parliament's cultural committee observing: 'Advertising and, more generally, promotional activities are invading all areas of daily life ... to the extent that the public is suffering unbearable commercial harassment against which it has little defence ... Sponsorship is more often than not a massive invasive presence ...' (*The Times* 7 September 1993: 33). Critic Alan Blyth (*Opera* November 1988: 1366) attacked ROH programmes for consisting substantially of advertising. John McMurray, Publications Officer (*Opera* January 1989: 28) retorted that the *Turandot* programme for 1988/89 season consisted of 35 editorial, 13 'House' and 24 advertising pages. In season 1986/87 the *Turandot* programme had been 23 editorial, 12 'House' and 27 advertising pages, as though to prove that the trend was in the right direction. He commented that there is no embarrassment about the amount of advertising revenues going into ROH general funds which pay for the house's activities, and again reminded us that without ads seat prices would have to increase further. 'Sponsors' logos have been appearing on CO programme covers for at least 15 years and most operagoers recognise that they are a fact of economic life'.

As for sponsorship, sponsors prefer low-risk, non-innovative activities.[35] Most of those who receive sponsorship do not dare to speak their mind for fear of losing it. Arts pages are generally hostile too, though space has been made for the case to be put. Richard Law (1987, 1988) for example, newly retired from a career in banking, asked 'Why should tax payers support those who consume an art form they themselves do not like?', arguing that had the future scale of state arts funding (£340 million in 1987) been foreseen in 1945, support would not have been as forthcoming or idealistic. Law (1987: 1136-37) attacked anti-sponsorship lobby assumptions: (i) that subsidies and Arts Council influence are necessarily good: (ii) that financial support from organisations whose ethics are concerned with the maximisation of profit is by definition bad: (iii) that subsidising seat prices will make opera a mass entertainment: (iv) that it is unreasonable to make those entertained to pay for it via the box office rather than by fellow citizens with little interest in opera:

(v) that it is reprehensible for audiences to flock to hear works in a familiar and intelligible idiom and to stay away from those they find rebarbative and difficult, and (vi) that it is praiseworthy for composers to write in the latter rather than former style: (vii) that it is morally virtuous of companies to play unpopular pieces to half-empty houses with unknown singers: (viii) less so to perform popular operas with well-known singers to full houses: (ix) that the unglamorous will be left out in the cold by commercial sponsors' propensity to favour the successful. Law attacked these assumptions as misplaced before proceeding to attack composers (and others in the arts establishment) 'encouraged by subsidies to acquire "hermitical tendencies": to retreat and preoccupy themselves with their material, to strain after originality at the expense of accessibility, even to express open contempt for their audiences' (ibid.: 1140). Glyndebourne, he claimed, does not receive any public money yet survives and develops 'because it puts on what its audiences are prepared to pay to hear'. He attacks the 'cosy world of arts administrators and their statist patrons' the arts establishment of amateurs, patronising the mass and the popular. The future is not assured by the provision of ever more money regardless of the wishes of the taxpayer who provides it, 'to contemplate with apparent equanimity the increasing isolation from public taste of artistic creation as evidenced by the only solid criterion' (ibid.: 1140). Glyndebourne audiences however, have the money to pay for what they want to hear at more or less cost price, and the collective interest to preserve the champagne, picnic, Sussex festival culture which is as much Glyndebourne as the opera. Indeed, when the opera becomes too intrusive, these well heeled natives get restless, as later chapters will record.

Reactions to Law (1987) were irate, reiterating arguments concerning sponsorship chasing repertoire safety, popularity and success as well as a London bias 'towards fat cat projects', 'not the sort of "middle-range" companies that enable young professionals to launch the kind of experimental concepts that breed future winners' and so on.[36] What appears to antagonise most critics hostile to sponsorship is that the pure 'creators' and works themselves become submerged beneath the logos of commercialism—on programme covers, posters, possibly emphasised by special staff uniforms or badges, garlanded promos across hallowed theatre facades—all of which occurred with the Midland Bank's sponsorship of the 1980

Covent Garden *Ring,* a revival of the 1976 production 'made possible by substantial donations from Commercial Union Assurance and the Baring Foundation'. Even small sponsorship sums can lead to excessive publicity for the source concerned, Blyth (1981: 114) found it 'faintly distasteful' that the WNO's visit to London in 1980 was advertised as Amoco Festival of Opera when Amoco contributed only 5 per cent to WNO's annual budget. There is also the danger of sponsors dictating repertoire, there would be little point in a corporate sponsor funding substantially a work 'unpopular' and/or rarely revived, but theatres like Covent Garden have several productions sponsored by support associations or trusts linked to them: for example, The Friends of Covent Garden and the ROH Trust. For the 14 sponsored productions given by The Royal Opera during 1993/94 sponsors were: The Nestlé Company and The Jean Sainsbury Royal Opera House Fund for *Guillaume Tell* (1990):[37] The Friends of Covent Garden for *The Fiery Angel* (1992): *I Capuletti e i Montecchi* (1984): *Il barbiere di Siviglia* (1985): *II viaggio a Reims* (1992): *La Damnation de Faust* (1993) and *Stiffelio* (1993): The Linbury Trust and Friends of Covent Garden for *La Bohème* (1974): The Royal Opera Trust for *Der Fliegende Hollander* (1992) and *Samson et Dalila* (1981): Citicorps Investment Bank Ltd. for *Porgy and Bess* (1992): Morgan Grenfell Group plc for *Otello* (1987): Forte PLC for *Madama Butterfly* (1988): Norwest Holst Ltd. for *Turandot*. The Midland Bank supports the Summer Proms and The Paul Hamlyn Foundation a week of performances for first time visitors.[38]

All companies rely on fund raising activities by various bodies which also link into social activities. During 1992/93 The ROH Trust raised £6.1 million gross, £5.7 million after deduction of administration expenses. £4.3 million was allocated to operations of the ROH £0.5 million to help in the elimination of the ROH deficit brought forward from earlier years. Galas raised £712,000 net of expenses. Such fund raising organisations necessarily need to attract those with money or those with friends with money, thus a greater reliance on private funding can only reinforce establishment connections and control at formal and informal levels, as symbolised by the presence of royal patrons and patronage: 'Her Royal Highness the Princess of Wales attended a *Welcome Back St. Petersburg* Gala, which was under the chairmanship of the Duchess of Abercorn, and Their Royal Highnesses the Prince and Princess of Wales attended *Otello*. We are very grateful for their support.' (ROH 1993c: 34). The ROH Trust has

Full, Premium and Patron ranked Members. Those contributing more than £5,000 included:

The American Friends of the Covent Garden and the Royal Ballet Inc. Bankers Trust Company: The British Council: Cable and Wireless plc: European Arts Festival: The Friends of Covent Garden: The Jean Sainsbury Royal Opera House Trust Fund: KPMG Peat Marwick: Legal and General Group plc: Lehman Bothers International: London Opera Festival: Midland Bank: Morgan Furze Ltd: The Paul Hamlyn Foundation: The Pacific and Oriental Steam Navigation Company: Richard Attenborough Trust: Royal Opera House Trust: RTZ Corporation plc: Sounds Like Birmingham: Union Bank of Switzerland: and Westminster City Council.

The Friends of Covent Garden publish *About the House* magazine—membership is about 20,000, it receives talks from members of the ROH staff plus celebrity interviews and has access to 'open' rehearsals (ibid.: 36). In 1992/93 £772,000 was donated to the work of the ROH. In New York the Met Guild also runs lecture programmes and a family participation scheme, *Growing Up With Opera,* which in 1993/94 gave 10 performances of *Il barbiere di Siviglia.* Shops run retail order and merchandising catalogue mailed to over 700,000 addresses, selling proprietary books etc. with titles such as *The Metropolitan Opera Guide to Recorded Opera* (Gruber 1993). The Guild ended in the black 1993/94 (after two years of losses) $28,000 after contributing $4.4 million to the Metropolitan Opera Association. Fund raisers during 1993/94 included galas and auctions at such hotels as The Four Seasons on 57th St., cabaret provided by mezzo 'star' Frederica von Stade, as well as the annual membership luncheon at the Waldorf Astoria with past 'diva' guest of honour Birgit Nilsson. The Lyric Opera of Chicago is aided by The Women's Board which 'for 37 years has supported Lyric Opera with its commitment, hard work and love'. In 1991 it raised $1.8 million. The Chicago Lyric Opera has over 33,000 subscribers per season, ticket sales and contributions reached new highs of $14.1 million and $10,390,000 respectively. 65 per cent of Lyric's expenses were covered by operating revenues.

Every company's promotional literature pays fulsome praise to donors and fund raisers, usually in a hierarchy of categories reflecting levels of contribution and labelled with references to degrees of precious metals and kitsch 'high' art. Scottish Opera's Annual Review for 1989/90 lists individuals, institutions, organisations, local authorities etc., without specifying sums involved, on a scale from Sponsors, through Benefactors, First Night Sponsors, Single Performance Sponsors, 21 Club-Gold Card Members, to 21 Standard Members, Premiere Patrons and lowly, but still worth a mention, Patrons (ibid.: 7-8). The much wealthier Los Angeles Music Centre Opera has ten Founding Angels to thank for ensuring that it finishes seasons in the black, and lists individuals, married couples, corporations, hotels etc. in its Yearbooks by amounts. Major Donors (1993/94) giving $100,000+ or, level two, $50,000+, and mere Donors in bands of $25,000+, $10,000+, $2,500+, and $1,000+.

San Francisco Opera (SFO) lists The Medallion Society of non-corporate donors topped by The Medici Circle: those giving $50,000 or more per year, followed by the Triple Gold Circle contributing $100,000 over three years, then the Gold Circle ($25,000 plus): Silver Circle ($15,000): Silver Circle second class ($10,000): Benefactors ($5,000): Sponsors ($3,000): Founders ($2,000): Sustaining Members ($1,000) and Supporting Members ($500). There are also donors making Tributary Contributions 'in memory of' or 'in honour of' someone. Corporate donors are listed in a similar hierarchy except that the top donorship status is membership of The Leadership Circle, followed by Public Support (three names only!). The Bel Canto Society includes all those who have 'with special generosity and foresight included SFO in their estate plans' (SFO 1993a: 51), whilst other named donors support particular projects. The SFO provides 'Preferred Seating ... assigned according to subscription length and level of support. Subscribers who request seats in preferred sections are expected to make an annual contribution to the SFO' (1993b: 29). As we shall see, in many cases the 'preferred seating' reward is on company boards. The New Israeli Opera Tel Aviv, disarmingly, lists donors as The Association of Opera Lovers ranked 1993/94 as Patrons (annual contribution NIS 11,000+) Honorary Fellows (NIS 7,000+) and Lovers (NIS 3,500+). Whatever language is employed, corporate and individual sponsorship of opera confirms, with the evidence of their spatial structures and seat pricing policies, the opera house as a stratified hierarchy of considerable economic detail and status distinctions, for the dead as well as living! The Met advertise for donors in its house journal *Opera News* through showing, in one example, an antique framed portrait of solidly middle-aged, middle class and, seemingly, healthy Caroline and Ron of Portland Oregon, both smiling into camera, she leaning over his right shoulder:

'A PORTRAIT OF GIVING'

Caroline and Ron have early childhood memories of their first opera experiences—the Metropolitan Opera Saturday radio broadcasts. 'Fortunately, both our parents loved the opera. We still listen to every Saturday afternoon broadcast and our favourite gifts to each other are tickets at the Met'. Caroline and Ron have decided to perpetuate their life-long commitment to the Metropolitan through their Wills. Because they are particularly interested in the nurturing of young opera singers, they have created in their estate plans a named endowment fund to support the Met's Young Artist Development Program. 'After receiving such pleasure from the Met, we want to give a significant and special gift—which for us is possible through our estates. We want to ensure the quality of Metropolitan Opera performances for the enjoyment of future generations'.

Over the years many Met family members have remembered the Met in their financial and estate planning. If you would like information on how you can include the Metropolitan Opera, as Caroline and Ron have done, please write or call David Martin Esq., Director of Planned Giving, Metropolitan Opera, Lincoln Center, New York, New York, 10023.

YOUR LEGACY TO THE MET

(*Opera News* 5 December 1992: 23)

'Although musical values in the United States have incorporated European artistic traditions, musical life was assured here only when it proved profitable and awarded social prestige to its consumers' (Martorella 1982: 41), even posthumously.

Industry Facts (iii) box office revenue and seat prices

A letter to *Opera* (April 1994: 399) noted that if a 1967 £1 could purchase approximately £9's worth in 1994, how come Royal Opera House seat prices have rocketed so? He notes that in 1967 a Covent Garden *Turandot* with Birgit Nilsson and James McCracken had seat prices ranging from 75p to £4.50, a Reri Grist-Giacommo Aragall-Cornel MacNeil *Rigoletto* from 40p to £1.90. 1994 *Rigoletto* prices ranged from £5 to £118. Another *Opera* correspondent (December 1990: 1403-4) noted '(In 1962) ... as an articled clerk on £17 a week, I could afford, and sat regularly in the balcony stall sides at 10/6d. Today at £48, such a seat would require a gross annual salary of £80,820. Some articled clerk!'. What audiences is Covent Garden attracting? The editor of *Opera* concluded 'Rich audiences, sponsor's audiences, audiences whose interest in opera may be marginal ... champagne louts ...' (Milnes 1989a: 269).

One of Covent Garden's anti-élitist defences for applying for Lottery funds has been to enable it to establish a £100 million endowment fund to enable lower seat prices. *The Royal Opera House Annual Report* of 1987/88 made the commitment to keeping 40 per cent of seats with 'relatively low admission prices' (ibid.: 5), often repeating the pledge to reduce ticket prices 'at the first opportunity' (*The Times* 19 April 1994). In 1984 a centre front stalls seat averaged £37, by 1994 £102, a 75 per cent rise taking inflation into account, making Covent Garden prices the second highest in Europe after the Salzburg Festival. The ROH seats 2095: in 1993 29 per cent of seats for opera were priced at under £22, 44 per cent for ballet. The average price for an opera seat was £62, for ballet £27. This average includes sometimes dramatically marked up prices for expensive 'stars' such as Domingo, Carreras, Pavarotti, Te Kanawa etc. In 1992/93 the value of these top priced performances (13 out of the total) equalled 9.4 per cent of total box office budgeted income. As discussed in the last chapter, top 'stars' for 1994/95 were Pavarotti and Domingo with identical price structures for their appearances in *Un ballo in Maschera* and *Stiffelio*: top Grand Tier prices of £267, Grand Tier Boxes seating four at £1068 and centre Orchestra Stalls at £197.50. Top prices for most performances, including *ballo* without Pavarotti, were £121.50: £486 (for Grand Tier Boxes) and £108. Front Amphitheatre Centre were £49.50 for Domingo and Pavarotti and £41 for most other productions.[39] The ROH like all companies, seeks to maximise seat sales, and succeeds to an overall 81 per cent plus of both seating and financial capacities though in all planning and financial senses it appears to be more secure than Britain's major regional companies.[40] The 1987/88 report reasserted: 'If we were to succeed in getting a substantial increase in our grant we would deploy it on reducing seat prices and tickets that we are finding hard to sell', argued Chairman Sir Angus Stirling, who continued by claiming that without subsidy increase 'seat prices will have to rise and operas by British composers and new operas will have to be cancelled', asking 'can Britain afford an international opera house like Covent Garden if the Government is not prepared to subsidise it as comparable houses abroad are?':

> It's the duty of the Arts Council to make the arts more accessible to the public, and we need more subsidy. We feel very strongly we should like to do everything we can to bring seat prices down. We want to be able to offer as wide a range of seat prices to as wide a range of people as possible ... We are considering a fund that would be invested, and would yield sufficient income to help sustain the operations at the Royal Opera House ... The Government must not be allowed to regard the Lottery as an alternative to the revenue subsidy. The extreme and persistent shortage of funding makes it impossible at the moment to maintain the quality of our work (Sir Angus Stirling *Independent on Sunday*, 4 June 1995: 10).

Comparable major international companies, especially the arch conservative in repertoire and character, the Met New York and Vienna State Opera (VSO) show higher capacity statistics. The VSO rarely fell below 95 per cent during season 1992/93 and frequently hit 100 per cent, the least popular single performances being of Tchaikovsky's *Queen of Spades* (89.56 per cent) and Janacek's *Katya Kabanova* (83.32 per cent). In most theatres demand is stable and outstrips supply through the deployment of forms of subscription scheme, 'a logical way to reduce the element of chance in securing a well-filled auditorium is to rely as little as possible on single seat sales' (Klees 1960: 671). At Covent Garden, subscribers get booking priorities and up to 20 per cent price discounts, which simultaneously exclude the irregular or uninformed potential consumer unable to commit themselves to regular attendances at particular performance three months in advance.[41] Most theatres acknowledge such problems notionally by retaining a small number of seats for sale on or near the performance date. At Covent Garden 65 rear

Amphitheatre seats are sold from 10a.m. on the day, limited to one per person, and when all seats have been sold, including the upper slips with the worst view of all (though some have music stands for students), standing places in the Stalls Circle are sold one and a half hours before curtain up. The latter are located and allocated in various ways in different theatres, but all tend to integrate with and materially sustain as a result, a particular relatively closed subcultural network of 'regulars' information, ticket exchanges through personal contacts, queuing rules etc. This hard-core 'regulars' subculture to be found in and around all the world's major opera houses will be discussed in more detail in the final chapter.

Large international houses employ a double hierarchy of seat prices, one determined by location in the theatre, the other by factors such as night of week, popularity of works, newness of production, the presence of 'stars' etc. With regard to the former, generally the lower the level and more central the seat the more expensive, with the possible exception of front-centre Grand Circle or Tier seats or boxes, being the most expensive (example house plans are given in Appendix B). Given the conventional nineteenth century horseshoe shape of auditoria, in which being able to see and be seen by the audience was as important as seeing the stage, there are a number of restricted view seats at all levels sold at discounted prices, a structural factor largely absent from newer theatres such as the Metropolitan Opera New York, The Hamburg State Opera and the Bastille Opera in Paris, built with £230 million of public money, although the size of most modern theatres brings its own seating drawbacks.[42]

Absolute prices change from year to year of course but the following examples demonstrate the price structuring employed. The Deutsche Oper Berlin is relatively straightforward, employing **A, B** and **C** categories which in 1992/3 ranged from 56DM to 11DM: 69DM to 14DM and 99DM to 17DM respectively. With at least three major companies in Berlin, perhaps competition keeps prices relatively low, for without such competition, the Bavarian State Opera Munich employs an **A-L** price structure in its main National Theatre, in 1993/4 a front 5 rows centre Stalls seat costing from 54DM to 312DM. A similar **Q-Y** hierarchy is used for the small (and beautiful!) Cuvillies Theatre, top seats ranging from 30DM to 225DM. The **A** range from this high of 54DM down to 7DM applied to recitals and orchestral concerts, as set against the **K** range during the main Season 252DM down to 18DM (for each performance of *Die Meistersinger von Nürnburg* and for the premiere of a new production of *Così fan tutte)*. The L range from 312DM down to 20DM applied to July/August Festival performances of a new production of *Tannhauser*, and further performances of *Die Meistersinger* and *La traviata*, the latter having been priced at I for non-Saturday nights and K for Saturday nights during the main season. These details are turgid but they demonstrate not only the complex pricing structures employed by major opera houses, but also the fine social distinctions which must exercise the minds and filofax of the Bavarian well-to-do. Small wonder too that those peering down from 'the gods' with the privilege of a 20DM restricted view believe, as compensation, that *they* are the 'true' opera lovers. They would have to, to participate in a stratified ritual in which they would otherwise possess little if any distinction at all.

Industry facts (iv): creativity in production choreography and design

The largest international houses tend towards a conservatism in repertoire 'star' casting, and production styles that suggests that thereby lies financial security in terms of revenues from non-subsidy sources: box office, and private and corporate gifts and sponsorship. To a certain extent this is negatively borne out by the experience of Britain's (and London's) second company, the English National Opera (ENO). Under the latter's *Power House* regime (Peter Jonas, General Manager: Mark Elder, Music Director: David Pountney, Director of Productions see Jonas *et al.* 1992), the ENO was noted, to use one of Covent Garden's 'aims', for its radical '... creativity in production, choreography and design' and programming policy, most clearly demonstrated by its 1990/91 'Twenty Plus' season which, apart from three Mozart operas mounted for the Mozart celebrations, included only works premiered in the twentieth century. Later the ENO acknowledged that: 'Whilst the more well known operas continued to attract higher attendances, less familiar works have not necessarily responded to marketing initiatives' (ENO 1993: 2). It is difficult to judge the impact of artistic policy challenges to repertoire conventions if, as in this instance, they coincide with an 18 per cent increase in seat prices and fewer performances than the previous season, but attendances did drop sharply during a season with a higher than usual number of 'lesser known' and 'new' works. The ENO is different to the ROH in many ways: productions are given in English, its pool of singers willing to sing in English is thus partially distinct, and although having its own company 'stars', some of whom sing abroad and at Covent Garden, plus some guests of international standing, it doesn't have the same capacity for constant remountings of familiar productions with changes of 'star' leads. These structural conditions could well explain the *Power House* style and success during, the 'yuppie' eighties and its fall from grace during the recession nineties. Whatever the causes 1992 ENO financial statements noted bleakly: 'box office income fell somewhat short of its target' (1992: 1), blaming the recession and regrettable though unavoidable seat price increases as the main culprits, not the possibility that the eighties production style had lost conventional middle class audience support. By 1993 the ENO had a deficit of £1 million. and an accumulated debt of £2.3 million. Audience figures had fallen by 6 per cent, some of the most adventurous productions doing the worst, for example 41 per cent for a well reviewed *Wozzeck*. By 1989 signs of desperation had crept into ENO advertising with a series of photographic images to which *The Times* responded 'Is this hard sell or soft porn?'[43] A sweaty male torso entwined with snake touted *The Magic Flute,* the ubiquitous Lesley Garrett 'in what Lorelei Lee would have called a "flimsy negligay" miming nameless pleasures' (Milnes 1989b in *Opera* : 1165), a stagehand in gay male beefcake pose, thumb hooked in belt and seductive glance at camera, advertised apparently very little for no opera names, dates, etc. accompanied them. *Opera* commented that the campaign was the latest betrayal by the company of its founder Lilian Baylis: 'given the price of such things (they) can hardly be cost effective for a company with a budgeted deficit of £300,000, what on earth is it all supposed to achieve? New audiences? Don't make me laugh' (ibid.: 1165). Jonas responded needs must when the Arts Council devil drives but rejected accusations of betrayal:

She (Baylis) believed in popular art for all people at popular prices. Her highminded principles were tempered by the reality of her ambition to build a broad-based British audience which would fertilise a British operatic tradition. It was she who urged us to be the missionaries of art and not rest until the work of our theatre is accessible to all (1989:1295).

The ENO also retorted that the campaign resulted from commissioned research to uncover the barriers preventing younger people attending opera, despite a peripheral interest. The research revealed that for them, titles, dates, casts etc. were:

> understandably meaningless ... Furthermore this section of the population has, through the broadcast media, attained a unique level of 'visual sophistication', and therefore are more likely to respond positively to the kind of advertising that creates an image or 'tone of voice' that dispels the numerous negative perceptions associated with opera. Ironically it is the attitude implicit in your Editorial that has kept younger people away from opera in droves, and it is only by firmly destroying ... negative perceptions of opera as 'élitist', inaccessible and probably boring as well, that new audiences are guaranteed. Judging by the coverage of ENO in the popular press—plus a quick look at the ENO audience—their current positioning appears to be an outstanding success *(Opera* December 1989: 1422).

By 1993 the ENO seeking to repair audience damage posted the London Underground with the announcement: 'Everyone Needs Opera':[44] '... a bizarre assertion at the best of times. Now at the worst of times it is almost hubristic' (*The Independent on Sunday* 18 April 1993: 9), for '... compared with the need for jobs and homes, the need for opera is a bit peripheral' (*The Times* 13 July 1993). Jonas replied:

> Perhaps I would have preferred 'Everyone Needs the Arts'. To those who think this impertinent I would reply that the arts are as vital as health, education, science, religion, politics. Remove them and you don't have a society ... Unless people in the arts are prepared to say their field is indispensable they deserve to be shot down. I don't think there ever was an eighties opera boom. You had a large growth in the eighties when the economy was moving. A lot of that growth has been consolidated. We knew we were priced a little too high for our market and it would affect us. But I certainly don't think there's any move away from adventurous opera productions. I believe that never again will the visual side of opera be taken any less seriously than it is now. Of

144

course when a recession comes the most adventurous work will suffer more than the comforting work because most people come to be comforted (*The Independent on Sunday* 18 April 1993: 9).

Graeme Kay of *Opera Now* accepted the recession argument to a degree but believe the ENO could not absolve itself of blame:

Latterly I've felt that productions were not just controversial but showed a complete lack of taste. *Die Fledermaus* was just plain tacky ... *Princess Ida* cheap and nasty ... recently they have been actively courting scandal rather than delivering interesting experimental productions which might attract controversy ... there has been a tendency for productions to develop in-jokes and self-parody, and that is deeply patronising to a loyal audience (March 1994: 9).

In *The Times:* (July 13: 35) Jonas described the Thatcherite '80s as a time:

when a very cold wind was blowing ... It was a bit like being a Vietnam veteran ... We sat there in the trenches in the heat of a vicious battle about public funding and the arts. But it taught us not to care about our own skins. It taught us to champion our organisations for better or worse. It taught us a lot about civil courage ... Mrs T was breathing down our necks and Rees-Mogg was hovering like some helicopter, spraying expressions of shame at every penny of public money being spent on the arts, and preaching that there was too much opera for the country to afford. The biggest load of bull ever spoken.

In the Jonas years state subsidy as proportion of ENO budget fell from 74 per cent to 49 per cent: 'I think the argument was based on false precepts, and it has now gone too far ... I admit we learnt a certain amount that was beneficial ... marketing techniques that brought benefits'.

Industry facts (v) Members of the Board

At the ENO the *Power House* label identified the triumvirate in control. In practice opera company power lies in the sometimes labyrinthine committee and board structures which bring together representatives of main funding forms and agencies and company personnel (see Appendix E). Some European houses are reputed to be controlled by Machiavels who arrogate power (Christiansen 1990 on Mortier at Brussels[45]), but generally artistic control rests with an ENO or Met New York style triumvirate answerable to or responsible to the governing board which, depending on the company's forms of financial support, is concerned with maintaining strong political links with the powers that be and/or with raising revenues. US company boards are preoccupied with fund raising, board presence determined critically by either personal gifts or access to networks of corporate and personal wealth, which reaffirm the class, status and political clout of those involved: 'In the cultural life of the US the board of directors enjoys unique status ... arts organizations ... rely chiefly on the private sector for financing. This is where the board comes in: its primary function is to raise money' (Price 1989: 8). And the amount of money needed is enormous,[46] in 1986/87 the ninety companies reporting to Opera America claimed expenses totalling $290.3 million, ticket sales, broadcasts, recordings and investments provided 55 per cent of this total, the remaining 45 per cent had to be raised. The federal government provided 2 per cent through the National Endowment for the Arts,[47] state and local governments a further 3.7 per cent, leaving 40 per cent to come from the individual and corporate sources referred to earlier, plus foundations, galas, retail outlets etc. Foundations and corporations give 11 per cent of total income. 'Corporations want a big bang for the buck. They want to be visible, to know where their money is going ... So opera companies must provide creative packaging of sponsorships and underwriting for productions' (Patricia Fleischer, Washington Opera quoted in Mauney 1989: 12). 'The quality of the performance is the most important thing. People don't give money to the individual soliciting it but to the company. We don't take donors for granted—we can't be arrogant' (Marilyn Shapiro of the Met quoted in Mauney: 13). Most donors, corporate and individual, like to be associated with a specific aspect of opera: education, a particular production, artist development, development departments try to match potential donors to upcoming projects:

The first priority is to build a track record of productions that people want to see. This increases the ticket sales, which in turn increase the donor base. Supertitles have been a positive influence in bringing more people to opera. We want to reach as many as we can (Russ Taylor, Seattle Opera quoted in Mauney 1989:12).

Opera is high profile and 'glamorous' and so opera boards tend to be drawn from the business, social and cultural élite, claims Price (1989) who describes five company boards in the US 'chosen at random',[48] amongst which the Met is 'unmatched for its prominence or elegance' anywhere. Its origins were social, 'the old Academy of Music simply didn't have enough boxes to satisfy the ostentatious demand of the nouveaux riches making their money in banking, railroads, real estate and the like'. Board members owned their boxes and interfered in policy all the time: 'one board member's wife requested that Jean de Reske sing *"Celeste Aida"* later in the opera as she did not like to get to the theatre before eight', clearly unaware that he omitted the aria altogether when he didn't wish to exert himself so early in the evening. Banning *Salome* after a single performance was another occasion when the board interfered in artistic matters.[49]

In 1976 the Met board was slimmed down into two tiers. The larger lower tier is made up of advisory directors, but power rests in the smaller upper tier of managing directors and executive committee of ten within, which is proposed by the nominating committee in consultation with the president and elected by the Board. The Met budget is over $100 million and the endowment is also $100 million plus. In 1989 the President Louise Humphrey, ex-first woman director of the National Bank of Cleveland stated 'I have simple criteria for board members "Give, get, or go". I want a well balanced board with different outlooks ... we have only two functions ... to hire the best general manager possible and to raise money to allow us to put on the best opera in the world' (Price 1989: 10). Run like an exclusive private club (similar descriptions are offered of the ROH Board see below), members of the boards and the Association (a large group affiliated with the managing and advisory directors in a mainly honorary capacity) can all submit names to the nominating committee. One benefactress, Sybil Harrington, has donated millions and, for her pains, had the auditorium named after her. It is rare for singers/musicians to be managing directors. Represented are Texaco which sponsors the famous Saturday matinée radio broadcasts, and

Chemical Bank which underwrites the early summer parks series of performances.[50] 'The paramount consideration however remains a deep interest in the art form'. Beyond setting budgetary restrictions there is no interference in artistic matters, though board members 'speak their mind on what they do or do not like'.

The big three controllers at the Met are currently President of the Board, Bruce Crawford associated with Omnicom advertising group, Artistic Director James Levine and General Manager Joseph Volpe, respectively involved with the company since 1976, '71 and '64. Volpe, appointed to this post in 1989, exceptionally worked his way up from starting as a carpenter, is responsible to the Board for whatever is produced. He and Levine collaborate on all artistic decisions, but Volpe has the financial responsibility. 'Every artistic decision is a financial one, and every financial decision is an artistic one' (quoted in Smith 1994: 14). Levine, as artistic director, initiates ideas and thoughts which are then long term feasibility studied and cost-tested. Proposals are then reviewed with Crawford as production funding is a board matter 'inasmuch as new productions are funded by either individuals or foundations'. Crawford is also consulted on other planning matters:

> Jim's responsibility is to be creative, to be abstract, to try to think and do whatever he can in the artistic area. I wait for Jim's initiative, and then we discuss the practical side of those ideas and we come to an agreement as to how to proceed (Smith 1994: 14).

Volpe has an Assistant Manager responsible for the administration of the artistic department 'She is in planning meetings with Jimmy, myself and (artistic administrator) Jonathan Friend, bringing to those meetings her experience and knowledge of singers, designers and directors'. She supervises television, the commissioning of new operas and domestic and foreign tours. It is Volpe's responsibility to set a standard for what is produced at the Met and how the Met is viewed by the public, company, and board.

> I pride myself on being supportive of everyone who performs at the Met, whether it be solo singer, chorister, dancer or orchestra member, because they need an environment where they can perform at their best.[51] This is one of the hardest parts of the job for it is not something you can do long-distance or second-hand.

I'm here four or five performances a week out of the seven, because it is important that you see first hand what is going on. The general manager must be here and involved in every aspect of what we produce ... I remember a performance when Placido Domingo was not feeling well, and when I went back to the dressing room he said 'Joe what do you think we should do?' That was the biggest compliment I could ever receive (Smith 1994: 15).

He tries to go down to the stage door to greet the most important artists on their first arrival of the season, and he attends virtually every performance, going backstage 'first to tell everyone to break a leg ... installing an intercom in his box so he can communicate with backstage as (in his opinion) needed' (Mayer 1990: 1415).

The social and financial contrast with the New York City Opera (budget $25 million in 1989) is clear: 'members are not here because it is chic—those people go to the Met' (Robert W. Wilson Chairman of a board of 30 and executive committee of nine which meets only when there is a 'problem', quoted in Price 1989: 11). The San Francisco Opera (budget $24 million 1989) board has three kinds of people: 'those who give and raise money, of course, but also ... workers' (ibid.: 11). In San Francisco board power over artistic matters is greater than in its New York counterparts not so much within the 75 strong boards as the 20 member executive committee. The chair of the Music Center Opera Association in Los Angeles is quoted:

The board needs wealth and connections, politically and socially, and it's very attractive to be a member. That's not to say a board seat is for sale—it isn't. A fifteen person executive committee takes the important decisions ... We are mostly satisfied with the repertory, but there was controversy with *Wozzek*. We ask advice from other companies and from individuals, such as our artistic consultant, Placido Domingo, but generally we don't interfere (ibid.: 44).

Dallas Civic Opera's board by contrast '... is a joint participant with the artistic staff in planning. We are a large organisation of about 250, many of whom don't come to the once a month meetings but will come to the annual opera ball'. This company's budget in 1989 was $5 million and the company mounted four productions, 'we must have a product that appeals to the public. You can't sell a bomb. And we do

149

like to have a Domingo or a Pavarotti who can stimulate the box-office' (Chairman Tony Copp quoted in Price 1989: 44). All board members must contribute $2,500 and serve a one year term renewable if they cough up the same again:

> A board member must bring a number of attributes to the position, foremost a personal involvement and caring for the institution, plus some basic knowledge. You have to have certain names to attract other names. Power and recognition come to those who know their own capability. They can't depend on an institution to find their own identity. Along with caring they must bring some expertise in a field with them. It's an unfortunate reality, but never forget we are in the *business* of art (Marie M. Ashdown ex-vice president of Met's Opera Guild Board quoted in Price: 44).

Despite the monetarist emphasis on meritocratic values and careers, as these Board lists suggest, and as the Annual Reports and promotional literature of the opera companies in the USA whose funding structures companies here are being asked to emulate, spell out all too clearly:

> In the world of the arts, the rich are always with us, exerting patronage and brokering power ... The old cycle—'go to war, make a fortune, become a patron of the arts'—hasn't changed much. Over the past decade a new generation of power brokers have come to the fore; men (and a few women) who by virtue of their wealth, position or personality, wield enormous influence on the crossroads where money and the arts meet central government (Rocco 1995: 22).

This much is clear with the ROH and ENO where a mere listing of the Boards in 1992/93 shrieks titles and establishment:

> The Royal Opera House Board of Directors: Angus Stirling: **Sir** James Spooner: **Sir** Alex Alexander: **Lord** Armstrong of Ilminster: **Sir** Christopher Benson: **Baroness** Blackstone of Stoke Newington: Vivien Duffield: Bamber Gascoigne: Robert Gavron: **Sir** Jeremy Isaacs: **Sir** John Manduell; **Sir** Kit McMahon: **Sir** David Plastow: Andrew Tuckey: Andrew Edwards. The Opera Board has in addition to some of the above: Irene Brendel: The

Earl of Chichester: Michael Scholar. The Patron of the Royal Opera is the **Prince** of Wales.

The ENO Board: **Earl** of Harewood, **Lord** Carr of Hadley; **Sir** Nicholas Goodison; Charles Alexander: Robert Boas; Paul Boateng; **Sir** Rodric Braithwaite; Roger Bramble; **Sir** Anthony Cleaver; **Dr** David Cohen; Mrs Donatella Flick; Mrs Robin Hambro; Mrs Sue Hammerson; **Lord** Justice Hoffman; David Mellor; Stephen Oliver; Ron Peet; **Lord** Thomson of Montieth; **Sir** Brian Unwin; **Lord** Weidenfeld; **Sir** Philip Wilkinson; **Lord** Wolfson of Sunningdale.

The ROH Board of 15 includes eight educated at Oxbridge, five at Eton, one academic (Master of Birkbeck), one 'heritage' administrator (National Trust/Courtauld Institute): two senior civil servants (Secretary of the Cabinet: Director H.M. Treasury) and eight company directors and/or chairmen linking such concerns as Morgan Crucible: John Swire and Sons: British Telecom: Shell, Carlton TV: Biotechnology Investment Ltd.: Trustee Savings Bank: Baring Brothers and Co.: House of Fraser: Lloyds: Reedpack Ltd. etc. These interconnections, and they are reinforced by detailed evidence of Royal Opera and ENO Boards, are consistent with Covent Garden's location at the cultural heart of Britain's ruling class: 'Britain is ruled by a capitalist class whose economic dominance is sustained by the operations of the state and whose members are disproportionately represented in the power élite which rules the state apparatus' (Scott, J. 1991: 151), including Covent Garden.
Why do such people turn to the arts in the first place? Donaldson (1987), whose husband was a member of the Board from 1958-74 claims: 'objectivity of judgement is more likely to be achieved by people whose personal ambitions lie elsewhere', more realistically, others claim 'Kudos as well as power, attaches itself to those who apply their talents and their riches to the service of the arts.' (Rocco 1995: 24). Lord Palumbo (ex Chairman of the Arts Council) presents the benign face of involvement: 'It goes back into the mists of time. Respectability, peer group acceptance, a feeling that having made money something should be given back to society ... (but) of course the act of patronage itself can be very satisfactory' (ibid.: 22). This peer group acceptance, socialisation and communality again reflect the ROH as at its core an exclusive club or 'Establishment dinner party'

(David Mellor, ex-National Heritage Secretary: 24),[52] 'and opera is after all only the continuation of (or prelude to) a jolly good dinner' (*Opera* November 1993: 1275), a club which finances and runs itself by all manner of informal as well as formal means. It has been claimed that the core of Britain's capitalist class comprises 0.1 per cent of the adult population, about 43,500 people who held 70 per cent of total wealth in 1986 (Scott 1991: 82). In 1990 there were 200 families with more than £50 million each amongst whom the names Windsor, Clore, Rothschild, and Sainsbury loom large. Rocco describes Lord Jacob Rothschild as a prime example of arts *animateur*: 'mover, shaker, puppet-master all rolled into one' (ibid.: 22). Sir Angus Stirling, Chairman of the ROH, argues that Lord Rothschild: 'is someone who does not like self-publicity. But he has great authority and his views certainly carry weight. He is someone to whom everyone would turn for advice. But he would never force his views on anyone' (Rocco 1995: 23). At Covent Garden two wealthy patrons dominate: Lord Sainsbury, former chairman of the Royal Opera; and Vivien Duffield, daughter of property tycoon Sir Charles Clore. Duffield is Chairman of the Royal Opera Appeal, which aims to raise enough funds to match whatever the Lottery provides plus an additional £100 million for the private endowment fund to underpin future artistic work and to stabilise or even lower seat prices.

> Sainsbury is a captain of industry, smooth and urbane. 'He treats everyone as if they were the under manager of his superstore at Penge' says one former government minister. Duffield, plump, plain spoken and the partner of another notorious *animateur* Jocelyn Stevens, former Rector of the Royal College of Art and now Chairman of English Heritage, can also be bullying. But she has far more of the common touch ... she is probably the only patron of the opera house to be part of the syndicate that buys lottery tickets ... Brazen Vivien Duffield may be but delicacy still cloaks the hard-nosed face of fund-raising at the opera house. Ever mindful of its patrons' sensibilities, Covent Garden has recently taken to calling the wealthiest of them its 'senior volunteers' and has rechristened its fund-raising drive a 'ladder of giving' (ibid.: 24).

Duffield and Sainsbury have already pledged to provide a large portion of the Lottery matched funds. 'It is unlikely that the full extent of their donations will ever be known. But together with other private donors, we are well on the way to meeting our matching target' (Keith Cooper, head of corporate affairs at the ROH quoted in ibid.: 24). 'As far as "senior volunteers" are concerned, Sainsbury and Duffield are up there with the gods. And to see them go about their business is an education into where power lies, and how it works in Britain, even today' (Sir Angus Stirling).

But even with their power it is no guarantee that either (or both) would get the replacement for Isaacs that they wanted:

> There is a tendency towards committee government. It is important to be seen to be taking all sorts of people, including minorities, into account. To be seen to be more democratic. We have changed our way of doing things at the Royal Opera House. I'm obliged now formally to seek the views of the chairman of the Arts Council and the Secretary of State [for National Heritage] on a number of things ... What it means in the end is that there is a sentiment in this country that prefers the compromise of committee deliberation to the bold confident decision of the individuals which involves a degree of risk. But it is the latter that has generally achieved great things in the past (Sir Angus Stirling quoted in Rocco 1995: 24).[53]

Opera is dramatised music with text. Opera is fetishised ritual, commodities conspicuously consumed as signs of lifestyle distinction and taste. Opera is 'high' art from which the general public should not be excluded, rather it should be encouraged to attend and appreciate. Opera is an 'industry' in crisis, forever lurching from one financial crisis to another despite its incorporation into audit culture. Opera appears to be more popular and commercially viable as 'opera' outside the opera house, politically contentious within, where subsidy retreat has offset efforts to make it more socially and culturally accessible by enforcing 'inaccessible' seat prices. 'Culturist' aspirations through state subsidy and influence may now be written off as part of British post war regenerative culture but they did at least challenge, naively admittedly, the élitist connotations and realities of opera in Britain, in London at least. The ascendancy of monetarist policies, requiring greater private and corporate funding, despite suggestions of meritocratic challenges to establishment power and lack of accountability, appears to have reaffirmed opera as a symbol, club, pastime for those with access to the substantial sums required to put it on. The opening of the Covent Garden season used to *officially* form part of the 'London Season' for 'Society' along with Queen Charlotte's Ball, The Royal Academy Summer Exhibition, The Royal Tournament, the Derby, Eton speech day and cricket, Henley, Ascot, Cowes Week etc., and though this Establishment calendar is now formally, like wealth concentration itself, somewhat modestly diluted, there can be little doubt that *informally* it still serves through these events and institutions to bind this dominant class together, represents its particular cultural outlook, 'life style and code of practice, and reinforce(s) the social closure ... exercised by the capitalist class as a whole' (Scott 1991: 94). Covent Garden is like any 'club' for such a closed and dominant status group: '... evening meetings over a drink or a meal at the club have been frequent and important sources of information for those involved in business and politics' (ibid.: 110). When the phrase 'mixed patronage' is used several meanings come to mind, not least that state subsidy for such élitist companies is wrong but such 'populist' policies are part of 'the necessary "concession" to other classes whose electoral and other support is necessary if the capitalist class is to maintain its general economic dominance'(ibid.: 82), and in any case for club members with wealth in millions, the club's future can be substantially assured by, if possible, millions of the general population's National Lottery money distributed by and through state channels also dominated by this very same class, to preserve what is then proclaimed a 'national institution'.[54]

The ROH's status, wealth and standing is some distance from that of SO, WNO, ON even ENO, but the élitist connotations stick to opera culture as a whole, and through their increased reliance on extra subsidy fund raising these companies are invariably drawn into being institutions also dominated by the local wealthy and those who have wealth connections. In 1982 Martorella commented: 'Opera, perhaps more than other performing arts, has had to work toward severing itself from its patrician roots and its image as an "élite" institution. A more realistic approach might be to acknowledge opera's élite position, and insure its aesthetic standards' (Martorella 1982: 79). The one does not necessarily follow from the other of course but Martorella's observation is perhaps inadvertently a provocative one for it would appear that currently in Britain behind the still deployed 'culturist' rhetoric, evident commercialisation of 'opera' outside the opera house, and media attacks on Covent Garden's élitism and unacceptable receipt of National Lottery funds, its élitism remains not only intact but through the expansion of Glyndebourne style dress coded dinner suited picnic sited opera in idyllic rural country house settings, as entrenched as it has ever been.

Notes

1. Even *Opera* magazine which takes a 'culturist' line on subsidies and the arts talks of opera and the arts generally as 'one of the few profitable growth industries' (September 1993: 1021). Intendant Hugues Gall talks of opera as a public service *'mission culturelle'* (Clark 1993: 144).

2. For an account of the Arts Council see Sinclair (1995). In his review Conrad (1995) states: '... it was too good to be true, flawed by its over-estimation of human nature. It began as an enlightened vision of renewal, but the practical realities ... were entrusted to the usual grafters, fixers and scramblers on the greasy pole. The result has been jobs for the boys (and girls) who concentrate their guile on denying money to artists'.

3. The Royal Opera, Sadlers Wells Opera (later English National Opera), Welsh National Opera, Scottish Opera.

4. For some, for example, Gerard Mortier when director of the Théatre Royal de la Monnaie Brussels, the enlightenment may well not be pleasing. He is reported as saying: 'I want to hold a mirror up to my country, so that it can see itself and realize its own mediocrity' (Christiansen 1990: 11).

5. For example Dupechez (1985) gives a detailed account of the Paris Opèra, the perpetual problem of making ends meet while catering for the persistently demanding Paris public. He concludes that the greatest director was Jacques Rouche (1914-45), and the greatest crisis the 'shipwreck period' of 1945-72. Opera organisation in Paris is a glory unto itself: for discussions on the new Bastille Opéra (Clark 1989) and its relationship to Paris' other opera houses (Chatelet, Opéra Comique, Palais Garnier, Salle Favart, Théatre des Champs Elysées Palais Omnisports for 'arena' stagings) see 'Opéra bouffe', *Opera* February 1989: 139.

6. For details of the effects of reunification on the arts (at the time there were 88 orchestras and 42 opera companies in East Germany for a population of 16 million) see Clark (1991a) who comments that the 'art for the people' philosophy was persisted with even though the state was bankrupt. Since reunification, rising ticket prices, service costs, falls (average 40 per cent) in audiences has led to the closure of some companies (Bautzen, Dobeln, Gorlitz) and a breakdown of repertoire, at Halle *'The*

Rocky Horror Show is a regular last minute replacement for *Fidelio*' (ibid.: 768). For similar details on Czechoslovakia see Clark (1991b and 1991c). By contrast the USA is now proclaimed operatically 'a land of plenty' (Heymont 1990: 20).

7.   Italian houses are in a permanent state of crisis. Opera houses are not crumbling due to terminal neglect. Central government has not stopped endowing them with large grants, standards of performance are not uniformly low, and opera companies are not all ran by incompetent would-be politicians. The crisis is to be found in the gap between rising costs and falling subsidies, between still impressive subsidies and a decline in the number of performances, and between the democratic rules of the Constitution and the political horsetrading they are sometimes used to licence (Jamieson 1994a). Falling subsidies have to be set in the context of 70 per cent plus of opera house budgets coming from the public purse—that is, in the 13 *teatri lirici*—public opera corporations—Milan, Rome, Florence, Palermo, Naples, Venice, Bologna, Turin, Verona, Trieste, Genoa, Cagliari and (oddity of oddity!) the Santa Cecilia Orchestra Rome, received in 1992 approx. £185 million, reduced to £179 million in 1993. An additional 20 opera houses including the Teatro Regio in Parma, classified as *teatri di tradizione,* rely on substantial regional funds. Seats in London or Munich are subsidised much less than in Italy. *Sovrintendenti* blame the public bureaucrats responsible for the day-to-day management. The theatres themselves are often not cost-effective—e.g. Bologna's Teatro Communale has 873 seats, La Fenice only 677 destroyed by fire in 1996—both scenically labour intensive—but both have wonderful acoustics and are irreplaceable! Jamieson describes the experiences of the Rome Opera until mid-1994 as 'A *Gesamtkunstwerk* o f mismanagement in which multiple strands of duplicity, profligacy and sheer ineptitude are woven into a single breathtaking narrative' (1994b: 32). In 1989 'special commissioner' Ferdinando Pinto was appointed to put the house in order and he cleared debts and even produced a small surplus. He stood for election as *sovrintendente* on a regular basis but instead the election of a Socialist Mayor, 'arranged' with the collusion of other parties, guaranteed some of the spoils i.e. a Christian Democrat, Gianpaolo Cresci, became *sovrintendente,* setting himself up as 'champion of simple opera loving Romans',

promising them what they really wanted and to defend them against intellectuals who had polluted their repertory with operas they had never heard of. Cresci dispensed with the services of an artistic director, planned productions of *Boris Godunov* and *Das Rheingold* were scrapped, *Toscas* and *Bohèmes* took their place. 'Rampant populism is not what is expected of a theatre receiving a £20 million. annual grant and since Italian intellectuals have no Anglo-Saxon inhibitions about proclaiming the inalienable centrality of *la cultura* to the civilized life, acres of earnest articles denounced Cresci's Philistinism, lack of vision and general ghastliness' (ibid.: 532). He employed more and more people to keep the unions happy, offered lucrative jobs to, and to buy, press reporters. Famous singers were unwilling to sing in Rome and so he paid Carreras 170 million lire ($106,000) to do so in a concert. Rome has 'the ugliest opera house in Italy' so he dressed it up with fancy floodlights and Persian carpets. Empty seats were filled by handing out free tickets. He did this and more without consulting the governing board and massive debts were acquired in the process. The opera receives an annual state subsidy of $31 million the projected deficit for the end of 1992/93 season was $37.5 million. The city council voted for his removal but instead the performing arts minister disbanded the board.

Eventually, in 1992, he found an artistic director to suit him— Giancarlo Menotti. Financial pressures led Menotti's first season's programme (1993/94) to be trimmed from 11 to nine and then six operas 'I get endless faxes from artists engaged to perform in Rome. Many of them will go elsewhere and I don't blame them. I can't give assurances. I have not the slightest idea if the season will take place.' The City of Rome saved the season with an impromptu gift of $12.5 million but machinations between the City and the national government to clear the remaining £25 million debt provoked a furious response from other houses which had just been informed of a cut of a total £21 million in their promised (and budgeted for) subsidy. The *sovrintendente* of other houses successfully issued an ultimatum—either cancel deals with Rome or we cancel our seasons immediately. In 1994 Cresci eventually resigned upon repeated requests from the newly elected Mayor, his place taken by Giorgio Vidusso an experienced musician with considerable administrative experience.

8. 'Just over a century ago, the critic of the *Illustrated Sporting and Dramatic News* wrote that "a very small sum extracted from the ratepayers would support a national opera, such as travellers find in every European capital but our own, and that the cost of a single ironclad, would endow such an institution in perpetuity". For "ironclad" read "Trident". Plus ça change, plus c'est la même chose'. *Opera* has maintained a very detailed coverage of funding issues in Britain during the past 15 years. It is impossible to refer here to all editorials and articles from this and other journals. For a considered account of play by 'half-time' see the Milnes' Editorial (*Opera* 1987: 496-7): 'The axe falls again', and for more recent details that of June 1993: 635.

9. For the artistic compromises of production sharing see Loppert (1992b): 'Making theatre is an organic business, a vital act drawing on the shared place, time and social background of its enactors and spectators equally'. Thus productions rarely travel well.

10. In the inter-war years for example: 'Highbrow-baiting was a favourite sport in the millionaire press, and it was taken up with enthusiasm on the golf links and in the smoke rooms of the commercial and county hotels ... Anti-intellectualism was also a matter of pride in the upper middle class. In the public schools, not withstanding a certain weakening in the cult of athleticism, the tyranny of the 'bloods' was unimpaired, and the budding of the artist or the poet was able to be treated with sniggering contempt. In the universities, aesthetes were persecuted by the boat club and rugger scrum hearties, debagging being the favourite Oxford punishment in the 1920s for those too immersed in their books' (Samuel 1983a: 35).

11. For example such as surrounded Deborah Warner's production of *Don Giovanni* at Glyndebourne in 1994. There will be further discussion about this production and the reactions it received amongst audience and within media in Chapters 6 and 8.

12. The ENO are not alone in arguing that it 'continues to find it difficult during this present and prolonged recession to raise adequate financial support from the private sector. Whilst 16 of the 19 productions were sponsored during the financial year and the membership of the corporate schemes was only just below the levels of the previous year, private sector funds are becoming

increasingly scarce' (ENO 1991: 2).

13.   The National Endowment of the Arts advised by the various
       arts councils and Partnership for the Arts, is not going to
       scatter money around promiscuously ... the total of state and
       Federal help for any organization should not exceed the
       amount of private support that organizations can raise. The
       people running American cultural organizations are not
       radicals; they are bankers, brokers, philanthropists, and
       businessmen who are as much exponents of private enterprise
       as anybody in the inner circles of the present Government
       (Schonberg quoted in Martorella 1982: 77).

14.   The Royal Opera House commissioned Price Waterhouse for a
       review of working practices, leading to them *Putting Our House
       in Order* (1993). Welsh National Opera annual reports are
       produced by Touche Ross a subdivision of Deloitte Touche
       Tohmatsu International who carry out the same duties for other
       companies world-wide including the San Francisco Opera. The
       English National Opera use Baker Tilly Chartered Accountants
       as auditors.

15.   *The 1992/93 Report of the Royal Opera House Covent Garden*
       includes accounts of Royal Ballet and Royal Opera performances
       which had included the cancellation of *Die Soldaten* by
       Zimmerman (misprinted as *Die Soldatenet*). The Report
       comments on the 'rarities': Porgy *and Bess, Die Frau ohne
       Schatten, Il viaggio a Reims, Alcina, Stiffelio, La Damnation de
       Faust,* the technical expertise of *Der fliegende Hollander,* the
       'style' of Pavarotti in *Tosca,* the *Otello* electricity generated by
       Solti, Domingo, Te Kanawa and Leiferkus. 'It seemed that the
       more the audience enjoyed *Il viaggio* the greater the critical
       bashing ...' Singers were singled out, either individually or in
       partnerships: Galina Gorchakova in *The Fiery Angel:* Giuseppe
       Sabbatini with conductor Daniele Gatti for *I Puritani:* Julia
       Varady and Christoph von Dohnanyi in *Der fliegende
       Hollander:* Domingo and Olga Borodina for *Samson et Dalila*:
       the 'unsurpassed combination' of Amanda Roocroft and Anne-
       Sophie von Otter in *I Capuleti:* Anna Tomowa-Sintow and
       Bernard Haitink in *Die Frau ohne Schatten:* Malfitano and
       Carreras in *Stiffelio:* Jones and Popov in *Turandot:* White and
       Haymon in *Porgy and Bess* and Barstow and Reiner Goldberg in

Fidelio.

Most companies produce a handbook promoting the forthcoming Season. That of the Frankfurt Opera is typical. After a brief introduction followed by photographs of the main concourse, the auditorium and backstage machinery, the new productions are introduced with casts, conductors, producers and other personnel and brief accompanying essays. A similar form is used to introduce the season's revivals, followed by a series of photographs from these already existing productions. The small concert programme follows, it in turn followed by a full list of all personnel. The handbook is completed by small black and white passport-sized photos of all the soloists due to perform. Singers even in the most 'democratic' houses cannot help but be the human face of opera. Here, listing is alphabetical and not hierarchical but recognition of the few 'star' names in this middle-ranking company (for example, Jochen Kowalski: Anna Tomowa-Sintow) leads to an inevitably hierarchical reading of the list.

The Lyric Theatre of Chicago's literature includes photos of some of the donors of financial gifts! The promotional literature includes the following: 'If critics see Anderson as a young Sutherland, fans compare her to Callas' (*Time*): 'Evenings any opera house would have been justly proud of ... *Elektra* and *The Bartered Bride* were given world-class vocal performances by Lyric Opera' (*New York Times*). As for advertising particular works: *Die Walkure* is described as 'A brother and sister fall in love—A daughter defies the commands of her father—A husband and wife forsake their marriage vows—There's chaos in the cosmos and the gods are not amused! Last season, our stage director had the Rhinemaidens swinging and swooping on bungee chords 40 feet above the stage—and the audience went wild!' As for *Tosca*: 'If Scarpia had known what else *Tosca* could do with a dinner knife, he would have ordered minestrone'.

16. 100DM in 1991, 700DM in 1992, 200DM in 1993. A sign of global warming?

17. There had been an enormous outcry (between The Arts Council of Great Britain and the ROH, in the media) over the ROH's policy of spending into deficit (£5 million) in 1990-91. The ACGB appointed a team of assessors and warned the ROH that it would have to be back in the black in three years. Lord Sainsbury,

then Chairman of Covent Garden (friend of the PM Thatcher) threatened to resign if funding was cut (i.e. lower than inflation). 'Someone somewhere decrees that London is to have an international opera house, and someone, somewhere declines to pay for it' (*Opera* June 1990: 644).

18. Warnock acknowledged the ROH as a flagship organisation of international renown, confirmed that it should receive substantial public funding, and praised its recent artistic achievements, accepted that the financial crisis was due in large part to the disrepair of the building, but criticised the accumulated deficit and the management which had run it up for deciding what was artistically right first and then counting the cost (that is, losing patience with persistent underfunding it budgeted for a deficit) later. Warnock did not address seat prices. The Price-Waterhouse report did, challenging ACGB to come clean about the reasons for subsidy 'to help make normal performances accessible to normal people', and to help with the costs of restoring the building. Its recommendations for streamlining led to 70 redundancies. But reports on opera funding in Britain are legion. On 27 January 1995 the ACGB released an edited version of its *Lyric Theatre Review* in which the displacement of the ROH and the ENO during refurbishments to their respective theatres was the main concern, but dealt with in ways which clearly gave the ROH priority, even flirted with the idea of dismantling 'the people's opera house' (ENO), and overall noted the reduced demand for opera in London (see Canning 1995b: 16).

19. Strikes editorial on the ROH 'black-out' strike, *Opera* (December 1985: 1352) quoted the cause as the orchestra's claim for 10 per cent rise against the offer of 8.5 per cent with the expected ACGB grant for 1985/86 being a rise of 2 per cent showing a shortfall of £2 million—following the 1984/5 shortfall of £750,000. The editorial also covers some of the negotiated issues then affecting the CG orchestra including long-service increments, time and a half for overtime (including) Saturday rehearsals etc and quoted Sir Claus Moser, then chairman of the ROH 'If "candle-end economies" (to use the Prime Minister's phrase) cause the Royal Opera House and other artistic restitutions to cut activities and standards built up over decades, both country and Government will lose much more than our

masters in the Treasury may realise'. He referred to the growing influence of the 'anti-arts Establishment' in belittling the Arts Council and the achievements of its clients. 'The remarkable success story of the Arts since the War would not have happened without public funding. The Minister represents the greatest sponsor of the Arts—the State—and in both the first and last resort, he and the Government must bear the responsibility for their future welfare.' The Orchestra of the ROH were involved in an industrial dispute during 1991/92 season. Scottish Opera chorus threatened a strike early 1995/96 season.

20. More accurately, on page ten, an *Evening Standard* leader of October 1992 described Covent Garden as 'A London asset ...' *Opera* editorial October 1985 detailed how in defence of opera's relatively high costs and thus subsidies relative to other theatrical forms, the broadcast of élite establishments to the masses (of ratepayers) is a major defence. This editorial appeared in the context of a then at least three year lack of agreement between chorus members equity, stars and BBC. Similarly during 1992/93 four productions seen by 2.7 million on television: 12 productions heard by 1.2 million on radio: five Midland Bank proms: 30,000 saw three Big Screen performances in the Covent Garden Piazza: 5000 heard *Samson et Dalilah* at Kenwood; 20,670 children attended 13 schools matinees.

21. The ENO's aims refer to 'the lyric art' rather than opera (ENO 1991: 1).

22. The ACGB pre-1990 got what money was allocated from the Treasury and distributed according to policies which the ACGB itself formulated (the 'arms length approach'). In 1990 with the appointment of property developer Lord Palumbo as Chairman by the government, and a government minister who directed rather than proposed Arts Council policy and who himself appointed a committee to see that it is carried out, a new structure 'improving accountability to the taxpayer' was set in place. The results of ACGB funding policies included several high-profile casualties, e.g. Kent Opera (see Platt 1990).

23. *Opera* (June 1988: 653) identified Covent Garden's need for an identity. The Met New York has the identity of a singers house, the Welsh National Opera as the nearest British equivalent to a European house ' a sort of 'Frankfurt am Taff', but what was Covent Garden's identity? Perhaps the 'Covent Garden

Experience' is the result of that search, i.e. red plush, Crush Bar champagne and so on.

24. *The Times* (5 May 1993) reported that as opera nights were more lucrative at Covent Garden than ballet nights, and given the deficit of £2.8 million ballet performances were going to be cut for season 1993-94 to 96 (of 15 titles) compared to 160 of opera (20 titles).

25. Please note that financial details refer to either The Royal Opera House Covent Garden, or each of its three companies especially that which concerns us, The Royal Opera.

26. The Royal Ballet remained the same size and the Birmingham Royal Ballet and Orchestra increased its overall strength marginally.

27. 'Although such patronage in the United States qualifies as a deductible business expense, most corporations use the charitable contribution' provision of the 1935 Revenue Act, which allows donations totalling a maximum 10 per cent of income to be offset against taxable profits. US arts organisations are registered charities' Cole 1990: 4). However, in 1993 this tax deductible incentive was removed leaving corporate donors to use the 1935 Act but private donors without any such provision, much to the concern of arts organisations.

28. In 1992 the Met's annual budget (approx. $115 million) was greater than that of the next five largest companies (San Francisco, Chicago, New York City Opera, Houston, Los Angeles) combined (see Smith 1992b:4).

29. In earlier figures (see Cole 1990: 2-6) the ROH had calculated total resource per performance' (i.e. dividing total resources by number of performances) showing (in £000s) La Scala Milan at £278: the Met £231: Rome £185: Florence £159: Paris £147: Vienna £146: Munich £103: Berlin £99: ROH £87: and ENO £71. However the ROH's higher proportion of cheaper ballet performances within this total compared with other houses somewhat reduces the significance of these figures.

30. The Australian Opera's 1992 expenditure breakdown shows 66.1 per cent ($20.8 million) on salaries and wages: 16.3 per cent (£5.1 million) on 'Other presentation and production': 10.6 per cent on marketing ($3.3 million) and 7.1 per cent ($2.2 million) on General Office and Finance (ibid.: 16).

31. The WNO appeared in Cardiff, Swansea and Rhyl during

1992/93 for three, two and one period respectively incurring travel and subsistence costs of over £85,000. Marketing costs for the whole season reached £344,023. The Company also appeared in England (84 performances) with several week long including repeat visits to Birmingham, Bristol, Liverpool, Oxford, Southampton and Manchester. Box office income from Welsh performances = £623,392, for English = £2,221,868.

Nine Local Authorities supported the WNO ranging from £87,000 Cardiff City Council to £8,500 and £5,000 respectively from Swansea City Council and Mid Glamorgan County Council. Birmingham City Council gave the second highest grant of £50,000. Sponsorship and donations came from 36 (+ other) sources and totalled £568,012 (less than in the previous Season when it was £642,699.) The biggest source was the Peter Moores Foundation £170, 049.

32. Scottish Opera also toured into England, e.g. to Newcastle, but as part of its decision in 1995 to go part-time (again seemingly without political or financial support from the SAC) all English touring was suspended.

33. The cast, piano accompanied, was made up of recent graduates from British, European and American music institutions, and the production was seen by over 5000 people.

34. The WNO has a Community and Education department which includes theatre tours, talks, and interviews and so on. SO's is called Opera for All. All three companies have Education Officers. The Royal Opera held over 50 introductory opera workshops in schools throughout the country reaching over 2,000 school children. The ROH Education Department 'subsidized' performances by the ROH and sold to students, young people, unemployed and other targetted groups on low, fixed incomes, prices from £3.50-£20 with over 1045 seats at under £12 in 1993, touted as 'a number throughout the season' actually numbered four in total, two opera (*Madama Butterfly* and *Die Zauberflöte*) and two ballet.

35. There are sponsorships which are by comparison enlightened: The Peter Moores Foundation (Moores is of the Littlewoods retail and pools family) has sponsored the recordings of many 'lesser known' works by Donizetti, Mayr and Meyerbeer, such productions as the Goodall *Ring* in English at the ENO, *Parsifal, Maria Stuarda* and *Julius Caesar* with Janet Baker. Peter

Moores also sponsors scholarships to the London Opera Centre such as Jane Eaglen, Rosalind Plowright and Simon Keenlyside. Moores is a great supporter of opera in English. 'I very much object to doing things that the government should be doing, and therefore try not to fill gaps that have been created by governments or local authorities withdrawing their funds ... I object very strongly that once you have raised the money, the government reduces their contribution ... The arts and the railways are automatically funded nationally in France, Italy and Germany, but art is not an English tradition, especially music ... there's space for getting off your own bum and finding extra money, but the majority of funding should be from the state' (quoted in Milnes 1993b: 290).

Hugues Gall, Intendant of Geneva Grand Theatre, agrees sponsorship is OK:

> as long as it is the icing on the cake. As soon as you increase your dependence on private funding, by raising seat prices or giving blocks of tickets to sponsors, you change your public. It becomes less popular and often less discerning. Opera requires harmony not just between stage and pit but also performers and public: it's a love affair you need a reaction on both sides. There's no point in having a public institution where the audience has little idea of what is being played. They'll applaud happily after every aria, and the next day they read from the critics that they have sponsored a piece of rubbish. In the long term you can't survive with a gap between the reactions of connoisseurs and the wider public. The artists wouldn't know for whom they were singing (Clark 1993: 145).

36. In 1989/90 Scottish Opera's sponsorship deals included £150,000 from IBM towards Berlioz' *Les Troyens* and £50,000 from North Sea oil and gas explorer/producer Amerada Hess Ltd for Weir's *The Vanishing Bridegroom,* which received much publicity at the time but which has yet to be revived.
37. An interesting party game might be matching sponsors to operas as here Nestlé and *Guillaume Tell.*
38. In 1995 July, immediately following the disclosure that the ROH had been successful with its claim on National Lottery funds, it announced that it was cancelling its schools matinees for 1995/96

because of lack of sponsorship. A sponsor was later found, the performances reinstated, only to be cancelled again at the end of 1996.

39. The ROH Trust Gala of *Stiffelio*, 11 July 1995 had a top price of £550 per seat (£187 basic price plus £363 donation), with comparable gradings through the rest of the house. In any company's accounts, artists costs are going to be important but in the large international house they remain closely guarded secrets shared by the 'stars' and their managements, rumours surfacing only when 'scandals' of specific seat price increases for particular singers are taken to reflect their higher fees. The 25th anniversary performance gala at the Met for Pavarotti and Domingo had a top price of $ 1000.

40. Smaller regional companies which, in Britain, do a certain amount of touring, throw the combination of commercialism and culturalism into quite different relief. Taking the WNO as example: the WNO per cent capacities for season 1992/93 (no. of performances in brackets) were *Il barbiere di Siviglia* 84 per cent (14): *Elektra* 61 per cent (16): *Ernani* 58 per cent (14): *Iphigénie en Tauride* 45 per cent (13): *La bohème* 89 per cent *(10): La favorita* 68 per cent (4): *Madama Butterfly* 88 per cent (20): *Pelléas et Mélisande* 95 per cent (4): *The Magic Flute* 98 per cent (3): capacity best venues played were Bristol 83 per cent and Liverpool 78 per cent (with a 2280 seater theatre) Oxford, Rhyl and Swansea all 77 per cent (the last with a 980 seater theatre). Lowest attendance was Manchester at 64 per cent. The WNO provide data for all operas performed between January 1981 and March '93. Of the 56 operas given the 10 most performed were: *Butterfly* (75 performances): *Bohème* (68): *Carmen* (68): *Barber* (63): *traviata* (56): *Tosca (55): Rigoletto, Der Freischutz* (57.81 per cent): *Wozzeck* (59.22 per cent): *Tamburlane* (60.89 per cent): *Elektra* (61.43 per cent): *Greek Passion* (61.94 per cent): *Jenufa* 62.25 per cent) and *Ernani* (63.61 per cent). In terms of yield per seat the top 10 were: *Tristan und Isolde: Pelléas et Mélisande* and *Le Comte Ory: La fanciulla del West* and *The Trojans.*

MNO Report for 1992/3: £11,933,600: Staff costs £5,640,662: Cost of reductions and performances £5,164,950.: Administration expenses £1,022,163. Surplus for financial year before transfers to reserves and benevolent fund £37,861. Itemisations of depreciation costs include premises, motor vehicles, trailers, equipment and fittings, computer, costumes and scenery, and so on. Box Office Income £3,168,640: Concerts/recordings £799,505. Sponsorships middle-scale companies, including individual production costs ranging from the main company's *Tosca* (£255,715) to the small *Macbeth* National Tour (£2,267) which travelled from Cardiff to Worthing, Richmond to Milton Keynes.

Audience statistics for Scottish Opera's 1992/93 Season show that the 50 performances in Glasgow (Theatre Royal capacity 1547) achieved overall an 83 per cent seat capacity ranging from 91 per cent each for *Il trovatore*, *The Magic Flute* and *Norma*, to 62 per cent for *The Makropoulos Case*. For the 15 performances given in Edinburgh (King's Theatre capacity 1300) overall 90 per cent capacity was achieved (57 per cent for *The Makropoulos Case*). Ten performances in Aberdeen (His Majesty's Theatre capacity 1363) managed only 56 per cent overall.

Opera North prides itself on its reputation for exploring the repertory as 'the liveliest company in the land' (*1990/91 Annual Review*). From 1990 to 1993 amongst the 33 productions (30 operas including three revivals) performed ON presented *Jerusalem* and *Attila* by Verdi, Nielsen's *Masquerade*, Dukas' *Ariane and Bluebeard*, Ravel's *L'Heure Espagnol*, Gerhard's *The Duenna*, Weill's *The Threepenny Opera*, Tchaikovsky's *Yolanta*, *Wozzeck*, *The Secret Marriage* (Cimarosa), Saxton's *Caritas*, Berkeley's *Baa-Baa Black Sheep*, Schreker's *Der Ferne Klang*, Chabrier's *L'Étoile* and Tippett's *King Priam*. Percentage capacity figures show that in 1990/91 12 *La traviatas* reached 100 per cent capacity and 11 *Così's* 93 per cent, in '91/92 14 *Butterflys* and 11 *Carmens* reached 100 per cent and 20 *Don Giovannis* 90 per cent, whilst in 90/91 3 performances of *Caritas* reached 43 per cent and *Der Ferne Klang* in 91/92 60 per cent. Of the 33 productions in these three seasons 16 reached 75 per cent of capacity or less. Performances are given in on average eight venues, some returned to two or even three times in the Season (e.g. Leeds and Manchester). Venues don't show significant differences but the times of year visited do, for example September and October appear to be less popular months for opera in Manchester and Leeds than other periods of the season.

41. Editorial *Opera* (June 1980: 526) 'The advantage of subscribing to an opera house are many: as well as the purely financial

168

advantages it means ... that the company will be sustained by the support of a regular critical and appreciative public to whom it can introduce the less *familiar masterpieces* (my italics) in the repertory, perhaps more regularly than before. A subscription scheme also develops a kind of camaraderie in the audience—talking to neighbours.' In *Opera* (February 1990: 146) 'I believe that an opera house that does not make all the seats available for every performance does not deserve any government subsidy, however small. A subscription policy means that the best seats in all parts of the house are taken by the same people. The British people are subsidizing the people who have the time and money to take out the subscription'. (D. Richards). This writer goes on to comment about the ROH scheme in which existing subscribers have priority over new subscribers, about difficulties in finding a subscription series which suits completely, and especially the difficulties for those who live some way from the theatre.

42. *Opera* (July 1985: 806) reported on the new massive opera house come conference centre, in Nice (L'Akropolis) which took three years to build covers 54,000 square metres in which the Apollo Auditorium with a stage 28m by 30.5m that is, bigger than that of the Paris Opèra. the auditorium is an enormous oval. The same issue (ibid.: 801-2) revealed the new Queensland Performing Arts Complex in Brisbane opened by the Duke and Duchess of Kent. Fifth of the Australian states to build such a centre—including a concert hall (2059 seats) a small studio (264) and a lyric opera house (2100). The proscenium is 48' wide by 30'6" high and 60' depth, with a similar space behind and another to one side. The pit is adjustable and able to accommodate from 30 to 90 players.

43. At more or less the same time the ROH too was using such tactics, advertising e.g. Puccini's *Turandot* as 'savage and erotic'.

44. Scottish Opera's pre-1995/96 season campaign was 'Get off your arias'.

45. But who, when he took over at Salzburg was formerly obliged to share power with an administrator Hans Landesmann and a 'President' Heinrich Weismuller, responsible for control of the budget. When director of Geneva's Grand Théatre, Hugues Gall had no resident music director, he chose repertoire cast and production team (see Clark 1993). 75 per cent of Geneva's

revenue comes from Geneva tax payers: 98 per cent attendance record, 50 per cent seats sold on subscription before season begins 'reducing his dependence on safe repertoire' (ibid.: 144).

46. See Martorella 1982 for a detailed account of the economics of opera in the USA at that time.

47. Government support for musical arts in the USA 'has been small and indirect. Through tax exemptions, land grants, urban renewal programs, park and recreation subsidies and Title II which provided funds through state education program' (Martorella 1982: 73).

48. The five large opera houses in the USA are, with their capacities, The Metropolitan Opera (3,600); Lyric Opera of Chicago (3,500); San Francisco Opera (3000); Seattle Opera House (2875); New York City Opera (2500).

49. Perhaps the cruelest interference took place in the 1940s when a board member objected to the 'unsightliness' of Marjorie Lawrence upon her return to the house in *Tannhauser* and *Tristan und Isolde* following a polio bout. The first woman on the board was Mrs August Belmont who in the Depression founded the Metropolitan Opera Guild for fund raising. The board showed its clout when the Met moved to the Lincoln Centre by making sure that the old theatre could not be bought by a rival, organising a quick sale and having it pulled down.

50. Manhattan Central Park: Queens Cunningham Park; Bronx: Van Cortlandt Park; Stanhope New Jersey: Waterloo Village; Brooklyn: Prospect Park; Brooklyn: Marine Park; Staten Island: Miller Field; Montclair New Jersey: Brookdale Park; New Brunswick New Jersey: Buccleuch Park; Pennsauken New Jersey: Cooper River Park etc..

51. In 1995 news broke (see Reid 1995) that Marta Brennan, assistant stage director at the Met, was suing the company in the first US case claiming heterosexual discrimination and favouritism given to young gay men. The board, claims Reid, is so worried about the Met's gay image, behind stage and in the audience, that 'it has spent much of the past year hotly debating the pros and cons of scheduling Britten's *Death in Venice ...*' (ibid.: 13). In the official papers filed Brennan declared 'I'm a 46-year-old heterosexual female. I believe that the Metropolitan Opera's general manager Joe Volpe, and executive stage director David Kneuss subjected me to a hostile work

environment ...' (ibid.: 13). In this article Volpe is described accurately but unnecessarily as 'a former carpenter'.

52. 'I never believed the British Establishment existed until I became a minister and started going to dinner parties where I'd be lobbied about the ROH' (David Mellor quoted in Rocca 1995: 24). Mellor, like all Heritage Secretary's has been berated by the high arts lobby, Conrad (1995) describing him as 'so vulgar he even knows how many CD's he has'.

53. On the internecine Board politicking of 1997 as the the Royal Opera House prepared to close for two years for renovations (see *Opera* July 1997, editorial by Milnes).

54. The ACGB periodically threatens removal of subsidy from smaller companies for example, Glyndebourne Touring Opera (GTO) *(Opera* December 1993: 1383). GTO, 'a company which fulfils all the requirements of excellence, accessibility and educational outreach' *(Opera* editorial September 1993: 1022) is part-subsidised by GFO which is self-financing. *Opera* talks of the 'yawning chasm 'between arts organizations and the body that is supposed to sustain them. ACGB has an amateur Chairman and is given funds to disperse by the Heritage Dept. as from 1995 the Heritage Minister was Virginia Bottomley. There is more in *Opera* (editorial September 1993) where there is talk of delaying tactics re: the impending Lottery, and talk of abandonment of the 'arms length policy' of the Government (National Heritage Secretary) to the ACGB and the arts. General pressure has been to spread alarm and despondency amongst the arts in general. 'The sole raison d'etre for the ROH being given money deducted from the wage packets of shop assistants in Bootle is that it is the nation's international opera show-case, and without it it cannot compete with similar institutions as the Met and the Bastille' (correspondent to *Opera* July 1991: 752).

4　The opera museum

museum n. orig. a temple, home or resort of the Muses: a place of study: a resort of the learned: an institution or repository for the collection, exhibition, and study of objects of artistic, scientific, historic, or educational interest: an art gallery (US): a collection of curiosities (*Chambers English Dictionary* 1988: 945).

Introduction

Whatever the forms and sources of a particular opera house's funding, worldwide the language of audit culture—'box office receipts', 'central overheads', 'overheads for maintenance and utilities', 'performance-related costs', 'aims and aspirations', 'enhancement funding', 'less VAT'—has become a prominent addition to existing multilingual discourses on music, text and drama, and one which confirms, rather than challenges, opera as 'museum culture'[1] underwrites opera as cost and efficiency conscious 'auratic' art within 'the culture industry'. 'Museum culture' refers to all aspects of the exhibition and consumption of 'high' art, and thus to much that will be discussed in subsequent chapters, but with reference to opera, the phrase is applied most frequently to repertoire content: the narrow and repetitive concentration on a small proportion of largely nineteenth century works by a small select band of composers. There is not complete stagnation: new operas are written, although they rarely find their way on to the world's main stages;[2] lesser known works are 'rediscovered' although these are usually by composers who are already known;[3] and sub-genres such as *baroque* and pre-*baroque* are unearthed,[4] but the exhibits are largely known and familiar. Curators busily reorganise, redisplay and recatalogue, creating an impression of 'newness', conferring on producers in particular the responsibility and power of reimposing the ideology of opera as 'high *living* art' on the duly, albeit at times, enraged but awe-inspired.

Despite dissenting murmurs from many in the business ('Opera is a museum of *living* art'—Nicholas Payne Director of Covent Garden BBC Radio 3, 24 March 1994), the vast majority of opera's exhibits date from between 1780 (Mozart's *Idomeneo* appeared in 1781, *Le Nozze di Figaro* in 1786: *Don Giovanni* 1787, *Così fan tutte* 1790 and *Die Zauberflöte* in 1791) and 1926 (*Turandot*). Hence Puccini's 'epitaph for an artistic epoch' (Ashbrook and Powers 1991: ix); essentially 'the operatic canon is closed, our attitude to the art necessarily retrospective' (Conrad quoted in Littlejohn 1993: 26).[5] For some, another work is of more significance in signalling the subsequent search for relevance of an art form under cultural and commercial siege. Boulez in a notorious 1966 interview by *Der Spiegel* ('M. Boulez you are the funeral orator of modern opera') favoured Berg's *Wozzeck* (1925) and later *Lulu:* 'since 1935 ... no opera worth mentioning has been composed ... Berg probably knew that he had brought a chapter to its close' (quoted in Christiansen 1985: 186-94).

> This less than two-hour ... traversal of the life and death of an obscure army private has become, over the years, a paradigm of the plight of the common man ... [an] unrestrainedly bleak view of humanity ... Berg's setting is ineluctably an outgrowth of nineteenth century music ... [it] may be twentieth century in its non-tonal orientation, but it is not serial, as many commentators like to call it, *Wozzeck* is a deeply human work, and in this respect it is nineteenth century in origin, set apart from the nihilistic plays that were bred following the First World War (Smith 1990).

Despite the attractions of clear demarcation lines marked by a single work, opera's crisis, which culminated in the *Turandot* or *Wozzeck* schism, can be traced through the accumulated works of its last major composers: 'Puccini ... Richard Strauss [and] Massenet really ended the development of opera. There have been lots of last gasps after them but they brought opera to its final fruition and somehow also its decadence' (Epstein quoted in Milnes 1992). The hard-edged phrase: 'the Opera Industry', is thus little more than a euphemism for new ways of marketing old products, persuading audiences to purchase newly wrapped *Kultur*, for a museum trying to pay its way.

So, how to judge the conservativism of this museum's collection? Given the ROH audit terminology encountered in the previous chapter, much depends on definitions of lesser known' and 'new' set against the measured repertoire core. Using the Littlejohn (1993) top 100 performed works for 1989/90, listed with additional data in Appendix A, the core is clearly mapped out, but definitions of 'lesser known' and 'new' are problematic and arbitrary. 'Lesser known' could mean outside this 100 but, given the entrenched stability of the top half over time outside the top 50 might be more reliable. Even so, either choice would conceal national variations. Littlejohn's 65 and 86, for example, are Lortzing's *Zar und Zimmermann* and Nicolai's *The Merry Wives of Windsor*, both owing their rankings to their popularity with German and mid-European audiences and rarely staged elsewhere. Tendencies towards the universal opera commodity *qua* singing, production and musical styles—much influenced by ease of air travel, shared productions and record company power—are still offset, sometimes resiliently, by such local tastes and traditions. Nor is the repertoire wholly static or always predictable as 'lesser known' works surface, establish long- or short-term vogues, and are possibly championed by particular performers and production exchange between houses. Mozart's current popularity is very much a development of the second half of the twentieth century. Faggioni's production of Massenet's *Don Quichotte* starring, usually, Ruggiero Raimondi, has appeared in many theatres over two decades, probably notching up more performances than all other productions of this work put together during the same period. Long- and short-term trends are thus not easy to judge, but using the Littlejohn 100 as a benchmark for the 1990s thus far show a continuing exploration of the (non-comic) *bel canto* works of Donizetti and Rossini, the advance of lesser known Verdi, Puccini, Massenet, Janacek and Britten, and that the growing interest by musicologists, specialist performers and recording companies in baroque and pre-baroque opera has not translated itself into equivalent mainstream audience interest. These trends lie tentatively around the periphery of a core repertoire, reshuffled from year to year but resilient over time. Given these qualifications I treat all works outside the Littlejohn 100 as 'lesser known', unless 'new'. The discussion which follows draws on details from some of the 28 companies listed in Appendix C, which show, for example, repeated productions of 'lesser knowns' such as *Maria Stuarda* (Donizetti) and *La fanciulla del West* (Puccini).

Just as many problems attend any definition of 'new'. Possible criteria are: dates of composition, or premieres, premieres in particular continents, countries or theatres. Opera dictionaries and guides (for example, Rosenthal and Warrack 1980: Kobbé, [rev] Harewood 1961) confirm that all are important in a work's provenance. Other sources, such as company publicity materials, suggest that the first ever staging is the criterion (*Opera Now* 1995). Given the length of gestation and production costs of new works these might be some time after compositions. Should an arbitrary time period—say 10 years after composition or 20, define 'new'? In 1961 composer Luigi Dallapiccola contributing to one of many post-war 'wakes' over opera, defined 'new' works as those by living composers (1961: 11) which, on his death in 1975, would mean that his *Volo di Notte* (1940) and *Il Prigioniero* (1950) thereby instantaneously lost their 'new' status. Michael Tippett is still alive, so is his *The Midsummer Marriage* (1955) still a 'new' opera? Should the 'newness' of musical, textual, dramatic language also be taken into account?[6] Sometimes this would appear to be the customary meaning of the alternative, and just as problematic, label, 'modern opera'. On the basis of earlier comments this could mean any work written in a post-*Wozzeck* (1925) style, whatever that might mean. Institutional guidance is not very revealing either: in 1960 the New Opera Company's London season included the first British staging of Schoenberg's *Erwartung* (begun in 1909, premiered 1924), which, compared with Britten's *Peter Grimes* (1945) is less conventional and audience-friendly. Corigliano's *The Ghosts of Versailles* premiered at the New York Met in 1991/92, although 'new' in many senses, is less than 'new' in musical, textual and dramatic terms. Whatever its meaning, 'new' is used frequently to justify opera's continuing contemporary cultural relevance.

Administrators, music directors and the like are deeply sensitive to the 'museum culture' slur, no doubt because current high profile debates about public accountability and accessibility of opera are conducted not only in terms of seat prices, but also in terms of vitality of repertoire, popularity of works mounted and styles of presentation. Their defensive rhetoric does not, however, clarify the definitional problems. James Levine, Met Music Director talks of 'the mistaken perception of opera as a post-*Turandot* dying art-form' referring to 'a huge spectrum of twentieth century works played by the Met and elsewhere: 'from Strauss and Janacek through Britten to *Pelléas*, *Bluebeard* and *Erwartung*' (Milnes 1995b: 896). However, these three are unfortunate examples, for although arguably musically, textually and dramatically 'new', they are of pre-*Turandot* vintage, premiered in 1902, 1918 and 1924 respectively. Perhaps Levine is echoing the suggestion implicit in the ENO's 'Twenty Plus' season, that 'new' or 'modern' operas are those composed this century—a hardly satisfactory solution. Alternatively there is a suggestion here that 'new' might be a euphemism for unpopular and financially risky.

If by 'culture' one means the norms and values of an institution as a whole, all that is learnt, shared, imposed on or disputed by those within, 'new' opera is evidently a highly negotiable label. Although opera has a continuing post-*Turandot* development including proclaimed 'masterworks' such as Schoenberg's *Moses und Aron* (1957) and Zimmermann's *Die Soldaten* (1965), the few relatively well established, widely performed, financially as well as aesthetically viable 'last gasps' of the past 70 years are in conservative musical, textual and dramatic languages—those of Britten, Poulenc and Glass rather than Nono, Berio and Ligetti. To many leading composers of the immediate post-war decade—Boulez, Nono, Stockhausen, Pousseur and Berio—the operatic form had no relevance; its grand houses, such as Covent Garden and La Scala Milan, were offensive costly monuments to the past which, Boulez metaphorically asserted, should be 'blown up'. Yet in the season of the Boulez/*Der Spiegel* interview (1966) 20 new operas were scheduled in West Germany alone,[7] a clue perhaps to the problematic meaning of *'new'* in any 'auratic culture'. The culture itself is given, ordered, ritualised, hierarchical and above all 'safe'; our attitude to it is reverent and retrospective. The quality of 'newness' in a work tends thus to be attributed, from a variety of concerned sources (performers, critics, audiences), to any element deemed 'unsafe' or threatening. Desertion of tonality is still 'new' for some, for others it might be lack of 'realism' or producer's 'idée'. However, the fetish of 'newness' is a core component of recycled commodification in a consumerist economy. All museums depend on the appearance of 'newness', set against and affirming the fundamental long-term security and value of its exhibits. In this sense, the most radical and subversive intentions of producers—whatever the short-term scandalous impact of their work—can only be conservative in long-term material effects. Their 'new' work is ephemeral judged against the thereby reified 'original'. 'The Covent Garden management must be delighted ... they not only have a *Ring* of unbeatable musical calibre, but a big opera scandal to boot; and, with luck, the publicity should sell the few seats left for the remaining three performances' (Canning review of Jones/Haitink *Ring* 1995d: 20). Thus, given the culture's conservatism and the 'industry's' economics, such elements of the 'new', including 'new' operas, may be modishly 'safe' in box office terms, in the short term, but justify yet another 'new' production in the long term.

Whilst majority opinion is that, barring 'last gasps', the museum is closed,[8] practitioners are desperately concerned to prove otherwise and occasionally there is sufficient high profile creativity on a grand enough scale to convince some that the beast is not fully dead. In the US the 1990s suggests one such moment. Bolcom, composer of *McTeague* (1993) states '... we all thought opera was dead and it's not even sick!' mentioning new works by, amongst others, Philip Glass, Anthony Davis, John Adams, John Corigliano, Ned Rorem and Robert Moran (Malitz 1992: 16).

The Littlejohn 100 adds further difficulties with its inclusion of 'musicals', *My Fair Lady* (1956) and *West Side Story* (1957), obvious snubs to Levine's and Bolcom's faith in opera as a still healthy art form in any purist sense.[9] The newest *opera* in the 100 is Poulenc's *Les Dialogues des Carmélites* (1957) at 95, musically and dramatically a conservative work which, for one critic, demonstrates the audience verdict on opera's development, the 1780-1926 era showing music and singing *qua* singing elements steadily ceding ground to the dramatic and the theatrical so that:

> ... the long debate closed with something like this: the best opera is the one that is nearest to a play with supporting music, But the complication is that the winner quickly lost legitimacy by losing opera's historic constituency. The cessation of melody pretty much finished opera off as far as any chance of appealing to a broad

public was concerned, and the extreme dissonance of the advanced modernists sealed the file. A few operas that are conservative in this respect have had some success since 1930, but in their conservatism they have done little to provide a jumping off point for new developments (Crutchfield 1991:54).[10]

1780-1926

Between the Mozart-Puccini bookends Littlejohn's list demonstrates the repertoire's conservatism: 29 of the top 50 operas are by five composers (Mozart, Verdi, Wagner, R. Strauss and Puccini); 30 of the top are 100 are by the first three; 62 of the top 100 are by ten composers (Rossini, Offenbach, Donizetti, Massenet and Britten in addition to the previous five). Three works date from before 1780—Monteverdi's *L'incoronazione di Poppea* (1642); Handel's *Giulio Cesare* (1724); Gluck's *Orfeo ed Euridice* (1762)—eight from after 1926 including the two 'musicals', a Lehar operetta, Strauss's *Arabella*, (like all post-*Rosenkavalier* Strauss operas, at one level a dramatised discourse on opera's struggle for survival), the Poulenc and three Britten *(Peter Grimes, Albert Herring* and *The Turn of the Screw).* In terms of popularity Britten appears to be the most popular composer of the second half of this century, his works strong on conventional narrative theatricality, most based on known literary sources (Melville, Mann, James), with recognisable structural components 'arias' and so on. In the list 89 works date from between 1780 and 1926 including eight by Mozart and 81 date from between 1814 and 1926. Indeed 54 of the top 100 and 31 of the top 50 date from between 1850 and 1909, showing an almost perfect distribution curve peaking in the 1860s and 1870s, falling away gradually to a sharp drop in the 1920s with *Wozzeck and Turandot*.

Opera company repertoires are not consistently conservative, as can be seen from details of large international houses such as Covent Garden, Munich, Vienna and the Met, middle-ranking houses such as Frankfurt, Hamburg, Bologna, Florence and Chicago,[11] and important national companies somewhat out of the international network such as the Stockholm Royal Opera. Of the 21 works presented at Covent Garden during 1993-94 (including Britten's *Gloriana* by Opera North); 14 are in this 100, eight of which are by four composers; (Verdi, Mozart, Puccini, Bizet), in the top 20; *Figaro*

(1), *Tosca* (2), *Die Zauberflöte* (7), *Butterfly* (9), *Rigoletto* (10), *Carmen* (11), *Aida* (15) and *Un ballo in Maschera* (18). Two works are in the lower 50, *Katya Kabanova* (55) and *L'Italiana in Algeri* (74). *La fanciulla del West* (Puccini): *Mitridate re di Ponto* (Mozart): *Chérubin* (Massenet): *Fedora* (Giordano): *Mosé in Egitto* (Rossini) and *Gloriana* (Britten) qualify as 'lesser known' by known composers. The Royal Opera presented one 'new' work by any criterion: *Gawain* (Birtwistle), premiered the previous season.[12]

Conservatism of repertoire depends on numbers of performances of works as much as the works themselves. During this season *Carmen* was performed 17 times, The *Magic Flute* 14, *Gawain* and *Fanciulla* five times each. Of the 179 performances, 83 were of the eight top 20 works and 107 of works in the Top 50. Programme planning requires precise assessments of just how many performances a work can sustain, with or without cast changes, during single and successive seasons: *Carmen, Flute, Aida, Rigoletto,* had at least two scheduled changes of casts.[13] 'Stars' may be drafted in to revitalise familiar productions—for example, *Tosca* (in the Zeffirelli production originally built around Callas and Gobbi in 1964) framed Anna Tomowa-Sintow's Tosca, a concession to this 'star' who with the Scarpia, Sergei Leiferkus, had originally been engaged to appear in a cancelled revival of the 'lesser known' and less popular *Prince Igor* (Borodin).

ROH General Administrator Sir Jeremy Isaacs, also aware of the 'museum' slur,[14] notes the need for repertoire variety but justifies conservatism by using 'shock of the new' to include the experience of a complete newcomer faced with even a standard repertoire piece such as a traditional *Tosca* (1994). When he talks of discovering 'new' works, he means the movement into the core repertoire of Janacek operas as well as the exploration of the 18 or so relatively rare Verdi works hidden behind the familiar 10. By the year 2000 the ROH will have performed in summer Verdi festivals (some in concert), all of Verdi's 28 operas, thus serving various functions: a musicological/academic one of completeness in critical editions; by a composer at the very heart of the popular repertoire; filling the summer months with an audience and income catching production; and providing 'newness' in a safe commercial package.

The Vienna State Opera (VSO) remains organised as a *repertory* rather than a *stagione* house, enabling the presentation of a greater number of works with several cast changes in any one season. During the 1992-93 season the VSO performed 40 works, only three of which were outside the top 100—Richard Strauss's *Capriccio*; Donizetti's *Maria Stuarda* and Mussorgsky's *Khovanschina*. Of the remaining 37 only one was outside the top 65; *Arabella* at 79.[15] Not for nothing does the VSO earn its reputation as the most conservative of all great opera houses, a conservatism which extends to staging and even dress codes for the *Stehparterre* (standing area behind the stalls).

If Vienna has a rival for this accolade then it is, *pace* Levine, the Met. Rumours abound that wealthy trustees are mainly responsible for this conservatism, although they claim otherwise. Virgil Thompson's opera, *Lord Byron*, was commissioned by the Met but then refused a production because 'It seems that both incest and pregnancy (among the high born) are considered bad taste' (Thompson quoted in O'Connor 1991: 164).[16] 'Elsewhere he wrote 'to criticize the visual investiture of Met productions would be like recommending a tailor to a patient dying of cancer', although even the Met stirs itself towards international trends. During the three seasons 1989-92, 49 operas were produced, 41 in the top 100 including all the top 20 bar *Butterfly* which has since received a new production and made up much lost ground. Of the eight others, six were 'lesser knowns' by popular composers—three by Puccini (*La fanciulla del West, It tabarro, Suor Angelica*), Rossini's *Semiramide*, Verdi's *Luisa Miller* and *Porgy and Bess* (Gershwin). Only two works could be defined as 'modern' (*Billy Budd* by Britten and *The Ghosts of Versailles*) and only the latter as 'new'. Taking into consideration productions in store, Levine states: 'Here at the Met we also play Weill ... have a Shostakovich, two Poulenc ... and a third Janacek, a fourth Britten', arguing that the Met commissions new works, revives, tours and televises them: '*Ghosts, Carmelites, Erwartung, Lulu, Mahagonny, Bluebeard* have all been transmitted: Name me another opera house, government subsidised or not, that does this' (quoted in Milnes 1995b: 896). This doesn't, however, alter the Met's overall conservatism, which is also reflected in its reputation as 'a singers house', in which the focus is on 'stars' and singing above all else, 'safe' enough in production and design terms to accommodate singers such as Domingo and Pavarotti for reputedly lower fees than they could claim elsewhere but who consequently earn considerable 'opera' spin-offs.

Major international houses' planning priorities involve schedules worked around the availability, years in advance, of premier artists and, sometimes in conjunction with them, new productions[17] which 'add excitement ... and if spaced out properly generate a ... momentum ... which helps ticket sales, and [other] ... aspects of the revenue side' (Joe Volpe, Met General Manager quoted in Mayer 1990: 1415). Volpe would like to present a commissioned work every two or three years, but:

> ... the more we work on planning, the more it becomes apparent how reliant we are on the standard repertory. Our public will buy *Bohèmes*, *Traviatas*, *Aidas*, and those will consistently do 95% of capacity or more. Sometimes we have too many performances of a standard repertory opera in consecutive seasons. I believe we should do only ten or twelve performances a year of each of the extremely popular works, to avoid subscribers seeing the same operas every year. We need more operas and fewer performances of standard works. Then we go from standard works to operas we would like to perform but which rely heavily on casting. There are certain works for which you need superstar casts to have necessary box office revenues. And still there are certain operas that, no matter what, won't sell the way we hoped—for example *Rusalka*. It could be that we did too many performances, but if you do a new production you cannot limit it to four performances. This season we are planning a new *Pelléas* and doing six performances, and we're doing six of *The Ghosts of Versailles*. It's a question of the mix of repertory—can we have more operas with fewer performances of each? This puts pressure on our schedule because of rehearsals. For season '95/96 the repertory mix is expected to achieve 90% capacity or better ...[18] When I say *Mahagonny*'s [Weill's *The Rise and Fall of the City of Mahagonny*] coming back people cringe, they say it doesn't do well at the box office. But if we do six performances I don't believe it's going to hurt our overall box office. It's a work we should be doing (quoted in Mayer 1990: 1415).

Isaacs of Covent Garden argues that there is a limit to a public's appetite for *Bohème* and *La traviata* and so on:

> ... however appealing, the best productions need a rest. Opera audiences who come to a theatre several times a season are entitled to a changing, lively, challenging repertory which mixes

the familiar with works they have not seen for ages—or have never seen before (Isaacs 1994: 21).

The Lyric Opera of Chicago in the four Seasons between 1991 and 1994 produced 32 works, 22 of them in the Top 100.[19] The other 10 included 'lesser knowns': *Don Quichotte* (Massenet); Bellini's *Puritani;* Prokofiev's *The Gambler;* Gluck's *Alceste;* and once again Puccini's *La fanciulla del West.*[20] "New' works were Bolcom's *McTeague* and Argento's *The Voyage of Edgar Allan Poe.* Given US funding policies the recent upsurge of American opera produced by large as well as medium and small companies, suggests that greater reliance on private sources does not necessarily mean the demise of 'new' works. European evidence, however, suggests otherwise. In the 1990-91 season the 12 most frequently produced operas by all US companies were, in order, Littlejohn's 9, 1, 3, 12, 8, 10, 7, 6, 11, 29, 4, 19 *(Opera News* November 1992: 32).

Italian opera houses present smaller seasons than is common or expected outside Italy, for many reasons not least parlous finances but also cultural misconceptions: 'We tend to think that all Italians go to opera. That's not at all true. It's more soccer that attracts the vast public and there are some opera houses where you think you are at a soccer game' (June Anderson quoted in Baker 1995: 18). In its 1993-94 season Bologna, with an admirable orchestra, shrewd management and a good chorus' (Jamieson 1994a: 35), presented only 49 performances of six works (eight if one counts Puccini's *Trittico (Il tabarro, Suor Angelica, Gianni Schicchi)* as three[21] only one of the latter *(Gianni Schicchi* at 82) and one other, Rossini's *L'Italiana in Algeri* (74), in the Littlejohn 100. The other six were the other two parts of *Il trittico (Il tabarro* and *Suor Angelica), Maria Stuarda* (Donizetti), *Il Caso Makropulos* (Janacek), *I Lombardi alla prima crocciata* (Verdi) and *Barbablu* (Offenbach). This is bold programming for whilst Janacek's *Jenufa, Katya Kabanova* and *The Cunning Little Vixen* have become increasingly popular in the past 20 years, *The Makropoulos Case* is musically and textually less accessible although here, as the title indicates, it was given in Italian and with Italian 'stars' such as Emilia Marty and Raina Kabaiwanska. This highlights an additional element in some major companies' attempts to stage 'lesser known', even 'new', works, performing them in the vernacular, and even when so doing, perhaps also using surtitles. Bologna's 1992-93 season was more conventional

(*Gotterdammerung, L'Incoronazione di Poppea, Simon Boccanegra, Adriana Lecouvreur* and *Rigoletto*) although the balance was still at the lower levels of the 100 (51, 71, 58, 53 and 10 respectively). This season also included a genuine rarity— *Amor rende sagace*, by Cimarosa. Florence is also exceptional, presenting in 1993 six works, only one of which was Italian: *La Cenerentola* (Rossini). The others were *Boris Godunov, Jenufa, Carmen, Die Zauberflöte* and *Die Frau ohne schatten* (43, 52, 66, 11, 7 and 76).[22]

In Germany, the Hamburg Opera during 1993-94 gave 116 performances of 19 works, all in the top 100 and 16 of which were in the top 50:[23] 59 performances were of the nine works in the top 20. Munich with the highest state funding of any German house, gave 166 performances of 29 operas (including the *Cavalleria rusticana* and *Pagliacci* double bill) in its two auditoria, the National Theatre and the Alte Residenztheater (Cuvillies Theatre). Twenty-four of the 29 were in the top 100 and 21 were in the top 50.[24] Dvorak's *Dmitrij*, Berlioz' *Damnation of Faust*, Schostakovitch's *Lady Macbeth of Mtsensk*, Penderecki's *Ubu Rex*, Eckehard Mayer's *Sansibar*, Hans Werner Henze's *Der Prinz von Homburg* and a Mozart double bill of *Apollo et Hyacinthus* and *II sogno di Scipione* were the unlisted works. The Penderecki and Mayer and arguably the Henze, qualify as 'new'.

National or cultural distinctions explain some but not all variations in 'lesser known' and 'new' presentations. The Royal Opera Stockholm in 1991-92 presented 19 operas, nine of which were in the top 100 and seven in the top 20 (1-4, 7, 11, 13). 'Lesser known' were *Maria Stuarda*, Mozart's *II Re pastore*, Suppe's *Boccaccio* (1879) and Haffner's *Elecktra* (1785). No fewer than six were 'new' and had a distinctly Swedish flavour (although German, Haffner's career was largely spent in Sweden) including *Backanterna* by Bortz and *Malin-Historiens portar oppnar sig* by Nilsson.[25]

Opera as 'a museum culture' implies not only a conservative repertoire but also the sociopolitical, ritual and economic traditions by which opera is auratic. Even when 'new' operas are staged in the conventional opera house, they immediately become incorporated into that culture. The problem for some therefore becomes not how to create 'new' operas, but how to liberate opera from the opera house:

> While opera remains primarily an historical artefact, the idiom
> will continue to be marginal, exotic, something to be squabbled

over by those whose proprietary interest rejects any notion of relevance... it is a battle between those who would keep opera locked in the museum display cabinet and those who insist that opera come out on the streets ... [the problem is] how to find room for new opera in a world which still sees Alban Berg as a contemporary and therefore difficult composer (Kimberley 1993: 787, 786).

This is a problem which some recent developments suggest is insoluble. Favourite composers' music may be posthumously forged into 'new' works such as 'Mozart's' *The Jewel Box*, drawn from some of his uncompleted comic operas (see Griffiths 1991). Alternatively, outside the opera house, familiar works may be pared down to their dramatic essentials as in the Peter Brook/Centres International de Créations Théatrales *Pelléas* and widely toured *(La Tragédie de Carmen*. Alternatively, 'unknown' substrata from before 1780 may be unearthed.

Moving the heart

During the mid-eighteenth century opera underwent a change of paradigm, not cataclysmic, but revolutionary over time. Existing dominant *opera seria* (or Neapolitan opera given that court's importance in elaborating and realising its principles), was a 'repository of manners' (Vieira de Carvalho 1995: 41) much as courtly ballads had been in the late Middle Ages (Elias 1983), existing in 'structural resonance' (Kaden 1984: 21ff), with the 'civilizing process' (Elias 1994) of the Enlightenment: 'The stately proportions, dignified formality, graced with arabesques that are themselves formalized, furnished an ornate counterpoint to the stylized living that the courts enjoyed' (Orrey 1992: 67). *Opera seria* in the eighteenth century was maintained by court cultures: Naples, Lisbon, St Petersburg, Vienna and by associations of aristocrats in Venice, Milan and London and so on (Bauman 1994: 47). *Opera seria* characters are distanced from their emotions, views and impulses; they don't act spontaneously but in accordance with a plan, their passions repressed by rational imperatives dictated by the responsibilities of roles played, above all those adopted for reasons of state, idealised in the monarch as enlightened despot:

Alexander the Great, resolute in war, magnanimous in victory; Titus removed, godlike, far above petty jealousy, extending an almost more than Christian forbearance and forgiveness towards those who had plotted against him ... (Orrey 1992: 67).

Musically this disassociation of outer behaviour from inner experience and feelings is mirrored by the enacted *secco recitative*[26] set against the emoted aria, the public face of convention displayed in the former, revealed and explained in the latter (Vieira de Carvalho 1995: 43).

Opera seria reflected the general control of nature by reason and rationality. Politics controlled human passions; magnificent sets and elaborate singing changed nature into high artifice (for example, the *aria da capo* of perfect symmetry), the ultimate human evidence of which was the *castrato*. 'In every respect the genre upheld a sense of dignity, stability, and decorum that lay at the heart of the culture sustained by the ruling class' (Bauman 1994: 47). The audience too was conventionally meant to show detachment, discretion and distance (Vieira de Carvalho 1995: 41-61). Increasingly this inherent artifice and stylisation was challenged by such writers as Algarotti, Calzabigi and Rousseau (Bauman 1994: 69-83), the latter using baroque to identify all he disputed in art: the extravagant and strange, magnificent and overstated, the opposite of what art should be—'*naturel*'. He repudiated ornamentation and the *castrato*, arguing that singing should be at the service of both the role being enacted and the character not the singer and *seem* spontaneous. The opera:

> ... should not astonish, but arouse interest, not aim at the marvellous, but ... at the natural by means of perfect illusion. And since there is no illusion without the involvement or engagement of the heart, then singing should be expressive not *baroque*. In opera the best music makes itself forgotten (Rousseau quoted in Vieira de Carvalho 1993b).

For Rousseau *opera seria*'s anti-democratic content was part of its artificiality, especially as manifested in grand and Parisian style, set against radical *buffo* works emerging from Italy such as Pergolesi's *La serva padrona* (1733). This was concerned with the romantic entanglements of maid and master and was originally an intermezzo in the composer's *opéra seria, Il prigioner superbo,* later achieving independent success especially at its first appearance in Paris in 1752,[27] inspiring thereafter French composers to develop *opera comique,* hitherto no more than parodies or primitive comedies in which music played a subordinate role.

On the grand operatic scale, the 'paradigm change', which united music and text in drama, was wrought by the reforms of Christoph Willibald von Gluck—dramatised with density and wit by Richard Strauss in *Capriccio* (1942)—with librettists such as Calzabigi and sponsorship from such influential figures as Count Durazzo.[28] Commencing his career in classic Metastasian *opera seria* (named after Pietro Metastavio the influential poet and librettist) Gluck pursued spontaneity and dramatic truth, still involving classical figures, but recognisable as characters not merely singers—gods perhaps, but with mortal feelings and dilemmas. The resultant engagement of audiences in the 'perfect illusion of reality' in *Alceste* (1767), *Iphigénie en Aulide* (1 774) and *Iphigénie en Tauride* (1779) was dramatic:

> ... those who have seen it represented could not keep their eyes a moment off the stage, during the whole performance, having their attention so irritated, and their consternation so raised, that they were kept in perpetual anxiety, between hope and fear for the event, till the last scene of the drama ... (Dr Burney quoted in Scholes 1959, vol 2: 93)

'... like a thriller, a superdrama!' (Vieira de Carvalho 1995: 47).

Until the French Revolution, opera remained largely concerned with the mythological and historical—gods, heroes, kings—ordinary mortals playing no more than subsidiary roles, if present at all. In Britain, Germany, Italy and France, ballad opera, *Singspiel, opera buffa, opéra comique* and the sentimental *drame bourgeois,* more accessible to wider publics, were by contrast more 'realistic' or mortal in their concerns and representations. Opera's very origins may also be so described, for they partly lay in dramatic madrigals such as Orazio Vecchi's *Amfiparnaso* (1594) which, using folk themes, attempted to translate into music 'earthy', popular *commedia dell'arte.* Composers of *opera seria,* especially through the incorporation of *commedia* episodes as light relief from heavy *seria,* sought to stifle any seriousness in such associations.[29] For practical demonstrations we may turn yet again to Strauss who in *Ariadne auf naxos* (1912/1916) parodied, and in *Die Frau ohne Schatten* (1919) reviewed this god-mortal dialectic. Arguably serious 'realism' was born out of the French Revolution. The rescue *opéras comiques*, popular in France in the 1790s, were based on *faits divers* drawn from the 'real-life' experience of the Revolution. These included Bouilly's libretto for Gaveaux' *Leonore, ou l'amour conjugal* (1798), Cherubini's *Les deux journées* (1800), and Beethoven's *Leonore/Fidelio* (1805/1814). *Fidelio*, though now part of the 'Beethoven legacy' and ranked amongst the highest of 'high' operatic achievements, was originally, considered unoperatic in the 'true' (that is, *seria*) sense, falling short of 'majestic illusion' and atmosphere of nobility because of its *opéra comique* format of spoken dialogue between musical numbers.

It is in Mozart's great works including two with clear *seria* pedigree: *Idomeneo* (1781) and *La clemenza di Tito* (1791) but especially the four which now feature in the top 10 of Littlejohn's 100—*Figaro, Così, Don Giovanni* and *The Magic Flute*—that the challenge to *opera seria* is most emphatically signalled. These are works in which characters are characters, not rigid symbols of station neglecting 'to ask just why two characters should find themselves at a particular corner of the palace, with a third character, accidentally there at the same time eavesdropping' (Orrey 1992: 103). The appeal to Mozart of Beaumarchais' *The Marriage of Figaro* was its ingenuity, logic and protodemocracy. The Countess and her maid Susanna are as joined in their character and narrative accord as they are separated by rank. In the same opera it is the Count's servant Figaro who has guile and wily wit, just as Leporello is the (street)wise counterpoint to his headstrong and driven aristocratic master, Don Giovanni. In these works the aesthetic battle between two versions of Enlightenment—the courtly concern for rationalised behaviour, repressed emotions, actions constrained by duty, hierarchies, detachment in art and life and so on, versus that of the cultivated middle-class—spontaneous behaviour, liberated emotions, the actions of humans according to laws of nature, involvement in art and life—has clearly been won by the latter in which opera takes on an altogether new function: 'promotion of culture, education aiming at the "promotion of humanity". It was by means of moving the heart that humanity in its entirety should be enlightened' (ibid.: 48). It is from this perspective that Smith (1990) judges *Wozzeck* as '... maybe twentieth century in its non-tonal orientation, but [also] ... a deeply human work, and in this respect... nineteenth century in origin'. If 'promotion of humanity' through 'moving the heart' is the epitaph for opera's core repertoire from Gluck/Mozart to *Turandot/Wozzeck*, is it one which rules out any significant extension of the repertoire back into *seria* territory and beyond?

The archaeology of opera

> Not so long ago, the way to enjoy a baroque opera recording was simple: Valium. Just pop a blue one, zone out and try not to grow restless with the out of tune strings and the singers who seem to be sight-reading. Even then there wasn't a pill big enough for some of those Jean-Claude Malgoire recordings on Sony; despite the presence of such singers as Arleen Auger and Ileana Cotrubas, they were still amazingly dreary (Stearns 1994: 34).

One noteworthy late twentieth century development has been the archaeology and commercial promotion of pre-Gluck opera,[30] despite inherent difficulties: 'In however favourable a light eighteenth century *opera seria* is presented ... considerable adjustment is demanded of present-day audiences before they can begin to enjoy it' (Orrey 1992: 78), or be engaged by it, spiritually, emotionally or musically. Pre-baroque works such as Monteverdi's *L'Incoronazione di Poppea* (1642) with no hieratical ruler to flatter, being given before a citizens rather than court audience in the republic of Venice, are freer in form and more directly engaging and adaptable to late twentieth century narrative precepts. Even so, the musical and theatrical conventions of such works pose a considerable challenge to performers and audiences largely preoccupied with mid-nineteenth century musical styles, vocal size, technique, 'realistic' narratives and the like—a challenge with which 'theorists' have been engaged for some time. In 1970 Donington, following an already burgeoning interest in this field (Noble 1969; Jacobs 1967; Maderna 1967; Rose 1965 and Donington himself 1965), predicted:

> Opera after Monteverdi and before Handel may be the biggest booty currently looming over the musicological horizon.

Musicological the area has to be for a start; for seldom can so many works of music, on so large a scale, have been so sketchily set down in notation. To fill out all that the few early prints and many manuscripts do not include needs the knowledge of a musicologist, the inspiration of a composer and the self-denial of a saint (Donington, 1970: 16).

Writing for *Opera*'s relatively specialist readers, he explains how to appreciate works from this era, referring to historical accounts of salon and mass audiences being frequently moved to tears by works which modern audiences and performers tend to treat coolly, as academically and historically fascinating, but not engaging in directly emotional or humanly inspiring terms. Donington added: 'Power is of the essence in 17th century opera. But what kind of power?' His answer: vocal power, suggests one means by which contemporary audiences may be engaged by recordings at least where the vocal style and weight considered idiomatic for works of this period are not lost in cavernous nineteenth and twentieth century auditoria.

The baroque movement cleansed our ears ... it had a lot to do with getting the muck off and sometimes going too far in the opposite direction towards ... a rarefied, smallish idea of things ... where 'authentic' equals etiolated ... I can't stand early-music singers who flout their weaknesses as strengths ... on the principle that the less voice you have the more 'authentic' you must be (William Christie of *Les Arts Florrisants* quoted in Milnes 1995a: 150, 151).

Talk of 'cleansing ears' and authenticity requires explanation to audiences used to nineteenth century conventions,[31] the cue for a barrage of 'new' knowledge:

In the 1500s polyphonic music already had used *canto di gorgia* [florid singing], *variazoni* [shadings or colouration] and the categories of voice we are familiar with today (*superius*), *contratenor altus* [contralto], *tenor* [tenor], *contratenor bassus* [bass], *mediu cantus* [mezzo-soprano] and *baritonus* [baritone]. Women, though, were not permitted to sing in church, so the sopranos and mezzo-sopranos were boys... or men who imitated the timbre of women's voices by falsetto (*falsetti artificiali*). The contraltos ... were tenors who used falsetto in the upper range,

190

and they are the true countertenors (singers billed as countertenors today are really *falsetti artificiali*, whose voices were sharp and not sufficiently flexible). Later even the countertenors were displaced by the *castrato contraltisti* (Celletti 1994: 11).

Celletti's piece is part of a whole edition of Met Guild's *Opera News* devoted to baroque, its origins, singing styles (Kellow 1994), countertenors (Randell 1994) and discography (Stearns 1994), in all a potent demonstration of the promotion of 'early' opera and the discursive barriers to be overcome if it is to be successful.[32]

The underlying message in such tutelage is 'don't be afraid', pre-Gluck works have more in common with the conventional operatic canon than differences, hence the stress on immediate contemporary audience reactions and on the chest voice as source of power, evidence that it is not musicological correctness but misunderstanding which has alienated modern audiences through having these works sung: '... with small or restrained voices... in a chamber style... their opera was public music and big music. Sensitive by all means, but robust as well' (Donington 1970: 17). As for orchestras and instruments, Donington surveys such sources as receipts for payment and manuscript listings, showing that in performance practice a great variety of instruments and rich orchestrations was employed. Recorded notation was string-based but left incomplete so that, during rehearsals, they could be added to brass and woodwind instrumentation (Rose 1965). It is the misleading sketchiness of manuscripts which suggests that Venetian opera was reduced to a string orchestra and *continuo* in order to save money after the public opera houses started opening there from 1637 onwards. Thus the parameters of 'authenticity' debates embrace orchestra size and depth, vocal weight and style and exuberant theatrical effects, drawing a deep response from audiences. While much has been accomplished in revitalising these works through the 'authenticity' of musical performance and of visual and dramatic archaeology there are doubts. Christie, who has worked with several 'radical' or 'adventurous' producers comments:

A lot of ['authentic'] work in the way of gesture and comportment I've found poorly digested and presented ... we have so little to go on, only iconographical evidence, with very few annotated scores with any indication of how singers came in and out and moved and behaved towards each other ... (Christie quoted in Milnes 1995a: 151).

Enhancement of the museum's collection through excavations of this field set in motion tensions and impose new sets of 'knowledge/power' distinctions within the existing discursive hierarchy: between musicologists, performers, critics, producers and audiences. More practically, what of the theatrical and box office potential of an artefact around which additional musicological barriers are raised? Remembering Adorno's attack on the absurdity of 'star' hype as consumers 'go into raptures' once informed that they are listening to a Stradivarius or Amati 'which only the ear of a specialist can tell from that of any good modern violin', it is unlikely that a contemporary popular audience could be roused to equal rapture by being told that Handel's *Radamisto* is a masterpiece. Nowhere perhaps, is the stratified character and competitiveness of opera discourses more succinctly demonstrated than here, nor the justification with which producers now dominate as key intermediaries between work and audience, but the extent to which more can be expected from a modern audience, trained to respond to opera as 'promotion of humanity' through 'moving the heart', on hearing a Cavalli or Rameau work for the first time is questionable. The 'authentic' resuscitation of baroque operas, as part of a strategy for revitalising opera in general, can only be of limited appeal, especially as when these works are produced in ways which attract modern audiences (for example, Scottish Opera's *Julius Caesar* produced by Willy Decker), involving some reorganisation of musical numbers, they are often promptly declared decadent by musicologists and critics.

If not in the theatre, in the recording studio the buoyancy advocated by Donington has been achieved:

> Names previously found only in detailed musicological texts are turning out to be substantial musical personalities, such as Michel Pignolet de Monteclair, Andre Campra and Marc-Antoine Charpentier ... Jean Marie Leclair, Marin Marais, Giovanni Pergolesi (Stearns 1994: 34).

These recordings are performed by specialists, including singers trained (based on specious interpretation of the evidence) '[in] an essentially non-legato style ... in which the core of vocal tone is allowed to drop out on weak syllables and diminuendos ... the roots of which lie in resonant cathedral singing' (Crutchfield 1991: 54).

... not Met singers, nor will they ever be, not only for the obvious reasons of size of voice and projection in huge houses, but also because of economics and unionisation of orchestral performers: ... it doesn't make sense to hire a specialised baroque orchestra when regulations require the regular orchestra to be paid, whether it plays or not (ibid.: 34).

Young singers can do this music often... just as well as mature artists; they can devote the time that's necessary to what I think is the most important element in this kind of work, and that is homogeneity of style. You don't get that with casts that cost a lot of money or that arrive one week before the show goes on.
(Christie quoted in Canning 1991a: 278).

Stearns, in a style which avoids music theory and musicology, suggesting through generalised adjectives how this unfamiliar music may be appreciated, guides readers towards the 'right' recordings by an imposing array of specialist companies with 'tradition' filled titles, and their individual leaders—William Christie (*Les Arts Florissants*); Mark Minkowski ex-member of the Christie ensemble (*Les Musiciens de Louvre*);Nicholas McGegan (*Philharmonia Baroque*); Rudolph Palmer (*Brewer Baroque Chamber Orchestra*); John Eliot Gardner (*English Baroque Soloists*); Sigiswald Luijken (*La Petite Bland*); Christopher Rousset (*Les Talens Lyriques*) and René Jacobs (*Concert Köln*)—and warns them off the 'wrong' including Harnoncourt (*Concentus Musicus Wïen*): 'A borderline case is Christopher Hogwood (*Academy of Ancient Music*) who understands this repertory but doesn't always translate it into a *vital* musical experience' (Stearns 1994: 34). The dabblings of non-specialists (Riccardo Muti, Richard Bonynge, Richard Hickox) are dealt with curtly, but Stearns accepts that Charles Mackerras' work for the ENO on conventional instruments conveys the *spirit* of the works. He concludes:

At least a viable performing tradition is being established. After years of casting about in the darkness with all manner of trial and error, [performance] models [have been created] that can accommodate big personalities while revealing the music. At the moment *baroque* opera promises to be one of the most exciting frontiers of the 1990s (Steams 1994: 38).

This 'frontier' implies 'newness', albeit retrospective and largely recordings-based, commercial as well as musicological, but not yet obviously theatrical. The consumerist intent spills over into professional jealousies in what is evidently a highly competitive field. Christie (Canning 1991a: 280) compares British baroque styles to frozen food: 'neatly packaged, inexpensive (comparatively speaking) tasteless in the bland rather than the vulgar sense'. But to be done tastefully in either sense, baroque costs! Christie champions stylish productions of *tragédies lyriques* because they stand or fall by the kind of lavishly decorated and costumed spectacles which the glory-conscious Louis XIV and his descendents expected. In 1990 a one-off 'period' production of Molière's comédie-ballet, *Le Malade Imaginaire*, with original music by Charpentier required a full company of dancers, soloists and chorus plus an acting ensemble on stage. The orchestra, including Christie, were dressed in lavish Sun King costumes, the whole costing millions of (state provided) francs. Few opera houses are equipped or funded to mount such productions, as is also found with much 'new' opera, Christie argues that student productions may well be the salvation of 'this connoisseur's, but musically important, corner of the repertoire' (Canning 1991a: 278). Indeed such productions could prove their salvation in the longer term by also providing trained practitioners:

> For years schools all round the world have been teaching the last half of the nineteenth century and the first quarter of the twentieth century, with a little bit of Rossini, Handel and the few Mozart repertory pieces. Now they've realised, especially in Britain, that all this Baroque stuff, this Handel, this Vivaldi, these Rameaus, well they're money in the bank. If young singers have a good sense of style and they are intelligent, there's a career in all that music (Christie quoted in Canning 1991a: 279).

Baroque opera may well have been promoted with some success as an opera commodity in the recording studio, but it remains, and is likely to remain, in a corner of the repertoire. It is rarely performed by known 'star' singers; its stylistic elements are too alien from dominant operatic nineteenth century musical, narrative and theatrical styles, and its form and unfamiliarity prevents it from becoming part of commodification at its most lucrative as 'opera' entertainment, part of mass culture, as background for advertising and so on.

Verismo

With Pavarotti's chart-topping hit of 'perhaps the best loved melody of all time *Nessun dorma*' (*The Readers Digest Magical World of Opera*, advertised in *The Sunday Times* 27 February 1994), the interaction between commercially lucrative 'opera' and opera house culture and economics is clear. It is also highly suggestive as to how, within the general culture, opera as 'promotion of humanity' through 'moving the heart' might be interpreted, through broad brush strokes of heroism, excitement, passion, transposed from mythical China to Italian football pitch. It is not insignificant that '*Nessun dorma*' is from *Turandot,* an exotic 'last gasp' of the subgenre which signalled the late nineteenth century peak of opera's mass popularity and, given the rapidly developing technologies of 'the culture industry', the inevitability of opera's demise—*verismo,* realism 'thrillers and superdramas' at their most operatically accessible, dismissed by arbiters of 'high' operatic taste as 'shabby little shockers'.[33] But in all cultural creations, not least this, the most artificial, realism is elaborate illusion.

Conventional 'high' wisdom on the nineteenth century operatic promotion of humanity through 'moving the heart' (*Gefülsverstandnis*) is that the greatest achievements were those of Wagner: 'the most accomplished achiever of the ideal of "perfect illusion" ...' (Vieira de Carvalho 1995: 50). 'By locating the miraculous in the human soul, he endows it with truth in the artistic sense and intensifies the world of saga and fairy-tale into the illusion of the absolute reality of the unreal' (Bekker 1924: 128), and as such, for his critics:

> ... sums up the unromantic side of the phantasmagoria: ... at the
> point at which aesthetic appearance becomes a function of the

character of the commodity. As a commodity it purveys illusions. The absolute reality of the unreal is nothing but the reality of the phenomenon that not only strives unceasingly to spirit away its own origins in human labour, but also inseparably from this process and in the thrall to exchange value, assiduously emphasizes its use value, stressing that this is its authentic reality, that it is 'no imitation'—and all this to further the cause of exchange value. In Wagner's day the consumer goods on display turned their phenomenal side seductively towards the mass of customers while diverting attention from their purely phenomenal character, from the fact that they were beyond reach. Similarly in the phantasmagoria, Wagner's operas tend to become commodities. Their tableaux assume the character of wares on display (Adorno 1991: 90).

But the wares are not of surface narrative value, but accurate reflections of complex inner, psycho-spiritual reality. With Wagner the conventions of the opera experience for audiences were broken. They were:

> ... not to be led to focus on narrative—which is a form of referring to external reality in an objectivist mode—or description, but to experience a number of scenes in a mode of presentation and reception which suspends any engagement in the natural structures of the objective world (Daschra *et al.* 1989: 28).

However, the capitalist dynamic does not protect aesthetic complexity but erodes it through market expansion, greater accessibility to consuming publics who, at the end of the last century, were increasingly socialised into the technological reproduction of not complex inner reflections of psychological 'reality' but reality itself. Wagner may have achieved the ultimate realisation in opera of the 'absolute reality of the unreal' (though Mozartians may well demur), but at a popular, mass level, *verismo* served Adorno's interpretation of phantasmagoria even more effectively. Vieira de Carvalho claims that Wagner's mature *Gesamtkunstwerk* would only be surpassed by the invention of the talking picture in the 1930s 'whose communicative patterns Bayreuth undoubtedly anticipated'. Soundtrack in the cinema 'gave an enormous technological boost to illusory arts' (1995: 51, 54), but photography, silent cinema and, later, 'talkies' were first and foremost popular, not 'high' entertainments, their themes drawn from realist literature and opera—indeed, cinema employed opera 'stars' and plots in their illusions of naturalism and realism. *Verismo* is not easy to isolate and define, but it grew out of late nineteenth century debates over the representation of 'things' in the arts in which naturalism confronted realism. The former is:

> ... unselective—or rather is selective only in order to present with maximum credibility the immediate scene ... its ideal aim [is] to produce a replica, thus preserving the present. Such a replica is impossible because art can only exist within the limitations of a medium. Consequently naturalism relies upon tricks of illusionism to distract attention away from the medium (vernacular, exact dialogue, facts that are unexpected in literature, illusionist effects of texture, highlights and so on). Realism is selective and strives towards the typical ... realism selects in order to construct a totality. In realist literature a man represents his whole life—though perhaps only a small part of it is described- and this life is seen or felt as part of the life of his class, society, and universe. Far from disguising the limitations of his medium, the realist needs and uses them. Because the medium is limited, it can contain within its own terms and create a totality out of what in life presents itself as uncontained. The medium becomes the palpable model of the artist's ordering consciousness. [Naturalism] ... is a submissive worship of events just because they occur ... (Berger 1969: 50-51).

Naturalism refers to a *style* of theatre in which the stage-setting, dialogue and performance of the actors seem 'life-like', realism to a kind of theatrical content. Naturalism reflects 'accurately' the surface of life; realism is concerned with the truth of the experience conveyed. Thus the two are compatible but not inseparable.

'Alternatives to naturalism become expressionism, poetic drama and so on, alternatives to realism, fantasy and melodrama' (Gascoigne 1962: 7). The limitations of the operatic medium for the portrayal of naturalism or realism are inherent and yet reviews of singers performances and productions are replete with judgements measured against both. For its critics, opera's artificiality is self-destructive: '... the idiocy of opera lies in the fact that rational elements are employed, solid reality is aimed at, but at the same time it is all washed out by the music' (Brecht quoted in Willett 1967: 133). Even fans concede: 'realism does not come naturally to opera' (Conrad 1977: 186), yet realism was increasingly demanded of a nineteenth century culture based not on dreams but 'facts', not imagination but 'reality', not elevated rhetoric but frank and accurate documentary style—a culture contemporaneous with the birth of sociology and the search for scientific means of understanding the workings of complex industrialising societies. Opera was inevitably affected by such developments despite resistance from some, such as composer/librettist Boito who as late as the 1880s claimed realism in opera to be inappropriate because 'music had no business trying to represent things' (ibid.: 64) a judgement which does not accord with the means of operatic understanding adopted by non-specialist listeners.

The *verismo* movement in opera was short-lived. Cooper hazards 1890-1910 (1974: 1043), but it wasn't that tidy. Its most innovative and typical examples were one-acters: *Cavalleria rusticana* (Mascagni 1890 with libretto by Zola, influenced by Giovanni Verga) with which the *verismo* school was acclaimed; *I Pagliacci* (Leoncavello 1892, subsequently customarily presented on the same bill, the two popularly referred to as *'Cav and Pag'*); and the first part of Puccini's *trittico, Il tabarro* (1918), characterised by brevity, concentration, 'brutal miniatures' (Hanslick 1963: 296) and concerned with contemporary, naturalistic, urban working class or rustic settings, dramatising episodes in the domestic lives of 'real' people of 'low life.[34] These works were received enthusiastically: 'violence, passion and sensationalism' (Martin 1972: 195), travesties of heroism (Conrad 1977: 186): 'terse' and 'intense': 'excruciating emotional climaxes' (Kimbell 1991: 625), 'no grand opera finales, no divertissements, no chivalric characters, period costumes' to capture a sense of "real" life ... it had to be terse to stay intense' (Morrden 1987: 195). Many, such as: *A Santa Lucia* (Tasca 1892), *A basso porto* (Spinelli 1894) and *Mala vita* (Giordano 1892) are now largely forgotten. It is with *verismo* that the sea-change referred to earlier by Crutchfield is signalled: the most popular operas were those 'nearest to a play with supporting music', although in *verismo* the 'cessation of melody' was yet to come.[35]

[There was] a shift of the centre of gravity of opera. In nineteenth century *melodramma* it was for the music to provide the tragic events. The deepening of character, and then with Verdi, of emotional and political problematic, was achieved through the enrichment of musical events. It was for melody, timbre, harmony to give a tragic sense to the banal verses with which King Philip laments the inconsolable loneliness of the powerful (*'Ella giammai m'amò/No, quel cor chiuso è a me/amor per me non ha!'*). From *Andrea Chénier* (1896) onward, the functions are reversed: the plot comes to the fore; the story-telling (*romanzesco*) seizes the attention, while the music declines to a subsidiary task, that of reinforcing the rhetorical act with rhetorical vocalism. Comparison with the immanent stylistics of commercial cinema, which provoke tears and laughter using devices whose efficacy is proportional to their elementarity, proves once again opportune (Tedeschi 1978: 97-8).

In *verismo* musical effects frequently relied on the use of familiar or 'real' folk tunes deployed as atmosphere or *ambientismo* (for example, *tabarro, fanciulla, Butterfly*). That the protagonists are 'ordinary' they themselves testify: In *La fanciulla del West*, Minnie is a self-affirmed nonentity (*'oscura e buona e nulla'*) whilst the bandit Johnson in the same opera is merely *'signor di Sacramento'*, but their tragedy is worthy of the gods. Some argue that these 'ordinary' heroes and heroines are more prototypes of the twentieth century obsession with 'showbiz gods', scandals surrounding film stars and royals, lived vicariously by the masses: 'ordinary' but nevertheless, artists, singers, actresses, actors such as Tosca, Cavaradossi, Canio, Nedda, Adriana Lecouvreur and so on (Conrad 1977: 194), but core *verismo* works also mark an operatic interest in rag-pickers, organ grinders and stevedores who visit Margot the prostitute.[36]
    The problem with defining *verismo* is that whilst *Cav, Pag* and *tabarro* qualify with their conjunction of veristic textual, dramatic and musical elements, many works of this period, including some referred to above, were veristic in some rather than all aspects. At their purest—if this may be said of a form often labelled corrupt—'ordinary' serious, tragic and dignified people, rather than *buffo*, expressed themselves in 'everyday' language and were invested with a grand opera importance previously the locutionary domain of mythological heroes, royalty, nobility and, by mid-century, the bourgeoisie (for example Verdi's *La traviata*—'Verdi's first foray into

realism' [Kauffmann 1990: 1131] and *Stiffelio*). In dramatic terms these two works were 'realistic' harbingers of what was to follow but, in both the characters still express themselves in the 'stilted and ornate conventional language' of opera (Arblaster 1992: 264). Most critically *verismo* required 'realism' in vocal reproduction, with the simulation of speech rhythms, subsequently damned for its destructiveness on vocal writing, singing technique and sustained singers' careers. In *verismo* what had hitherto been considered vocal aberration became instituted as style. The creators of Turridu and Santuzza in *Cavalleria rusticana*, husband and wife Roberto Sagno and Gemma Bellincioni, soon abandoned their usual lyric repertoire, their voices subject to wear and tear from the required intense, highly inflected style and 'over-emphatic delivery' (Scott 1979: 80), punctuated with ironic laughter, screams and sobs—'It has muscles of steel. Its force lies in the voice which does not speak or sing: it yells! yells!: yells!' (Mascagni on his *Il piccola Marat* quoted in Carner 1958: 259)—as recordings by such specialists as Tina Poli-Randaccio, Carmen Melis, Juanita Caracciolo, Gilda Dilla Rizza and Magda Olivero demonstrate (Ashbrook 1994: 441). Melis had all the 'devices of *verismo*: the dolent and fluttery tone, sudden lurches in the line, exaggerated and pinched sounding *subito* pianos, and a quantity of aspirates and sobs' (Scott 1979: 81), whilst tenor Lauri-Volpi described Dalla Rizza's voice as: '... characterised by gutteral and nasal inflexions, imperfect technically, responding to the demands made of it by the actress, who employed it rather to express the emotions than for purely musical effects' (1977: 62). In the complete *Fedora* recording of 1931, when not yet 40, she sounds considerably older. This vocal (visual, dramatic) *verismo* style lived on to affect and contaminate all twentieth century opera and, musically, many pre-*verismo* works with proto-*verismo* dramatic appeal such as *Carmen* and *La traviata*. Many works were *verismo* in musical style but not setting *Adriana Lecouvreur* (Cilea), *Andrea Chenier* (Giordano), *Guglielmo Ratcliffe* (Mascagni), Zandonai's *Francesca da Rimini* and *I cavalieri di Ekebu*, Puccini's *Tosca* and *Turandot*. Others were *verismo* in theme but not musically: *Peter Grimes*, *Jenufa, Intermezzo, Wozzeck* and *Lulu*.

The initial impact of *verismo* on London critics seems to be that it was viewed as a relief from Wagner. Arundell (1980: 373) reports that immediately prior to *Cavalleria rusticana*'s first London appearance (19 October 1891) '... the feeling had been growing that ingenious compositions full of interwoven themes and kaleidoscopic modulations had been too prominent ... and there was a danger that simple melody as such had been swamped'. *The Daily Telegraph* critic was weary of musical mazes 'through which the ordinary man needs a guide, the world, we cannot but think, is hungering for a great melodist... with the skill of a master and play upon the feelings by its most direct appeal'. *The Times* spoke of the 'wonderful success' of the opera, the number of encores given, a practice deplored in more than one paper as typically Italian. *The Whithall Review* noted: 'this opera of Mascagni's, consisting of one act, suffices in an Italian theatre to fill up the entire evening, so numerous are the encores' (Arundell 1980: 375). These reviews, although they did not use the term *verismo*, recognised this as a new type of opera. *The Times* stated the work to be less remarkable for its melody 'than for a complete appropriateness to the situation and character'.

Pagliacci was first given at Covent Garden on 19 May 1893. *The Daily Telegraph* commented on rumours that the story was based on actual facts:

> Whether that be true or not matters nothing: the great point is that the poet-musician discerned the signs of the times in regard to operatic libretti. We appear to have done for the present with legendary heroes and cloudy myths. These personages are too far removed: they are not flesh of our flesh and bone of our bone. Nowadays the demand is for 'human documents'—for characters in tale and drama that are our kin, our exaggerated selves (quoted in Arundell 1980: 375-6).

With the first staging of a Puccini opera, *Manon Lescaut*, in London (14 May 1894), references were made to the *verismo* manner in scoring and singing: '... there is a sense of straining ... here and there even of that hysterical mode of uttering, which becomes so wearisome in Mascagni's music'. (*The Times*, quoted in ibid.: 378). *La Bohème* was widely praised, although some found a 'slight plot' (*The Morning Post* quoted in ibid.: 381). *Tosca* (12 July 1900) was staged in sets based on photographs of the originals so that, in Act III, there was 'so much illusion that *Tosca*'s suicidal leap from the parapet becomes quite horrible' (*The Times* quoted in ibid.: 383). *The Daily Telegraph* critic after *Tosca* was forced to comment in detail on melodrama's survival on the opera stage.

Illustrative, for the most part, of primitive passions, and appealing as it does to the lowest as well as the most powerful human feelings, that form of art must needs be attended by blood. To this end the librettists call in the demons of Jealousy and Revenge- ghastly shapes which, if there were no public taste for horrors, would at least be banished from the stage. Now this is all very crude and elementary, as an adjunct to art. Moreover it is very cheap ... (Arundell 1989: 383-4).

Verismo in general was the culmination of nineteenth century performing developments: larger theatres, mass audiences, bigger orchestras sunk in pits before the proscenium arch, pressure on singers to 'thrill' through vocal excess, 'emphasizing volume and expressive intensity, causing overextended singers to declaim and shout, even mime in default of being able simply to sing' (Morrden 1987: 194). It reflected the growing democratisation of culture, the emergence of popular, mass entertainment, by an art form incapable of competing with emergent photographic, cinematic and literary alternatives in providing 'thrillers and superdramas' to meet the public taste for 'cheap', 'crude', 'elementary' horrors. The social significance of *verismo* cannot be understated. *La traviata* (Verdi 1853) and *Carmen* (Bizet 1875), were important precursors, the former with 'a purely domestic background, no intrigues, no duels, none of the trappings of high romance ... avant garde' (Osborne 1969: 266). The music was not *verismo*; the theme of a TB-stricken 'high class' courtesan was. Indeed the fiasco of the first performance was partly due to the audience's expectations being too realistic in ways which increasingly stalk opera throughout the twentieth-century— 'The first night audience laughed at the thought of Fanny Salvini-Donatelli, an extremely stout lady, dying of consumption' (ibid.: 266)—nor were the Venetian audience used to seeing a 'modern' theme, although fearing hostility, Louis XIVth costumes were used. The veristic elements of *Carmen* (1875), still technically an *opéra comique* by reason of its spoken dialogue, proved incomprehensible to opéra comique patrons who felt that the respectability of this state-subsidised theatre was sullied by 'Castilian licentiousness', but Bizet refused to 'have the story prettified, its savagery and cruelty diluted ...' (Orrey 1992: 156-7). The outcry which greeted *Carmen* demonstrates the social tensions in an oeuvre which threatened social, moral as well as musical 'auratic' conventions, particularly because in *verismo* 'heroines' and especially 'anti-heroines' take centre stage, Violetta and Carmen were prototypes for Manon, Tosca, Musetta, Lodoletta, Mimi, Butterfly, Iris, Zaza, Minnie, Santuzza, Lola, Nedda, Liu and Turandot.[37] It is debatable whether there is much mileage in claims that these male composers based their 'realism' on 'passive women of inferior status as objects of sexual desire' (Plaut 1993: 247), for most heroically demonstrate an independence of spirit in response to circumstances, but that they are objects of social interest and significance there can be little doubt.

Verismo remains the 'social bad conscience' of 'auratic' opera. If, as Bakhtin argues, literary history is a running battle between 'high' forms such as epic and lyric poetry, which seek to impose a single monological voice of authority, and 'low' forms such as the novel, which sustain an open-ended dialogue of social codes, thus having powerful subversive effects on the ruling ideology of their day, *verismo* represents a similar 'dialogism': as a 'cultural apparatus, [it] ... embodied the adjustment of reality to the social presence of *the masses*. ... a technical realization of a political demand' (Mowitt 1987: 185). It was and remains, in terms of 'high' criteria, of low quality, low taste, poor music and cheap entertainment, popular not because it was identical with reality, for no art can be, 'but rather proceeds along a parallel plane ... the work of art itself ... (be) a subversive gesture' (Brustein 1965: 8-9). *Verismo* composers have suffered the same fate as 'realists' in other arts: 'unintellectual and uninventive' (Panofsky 1970: 324), though 'vigorous and popular' (Berger 1969: 51), their broad appeal synonymous with the 'uncultivated' (Rosenberg 1970: 62), stimulating in response aesthetic and social closure on elite grounds, as lower tastes became catered for elsewhere.[38] The fetishisation of opera as 'high' hallowed tradition paralleled the growing 'mechanical reproduction' challenge to theatrical realism:

> While waiting for the film properly speaking... there existed already a horde of spectators looking for the same sensations and celebrities as the *melodramma*: the thrill of the future of the *Great Train Robbery*, the wonders of the yet to be borne *Last Days of Pompeii*, the pathos of *Broken Blossom*. Before the spread of the film the genres were ready—adventurous, spectacular, pathetic—and the recipes to cook them were in place, the principle—means of doling out of effects—as well as the choice of

plots. The *melodramma* in short, opened the way for the film which was to become, in the twenties and afterwards, the *melodramma* for everybody, reduced to its most elemental form and industrialized according to the rules of commerce and the needs of society with universal suffrage (Tedeschi 1978: 95).

A future for opera?

[By 1900] the most important and influential among the younger composers had turned away from realism, and in many cases ... from opera as a form. The most striking example of this revulsion was Debussy's *Pelléas et Mélisande,* which in its turn largely determined the character of Dukas' *Ariane et Barbe Bleu* and Bartok's *Duke Bluebeard's Castle.* Ravel, Schoenberg and Stravinsky all avoided suggestion of realism in their operas (Cooper 1974: 1044).

Later Weill toyed with operatic illusions of reality to alienating effect. Schoenberg, Stravinsky and Weill with Brecht reassessed opera through dodecaphony, neoclassicism and 'epic' theatre respectively. Mascagni, Puccini and Richard Strauss continued to seek an operatic future continuous with nineteenth century tradition, the former reworking verismo (*Iris*), reworking *commedia del'arte (Le Maschere)* experimenting with operetta (Si), reinvoking romanticism *(Guglielmo Ratcliffe),* retreating finally to epic classicism *(Nerone)* (Stivender 1988). Similarly Puccini, after the *La fanciulla del West* experiment: '... a whole evening of almost exclusively Pizzettian declamation against a colourful orchestral background, and his attempt to strike into a more popular vein with *La rondine* reversed into the Grand Italian Tradition' with *Turandot* (Ashbrook and Powers 1991). Strauss, once over the psychorealism of *Salome* and *Elektra,* produced works which looked over their shoulders at *commedia* and *opera seria (Ariadne auf Naxos),* Mozart *(Der Rosenkavalier),* operetta *(Arabella, Die schweigsame Frau),* autobiographical realism *(Intermezzo)* and complex symbolism *(Die Frau ohne Schatten),* struggling to make classical references relevant and entertaining to bourgeois audiences *(Daphne, Die Aegyptische Helena, Die Liebe der Danae),* epic history *(Friedenstag),* discoursing lastly on the essence of modern opera, Gluck's reforms, in *Capriccio*

(Mann 1964). For many younger composers the conventions of opera were moribund, decadent and epitomised by Korngold's *Die tote Stadt* (1920) and *Das Wunder der Heliane* (1927):

> ... he knew how to write an opera for the audience of his time. It made much of grandiose, over-blown, big band kitsch in the manner of Richard Strauss, with additional bows to Puccini, Wagner, Debussy and Lehar. It dabbled freely and modishly in amorous exorcism, surface eroticism, postcard piety, boulevard psychology, soppy surrealism and Grand Guignol grotesquerie... the opera did enjoy considerable esteem, for a while, as a masterpiece of junk (Bernheimer on *Die tote Stadt* 1985b: 1383).

Alternative routes were more adventurous. In the 1920s Brecht with Hindemith, Eisler, Dessau and Wagner-Regeny became linked as members of the 'socially oriented movement', promoted by publishers Schott and Universal-Edition and 'exhibited' at the Donaueschingen and, later, Baden-Baden Festivals. This movement employed many of the musical ideas associated with Satie, Milhaud and Stravinsky, its theatrical and/or operatic elements associated with those of Cocteau who, like Brecht, had a strong influence on the form, orchestration and general approach of his collaborators. Musical objectives were lightness, melody and clarity, reactions against the rich works of Mahler and Strauss, their methods a return to classical models but tied to the trenchant, 'natural', lively and still uncorrupted language of jazz. Stravinsky set the agenda with his chamber opera *Renard* (1915), intended to be played by clowns, dancers or acrobats, on a trestle stage with orchestra behind. *L'histoire du soldat* (1918), for narrators, dancer and seven musicians, had a jazz influence as clearly had *Ragtime* (1918) and *Piano Rag-Music* (1919). Cocteau in *Le Coq et l'Harlequin* (1918), advocated the clear, accessible, popular musical style found in his earlier Diaghileff ballet *Parade* (1917), Satie's music 'like an inspired village band', included a *'Rag-time du Paquebot'* and slogans shouted through megaphones (Cocteau 1921: 57). Milhaud's *Boeuf sur le Toit (The Nothing Doing Bar)* (1919) also used a slimmed down orchestra to accompany a cast of clowns and 'interesting characters': 'a Boxer, a Negro Dwarf, an Elegant Woman, a Redhead dressed like a boy, a Bookmaker, a Gentleman in Tails' (Milhaud 1949: 116).

French composers continued to experiment with such *depouillement* or stripping down, freely employing jazz and 'negro' elements and flirting with popular composers such as Cole Porter who studied with Ravel. In all, the division between 'low' music and the new anti-Wagnerian aims of young 'classical' composers were for a time very close. Inevitably this trend did not, could not, express itself in orthodox opera, although in the Donaueschingen and Baden-Baden Festivals German composers furthered French experiments in works such as Krenek's jazz operas *Der Sprung über den Schatten* (1924) and *Jonny spielt auf* (1927). The populist intent is clear from the use of such terms as *Gebrauschmusik* (originating with Satie's *musique d'ameublement:* musical furniture, to be listened to with half an ear) and *Gemeinschatsmusik*—respectively applied or functional music and popular, amateur community music—both seeking answers to the fundamental aesthetic question 'What ought music actually to do?'. There were experiments with film soundtracks (which provided functional music in a technical as well as contextual sense until sound recording replaced the necessity), mechanical music, potted opera, radio music, almost anti-music (Milhaud's *Machines Agricoles* of 1919 being random settings of farmers and seedsmen's catalogues), music for the young and for the amateur. The objective was not the democratisation of existing 'auratic' art, but its subversion through intellectualisation of the people's 'natural' 'repetitive' music, as in Empson's sense of 'pastoral' producing 'a puzzling form which looks proletarian but isn't' (1966: 13). As with *verismo*, emphasis was on popular as 'true' because 'natural', guileless, set against the serious and sophisticated as 'untrue', but musically rather than dramatically:

> ... jazz has played a considerable part in the rhythmical, harmonic and formal liberation which we have now attained, and above all in our music's steadily increasing simplicity and intelligibility... So-called 'cheap' music, particularly that of the cabaret and the operetta, has for some time been a kind of *gesticht* music (expressing externalized attitudes, almost 'natural' in the sense of unscripted or rationalised). Serious music however still clings to lyricism and cultivates expression for its own sake (Weill quoted in Willett 1959: 130).

Thus Weill and Brecht employed comparable arguments to critically engage with and reform opera, not by embracing the ultimately conventional 'grand opera' means employed in the high-flown though still radical, works of Hindemith and Krenek, upon which institutionally, 'the Press etc. [can] impose their views as though incognito' (ibid.: 131), but by comprehensive critique of what Brecht called 'culinary opera' (opera whose suppositions and presentation flatter the audience and confirm their complacent acceptance of art as simply an evening out). From 'ballad'—slimmed down works such as *Die Dreigroschenoper*—to more obvious parodies of the full-blown 'culinary' thing such as the (originally) large-scale *Rise and Fall of the City of Mahagonny*, Brecht's intent was 'to make strange *(verfremden)* the social gesture that underlay all the events *(vorgange)*' (1977: 212). As Brecht defined 'social gesture' as 'the comic and gestic expression of the social relations in them by which people of an epoch live' (1977: 212), the meaning of *verfremden* becomes clear: what is familiar, obvious, known in social relations should be viewed as unfamiliar, not obvious and unknown, and in this way something to be questioned, rendered problematic and changeable. Within such an aesthetic, music mediates rather than engages the passions, awakening in audiences their rational faculties as 'thinking spectators' (1977: 21) instead of enrapturing them—the 'promotion of humanity' through (dis)'engaging the heart'. Unlike the Wagnerian brief of achieving 'the perfect illusion', Brecht sought to shatter illusions and corresponding identification strategies through the 'separation of elements'(1977: 113).

In retrospect Brecht believed *Mahagonny* to have been a mistaken and doomed attempt to modernise the content and mechanise the form of opera without querying the 'apparatus' or the social functions which it performed, so he sought to 'more and more emphasize the didactic at the expense of the culinary element' (quoted in Willett 1959: 133), challenging 'art for art's sake' ideologies, playing down the artists or composers 'star' individuality, exploring music with set and fixed functions, meanings and uses, democratising music as an open and shared experience which necessarily required a simplification of musical means and discourses, emphasising music especially for the young or schools[39] and rejecting of music as an empty, individual, internalised, emotional experience.

These attempts to find a future form and relevance for opera suggest the museum doors were shutting some time before the premieres of *Wozzeck* and *Turandot*. The subsequent twentieth-century concern has been with whether all the valedictions have been justified, whether, as Poizat (1992) states with regard to another signal work, 'after *Moses und Aron* opera can go no further ...'.[40]

'The end of civilization as we know it'?

And yet how hard it has tried—is still trying. Earlier in this chapter reference was made to the assertion that the problem with contemporary opera is not the creation of new works but the liberation of opera from opera house, auratic, culture. If opera has been 'liberated' in a 'democratic' sense it has been at its 'low' populist incarnation in Shaftesbury Avenue and Broadway big business spectacles, *Cats, Les Misérables, Phantom of the Opera* and that pale copy of *Butterfly, Miss Saigon*. Most 'new' operas are also liberated from the opera house, but into studio theatres, music colleges and television, not as more democratic alternatives to culinary opera as Kimberley's phrase 'out on the streets' suggests, but rather into spaces and rituals as socially and culturally inaccessible to wider audiences as those of the conventional opera house—indeed even more so, given the inevitably challenging musical, textual and dramatic form and content of 'new' works. This text has throughout been concerned with opera as hierarchies of discourse linked to institutional organisation, ascribed sociopolitical meanings, and degrees and means of access. So too with 'new' opera the principal problem is gaining access and making sense of it musically, dramatically and socially given its institutional marginalisation. It may often be sponsored through specialist extensions of mainstream opera companies but its publics are a 'tiny though worthy minority' (Milnes 1989c): even when grand-scale works are performed on major stages *Gawain*'s audience is not *Bohème*'s. 'New' opera's box office appeal is limited, its success unpredictable, revivals unlikely when set against costs, hence the preponderance of small-scale works performed in 'experimental' spaces. New opera rarely integrates with the standard operatic experience of ritual, 'stars', entertainment and so on. Of course, there are exceptions, especially large-scale commissions as symbolic gestures for state occasions, opening of new houses, even Corigliano's *The Ghosts of Versailles* providing 'star' roles[41] but, like all exceptions, these prove the rule. Yet the rule would also appear to be that opera companies must deploy 'new' opera discourses as defences against attacks on its museum culture and as ritual and club entertainment for the privileged.

Typically in London, sponsoring schemes linked to the ENO (Baylis Programme) and the ROH (the Garden Venture), funded by the Arts Council and subscription encourage young composers to write operas as though:

> ... more must mean better... writing operas is intrinsically A Good Thing for all concerned. The more operas staged, the more composers given a taste of what writing music theatre entails, then the more vital everyone can be seduced into believing London's musical life must be ...[42] (Clements 1989a: 801).

Unfortunately quantity does not mean quality claimed Porter (1993b), after reviewing 20 new operas in London in as many days: five were given in one evening as ENO Soundbites! at the Donmar Warehouse; four by the Opera Theatre Company of Dublin; six by the Garden Venture at the Riverside Studios and four at the Britten Theatre of the Royal College of Music as New Visions, New Voices, again a result of the ENO's Baylis Programme (sponsored by British Gas!). A call for operas '... which are truly contemporary: ... based on original ideas from unusual sources ... with lively contrasting and challenging musical styles', received 103 responses of which these four at the Britten Theatre were deemed the best:

> I sat glumly wondering whether *Les Miz* and *The Ghosts of Versailles* with dashes of seasoning of *Klinghoffer* and *Akhnaten*—not *Gawain* and *Inquest of Love*—represent the new wave of contemporary opera: what the public wants, what Intendants with an eye to the box-office will gladly perform. I felt out of touch and out of tune (ibid.: 899).[43]

For Porter, inaccessibility is a key issue: inapt spaces; inaudible words (whether the fault of conductor, composer or singers); and brevity— many were very short, no more than 12 or 15 minutes, 'but short operas are harder to write than longer ones, every phrase has to carry its weight', (ibid.: 904).[44] Accessibility is not only a problem for critics: composers may not feel able to write a 'new' opera, singers to sing it, companies to stage it, audiences to find it, respond or categorise it. Even musicologists have their problems and, given their role as disseminators of authentic 'knowledge', this proves crucial, as their terminology becomes opaque and unilluminating.

It would be so easy if contemporary music could be divided up into neat little packages into which composers with shared aesthetic and a congruent approach to music theatre could be consigned together. In one basket would go all the neo-romantics; into the next the unreformed serialists, into yet another (preferably well insulated from the rest) minimalists. But it doesn't work like that any more, or rather it does but in a negative way, for all the interesting composers writing operas at present seem to be precisely those who would never fit happily into any categories one could care to invent—Weir and Turnage, Birtwistle and Gerald Barry (Clements 1990: 804).[45]

The new works most likely to be 'known' in any sense are those presented in conventional opera houses as part of the normal season, usually requiring special sponsorship support, given inevitably lower box office returns and, frequently, given the time and expense of writing full-length large-scale works, which are commissioned, for otherwise composers are reluctant to undertake them. Even when commissioned there is no guarantee that a work will be performed as Virgil Thompson discovered. Robert Moran composer of *Desert of Roses* (1992) and *From the Towers of the Moon* (1992) states: 'I was not going to write one unless I had a commission, because they sit around on shelves like beached whales' (Swed 1992: 112). One commission often leads to another: for example, Alexander Goehr's *Arden Must Die* (1967) for Hamburg State Opera; *Behold the Sun* (1985) for Duisburg Deutsche Oper am Rein (as *Die Wiedertaufer: The Anabaptists*); and *Arianna* for the ROH Covent Garden (1995).

As might be expected, the more conservative houses take the fewest 'new' risks. Alfred Schnittk's *Gesualdo* (1995) was the first Vienna State Opera commission for a very long time. Corigliano's *The Ghosts of Versailles* (1991), originally commissioned for the 1983 Met centennial, proved a popular success on account of its use of 'stars', and clear narrative based on characters from Mozart's *Le nozze di Figaro*. Described as a 'grand opera buffa', it was the first premiere staged by the Met since Barber's *Antony and Cleopatra* opened the Lincoln Centre home in 1966, a grand 'new' opera starring Leontyne Price, given a lavish realist production by Zeffirelli which, by critical accounts, swamped it. As these Met examples suggest, commissioned operas, such as the staging of *Gloriana* (Britten) by the ROH Covent Garden to mark the Coronation of Elizabeth II, serve symbolic and ritual moments well within the 'auratic' tradition. The Met commissioned Philip Glass's *The Voyage* (1992) to commemorate the 500th anniversay of Columbus' 'discovery' of the New World, which Glass tailored to the Met's resources: using a large orchestra, chorus and so on. Sallinen's *Kullervo* (1992) was commissioned for the opening of the new Finnish National Opera, although the late completion of the latter meant a premiere in Los Angeles. Festivals also provide the resources for newly commissioned works, especially Schwetzingen, Munich and Glyndebourne. Given the problem of costs it is not uncommon for joint commissions to be made, such as with *The Death of Klinghoffer* commissioned by six companies. Siegfried Matthus has had commissions from Dresden Semper Opera, Santa Fé, Schwetzingen Festival. Houston Grand Opera was joint commissioner with the BBC of Tippett's *New Year* (1990). Smaller festivals also commission—for example, Gerald Barry's *The Intelligence Park* for the Almeida Festival, premiered by the Opera Factory in July 1990. Competition prize-winning proves another common means of acquiring a professional airing, even recordings depending on the status of the competition. Casken's *Golem* won the 1991 Britten Award for Composition and has been recorded.[46]

Reviews of new works invariably seek to access them by means of recognisable musical signposts or quotations which mere audiences cannot be expected to pick up. On *Ghosts* one critic claimed that critics 'recognize the many quotes from Mozart and Bach, Rossini, Verdi, Mussorgsky, Richard Strauss, Auber and so on, ad infinitum, [unlike] the general public who merely know when they are being entertained and even, in the final 40 minutes moved' (Mayer 1990: 307). Judith Weir's *Blond Eckbert* (1994) is:

> ... a fairytale in form but a psychoanalysts case-book in content ... of the quality of Weir's score there can be no doubt. She is a composer who postmodernistically respects rather than rejects the past ... She takes what she needs from the past and transforms it into her own admirably economic musical language. *Eckbert* lasts less than 90 minutes and as with Janacek you feel that there is not one note that does not need to be there ... Horn calls herald a *Schone Mullerin* style Lied; a rippling Mahlerian figure conjures up the forest trees rustling ... It is cunningly put together, with telling motives, splashes of orchestral colour and natural-sounding speech melody combining to unfold a narrative in a

coherent and gripping manner (Milnes 1994a).

It is hard to believe that readers of reviews are meant to be any the wiser about form and content: 'Holler's *Die Meister und Margarita* (1989) makes extended use of quotation and pastiche [and thus] inevitably recalls Zimmermann's *Die Soldaten'* (Clements 1989b: 84), the latter a work of 'atonal twentieth century angst' (Reise 1991: 18), incorporating parody, pastiche, pop, synthesisers and jazz through the use of a combo in the night club scene. Many 'new' works are berated for being anything but: '... the watered down blend of middle-of-the-road pop and fired musical theatre clichés ... constituted the score' (Clements 1989b: 801 on Weldon/Sekacz *A Small Green Place*). Tippett uses jazz references in many of his operas and he claims that *New Year* was influenced by the TV series *Fame* (Pettitt 1990). Turnage in *Greek* acknowledges the influence of Britten and Puccini, Stravinsky and Henze. John Metcalf's *Tonrak* has 'echoes of Donizetti, Britten, Tippett, Vaughan Williams and Berg' (Milnes 1990c: 869). Lambert's *The Button Moulder* (1990) uses 'folk music, evocative yet never quite definable, [which] intercuts with the pounding pulse of rock and the earthy organum of the middle ages ...' (Finch 1990: 876). *Melissa's Maelstrom*, one of four prize-winning works given at the Britten Theatre of the RCM in 1993 possessed a '... musical idiom [which] ... hardly transcended Andrew Lloyd Webber' (Porter 1993b: 899).

If musical means of access prove elusive, familiar textual sources may not be. Blake's *The Plummer's Gift* has characters and situations which are staples of British drawing-room comedy enriched by Pinter and Ayckbourn. Holloway's *Clarissa* (1990) is based on the Richardson novel of that name. Many are drawn from Shakespeare—for example, Barber's *Antony and Cleopatra* (1966), Oliver's *Timon of Athens* (1991), Reimann's *Lear* and a range of classic literary sources from Lenz's *Die Soldaten* and Buchner's *Wozzeck* to Steinbeck's *Of Mice and Men* and James's *The Aspern Papers*. As musical elements in museum opera become part of a general culture's musical stockpile, so too 'new' works based on known sources utilise a literary stockpile. Clements (1989a: 281) comments:

> [*Lear*] seems to rely heavily on its cultural inheritance to elicit an
> emotional impact. If such sources serve as positive means of

access, biting, contemporary, modishly new language may prove the opposite as Tippett in his own libretti has often shown: 'Wow! This chick wants balling' *(The Ice-Break* 1977).

Perhaps surprisingly 'new' opera demonstrates its detachment from the institution proper in a production sense too, for unlike the top 100 now reproduced as commentaries on the 'known' originals, producers of 'new' works have a greater responsibility to original staging instructions. Radical productions are possible only when the traditions and conservatism are strong enough to survive. Clements gives the premiere of Maxwell Davies' *Tavener* at Covent Garden (1972), Chereau's Paris production of Berg's *Lulu* (1979), Holler's *Die Meister und Margarita* (Paris 1989), and the Almeida Festival London premiere of Casken's *Golem* (1989) as examples of productions which did not serve the works presented, although he pithily adds:

> Sometimes fidelity is a dubious privilege: had *The Making of the Representative for Planet 8* not been treated to such an inadequately literal presentation in Houston and then the Coliseum (London) ... more might still be sheltering under the illusion that Glass's operas have genuine musical worth. (Clements 1989b: 1183).

That there has only been one revival of Tippett's *The Ice-Break* at the ROH since the 1977 premiere is also blamed on the insane clutter of that production, rather than the 'trendy' libretto. Returning to the earlier point by Crutchfield that 'new' works succeed more as theatre than as music and singing, with the abnegation of music in the face of drama, *recitative* and *sprechgesang* with, by 1926, music's virtual obliteration, not all composers agree. Bolcom states:

> ... verbal communication is not the front line in opera. Think of characters like Don Giovanni, types so universal and understood that people can put different spins on them, from Molière to Richard Strauss to Byron to Bernard Shaw. They can do that because we all know that Don Juan is a driven womanizer. The operas I am thinking of as archtypal are all like this. They aren't wordy. They involve jumping off the parapet, all the big emotions. The basic communication level is really not verbal, because it

doesn't need to be (quoted in Malitz 1992: 16).

If known literary sources are not used as the basis of libretti, then newsworthy events or characters provide alternative means of audience access for example, *Nixon in China: The Death of Klinghoffer* (during the hijacking of the Achille Lauro), Harvey Milk Nono's *Intolleranza 1960* and *Intolleranza 1970* which depicted the exploitation of immigrant workers and his *Al gran carico d'amore* (La Scala 1975) which celebrated the Paris Commune. Modern music *and* strong messages are too much for some: Mayer described Goehr's *Triptych* as 'three pieces related at bottom by their intellectualized isn't-it-awful approach to human existence' (1992: 309). Many instruct on twentieth century heroes and heroines or link into fictions with strong national sentiments: Thompson's *The Mother of Us All* concerns the life and work of American suffragette Susan B. Anthony. Bolcom's *McTeague* (1992), set in San Francisco of 1899, is based on the Frank Norris novel.

Throughout the century the impact of experiments with the 'new' have been deemed anti-opera, or more generally anti-art. Milnes's review of the John Adams (composer) Alice Goodman (librettist) and Peter Sellars (producer) *The Death of Klinghoffer* in Brussels (1991), responded to *The Spectator* headline cliché, 'The death of opera': '... if opera's future is to be as actionless oratorio in which everything is amplified and scarcely a word heard, then opera could perhaps be described as having at least caught a slight chill' (1991: 494). No action, minimal characterization '... and the use of titles for English language performances really is the end of civilization as we know it' (ibid.: 496). Glass's *The Voyage* (1992) has action 'more psychological than physical' (Nott 1992: 12), and the Glass/Robert Wilson *Einstein on the Beach* proved just as mystifying. In the first scene:

> For perhaps five minutes the stage is static, except for one person moving backward and forward with angular gestures, and someone writing on an invisible blackboard ... Suddenly a paper airplane darts across the stage, or a band of white slowly winds down the backdrop. At the side a girl stands on one foot (for twenty minutes) with a conch shell to her ear (Smith 1977: 48).

Einstein evidently takes the stage as a violinist but not on a beach. There are scenes on a train, in a law court, in prison, in bed, in a spaceship, and there are connecting interludes mysteriously called 'Knee Plays'. The whole comprises four acts and nine scenes, which last some five hours of evolving ostinatos (mercifully reduced to fit on eight LP sides). It is clear that what attracts the audiences to return to Glass's operas is their literally entrancing music, which suspends the activity of the intellect while keeping the ears thoroughly alert and busy. This combined with fascinating abstract stage pictures, held my interest completely in *Akhnaten* and for a while in *Satyagrapha* though because it was on the telly at home I did not concentrate on it all the time. *Einstein on the Beach* without any stage spectacle to accompany it means very little to me. What, I keep wondering, is happening now? Why do the voices declaim simultaneously—are we not to share in the secret? How is Einstein involved in the trial and night- train and the rest? So many questions to which the music ... does not supply enough answers (Mann 1985).

Anti-opera can mean obscurantism in other ways. Barker's *La Malanchine* (1989) has a text in a mixture of Latin, Spanish and Nahuatl. American John Cage's works are simply 'anti': 'The Europeans have been sending Americans their operas for the past 150 years and now I'm sending them all back.' His *Europera 3* involves six operatives wielding a pair of early electric gramophones on which they play their selection of past great opera extracts from old 78s whilst two pianists play extracts from operas mainly in Liszt transcriptions; six peripatetic singers in evening dress every so often ping their tuning forks and break into aria and there are periodic thunderclaps of electronic mayhem, all under the glare of an elaborate lighting plot.

Despite the grand opera implications of much of the above, most 'new works are small and efficient in terms of resources. Zimmermann's *Die Soldaten* however:

... has treacherously difficult and complex vocal and instrumental parts, a huge cast, personnel traffic nightmares, simultaneous scenes and a warehouse full of percussion and electronic equipment. One European production is said to have involved 377 vocal and 33 orchestral rehearsals. In an American society notoriously tight with its arts budget, these complexities explain why *Die Soldaten,* despite its high artistic reputation, has had to wait so long for its New York premiere (Reise 1991: 18).

Similarly, 'Charles Lamb famously thought that "The Lear of Shakespeare cannot be acted". The key question is whether the *Lear* of Reimann can be sung' (2 1991: 585). On economic and aesthetic grounds 'small' has its virtues. Casken's *Golem* requires eight singers and 11 players, Harbison's *A Full Moon in March* is 30 minutes long and scored for four singers and eight players. I don't think, however, that economies of scale determined Judith Weir's *King Harald's Saga,* a three-act epic of nine principals and a chorus of the Norwegian army, all sung by a single soprano, unaccompanied, who introduces each act with a brief account of what is to happen, the whole thing lasting 10-11 minutes. Sally Beamish's *Ease* (1993) is scored for viola, flute, clarinet and typewriter, the significance of the latter being the subject-matter—an encounter between Emma Bovary and her first translator Eleanor Marx.

Christie's comments on the talents of student singers for extensive work on early operas which they thus present with unity of style and commitment also apply to 'new' opera. 'Put [established] singers on the stage and start making them act spontaneously—all you'll end up with is banality' (Virgil Thompson quoted in O'Connor 1991: 163). In 1991, Goehr's *Tryptych* was presented by the Manhattan School of Music which in 1990 had given the US premiere of Matthus's *Cornet.* Christoph Rilke's *Song of Love and Death* was originally commissioned for the post-war reopening of the rebuilt Dresden Semper Opera. Bruno Maderna's *Satyricon* (1973) was 'composed' through exercises with students at the 1971 Tanglewood Summer Festival.

Small means beautiful, means children, and 'new' opera has continued to involve children early in opera, although the risk is yet another version of the common one—how to talk *to* and not down to them. Britten's *The Little Sweep* and *Noyes Fludde* are exalted examples which have survived longer than most, which will include, one suspects, the Weldon/Sekacz *A Small Green Space* (1989), with its 'wincing sentimentality ... [and] hand me down accessibility of its music' (Clements 1989a: 801). Matthus's *The Never-Ending Story,* and Lambert's *The Button Moulder* (1990), are other examples whilst *The Queen of Sheba's Legs* by Grant (1991) involved children in writing and performance, spaces being left in the score for their contributions and over 250 being used on stage.

Very few 'new' works receive second productions or revivals, although so socialised are we into opera as an industry of revivals, we may be forgiven for not realising that Handel's operas were typically not revived during his lifetime (Ivry 1989: 20). Corigliano comments that premiere productions have to be 'just right', for new operas rarely get a second chance (Nott 1992: 10). Casken's *Golem* is an exception, receiving three productions in as many years (Almeida Festival in London, Opera Omaha [1990], Northern Stage, Newcastle [1991]). Blake's *Toussaint* premiered by the ENO in 1977 was revived in 1983 and as a result of this 'success', *The Plummer's Gift* (1989) was commissioned. Barber's *Antony and Cleopatra* was never revived at the Met, supposedly due to a 'press overattentive to the social glitter of the occasion' and an overelaborate production: 'in one scene there were three horses, two camels, an elephant and 165 people on stage' (Heyman 1991: 56). It was remounted by the Lyric Opera of Chicago in 1991.

All of the above suggests that, in terms of institutional practice, 'new' opera is tangential to repertoire, audience taste, ritual and so on. But 'new' opera is apparently very important as a defence against opera as moribund artefact—a proof of opera as a still creative art form within a singular auratic tradition. Clements says of Birtwistle, the composer of *Gawain* (Covent Garden in 1991): '... [it was] as if he had been characterised overnight as a composer of operas that could be recognised as belonging to the great tradition, rather than someone whose inventions for the stage were at best tangential to it' (1991b: 874). However, in terms of form and content, which for many is the acid test of opera, 'last gasps' is all we now get:

.... one of the problems with contemporary opera is that the music must be vocal. If when you go to the opera there's not a sense of *vocalita*, then something's wrong, I'm not saying you have to come out humming the tunes, but there must be a vocal approach' (Epstein, see Milnes 1992: 522).

Notes

1. The Arts Council grant in 1993-94 was £19.5 million. 'If there is no increase then seat prices will have to rise and operas by British composers and new operas will have to be cancelled' (Sir Angus Stirling *The Independent on Sunday* 4 June 1995: 10).
2. Covent Garden and the English National Opera have used various schemes such as The Garden Venture and the ENO's Contemporary Opera Studio. For a discussion of both when first established see Judd (1988) and Bredin (1988). See Kimberley (1993) for an account of the association between the ENO's Contemporary Opera Studio and the Almeida Theatre.
3. Except that, in series like Decca's *Entartete Musik*, attempts are clearly made to promote 'forgotten' or 'banned' music. Political reasons for works being 'lesser known' perhaps have their own financial cachet.
4. Despite widespread use, baroque, borrowed from architecture, is not usually given precise operatic definition. As a musical period it is applied to late seventeenth- and early eighteenth century works, broadly speaking from Lully to Handel.
5. Innaurato (1992a: 9) describes *Turandot* as more accurately looking forward to 'event musical theater like *Phantom of the Opera*'.
6. Some operas take a very long time to gestate. Holloway's *Clarissa* (1990) took 20 years between genesis and premiere and 14 years between completion and first performance. Maxwell Davies' *Tavener* (1972) reached its Covent Garden premiere 16 years after conception.
7. Nono was the first to break ranks through his desire to give a more vivid articulation to his political ideals with his two-act *Intolleranza 1960* later revised as *Intolleranza 1970*. Stockhausen eventually took up the operatic challenge the series '*Licht*' to be performed on seven consecutive evenings, *Donnerstag* first performed at Covent Garden (1985) preceded by *Samstag* at La Scala (1985) although a fragment of *Dienstag* had been given in concert form as early as 1977 and similarly, other components of later works in the cycle were first performed in the concert hall. Many of his earlier concert works were performance art requiring theatrical elements in their presentation: that is, as 'visible music' (for example, *Momente* 1972) was scored for a

large chorus, soprano and orchestra and required the performers to enter via the auditorium ('Listen to the Moments. Music of Love' summons the soprano) from the side aisles, chanting and murmuring until joined by the conductor when the performance begins.

8. 'I can see operas that mean much to me by Monteverdi, Handel, Rameau, Gluck, Mozart, Verdi, Janacek, that my grandfather had no chance of seeing. When radio, records (commercial and 'prime') and videotapes are taken into account, scarcely a corner of operatic history has not been opened to live exploration' (Porter 1990).

9. *Fiddler on the Roof* appears to be especially popular in middle Europe and Germany.

10. In this context Crutchfield makes the point that radical deconstructionist productions are pernicious and misplaced. The problem is not to revive the operas as theatre but to reintroduce musical parity at least with words and theatre.

11. Although the latter's own publicity claims: 'recognised internationally as one of the truly great companies of our time' (LOC 1993: 1) and regularly praised as outstanding in seriousness of purpose and achievement, its seasons are short and limited.

12. The previous premiere had been Tavener's *Therese* (1979) although in the meantime the ROH had presented productions of Berio's *Donnerstag* and *Un ré in ascolto*, *The King Goes Forth to France* (Sallinen).

13. *Aida* had almost nightly changes due to a series of illnesses but, for 'regular' operagoers, unscheduled appearances are part of opera's excitement and occasionally bring rare visits to a theatre of 'stars'. Christa Ludwig made her only Amneris appearance (in *Aida*) at Covent Garden under just such circumstances.

14. For a discussion on repertoire planning and so forth at the ROH under Isaacs, Haitink and Findlay, see *Opera* (April 1988: 402-10 and May 1988: 531-37). The Warnock Report (1991) included as one of its recommendations long runs of popular favourites. For a discussion of the particular issues facing the Bastille Paris and the Teatro de la Monnaie Brussels see Lannes and Nusacc (1986a, 1986b).

15. The other 36 were Littlejohn's 1-9, 11, 14, 18, 20, 22, 23, 25, 27, 30, 32, 35, 39, 40, 44, 47, 51, 55, 57, 61, 62, 64.

16. But cost is most likely. In 1990 the San Francisco Opera cancelled its commissioned Hugo Weisgall opera *Esther*, citing costs of 'a Meyerbeer sized project'. Meyerbeer's name is synonymous with the biggest, most lavish, longest of French 'grand opera' of the nineteenth century. His works (for example, *Les Huguenots: L' Africaine*) are rarely mounted now but works by others in Meyerbeer style, such as Verdi's *Les Vepres Siciliennes*, have become increasingly popular.

17. In general it would seem that core repertoire works are given new productions around the availability of a 'star': works which *should* be done have few such constraints, although the Met's mounting of *The Makropoulos Case* for Jessye Norman is an exception. Given the long-term character of such planning problems arise when new youngsters are the focus of planning and fail to last the course.

18. Martorella (1982: 61) reports that during the 1960s attendance at the Met dropped by 20 per cent. The strike (1969-70), general inflation, 'the middle class flight into the suburbs' and higher ticket prices contributed to the decline. Critics are inclined to blame administrators more than others involved in the industry for their 'museum mentality' (Mayer 1992: 308).

19. 1, 2, 5-11, 18. 20. 25, 27, 28, 31, 32, 40, 44, 50, 60, 67 and 92.

20. With its 'spaghetti western' atmosphere, this latter work has an obvious appeal to American companies (it was premiered at the Met in 1910 with Emmy Destinn and Enrico Caruso), as indeed do several other works less likely to be encountered in Europe or elsewhere, such as *Susannah* (Floyd), *The Ballad of Baby Doe* (Moore) and *The Mother of Us All* (Thomson).

21. It is rare for all three to be given in the one evening. They are a disparate threesome and, with two intervals, constitute a relatively long evening. *Il tabarro* in particular appears to be becoming a popular alternative to either *Cav* or *Pag*, breaking up these 'terrible twins'.

22. For its 1993-94 season, for financial reasons, Florence resorted to concert performances for three of five works given.

23. 1, 4-9, 13, 15, 23, 25, 26, 31, 32, 37, 40, 54, 62, 67.

24. 1-9, 16-18, 23, 31, 34, 35, 37, 41, 43, 44 and 48.

25. The other three were *Pelle Svanslos* by von Koch, *Gustaf Wasa* by Neumann: *Don Juan Freestyle* but amongst them was also *The Aspern Papers* by the American, Argento.

26. *Secco recitative:* the dramatic declamatory portions of opera in which the plot is advanced, as opposed to the reflective outpourings of arias.

27. *La serva padrona* appeared five years later than the British ballad opera, *The Beggar's Opera,* and eight years after Telemann's *Pimpinone* which can be traced back to a Venetian origin in Albinoni's *Astarto* (1708).

28. Loppert (1992a: 456) gives the ballet-pantomime *Don Juan,* based on the Molière play, as the key 'reform' work. It was premiered in 1761 at the Burgtheater Vienna.

29. Monteverdi and Cavalli interwove short comic scenes of everyday life between the main acts of their mythological/ historical works, but it was only towards the middle of the eigteenth-century that *opera buffa,* as a separate form, was created in Naples and operatic 'realism' was born.

30. Although it should be noted that Gluck's own works have great difficulty in holding core position in the repertoire, only *Orfeo ed Euridice* at 46 appears in the Littlejohn top 100.

31. As Shewan (1991) has pointed out, 'authenticity' in production has lagged far behind partly because there is little source material to work from.

32. For example Donington quotes singing teacher Giovanni Maffei:

> It is necessary to explain many arts of nature, to know the finest ones *(bellissimi),* and above all how many things the voice is required to do, and to what power of the spirit *(potenza dell'anima)* the voice is brought ... the motive power of the chest *(potentia motiva del petto)* are the main causes of the voice ... [the voice] must issue forth with violence *(furia),* which when one breathes naturally does not happen (Giovanni Maffei, 1562, quoted in Donington 1970: 17).

The following extract also from Donington illustrates how instruction of readers can easily become more an assertion of the superior knowledge, and power, of the writer:

> What are we to make of an editor [Maderna], who ignoring Monteverdi's instructions to play the opening toccata thrice in concert D (for written C, because baroque mutes raised

trumpets by a tone), expands it, keeps it incorrectly in C major, transposes the first following strophe from D minor (concert and written pitch) to G minor for a smoother transition, leaves the second strophe unaccountably in D minor and smooths *that* by altering the intervening ritornello, transposes the third and the fourth strophes, and ends by leaving the fifth strophe in Monteverdi's key, which is however no longer the key of the first strophe and therefore unbalances the closely knit strophic form more insensitively than ever? (Donington 1970: 20-21).

33. It is a given that music follows the visual arts with regard to specific and major aesthetic movements (Kramer 1990), and this appears to be no less true of opera's development, but the *crisis of realism* in opera, or *verismo*, dating from the 1880s indicates a watershed that pre-dates its appearance in other musical forms, perhaps because, being a multi- or hybrid medium, opera was forced to come to terms with theatrical and literary realism, earlier than 'abstract' music.

34. And literally 'lowland' as in a German variant (by Glasgow-born D'Albert) *Tiefland* (1903).

35. Kimbell (1991) doesn't agree: 'There is scarcely a number in the score that is not startlingly almost truculently primitive in musico-dramatic terms.'

36. *Mala vita* (Giordano) also focused on lumpen working-class subjects, including prostitutes. Realism in the visual arts of the same period consisted of 'homey scenes of the folk and its heroes, religious images of miracle and martyrdom' (Rosenberg 1970: 49).

37. Manon (Massenet) Manon Lescaut (Puccini) Tosca, Lodoletta, Butterfly, Iris, Zaza, Turandot, are eponymous heroines. Musetta and Mimi are in *La Bohème* (Leoncavello and Puccini versions), Santuzza and Lola in *Cavalleria rusticana*, Nedda in *Pagliacci* and Liu in *Turandot*. The use of 'pure' versus 'impure' images of women in these operas cannot be underestimated as reflections of women's changing role in society. This is another characteristic of *Carmen* (counterposed with Micaela) which justifies defining this work as *proto-verismo*.

38. Only Puccini, and then latterly, being treated with due regard, but, whatever the musicological justifications for such condemnation, one cannot but help feel that its crime was to

throw into crude focus the sociodynamic tensions of late nineteenth century culture.

39. School operas flourished—for example, Brecht and Weill's *Der Jasager* and *Der Lindberghflug*, Hindemith's *Wir bauen eine Stadt* (1931) and Milhaud's *A Propos de Bottes* (1932).

40. The first two acts were completed by 1932. It was premiered still uncompleted in 1957, six years after Schoenberg's death.

41. *Ghosts'* roles include a dramatic soprano, lyrico-spinto soprano, coloratura soprano, Verdi baritone, Mozart baritone, romantic tenor, character tenor, character mezzo and so on, which will attract 'star' artists who 'don't usually fool around with contemporary scores' (Mayer 1992: 306). Casken's *Golem* is described in one review as presenting 'grateful writing' for the singers' (Crichton 1991: 1489).

42. It would be so much easier then to open this music up to wider publics, to commodify it. Newspapers (especially Sunday broadsheets) have spent a considerable amount of time and space promoting opera, ballet, concerts and even modern composers, giving brief summaries of works, reduced priced tickets and so on *The Sunday Times* (30 January 1994) in its 'The Culture' section reported that *The Sunday Times Modern Classics* CD had entered the Gallup classical chart at 10. In this edition three composers, James Dillon, Mark-Anthony Turnage and Luciano Berio are featured. Turnage's *Greek* (1988), based on the Berkoff reworking of the Oedipus myth set in London's East End, and Berio's *Passagio* (1962); *Opera* (1970); *La vera storia* (1978) and *Un ré in Ascolta* (1983) staged at Covent Garden in 1989 are referred to but not described. Indeed words signally fail in such exercises (for example, on Dillon):

> ... however rebarbative the musical surface of tangled rhythms, multiple *glissandi* and trills, and fastidious and extreme dynamic shadings appears to most listeners, its exponents, Dillon included, would argue that they are making a vitally serious point about modern culture, protesting about the infringement of media control and mass communication on the high ground of European culture.

Right! Hence no doubt the CD.

43. The works given in The Garden Venture programme 1989 were:

223

Caedmon by Edward Lambert; *The Uranium Miners' Radio Orchestra Plays Scenes from Salome's Revenge* by Andrew Poppy; Michael Christie's *The Standard Bearer*; Peter Wiegold's *Last Tango on the North Circular*; Kenneth Chalmers' and Penelope Hayes-McCoy's *Soap Opera*; Jeremy Peyton Jones *The Menaced Assassin* and Priti Paintal's *Survival Song*.

44. Porter considers press verdicts—for example, *The Times*:

> Even the most patient and benign might be thinking it is time for the Garden Venture to produce something interesting, substantial, and worthwhile... Who commissioned the four non-starters? Who read the scores and thought they should be put on before a paying public?' *The Financial Times:* 'For so much devoted and costly labour, a meagre result ... Once commissioned are the composers left fancy-free to pursue duff ideas?'

45. Critics do try to understand: Clements talks of *Donnerstag* as 'a curious amalgam of autobiography and mysticism: there can be no doubt that in the character of Michael, played by a tenor, a dancer and a trumpeter, there is a good deal of the young Karlheinz' (1985: 991). Michael's journey around the Earth in Act II is called by Clements 'a 48 minute concerto for trumpets and orchestra ... a musical voyage in which the triumphant Michael travels the world, encountering a variety of different musics which are woven into a splendid tapestry of sound'. To justify its position in the opera, the whole piece is given theatrical trappings: Michael plays his solos from atop a giant globe, while the orchestral musicians cluster around the south pole, dressed— at least in the premiere production—as penguins. It is a strange confection indeed: 'Those who look for any meaningful fusion of dramatic action and musical are likely to be disappointed.'

46. A surprising number of new works are recorded: Tippett's *King Priam* (Chandos), *The Midsummer Marriage* (Lyrita), *The Ice Break* (Virgin Classics), *The Knot Garden* (Philips) and *New Year* (Virgin Classics) have all been recorded, but this is not surprising for such an illustrious composer. Casken's *Golem* (Virgin Classics) and Sallinen's *Kullervo* are also recorded, the latter not uncommonly before its premiere.

5   Singers' opera

Any musician has a tendency to fill up whatever room he is in but the opera singer is especially permeating. He just naturally acts at all times as if he were singing solo on a 200 foot stage. His gestures are large and simple: and he moves about a great deal, never looking at anybody else and never addressing a word to anybody privately, but always speaking to the whole room (Virgil Thompson quoted in Meyer 1986).

Introduction*

Rosselli (1992a: 1) establishes the traditional bad reputation of the opera singer, male and female, quoting composer Bellini, amongst others, in support: 'She is a singer and therefore capable of anything' (Bellini 1943). Whilst 'opera singer' should now be little more than a professional job title, hints persist, particularly in the media, of extra-curricula larger-than-life, 'behaving badly' qualities, especially of stars, *prima donna* and *diva*: 'vain, extravagant, demanding ... the best opera singers have always been stars' (Rosselli 1992a: 1). Rosselli tells us that the phrase *virtuosa canaglia* ('singing rabble') had a career of several centuries: '[they] suit ill with that part of society which has decent principles' (ibid.: 2). As this 'rabble' became schooled, trained, institutionalised and ranked into professional chorus, secondary soloists, *comprimari* stars, superstars, *diva, prima donna, prima donna assoluta*[1] and so on, the terms *diva* and *prima*

---

* In this chapter, which is based on numerous media interviews with singers, references are to the singer, not the interviews. They are marked by an * after the name and the sources are listed in Appendix F.

donna, though losing some stigma, as for example, 'a sort of courtesan, idling her way through wealth and fame' (Christiansen 1984: 9 quoting Mayhew 1862), have nevertheless retained in popular culture connotations of 'vanity and capriciousness' (Rosselli 1992b), extravagance and being 'difficult', which sit paradoxically alongside the mundane career experiences of most singers: scholarships, competitions, lengthy training in all aspects of performance, work shortage, dealings with agents and managements, short-term contracts, auditions, excessive travel, pension schemes and so on. *Prima donna* tantrums may be the exception rather than the rule but representations of operatic stardom still flourish, partly because as loud claims are made that *prima donna* are, if not yet extinct, doomed to extinction, stars are simultaneously being created and marketed to operagoers, news media and especially record consumers. Commercialisation into wider 'opera' entertainment markets, the current dominance of television executives and accountants in opera house managements, reliance on box office receipts in the face of retreating subsidies and record company power serve to sustain and recycle the opera singer as 'star' ideology—an especially potent means by which opera is commercially transmuted into 'opera'. Meanwhile enhanced producer power requires 'more compliant singers than larger than life characters who may be difficult and have too many ideas of their own' (Moshinsky 1995: 20). In all these respects it is agreed that opera singers, apart from a few superstars, have lost the almost autocratic power that underpinned *prima donna* status in its prime, and yet opera is, for many consumers, first and foremost its singers and stars: 'The *condito sine qua*, the ace card with which to make a world wide public love this "organised madness" is the singer—his or her bravura' (Stinchelli 1992: 9); '... opera's fundamental power lies in the singing voice' (Christiansen quoted in Milnes 1990a: 143)

As with other aspects of opera, contemporary discourses on the opera singer are mostly pursued in the context of a false, foreshortened, largely nineteenth century 'tradition'—especially from the second half onwards—in increasingly recorded photographic and phonographic forms. Contemporary singers are judged against an earlier reified 'Golden Age', a never-to-be-recaptured era of unquestionably great vocal talents, justifying their fame, fortune and dominance over their contemporary stars in other media. It often appears that any one generation's 'Golden Age', is that of the immediately preceding generation, or more generally that of all prior generations. Yet again, in this technological sense, the onset of 'realism' and the technological means to reproduce it combined to attenuate operatic history, covering earlier reputations of immorality, vulgarity and lack of respectability with a patina of respectability—of 'the Grand Tradition' (Steane 1975) as further validation of opera as auratic art.

In this chapter I shall not replicate existing valuable histories of the opera singer (for example, Rosselli 1984: 1992a: 1992b), the nineteenth century institutional contexts in which they performed, or their constructed 'tradition' (for example, Fulcher 1987: Levine 1988), rather I concentrate on current representations of the changing role, career and status of the opera singer in the late twentieth century opera industry in which, for many, the term 'star' is now applicable to only a very few 'dinosaurs', judged by the criterion of excessive 'in-house' power. *Mezzo-soprano* Anne Howells who pursues a very considerable international career and who one would have thought to be unquestionably a 'star', claims not to be so in this older established sense:

> ... people in my stratum of the business have to sing roles they don't necessarily want to in order to make a career. I'm not in the luxurious position of being able to say 'I won't work with her' or 'I want him in the cast' (Howells* 1989: 273).

Agents, and now recording companies, are frequently rumoured to also impose a package of artists on managements prepared to pay for a 'star'. Others use 'superstar' for a yet more elevated stratum whose excessive 'in-house' power is matched by high profile media marketing, interviews and advertising, a stratum likely to elicit purist disapproval.[2]

> The concept of 'superstardom' is questionable ... to me as a human being. Perhaps it suits some people, but I'm not ... sure ... the lifestyle ... would suit me. I really most enjoy doing worthwhile quality work with good colleagues and good musicians. That to me is career satisfaction, not whether all the hype and publicity machines get you into the newspapers every five minutes (Soprano Yvonne Kenny* 1992: 1393).

Future 'stars'

Despite such reservations, whether called singers, stars, superstars, diva or *prima donna*, singer status to the point of stardom clearly dominates careers. How could it not when, from the outset, singers compete for attention, prizes, scholarships, funding and schooling on the basis of signs of future stardom and proof that they have the fighting spirit necessary to achieve it? Marc Belfort, Director of Zurich's International Opera Studio identifies qualities required for a singing career as:

> Great survival instincts! A good technique is important, and natural beauty of voice ... An individual sound is important. There is also personality ... charisma, the ability to communicate emotion and atmosphere ... This is a profession in which to be even mediocre you have to be sensational (quoted in Driscoll 1993: 27-28).

Peggie (1993a: 32) agrees that—in addition to 'raw talent', 'musicianship, expressive maturity, stage presence, physical awareness and the desire to communicate', material matters of financial support and security—necessary qualities are those which 'apply to any kind of achievement: commitment, hunger for success ... nose for publicity, self marketing abilities ... indestructible confidence and luck'. From the outset then, the shadow of hoped for and/or potential 'stardom' falls across all aspirants: 'great survival instincts', 'personality', 'charisma', 'indestructible confidence', 'intensity', 'a nose for publicity' allied to 'natural beauty of voice' and 'raw talent', 'larger than life' qualities which cannot be contained by an auditorium or college studio and may eventually expand into the media as focus of news, profiles, anecdotes, gossip and rumour. The social construction of the opera singer is a rich tense blend of professional/rational versus irrational/mystifying/charismatic contradictions. Behind the rhetoric of 'God-given' 'natural' gifts, careful and rigorous training is required to nurture and maximise them. Although from the outset 'larger than life' qualities are reified, it is a bruising career for the most ambitious voices, rather than the greatest and there is great stress on professional training, career patience and control: 'No singer could possibly hope to succeed in the highly competitive world of international opera if (s)he didn't start out with complete belief in his or her worth and wholehearted determination to reach the goal' (Peter Glossop*: 1969: 386). While career progress can bring great material rewards, the singer should be first and foremost a servant of the music, the composer, the conductor and now producer, but the greatest servants are the 'biggest stars'—established stars, retiring stars, 'rising stars', 'overnight sensations', 'recording stars'. The majority of singers active in opera—chorus members, debutantes and supporting artists—tend to be absent from these representations because the star is the public face of opera, the focus of immediate and outstanding attention. Not surprisingly, for some, the pressures become simply too great; nerves rather than voices fail (for example, Anita Cerquetti and Linda Esther Gray).

Despite the persistent 'raw talent'/'mystery of voice' myth, training is increasingly professionalised. Clive Timms, head of Opera Studies at the Guildhall School of Music states: 'It is becoming less and less possible to go it alone ... What do you do with raw talent? When do you do it? How do you do it? How long will it take? And what happens if it goes wrong?'(Peggie 1993a: 32). Voices mature at different rates and ages, Peggie stresses the uniqueness of each voice as an instrument which also varies by time of day, month, climate and with age. Singers unlike athletes, with whom they often compare themselves, 'experience their physical manipulation internally'. It is therefore much harder to feel or see what is going on 'except by recourse to imagery or metaphor. What is more they must aim blind so to speak' (ibid.: 32), meaning that, as with our speaking voices, what we hear is not what others hear.

While opera singing has become more professionalised, professionalisation can only go so far before it hits the essentialist 'mysteries of the God-given', 'impossible to fully understand, describe, control' wall. Finding the right teacher is thus also always problematic because the teacher/pupil relationship cannot rest on rationalised technical criteria alone; there must be a personality as well as a vocal relationship. The 'mystery' is compounded by 'there being as many opinions about training opera singers as there are teachers' (ibid.: 33). It is questioned whether instructional texts on singing can be usefully written for or read by students, given the use of 'imagery and metaphor'. Peters (1989: 1276) in her review of Salaman (1989) comments:

She explains in layman's [*sic*] terms how to achieve throat opening, good posture for singing, proper support and breathing and the mysteries, because they are given foreign titles, of *vibrazione* and *messa di voce*. These last two are difficult to explain in print, and full comprehension, like so much else in singing, would depend on a practical demonstration ...

In his review of Winsel's *Anatomy of Voice*, Lockhart states 'it is almost impossible to write anything on this subject which will not receive a different interpretation from every reader. Indeed there is no doubt that reading such books can do great harm to students' (1966: 644). These texts for pupil singer and teachers reiterate the general strengths which singers need to sustain careers and the exercises which should help them to 'overcome tension both physical and mental, lack of self-assurance, diffuse concentration, the inability to question' (Balk 1985 quoted in Peters 1989: 1276).[3] Horne* (1995: 43) explains how even basic terms are difficult to use and understand: for example, 'bring the voice forward':

O.K. so they'll place it in their noses. And then they don't get a proper amplitude to the sound. It will just be a very nasal sound. So fine, it's forward, but you can't just say 'Place the voice forward'. My former husband Henry Lewis came up with a wonderful corollary—it's like having a pencil and you have the eraser on your vocal cords holding them just in the right place, and then you have the point of your pencil at your nose, so that you have that feeling, that your vocal cords are at their right placement, and its coming out in the mask at that point. And that's what it should be. That's what they call a pointed tone, and maybe that's what is meant by 'placing it forward'. But you've got to have that resonance in the head, in the mask.[4]

Pleasants (1989: 88) recalls a discussion with Dame Eva Turner and others with a common interest in opera when Dame Eva observed that:

Madame So-and-So's vocal problems were being caused by 'carrying her chest too high', was greeted by many present as though she was referring to Madame So-and-So's embonpoint. If so many in so musically sophisticated a circle would not know immediately that Dame Eva was referring to Madame So-and-So's handling of the 'passage' or transition from chest to middle register, what of the poor layman exposed in reviews and in conversation to the jargon of vocal comment and criticism? How confusing and bewildering it must be!

Pleasants then gave (ibid.: 88-95) an excellently clear guide to basic vocal terminology and their applications.

When stars comment about their early training they invariably relate such doubtless apocryphal tales as that of Nicolai Porpora keeping the *castrato* Gaetano Caffarelli singing the same sheet of vocal exercises for six years and then dismissing him with the comment 'you are now the greatest singer in the world'. Rïse Stevens recounts that for the first year of her training by Anna Schoen-Rene, she sang nothing but scales (*1988: 14). Student singers today, however, are likely to be more institutionalised than in the early days of Stevens's career: 'The hazardous voids, between private singing lessons, amateur gigs, competitive festivals, serious training and the first contract are gradually being filled out' (Peggie 1993a: 32). In Britain there are more than 100 graduate singers each year, 'the growing number of graduate courses and growth of small-scale touring companies providing a *de facto* apprenticeship system' (ibid.: 32). Particular mainstream conservatoire experience and the backing of prestige courses such as the Britten-Pears School, Brereton or Clonter Farm Opera, provide a pedigree which those not so fortunate have to work all that harder to overcome, not least in establishing all important future contacts. Conservatoires should maintain vocal health: 'fully fit, properly coached and kitted out with all the most up-to-date-musico-dramatic skills' (ibid.: 32). Admission is normally by audition and to degree courses by meeting normal 'A' level or equivalent entry qualifications. Inevitably 'raw' vocal talent is not always matched by academic qualification, students on courses at both may be of normal undergraduate age or 'mature' and in their thirties. Courses will not normally be exclusively geared to opera singing either although the exception is the Royal Northern College of Music, the only conservatoire in Britain with a self-contained opera studies department distinct from a school of vocal studies. Opera singers now require general stagecraft skills, movement and acting, to add to the vocal. The Guildhall School of Music has a postgraduate department of opera studies 'run virtually as a production company' (ibid.: 33). Intake is limited currently to 24 per year, approximately one-third of whom are from abroad, aged between 21 and 28 for women and 21 and 32 for men. Students admitted have fully trained voices in preparation for two years' intensive training.[5] Journals such as *Opera*, regularly list international singing competitions, and cover the results of the most important (for example, in Britain the Kathleen Ferrier Memorial Scholarship), although 'In many instances the competition route becomes an end rather than a means. Some young singers enter every audition open to them, taking prizes, yet never succeeding in translating their talent onto the lyric stage' (Poole 1989). *Opera Now* (December 1995: 46) lists 58 singing competitions in 17 countries, including the high media profile bi-annual Cardiff Singer of the World Competition, featuring singers who are often already soloists with major companies, with considerable competition experience and, as past competitors have demonstrated, already on the edge of operatic stardom.

Few singers now serve apprenticeships in the chorus,[6] however; the development of more formal professional training and qualifications through academies and conservatoires, as with other professions, means that entry into solo careers is increasingly direct rather than by working up from the ranks: 'If you want to be a general, you don't join the army as a private' (drama coach Dudley-Long quoted in Peggie 1993b: 34). Given the 'irrational/charisma' side of opera singer ideology, the dangers of professionalisation are clear. Through training, conservatoires may eradicate or flatten individuality of voice, ambition and 'star' potential, especially where courses are broad and for extended periods. The ambitious will look outside the routinised collective work of the college, to limited exposure before the public, to be noticed and make contacts for further long-term work, perhaps abroad, in which case guides to foreign institutions (from company lists, agents fees, audition details) are available (see Maddison and Sullivan 1991). In the 1980s before reunification it was estimated that 2000 US singers auditioned each year for German houses (Midgette 1993b).

Chorus work seldom provides a gateway to stardom, requires a heavy schedule in which individuality is further constrained, although much depends on the size of chorus and company; at Glyndebourne, for example it is small, prestigious and limited to the summer months rather than the full season from autumn through to summer. Some teachers will not allow their students to apply for chorus work even though it appeals to the aspiring singer by providing financial security, but this very security is often depicted as a trap, inhibiting ambitions and development towards solo work. Until the financial crisis following German reunification hit subsidies, the many smaller houses there provided valuable 'finishing schools' for young singers.[7] The anachronisms of opera singer ideology, involving the imposition of increasingly routinised learning procedures on the resilient ideology of 'unique' 'mysterious' resources, and 'charisma' of future stardom, is well summarised by John Mitchinson head of vocal studies at the Welsh College of Music and Drama: 'It takes 25 years to create an overnight success' (quoted in Peggie 1993a: 32).

Film stars opera stars

Dyer notes how film stars 'form the basis of probably the larger part of everyday discussion of films' (1979: 1), and the same is true of opera stars and opera. Indeed throughout the first half of this century many opera stars became film stars. Opera held a deep fascination for early cinematographers, for technical as well as social reasons, ranging from the legitimisation of this new art form through incorporation of elements from the most accessible of auratic forms, even though what was initially reproduced was opera reduced to piano accompaniments to 'silent' films. With the appearance of soundtrack technologies, opera faced the further challenge of accurately reproducing the complexities of operatic sound: orchestral and vocal.

One of the earliest full-length (46 minutes) silent films was Gounod's *Faust* (1903), featuring the Royal Italian Opera of Paris, and versions of *Rigoletto*, *Il Trovatore*, *Aida*, *Manon*, *Manon Lescaut*, *Parsifal*, *The Marriage of Figaro*, *Salome*, *A Life for the Tsar*, *Eugene Onegin*, several *Carmen*'s (that of 1919 starring Pola Negri) and Wagner's *Ring* (in two hours!) followed in quick succession. Shown initially with a piano accompaniment, then with a pit orchestra, experiments with synchronised playing of early recordings proved unsuccessful. The zenith of 'silent' opera films was probably *Der Rosenkavalier* (1926) for which Richard Strauss provided a special orchestral transcription. With 'talkies' there was much to prove in sound reproduction—so much so that by the mid-

1930s some studios suspected overkill, advertising their latest products as 'films without music'.

From more or less the beginning the film industry recruited opera stars to give glamour, status, and audience appeal. In 1915 Met star and great beauty Geraldine Farrar made three films including *Carmen* (directed by Cecil B. De Mille). When Farrar travelled to Hollywood by train, her female fans, 'gerryflappers', waited at each station, 5000 school children greeting her at her destination. Farrar made 15 films between 1916 and 1921. Mary Garden, the first Mélisande in Debussy's opera, also made silent films (but in Manhattan), including one of Massenet's *Thais*, whilst in 1918 Caruso also made two silent films—*My Cousin* and *A Splendid Romance*—neither particularly successful. The first experiments in sound cinema (that is, to audiences) featured opera stars Marion Talley (*'Caro nome'* from *Rigoletto)* and Giovanni Martinelli (*'Vesti la giubba'* from *Pagliacci*), a year before *The Jazz Singer* appeared. In the 1930s many opera stars were also Hollywood stars. Grace Moore's first film was *A Lady's Morals*, in which she played opera star Jenny Lind; her *One Night of Love* for Columbia (1934 including arias from *Carmen, Butterfly, Martha* and the like) was the second biggest grossing picture of the year, winning six Oscar nominations: 'La Moore ... Toujours La Moore' (*Photoplay*). When commentators speak of 'crossover' as a recent marketing ploy these early century moves by opera stars into popular cinema should be remembered. More Moore operettas followed: *Love Me Forever, The King Steps Out, When You're in Love* and *I'll Take Romance*. Killed in a plane crash (her last film in 1939 was of the opera *Louise* with Georges Thill), Moore became the subject of her own biopic, *So This is Love* starring Kathryn Grayson. *The Merry Widow,* made in the same year as *One Night of Love* starred Jeanette Macdonald, demonstrating the overlap between film stars who could sing and singers who could act. RKO signed up Lily Pons for such films as *I Dream Too Much* (nicknamed *I Scream Too Much*): Paramount used Gladys Swarthout for *Give Us This Night* (1936) and *The Champagne Waltz* (1937), and Twentieth Century Fox used Lawrence Tibbett, whose first film had been *The Rogue Song* (1930) for MGM for which he also received an Oscar nomination. Nelson Eddy began as opera singer but, following the success of *Naughty Marietta* (1935) with Macdonald, never returned to the stage. The most unlikely film stars also sang arias, Mae West's rendition of Dalila's *Mon coeur s'ouvre à ta voix* in

234

Goin' to Town, was a high point[8] (MacKay 1991: Fawkes 1994).

Film stars have been described as a group 'whose institutional power is very limited but whose doings and way of life arouse a considerable ... sometimes maximum degree of interest' (Alberoni quoted in Dyer 1979: 75). By institutional, Alberoni means in formal and wider political arenas, but opera stars have always held considerable power *within* the operatic institution, for the kinds of reasons Howells and Kenny have described. For Alberoni the stars phenomenon rests on a bureaucratised, structured social system which ensures the existence of social roles defined by objective hierarchically ranked criteria, reflected in a developing consumerist economy, able to market the unique and rare few, who become consumed, 'known' and recognised by the many. Within a 'high' art medium such as opera there is a heightened tension around stardom in these terms as it tends to undercut the art form itself:

> Our entire society is completely captivated by celebrity, especially in America. For all its benefits, that preoccupation is a cancer in a lot of ideas—not just in opera [whose] ... public is more interested in visiting a famous personality than really understanding the art form. Popularity through television is often confused with fame and notoriety ... fame is simply the geometrical proportion whereby more people know who you are than you know who they are (Baritone Thomas Hampson* 1989: 10).

To ideologies of 'fame and notoriety' are appended 'myths' of apparently effortless rapid upward social mobility, so that stars, though 'unique', may come from any class, may be 'anyone' or 'no-one', for that is what stars tell us they originally were, and indeed, in many respects when out of costume and spotlight, claim they still are. Costumed, whatever their role, they remain sufficiently detached to be recognisable as 'themselves'. Major opera houses are large, the 'cheaper' mass audience some distance from the stage, but singers can develop and deploy aural characteristics, equivalent to film star 'close-ups' through vocal colour, technical idiosyncrasies and 'acting' mannerisms: 'the flick of an eye can express volumes in a film close-up, the movement of a voice likewise in a theater' (Innaurato 1993: 14). 'Close-up' is an appropriate term to describe recording stars and their record companies' marketing of their vocal identities combined with photographs in adverts, the former sometimes difficult to replicate in the acoustics of a large theatre. All opera stars of whatever type conform by degrees to the cinematic and 'soap opera star' model,[9] their 'individuality' cosmetically packaged.

Alberoni argues that stars are uniquely privileged for they are not envied or resented; people believe that anyone may become one if suitably gifted, that they have earned their stardom by being so blessed that they have not had to work, perhaps deviously for it—indeed they are rarely depicted as working at all. In the process stars become symbols of fetishised egalitarianism and openness. Although few stars have access to what Alberoni calls 'real' political power, they exert considerable influence of a normative and material kind, through ideal images of well earned 'success', how to be and live the lifestyle of a star, and of opera's auratic qualities matched by wealth, status and glamour. As the culture industry develops, stars increasingly depend upon a mature consumerist economy—a consuming population able to consume *them* via all manner of reproduced commodity means—in time defined as leisure not work, and in a culture increasingly underpinned by a global consumerist market. True, even in opera, national stars residually survive (until recently in the old Soviet bloc, now rapidly being drawn into the world market,[10] or for reasons of physical distance—for example Australian singers, such as Joan Carden* (1994: 415) who even so stresses that 'Australia is not as cut off from the rest of the world as some people ... think'), as do some 'in-house' company stars, but the greatest stars are now stars worldwide—stars of recordings, videos, laser discs and celebrity concerts which may be consumed anywhere. Perhaps as the distinction has been made here between opera (the cultural artefact in performance) and 'opera' (commodified entertainment fragments outside the opera house), so too one should differentiate between opera stars and 'stars'. These *may* be the same singers, but their treatments differ considerably according to the contexts in which they are promoted, their earning power varying according to the demands of their different, at times overlapping, audiences (Morin 1969).

As noted in earlier chapters, 'superstar' fees have become a thorny issue in discussions of the industry's finances and are perceived by some as eating up unjustifiable proportions of production costs and diminishing subsidies. Alternatively, it is argued that high box office demand for such stars, despite their higher fees,[11] translate into higher seat prices which not only enhance their value in both opera and 'opera' markets, but also stabilise the former by being 'guarantors of "sell-outs"' (Schickel 1974: 27). It is those who achieve 'opera' star status (Bartoli, Te Kanawa, Domingo, Pavarotti, Carreras, Norman and possibly Battle[12]) who most resemble film stars, retaining considerable power within and transcending the institutional restrictions of opera, and becoming 'standardised products ... insurance for large profits' (Powdermaker 1950: 229). Te Kanawa provides an ideal contemporary example:

Even though careful about her privacy, beetle-browed opera fans mosey on down and hang about the entrance to her estate. The regulars are not too creepy, she explains, but you never know when a fruitcake packing an axe might turn up. We get such weirdoes coming to the house, genuflecting at the gate. Nutters ... 'I'm your greatest fan'. 'Those are the scariest words in the English language' ... Her friends, rather tactfully, describe her as a *truthful* character ... : 'I don't need people to tell me how good I am. I know what comes out of my own throat. But if someone says your hair is a mess, you didn't sing very well last night, I suddenly think, I don't need this person around me. I tend not to be around too many people who have negative attitudes about me'. These include producers who want her to work in the afternoon—she likes to rehearse in the mornings only—and assorted amateurs. Five years ago she refused to go on stage at the Met unless the management removed Hei-Kyung Hong, a young Korean due to sing opposite her in Così fan tutte. Naturally the cowed bosses did what the diva wanted ... 'In the end I was proved right. The girl was not ready to play the role' ... material gains from her performing and recording career are obviously vast: My mother told me never to talk about money. You have already asked me one question about my stage dresses (made by Gary Dahms, £2000 each min.) and that is as far as you can go. You earn what you earn. There are some nights when I don't earn a penny but no one talks about *that*. They always talk about the high ticket price ... I'm not embarrassed about being paid a lot to do a job' (Moir 1993: 8).

The last century in the history of the opera singer is largely a history of technological developments and expanding markets so that now, through TV, video and laser disc, opera stars are manufactured and sold in ways comparable to those employed in popular music, leading

237

many earlier stars to regret 'I was born too early' (Lisa Della Casa*1995: 17). Te Kanawa sings on stage relatively infrequently, records a great deal and through media coverage and advertising, has a very strong 'opera' presence.

On stage the extent to which stars may now display themselves is circumscribed by the the power of management, colleagues, conductors, producers and so on and by levels of recorded as well as 'live' knowledge and experience possessed by audiences, by which they will be relatively judged. Analyses of film star relations with audiences in terms of 'emotional affinity', 'self-identification', 'projection' and 'invitation' (Tudor 1974) are probably of less relevance to stars of the more artificial opera, although fanaticism in opera audiences can reach similar levels of obsession (see Koestenbaum 1993). In all fields: '... the role of the star [may] become "psychotic": it polarises and fixes obsessions' (Morin 1960: 164). Past opera stars undoubtedly excited such 'psychotic' reactions and many continue to do so.[13]

The 'ideal' singer

To organise and contextualise the many individual singers' accounts which follow it is necessary to employ an 'ideal type' of opera singer iconography. In the telling, many singers appear to be close to 'ideal', so consistently patterned and recurrent are representations of them in media and (auto)biographies. Much depends on the generation of the singers concerned, those active until the 1960s being especially likely to bemoan the fate of the *prima donna* (see Rasponi 1984: 1), but whilst jet travel, recording techniques and performance schedules have dramatically altered the means and forms by which 'stars' may be constructed, technologically reproduced and sold in the expanding world market, the parameters of opera stardom have remained remarkably stable. Media coverage of contemporary singers, whilst acknowledging commercial and marketing developments such as the 'milestone' first solo recording of 'new stars',[14] nevertheless proceed to reproduce the latter much as they did the old. An 'ideal type' is a necessary tool because it is impossible to discuss every empirical example (Weber 1949: 81-112). Similar in purpose to Durkheim's 'average type', Weber's 'ideal type' provides a means of attaining some kind of generalisation while at the same time remaining as faithful as possible to the facts (Rex 1961: 9) but, unlike an 'average type', an 'ideal type' is not intended to be descriptive but explanatory; it is 'a construction of certain elements of reality into a logically precise conception' (Gerth and Mills 1967: 59). The 'logically precise conception' of the opera singer appears to be largely applicable to both males and females, allowing for some variations in their realisation, the reiteration by the former, for example, that being an opera singer does not mean being any less masculine, whilst the glamorisation of females and integration of career into marriage and motherhood takes a prominent role for the latter. With the exceptions of The Three Tenors and, on occasion, other males, the emphasis is on females of the species. Throughout opera's history, according to cultural, musical and theatrical style and fashion, tenors, *prima donna*, or earlier, *castrati*, have held particular positions of dominance, but these are precisely the kinds of variations which may be systematically located by the use of such an 'ideal typology'. For evidence I have referred to a wide range of sources including critiques of recorded evidence (for example, Scott 1977; 1979; Steane 1974; 1991; Douglas 1992): singers' autobiographies[15] and biographies,[16] and in particular a large number of interviews in specialised as well as mass media, signalled in their referencing, as has been done thus far this chapter, by* and listed separately in Appendix F alphabetically under singer, not author. Inevitably the emphasis is on 'stars'; only on rare occasions are singers of supporting roles, 'house-singers' *(comprimarii)* interviewed. What is of interest in all these accounts is not the accuracy of what is being reported, which cannot be tested, but the imagery and reasoning employed. Rasponi (1984) claims that the true *prima donna* is no more. By comparison, for Christiansen (1984: 9), the line continues unbroken: *prima donne* are still 'at the centre of the magnificence and scandal of opera, ridiculed, reviled and worshipped'. The greater the star the more opportunities to encounter them throughout their careers in various sources, including those where the gossip and innuendo are largely important in contributing not only to opera fan subcultures which thrive on 'inside' knowledge (for example, Mordden 1989; Vickers 1979), but also publicise opera stars as personalities to wider publics. In a great proportion of all of this material, discourses take on 'the trashy cadences and idioms of divaprose' (Koestenbaum 1993: 84). Koestenbaum is primarily concerned with the females of the species, but in truth *divaprose* applies to the iconography of males as well as females and consists of:

> ... sentences of self-defence and self-creation ... often banal: an ordinariness touched by sublimity ... to amplify (the) self ... amusing ... pathetic ... because they are so often no longer household words ... it never offers a new or surprising fact ... it is succinct, epigrammatic, an acquired dialect ... (1993: 85, 131).

In a text for, hopefully, sociologists without knowledge of opera as well as operamanes with a wider concern for the context and meaning of their obsession, the conjunction of, and need to illuminate, 'acquired dialects' is becoming a persistent theme. Of course unless one is an opera enthusiast one will not recognise most of the singers' names referred to below, but it is their collective rather than individual 'presence' I wish to focus on. Unfortunately, without academic references it might be believed that I am merely 'impersonating' divaspeak—hence the references in Appendix F and the main bibliography. For those interested in brief biographies of singers, the dictionaries listed in the Introduction should again prove invaluable. For those wishing to encounter a densely packed summary of 'ideal' characteristics from singers themselves see McGovern and Winer (1990). So what are the elements of this 'logically precise conception' of the opera star?

- Humble beginnings, so at odds with adult success and stardom.
- Natural 'unique' vocal talent of which everyone not least the singer was aware from the outset, described as 'God-given', 'a gift of Nature' and so on.
- An individuality of voice, sound, technique, though difficult to describe.
- A natural determination from an early age to do well, a fighting spirit to realise ambitions established at an early age.
- ... requiring sacrifices also from a (usually very) early age.
- But singers possess other natural talents thus requiring the taking of the decision to pursue singing rather than for example, chemistry or taxidermy.
- The singer's background did not discriminate between opera; other forms of music making, even popular entertainment were present—a reflection of its 'ordinariness'.
- Despite natural talent and determination to succeed (and the

certain knowledge of eventual success), hard work (whether in schooling or at maintaining faith and persistence) is required to get established.

- Persistent training and schooling are necessary after success and stardom ...
- ... yet with a certain self knowledge of vocal abilities and potentials beyond that of any teacher, as to what new roles to take on, in which theatres to accept engagements, how many performances to give per year, what to record, the speed and form of career development and so on.
- Frequently a personally based knowledge of one's own voice and voices generally is claimed which challenges existing and conventionally accepted wisdom re *Fachs*[17] and so on.
- The need in interviews to use a 'dazzling' array of terms (for example, *Fachs*) to demonstrate technical knowledge with the effect of maintaining the 'mystery' and distance of singing, singers, opera, from the public.
- 'Serious' researching of a role including background reading on historical periods and characters.
- ... but once knowing a role (and the grander one gets), resistance to alternative interpretations, to the need to be directed or rehearsed in every production ...
- ... usually defended as 'knowing better' by stars, completely committed to their art, who see themselves as its 'servants', with a duty to the composer and their audience, to use their naturally endowed gifts wisely, to maintain tradition.
- A grand, imposing, larger than life manner befitting an opera star, off and on stage ...
- ... and divas at whatever age, if not beautiful, become 'beautiful' through being commodified in some glamorised way or another.
- They are the perfect colleagues to all involved from co-stars to stage hands, properly treated with appreciative (small!) gifts.
- This generosity to colleagues extends beyond performances to interviews.
- The star is however a perfectionist, cannot tolerate poor performances or lack of commitment from colleagues, thereby giving rise to reputations of being difficult or unreliable, and veiled criticisms in interviews about which they do not wish to say more ... but often do.
- The greater the star the less likely they are to appear in 'crazy'

modern stagings and costumes (except maybe of Wagner). In any case they are less likely to be expected to, given the major houses in which they normally appear are, in standard repertoire at least, conservative in their production styles.

- Nor are they likely to appear in modern works.
- All of which is charmingly explained in relaxed, natural and un-*diva*-ish interviews conducted by deeply reverential interviewers.
- Opera singers' lives are demanding and require sacrifices in terms of resting, especially the voice, diet, sleep, exercise, medicines. Comparisons with top athletes are often made.
- The sacrifices are especially marked for females, in terms of their 'private' lives, marriage, having children, remaining married and so on.
- However, a fulfilled private life is claimed by many, again especially by females, to be the perfect preparation for enacting the same emotions on stage, and for overcoming the loneliness of non-stop travel, hotel rooms and the like.
- Longevity of career is retrospective proof that one's judgement about all the above was right all along. The early demise of 'foolhardy' younger stars is a yardstick of that judgement.
- Singers are very superstitious having 'unlucky' as well as 'lucky' opera houses, partners, roles (lucky ones of the latter being described as 'calling cards' for first appearances at the world's top houses), even 'star signs' and so on.
- Public rivalries and battles with other singers and administrations, are the stuff of the media opera star: Lehmann v. Ursuleac; Martinelli v. Pertile; Callas v. Tebaldi; Callas v. Bing (Met Administrator); Callas v. Sutherland; Callas v. Meneghini; Callas v. almost everyone; Nilsson v. Bing; Sills v. Bing; Bing v. almost everyone; Pavarotti v. Domingo and so on (see Canning 1995c).
- For true stars the surname is sufficient, Nilsson, Te Kanawa, Norman, Domingo, Pavarotti, Carreras, Battle, though rarely additional titles may be used for example, *la Divina* (Callas), *la Stupenda* (Sutherland). Operamanes suggest intimacy with idols by using first names: 'Joan says ... ' 'Kiri thinks ... ' and so on. Some singers are known by nicknames: 'Flott'; 'Blodwyn'; 'Big Lucy'; 'ENorma'; 'Monsterfat'.
- Older singers invariably lament declining standards of singing and performing, and that there are no longer any personalities or

voices. Recording companies, jet travel, general pressure to achieve great success too hurriedly—and to earn are all to blame.

- Declining standards means fewer (if any) great *maestri* but 'stars' claim great admiration for the last survivors for example, Solti, Haitink and Kleiber.
- Nor are there 'companies' as in the old days, when a stable collection of stars in the great houses remained in place for a season.
- Seeing opera at a young age, being immediately transfixed and enraptured and establishing a passion which has not faltered, is a major defining experience.
- After retirement or late in career, teaching—passing on one's knowledge and 'interpretive gifts', learnt first-hand from legendary names of the past—becomes a 'duty', a 'heavy responsibility'.
- Each house has its (albeit modest, young and/or local) stars, especially of its own nationality.
- Stars and their voices are 'typical' of their nationality, region, ethnicity or 'race', but alas this too is disappearing.
- Some 'opera' stars are minor opera stars but big commercial 'stars'—for example, Lesley Garrett.
- Increasingly stars become stars for other status reasons as well as those of commercially constructed kind, they sing at royal weddings, celebrate the opening of major sporting events, advertise Rolex watches, or are 'exotic'—that is, 'black', oriental and so on.
- Unless 'black', opera stars seemingly know nothing about politics; opera has nothing to do with politics. Jessye Norman claims that every time she performs in public it is a political act,[18] Elisabeth Schwarzkopf that she was too busy learning roles in Germany to know what was going on in the lead up to and during the Second World War, even though she 'guested' in occupied opera houses (that is, occupied by German opera companies) such as the Paris Opera.
- Proof of 'stardom' is a curriculum vitae including most, if not all, of the world's great houses and festivals: La Scala Milan, The Met New York, Royal Opera House Covent Garden, Vienna State Opera, the Bavarian State Opera Munich, Salzburg, Bayreuth Festivals and so on.
- Many 'new' stars become stars as the result of being 'overnight

sensations', often stepping in as replacements for the announced star—and thus stardom continues ...

As a brief typical example: 'Teresa Berganza made her debut in 1957—by 1967 she was one of the leading singers of her time'. Within a year '... she had sung at all the major ... houses'. Her voice 'difficult to describe' is 'a true Rossini *mezzo-soprano*. The colour darker than a soprano's but with flexibility, wide even range, easy top and agility, and she can produce a wide range of colours, her musical imagination is 'vivid', 'intelligent phrasing' served by 'Latin wit, brilliance and warmth'[19] (Berganza* 1967: 193). Also with 'Latin wit, brilliance and warmth' is Victoria de los Angeles. Aged 70, she stands back as simultaneously a high priestess and a nobody:

> 'People come to me and embrace me, even in the street,' [she] coos with a blend of bemusement and delight. 'They touch me. This touching! Sometimes after a performance I put a table in front of me, because it's too much ... I am now as I was when I was twenty ... I was nobody and I am still nobody. I am a human being like others you see and people feel this. They feel "Victoria is like us, except she sings". That I think is ... true life ... other things are all vanity' (de los Angeles*1995: 12-14).

Born in Barcelona (1924), daughter of a university caretaker, 'We were a very happy family ... always singing' (*1990: 54-6). The Civil War came and with it air raids, deprivation and hunger: 'It was a terrible time ... but I always think about music, singing with my mother, my sister, my uncle'. The university was used as a hospital for the wounded: 'I sang to them. I was too young to understand the politics—or the dangers. I just sang. It was what I felt I had to offer' (ibid.: 54). After the war she went back to the Conservatoire at the behest of her sister:

> I didn't even know what an opera singer was. We were very poor, and such a world did not exist for me. But I wanted so badly to make music. I never had the ambition to be someone, to be a name. I just wanted to learn music, and it was very, very easy for me to learn to sing (ibid.: 55).

Her reputation spread quickly; when she took examinations the public crowded in to listen. It was clear that she was going to be 'a great glory for Spain'. Her repertoire was 'surprisingly' wide (*La traviata*, Elisabeth in *Tannhäuser*, Rosina, Nedda, Butterfly, Santuzza and so on). Of her colleagues she speaks ill of none and remains close to the realist producer, mentioned with affection by many of the older generation: Franco Zeffirelli.

> He has music in his bones; he knows entirely what he wants to do. I am not in sympathy with many opera directors today—they may be fine as theatre people, they may be able to do Shakespeare and Ibsen brilliantly, but they do not know and feel the music—and then, no matter how cleverly they interpret the libretto, there is something that is awry. With Zeffirelli this is never so (ibid.: 56).

'She dispels the cold formality of even the largest concert hall as she walks to the platform with a springing step and a ready smile: an alluring figure who seems to personify everything that is warm and exotic in Spanish temperament', her whole manner, not just her voice 'of freshly mined opal', suggests that she has come 'to sing for her own pleasure as well as the audience's'. Throughout her life she has been 'a loner, fiercely guarding the privacy of her own life, in which there has been much pain', and although the operatic side of her career has been curtailed, hers remains 'one of the best loved voices of the century'(de los Angeles*1995: 12-14). As with all female singers 'the voice', 'the body' and procreativity present a great tension:

> To have children changed my career completely. I had my first child in 1963 ... When first married the doctors told us I would never have children. So in the Fifties it was easy for me to have a career that required spending six months in America, singing opera at the Met, Boston, Chicago, and thirty or forty recitals all over the States. It was exciting ... very hard work, but I had always worked hard. Then ... my first child came, it was the most important thing in my life. From that moment on I was not only someone who goes around singing—I was a mother and I had to think about the child. So I began to say no to engagements requiring long absences from home.

She recounts how she gave up opera almost completely for the kinds of guilt feelings common to stars also mothers (wrongly she feels in retrospect), and like other singers (Marilyn Home [*1995: 13] 'singing is half athletics and half art': Gwyneth Jones 'an opera singer ought to live like a sportsman'[*1970: 106]) remarks:

> ... it was like an athlete going out of training—you lose the energy, you lose the stamina.. Opera is very tiring, it's not the singing. It's the rehearsing, waiting, costumes, it takes a lot out of you. Also its not as rewarding in some ways as recital work—not in the way of communication with the audience (*1990: 55).

A skilled pianist de los Angeles prepared her roles without teachers or répétiteurs, and encourages pupils to 'search for yourself in yourself (*1985: 14). Though sopranos and a smaller number of mezzos are most likely to be constructed out of such *'divaspeak'*, males are not exempt. James McCracken as Otello was credited with:

> ... deeply felt subtlety (due) to his own vulnerability ... freshness of interpretation ..., illumination ... a great singing actor ... born not just made ... However he may think out a part intellectually—and detail after detail shows his careful study of psychology and character—he reacts so spontaneously on the stage that no two performances are exactly alike ... He is disciplined and unselfish ... He has what is unfashionable these days ... a tremendous girth, but he is also tall with great stage presence ... The voice is of noble quality and of singular sweetness (*1967: 8-14).

Son of a fire brigade chief, his rise to stardom was slow, failing several auditions but singing small roles at the Met between '53 and '57. Married to *mezzo* Sandra Warfield, in '57 the left the Met for Europe 'Their slow progress from semi-starvation to leading roles in important houses is now operatic history'. The breakthrough was the first night of *Otello* in Zurich in 1961: 'His triumph was instantaneous'. Off-stage:

> ... genial, conspicuously un-jealous of other artists, even in his own parts and generous to a fault. He has a warmth and largesse of spirit apposite to his titan frame, and a humour as well as artistic generosity that make him popular around the theatre. His Irish temperament, inherited from his mother, is doubtless the galvanic lever to his emotional temperament on stage; off stage, it

merely provides the occasional (and rightful) blaze that sparks and goes out quickly ... he has immense reserves of vitality and artistry ... (ibid.: 13).

Tenors, like all singers, especially in critiques of recordings, are summarily reduced to 'mystifying' base qualities: 'you will go to Gigli to find a smile in the tone, Pertile for earthy histrionics, Martinelli for heroic glint, di Stefano for romantic fervour. With Bjorling it is refinement of *legato*, stylistic probity, sensitivity of phrase ...' (Blyth 1985: 994). Whatever the qualities of 'the voice', careers depend on its careful maintenance.[20]

When I was studying in New York before the First World War, we ridiculed the Italian singers of the Met including Caruso, for enveloping themselves in fur coats and covering their faces ... with thick woollen mufflers, even when coming out of the stage door (to) walk only ten steps to a taxi ... They would not even tell the driver where to take them .... the prima donnas covered their heads with a big shawl so that we could not distinguish who was who ... Caruso would not talk to anyone in the street, Bori, Galli-Curci and Barrientos would not enter a room where someone was smoking, on the day of performances Caruso received no visitors nor would he answer the phone ... Pertile would only speak to people if he was sure he was not in a draft ... tenors (when they did speak) ... spoke a bit nasally so as to keep a high resonance even in speech ... (Radamsky 1967: 101-2)

Present day singers have to be even more controlled, jetting all over the world, giving performances in different climates and theatres with varying (or no) air conditioning. Singing in *La fanciulla del West* at Covent Garden during a heat wave:

It was unbearable. I was completely clothed in wool, a woolly dress with long sleeves, leather boots, woolly stockings and shawl, and no air conditioning. The dressing rooms at Covent Garden ... have no windows, and no air. It's very bad for the voice. You're completely dried out before you get on stage (Gwyneth Jones,* 1994: 24).

Marilyn Horne (*1990: 11-12) however, doubts whether the pressures of jet travel, as long as 'it is well measured', affect singers as much as is usually supposed:

> ... singers in the early ... nineteenth-century ... sang performances back to back of completely different operas. Malibran sang in the same night *Sonnambula* and *Fidelio* on a double-bill. Now obviously there had to be great cuts because it would have taken forever. Maybe they were sung differently, we have no way of knowing. But it must have been pure hell to take a coach and four or six from Paris to Moscow (Horne* 1990: 11-12).

'Now with jets, similarity of repertoire all over the world and general tendency to perform in the original language the great singer must be a citizen of the world' (Régine Crespin* 1963: 228), especially to promote him or herself as 'opera' as well as opera star. Snowman (1985) reveals Domingo's exhaustive and exhausting itinerary in which the singer 'courts the pop field', 'massages' his television image and controls 'as far as he can' his recording business. Consistently available and 'bonhomous', Domingo has 'almost a politician's gift for befriending everyone in his orbit, where he is as likely to talk of football as opera'. As though scared of unmanly implications, male singers are frequently presented as 'real' men; hence it appears perfectly appropriate, indeed 'natural', that football World Cups be launched by The Three Tenors. Snowman concludes that stars' lives are now better than they were, although 'the pursuit of perfection has eroded individuality and spontaneity', despite the survival of 'uniqueness' and 'perfectionism'. For baritone Renato Bruson (*1979: 212-20) it took: 'years of hard work ... beset by straightened circumstances, punctuated by many bitter experiences to achieve "star" status'. Bruson originally studied for a diploma in industry. Orphaned when young, he 'still bears the traces, in being unsociable, reserved, shy'. In 1968 he went to the Met, but after only eight performances left 'because of the "routine" presentations, a decision not well received by Administrator Bing'. The year 1975 was his career watershed, when he became a star 'in direct competition with the more expert and tougher Cappuccilli'. His demeanour is described as one of 'severe cordiality ... His has been a triumph of the will, fashioned day after day with a tenacity that does him credit [but] Bruson has too heavy an itinerary, one taken on through lack of confidence ...'

'Unique', 'superhuman', 'extraordinary', 'intensity'

'Natural', 'elemental', 'gifts', 'preordained' and so on are the terms singers and their biographers deploy to explain the inevitability of opera stardom.

> 'Someone is born with that gift to sing, and it's just a question of what is done with it' (Horne *1995: 13). Montserrat Caballé: 'I was born with a voice' (Matheopoulos 1991: 61). 'I was born for my profession' (Tomowa-Sintow 1983: 231). [Leonie Rysanek] 'was almost born singing and acting' ... 'One has to be born with this talent of giving everything you have—it can't be learnt' (Rysanek*1994: 16). Birgit Nilsson (*1960: 602) had a 'God sent voice and great artistry a voice that recurs only once or twice a century, extraordinary range, beauty and power a natural gift'. Chris Merritt is 'a tenor with the capacity to make history' (*1992: 11). Mario del Monaco was (*1962: 373) 'freakishly blessed at an age when the vocal cords are still not properly formed with a tenor voice which ill matched his frail physique'.

Whatever the voice, what one does with it is also likely to be not of this world. Del Monaco continued:

> ... my method is a very controversial one, it involves rather violent, if not actually superhuman muscular exercise of larynx and palate'. Natural career development is inevitable too: Wolfgang Windgassen (*1962: 591) 'grew into the *heldentenor* category, carefully and naturally', developed his breath support naturally, 'dramatic singing is not for him a craft that can be mastered with a few tricks. It is a form of expression of the soul and spirit.' Natural gifts still have to be humanly realised: 'Everything God gave her [Regina Resnik] is deployed with the highest degree of intelligence, to create an organic whole.. [her] greatness is deservedly achieved by sheer merit, art and guts' (Resnik* 1963: 17). Jon Vickers'* voice is 'unique', able to 'caress the smooth legato phrases of Verdi with expressive warmth, or flash the bright heroic gleam of Wagner' (1962: 325). Josephine Barstow's* voice 'is one of remarkable timbre and power of expression' (*1974: 859); Joan Sutherland's was: 'from the first ... naturally placed' ... 'This gift of acting with the voice was ... her

very own special quality' (Frida Leider* 1975: 736). If it is not the voice that is natural it is 'instinctive musicianship' (Mirelia Freni, Matheopoulos 1991a: 85). The theatre itself is 'a mystery' (Barstow: 36), where miracles may happen: 'that sort of trance when all of us feel we are not wholly there' (Caballé* 1975: 61). Caballé 'has an instinctive feeling for what is right, a natural perceptiveness ... a performer serving the composer by communicating his ideas with all possible fidelity and dedication. Sensitive musicianship goes hand in hand with her instincts' (*1975: 343). And when the raw material is not unique or perfect, and critics *can* be barbed,[21] singers deploy those superhuman 'guts' to triumph: Giulietta Simionato's 'exceptional vocal and artistic attainments have been aided by sheer strengths of will ... repeated triumphs over the natural limitations of her voice, guided by a fertile mind ...' (*1964: 88). Amidst all the attention paid to 'natural' 'mysterious' abilities teachers and critics have a hurtful tendency to speak of 'the voice' as though detached from its owner (Carden* 1994: 416), yet other singers talk in precisely these terms: 'I'm a great one for letting the voice tell you what it wants to do' (Dennis O'Neill* 1994: 24). Beneath such accounts lies that uniqueness which must be retained at all costs: No matter how hard one is schooled '... never try to get rid of the baggage of natural attributes that constitute their individuality' (Leontyne Price, Matheopoulos 1991a: 164).

Superstitions reign:

June Anderson (*1993: 25) is pleased she is a Capricorn 'because there is a serenity within me which keeps some sort of balance'; Edita Gruberova also has 'Capricornian patience and persistence' (*p.98); Ragnar Ulfung (*1975: 839) has that 'Piscean quality of being both reserved and yet also scintillatingly talkative ...'; Shirley Verrett (*1973: 585) 'wanted my life to be the way I planned it. Maybe it's because I'm Gemini with Cancer rising'. Not for Maria Stratus are the good luck charms used by other singers—teddy bears, photos of relations. She brings to her dressing rooms 'a flour sack in memory of the bed linens her mother made from such materials' when she was a child; Marie McLaughlin's friends and family 'light candles for me whenever I sing' (*1993: 1391). Ethnic stereotyping is rampant: Catherine

Malfitano has Sicilian blood on her father's side, Russian and Irish on her mother's 'so its a bit hot-blooded all round, with some of that strange melancholy from the Russian, and a kind of crazy arrogance and humour from the Irish' (*1993: 1145). Julia Varady is Rumanian but calls herself Hungarian '... she has the quicksilver character, the quick-witted charm of her nation ...' (*1992: 646), though which one we are not told; John Lanigan (*1971: 21) owed his dogged determination to being Australian; Alberto Remedios, though from Liverpool, owed his vocal qualities 'to his Spanish grandfather' (*1973: 15): Leyla Gencer says that 'like all Moslems, I am lazy and a fatalist, instantly resigned to adversity' (*1972: 692), although her interviewer disagrees—'she has always fought tooth and nail.' Régine Crespin, French, inherited from her Italian mother 'Latin vitality, sincerity, and forwardness of acting' (*1963: 229), so that, as Kundry, in *Parsifal*, 'all the passion, warmth, femininity, tenderness, were still there but endowed with some elemental strength'; Jones is 'grateful to be Welsh. We're dreamers with a capacity for childlike simplicity and fantasies ... sentimental, warm and religious, and they believe in things being preordained, as I do' (*1990: 12). Fiorenza Cossotto agrees: 'Our destiny is written for us' (Hines 1982: 70). As for Grace Bumbry 'Fate took a hand in her career as early as high school' (*1970: 506). Singers have unlucky theatres which they can do little about; for Leonie Rysanek (*1994:15) and Hildegard Behrens (*1991: 502) it is Covent Garden.

Whatever the origins of stardom star quality would appear to be there for all to see: Ruggero Raimondi has 'charisma ... and an actor's instinct' (*1994a: 539); Pavarotti has 'what Rosa Ponselle defined as "that something impossible to describe which is the ability to communicate in just the same way as Caruso did"'! (*1981: 123); and the charisma is gender-differentiated: like Lehmann (Lotte), Crespin has 'elemental feminine projection' (*1963: 228).

Given the hands dealt by God, Nature and the planets, it sometimes takes a surprisingly long time for mere mortals to recognise the star in their midst:

The career of Caballé emphasises two important facts of operatic life that we are sometimes reluctant to acknowledge: the enormous part that is played by chance, and the inability of audiences and management (not critics note!) to appreciate superlative talent when it is positively blazing under their noses (Caballé* 1975: 342).

All in all it is very humbling: 'It is my duty to fulfil my potential' (Amanda Roocroft* 1994: 22). For all the iconographic emphasis on raw talent and superhuman powers of interpretation, humble duty and so on, family backgrounds testify to the importance of socialisation and material circumstances, singers and journalists seldom recognising the contradiction. Two themes consistently emerge. For the great majority the early years were distinctly formative in providing a musical ambience, in the form of exposure to music and music-making of some kind, with much encouragement to enjoy music and perform. The majority of singers refer to a *musical* career appearing inevitable before the later realisation, often at music school or college, that singing would provide that career rather than piano or violin. In a few cases the supportive background is theatrical rather than musical, the expected future being in the theatre, until a similar transformation occurs. In Europe musical and theatrical backgrounds normally result from comfortable middle-class circumstances and the presence of family members of professional or semi-professional musical status, although in Britain working-class choral traditions have been highly influential, particularly on the Welsh and Northern English. In the US black artists from whatever class refer to a similar musical environment provided by the Gospel tradition and, in both instances, the connection between music-making and religious observance provided a constant ritualised organisation of music as spiritual expression rather than as diversion or entertainment.

The second recurring theme is not necessarily discrete from the first, wherein, as with Spanish singers of the Civil War generation, a settled comfortable home is shattered by war or some other cruel intervention. For whatever cause, this second theme is of great hardship and the need to overcome it to survive or, less extremely, the need to pursue singing as the one feasible means of upward social mobility. It is noteworthy that the issue of social class in accounts of backgrounds is rarely directly addressed. It would appear that this is due to singers' implicit belief that, like actors and academics, they are 'classless'. This reflects the constant battle to counter claims that opera is élitist as well as their essentialist belief that, despite all the evidence to the contrary, opera singers are naturally gifted creatures to be found at random throughout the population, and that 'talent will out'. Social class under such circumstances becomes at least irrelevant, at most an embarrassment. There is also more than a sense of relative, rather than absolute, hardship in such accounts and the standard against which judgements are made remains solidly middle-class.

Claire Watson's mother was a cellist, her grandmother an 'excellent pianist' (*1970); Christa Ludwig's father a tenor, her mother a contralto (*1973); Cecilia Bartoli's parents were both singers (*1992); Helga Dernesch's father played the violin and her mother was an amateur singer (*1973). Both Domingo's parents were singers with a Zarzuela company (*1972); all of Ileana Cotrubas' family 'sang and made music as a matter of course' (*1976: 429). Elisabeth Söderström's mother 'was a piano prodigy, her father a fine tenor' (*1969: 18); Heather Harper's father was not musically talented but could play the piano by ear (*1971: 595); Te Kanawa's adoptive mother's house 'was enormous, lots of get togethers, lots of music not necessarily classical, lots of singsongs' (*1981: 680); Lucia Popp never knew 'a time when she wasn't singing. As a child her life was full of music. "My mother had a beautiful soprano"' (*1982: 134). Yvonne Minton (*1977), Kirsten Meyer (*1973) and Anja Silja (*1969) whose mother was an actress and grandmother a singer, are amongst the many with similar family backgrounds,

Few had, as did Brigitte Fassbaender, an international opera singer, Willi Domgraf Fassbaender, as a father, but even this is regarded by her as evidence of the natural not social creation of her as a singer.

> I feel a great deal must be in the blood: at first I was obsessed by the theatre and wanted to be an actress like my mother [Sabine Peters] ... I was not really interested in music, rebelled against teachers who expected great things of me because I was the daughter of a *Kammersänger*... I was only vaguely aware of the great musical personalities visiting the home: Hotter, Berger, Cebotari ... then when I was finishing Gymnasium in Berlin I began to discover my voice. One of my school mates was Isolde Schöck [daughter of tenor Rudolf]. She was studying singing, so I thought 'Her father is a singer, so is mine. She is taking lessons, so

253

why don't I?' (Fassbaender* 1981: 791),
Parents invariably liked their 'gifted' children to show off (Ghiaurov* 1977: 941). 'There was always a lot of vocal music lying about' (Elisabeth Connell* 1988: 670), which would, regardless of type of voice required, be sung, leaving many, females especially, to mistakenly identify themselves as either *mezzos* instead of *sopranos* or vice versa ... Few singers are ascribed 'a charmed life', as with Anne Sofie von Otter (*1991: 627), whose father was a Swedish diplomat. Welsh singers mentioning the choral and competition background of *eisteddfodau* include Jones (*1970) and O'Neill (*1994a), while Bumbry (*1970) and Verrett (*1973) refer to their Gospel backgrounds: the former's father being a St Louis railway clerk. Verrett (ibid.: 585) tells how she was forced to split from her family of Seventh Day Adventists, because they disapproved of all forms of entertainment including opera: 'God was the one who gave me the vocal gift and I had to use it to the full.'

Others claim desparate home backgrounds with severe handicaps to overcome—hardly conducive to a career in opera. Caballé's was another home bombed during the Spanish Civil War, when she was only four, reducing the family to poverty; she 'darned other people's socks to supplement the family income' (*1975: 342). One of her earliest memories is of being given a recording of soprano arias which 'she sang along with around the house'. Katia Ricciarelli's childhood was 'marred by tragedy'; her father died before she was three (*1990): Eva Marton's Budapest had been destroyed in the war 'My parents had to start from nothing' (*1990); Sergey Leiferkus is 'from a very poor family. My father died when I was very very young and I started to work in a factory when I was 15' (*1990: 175); Vladimir Chernov worked on a collective farm: 'there was no formal music, but you could hear singing every day' (*1994: 10). Samuel Ramey is 'just a boy from Colby Kansas' (*1990); Gruberova's 'father was a workman, her mother took in washing' (Matheopoulos 1991a: 97); Cossotto's parents 'had to work hard just to eat' (Hines 1982: 70); Stratas 'survived tuberculosis as a girl in the Toronto slums', having also been autistic (*1994: 1146;: Leonie and Lotte Rysanek as children 'sold flowers in Vienna cafés to supplement the family income' (*1994: 17). Most singers however come from urban and rural middle-class backgrounds. Anthony Rolfe-Johnson, Ben Heppner, Jerry Hadley, Paul Frey and Bryn Terfel are all from farming backgrounds. Birgit Nilsson's home was 'a delightful farm in

Sweden', where 'she was given a toy piano aged 4 by a labourer' (1960: 602).

Alternative careers beckoned: Hines (*1991: 31) could have been a chemist or a mathematician, Eva Marton (1990) an international volleyball player, Chris Merritt (*1992: 6) a lawyer and Bruson (1979) could have 'worked in industry'. Verrett (*1973) originally worked in real estate; Remedios (*1973) as an apprentice welder at Cammell Laird; Janet Baker (*1970) was a bank teller. Gabriel Bacquier (*1982) began as a commercial designer but, during the War, had to find alternative employment. Windgassen (*1962), despite his mother being related to Eva van der Osten, the first Oktavian in *Der Rosenkavalier*, started at the Stuttgart Opera as a technical assistant and scene shifter and although later singing at all the world's leading opera houses, '... stayed true by still being a member of the Stuttgart Opera'. Italian Cesare Siepi (*1962) who won a scholarship to Milan but held on to his job as a bank teller, was heard at a teacher's soirée by an impresario who encouraged him to flee to Switzerland in 1940. Vickers (*1982), youngest of six children and his father a headmaster, was a Woolworth's trainee manager before working for the Hudson Bay Company and then winning a scholarship to the Royal Conservatory of Music, Toronto. Older singers especially thought it prudent to have a more secure occupation than singing, even if successful at the latter, Derek Hammond-Stroud (*1985: 1356) was for some years simultaneously an optician; Graham Clark (*1992: 1283) was a lecturer.

Even when embarked on careers, several singers, especially of older less professionalised generations with more varied and distinct vocal and personal personalities, recount triumphs over early criticism: conductor Leo Blech called Nilsson 'unmusical'; Olivero was told 'She's a complete nothing' (RAI executive quoted in Hines 1982: 204) with 'a small and limited voice'; 'this girl has neither voice, musicality, nor personality. She has nothing' (Tansini quoted in Rodolphe). Many mention the negative effects on their confidence brought about by such critical onslaughts which are not confined to their voices: 'as soon as a singer enters the opera house they correct your Italian, correct how you walk, how you dress ...' (Carol Vaness* 1989: 424). Lack of confidence is even attributed by some to their nationality: 'By nature the Irish have no confidence for they are born saying "sorry"' (Ann Murray* 1988: 916). It is claimed that American and British singers especially have limited confidence because they lack fluency in the languages they sing: Felicity Lott (*1989) although already established internationally as Arabella, Countess in *Capriccio* etc. could neither understand nor speak German. Black singers all report their colour to be the basis upon which their competence and confidence is challenged (Willard White* 1989b: 25).[22]

Opera singers depend on the guidance and inspiration of teachers, conductors and, increasingly, producers. Yet some vocal exercises and learning are accomplished best without a teacher's baleful influence: del Monaco (*1962) had an early teacher, as seemingly did most, who 'almost ruined his voice', leading him to reject teachers thereafter: 'my tape recorder is my teacher'. Felicity Palmer's first teacher 'bless his heart, didn't know how to teach singing' (*1994: 1031). She later studied with Marrianne Schech, 'an absolutely wonderful lady, but not a very good teacher'. Beverley Sills called Mary Garden, her teacher 'the meanest woman I've ever met' (*1970: 48). Travel prevents regular use of Toczyska* 1989: 18), whilst others 'anticipate what a teacher was going to tell me. And I said "Why am I depending upon someone to tell me what I could say to myself?"' (Studer* 1990: 16). Discovery by, or work with, a mentor is frequently claimed: for Nilsson it was conductor Fritz Busch; for Amy Shuard, Rita Hunter and Pauline Tinsley; for Gwyneth Jones it was Eva Turner; for John Tomlinson, Otakar Kraus.

Mentors of whatever kind can only teach you so much, however: Gwyneth Jones (Matheopoulos 1991a: 120) claims: 'the most important thing of all is having a fulfilled personal life ... you have to know the feelings you are portraying on stage ... Someone who hasn't known love cannot convey it convincingly.' Jones, with numerous others such as Fassbaender, Popp and Lott, recognises the remarkable influence on her of conductor Carlos Kleiber: 'He is a perfectionist and it is vital to him that you do it exactly as he wants' (ibid.:19), sending 'Kleibergrams' to singers after each performance identifying what should be improved at the next. For Barstow, Baltsa, Dernesch and Tomowa-Sintow, Herbert von Karajan fulfilled a similar role: 'I trusted him completely and felt utterly safe in his hands as an artist because he knew exactly what he was doing ...' (Barstow* 1992: 37). In Britain, Goodall was held in similar regard, especially for those who specialised in Wagner: Hunter, Remedios and Anne Evans. Older stars such as Licia Albanese (*1990: 46) mention Serafin and Toscanini in the same way. Whilst such conductors are clearly valued by opera stars, so too now are some directors, and not just conservative realists such as Zeffirelli. Lella Cuberli (*1989: 18) mentions Strehler, Chereau and Ponnelle; Jones (*1990: 11) cites Serban and Everding who have guided her to her interpretation of Elektra which 'survives and is deeply present wherever she sings the opera'. Even in an 'advanced production (by Nuria Espert in which Elektra lived in an old car) 'I was able to do it because my character remained the same'. She refused, however, to do a staging where she was meant to shoot Aegisthus with a pistol: 'I'm not old fashioned but one has to deal with the wishes of the composer.' In the age of what tenor Gerry Hadley calls cynical postmodernism in production, stars, once stars, are likely to jib: 'I will not sing Leonore [in *Fidelio*] on stage—the productions are always mad today' (Marton* 1990: 280).

As for stars' dramatic talents, critics are inclined to remind us that little has changed in the age of 'produceritis':

> Bumbry [as Cassandre in *Les Troyens*] took us through her limited repertoire of masonic gestures—one arm south-west, the other north-east; one arm due north the other at her throat ... and swung her train round to perfunctory effect (Christiansen 1990: 518).

Such antics are unnecessary even for the larger less physically mobile of singers who through a sympathetic presence and dignity may emote sufficiently well through the voice to meet the requirements of a role's dramatic 'intensity'. Shuard's Santuzza was: 'moving, tragic, [had] wonderful intensity, [the] heart rending, beauty of a tragic heroine, grief and intensity of feeling, noble' (*1975); Barstow (*1974) has 'dramatic intensity'; Jones (*1994: 22) 'great dramatic intensity; Vickers (*1994: 32-4) 'incomparable intensity ... one of the few to match Callas in the magnetism of performance'. Perhaps 'intensity' is due to having, as Tatiana Troyanos claimed, the 'fearlessness to make you exciting on stage' (1985: 270), or like Dernesch 'a peculiar charisma ... and a natural stage presence' (*1973: 408-10), inspiring her interviewer to note that 'singers divide into the intellectual and the intuitive. For many technique is everything ... others move an audience without really understanding why' or, like Cotrubas, 'distinguished by her ability to make an audience's heart beat just that much faster ... which she achieves naturally and sympathetically' (*1976: 428). More specifically it is the combination of acting and singing to an unsurpassed degree: 'actor/actress singers' such as Gencer (*1972: 695); Watson who 'completely identifies with her roles' (*1970: 1006); Pauline Tinsley who has always 'complete absorption in character' (*1982: 266); Baker 'a unique actor and exemplary singer' (*1970: 581); Silja: 'There is no boundary between what she acts and what she sings ... a completely musical-dramatic thing' (*1969: 194); and Agnes Baltsa who 'has a way of imprinting each character she becomes with a distinctive individuality through her own association of words and music, each shaped and stimulated by the other ... [her] performances are never predictable' (*1985: 483). Windgassen '... created characters as a whole by penetrating their psychology. Towards this end the actual singing is only one means among many, controlled, intelligent and methodical ... [he] was often close to tears in performance' (*1962); 'her character studies are so real, like meeting actual people' (Resnik's* 1963:14): Crespin's 'elemental feminine projection' enables the audience to 'sense the flesh and blood present behind the stage conventions' (*1963: 228). Baker claimed that 'Everything you do must mean something both to the artist and the audience. Whatever I'm interpreting ... must be reality. If you can achieve that other things will come naturally' (*1970: 395). The greatness of Domgraf-Fassbaender lay in his 'ability to use singing as a means of expressing tangible human emotions. His character portrayals were natural and convincing ... with penetrating intensity', the selfsame qualities possessed by his daughter (Fassbaender* 1981: 789). There is a real sense here of actor-singers being the truest servants of their art, rather than the sometimes more famous stars. Popp (*1982: 132) had 'the attributes of a true artist, rather than those of a manufactured or over glamorised star, by the essential musicality of her performance'.

Talk of fearless intensity and charisma suggests an emotional involvement which might reduce singers to tears or worse:

> I vividly remember the end of the second act of La fanciulla del West in Rio de Janeiro in 1964. I was laughing hysterically when the curtain fell and something snapped inside me. I stopped laughing and fell to the ground. I didn't faint. I was in a state of trance. They picked me up and Laura Guelfi, the wife of Giangiacomo, who played Rance, started to slap me in the face, apologising all the time. I managed to go for the curtain call but felt like an automaton and kept repeating a sentence over and

over again (Olivero* 1994: 15).

Olivero, the most famous Adriana Lecouvreur, likens this experience to Adriana's words *'umile ancella del genio creator'*? ('one must annul one's own identity and recapture the inspiration of the composer'). Vickers sees the danger of such a commitment, referring to Wagner's reaction to the intensity of Tristan's Act III extended scene: 'What have I done? What have I done?'. When Vickers was asked what effect this act had on him during and after the performance, he replied:

> Oh nothing, nothing at all ... when I prepare a role, I prepare it in a completely objective way. If when you sing Tristan you allow yourself to get caught up in the emotion of the opera, you will not survive. All the human emotions which are felt are automatically reflected in the human voice, and if you did not have a little policeman who said 'so much and no more' ... then you'd tear your voice to ribbons ... You cannot surrender yourself to emotions (Vickers* 1982: 362).

Stanislavski noted that, if an actor claims:

> 'I entered into my role so completely, I was so powerfully affected by it that I began to weep and could not stop', (s)he must be warned that '(s)he has taken a wrong turn. This way lies hysteria ... not art. We must understand emotions (but) have a technique to control them ... the creative capacity of a singer or an actor is a *science*, which like other sciences has to be developed through study (Cannon 1982: 1111).

Some certainly feel that Olivero's way was hysteria, but in its own terms it was controlled and undoubtedly highly effective.

'Ordinary'

Except when dealing with the 'difficult' superstars, opera singer discourses trade in glowing personal as well as artistic qualities, to demonstrate that no matter how divine the gifts, how superhuman 'the guts', how unique the intensity, opera singers can sit down and have a cup of tea with the rest of us, albeit gingerly because they remain superhuman people, their steely eyes set firmly on success.

It is said of Kirsten Meyer 'It is not a *prima donna* act, she just is a special human being' (*1973: 879). Dolora Zajick 'hardly conforms to the conventional image of a *prima donna*' (*1994: 15). Martina Arroyo is 'one of the most intelligent singers' and 'has sincerity and warmth' (*1991: 27). Watson 'has a shy and retiring nature and yet she knows exactly what she wants' (*1970: 1006). Jones 'has always had a fighting spirit' (*1970: 102); Schwarzkopf 'frank tenacity, will, guts, stubbornness' (*1976: 317). Merrill was '... quiet, thoughtful, serious, but with a streak of dry humour' (*1992: 7); Nilsson is characterised by 'amusing stories, gaiety, endless wit, warm human feelings, great generosity towards relatives and fellow artists ... delightful sense of humour, wonderful friend, charming, most prolific letter-writer, kind to colleagues (famous and not so famous), always full of pranks—on and off stage ...'(*1960:607); Shuard is 'the most un*prima donna* like person I have ever encountered ... unspoilt, uncomplicated, generous hearted, down to earth, sense of humour ...' (*1975: 542); Sutherland has: 'unaffected friendliness, gentle gaiety' (*1990: 1284); Ramey is 'normally retiring ... [but] not afraid to speak his mind' (*1990: 11). Hunter 'strikes one as direct, warmhearted, level-headed' (*1976: 20); Tebaldi maintained 'the image of not being a *prima donna* at all against a reality of always getting her own way' (*1992: 17).

The reification of these singers knows no bounds: Vickers is described as of 'moderate height, sturdily built, broad frame, fair hair, gentle blue eyes, friendly personality and charm tempered with determination ... tough but incredibly tender hearted, ruthlessly dedicated worker ...' (*1960); 'To meet him [Donald McIntyre] you might think him a rugby player' (*1975: 529); Norman Bailey is 'obviously a very practical man, clever with his hands and adept at making things' (*1973: 779). Resnik 'with herself ... colleagues, friends, and her art: finds it hard to hide her feelings for she is quick, emotional, devastatingly witty, furiously for/against a particular person. She does not suffer fools gladly, completely without "side"' (*1963: 15). Crespin 'discovered herself—became conscious of her true aims and brought to the sheer power of the voice all the formidable power of a free mind and a free heart' (*1993:12)

For females especially appearance is regularly commented on: Troyanos 'an awkward if not ugly duckling at the start, has grown into a considerable swan, a handsome lady' (*1985: 272); Sutherland

'... a chubby and undemanding baby, grew into a plump little girl with a sunny disposition ... there was nothing narrow about her taste in music ... as familiar with the Page's aria from *Les Huguenots* as with ... "Daisy, Daisy"' (Major 1987: 11-15); Siepi 'tall, handsome—he must know what he is doing and why, (with) athletic build, he is elegant, quiet, easy manner, grand singer, without imperiousness and vainglory, singularly untheatrical, quiet, intense off-stage manner' (*1962: 210). Material possessions are also important: 'when a boy his dream was a flat in Milan with a white telephone. Now he has achieved far more—he likes to be photographed at the wheel of his red continental ('the only one in Italy') or diving into the pool at his Hollywood style villa' (del Monaco 1962: 374). Expensive consumer goods go with opera stars. Maria Ewing is suited to her Hollywood 'hillside manse ... this grand domicile with its floor-to-ceiling windows $36,000 a month' (*1993: 18); Siepi liked 'minor gambling, social dancing, brandy and football' ... never been snared by a woman, 'most eligible bachelor' of the New York musical scene. 'I never got married because I am very respectful of the institution of marriage and I consider myself immature for it. I would make a victim of my wife' (1962: 211). Even career decisions exhibit the mark of rare genius: 'In October 1955 Resnik retired from public life with a courage, determination and self-judgement rare in any artist' to restudy as a *mezzo* because of her inner certainty—'the touchstone of the true artist' (*1963: 14). Retirement and/or giving up particular roles is also a sign of cleverness: 'I could have gone on singing Sieglinde much longer but I would not want anyone writing that she could be Siegmund's grandmother. Nor do I think you should go on stage and sing Salome when you're 55 or 60' (Rysanek* 1994: 18). 'Cleverness' or 'knowing' as a profile of John Tomlinson (*1990) calls it, is claimed on behalf of, if not by, many stars although there are also frequent self-berating attacks from those who felt they had made, or been made to make, wrong choices over productions, roles, even *Fachs* (Plowright* 1992).

Few singers bring the moral, ascetic, anti-entertainment critique of Vickers to their work:

Opera is 'a moral institution ... if it's not that it's nothing because it's lousy entertainment'. Opera is the great form of theatre, its personality is still in its adolescent stage. It has yet to grow up to realise the latent moral and dramatic force inherent in its nature.

Much of the fault lies with singers who use opera to glorify their own talent big or little rather than use their talent for the benefit of opera, as an expression of human drama through musical means ... when opera is restricted by (such) singers ... it is reduced to mere entertainment and I for one would sooner go and see Rex Harrison in *My Fair Lady* (*1962: 233).

For Vickers, opera's prime concern is drama: 'a role [is] an opportunity for a performer to reflect those facets of a character's personality which are strongest in the singers personality: and therefore no two performances can or should be the same'. By contrast Sutherland (*1990) is out of sympathy with those who scorn 'canary fanciers'; 'virtuosity is always exciting' and inspires—'her artistry has helped foster an interest in Handel operas'.[23] After her Lucia debut at Covent Garden inevitable comparisons were made between her and Callas. Sutherland was considered 'a mere virtuoso with a beautiful voice'; Callas by contrast was 'powerful, fierce, assertive, personally militant', whatever that might mean. Sutherland '... would always consider engagements for contemporary works provided that the role was grateful to the voice'. In fact Jennifer in Tippett's *The Midsummer Marriage,* which she created, is the only modern role she sang: 'I wish we all had a better idea of what it was about.' Della Casa had similar feelings about her creation of the three heroines of von Einem's *Der Prozess*: the first woman had black hair and was 'a dried up spinster'. The second, blond and 'under a vulgar exterior almost holy'. The third, a nurse, had red hair. 'At the end I combined all three women—the head of one, the costume of another, and I forget what of the third. It was all a bit too intellectual for me' (*1995: 17).

Retired stars, whether they teach or not, and most do, regularly take over key positions in the institutions of singing and voice training, even opera companies: after retirement Rosa Ponselle ran the Baltimore Opera (*1977: 13); in Marseilles Jose van Dam has his own *Ecole de chant* (*1993: 6); in Russia Irina Arkhipova (*1995: 389) is president of the Irina Arkhipova Foundation for 'young artists'. In the US Horne, Phyllis Curtin, Blanche Thebom and Licia Albanese are amongst those with, or having once had, such responsibilities. Thebom runs an annual seminar for girls aged 10-20 covering acting, movement, dance, make-up, as well as singing. In 1990 Albanese was head of the Puccini Foundation which helps young singers battle against conductors and producers: 'They want you to sing in a straitjacket, every gesture always the same, every costume the same. In the recent *Carmen* at the Met, Maria Ewing was dressed like a *comprimario*' (*1990: 10).

The mass and specialist media are constantly on the look-out for 'extraordinary' new talent as potential stars.[24] Singers on the edge of stardom, or for whom future stardom is predicted, are constructed out of the same lexicon, but with an additional material sense. Jennifer Larmore says of her 'calling card' role Rosina:

> It's a big part of me ... even now my interpretation is still developing. When I recorded the role I had already sung it more than 250 times, and by then I [understood] that Rosina is a challenger ... I've spent a lot of time in Spain, I know how the ladies are there. They have ... outward gentility but tremendous inner strength. Rosina's basic sweetness conceals a hard core. [Larmore's] ready smile ... relaxed graciousness and unerring sense of propriety seem to come naturally ... (*1995: 14-17).

Larmore is tough at the centre which translates into imposing lofty standards on her own work and productions with which she's involved: 'As long as audiences want to see me do Rosina I'll do it ... but I realize I'm growing out of Rosina'. She adds that 'it's natural and healthy for that to happen. As a personality in my everyday life, I used to be Rosina, but I'm not anymore. I'm now Isabella in *L'italiana in Algeri*, a woman who knows where she's going.' 'New' stars are part of the grand tradition: 'The first time I heard her *Barbiere* recording, I found myself imagining that this might have been the sound of opera singing in the first half of the nineteenth century.' Already Larmore publicly eschews the teacher: 'Actually I haven't been in a voice studio in, well, in all my life practically! I just had a natural voice. I was the little kid with the loudest voice.' She practised piano and flute, played in a band, sang in the school and church choirs and 'listened to Met broadcasts every Saturday. I just wanted to sing.'

At Westminster Choir College, Princeton, Larmore was supposed to take voice lessons 'but my singing teacher said right away "You have a natural voice and the best thing I can do for you is to leave it alone"', which she considers lucky: 'He could have screwed up what I had, which was a healthy all-round voice and natural *coloratura* ... in place since I was 14. I didn't need to learn how to sing ... it came as naturally as talking' (ibid.: 16). Larmore is typical of a number of US artists who have made their reputations and learnt their craft in Europe, but 'it's still true that singing at the Met has got to be the dream of every American singer' (ibid.:17). She enjoys the business aspects of her career, taking an active interest in its development likening her first American performances to 'opening up a new market ... My rule is not to accept any role that will not show me to advantage, that will not bring tears to your eyes when I sing it ... The roles I'm moving into now—Carmen, Adalgisa—are growing organically out of *me* as the woman I now am.' Her favourite singers are Eva Turner and Irina Archipova 'for their electricity, passion, strength, stamina, durability'. Passion in performance is a necessity not a luxury. She and husband, singer William Powers, ruled that they should not be separated for more than a month and a half at a time 'which seems to work well for us. We've been together fourteen years and it's only in the last eight that being apart has become a big deal. Then too you have to find time to get back to your roots' (ibid.: 17).

Andrea Gruber was identified as 'surely a star' (*1990) because the taxi-driver taking her to an interview at the time of her operatic debut (Glasgow in *La forza del destino)* recognised her ankle-length mink. In interview she gave a 'characteristically tough, cool assessment of her own performance', a 'native New Yorker, where they learn to look after themselves early', she had originally wanted to be a flautist: 'I always knew I'd be a musician' (ibid.: 30), but once at summer school 'l auditioned for all the singing stuff', and in her third year she was told that she was gifted. After four years at the Manhattan School of Music 'singing nothing but *lieder,* she realised that her voice was 'huge, unruly'. She learnt with Ellen Repp, 'a remarkable woman ... who had been a great Wagnerian singer ... I'm a Wagner nut'. Miss Repp is likened to 'some Bette Davis character', forcing Gruber to get right Mozart's *Das Veilchen.* 'Your throat is different every day, that's why people think singers are temperamental or crazy. Imagine what it's like to have something so vital to you that can alter every time you open your mouth' (ibid.: 33). She describes 'Jerry Levine as my mentor and friend'. Although at this time not having sung there, she is described as a Met singer 'I grew up at the Met', where qualities other than the voice are also no doubt appreciated: 'not a great actress, when not singing her acting amounts to "responding"' (ibid.: 34). Her first four Leonoras took place in just ten days. She and her mentors were aware of the dangers: 'We turn down a lot of roles and will keep monitoring how my voice responds; it's still growing. I don't take unnecessary risks ... I'm a perfectionist ... People have called me stubborn. I do have very clear ideas of what I want to do' (ibid.: 32).

All of which suggests that the *prima donna* of yesteryear is still very much here in the making. Can this be the case? Hasn't the socioeconomic environment for women changed significantly in the past 30 years and hasn't this affected the operatic *prima donna*? Instead, it appears to have contributed to a changing, rather than disappearing, *diva*. Nearly 30 years ago Anja Silja was described as:

> ... truly a child of our time. She likes leather clothes and provocatively short miniskirts and with a craze for fast cars—she has had a Fiat sports car, a Thunderbird and a Jaguar. Once when she was singing Venus at Bayreuth, who appears only in Acts 1 and 3, she unwound during the second Act, by tearing through the district in her car, out into the remote little place where she lived during the Festival and played golf with the boys of the village ... (*1969: 107).

Cecilia Bartoli has perhaps been the most cannily constructed female star commodity of recent years—young and sexy, her throat 'one of the biggest potential gold-mines in the opera and concert fields today' (1993: 10). We are some distance from the following critic's strictures on Sutherland reviewing her Agathe in *Der Freschütz:* 'She must learn not to present her face to the audience in full profile as many another singer with a prominent chin has had to: in other regards her aspect is agreeable, for she is quiet, natural and unmannered' (Smith, *Opera* July 1954).

Callas and Sutherland are amongst the many to become 'overnight sensations' in the source material—an almost requisite *rite de passage.*

The same has been said of Gwyneth Jones (replacing Leontyne Price in *Il trovatore* and later *Fidelio* in place of Nilsson, both at Covent Garden): 'It's a wonderful sensation to win over an audience under such circumstances ... You can't blame them they've paid to hear Nilsson and what do they get? Miss X who they've never heard of (1970: 104). Others achieving overnight success have been Rysanek (replacing Callas in *Macbeth* in New York); Te Kanawa (a last-minute replacement for Stratas' Desdemona in a Texaco Met matinee broadcast of *Otello*); and Behrens (a last-minute upgrade from First Bridesmaid to Agathe in *Der Freischütz*).

Callas and beyond

'There was something feverish ... in her nature and her art', wrote Henry Chorley, 'which dazzled while it delighted. In her nature and her art: the singer as personality, the impersonator who reveals herself as well as her characters ... it was Malibran above all who developed the notion of a compulsive performer, not husbanding her talent but spending it, and so intensely that she consumed herself (Mordden 1989: 115).

Maria Callas was more than *prima donna* archetype, for physically, vocally, and materially her career marks the movement of the late twentieth century female opera star into consumerism, cosmetic market and culture. 'Not since the time of Alfred de Musset, Theophile Gautier and Heine has a singer aroused such interest, not only in the musical world but in the whole world of art' claims D'Amico (1970: 809) adding: 'I find nothing wrong in the tendency to transform the object of one's admiration into something mythical' (ibid.: 807). Twenty-five years later 'The Callas industry is unstoppable' (Canning 1993b: 26) and Moshinsky (1995: 20-21) also uses Callas to epitomise the *diva*: a woman who, though famous as a singer, is lionised through expensive clothes, jewellery and lifestyle—'they are separated from ordinary mortals by a tradition of extravagant and often jealous behaviour'. Atrue *diva*, she has transcended mere mortality: 'divas have a priest-like separation from ordinary life', the basis of which is the voice. Treated as though objectively separate from the rest of their beings, the voice has primacy and all else by comparison must suffer, including the *diva* herself, through her wracked personal life. D'Amico (1970: 808) attacks those who claim that Callas's ascendancy was due to organised publicity, that she was 'little better than certain film stars whose physical rather than professional qualities have enabled businessmen to transform them into lucrative properties!', her testament speaks for itself; 'she remains the line of comparison every soprano must meet' (Mordden 1989: 198). Like:

> ... Patti, Lind, and Melba she was known to a far wider public than that which frequented the opera house. No other singer of the day challenged her supremacy; none could match her ability to win frenzied acclaim from the most critical and even hostile audience; none could match the astonishing series of scenes, scandals and triumphs that marked her progress to the top. She was responsible more than anyone else for the rehabilitation of the *bel canto* repertory—the long neglected operas of Bellini, Donizetti and Rossini—and in works such as *Tosca* and *La traviata* she set standards for the age. She was an untiring worker and seeked 'sic' after perfection, a true professional in the best sense of the word ... (Rosenthal *The Observer* 18 September 1977).

Her major breakthrough was as late replacement for Margarita Carosio as Elvira in *I Puritani* at La Scala, a week after singing the *Walküre* Brünnhilde in Florence. To move between two such different roles, to deploy her technique and what, for the time, was considered a large voice in the 'delicate' role of Elvira assured a triumph. What was the secret of her art? What made her performances so memorable? In the first place each role she undertook she perceived as an organic whole—music, text, acting were all of a piece: 'She was *melodramma*' (Guilini 1977: 1015) and, although there have been and are singers with more beautiful voices, few have the ability to recreate for an audience the notes in the score as if 'written specially for her, as if we were hearing them for the very first time'. It was this plus her ability to 'phrase the music like an instrumentalist and declaim the text as if singing were just as natural a means of expression as the spoken word, that made her unique' (ibid.: 18).

For many her voice was 'certainly ugly ... and yet I believe that part of her appeal was precisely due to this fact ... because for all its natural lack of varnish, velvet and richness, [it] could acquire such distinctive colours and timbre as to be unforgettable. Once heard it was immediately recognizable everywhere' (Celletti 1970: 811). The voice had attack even on high notes: 'the general public does not know whether it's an E, an F, or a G; but it does realise the note is very difficult to reach, that it has broken a sound barrier' (ibid.: 812). She relayed all these vocal qualities as a 'seismic shock' (Gara 1970: 814) in performance, 'total illumination of the character portrayed ...

a totally conceived dramatic interpretation ... She creates real people ... through the complete fusion of singing and acting' (D'Amico 1970: 819). 'Callas is in all these respects entirely of her time' (Gara 1970: 817).

To suit to her fame and subsequent significance Callas transformed herself physically. When young she was very large, with poor eyesight and other health problems: 'In 1953 she was not beautiful' (ibid.: 817), but became 'the most beautiful elegant young woman', 'only then did the tabloids sit up and take notice' (ibid.: 809) and she became 'hot copy in society gossip columns' (Mordden 1989: 197). For Giulini it was Callas's new slim figure which enabled her to become a convincing actress. Her tireless dedication was to her art not her career; indeed for many she sacrificed herself as a consequence. Her vocal technique and broad repertoire clearly made her exceptional but it was her new-found beauty, as well as fame, which gained her access to high society, mass media and career distractions, leaving her open to the inevitable press attacks. 'Another Callas walkout' a regular headline, as when she allegedly abandoned the final La Scala *La Sonnambula* at the 1957 Edinburgh Festival to attend gossip columnist Elsa Maxwell's Venetian ball. It seems that her appearance had been advertised by La Scala's management without her agreement.

> But who could blame her? She had dedicated herself to her art and now wanted to enjoy life. However it was impossible to achieve a 100% dedicated performance unless she was prepared to give up the new life she had discovered. That was the tragedy of Maria Callas' (Guilini 1977: 1016).

Giulini argues that, because of her, to some, unlovely voice, she always faced sections of audiences hostile to her, and so every performance was a battle for which she showed rare courage. There was nothing comfortable about Callas; 'she drove colleagues and managements almost as hard as she drove herself, and she played safe over nothing except in her insistence on meticulous rehearsal' (Harewood 1977: 1017). She is 'the legendary tigress' (ibid.: 1019): 'the whole world followed her every move'; 'She was a *diva* [and] goddesses never die' (Liebermann 1977: 1019).

In her late career Callas crystallised the ambiguous qualities imposed on late twentieth century opera stars: individuality of voice and technique, dramatic intensity, vibrant articulation of text, photogenic beauty, wealth, glamorous lifestyle, media interest—qualities which encompass the opera star as 'opera' star commodity in the most complete form possible. Since, there have been great singing actresses such as Varady and Barstow, great vocally intense singers of a less dramatic persuasion such as Norman and Tomowa-Sintow, imperfect vocalists with charismatic and dramatic appeal such as Baltsa and Ewing, but none has achieved the public interest or notoriety of Callas. By contrast, Te Kanawa and Kathleen Battle, with superb voices, have been subverted into glamorised cosmetic stardom to sell themselves and other 'conspicuous' products, subjected to inappropriate brush-stroked garb and glamour to advertise their latest CDs. The one quality which potentially unites all such singers' claims on *diva* status is 'being difficult, having a tantrum'. Callas's popular reputation reinforced this superficial view, her defendants claiming perfectionism as the reason.

Horne cancelled her final performances at the Met in *Semiramide* in 1993 because:

> I did not like the way it was truncated, the way it was being conducted... at the time a lot of people said 'oh you should really make a *cause célèbre* out of this, go to the press and make a big deal'. But I said, 'no this is not my style' (*1990:13).

Similar defences were made for René Kollo's (*1989: 1420) much publicised 'walk out' on von Karajan's Salzburg *Lohengrin*: 'I was never allowed even to touch Elsa!' Ewing is perceived as so fragile, 'they're all afraid she'll break if anyone tries to direct her' (*1993: 19). More notorious and noteworthy are bad behaviours such as Bumbry's stately parade through the central foyer of the Bastille Opera Paris, during the interval of the opening night of *Les Troyens*, still wearing her Cassandre costume from the first half, before the second in which her rumoured arch-rival, Shirley Verrett was the Dido.

Such stories of *diva* rivalry are media gold dust. Callas and Tebaldi provided much copy along these lines: Callas in the audience for a Tebaldi *Tosca* at La Scala, as Tebaldi entered, distracted everyone by dropping her gloves and calling the ushers to find them. Listening to a broadcast of one of Tebaldi's recordings, Callas remarked 'What a lovely voice! But who the hell cares?' (Mordden 1989: 204).

Tebaldi shrugs with just a touch of ennui, but ever the lady she speaks 'Callas hated me, and I don't know why. Some have suggested it was because I had a smooth time of it, and she had to struggle. Everything I did, I did myself. She had her rich husband, and society figures, such as the designer Biki, to push her. Aside from recordings, our repertories were almost entirely different. When she came into mine with Maddalena, Fedora and Butterfly, she had no success. I loved her as Norma, Elvira in *I Puritani* and Lucia (Tebaldi* 1992: 18).

Surviving feudsters claim not to have been party to, nor to have understood, the feud. Viorica Ursuleac said:

I always loved Lehmann for her intensity and fire on stage... alas it was not reciprocal... I forgive her all the harm she caused me. I believe her hatred for me originated when I exploded on the Viennese horizon with my easy top register just when she was beginning to have a difficult time with hers ... (Rasponi 1984: 136).

But *divas* don't need other *divas* to be *divas*:

... security measures at Heathrow are popguns compared to the state of alert backstage at the Barbican while Jessye Norman is in residence for the next couple of weeks. Large areas have been cordoned off and all other performers inconvenienced in order to protect the American soprano's monumental need for privacy and sterility. 'We have promised to undertake the following special conditions', wimps an internal Barbican memo, 'Smoking has been banned in all parts of the hall and backstage, even behind the closed doors of the individual dressing rooms'. Any artist gasping for a fag is officially being sent to the choir rooms. But this sanctum is frequently closed and choristers are being forced to climb all the way to level 1 just to get their frocks on. Tougher still the artists bar has been shut on Norman's orders because it is within eyeline of her dressing room ... she has also insisted on the evacuation of the main conductor's green room sending Sir Colin Davis to inferior accommodation. What Jessye Norman gets today, Kathleen Battle will want redoubled. Opera stars have always had their little ways. But Dame Joan Sutherland never found it necessary to impinge on her colleagues civil liberties and she was the last of the genuine divas, who spent the better part of their lives emoting out their roles on the opera stage instead of skimping the voice for half an orchestral concert. Jessye Norman is a major artist in an age of weak management, the more they acquiesce to her demands, the more unreasonable she becomes (*The Daily Telegraph* 14 March 1994).

Offstage antics are more rewarding. Teresa Stratas's affair with Zubin Mehta 'was in the gossip columns on five continents' (*1994: 1146) and, of course, *divas* getting above themselves are manna from Reuters—for example, Kathleen Battle phoning her agent from the rear of her limo, ordering him to tell the driver to turn down the air conditioning. Battle's unceremonious highly public 'sacking' from the Met after 'bad behaviour' during the rehearsals for *La Fille du régiment* in 1994 (Page 1994), appears to have put *divas* in their place, at least at the Met.

Rasponi (1984), Innaurato (1989) and the estimable Vera Galup-Borszkh (*1991, 1994) claim true *divas* to be no more. Rasponi's text is a litany of *diva* despair at the passing of time: 'I am a relic of another age, my world is dead and buried ... I am convinced every opera house will have to close down for a while and make a fresh start' (Gilda della Rizza quoted in Rasponi 1984: 121); 'I am very detached from the past. It all seems to have happened in another existence. The present is so ugly and uncertain, the revolution of values so distressing' (Iva Pacetti quoted in ibid.: 197); 'Today's critics hate singers and consider them of no importance ...' (Ester Mazzoleni quoted in ibid.: 195): 'We did not have the mentality of today's singers who want to sing everything and alas are allowed to do so' (Gina Cigna quoted in ibid.: 215).

The old system very much resembled the film studios. Opera houses signed actors to long-term contracts, and it was a big investment they were making. There was very definite guidance, great care taken to protect them. At the opera for all its faults and rigidity, we were led, we were made to take one step at a time, we were protected. Monsieur Rouche always discussed each new assignment with me, explained why he thought I could take it on. But he never imposed anything on me. Don't do what may make you nervous'. That was good, common sense. Where do you find this today? (Germaine Lubin quoted in ibid.: 605).

These sentiments are echoed by contemporary stars. Wagnerian tenor René Kollo (*1989: 1415) states in one of his 'Letters to my daughters':

> When you are 20 and want to go to the opera, there won't be any left. 'Why?' because the rising generation is not encouraged, but prematurely ruined. Young singers take on parts that are too big too early ... Nobody is really concerned about the singers, nobody fosters them, with care or introduces them to new parts when the voice is ready for them. Instead an Administrator needs some successes and throws the singers in too quickly, because he is only in his job for 4 to 8 years, and has to make a reputation faster than is really possible. The singers are the casualties. Administrators and producers just see them as voices to be used and discarded. They no longer love them.

Producers of the modern school are also attacked for their 'shenanigans' (Maria Caniglia quoted in Rasponi: 1984: 598), their power so great singers rarely resist the demands made by them or by exploitative agents, theatres and record companies. The result? 'Too many of our "stars" just aren't very good' (Innaurato 1989: 22) because without new operas—without opera as a live rather than museum industry—singers no longer sing new works. He explains the acclaim for cult soprano Magda Olivero during her late career appearances in the United States as a response to a singer who was one of the last, possibly *the* last, great creative *diva* in opera, singing roles new when she first learnt them by composers such as Giordano, Alfani, Zandonai and Cilea. Few singers today have that experience, even the Britten creators are now largely retired. For Innaurato, opera, as part of the culture industry has institutionalised conservatism: 'when jet travel means many of us can can go and see Michaelangelo, why indulge anything new?' (ibid.: 71). For Rasponi the demise of the *prima donna* lies in a too rapidly changing institution: early debuts, hectic careers, lack of permanent ensembles, inexperienced conductors, jet travel, unscrupulous managements, agents and recording companies, lack of control and sense by singers whose 'craze for cash knows no bounds'. Properly 'Singing is an expression of life, and if you have no time for your life, how can you sing? Quality always needs time, not only in music but in life itself' (Averino 1991: 53) but, in practice, for whatever reasons, singers tend now to follow the experience of Waltraud Meier (*1991: 886) who learnt and performed 35 roles in the first four years of her career, or of Sharon Sweet (*1993: 22) whose stage debut was 'more or less' Elisabeth in *Tannhäuser*. Rasponi's *divas* reify and represent the end of a Golden Age largely recorded, and hence dominated, by 'golden names' such as Lilli Lehmann, Emma Calve, Luisa Tetrazzini[25] and so on. Numerous sources testify, however, that earlier practices were by no means consistent with golden memories. Henstock's (1990) biography of Fernando De Lucia describes how, like other top singers at the turn of this century, his subject behaved in a cavalier fashion, transposing, rewriting, rearranging music, singing no less than five encores of *'La donna è mobile'* if the mood took him, and biographies of others demonstrate how many of the great singers of this Golden Age suffered early career decline. Lawrence Tibbett's and Margaret Sheridan's careers were all but over by their early 40s (Farkas 1990; Chambers 1990).

The problem now is not only early destruction of voices but the disappearance of certain types, mainly those unsuited to recording technologies and lighter semi-pop repertoires: the dramatic soprano, contralto and *heldentenor*. Technical expertise is probably greater than ever, but vocal individuality is on the wane. Horne suggests the reasons relate to the fact that opera singing has to compete against other more lucrative forms:

> Singers no longer have power within opera, but in the culture industry as a whole [they] clearly do, and the career possibilities of non-operatic singing have had a keen effect on (some) singers within opera: When opera was the main entertainment of the day, it was a horse of a different colour. We've got entertainment all over the place, such as it is. I'm not one of those people who believe in the genius of rock. But I do believe in really talented composers like Paul Simon. There's a lot out there to steer a talent in a different direction. When you think of the vast sums of money rock singers make, maybe some [who] might have gone into opera seventy five years ago are doing that now (Horne*1994: 13).

James King (*1991: 17) claimed that he and Vickers were the 'last of the bunch' of *heldentenors* and that consequently singers sing roles which are too heavy for them too early in their careers and in theatres which are too large. Singers who are exceptions to this trend recognise their unfashionable status as survivors of an earlier age: 'so unused are people to our sort of sound ... especially conductors [they] don't know how to react to them' (Ghena Dimitrova quoted in Matheopoulos 1991a: 73). So scarce are the voices to fill the larger halls, so advanced the technology and the expectations that advanced technology bring, so large are some of the newer opera houses, the sacrilege of opera house amplification (or 'aural enhancement') is now actively explored (Smith 1992a: Betley 1992: 24); some singers including Horne (*1994) believe that it is already the 'dirty little secret' of many large houses. Small wonder that the last *prima donna* interviewed by Rasponi 'were disoriented and frightened that the entire operatic structure is coming apart'.

However, contemporary *prima donnas*, despite their status being more likely due to the recording studio than the opera house, still claim to be part of the the same 'ideal' values: Cheryl Studer describes playing small roles in Wagner alongside great artists such as Astrid Varnay, Jones and Ingrid Bjoner: 'It wasn't their singing so much as their presence that was so inspiring.' Now cosmetic consumerism appears to demand nothing less than the brush-stroked beauty of a 'beautiful' voice:

> Not all these women were perfect singers—or artists, as they preferred to be called—but each of them was a personality in her own right, having reached this state through strict discipline, hard work and uncanny instinct ... they became stars through their search for perfection and their never-ending sacrifices... sometimes on the strength of a handful of roles. In the second half of her career Schwarzkopf cut her repertoire to six roles. Teresa Berganza became a celebrity with a very limited number of Mozart and Rossini roles ... (Rasponi 1984: 589).

Now 'we live in a much more visual age in opera' (Horne* 1995: 12) which leads to 'pressures of glamorising female singers' (Rasponi 1984)—'they have to look good' (Rysanek* 1994: 17):

> All these girls have a mania for remaining thin, so that they do not have a body that allows them to have the proper diaphragm ... the smallness of the voices seems to be related to the muscular frame, which seems to be practically non-existent (Hilde Konetzni quoted in Rasponi 1984: 99).

274

Much nonsense has been written in recent years about the streamlining of *prima donnas* and how the public will no longer accept singers who, because of their size, do not lend credibility to their characterizations. Nothing could be less true: the two biggest money-makers before the public today are Caballé and Pavarotti ... Marilyn Horne, Rita-Orlandi Malaspina, Margaret Price and Rita Hunter are [also] large ladies who have all the engagements they want (Rasponi 1984: 595).

In 1988 'fatness' became an operatic issue following producer Nicholas Hytner's appearance on television (BBC1 *Omnibus*: The Poisoned Chalice) envisaging his ideal future world of opera free of fat singers. Loppert (1988) noted the popular belief that opera singers of an earlier age were both fat and bad actors, that good acting requires slim bodies and that larger singers are incapable through voice and deportment of transforming, what is, in any case, the improbability of opera into something distinctly probable to audiences which have come to hear as well as, or rather than, watch. Deborah Voigt (*1992) states: 'One company has shown very little interest in me because of my size. That's their problem. I don't think I have trouble with acting ... I wonder if Jessye Norman is asked these questions.' In November 1995 Jessye Norman was reported to be sueing *Classic CD* magazine for $3 million for an article which combined attacks on her size with others which ridiculed her 'and all persons of Afro-Caribbean descent' (*The Guardian* 3 November 1995: 1). Studer too (*1994b) claims that 'producers have boycotted me because of my size'.[26] Koestenbaum states '"fat" in *diva* iconography means "Presence"' (1993: 102) but, for modern producers, it means 'unbelievable'. In 1988 Pilar Lorengar, at the end of an illustrious career, was pilloried by critics for her San Francisco Manon Lescaut because of her age and her size (*Opera* January 1989: 26).

Other pressures towards a 'false' cosmetic realism are also recognised. Asian singers (for example, Hayashi, Watanabe)[27] have found themselves repeatedly hired as Butterfly or Mascagni's Iris, and black singers hired to sing Aida (Leontyne Price, Arroyo, Weathers, Bumbry, Mitchell, Davy) and Eboli (Bumbry, Verrett). Matheopoulos (1991a) is typical of those ascribing to black singers dubious 'racial' qualities: Marion Anderson had 'a Negroid sound'; Grace Bumbry 'sensuous colouring and smoky timbre ... spiritual quality and a visceral passion ... characteristic of black artists' (ibid.: 257). Christiansen (1984: 231) describes Leontyne Price's voice as 'husky, dusky, musky, smoky, misty (on a bad day foggy!)—and a palpitating pagan sexiness'. On stage white singers are berated for blacking up as Otello or Aida, yet black singers would have highly restricted careers if forced to conform to the same 'theatre is 'naturalistic'' reasoning. Even 'trouser' roles[28] cause some problems to producers and conductors who try to recast them with men:

> Mehta says he cannot stand female Orlovsky's. Well, of course, composers will keep making these elementary mistakes, and how lucky we are with musicians like Mr Mehta who know better and can tidy them up. I look forward to a tenor Octavian, bass-baritone Cherubino when he gets around to giving us his *Rosenkavalier* and *Le nozze di Figaro* (Milnes quoted in Rasponi 1984: 596).

Ira Siff of La Gran Scena Opera Company should know a *diva* when he sees one for *he* is one: Vera Galupe-Borszkh:

> What I was interested in ... was that someone like Nilsson or Sutherland, the great *divas* of my time, were enormous physical presences ... The people I really admire ... make a statement of strength underneath the costume. That's what I see in the people I worship—Olivero, Rysanek, Scotto. Some gigantic assertion of power. And underneath that... tremendous vulnerability and emotional neediness. That combination is what I find touching, and it's what makes a *diva*. Occasionally you have a sane one like Joan [Sutherland] ... [but] ... what's interesting for us are the *insane* ones, of which there are fewer and fewer. You're not going to get much mileage out of the current crop. [Asked about Te Kanawa and Battle] I have tremendous respect for these people, anyone who can sing like that and attain that kind of career ... However I am upset by what the gifts they have are being used for... The time they're caught up in, they haven't created singlehandedly. It's a time of technology ... and therefore the art reflects it being a cold technological time. They are technically so adept. No-one works anymore who can't sight-read his way out of a locked trunk. No one works anymore who's going to risk expressiveness to make an uneven vocal statement. So this is a

time when you can't have a voice like Leonie's [Rysanek] on a flawless piece of CD equipment. It doesn't mesh. And this homogenized international thing, where you don't have Italians singing in Italian, and so forth is a pit ... in the 1960s (the end of the era) you could have a catharsis at the opera-house. You could go to a Rysanek-London *Der fliegende Holländer* or a Callas-Gobbi *Tosca,* and leave wasted. Now so many singers just have a generalized idea of what something is about (Siff 1991: 28-31).

Support for this final point comes from a *cause célèbre* interview in *Opera News* (2 February 1991) with three American sopranos (Dawn Upshaw, Cheryl Studer and Patricia Schuman), who claimed not to be interested in recordings of past great singers, although Studer (*1993b) later claimed to have been misunderstood. Belfort, director of the Zurich International Opera Studio also professed himself '... amazed that even the best singers I have possess no knowledge of the great singers of even my own generation' (Driscoll 1993: 28). 'I know Schwarzkopf sang Elvira, but I don't think about that. I wonder if the audience really cares' (Schumann* 1991: 11). Such attitudes, and the American training, leads to 'bland generalized singing [which along with] opera's increasingly museum core is also responsible for the emergence of Producer's Opera' (Siff 1991: 30). There are many young American female singers, especially sopranos, now on the international circuit (Vaness, Anderson, Studer, Upshaw, Schumann and so on) who though technically highly proficient and with pleasing even 'wonderful voices [which] seem to be able to sing anything—like Studer.[29] What we miss are great personalities' (Rysanek* 1994: 17). Phyllis Curtin and Will Crutchfield (1991) describe the American singing style as being the ability to be adaptable and multipurpose, to emulate other styles. Even so new stars are constantly compared with past stars: Nicolai Ghiaurov when he first sang in the West (Paris 1955) was considered a 'new Chaliapin', Roberto Alagna is now the new Pavarotti'. All great stars have their copies; Lucia Aliberti and Tiziana Fabbriccini are both modelled on aspects of Callas we are told; June Anderson on Sutherland.

Recording requirements are in great part responsible for these anodyne characteristics. Kollo (*1989: 1419) believes that a developing voice 'needs to sing everything', but recording companies impose a narrow range on singers which he considers is unnatural and also accustoms the listener to a sound which is unlikely to be replicated in opera houses where the ideal voices when recorded sound ungainly or, perhaps, blemished. Callas's great success would probably not be possible now with the cosmetic sounds which recordings have imposed on our ears. Exciting theatre performers generally disappoint in the recording studio, their voices too 'fat', their mannerisms too exaggerated. In addition, studio recordings are often 'put together piecemeal', spliced from takes of variable lengths recorded not necessarily in the correct order, sometimes over months or even years (for example, the von Karajan *Lohengrin*). As late as the 1960s several singers were reported as being unhappy with recordings—for example Siepi did not like the 'cold re-take and splicing procedure [with] its insistence on elusive perfection' (1962: 90). Mordden names other singers who suffered from the recording studio: 'Marie Collier, like Fremsted and Mary Garden, a great performer but not a phonographic singer. Her Minnie and Elena Makropulos are legendary—but opera history is "written" in recordings now, not in legend' (1987: 274). Jones also is 'an unreliable recording artist' (ibid.: 144) for reasons explained in a letter to *Opera Now* (August 1994: 14):

> I have done my best to collect all of Dame Gwyneth Jones' recordings and, to attend her performances. Her superb voice does not sound nasal like Nilsson's or 'cow-like' (Callas), and rarely does she sing under pressure like Marton. Ironically, what I adore in her voice the critics find unpleasant: Gruber (1993) unfavourably criticises her recordings by ... characterising her voice as 'wobbly' and 'squally'. Are these terms Jones' trademarks? Although I am not quite sure what they really mean, the Welsh diva's 'wobbles' and 'squalls' are a delight beyond expression. So much for you critics.

But as the sadly deceased soprano Claire Watson explained:

> ... vocal production today is in a state of revolution. They are doing away with the *vibrato;* the sound must be concentrated and smooth ... recording companies now rule, and, unfortunately, singers use the same technique before the public as they do in front of the microphones. The more like an instrument the better chance the voice has to record well. Take Schwarzkopf and Streich—they are perfect for recordings. But Gwyneth Jones has too much

vibrato, and as a result she records far less than the others who cannot compare to her vocally (quoted in Rasponi 1984: 402).

Notes

1. *Prima donna* ('the first lady') means the leading female star. *Prima donne* is the correct Italian plural but in English-speaking countries prima *donna* is also used as a plural. *Primo uomo* (It. 'the first man') emerged at more or less the same time in eighteenth-century *opera seria* and referred to the character rather than the singer and thus was applied to *castrati* (see Heriot 1975)—female, as well as male, performers of male characters. In *opera seria* with a cast of between six to eight, two usually female, the *prima donna*, usually a soprano, usually had the larger part. If both women's roles were of equal importance the term *prime donne a vicenda* (It. 'co-equals') was used. (For a discussion of the full range of such terms see Rosselli 1992b.)

    Steane (1991) gives an excellent guide (with examples) to the different vocal categories. Opera magazines and journals instruct in types of singers as well the technical language by which to describe them. Steane has detailed main types for *Opera Now*. As an example see his essay on the *leggiero* Light Soprano or Soubrette (June 1990: 18-21).

2. The distinction is commonly made between stars and superstars, but there is disagreement as to who should be categorised as the latter. On balance, drawing on high public profile, relative earning power, power in staged productions, recordings and so on, the following would qualify by most accounts: Kiri Te Kanawa, Jessye Norman, Kathleen Battle, Cheryl Studer (perhaps for studio rather than stage performances), Cecilia Bartoli, Luciano Pavarotti, Placido Domingo, José Carreras.

    Female superstars reified as *prima donna assoluta*, are now extinct. This term has almost entirely retained a purely artistic reference, free of the non-musical connotations of diva. Rosa Ponselle was by common consensus a *prima donna assoluta*. Recent singers to come closest to attaining such a status have been Joan Sutherland and Marilyn Horne and, before them, Maria Callas and Renata Tebaldi.

3. For student texts on relearning and training see Goldovsky and Schoep (1990) on soprano arias and how to act as well as sing them, and Mattei (1991) on Italian pronunciation for non-native singers. For a collection of singers and others on the techniques

of singing opera written for a wider than expert audience see Hines (1982).

4. Horne (*1995) claims 'singing is internal'. The singing is going on 'in the mask', 'resonance' 'which I never had to seek, it was nature's gift' (ibid.: 14). 'Young singers today place their voices in their throats and thereby lose resonance' (ibid.: 43). Horne also states that young singers should not copy her cadenzas—except maybe for practice—but they must find their own way. 'Cadenzas show off what you do best—leave out anything you can't' (ibid.:14).

5. The following institutions offer specific performance training for would-be opera singers: Admission is always by audition, usually held between October and January. Previous experience can often count for a year or more's exemption, but serious applicants should be prepared to commit up to six years' training: Birmingham Conservatoire; Guildhall School of Music and Drama, London; London College of Music; London Royal Schools Vocal Faculty; National Opera Studio, Morley College London; Royal Academy of Music, London; Royal College of Music, London; Royal Northern College of Music, Manchester; Royal Scottish Academy of Music and Drama, Glasgow; Trinity College of Music and the Welsh College of Music and Drama, Cardiff.

    On recent attempts to analyse the economics of singing and training see Towse (1993).

6. Elisabeth Schwarzkopf (Berlin), Josephine Veasey, Charles Craig, Geraint Evans, Michael Langdon (all Covent Garden London), Tatiana Troyanos (in *The Sound of Music* o n Broadway!), Janet Baker (Glyndebourne) are past examples, Giovanna Cassolla (La Scala Milan) is a rare recent example of a star beginning in the chorus.

7. The possibility of US singers training in a system with many native German singers fighting for work in fewer theatres in receipt of lower state subsidies since reunification, see Midgette (1993a).

8. In Europe, Tauber, John McCormack, Maria Cebotari, Gigli, Jan Kiepura, Martha Eggerth, Conchita Supervia, Tito Gobbi, Hans Hotter and Chaliapin (in a musical version of *Don Quixotte* with music by Milhaud, not Massenet) were amongst the many who made films. Other opera singers to be used by Hollywood

included Dorothy Kirsten, Blanche Thebom, Rise Stevens (*The Chocolate Soldier* [1941], *Going My Way* [1944] with Bing Crosby), Lauritz Melchior, Ezio Pinza (*Carnegie Hall* [1947] with Stevens), Roberta Peters, Helen Traubel, Jan Peerce (*My Imperium* [1951] with Lana Turner, *Strictly Dishonourable* [1951] with Janet Leigh), Jarmila Novotna and Licia Albanese. Patrice Munsel starred in a biopic of Dame Nellie (*Melba* [1953]), Robert Merrill in *Aaron Slick from Pumpkin Crick* (1951) for which unsanctioned indiscretion he was banished from the Met roster for a year. Even Kirsten Flagstad committed her Brünnhilde 'Hojotoho' to celluloid in *The Big Broadcast of 1938* between sketches by Bob Hope and W. C. Fields. The Marx Brothers in *A Night at the Opera* clearly had a great deal to work from (Mackay 1991; Fawkes 1994).

9. 'Soap opera' was originally a daytime radio serial with frequent advertisement interruptions (US); it was reputedly difficult to tell when the 'soap' ended and the 'soap ads' began.

10. The post-Soviet glut of exceptionally talented and individual singers (Prokina, Gorchakova, Guleghina, Hvorostovsky, Leiferkus, Chernov and so on), is surely due to a system whereby singers have trained and learnt, before international appearances, in a slower, traditional manner. These singers now appearing in the West do not accept that the Russian system was necessarily that much better: 'You have ten performances a month or one for the same salary. In those conditions it is impossible to make progress ... There are many baritones and tenors in the company. Each must work' (Chernov* 1994: 11).

11. Scott (1972: 592) notes how 'a commercial opera company' is unthinkable, and indebtedness merely grows. One aspect of expenditure which could be tackled is singers' high fees: 'The history of opera is full of demands made by its stars.' In the 1880s Patti was earning at least $3000 per performance. Fees are not merely a matter of money but of prestige, Melba always insisted at Covent Garden that she be paid more than any other singer. Traditionally the biggest fees were earned in the US provinces. It was there on tour with P. T. Barnum (of circus fame) that Jenny Lind laid the substantial foundations to her fortune. Even as late as the 1920s, when opera was losing ground as popular entertainment to jazz and the cinema, Hurok paid Chaliapin $3500 per Mephistopheles. Scott reports that the Golden Age of

Fees was at the beginning of the nineteenth-century when, for example, Angelica Catalani (La Catalani) (famed in equal measure for her talent, tastelessness and rapacity) earned $2000 per performance. In those days opera paid handsomely and her fee was directly related to box office receipts. It is in this salient fact that the fees of today's singers differ. In 1971 *Time* Magazine reported that Beverley Sills' concert fee was $10,000 which led a rival to immediately double her own. What is alarming for opera is not that the fee is large but that it appears to be fixed quite arbitrarily. If, as in 1972 at Covent Garden, only 50 per cent of costs are met by ticket sales, then subsidies are attacked for, far from democratising opera, they merely pay already wealthy singers. Scott suggests stars be paid a percentage of the takings which he believes would prove a very chastening experience.

The weakest apologia for high fees is that a star's career is a short one. This may hold some water with contract or 'house' stars who sing a great deal more anyway and for a fixed lesser wage. An untimely loss of voice could remove all earning power. 'Few other professions offer such little security, certainly none which require so much rigorous preparation, study and discipline' (Scott 1977: 596). Better to put subsidies into pension schemes.

Scott advocates unilateral action by all managements of 'star' houses, where reputations are made and maintained, and where recording companies require that they sing. The whole fees issue is shrouded in mystery; there is a conspiracy of silence.

When Bing arrived (at the Met), the top fee paid was $1000 no matter what the name or fame. The advent of Callas broke the overhead barrier—her fees (plus those of a few others) went up to $1750. Nilsson and Sutherland may have begun at that figure and Corelli came in at a new high of $2750. Because of their glitter a thousand or more has probably been added to the cheques of Tebaldi and Sutherland and the other crown-wearers. By 1968 the top price was $4000. Outside the Met, Corelli commanded $10,000 for a southern *Aida*, Sutherland $8000 for herself and $2000 for Bonynge for a provincial *Traviata*. In the 1930s at Covent Garden Gigli's fee was £400 per performance, Grace Moore's £300, Lily Pons' £250, Rethberg's and Lotte Lehmann's £150—all tax-free. Met stars are still reputed to earn less than elsewhere but they more than make up for that with increased prestige and 'opera' spin-offs.

12. Contemporary publicists for opera singers in the US, view the decline of the *prima donna* as also a decline in arts page and general press space being devoted to them, television having drained the power of both, through interviews such as CBS' *60 Minutes* with Pavarotti at his home (see Muir 1993: 15). Cecilia Bartoli is one exception: '

   Yes, by today's standards, but in the old days you'd be reading about her in the paper much more often than you do now, in sections other than the music papers. You could do things with personalities in former days that you can't do now (Alix Williamson quoted in Clark 1993: 21).

13. With, for example, the 'Gerry Flappers' (female fans of Geraldine Farrar in the 1910s and 1920s), and arguably from the nineteenth through to the late twentieth centuries for such minorities as gays and lesbians (see Koestenbaum 1993).

14. This phrase is used in the EMI advertisements for Ruth Ann Swenson's debut solo album: 'We have seen the future and it is positively *golden ...*' *Ruth Ann Swenson: Positively Golden.*

15. Amongst the many: Tito Gobbi (1980); Placido Domingo (1982, 1992); Renata Scotto (1984); Beverley Sills (1988); José Carreras (1991); Luciano Pavarotti (1981. 1995); Janet Baker (1982); Michael Langdon (1982); Robert Tear (1990); Thomas Allen (1993); Geraint Evans (1983); Marilyn Horne (1983); Galina Vishnevskaya (1984); Rita Hunter (1986); Hermann Prey (1986). Reissues of past singers are also numerous: Tito Ruffo (1977); Paolo Silveri (1994); Eleanor Steber (1994); Mirto Picchi (1982a, 1982b); Isobel Baillie (1982); Frida Leider (1966).

16. Amongst the many: Roberts (1982) of Victoria de los Angeles; Braddon (1974), Greenfield (1972), Adams (1980) and Major (1987) of Joan Sutherland; Stassinopoulos (1981), Segalini (1983), Stancioff (1987), Remy (1978), Ardoin (1988), Kesting (1992) and Scott (1991) of Maria Callas; Haberfeld (1991) of Gwyneth Jones; Fingleton (1983) of Kiri Te Kanawa; Pullen and Taylor (1995) of Montserrat Caballé; Dusek and Schmidt (1993) of Leonie Rysanek; Blyth (1973) of Janet Baker; Casanova (1982) of

Tebaldi; De Franchesci (1982) of Stignani; Elsner and Büsch (1986) of Pilar Lorengar; Turing (1983) of Hans Hotter; Paolucci (1991) of Beverley Sills; Scott (1988) of Caruso; Jefferson (1988) and Glass (1988) on Lotte Lehmann; Pugliese (1991) of Gigli; Borovsky (1988) of Chaliapin; Campion (1993) and Leonard (1988) of Kathleen Ferrier; Henstock (1990) of Fernando de Lucia; Chambers (1990) of Margaret Sheridan; Farkas (ed.) (1990) of Lawrence Tibbett; Pugliese (1993) of Toti Dal Monte; Cone (1993) of Patti; Headington (1992) of Peter Pears; Vercher Grau of Antonio Cortis (1990); Rubboli of Gino Bechi (1990); Turnbull (1991) of Joseph Hislop; Castle and Tauber (1971) of Richard Tauber; Leonard (1988) of Oda Slobodskaya; Werba (1986) of Maria Jeritza; Fitzlyon (1987) of Malibran; Vogt (1987) of Flagstad.

See also Pleasants (1983) *Great Singers From the Dawn of Opera to our Own Times* and Rosenthal (1965) *Great Singers of Today*.

17. *Fach* means vocal categories in terms of range and weight of voice, of which in the German system there are 22 from *hochdramatische Sopran* to *seriose Bass*. For a detailed discussion of types of voice see Steane (1991). At agency auditions singers are immediately labelled. Several singers change *Fach* during their careers, Horne was once a *soprano* and later a *mezzo-contralto*; King was a *baritone* and then a *dramatic tenor*; Jones a *mezzo* before becoming a *spinto* and then *dramatic soprano*.

Despite such categorisations several star singers claim to be without a fixed *Fach*: Stratas merely sings one role at a time, in different registers—'my voice is an extension of my soul' (*1994: 1148), and the same may be said of Maria Ewing. Varady too is 'one of those special singers who fits into no specific category'(*1992: 651).

You can never generalise about voices. Just because Joan Sutherland—who was a *dramatic coloratum*—sang this or that role, it doesn't mean that every *coloratura* can sing the same repertoire. Semiramide and Lucia are very different—completely different—Rossini anyway, is different from any other *bel canto* composer ... a completely different style (Studer* 1993a).

285

18. Black singers have not generally been overtly political about racism, militant or otherwise (see Story 1990), but it is difficult to imagine how covertly they could ignore the evidence and experience of discrimination (for example, Marian Anderson at the Met and Grace Bumbry at Bayreuth) only recently openly expressed by singers such as Norman, White and Simon Estes. See note 22 below.

19. Critics describe singers' voices through metaphor for example, Te Kanawa's (*1994) as 'cream', 'sauce vanille', 'vanilla ice cream': 'It's a voice noted more for easy flow than for brilliant accents or cutting edge'. This article states:

> Critics, like teachers, in their heart of hearts are more impressed by hard work than by natural gifts ... What they value is interpretation, especially when the performer can't get a free ride on natural good looks or good sounds. The Callas legend established a vogue for harsh timbre, overdriven resources, wobbles worn like a purple heart. The problem is that these qualities were misinterpreted as proof of dedication to the vocal work ethic. Te Kanawa has never seemed to suffer for her art' (ibid.: 16).

She is all line, smoothed out, she is unresponsive to the text. Her most influential singers are Tebaldi and Crespin—because they had no imperfections. Of the Schwarzkopf Germans Te Kanawa hates their affectedness: 'It's so untrue.' The writer uses McLuhon's 'hot' and 'cool' media descriptions to illustrate Te Kanawa's difference from Schwarzkopf. 'Hot' medium means high definition—communication packed with data—every detail with its share of information and every vowel and consonant heated up by intense and hard working performers. 'Cool' is what Te Kanawa is—leaving more space for audience reaction.

20. It is remarkable how many singers admit to smoking, or to having smoked: for example, Leonie Rysanek (*1994: 171) and Dennis O'Neill (*1994a: 291).

21. In the otherwise gushing fanzine *Opera Now*, Steane's series on 'Singers of the Century' provides refreshingly detached accounts of past and retired singers, sample Jon Vickers (*1994).

22. There have been, and increasingly are, a large number of black

opera singers, particularly Americans. Before Marian Anderson many a fine black singer (Paul Robeson, Roland Hayes, Jules Bledsoe, Todd Duncan, Ellabelle Davis, Dorothy Maynor, Anne Brown and Muriel Rahn) had to content themselves with concert careers—their paths to the Met blocked (Bernheimer 1985a: 755).

The story may be apocryphal but I doubt it. A great diva basking in the twilight of a long career, was singing Tosca one night at the Met in 1961. Before the performance, her dresser asked if she had yet heard Leontyne Price, who had just made a sensational debut as Leonora in *Il trovatore*. The great diva, herself a celebrated if fading exponent of the same role, quivered a few chins in lofty disapproval. 'Ah, yes' she purred 'Price, a lovely voice. But the poor thing is singing the wrong repertory.' The dresser registered surprise. 'What repertory' he asked, 'should Price be singing?' The great diva smiled a knowing smile. 'Bess', she purred. 'Just Bess'.

Price had sung Bess, she had also been in Virgil Thompson's *Four Saints in Three Acts*, and *Aida* 'but Leonora was her Met debut role because it suited her and make up could see to the rest. No-one had complained of whites blacking up as Aida, Otello, or playing Butterfly. Bing had had resistance from the Met board in 1955 when Anderson sang Ulrica—as Bernheimer states 'an old gypsy role that easily accommodates dark skin. Price did not mind singing Aida—'she is not a slave girl, she is a captured Princess. She is of noble blood.' B. H. Haggin, the respected critic, is quoted by Bernheimer from one of his essays in *Music and Ballet* (Horizon) recounting a *Don Giovanni* of 1974 with Price as Donna Anna:

Price presented with her Donna Anna the same obtrusive incongruity as previously with her Leonora and her Pamina ... but not with her Aida: when I look at what is happening on a stage my imagination still cannot accommodate itself to a black in the role of a white.

But as Bernheimer states, the imagination is as taxed surely by the old in the role of the young, or the fat in the role of the skinny. Opera in this sense is the epitome of 'camp' (see Sontag

1967; Babuscio 1977) given the superimposition or conjunction of seemingly incompatible and incongruous elements: age and youth; size and age; singing instead of speech and so on. Simon Estes, after a Bayreuth *Dutchman*, and Amfortas claims that he was not chosen for the Solti-Hall Ring because of his colour (see Fay 1994). Solti and Hall denied this strenuously, stating that they found the voice insufficiently pleasing:

> Hall might indeed have been troubled by the idea of a black Wotan surrounded by a large family of white singers. He did not object in principle to a black Wotan as long as there were black singers among his daughters, but he felt Este's audition relieved him of the need to make such a choice (Fay quoted in Bernheimer).

Willard White has subsequently sung Wotan for Scottish Opera and elsewhere.

For Porgy and Bess apparently the Gershwin estate insists on an all-black cast but Bernheimer quotes a Zurich production in German with all whites blacked up—*Bess, nun bist Du meine Frau'*.

The racial credibility gap may have to be softened by producers—Bernheimer mentions the NY City Opera *Ballo* with Willard White as Count Ribbing, the only black at the masked ball but with only a half-'domino' mask to cover his eyes: 'The problem was a problem of course only for those who want to take opera seriously as drama.'

Some critics objecting to the black sound of Cynthia Clarey as Nicklausse in a Berlin *Hoffmann* were taken to task by Dr Geerd Heinsen of *Orpheus* magazine: 'her tone quality is too Negroid for the vocal line.' 'But' he qualified 'that is a matter of taste.'

The editor of a French music and opera magazine, referring to Leona Mitchell in the Verdi Requiem observed 'The voice is very beautiful but she is too lazy to use it properly. All black singers are lazy.'

Are black voices recognisable? Robert Rushmore (1974) thinks so 'The only truly recognisable American voice, or used to be anyway, belongs to the black singer—though I may be accused of racism for saying so.' He cites Price's voice but also that 'this is beginning to change as blacks become more assimilated into

American culture'.

McCann (1953) observed, 'Frequently the range of a Negro singer can be developed to outdo any white singer's range'. She states that the *tenorino* voice (counter tenor) is peculiar to blacks, adding that, with appropriate training, the black *tenorino* can develop into a castrated virtuoso. Mordden (1987) calls Price a role model for all black singers: 'an example of how to do justice to opera and oneself, how to spend commitment and take one's time.' In describing her voice he states 'her Verdian timbre is so authoritative that it has become the sound around which modern Verdians navigate'.

> Price ... brought back uninhibited splendour, Price's voice has an unmistakably individual fragrance—husky, dusky, musky, smoky, misty (on a bad day foggy) and a palpitating pagan sexiness. It is not the voice of a good girl ... throughout the 1960s cut-Price imitations followed her thick and fast, as the black *prima donna* became fashionable rather than merely acceptable (Christiansen 1984).

Rosalyn Story (1991) profiles another famous Aida, Martina Arroyo, including stories from the latter about black singers who once successful become whiter than white: 'Once one of her colleagues, another black soprano, who had taken up residence in Germany, remarked in her most patrician manner "In a few days I must be going back to the Fatherland" Arroyo retorted "Oh so you're going to Africa?"' At a dinner party another black artist's affected European accent became so pronounced as the evening progressed that Arroyo was tempted to call for an interpreter. Arroyo's response: "Have some more chitlins girl."

23. Te Kanawa is very pro surtitles: 'If people have been a little slow to warm to *Arabella* it's only because they can't understand it, and I don't expect everyone to. That's why you need titles, if we are ever to get more people into the opera house.'

24. In *The Times* (30 November 1994: 36) Hilary Finch responded to the 'mournful cry "There are no great voices around any more"' by naming ten young names to watch: Jane Eaglen, John Mark Ainsley, Bryn Terfel, Juliane Banse, Galina Gorchakova, Simon Keenlyside, Elena Prokina, Cecilia Bartoli, Amanda Roocroft, and Roberto Alagna. Bryn Terfel has already proved a major

star sensation attracting such headlines as 'Welsh farm boy thrills the New York Met set' (*The Independent on Sunday* 4 December 1994). This article stated:

> It usually takes death, scandal or a difficult *diva* to turn new singers into front-page news, but the front pages is where Terfel has found himself, rivalling Cecilia Bartoli as the most talked about singer in town. At a time when singers are hot in the classical music business—about half the best-selling recordings are by singers—the appearance of a new, possibly great one, is bound to cause excitement .... He has no publicity agent ... *Newsweek* was in raptures last week ... they adore the way he ambles up Broadway in jeans nibbling cheese biscuits ... and that he invited over 74 of his relatives to hear him ... New Yorkers revel in the fact that Terfel was raised on a small cattle and sheep farm ... it doesn't matter they can't pronounce his name (it is *Tair-vel* announced the *New York Times*) ... Cecilia Bartoli is undoubtedly a major star already too, and others left off Finch's list vie for attention, especially Angela Gheorghiu.

25. Tetrazzini was a 16 year-old in the audience at the first performance in Florence of a new production of *L'Africaine*. The conductor announced that the soprano was ill, Tetrazzini jumped up and said she could sing the role. He agreed to a day's rehearsal, but then accepted that he should have let her go ahead on the first night anyway—so good was she. She made her London debut in the late autumn (that is, 'low') season of 1907. The press had not heard of her and she was given a perfunctory welcome; indeed Covent Garden offered her £300 to stay away. After the first night of *La traviata* there was no risk of empty seats in front of this 'Voice of the Century'.

Critics tell us what her recordings cannot do justice to—she was a fine actress. Also being around at the time when recordings were being made meant that she could be heard in the home. Pearl's complete edition includes 96 arias, although to 'hear' the voice one has to tolerate 'acoustic recordings'. 'Agility, leaps, trills, rapid runs, and extremely high *fioritura* are executed with ease and great beauty of tone. In her guide to the art of singing Tetrazzini stressed relaxation and ease of production, almost on equal terms with breath control. The writer states 'The quality of a singer's voice is difficult to invoke in words' (ibid.: 49).

26. It is perhaps rather ominous that so many rich foods have been named after *divas*: Peach Melba, Turkey Tetrazzini, Coupe Fremsted, Chicken Ponselle, L'Aile de la Bresse Sutherland, Beignets Soufflés with Sauce Callas, the Galli-Curci Prima Donna Cocktail (a tablespoon of strong coffee mixed with milk sugar and ice), Melba toast.

27. Elliott (1992) reports on Asian singers now making an impact in international opera: Haijing Fu (China) has sung Germont at the Met and Houston. Hei-Kyung Hong (Korea) has been at the Met since 1985, Juliette for Canadian Opera. Taro Ichihara (Japan) has sung the Duke in *Rigoletto* and in *Ballo* at the Met. Hong Shen Li (China) debuted in 1992 as the Steersman at the Met. (Others were Sumi Jo, Young-Ok Shi, Deng, Yasuko Hayashi, Yoko Watanabe.) The article claims there will be a 'Pied Piper' effect as successful singers return home to teach. In the early 1950s Chinese singers were enrolling at the Juillard—their training Russian-based. By the 1980s their technique was world-class—'they just lacked some theory, interpretation, performance practice issues'.

Elliott talks of Phyllis Curtin who has taught in Beijing: there is vocal talent but it is not sophisticated; recordings are a major source of information—a bad thing, because then people do not think these are mature interpretations for young voices—so they need retraining. The 'cultural isolation' of the Chinese leaves the singers without necessary experience. Koreans have more experience of Western culture. Hong went to study in the US when she was 15. There is the language difficulty as well. They must also learn to move too in an alien cultural milieu which leads to a credibility gap 'because they look different'. Language is thought to be their biggest hurdle 'they are not verbally distinguished'; 'Koreans have wonderful vowels'. Many Korean and Japanese women have trouble projecting because of cultural reserve (but what of Watanabe and Hayashi as Cio-Cio-San?). 'One conductor who saw both Fu and Li told Meyer (manager of both for IMG artists) apparently without malice, that the difficulty was 'he couldn't really see their eyes when they sang, and eyes communicate so much'. Meyer believes that people think that because the singers are Asian, they don't know what it is they are singing about.

Li reports that he sang Goro in Western Opera Theatre because an Asian singing Pinkerton would look funny: 'Opera is a European culture, and they prefer to use their own people. If I audition for a job against a Caucasian who sings at the same level-voice, technique, language—they will choose him instead of me .... we just need to work very hard.'

According to Ardis Kranik, artistic director of Lyric Opera in Chicago, 'There is no racial barrier in opera. There can't be, if you sing we take you.' 'At the Met we do not take account of anybody's race or nationality when we cast them. But just as with Western singers, we do weigh rather carefully whether someone's vocal and physical "type" makes them suitable for a role ... When Ichihara does the Italian Singer in *Rosenkavalier* we can't put a white powdered wig on him, because it would look wrong, even though it's correct for the period. We have to put a black wig on him, which is stylistically incorrect but the better thing to do.' An Asian sound? 'They sing with incredible pingy clarity' (Mathew Epstein). 'All our voices are very, very clear' (Hong).

28. 'Trouser role'; 'breeches part'; *travesti*; male characters sung by women—for example, Oktavian *(Der Rosenkavalier)*, Cherubino *(Le nozze di Figaro)*, Prince Orlofsky *(Die Fledermaus)*, Siebel *(Faust)*.

29. Studer (*1991) is described as 'the darling of the record industry. Exclusive to DGG—or at least "exclusive" in the sense that the yellow label has first refused on her first recording of new roles—Studer is none the less courted by every major international classical label'. By mid-1997 Miss Studer seemed to have disappeared from the opera stage.

6 Producers' opera

We're getting 'concept' opera by the truck-load these days, which to me is a bit like putting a crew-cut on Michaelangelo's David (Dolora Zajick* 1994: 15).

Introduction

Rosenthal's description of the past 250 years of operatic history as successively the Reign of the Singer (until the end of the nineteenth century), Dictatorship of the Conductor which ended during the last war (Mahler in Vienna, Toscanini in Milan, Krauss in Munich, Beecham at Covent Garden 'made sure producers and designers did not ride roughshod over composers. They were also the artistic directors of their theatres, where are today's?') and the Age of the Producer unfortunately still with us' (Rosenthal 1979: 528), was devoid of material contextualisation or explanation. Fifteen years on and artistic directors are audit-haunted managers whilst producers (now with movement specialists, choreographers and designers), have their power yet further enhanced: we have 'conceptitis' (Pleasants 1989), 'interventionist', 'postmodernist', 'radical', 'deconstructionist', 'produceritis', 'Pountneyfication', 'Aldenorrhoea' (Jonas et al. 1992: 16), we speak of Chereau's *Ring*,[1] Sellars' *Flute*, Alden's *Macbeth*, Visconti's *Don Carlos*, Zeffirelli's *Traviata*. Opera has been transformed by 'a surge of theatricalism' (Inglis 1993: 35) and, as these epithets imply, a surge of tensions and conflicts from all sides of the stage and proscenium. These disputes, often deeply acrimonious and frequently superficially reduced to conservative versus radical (Jonas et al. 1992), are disputes over the sanctity of works, rights of control over them and to the transmission of knowledge and interpretations of them to audiences and other members of the laity. Defence of the 'pure', 'original' work as written, directed and performed, is frequently used to signal an attack on producers who impose their radical *'idée'* employed as attempts to make works meaningful to modern audiences, to liberate them from culinary practice and museum dust. For such defendants the stance is reverential and traditional according to the musicological dierarchy outlines in Chapter 1, whereas the perspective of 'radical' producers is not reverential but referential to extra-musicological discliplines: literature, cultural studies, philosophy, political ideologies of various kinds, Marxist, 'post-modernist' and so on. Both sides claim the greater understanding of the 'truth' of the 'original', the former through an emphasis on meticulous 'authenticity', the latter through their claimed ability to release the 'spirit', 'essence' or some such hidden behind 'auratic' convention, age and familiarity.

The intellectual justifications of 'radical' producers are drawn from various sources such as Kristeva (1980), which argue that there is no primary, authoritative text, texts remake themselves and are remade in performance. Producers thus realise works through their 'intertextuality': 'the transposition of one or more system of signs into another, accompanied by a new articulation of the enunciative and denotive position' (Roudiez 1980: 15). Thus at each stage in a text's fissured and discontinuous history it enters into new relationships, it meets other texts and changes as it is placed in these new positions, no privilege should be accorded to the 'original' text, nor deference paid to the false history of continuous tradition. A text, be it literary, cinematic or operatic, is multi-accented, polyphonic, and the possibility of reaccentuation of what functions as a sign in society is always there (Bakhtin 1977). Modern producers open operas up to a new kind of examination, presenting audiences with new ways of seeing. The 'radical' producer thus activates the audience in ways which undermine critics, values and authority in fundamental ways.

Strategic marshalling

Until the Second World War: '... the idea of "production" was generally slight ... consisting more of strategic marshalling and positioning of forces against the geography of the set than the realisation of the director's ideological vision of the opera in question' (Christiansen 1984: 166). British practice was apparently little more elaborate by the 1960s. Writing in *The Daily Telegraph* after critical comments had been made of The Carl Rosa Opera Company's lack of named producers for their 'productions', Mrs H. B. Phillips 'revealed with pride that a producer is actually regarded as superfluous in her company. All its members, we are to understand, may contribute to an attempt at staging the work according to the composer's known wishes' (Warrack 1960a: 706). Dennis Arundell's first-hand account demonstrated what a producer might then have been preoccupied with. Eager to dispel the:

> ... common belief among non-technical enthusiasts that a theatrical producer is solely concerned with the movements of the actors (with some share in the lighting when a 'lighting expert' is not employed) ... now that entertainment has become an industry, the producer's role consists of the welding together of opera's various elements: ... of course he is still responsible for the movements on the stage (which includes arranging that the conductor can catch the eye of the singer at necessary moments and that awkward positions are avoided for singers doing tricky vocal passages), but he also has to see that excellent scene designs are practical both for the stage and for the action, that the lighting gives prominence to a character without either falsifying the general effect or dazzling the singer's eyes unnecessarily, and that striking touches of production do not distract from a leading character or action. Moreover, he is responsible for checking the construction and painting of the scenery and the choice of materials, and the cutting and the making of the costumes ... is involved in planning at an early stage, has some say in casting (though not for revivals) (Arundell 1961: 631-3).

Arundell's examples of the producer's challenge are limited to where the candles should be placed in *Tosca* Act II so that Tosca may follow the original stage instructions for their placement at the Act's close by the body of Scarpia, not adhered to in most productions because the time allotted appears insufficient, and in Act III where Tosca should stand when the firing squad is assembling to execute

Cavaradossi, so that she is close enough to comment to him after the firing, the soldiers cannot apparently hear her, but enables the audience to clearly do so. He adds that producers ought to be generally skilled practitioners of all theatre arts as well as psychotherapists for inexperienced artists, however he warned:

> ... many producers tend to be obtrusive themselves and to show how clever they are with this bit of business or background movement that is distracting ... others are careless about style of period (I recently saw Almavira in the first act of *Il barbiere di Siviglia* with neither cloak nor hat), and some from the straight theatre seem to have insufficient knowledge of musical problems (ibid.: 636).

Prosaic though this sounds, for contemporary critics of 'produceritis' it is nail hitting visionary stuff, for what a long way we have since travelled! *'La forza del destino* set during the Spanish Civil War ... Norma singing *"Casta diva"* from the turret of a tank, Rigoletto as a New York bartender, Carmen a Cuban guerrilla, Aida pushing a mop, Butterfly expiring as the nuclear bomb is dropped, Gluck's Orfeo losing Eurydice in a car crash...' (Littlejohn 1992: 141-2), Isabella arriving in Algeria as an air hostess on a crash landed Boeing: Iphigenia in a Tauris furnished with a Steinway grand plastered with travel labels, she on buskins a metre high, bald, white faced ... a giant bird wing hovering above: *Macbeth* witches as 'dear little old ladies (not all women) in floral print dresses with handbags and pudding-basin hats, bustling about officiously as if organising a Women's Institute cake sale' (Milnes 1990b: 646): a Ruth Berghaus *Die Entführung* (Frankfurt 1981) in which 'the physical and psychological confinement of the harem was represented by an empty white box set which at critical moments heaved and rolled' (Millington 1992a: 420): *Don Giovanni* set in a shabby Seville hotel corridor as the city rapidly sinks 'beneath a flow of black volcanic lava that inexorably engulfed the hotel' (Forbes 1984: 919). What price the Barber's cloak and hat now? Clearly the escalation of producer power has been rapid and extreme.

> ... when I started out ... the director was not a star ... he hardly existed at all. The conductor ran the show ... they were more like acting coaches and stage managers than the czar producers of

today. As luck would have it my professional life runs parallel to the emergence of the director as prime mover of the production (Herbert Graf quoted in Rizzo 1972: 25)

As a result of this earlier lack of power there was a dearth of new productions, limited stage rehearsal time, 'the effect was a good deal less than theatrical' (ibid.: 15). Ten years after Graf's comments, and despite the work in North America of early 'radicals' such as Frank Corsaro,[2] Martorella still noted in this conservative North American context, that the emergence of 'czar producers' had been slow, due to opera being a museum: '... his creativity and novelty are not accepted as they are in the world of the theatre, where he is directing new works and more than likely working along with the author and producer from the inception of the play' (1982: 170). By the mid 1990s few, if any, opera houses have avoided, or not resorted to, the scandal of a 'radical' production, press headlines, letters to the music and mass media, performance disruption, cancelled subscriptions and even fights in the stalls (Milnes 1989d). Consonant with earlier discussions, large international houses employing star singers and conductors, relatively insulated from straight theatre influences and personnel, required to revive productions frequently over several seasons with numerous changes of cast and little rehearsal, dependent on private, corporate, and box office finances rather than subsidies, manifest the least evidence of the phenomenon. The most radical companies are likely to be smaller, with stable rosters of singer/actors, producers with strong straight theatre links, probably larger subsidies, with or attempting to create 'new' audiences, whether by reforming the 'old' or attracting the 'new'. Again, these are 'ideal' poles of a complex continuum. The New York Met and Vienna State Opera are closest to the first set of criteria, Munich also an international house, enjoys large subsidies, is part of post war radical German theatrical culture, deploys some 'stars' but since Jonas' arrival trailing British producers with ENO connections in his wake, frequently in radical productions. What also needs to be remembered is that the increase in producer power has been across the conservative-radical spectrum, and that 'radical' is time and place specific. Radical productions draw the sting of attention, but, with familiarity, their signs and devices become new conventions: it has become commonplace for producers to set operas in the period and location of their composition hence the abundance of 1876 *Rings*,

*Aida*s as spectacles celebrating the opening of the Suez Canal, Strauss operas set in bourgeois salons during the 1910s and 20s. The French Riviera (for comedies) and fascist dictatorships (for tragedies) have become other favoured clichés (Littlejohn 1992: 141). Meanwhile some of the most powerful of producers (in terms of prestige, earning power in international houses) are amongst the most conservative, as suggested by the paeans of praise heaped by *divas* on Zeffirelli whose ROH *Don Giovanni*, of meticulous, painstaking, period 'realism', was described by Victor Gollancz as of 'offensively obtrusive over ornateness' [1966: 59]. Whatever the forms of producer-power nowadays, and there is no universal capitulation to 'postmodernist' irony and 'repertoire of bizarre and shocking images (with) ... subliminal appeal' (Millington 1992a: 420),[3] it is now harder to get away with just throwing productions on stage for singers to walk through. Quite what the difference is between 'walking through', 'operatic acting' and 'acting' is not always clear. Mackerras (1990: 172-3) claims that 'operatic acting' was appropriate acting: 'everything went downhill when in the '60s directors from the straight theatre were invited to stop all that "nonsense of big gestures"'. In contrast after the telecast of the Boulez/Chereau *Ring* from Bayreuth Milnes commented: 'One thing is for sure, none of the millions of operatically uncommitted viewers who have followed this first *Ring* telecast almost as if it were a soap opera will ever again be able to say that opera singers cannot act', continuing that 'we will all grow more impatient with what so often passes for "acting" in opera houses' (1983: 140).

The origins of the Age of the Producer have been credited to various mainly negative factors: the decline of the cult of the diva and the individuality of vocal expression though not technique; the demise of the autocratic, charismatic conductor 'who fashioned productions in his own image'; financial pressures imposing simplified, generalised designs; a testiness with which producers of the straight theatre have felt when dealing with opera as a genre and opera personnel as a breed; continuing technological developments and competing pressures in the shadow of cinematography, however, two are particularly significant, both concerned with 'renewal': specifically, but with widening consequences, the post-war renewal of German operatic culture, and generally the failure of opera to 'regenerate its form or repertory in accordance with the needs of the age. The survival of an antiquated, obsolete genre has necessitated renewal in terms of presentation' (Millington 1992a: 1122-9). But first has this contemporary power of the producer compared with earlier periods, been overstated?

From preceptors to Czars

The history of stage and costume design is well documented but that of opera production 'difficult to uncover', partly because it has only 'drawn attention to itself with the late twentieth century emergence of "producer's opera"' (Savage 1992: 1106). As opera is music '... unified pleasurably with plot, language, musicianship, gesture, dance and decor...' (ibid.: 1107), it was, from its origins, lengthily rehearsed,[4] following detailed stage instructions provided by composers[5] and/or poets,[6] under the directorship of preceptors or *corago*.. 'charged with coordinating, advising, teaching and animating the artists ... something of a blend of the modem impresario, director and stage manager' (ibid.: 1107). In Rome until the middle of the seventeenth century, the Barberini theatre, the mainstay of opera, employed ever more flamboyant scene changes and machinery effects so that 'Already in 1637 the architect Giutti di Ferrare took obvious precedent over the poet (Rospigliosi) and the composer (Michaelangelo Rossi) in the vaguely moralizing opera *Erminio sul Giordano*' (Donnington 1981: 213). With the appearance in Venice of commercial opera in the 1630s,[7] and as opera responded to audience and singer demands for greater vocal display with a commensurate loss of homogeneity in performance styles and values, the various *corago* directorial tasks became fragmented between numerous functionaries: designers, fencing masters, machinists and so on, singers being left much to their own devices. These *corago* were not producers in the modern sense, indeed Kimbell (1991) does not employ the term, nor indeed does he refer to production but rather to 'stagecraft and scenography' (ibid.: 30), special emphasis given by him to the critical 'art of the machinist' (ibid.: 129-33). The desire to emulate the stage practices of the Ancient World and the employment of perspective created 'Vistas (which) drew (the audience) into dreamlike realms of enchantment, miraculous transformation scenes and prodigious machines, superb costuming ...' (ibid.: 30).

Opera seria, preoccupied with the highly formal routinisation of a few limited emotions, was dependent on vocal expertise from singers usually perfunctory as actors in ritualised stagings by the same few specialists rigidly following libretto instructions. Singers required little rehearsal time but were expected to adhere to *seria* acting conventions – dignified stance, 'rhetorically eloquent gesture and expressive face-play' (Savage 1992: 1114) – to conceal the physical efforts of virtuoso performance, amidst stultifyingly ritualised *merveilleux* (extravagant illusions employing a heightened vertical axis of the stage) and elaborate deployment of large chorus and *corps de ballet* in symmetrical artificiality. By these criteria opera production in France in the eighteenth century was ultimately dominated by the 'director at his most absolutist ...' (ibid.: 1110), Lully,[8] who fashioned his cast's every movement, gesture and deportment as was common in presentations of plays by Corneille and Racine, protected through the acquisition of copyright and use of printed scores, enabling frequent but fossilised revivals. Absolutist *director* here highlights a possibly valuable distinction between director as strategist and producer as interpreter not often made in current debates:

in the main the preparation, rehearsal and performance of *tragédie en musique* and *opera-ballet* in the first half of the 18th century seem to have involved not so much an organic, chemical compounding of the arts, as a benign convergence of them. In the performance itself, for instance, principals graciously sat out of harm's way during the inset fêtes; the dancers often wore masks, which set them apart from all other performers; and, once settled into their U-formation, the chorus rarely moved, even when the words they were singing might be thought to demand some physical agitation (if only the unfolding of their much folded arms) (Savage 1992: 1111).

Gluck's reforms were marked by simplicity, slimmed down arias, to enthral move and edify, asymmetry in stage deployment and design, unmasked dancers, actively participating choruses and a concern for theatrical 'natural acting', the 'total impersonation of roles' (ibid.: 1115) through characterisation, exemplified by Guadagni the creator of Gluck's *Orphée*, although 'Personal vanities, audience enthusiasms and the staying power of the traditions and conventions of *opera seria* all dictated that few singers went as far as Guadagni...' (ibid.: 1116). Under the stewardship of, usually, the theatre's resident poet, opera became a form involving a 'carefully monitored synthesis of theatrical arts, blending together to present a heightened virtual actuality' (ibid.: 1116) out of which emerged the stage works of Haydn and Mozart. At the Esterhaza Court Haydn worked as musical director with Pietro Travaglia, principal scenographer and lighting designer, Nunziata Porta, theatre manager, and Prince Nikolaus, artistic director and financial controller, who also had a say in casting, a breakdown of responsibilities similar to that of other Court theatres of the time. Singers were expected to 'act' but their 'acting' was very much of their own making.

In the late eighteenth and nineteenth centuries, French tradition was maintained in terms of these broad characteristics and emphases. *Régisseurs* were responsible for putting together, in consultation with other key participants, production books to plot out every minute detail to facilitate revivability and durability. In Italy poet-directors, such as Salvadore Cammarano and Franceso Maria Piave, responsible for rehearsing, directing, some aspects of stage-management, costumes and so on were broadly reliant on the traditional stagecraft techniques and practices outlined above. Mozart's librettists took the producer's role if possible in the presentation of his works (for example, Schikaneder for *Die Zauberflöte* and da Ponte for *Don Giovanni*, *Le nozze di Figaro*, and *Così fan tutte*), but Mozart took an active part in the absence of librettist Varesco, in supervising the German translation of the Italian original of *Idomeneo*. The singers however, were left to their own *seria* devices though no doubt Mozart schooled them towards the theatrical effectiveness he held to be so crucial.

Savage (1993: 1118) refers to the writings of Christian Schubart and his Goethean concept of Total Theatre which looked forward to the autocratic theatre-company manager school to reach its zenith in Wagner's Bayreuth but with such forerunners as, as implied, Goethe at Weimar (1791-1817) and Carl Maria von Weber in Prague and Dresden (1813-16, 1817-26). Weber's pursuit of a synthesis of theatrical elements was based on a comprehensive knowledge of them all, including auditioning and employing chorus and soloists for their acting as well as singing abilities and supervising the dramatic read through of libretti so that all understood it and their own particular contribution (if they didn't a *'literator'* was on hand to explain). At the centre of Weber's conception of total theatre was the committed, role living, singer-actor epitomised by Wilhelmine Schröder-Devrient.[9]

With the progressive commercialisation of opera, bureaucratisation of administration, growth in size of theatres and scale of productions, technically improved expertise in all aspects of stagecraft, there is a steady differentiation of specialist roles at all levels and in all departments of the institution. It is with the closing of the museum doors however, that the producer begins to emerge, alongside questioning composers and librettists, as key interpreter of the 'new', politically suspect, and aesthetically dated and familiar.

In earlier chapters I referred to theoretical and practical critiques of opera as genre and sociopolitical institution which emerged after and during opera's 'crisis of realism' including *'dépouillement, Gemeinschaftsmusik, Gebrauchsmusik,*[10] and those of Brecht/Weill. The latter's *Threepenny Opera* is a 'ballad' opera, in 'popular' style for reduced forces and 'singers' primarily actors, most of whom were unable to read music: ('exactly why I was chosen' [Lotte Lenya quoted Willett 1959: 131]), their 'arias' commentaries on a dramatically lucid text, the singers required not to sing melody 'blindly' but to 'kind-of-speak against-the-music' (ibid.: 132), whilst the grander scaled *Rise and Fall of the City of Mahagonny* paid a more 'conscious tribute to the idiocy of the operatic form' (Brecht: 133). Inevitably such critiques, expressed through new works, signalled the need for comparable production and performance critiques for the standard repertoire. Amongst the earliest 'design' critiques were those to emerge in the 1920s at the Bauhaus influenced Kroll Oper, Berlin under Otto Klemperer, which engaged artists such as Dulberg, Moholy-Nagy, Strnad, Schlemmer and Caspar Neher. Other non-representational set design, employed especially in the interpretation of Wagner's works, by such as Max Reinhardt, Alfred Roller, Gustave Wunderwald, Hans Wildemann, Ludwig Sievert and Adolphe Appia, became familiar in German and Austrian houses before the Third Reich cultural clampdown. Elsewhere Stanislavski's Opera Studio productions were modest but innovative models for the post-war work of Felsenstein. For Stanislavski, as a man of the straight theatre, accurate and truthful words clearly enunciated were especially important, leading at times to excision or revision of libretti deemed either irrelevant, too traditional, or too complex for singers to perform and/or audiences to understand. Thus the epic and usually opulent *Boris Godunov* 'needs to be based on dazzling diction ... There is very little staging involved. Everything is based on the words in the phrases' (Cannon 1983: 714). Stanislavski's 'method techniques' downplayed rehearsals in the literal sense of repetition, constant going over of text and music leading to insensitivity to both, rather he sought a probing examination of a work's conceptual (historical, political, emotional) context:

> ... with every performer having an intimate knowledge of the verbal and musical text. He had the music repeated until each performer understood his part within the context of the whole work. A shared relationship with the music was the basis for everything: Not a single superfluous move outside the rhythm of the music' He told Tatyana (*Eugene Onegin*) 'Listen to the overture. Right there your role begins. Your music is there and all the questions you put to life' (ibid.: 717).

He asked his Mimi to write down her life history until the moment she enters Rodolfo's room and to express the *desires* which logically lay behind all her actions. Yet he worked from the score (*La Bohème* Act 2 was broken down into 23 units of bars of music) to develop character's 'objectives'. For example, with regard to Mimi and Rodolfo's first meeting:

> Now what are the principal landmarks in this scene? ... 1. Darkness. You wish to light your candle. This is an easy objective. 2. What would happen then if you had a dizzy spell? 3. Act so that he would not notice that your head is swimming. 4. Relax all your muscles to fall. 5. Look at the divan. 6. Note what the room is like. 7. What sort of young man is this? 8. Study him, this is a whole scene in itself. A whole chapter. And you Rodolfo what are your objectives? 1. Hurry to write your article. 2. The knock at the door. Must get rid of any importunate caller. 3. You see her, wish to look at her closely. 4. She faints, she is ill. You must help. You are now a physician, a nurse. 5. Light her candle. Escort her to the door (quoted in Cannon 1983: 719).

Such techniques clearly require long rehearsal periods and flexible singers, conditions which in international opera rarely occur outside festivals and one reason Peter Sellars gives for his rare productions in mainstream repertory houses (Clements 1995), but such meticulous dissections of popular repertoire pieces such as *Bohème* have become standard preparations in 'the new singing theatre' (Bawtree 1990).

The major post-war momentum for the radical reappraisal of opera production and the advent of the Age of the Producer, derived from post-war German cultural reconstruction: 'As in many areas of thought and cultural expression ... the end of the war marked the beginning of major change, in which virtually every aspect of music was transformed' (Kerman 1985: 20).

> Most of the stages had been destroyed by bombing, scenery and costumes had been burnt and people were sitting muffled up in draughty, unheated auditoria ... it would have been grotesque to revive the traditional illusions associated with opera under these circumstances. The magnificent scenic deceptions put about by opera had vanished along with the vulgar theatrical palaces of the Hitler regime ... It was no longer money or sets which determined the worth of a particular work. People just wanted to see human beings on stage and hear music which would help them carry on (Liebermann 1983: 134-5).

Liebermann describes how this altered the presentation completely, the 'hour for a heightened sense of truth and reality' had come, even the splendour of singers voices took on a secondary role, even the very word opera was used with suspicion, 'Music theatre' preferred indicating that opera should 'be acted as naturally as a stage play' (ibid.: 135),[11] a new generation of singer actors appeared, new works emphasised intelligibly sung dialogue rather than arias, 'the founders of "music theatre" ... on the lookout for artists capable of helping to sweep away the dust and stuffiness of all the clichés traditionally associated with opera' (ibid.: 136).

Important influences on these post-war German developments were Gunther Rennert and Oscar Fritz Schuh, but two centres were especially influential for opera's reconstitution. First, from the first post-war Bayreuth Festival of 1951 Wieland Wagner's 'symbolist cleansing' (de-Nazification) of the Wagnerian canon: 'Bare cyclorama-backed stages, *Die Meistersinger* without Nuremburg, the starkness of the stage ... matched by an equally non-romantic approach to the music' (Hartford: 1979: 14) under the musical direction of, 'Kna' or Knappertsbuch apart, conductors outside the pre-war tradition. Second, the 'ultrarealist' (or 'socialist/realist') style of Walter Felsenstein and the Komische Oper East Berlin and now in somewhat routinized form 'as likely to turn up in Cardiff or Long Beach as Kassel' (Littlejohn 1992: 142). Superimposed, by socio-political necessity, on opera's base requirement: 'The survival of an antiquated, obsolete genre has necessitated renewal in terms of presentation' (Millington 1992a: 1122-9) the innovations of both have been globally influential. From Wieland Wagner we see born out of necessity, a producer severing a specific culture's auratic interpretations, the deployment of universal symbols in place of debased German signifiers. 'Detachment from' and 'interpretive power over', have become the founding defining criteria of 'radical' opera production of 'museum' pieces. The degree to which both are exercised varies considerably, sometimes cynically or ironically, at others chaotic and mystifying, but throughout there is a sense that productions are commentaries on, rather than interpretations of, the works so treated, given to audiences by equal degrees expected to have sufficient knowledge of the originals to recognise the commentaries.

From Felsenstein there has been inherited intricate immersion in works allied to an 'interpretive power over' deployment of socialist-realism, which has in turn blossomed into deconstructionist exercises of a complexity (for example, in the work of Ruth Berghaus[12]), that makes the continuing straightforward separation of these two postwar paradigms and the reduction of the latter back to their socialist origins, hazardous and if possible at all, only through intense additional 'homeworld', not on the opera itself but on philosophies of intertextuality and so on. Despite these differences, both required of their singers dramatic skills and engagement at odds with the pre-war 'star' system. The latter survives to a degree, as we have seen, but singers are now judged by their dramatic as well as vocal skills. Both also require the complete integration of all theatrical elements, especially developed stagecraft, extending the producer's power base from 'power over' the work to overall production control. Other factors contributed to this movement of producer to centre stage. Pre-war opera organisation had been 'ensemble' based, 'stars' attached to companies for whole seasons, singing important supporting as well as lead roles, the rapid expansion of air travel drawing 'stars' out of such commitments towards international careers also important for expanding recording markets. With opera productions increasingly dependent on 'guests' rather than 'residents', a strong theatrical, as well as musical, power was required. Also given the cinematographic and televisual technological developments of the past 50 years, audiences increasingly demanded more of opera as spectacle, so that whether conservative or radical, opera production jostled with musical realisation for dominance. Within such a changing socioeconomic context the dispersal of these originally German innovations in the post war period has had much to do with the training of 'disciple' producers in both centres, professionals with the technical expertise to put their ideas into practice. Underlying the post-war institutional capitulation to producer power however, has been opera's constant requirement for renewal, not in the merely aesthetic sense suggested by Millington, but in the sense of commodity fetishism, opera as an industry, as a market, can only survive through the sale and purchase of the 'new', whether 'new' theatres (studios, arenas), 'new' operas, 'new' stars (singers, conductors, producers, designers), 'new' productions, 'new' scandals. Behind this facade which fetishises the new, opera as auratic art remains firmly in place. Producer Richard Jones comments:

> There are more great plays than operas and because we all know the thirty or so great operas very well the pieces become as much about the idiosyncrasies and imaginations of the men and women who direct them as the composer's imagination. This is a recent historical development and it has to do with the fashion for opera, the commodifying of singers and directors and opera as a sort of late 1980s culture snack. I'm aware of, and have difficulty with, the rather decadent fact that operas written to provoke political passion in the nineteenth century: Verdi's *I Lombardi* and *A Masked Ball*, often only arouse aesthetic passion in twentieth-century productions (Jones in *Opera* 1990: 56).

Wieland Wagner

It is appropriate that post-war producer dominance should in part commence in Bayreuth, for it was there in 1876 with the first Festival that modern opera production was established. Wagner placed great emphasis on improvisation and interpretation in performances in which singers were encouraged (expected) to interact with each other rather than play to the audience, in three dimensional illusionist sets of mood and atmosphere, designed to achieve 'ideal' performance conditions and results, the latter 'ideal' in ways all too open to political exploitation by the *Reichkammermusik* during the 1930s and early 1940s (Lang 1945: Levi 1994: Spotts 1995). Wieland Wagner had to explain and justify his intentions however:

It would be unjust to condemn us, the so-called sceptical generation, as simply destructive. We have seen and experienced things that our fathers and grandfathers were powerless to prevent: acts of destruction which go far beyond human imagining. If one wants to build a new house one must first dig up the ground in which the foundations are to be laid. My generation has been and still is concerned not to luxuriate in aesthetic conceptions as if they were defined immutably for all time, but to seek out the inner laws, inherent in a work of genius and to interpret uncompromisingly as we find it mirrored in our own souls ... (our) scepticism demands that (our artistic tendencies) should keep clear of fixed ideas (quoted in Gollancz 1966: 109-13).

Superficially 'fixed ideas' are what auratic art and the museums which house it depend on, unfixed ideas, producers ideas, by definition arrogant and presumptuous at best, at their worst blasphemies. The fetish of the 'new' is thus for producers and opera houses a tense balancing act. Wagner's Bayreuth *Ring* (1965) earned this response from Gollancz (1966):

The producer must never outrage the musical dramatic intention, the something 'given' in point of either general atmosphere or detail. The producer must never so obtrude his visualities (things seen on stage) as deliberately to focus a preponderance of attention upon them. What opera should aim at is the nearest possible approach to a unity of appeal: but even if this were fully achievable (as it is not), of the elements within such a unity, the music, by reason of its innate kingship, should always be *primus inter pares*, like a flower on a flowering tree ... the music must never be sacrificed to the stage (1966: 51-2).[13]

307

Wagner observed that conventional critics of opera production are rooted in their youthful experiences, and in particular that generation of the 1950s and 60s brought perceptions to the opera house that were 'as though the war had not taken place', TV, radio and film not invented. Not that critics were uniformly hostile: 'The achievement of the new Bayreuth lies in the taking of Wagner's art in an ultimate, fully transcended aspect and actually succeeding in putting it on the stage' (Warrack 1960b: 730), but Warrack thought the Wieland Wagner achievement to be a temporary measure forced upon Bayreuth in 1945, keen to deepen Wagner's German Romanticism ('... all that is most valuable *in heil'ge deutsche Kunst'* [ibid.: 729]), below the purely national associations that the Third Reich had exaggerated. 'In a metaphysical sense Wagner had to go underground. But, and this is the crux of the matter — the completeness of a great work of art is that it should speak to all centuries and all nations from it's own century and nation ...' (ibid.: 732). For conservatives the 'speaking' is primarily done by the music, but this cannot be sufficient for producers seeking to erase or unsettle residual, political but by implication, any lingering established meanings or associations. In the case of post-war Bayreuth the producer's goals were mainly clear to critics and audiences, as 'producer's opera' has not always been since. Even so the first post-war *Ring* left Warrack with an experience later echoed by many audiences: 'One feels oneself at times attending a lecture ... rather than being confronted with the total experience' (ibid.: 736). For Warrack the 'total experience' was unquestionably tied up with the distinctly German feelings, instincts and emotions of the original, their translation into universal symbols sacrificing the unavoidable socio-historical essence which gives them their inner meaning. This tension between enabling audiences to universalise meanings from a 'true' representation of the original and the imposition of an interpretation of the work's 'essence' behind which the original work lurks, has subsequently proved elastic to breaking point.

There is no point in trying to make medieval Nuremberg a universal experience — its charm lies in its very Germanness. Siegfried lies dreaming in a German wood; it is to the Rhine and not 'a large river' that he journeys; Nibelungs and Mastersingers belong to German legend and history and not to the world's; and the *Festwiese* lies outside the walls whose remains still cast a broken ring round the city of Nuremberg (ibid.: 737).

Until hit by Felsenstein graduates, Gotz Friedrich, Joachim Herz, Harry Kupfer and others of the East German school of 'socialist realism', the universalising humanist 'symbolist' style at Bayreuth and elsewhere became a viable means of presenting, hearing and seeing Wagner's works, but to the latter the 'total experience' of Wagner also lay in German cultural history, not the folksy charm of Nuremburg, but its wider capitalist/racist culture. Wieland Wagner's productions may have upset the most conservative opera audience in the world, through their unfamiliar scenic and dramatic styles, but they did not challenge them ideologically, they were not made to politically think about their recent past.[13] Friedrich et al set out to do just that, and with great success. Hartford describes how audiences arriving at the Festpiele for Chereau's nineteenth century industrialising capitalist Ring were given leaflets, encouraging demonstrations, by the *Aktionskreis fur das Werk Richard Wagners e.V* and yet 'I have never seen a *Ring* with so much human emotion' (1979: 17). While the Chereau *Ring* is usually seen as the demarcation line at post-Wieland Wagner Bayreuth, it was preceded by Götz Friedrich's *Tannhäuser* (1972), with frank eroticism which shocked, in the Bacchanale (choreographer John Neumeier), Tannhauser disappeared beneath Venus' skirts for several minutes while she sang with orgasmic pleasure. Like most when new at Bayreuth, the production was greeted with howls of displeasure but became a classic, a 'fate' to also befall Kupfer's *Dutchman* presented as Senta's dream. Senta remained on stage throughout as a furtive obsessively intense persona whose final plunge is more an act of demented suicide than romantically redemptive love.

Apart from the New York Met's attempt to return to Victorian values with its Schenk, Schneider-Siemssen production based on that of Bayreuth in 1897 (Mayer 1989: 659), Wagner's *Ring* is now invariably the site of hyperactive 'energetic resonance'. The 1989 Bayreuth 'ecology' production:

in which the world had been destroyed and nature with it, left only a grey 'rutted' street ... a neon rainbow lit one leg of Valhalla, which the gods ascended in a crane ... the gods wore silver plastic raincoats and Stetsons and carried plexiglass luggage. Donner's plexiglass hammer, an 'art work', perhaps explained why his costume resembled the work of the late German artist Joseph Beuys. Status gave Wotan's family fur lapels, and the left lens of the head god's glasses was blacked out. The Valkyries ride took place on firemen's steps, down which the warrior ladies tiptoed ... Mime's cave looked like a stranded submarine ... Fafner's a tangled mass of cables and half destroyed structural girders ... Hundreds of TV antennae onto which the Norns had strung their rope, occupied the first look at *Götterdammerüng* ... skyscrapers suggested Gibichheim ... teenybopper Rhinemaidens cavorted in the tubes of what seemed an oil-drillng platform. When the immolation smoke began to clear, five groups of yuppies were seen, dressed for cocktails, watching the news on TV screens reporting the strange fire and subsequent flood. A little boy in evening garb led a little girl into the wings with a flashlight, and Alberich ... watched it all from the proscenium (Helme Sutcliffe 1989 40-1).

Jonathan Miller (1991: 25) expresses misgivings about Wagner the man and the social and political thinker, which demand a strong producer's interpretive hand:

Today we don't have a very subtle relationship to (Norse myths) ... so there's got to be a way of transforming them ... I think the Patrice Chereau *Ring*.. was very successful. I'd like to do a *Star Wars* version of it. That is our modem myth (already dated!), and that way I think it would work ... the music for *Star Wars* borrowed so much from Wagner ... It is amazing how many of the figures *in Star Wars* also appear in the *Ring* ... Luke Skywalker is Siegfried. In fact these apparent similarities may have been quite deliberate in creating *Star Wars,* so the thing to do is to exploit that, to make a point of the ripoffs.

Felsenstein

In the long term, as the above comments suggest, the Felsenstein watershed has probably been the more significant and influential, perhaps more so in the sense that with his founding of the Komische Oper in East Berlin in 1947, he established the principles and practise of *musiktheater* from which key disciples flowed. Felsenstein's goal was the painstakingly 'realistic' presentation of repertory operas and operettas, sometimes involving six months of rehearsal within which the vital interrelationship between music and drama was meticulously pursued, so that the score 'becomes a visible and living experience' (Friedrich 1955: 55). As Lord Harewood commented on the opening of the rebuilt Komische Oper in 1967:

> His admirers see him as the man who has most intuitively, insistently, consistently, since the war interpreted through his productions a score of the world's greatest operas. His detractors find the emphasis too firmly on stage happenings and away from musical performance and criticize the singers in his company as often vocally inadequate to their roles (1967: 109).

Götz Friedrich provides a revealing description of Felsenstein's methods:

> The main principle of (his) ... productions is that he does not claim them as being original, or novelties: ... his aim is to remain the servant of the composer and the poet. Accordingly he always takes pains to establish the definite basis and "rhythm" of each opera. with each new production, the temperature of the rehearsals is changed — to each singer he behaves differently, and tries to come to terms with each artist's individuality. Felsenstein demands that the actor himself should feel, think and act in a way that responds to the situation. The truth of the expression is in the music ... only the score can be the basis of the stage production, and ... scenic experiments which originate, not in the score, but in the producer's own vanity, are to be condemned (Friedrich 1955: 49).

Friedrich stresses Felsenstein's humility, experience, responsibility and vocation creative in the highest sense 'which produced an opera company in which neither producer, singer, nor conductor think of themselves as the protagonists; but one in which the composer and librettist reign supreme. Artists were expected to *be* not to perform the actions and emotions of, the characters they portrayed: 'Please don't try to be the Queen (of the Night) ... only try to strive for something that the Queen strives for' (ibid.: 50). Singing is not an end in itself, the singer should hate Sarastro: 'You must not *imagine* that you are hating Sarastro ... you must hate him *actually*, not as a fanciful picture but as a known reality!' (ibid.: 50), and to encourage the singer, Felsenstein took her to the footlights and pointing at the auditorium asked her to imagine that she was seeking to convince a sitting tribunal which she succeeded in doing 'furiously', he then rehearsed time and again the singer's attempt at strangling Sarastro to create the right physical sense of hatred. 'The seizing itself is not important, but the motive of the seizing' (ibid.: 50). Thus singers engaged in exercises beyond the eventual task of performing roles and singing arias, to realise the psychological state of the characters they were (rather than they were playing), to enunciate clearly the text as well as sing it and the music, as they drew on their own emotional reserves and experiences:

> Gradually the singer captured the real physical feeling he required. Then he gave her a new lesson: an evening party, she has come in her gala-gown, set with costly diamonds, to unmask among the assembly the man who has raped her daughter: 'You wish the participants to kill the offender on the spot, therefore you have come, therefore you have dressed so beautifully!' She considered and then began to play: 'You know who it is? There he stands! This vulgar beast — you brute, brute!' (ibid.: 50).

And so, concluded Friedrich, the whole of Felsenstein's *Zauberflöte* is ruled by this sublime *unity of music and text*, a unity which took six months' rehearsal, meticulous application of Felsenstein's complete control to the realisation of the 'concept'. Bawtree (1990) has noted that the validity of this approach is now 'in principle' accepted, but few theatres can afford the rehearsal time, few 'stars' would willingly submit to such training, and the reliance on ensemble often led to illness cancelling performances, rather than hasty replacements (Lord Harewood 1967: 109). Felsenstein rarely worked with 'star' conductors and amongst his singers, though of a high musicianship, great voices were rare. 'His example gave opera producers a Mercedes to drive but did not tell them in which direction to drive it' (Jonas et al. 1992: 16), and commitment to these principles does not mean agreement as to how to put them into practice, how, for example, to interpret and explain the Queen of the Night's motives upon which such rehearsal techniques hinge. For Lord Harewood, Felsenstein's *musical* insight:

sets his performers problems that they find hard to solve, not because his demands are unmusical but because his musical ambition, like Callas', attempts to reveal the composer's thought at its purest and most intense, without compromising with the limitations of technique, without allowing performing art to degenerate to the level of say politics, which has been described as the art of the possible (1967: 110).

Wieland Wagner's and Felsenstein's influence on post-war opera production has been significant in several respects: both asserted the relative importance of drama and text, although it is debatable whether this was at the expense of the music, it was certainly a challenge to the dominance of conductors and the 'star' singer system. Both asserted the producer's dominant role as interpreters, commentators on works (rather than monitors of correct candle placement, cloaks and hats), thus establishing the basis for subsequent drift into what many producers call 'ironic detachment'. The greater the distance from which such commentaries are made the greater the reliance on audiences possession of sufficient knowledge of the original to be able to 'understand' (or be unsettled by) the producer's 'concept' or *idée*. Both sought the 'essence' of works in ways which were likely to be at odds with those of dominant musicological discourses, hence the subsequent bifurcation of musical and production paradigms, the former driven by 'authenticity' the latter by 'political/philosophical insight'. Both, though in different ways and to different effects, were motivated by political ambitions and constraints, Wagner in particular releasing the legitimacy of universalising symbols potentially applicable to all standard repertory works. Both echo the original composer, composer and singer culture as mere 'servants' of the work in question. Both reaffirmed the successful producer's need for specialist technical assistance (set design, costume design, stagecraft and stage technology, lighting, movement, and in part eventually 'miking' and surtitles). Both established an international market for producers with careers comparable to those of singers, and established opera as a museum not necessarily 'safe' for the 'aura' seeking visitor (critics or audiences). Both set in motion a 'producer's opera', which eventually, through what has been called 'postmodern' intertextualisation, has become so apparently detached from the original, it has tended to impose a new élitism of mystified opera knowledge on a laity unable to fully comprehend it.

Producers versus critics

Audiences have been challenged by much 'producer's opera', so too have critics (mere 'kerb-crawlers' and 'pimps' according to Jonathan Miller: Richard Jones is more sanguine: 'Someone's got to do it and it is far better to have a passionate critical forum than none at all' [Jones 1990: 561]). Throughout the 1970s and 80s British critics registered their perplexed conservatism with regularity. Shawe-Taylor (1979: 612) attacked Scottish Opera's *Rigoletto* by the then little known David Alden as 'a tasteless travesty of the work it *pretends* to interpret' (my italics), which opened with:

> an orgy *à la mode,* male courtiers in shiny black leatherette, bare midriffs ... boots. ... spurs ... whips ... the lot. Monterone's daughter had a bald wig, Monterone was strung up on a chandelier ... it does not work, at every end and turn it contradicts the music (another example of) the modem opera schizophrenia of musical authenticity and wanton perverse theatricalism.

Rigoletto, in Britain at least, has received much 'interpretation' but it should be remembered that it suffered 'interpretation' (censored) before its premiere, Verdi originally identifying not the Duke of Mantua but King Francis I as its central debauchee (Rubsamen 1941: 32). Of a Welsh National Opera *Rigoletto:*

> It sometimes seems that the WNO deliberately searches for a producer of a specific opera who has little faith in the work ... And why must these producers come from abroad, usually from behind the Iron Curtain? I think we should be told. Lucian Pintile more or less scuppered *Carmen,* so the management seems to have alighted on the idea of handing him *Rigoletto,* and letting him do his worse with that ... the courtiers (were) drag queens,.. the Duke warmed up for seductions by way of a work-out in terracotta combinations, Rigoletto petted Gilda *unhealthily* in Act I, the latter sat on a pile of coal in Act III and revived from her death throes in Act IV to climb a ladder in white trousers, shirt and boots

314

(my italics) (Blyth 1985a: 824).

Such criticism, resting on xenophobia, 'pretence' at interpretation, lack of faith in the original, suggestive of conspiracies, has been echoed especially outside London where opportunities to regularly see and hear works in the standard repertoire are limited, as is therefore the 'experience/knowledge' residue against which 'radical' interpretations play: '... whether it is the job of a provincial company so often to present distorted ideas is another matter, particularly as this is now the rule rather than the exception' (ibid.: 824). This 'provincial' company has been responsible for several important directorial debuts in Britain: 'Kupfer (*Elektra*), Berghaus 'in a vindictive feminist *Don Giovanni*', Jarevelt in a high-tech *La traviata*, Pintile in the *Carmen* played by guerrillas during a Latin American revolution' (Conrad 1989: 18).

> Please Mr Alden just listen to the score the story of *Ariodante* is domestic and, for its period, simple. There is no magic, no fantasy; just the template opera plot of a frustrated marriage where events keep the lovers apart until they have passed through some crisis that empowers them to build their relationship anew, on more solid ground than sighs and stolen kisses. The three acts have a clear dramatic contour — joy, despair, joy — and the score defines its peaks and troughs. But Alden ... knows better than the score. When the music dances with prematrimonial pleasure at the end of Act I, Alden's production darkly tells the audience it will end in tears. The same thing happens in the *lieto fine* of Act III: on comes a troupe of lunatic refugees from the bedlam scene of *The Rake's Progress* to tell you there's no happy ending after all — just the bruised memory of events which, Alden has decided, witness the abuse of women. Now this is interesting. It makes engrossing theatre and looks good on stage. But its the wrong opera—that is the opera Alden wanted to direct but not the opera Handel wrote: and although such conflicts are potentially invigorating when a piece is known and tired from over exposure, they betoken arrogance in a rarity like *Ariodante* where the fundamentals of the piece are unfamiliar. Alden's killer instincts would be better trained on *La Bohème and Madama Butterfly*. (White 1993: 24).

'Known and tired from over exposure' suggests that the critics

315

constituency is a fairly narrow one. Alden's design and production mannerisms have become readily lampooned as their own strait jacketed convention: modern dress, lavatories, naked light bulbs, tilting rooms, lone chairs 'meaningfully overturned' Louis Quinze for *Ariodante,* sparseness, the 'ticks' of a self promoter: Alden however defiantly accepts that his productions are ...

> ... about self. This is the big problem, with people accusing you of presenting yourself on stage, and not the piece. To me that's what the director's supposed to do, that's his job — a fusion of expressing yourself instinctively with the opera. The opera itself, and my relationship with it, is the most important thing (quoted in Inglis 1993: 35).

His intention is 'to take these pieces and do them in a very personal and vivid way ... these intense music dramas have to have an explosive effect in the theatre, because it is part of the velocity of these scores' (ibid.: 36). He receives brickbats from opera critics he claims because they are essentially *music* critics with a poor sense of the visual and the theatrical, and of opera production. As such they are committed to the ultimate existence of works outside the theatre, textually as well as musically. David Pountney, Director of Productions at the ENO, has also been the target of critical phlegm, even when producing modern works. Paul Driver attacked Pountney for not taking Tippett's symbolism seriously in the ENO production of *The Midsummer Marriage* and for using 'as many additional symbols of his own "flung in like alphabet-vermicelli"'. Pountney has turned an opera remarkable for what Robert Donington terms its "autonomous symbolism" into a one-dimensional frieze like display of random symbols, resembling a producer's lurid dream of Durer's "Melancholia II"' (1985: 826-8). Critics references are thus inclined to climb on each other's shoulders to claim discursive superiority over such upstart practitioners.

Rumbustious, iconoclastic

Pountney, Jonas and Elder defend their regimes' constant questioning and reinterpretation of opera's action and image as lying '... at the heart of the nature of opera itself' (Jonas et al. 1992: 16), but describe the origins of the *Power House* production style as an unexpected consequence of Lord Harewood's attempts to expand the repertoire into non-standard territory at minimum expense through what became known as the Norwest Holst series after it's sponsor (1992: 15).

> The brief of the series was that it should contain rarely performed large-scale works by major composers. *Rienzi* (Wagner), *Mazeppa* (Tchaikovsky) and *Moses* (Rossini) were performed ... the ones that got away were Schubert's *Fierrabras* and Schumann's *Genoveva*. The productions were done on a *very* low budget, the chorus were not required to memorize their music (removing pressure from their crowded schedule) and the shows were not designed to be revived ... The very low budgets meant that anything pertaining to grandeur or spectacle had to be realized in a more or less ironic way, and the lack of the threat of a revival unleashed in Hytner, Alden and Warner a spontaneous and irreverent bravura that made enormous impact. (1992: 15).

The triumvirate described this ENO style as 'rumbustuous, iconoclastic' (borne out by 'nervous reminiscences of chain saws, raked stages, green blood ... chairs' (Milnes 1993a: 73), and different to other contemporary variants of 'interpretive theatre' including the 'highly aesthetic and intellectual deconstruction techniques current in European music theatre' (ibid.: 16). With their producers (Vick, Alden, Albery, Hytner, Jones, Freeman, Pountney himself 'truly polemical and controversial' [Canning 1993a: 782]), the 'lot of controversial productions 'was quite deliberate' (Pountney 1993: 777):

> We believed in opera as a total theatrical experience that demanded a dialogue with an engaged, committed audience ... I have argued all along that the case for 'interpretive' production based on abstract, non-representational design, derives from the nature of music itself (ibid.: 775). Music is abstract. How often can we agree on what a piece of music is about? Yet music is precisely notated, down to the last detail. All good musical performance rests on the tension between the exactitude required simply to carry out these instructions and the creativity necessary to bring them to life (in Jonas 1992: 20). (We wanted) a synthesis of taste to guide our productions (rather than a house style). Without that a

theatre becomes too diffuse: the world wide tendency to acquire productions 'off the shelf' testifies to that (ibid.: 777-8).[14]

For Milnes however, the regime ended in self indulgence (for example, *The Excursions of Mr Broucek* furnished with lots of in-house jokes) and condescension (the sweaty stage-hand adverts 'a conscious and ... condescending attempt to win an imaginary new audience to replace the fuddy-duddy oldsters whose sclerotic reactions were holding up the progress of opera production' [1993a: 783]), towards a shrinking audience, disengaged and alienated by too adventurous programming. Echoing earlier comments by *Opera's* previous editor, Milnes suggested that some of the more wayward productions might, nay should, have been halted at early, economically viable stages, once their clear waywardness had been noted, but similar comments on the lack of superintendent control have been made of other theatres not least the ROH where recent *Les Huguenots, Médée,* and *Il viaggio a Reims* have not reappeared once past the first series of critically badly received performances.

Whatever the disaster however, productions are disposable, the work still there. Action and images have to be reinvested for each production, they are of the moment, subject to the dictates of fashion, and so on and take place on a stage, part of a theatre of the imagination, not imitation. Conservatives, hostile to interpretive theatrical trends tend to be so in terms of fetishised 'realism' or 'suburban naturalism', what should Amelia wear in *Ballo,* how should Brünnhilde dress? Dennis Arundell might have some precise answers but most in the audience surely do not, and yet no theatrical performance can be 'real' or 'natural', especially of the most artificial, opera, where characters sing, must act in ways that enable them to sing, express their sung feelings through actions inevitably liberated into larger than life statements of themselves. 'Modernization' appears to be a common problem. Miller, who claims that his 'interpretation' probes works from a psychological rather than political or emotional perspective: 'the music is the most important inspiration ... because it's the dramatic diction of the work' (Loney 1991: 21), comments:

If we modernize everything, it's simply like tourists going from the United States to France — and insisting on eating hamburgers. We go to other places and ... other times — to experience the difference ... I'm very much opposed to the idea of transposing (Mozart's) operas to modern times. Mozart doesn't work that way ... you simply cannot be a *Theater-schlepper* packing a work of art in a truck and driving it two centuries up the freeway. That not only patronizes the audience but it's also an example of what T S Eliot calls 'overvaluing our own times'. The danger ... is that what the artist intended becomes distorted or falsified in the desperate attempt to make the work 'relevant' (quoted in Loney 1991: 21).

Desperation is also a relative concept. Miller observed that although one might have some reason and excuse for altering the period of *The Magic Flute*, as he did with his Scottish Opera production set at the time of its composition, generally 'one can't reasonably or interestingly do it on operas composed before about 1820. Up to that time there are really only two periods chosen by composers: the remote biblical or mythical past in order to be serious, heroic and grave, or their own period in which to be satirical, comic and realistic' (ibid.: 18). The three Mozart-Da Ponte operas *(Così, Figaro* and *Don Giovanni)* are of the latter type:

... absolutely, explicitly set in their period ... the intervening 2000 years is left scrupulously unexploited and unoccupied so there's a simple — one might say a semiotic — distinction there. And you would be unwise not to pay attention to the reason for setting it in remote antiquity or the eighteenth century. After about 1820, these intervening 2000 years are promiscuously colonized, and colonized without any semiotic significance: there's no particular reason for setting *Anna Bolena* in the sixteenth century, other than that the story happens to take place then. There's no particular reason for *Rigoletto* being in sixteenth-century Mantua other than the fact that that's when it nominally seems to have taken place, but it makes no difference to the music nor the dramatic genre of the work ... It's pantomime history. The Gonzaga world which *Rigoletto* nominally refers to was quite unlike Verdi's version of it. I mean anyone who thinks that these things are really from the sixteenth century is historically an ignoramus and that unfortunately is what most of the critics who complain about it are. They are loosely anchored in this Madame Tussaud past for the purpose of using an exotic tableau, and since they are so

319

loosely anchored there is less constraint about moving them. It may sometimes be best of all to put them in the period in which they were written or, if necessary, to shift them forward to a period in which they have a more energetic resonance (Miller 1992: 18).

Madame Tussaud past or *haute couture* present? Despite his erudite prognostications Miller in 1995 drove *Così* up the freeway and straight into the Armani collections at Covent Garden. Several newspapers sent opera and fashion critics along, the *Guardian*'s latter 'was full of praise for the apparel but thought the opera "rather silly"' (Loppert 1995: 267). Miller is a theatre director as well, as are most of the new school of producers, and their theatre backgrounds leave them ill-prepared for, and impatient with, opera in most of its institutional aspects: '... it's like being an anthropologist, examining some alien tribe. I try to communicate with these opera singers and their customs, but they remain alien creatures, and I am not of their world' (Deborah Warner 1992: 12-15). Warner was disconcerted by how opera works: 'It's just miraculous that every performance doesn't sink into catastrophe ... why aren't there any previews? I haven't gone from a dress rehearsal to a first night since I was in a school play. I'm not sure I should be here at all' (ibid.: 12). In certain areas of the repertoire especially, straight directors step at their peril as Terry Hands discovered after his Covent Garden *Parsifal* (1979) 'fiasco' (Hirst 1979: 548), *Opera* critic Warrack berating him for never even having seen a Wagner opera let alone produced one prior to this 'disaster'(Warrack 1979: 605). Bill Bryden received similar brickbats for his succeeding ROH *Parsifal* (1989), also for not having seen a production or having heard all the music. He set *Parsifal* in a 1940s West Country community who mount their own production wearing cardigans and waistcoats and with 'the women looking like throwbacks to Celia Johnson' (Bryden 1990: 62). Nuria Espert observes: 'In opera, unless you are a traitor to the music, you are much less free than you are in the theatre ... in opera the director's role is to hear the composer's indications for the *mis en scène* and translate his music into images. Some of my colleagues may not be happy with this definition, but I think this is our real role' (Matheopoulos 1991b: 24), a 'real role' disputed by some and by others accepting it is not one they are prepared to tolerate. Sellars for example:

One of the exciting things about opera is that you have more information than in any other imaginable art form, because music is so imprecise. It's very hard for straight theatre to get beyond 'a table is a table', whereas in opera clearly everything is a metaphor; music insists on the immateriality of the world (quoted Clements 1995: 1262-63).

But unless the music is completely rescored, there are material and metaphorical constraints surely? Peter Stein, another WNO coup (*Otello* 1986 and *Falstaff* 1989) like Peter Brook renounced opera after an initial skirmish with stubborn singers and obstructive administrations. Bayreuth offered him its centennial *Ring* but when Stein proposed a digest version of two and a half hours 'to ensure the drama wasn't submerged by music', the job went to Chereau (Conrad 1989: 19). When Stein did undertake a *Ring* he got no further than *Das Rheingold* when Theo Adam, the Wotan, refused to don his tuxedo. 'The singers showed me how they'd done it for the last hundred years'. He told them 'OK do it that way', and decided that 'habit-ridden opera had no use for directors who want to explore motives, and recreate the drama. "It is impossible ... in Berlin in 1984 to motivate people in the opera to do real theatrical work"' (Conrad 1989: 19). Stein suspected the problem went deeper, lying in the very notion of music drama. Drama depends on improvisation, music is preordained by the notes in the score. How can actors respond as the emotional situation requires if they have to hasten on in obedience to the musical measure? For *Otello* WNO offered Stein a cast with no preconceived ideas and a three month rehearsal period. The alliance of Verdi and Shakespeare intrigued because of the distance between their theatrical forms, between the Renaissance arena and the illusionism of the nineteenth century opera house, whilst both are derived from Greek theatre:

In *Otello* he found a way of representing this complex history on stage: in his conception the opera happened simultaneously in Verdi's 19th century, Shakespeare's Renaissance and classical Greece, which the Renaissance had rediscovered. Iago was a Victorian pantomime devil, playing with curtains of infernal red, yet the boxed set (opening onto a foamy sea) copied the ideal town plans of Renaissance architecture, while the chorus functioned as the judicial voice of the community, as it does in Greek plays, and the moral ground of the drama, reconvening to witness Otello's collapse at the end of the third act and his death at the end of the fourth (Conrad ibid.: 20).

As for his approach to the singers, 'Stein dreamed of a performance in which the tenor would genuinely imperil his voice in the service of the drama: "The singing stops, and the rest is sighing or animal cries, or silence"' (ibid.: 20). Not surprisingly, few 'stars' will imperil their voices or careers in such service to drama.

Producer/designer

Contemporary opera producers tend to work closely with regular designers on a production's development. Alden's frequent designer is David Fielding, he comments: 'My primary relationships have been with designers ... more than singers, more than conductors' (Inglis 1993: 35), indeed the division of roles is no longer clear cut to Alden: 'Most directors who have become famous have a real vocabulary of movement. They have a visual choreographic and design style, and an instantly identifiable use of shapes and colours. Directors need all that for very personal productions of classics' (ibid.: 35), and designers move for similar reasons into producing (in 1994 Fielding directed *Capriccio* for Garsington Manor's summer outdoor festival), though rarely successfully:[15] 'As with most designers turned producer (Erich) Wonder's lack of Meaningful movement was either filled out by gags or visual effects...' (Sutcliffe *Ormindo* Hamburg 1984: 907). Despite their experience of creating hostile responses in audiences 'We weren't ever preparing to alarm or shock anybody' (quoted in Milnes 1988a: 1290), Alden and Fielding claimed growing ENO audience support: 'There's been a stylistic change in types of opera production, not just in ours ... We happen to have come along at a little historical moment ... following in the footsteps of a huge wave of similar productions in Europe' (ibid.: 1290). Once their first collaboration, the Scottish Opera *Rigoletto* (1980) referred to above, had attracted so much scandalised attention they believe that audiences were thenceforth scripted to expect and experience the same. Their combative subversive approach is justified on grounds that:

322

... one's still essentially dealing with works from the past, and dealing with something that until recently was tied to establishment areas within society, something that has usually spoken to an élite, whether an aesthetical élite or a social one, and even now when you're doing opera you're talking to a certain definable audience. You're also dealing with works of art from the past. When you're directing a piece written in 1883, there's a whole world-view that the piece was expressing and confronting and supporting or attacking, but nonetheless it's about a certain age. When you do it 100 years later in another age for another audience, half of you inevitably has to be extremely ironic and detached from the work, because of the implications of how the world has changed and because of the irony of doing a piece which is based on a musical harmony that was part of the world then and is absolutely, sadly and interestingly, not part of the world now (ibid.: 1291).

Thus inevitably distanced, at least in part, a degree of detachment and ironic voyeurism are necessary. Confrontational productions ensue, especially through the use of minimalist designs, which seek to express the music through reference to its visual equivalents. As with Sellars, Alden and Fielding have, somewhat similar, 'design tics' (ibid.: 1294): for *Macbeth* 'the wonky bedstead (here sticking out of a wall 15 feet up), a baritone in vest and braces, slouch hats, suits, costumes ... all spanning the centuries and set within walls that tilt vertiginously' (Milnes 1990b: 646), strip lighting, restless lighting, overturned chairs, the reductive use of large strange symbols such as the giant hand in *Boccanegra*. Alden claims that producer/designers are re-presenting themselves each time they mount a production: 'one is essentially painting one's own painting over and over again ... you're dealing with your own inner landscape ...' (quoted in Milnes 1988a: 1294), precisely the kind of comment which angers traditionalist critics who feel the producer/designer's landscape takes precedence over the wor ks. The opera producers praised by Alden and Fielding: Berghaus, Chereau, Kupfer are 'essentially de-constructing ... alienated from the ground out of which those pieces grew' (ibid.: 1294). However both accepted that from their predominantly middle class audiences (all three in this conversation misapplied the term *bourgeois* for middle class), the general response to their poems that are collections of images 'which are all very specific and blend together into a whole rather mysterious event' (ibid.: 1296), was rational rejection rather than the emotional acceptance sought. Milnes' concern is that at certain moments the audience is forced to respond in anger, mystification, laughter, confusion, to such a degree that they stop listening to the music. Alden responds: 'I don't like homogeneous things on stage. I think they're boring, and I don't like a production that is a perfectly pasteurized event' (ibid.: 1297). Milnes does, however, expect to understand what is presented to him, not unreasonably if *not* understanding leaves him and others unable to concentrate on what follows. In the Elder/Pountney/Laziridis *Macbeth:* 'The only design idea I didn't quite grasp was the tableau of naked people (models) sitting in the shrubbery; something to do with Birnam Wood I suppose, but momentarily disconcerting in an evening whose effects were otherwise spellbindingly clear' (Milnes 1990b: 646). The onus on critics to now convey to readers production as well as musical details and sense is often beyond them. Despite Milnes' doubts in this interview, by the time he had witnessed Covent Garden's John Cox directed *Capriccio* of 1991, updated to the time of composition and dominated by the clothes of couturier Gianni Versace as a vehicle for Te Kanawa and the international brigade, they had evaporated:

> In the past I have loved Strauss's last opera with indecent fervour ... and often ... admired Cox's way with it, but.. I was bored, irritated and impatient, and I felt I never wanted to see it again. That's putting it too strongly, but I would like a year or two off and then a completely fresh look at the piece, by Harry Kupfer say, or David Freeman, set in Hitler's bunker in 1944 over Kaffee and Kuchen, or — shock horror, sensation — set in a chateau near Paris at the time of Gluck's reforms in the 1770s. Now that *would* be something ... (Milnes 1991a: 269).

Richard Jones who has been instrumental in bringing the Brothers Quay into the opera house (*The Love of the Three Oranges* [with scratch 'n sniff cards] at Opera North/ENO in 1990, Tchaikovsky's *Mazeppa* for the Bregenz Festival/Amsterdam 1991, *Un ballo in maschera* Stuttgart 1991) also claims that directors have got to like designers (but presumably not dress designers): 'they've got to be literate and let you do a lot of the designing — as you must let them do some of the directing so that the relationship becomes 'seamless and you don't know where one person's work begins and the other's ends' (1990: 56).

It is presumably because producers do not have the complete 'czar' like power they are credited with that some establish and work within their own companies. Stein is one and Peter Brook another. Some feel that producers like Brook subvert opera through their somewhat anti-opera productions and the notoriety their own status gives them. Milnes commenting on the telecast of Brook's *Carmen* stated:

> The main point of interest is the hype, the process by which a minor happening in a suburban theatre in Paris has been blown up into an event of world shattering significance and, even worse, accepted as such ... Brook sadly out of touch with current developments is unable to separate Bizet's *Carmen* from old-fashioned performance styles. Opera has never been in the business of detachment...' (1984a: 570-1).

Well it obviously is now. On the other hand the whole ethos of big-house opera remains anathema to some producers, even those who occasionally work in them, such as David Freeman of Opera Factory (quoted in Clements 1989d: 1299):

> I don't think you can just drop in a lot of ingredients as large opera houses by and large do ... You only have to look around and see the result — something bad comes out nine times out of ten ... and your talking about megabucks ... go to Hamburg, Paris, Covent Garden, the Met, La Scala, and see the same travelling circus of tired old performances rammed together — a production equals a set of costumes and that's all it is — and sometimes they're even praised for being 70 years old. It's museum art taken to its logical conclusion.

'You ain't seen nuttin' yet'

Defence of 'radical' productions through intertextual reinterpretations of works is all very well, but as with so much musicological analysis, what is usually forgotten is that opera is an institution, theatres and companies have traditions, audiences who pay and who must be retained, indeed opera's audiences are in several senses retainers of a certain age and outlook. The ENO's *Power House* 'rumbustious, iconoclastic' style aroused tensions around the use of subsidies, disrespectful attitudes to works, the company's origins (Sadlers Wells/Lilian Baylis) and 'loyal' audiences who, to an extent, feeling betrayed, took their loyalty elsewhere. The works do not exist in any absolute original sense but when intertextuality extends to a similar perspective on opera houses, opera audiences, then it does so at it's peril, for specific theatres and their audiences are part of the 'live' experience. Thus the impact of Alden and Pountney at the state subsidized relatively cheap broad audience based ENO differs distinctly from that of a Sellars or a Deborah Warner at the most élite, privately funded, Glyndebourne Festival. It was in 1990 that Sellars produced *Die Zauberflöte* at the latter, eliciting the first booers to grace the Festival. Glyndebourne knew what to expect from the already (in)famous Sellars: 'Hang around, oh timorous UK readers given the vapours by Alden- 'n Fielding ... or the work of quaint old fashioned David Freeman, you ain't seen nuttin' yet' (Milnes 1989c: 11), that is his American Mozart/Da Ponte trilogy at the PepsiCo Summerfare at Purchase New York State in 1989e.[16] *The Marriage of Figaro* set in Trump Tower where the Almavivas have a penthouse, Figaro is their chauffeur. Cherubino sings *'Non so piu'* 'whilst humping' his mattress, and the Act I chorus are Trump's office staff presenting their employers with Christmas gifts and so on, Don Giovanni is a drug addict/dealer/rapist in Harlem, Donna Anna a wealthy white woman buying heroin to 'shoot up', Don Ottavio a local police officer, Giovanni's palace an all night disco, the Don and Leporello played by twin black singers Eugene and Herbert Perry; *Così* set in Despina's Cape Cod Diner where Don Alfonso is, as the programme noted, 'a Vietnam veteran having trouble holding on'. His hiring must therefore have been to elicit the response the production largely received. Sellars accepts such opportunities for political as well as aesthetic reasons:

> I think one's task is to engage with every element of this society. And to me that means Glyndebourne as much as street theatre in East Los Angeles. If you're not addressing the power structure then you're leaving a major part of the world unaddressed, and the opportunity to work at Glyndebourne and Salzburg, and through Salzburg to address people who can afford $400 a ticket is

very important because if you don't get to them, nothing's going to happen. If it's any consolation I think I'm as hated in the streets of Los Angeles. I don't do any of this to win a popularity contest (quoted in Clements 1995: 1260-61).

Sellars' credo on opera production is gleaned from programme notes: 'What the audience sees is more important ... than what it hears, because we think in images' (Littlejohn, 1992: 132); 'That a system of contemporary references is an essential ingredient to the functioning of these pieces seems relatively obvious' (Milnes 1989e: 11). For Milnes, 'wonderfully designed' (by Lobel for *Così* and *Figaro* and Tsypin for *Giovanni)*, competently sung, these totally gripping theatrical experiences were 'dangerously persuasive', dangerous because the sung Italian was at odds with what occurred on stage, Sellars' programme plot lines being the productions' *idées fixe* rather than those inherent to their libretti. 'It is better then that words are not understood' (ibid.: 12). The productions presented Sellars trademarks: visible stage machinery as part of the sets, dramatic fighting shifts, circus-like *coups de théâtre*, the use of contemporary symbolic props such as ball-point pens, Big Macs, machine guns, dramatic pauses in music and action, precisely choreographed and stylised movement — crawling, heads sticking out of floor traps, the use of arias as intense releases of nervous energy (Mozart is already full of conceits, women singing that they hate the man they really love, or vice versa, to add others such as Donna Anna's *coloratura* outburst at the close of *'Non mi dir'*, due to a heroin injection 'strained directorial deceits' [Littlejohn 1992: 148]), arias sometimes substituted for the correct ones to be in accord with Sellars' interpretive vision, performed by singers self-consciously not engaging with audiences, by facing away or to the wings, in short subversion of the music and texts from which the performances were drawn.

The *Flute* at Glyndebourne, set against photographic backdrops of Californian freeways, townscapes, filling station, sun-drenched beaches in 1950s B-movie technicolours, Tamino was a junkie, Sarastro the guru of a post hippy cult. The spoken dialogue was replaced by brief cryptic words and comments projected onto a screen bisecting the stage, not sub- or sur- but mid-titles. Some critics welcomed 'The invitation to Sellars (as) a stroke of genius that will delight all but a few prejudiced old buffers. It sets a new standard for Mozart at Glyndebourne'(Sutcliffe 1990: 52), most were hostile:

'probably the flattest, laziest, emptiest piece of work in festival history' (Loppert 1990b); 'An evening of crashing terminal boredom' (Canning 1990); 'not ... outrageously novel but ... everything about the production is so pathetic' (Henderson 1990). Apart from Sutcliffe: 'The keynote of the production is an unfussy simplicity, right through to the final scene', Michael Kennedy also responded positively 'I found myself unexpectedly moved and entranced'.[17]

Sellars, more than most, exposes the greatest tension in 'radical' production techniques, the setting may be changed relatively easily, the musical original or convention may not be known to audiences when they hear arias out of sequence, or from quite different works, but if they understand the words sung, how are they to make sense of contradictory actions? The answer is anti-text, usually through performance in the original language but with surtitles drawn not from the libretto but the producer's production. For his Chicago *Tannhäuser* (1989), which opened in a seedy Las Vegas motel Venusberg and in which Tannhäuser was a televangelist the surtitles consisted of three different translations each in a different colour: white for more or less literal translations of the original libretto, blue for quotes from various contemporaries of Wagner and red for 'raunchy interpretations of Wagner's own subliminally sexy text' (Samachson 1989: 431). When the three Mozart productions were broadcast on television in 1991 they were given Sellars' own subtitles: 'a slangy phrase, or sentence if one is lucky ... threadbare, not just musically but intellectually' (Clements 1991a: 614).

Sellars' 'system of contemporary references' is apparently somewhat casually arrived at. Adrienne Lobel, designer for the Glyndebourne *Flute* describes how, on a recent trip to Thailand, Sellars had seen a group of travelling actors. 'They used really cheap theatricality — bright lights, simple back drops, without big effects ... (there was) ... a fascinating incongruity between the ancient and the "tacky" modern' (Clarke 1990: 54). Lobel continued: 'We saw that LA has the "tropical" quality of Egypt and is also very remote culturally from Sussex! It is rather what Egypt would have been for eighteenth century Vienna. Having made that decision all the other elements fitted into place'. Lobel hates LA, grew up in New York, and now lives in Britain so: '"the incredible reality of AMERICA" that she creates on stage in fact has a rather ironical detachment' (ibid.: 54). But this is not simply updating: 'My productions are never updated ... I hate updatings as a gambit ... it's cheap and vulgar ... obnoxious and not to the point' (Sellars quoted in Littlejohn 1992: 142), rather he is 'juxtaposing cultures', setting up 'visual counterpoints' to the music to 'stimulate the greatest possible intensity and range of response', without obliging either actors or audiences to think their way into another century, instead he recasts works in their 'image language' or 'systems of reference'. The intention is not to update but to test or reflect the present against the works of another age, thereby arriving at the core of the work 'the character's emotional plights as revealed in the score ... I believe very strongly that the point of the theatre is to make people notice the present. Most people go to the theatre to escape the present' (ibid.: 142). Fine, except that political correctness now frequently protects audiences from unpalatable but nevertheless core elements in some works:

> ... what about Monostasos, the villainous black servant of Sarastro, who does try to rape the beautiful and fair Pamina ... ? "Of course there are now racial problems which make it difficult to do certain operas, and indeed certain plays. It is very hard to manage Monostasos. It's also hard to do *The Merchant of Venice* ... Today there are all sorts of problems which could not have been anticipated when these operas and plays were created, so we have to find ways of doing them without gratuitously offending the audience. I sometimes think it's quite a good idea to offend an audience — but not gratuitously (Miller quoted in Loney 1991: 23).

So 'offending the audience' in some ways is acceptable, in others it is not.

Producer versus producer

The debate about opera production in Britain became finely and furiously focused with Moshinsky's article 'Verdi: a pox on post-modernism' in *Opera* (October 1992). Moshinsky is not a conservative, but he is less of an 'interventionist' than many. He has expressed his perspective on opera production in various pieces, for example regarding *Tannhäuser* he has warned about making it 'a mere historical pageant ... a performance of the stage directions, not of the inner spirit of the opera. We know what Wagner's intentions were but I don't think they are artistically valid any more' (1984:

963).[18] Moshinsky claimed that he adhered to the Wieland Wagner maxim that, in the age of Matisse and Picasso, one couldn't adhere to the visual taste of Wagner. 'Fidelity to a composer, not maintaining the letter of their instructions but the spirit of the opera drawn from some essential dramatic thread inside. In order to make works live for the audience and artists' (ibid.: 967-8). All producers presumably have this as their goal, but over ten years later Moshinsky had become wary of more extreme manifestations of production. Stating his credentials as a producer who has 'fallen in love with the operas of Verdi.' (ibid.: 1164), he expanded thus:

> His operas have the pulse of feeling and far transcend the operatic conventions which they use to express their ideas. The most extraordinary aspect of Verdi's output is its range. He is not only a composer concerned with the expression of passion in dramatic form. he is also a wide-ranging thinker who used the rather crude forms at his disposal to dramatize ethical and social questions. Verdi was a moral philosopher and realist of great perception (ibid.: 1164).

For Moshinsky Verdi's importance was as an operatic chronicler of the emergent post-Napoleonic capitalist society (Kimbell 1991), addressing politics explicitly (*Simon Boccanegra, Don Carlos*) socio-sexual values such as adultery (*Stiffelio, Un ballo in maschera*) sexual exploitation (*Rigoletto*) and prostitution (*La traviata*), as they impinged on family life. For Verdi the 'direct and almost artless presentation' of the human condition employing 'long narrative, multi-plot structures, easily achieved verisimilitude of character, the epic and humanistic point of view' (ibid.: 1164) was rooted in a historicism only at times apparently subverted by arbitrary changes in the setting of an opera 'to the most ludicrous' epoch, in order to circumvent censorship, and by 'his attempt to heighten dramatic conflict ... (by resorting) to the most unbelievable coincidences ("you mean you burnt the wrong baby?")'.[19]

For Moshinsky, contemporary solutions to the problems of presenting these works ironically through 'the use of expressionism and surreal post-modernists is at one with other artistic developments, the pressure is on us to '... treat the great works of the past ... from a new and oblique angle. We should "quote" them, not involve ourselves in their great emotions. Modern theatre productions now aim at deconstructing the past: we should treat the classics as familiar cultural icons which can be taken apart and reassembled in new forms. We should keep an ironical distance between them and us. Perhaps we should even debunk them' (ibid.: 1165). Thus the music 'kept as a sort of live sound-track' becomes divorced from stage spectacles which are critical commentaries on the 'stupidity, of all those tired old Italian opera devices ...' (ibid.: 1164) The aesthetic goal is greater relevance for the (post)modern audience: 'The true modern producer, then declares his distance from the past and aims to reform the operatic stage by debunking its narrative methods' (ibid.: 1164).

For Moshinsky however, the dilemma is that of someone wishing to engage others 'directly' with Verdi's liberal realism: 'Why are directness, clarity, truth and simplicity not fashionable in Verdi production? Must these virtues be considered inherently "culinary"?' (ibid.: 1166). He was not advocating a return to the worst kind of traditional routine, wherein even so the kinds of extraordinary creative characterisations such as those by Callas and Gobbi were still able to shine, but rather a return to the direct experience of realism, and it seemed, in general performance terms to operatic conventions, away from the colonising performance 'self-conscious' conventions of the non-lyric stage, experimental theatre, film, television and so on, the 'steeply raked stage' 'whereon the opera can be presented as if in quotation marks' (ibid.: 1167). Blind traditionalism was not what was being advocated. Visconti's *La traviata* at Covent Garden changed the date of the opera to that of its composition and set it in 'unrealistic' black and white, but Visconti sought the heart of the drama, not to deliberately effect irony. Moshinsky advocates a return to the dominance of the singer, characterisation, action, dramatic situation, and away from the alienating commentaries of designers and producers 'forced to remind the audience of (their) presence' (ibid.: 1166).

... the time has come for a 'post-ironic' approach to production. this is the way to rediscover and reveal the human richness in Verdi's operas ... symbolism and post-modernism, imposed from the outside are antipathetic to the very core of Verdi's work. The time has come to turn away from conceptualism to something altogether more human and performance-friendly (ibid.: 1168).

331

Pountney responded vigorously (1992b): 'why should he have a complex about doing what he believes in?' Moshinsky had a successful career of several Covent Garden productions generally well received by critics: 'So what is his problem?'. His terms of reference and motives are unclear: 'I don't think I have ever seen a "postmodern" production of a Verdi opera, and I am not sure I would know if I had', but he then proceeds to defend Alden's productions at the ENO of *Simon Boccanegra* and *A Masked Ball* as getting 'so close to the powerful heart of a genius like Verdi' (ibid.: 1394). Neither were concerned with irony, but with the release of raw emotional intensity in his performers which 'drives them towards a miraculous reinvention of high melodramatic style'. He conceded that Alden's *Boccanegra* had been 'wildly controversial' but that it 'so faithfully captured Verdi's emotional aesthetic' (ibid.: 1394). Nor is a raked stage a device for irony, but a means for projecting the performers and their emotional expressions directly towards the audience, heightening the sense of danger, 'of vertiginous excitement, and hence the visceral communication of emotion, which is at the heart of Verdi's work, and which is the very opposite of irony' (ibid.: 1395). Verdi's works are not realistic in the historicist sense of traditional costume dramas with logical linear narratives, rather they are made up of sequences of vividly etched melodramatic incidents. They seem absurd when presented as realistic narratives, this is why Verdi's plots are so often the butt of silly jokes. 'If you approach them with the expectation of a well-made drawing room play, of course they seem absurd' (ibid.: 1395). Pountney finished with a flourish pointing out that conservative productions need not however be bland: 'Strehler's *Boccanegra* wasn't, nor was Stein's *Otello*. Achieving a production like that would cure Elijah's pox in a trice!' (ibid.: 1395).

Critic Sutcliffe also took up cudgels against Moshinsky, reminding him that he had been a dealer in Brechtian alienation earlier in his career and that he now aimed to be the poor man's Visconti, or the intellectuals' John Copley.[20] Verdi's interest was in the human condition because of the musical and dramatic process which engenders it rather than because of their historic realism. Sutcliffe however, unlike Pountney, appeared to understand the meaning of post-modernism: 'Post-modern architecture is certainly a witty gloss on utilitarian commercial principles. But quotation, borrowing, intended syllogism, have long been part of the creative artistic process. Is not adaptation, owning and transferring to a new context what another has created, the essence of performance?' (1992: 1395). Nor do productions which employ postmodernist irony result in alienated objectivity amongst their audiences, on the contrary they are but different means towards the same goal, the representation of the work's emotional force. He asks then a question which casts more doubt on the meaning of Post-modernism: 'Is not "totalkunstwerk" an inherently postmodern phenomenon? Sung dialogue, monologue and ensemble do not portray accurately the process of human discourse, but the resolution which is its outcome. Rather than mimicking normal communication, they confirm passionate currents below the surface. The greatest benefit of combining music and words on the theatrical stage is the varied and often quixotic associative potential of the mixture' (ibid.: 1396). So opera, arguably *the* art form of the modern era, locked behind its museum doors, becomes the ultimate postmodern artefact in the hands of the redeeming producer, who against the 'neutral approach with bland stars seriously under-directed in a decorative, historically correct environment ... illuminate the meeting-point between the present day context and received music and drama which is the essence of live theatre — and therefore of opera' (ibid.: 1396).

Not in North America it isn't – apart from Speight Jenkins in Seattle, Peter Hemmings in Los Angeles, John Crosby in Santa Fe and David Gockley in Houston, 'otherwise American audiences and practitioners in opera lack vision' (Zambello quoted in Ellison 1992: 43). It is also largely a matter of economics: 'This is a production (Met 1989 *Aida*) that has to last fifteen to twenty years. We have to present Verdi's *Aida* not invention. Inventions are fine for three or four years, but the only thing that is going to last is a clear presentation of the story, dramatic interaction of the characters. It has to be clean, powerful' (Sonja Frissell quoted in Paolucci 1989: 15). In such houses, when risks are taken in production, the conceits become permanent embarrassments if costs are to be maximised. The Met's Ponnelle *Der fliëgende Höllander* (1979) which showed it as the Steersman's dream, the Steersman and Erik sung by the same tenor, and was greeted as a 'grotesque perversion' by Patrick J. Smith, *Opera*'s critic, for it made 'the characters/opera peripheral, puppets in a dream world ... thought and human emotions banished, no sacrifice, redemption, transfiguration ...' and so on, was still being revived in 1994. As Smith said after the première: 'Since the production is meant to be shared between San Francisco and New York we are condemned to traffic in this baggage for as long a period as the Dutchman was condemned to sail the seven seas' (ibid.: 585). Zambello's 'deranged' *Lucia di Lammermoor* at the Met was also badly received. It started with an initial vista of apparently literal Scottish mist and moors but succeeding scenes become increasingly unrealistic 'visually tracing' the gradual disordering of Lucia's world, 'the disintegration of her mind. Even the natural elements seem corrupted, so her water becomes blood, stones become tombs and are seen at increasingly skewed angles, as if they're sinking into a marsh' (Ellison 1992: 44). Zambello's reasoning is of the 'retrospective imposition of Freudianism' on pre-Freudian culture school.

> We're going after the mood and feeling of the piece more than the specific historical period. We've taken our cue from the music, from the high romantic climate surrounding Donizetti when he wrote *Lucia*. We've tapped into the watercolors of Victor Hugo, the reverse photo imagery of Simon Marsden and, perhaps most of all, the hallucinatory atmosphere of Edgar Allan Poe. You see *Lucia* is not just this quaint family drama set in a picturesque Scotland. It's primarily a story of psychological terrorism set in the subconscious (ibid.: 44-6).

Zambello, on being called a 'deconstructionist', responds: 'That's just a fancy postmodern term for "reexaminer"' (ibid.: 45), and Miller too hints that much 'radical' producer rhetoric is less dramatically new than some would have us believe: 'I don't think there's such a thing as post-modernism. It's simply a name for what's happened in the last ten years' (Loney 1991: 21), but Zambello does deconstruct:

> All it means is that I like to take a piece of work apart, like when you were a kid and took a toy apart to see what was in it and how it worked ... My job is to tell a story in the clearest way possible. But 'clear' and 'literal' are not the same animal. Opera is a stylized art form and we Americans are caught up in literalism. When we try to make opera realistic, try to make it function like a TV situation comedy, we fail it ... Ultimately it has to be the psychological landscape that has to be realistic, not the pictorial

one. Directing standard repertory, you have to spend half your time stripping away preconceptions (quoted in Ellison 1992: 46).

As well as a 'deconstructionist' Zambello is tagged a 'feminist': 'What I'm trying to do as a director is challenge people to take a closer, fairer look, at these great female opera characters. So much of the power and popularity of opera is based on these incredible women, but ironically we have locked them into this nineteenth century helpless-victim role' (ibid.: 46). In one sense this is a curious remark for if after one strips away the preconceptions of a piece, take apart the toy, and find a typical nineteenth century heroine as victim what is your responsibility as a producer? Reveal this victimisation in a psychological landscape of relevance to today's audience or, because one ideologically rejects that this be so, reconstruct the heroine as someone other than a victim, rather than reexamine? In contemporary debates about opera production this would appear to be the very fine line between protagonists fighting over the property rights of producers and their great power in the institution. For Zambello like all theorists, whether study-bound or stage active: 'The operas that interest me most are the ... *Gesamtkunstwerks* where words, music, ideas and action combine to trace a spiritual journey' (ibid.: 47).

Alden relates how the creative process, which starts with the producer and designer some two years before performance, is not just a process of ideas, but also one of budgets and deadlines with the rehearsals when they commence, 'intuitive' (Inglis 1993: 35) in a context of elaborately planned staging:

Let's be honest, music isn't very intellectual. It's about instincts, emotion, energies. Opera, especially nineteenth century music, is oceanic- great waves which you learn how to control, how to surf. It's like a drug, a passion, with a latent, emotional, erotic, tense sub-text. I try to unlock the energy of the score and the intellectual tension of the music (ibid.: 35).

Alden's descriptions of rehearsal techniques with singers are replete with references to 'instinctive response', 'tight emotionality', 'singers feeding off energy and movement style' (ibid.: 36-7) engendered by balancing extreme precision and clarity with the open and rather improvisational, often changing whole scenes at the dress rehearsal 'to throw something into the works to generate extra tension. They have to roll with it.' (ibid.: 37).

> Mistakes are marvellous on stage ... one of the joys for me in rehearsal is watching people in breaks doing something personal outside of the scene, and thinking 'ohmigod, this is better than everything we've been working on for three weeks, he's just got to do this'. Something like taking a glove off, or a shoe off. Things like that happen all the time, and when you censor yourself and try to keep everything under perfect control, then the great human weirdnesses and oddities don't get on the stage where they belong (quoted in Milnes 1988a: 1300).

Zambello however, stresses: 'a trusting, nurturing environment where everybody feels safe to contribute as much of themselves as possible, where anything goes in rehearsal. It's my job not so much to "direct" but to edit ... I suppose in a way that's a feminine approach — a function of being a woman director, or just being a woman period' (Ellison 1992: 47). The emphasis is on theatrical tension and large emotional scale but little reference is made to singing values, or indeed the combination of voice, singing ability and charismatic individual acting abilities of the Callas, Gobbi school, and whilst the Alden/Sellars theatricalism has developed dramatically it can only succeed in theatres of a particular regime, with a particular set of priorities perhaps enforced on them because their relative economic and political strengths result in the absence of more traditional productions and audiences, and top, star singers. Tito Gobbi commented: 'Naturally fresh angles must be sought in presenting a work which has been performed many times before, but these must be within the frame of the period and the composer's intention, the truth is that most great composers were great men of the theatre too. They do not require to have their masterpieces rehashed for them in one eccentric form or another' (quoted in *Opera* June 1979: 528). Renata Tebaldi added: 'Singers are quite secondary, conductors and stage directors come first. The public go to see the production of Ronconi or Ponnelle. In a short space of time, producers have managed to destroy the individuality of the artist' (ibid.: 528). Conductors too may object to productions, at the first night of Petrika Ionesco's production of *Boris Godunov* in Geneva (1983) the audience booed the producer and the conductor joined in. Yuri Aronovich reportedly picked up the score and 'copiously kissed it' (Pitt 1984b: 900). Although the conductor has the final say in the pit and control of the live performance, music rehearsals prior to the producer's arrival are in most houses a thing of the past, further weakening the prior importance of the conductor. But the status of the producer matters: 'Power games are one terrible aspect of this business, but unfortunately it's not until you get into a position of power that you can really build a harmonious work environment' (Zambello quoted in Ellison 1992: 47). Kiri Te Kanawa is a typical 'star' in her attitudes to rehearsals:

> I don't like new productions that take six weeks rehearsal time any more ... It takes 10 to 12 days for me to do *Arabella*, I can do *Bohème* in ten days, Placido (Domingo) takes 2 days for *Otello* and when I sing Desdemona with him, all I need to know is how he is going to throw me on the bed, how he is going to throw me on the floor (*The Daily Telegraph* 25 February 1994: 15).

Miller (1991: 20) contrasts the director's relative powers in large international, as opposed to small, companies. In the latter 'you can choose the opera in the light of who you've got and you're not exhausted by being part of a huge, rolling repertoire' whilst in the former the casts (are) usually chosen independently of the director. Miller criticises 'big stars':

> They often arrive too late, they've done the part many times before and they have a fairly standardized understanding of how it's to be done. Often they can be very difficult to sway, but not always. Leonie Rysanek, for example, with whom I worked on *Katya* (New York Met) was only too eager to be told ... 'Look please tell me. This is your production and I want to be made new again with this role. I've done it many times, I don't want to do the same. Tell me other things about it that I don't know' ... but other people think that it's impudence in a director who hasn't done it before to have ideas. Singers who arrive too late haven't got time to do more than unpack a standard version of the work ... when Domingo came to do *Fanciulla* (La Scala Milan) he arrived not much more than four days before we opened. And several other

337

performers didn't arrive until ten days into rehearsal: the diva Casolla, didn't arrive until ten days in, and then her tenor wasn't there and I said you have to imagine, and she said *'Sempre, sempre imagine!'* And I think that expresses the predicament which is almost universal: people fly in at their convenience, and those who have either had the courtesy or the lack of power not to arrive late are put in the invidious position of having to imagine the as-yet-unarrived person they are meant to be playing opposite ... that's one reason why international opera is usually dramatically so second-rate. It's thrown on.

Miller clearly prefers working with an ensemble with everyone present from the first day and with works like *Katya* this is possible even in the international houses, however he claimed that he did have 'very great difficulties' with the Met Katya herself, Benackova,

These are not the kind of singers Richard Jones could find himself working with. He works with stars, 'stars' could not tolerate his sometimes very radical approach:

> Sometimes singers say to you. "I want to improvise this", or "I should really be living this". A lot of people get fucked up because they think that actually experiencing something on stage is like theatrically signifying it. I suppose I like things to be truthful and magnified. It's easier to work with singers who enter the rehearsal room approaching their work on a more unconscious as opposed to methodological level. Opera is about surrendering to a theatricality and time-scale which isn't like an every-day exchange, which is what is so brilliant about it (Jones 1990: 56).

But this is not what is so brilliant about 'it' for audiences or critics as Jones has found in their responses to much of his work, not least his Covent Garden *Ring* cycle (completed 1995), and for all their theorising the 'radical' producer of necessity shares the stage with Domingo and Te Kanawa doing their Otello and Desdemona before audiences who want their voices as much if not more than 'psychological re-examination', audiences who want spectacle not least in arenas such as Earl's Court and Wembley in London and the Palais Omnisports in Paris, indoor equivalents of the Roman arena opera of Verona and Caracalla Baths in Rome. For some producers it is a matter of cutting the cloth of all environments (Zambello produced *Tosca* at Earls Court) but many would resist the challenge of producing *Carmen* in the former 14,500 seater venue in June 1989 as 'a football match'. Steven Pimlott did not resist but encouraged:

> the audience could buy Carmen T-shirts at the door ... in the round, first and foremost to bring the audience closer, so that they feel more involved and see more. It will of course be sound-enhanced, so with luck people will hear clearly. We want to make the audience very much part of the experience itself, and hope that a communal excitement will be generated in that way (1989: 664).

Inevitably this kind of production emphasises the spectacular: smugglers, bullfighters, soldiers and so on the *Fiera* side in *Carmen*, with a chorus of 150, 80 dancers, 100 children, and a competition between singers for performances being daily they require multiple casts, possibly encouraging audiences to attend more than once. As with Alden however, choreographic references[21] abound although in this instance more in the football match sense: 'At Wembley you're millions of miles away from the players yet you can see every detail of their footwork' (ibid.: 65). Pimlott says of himself 'I am not the sort of producer who starts with a concept of a piece. The danger then is that everything has to be forced into it ... (and with a piece like *Carmen*) you have to be 100% inside it and not try to pass comment' (ibid.: 66). Clearly presenting emotions, reactions, motives indeed any of the Alden/Sellars type theatrical tension could not be accomplished in such an environment, not that the audience aimed at would expect or applaud it.

Millington claims that: 'Shifts in public taste will no doubt continue to foster experimentation. In a postmodern age, uncertain of its cultural identity, iconoclasm and traditionalism seem destined to co-exist, giving rise to a multiplicity of stylistic approaches for some time to come' (1993: 1129). This is not the place to enter into, or even resolve, the labyrinthine debates about postmodernity and postmodernism, but Millington's conclusion seems a singularly inappropriate one in that the material base of opera as an industry and of opera's development as an auratic art of status distinction for those who differentially consume it is simply ignored. In a consumerist world of retreating subsidies and advancing marketing of opera, 'radical' producers provide but one fetish of 'newness' to set alongside all the others. Outside the opera house 'new' singers, C D recordings, videos, films: audiences experience 'newness' through a variety of commodified means, but in the opera house 'newness' is largely the producers preserve, for where else would it come from?

Notes

1. Although when first mounted there was much talk of Boulez' *Ring*: 'extremely fast, unyielding ... the score is purposefully drained of all colour and expression' (Milnes 1983: 139).
2. Frank Corsaro studied at the Actors Studio New York and his productions bear the imprint of this background. With a reputation in notoriously conservative North American opera for his 'radical' changes of locale and period, his work by current trends is conservative.
3. Donington (1990: 43) asserts that 'radical' producers employ 'new trickery' and that 'really there is no substitute for the sober norm. We do not want the producer to stage what he (sic) may think the symbols mean. We just want him to stage the symbols'. But how can symbols exist without thought?
4. For example, as with Monteverdi's *Arianna* (1608) produced at the Court Theatre Mantua, Arianna's lament being the first popular aria 'to sweep all Italy' (Martin 1972: 113). Goehr's reworking of Monteverdi's *Arianna* symbolically relevant to all aspects of opera dealt with in this text, was premiered at the Royal Opera House Covent Garden October 1995 (producer, Zambello).
5. For example, Cavalieri for *Rappresentatione di Anima, et di Corpo ... per recitar cantando* (1600).
6. Such as Rospigliosi, Mateo Noris and Rinuccini the librettist of Peri's *Dafne* (1597), and *Euridice* (1600) and Caccini's *Il Ragimento di Afolo* (1600).
7. The Teatro Tron di San Cassiano was erected in 1637 by a nobleman who rented it to an impresario to manage at his own risk. By 1641 three other opera houses had opened, the latest called 'Teatro Novissimo' (Martin 1972: 117), and by 1678 there were more than ten. Here as well as elsewhere in Italy, the expansion of Court and commercial performances ranged from the lavish and spectacular. Savage (1992: 1109) tells us that the 'souvenir wordbook' for Melari's *Ercole in Teba* (Florence 1661) contained 40 pages on the production's splendours, including a description of 'a well conducted battle between two 30 strong armies of *"comparso"*,' (non-singing chorus, all named), to resident and touring *commedia* troupes. In the last quarter of the seventeenth century, at least seven new operas were produced

each year in Venice and in some years (for example 1682-3) as many as 12 (Ivanovich 1681: 392), so that by the end of the century over 350 productions of opera had been staged in Venice alone, where opera became a major tourist draw (Kimbell 1991: 115). To cater for popular demand, various venues were created out of existing buildings such as large old warehouses (Glover 1982: 103). Commercial opera: 'run for profit could not afford to indulge in costly machinery and great choruses, it won its popularity partly as a manifestation of civic, rather than individual power: opera meant no less a symbol to merchant princes than it did to Mantua, Florence or Ferrara, and in a short time Venice, where it was a recognised declaration of political authority and wealth' (Raynor 1972: 169). It was in Venice's commercial theatres that *commedia dell'arte* were at first allowed to appear at various moments in the opera, even serious and solemn moments to cheer them up. Later their appearances were limited to the final scenes of each act, whilst later still they appeared in *intermezzi* which became popular in themselves. The first complete comic opera it is thought was Monteverdi's *La finta pazza Licori* in Mantua in 1627 (Rosselli 1991: 213).

8. Royal ordinances of 1713 and 1714 established conditions governing size of company, salaries, repertoire planning, casting, vocal and movement instruction, stores and finances, for example all under the control of the inspector general to the company.

9. Wilhelmine Schroder-Devrient (b.1804-d.1860). First an actress then singer, she sang Fidelio in the presence of Beethoven. Reputationally 'she overcame marked vocal deficiencies by the power of her acting and declamation' (Hamilton 1987: 330). Nicknamed the 'Queen of Tears' because of her ability to cry on demand on stage, she created three Wagnerian roles: Adriano in *Rienzi,* Senta in *The Flying Dutchman* and Venus in *Tannhäuser.*

10. *'Dépouillement'* specifically used by Ravel to describe his 'stripping-bare' of musical forms which started with his violin and cello sonata of 1920 and which is operatically manifest in *L'Enfant et les sortilèges. 'Gebrauchsmusik'* and *'Gemeinschaftensmusik'* respectively refer to the social and aesthetic ideas which informed the Donaueschingen and Baden-Baden Festivals up to and post-1927 respectively: that is 'applied

or functional' music and 'amateur' or communal music as answers to the question 'What ought music to do?'

11. Midgette (1993b: 24) discusses an alternative term *Regietheater* 'a disputed term and concept' meaning opera as 'undistinguishable from all other theatre or some such' and/or 'modern' theatre, making theatre modern (radical/shocking). McMurray (1989: 452) uses *realitisches Musiktheater*. This takes us back to the debates about realism in opera: the heart of music theatre is to turn music-making and singing on the stage into a communication that is convincing, truthful, utterly essential. All problems of drama and of staging are secondary to this. Music theatre exists when a musical action with singing human beings becomes a theatrical reality that is unreservedly believable. The dramatic happening must take place on a level where music is the only means of expression. The performer must not give the effect of being an instrument or a component part of the music that already exists, or of a marionette being manipulated by the music, but that of being its creative fashioner.

12. Ruth Berghaus (see Bertisch 1990) studied dance and choreography at the Palucca school in Dresden, was engaged by the Berliner Ensemble in 1964 as production and choreographic assistant, taking over direction of the company on the death of Helene Weigel in 1971, holding this position until 1977. She married composer Paul Dessau in 1954 and worked on productions of his operas, for example *Puntila* and *Einstein*. From 1980 she worked in Frankfurt (am Main) with Michael Gielen, where many productions, for example the *Ring* were scandals at first but became very popular. After the 1985-87 *Götterdämmerung* applause lasted for 65 minutes. In this text, singers William Cochran and Gabriele Schnaut testify to her inspiring direction.

13. (Boulez *Der Spiegel* 190) 'Wieland Wagner was the only producer that I have known who has stimulated me into collaboration' (but Brook and Bergman are possible). He also attacks opera house (modern as well as old) lay-outs, stage auditoria arrangements and so on. which apart from anything else mean that modern operas have to attract sufficient public in large houses to make them pay. 'If anyone asked me to conduct *La forza del Destino* I'd sooner go for a walk' (Christiansen 1988: 186-94).

14. Ian Judge, for example, was asked by Pountney to direct *Faust* (at the ENO in 1985) 'as a musical — bringing musical comedy techniques to the opera stage' (Forbes 1993: 403).

15. Beni Montresor designs for other producers as well as produces himself. Designer John Conklin studied under both Wieland Wagner and Walter Felsenstein (see Osborn 1992). For insights into the particular role of the opera costume designer see Schmidgall (1989) on the work of Rolf Langenfass.

16. Sellars' Purchase Company represents the kind of company conditions set out by Bawtree (1990) for opera as Music Theatre or New Singing Theatre. David Freeman's Opera Factory companies do likewise. The first Opera Factory was established in Sydney in 1973, today Freeman has two companies, one in Zurich (1976), the other in London (1981). In addition to Opera Factory Freeman has produced for the ENO during the Pountney-Elder Jonas regime (*Orfeo*, Glass' *Akhnaten* and *The Mask of Orpheus*) As suggested by this brief list, Freeman's interests are classical and modern works (Opera Factory productions have included Birtwhistle's *Punch and Judy*, *Yan Tan Tethera*, *The Beggar's Opera* and the Da Ponte-Mozart trilogy) rather than the romantic which dominate conventional repertoires, although he has expressed interest in some romantic works: for example Wagner and *Traviata*. Sellars (Clements 1995) is very similar in his specialisations and desire to be able to produce nineteenth century works (apart from *Tannhäuser*) especially those of his great idol Verdi. Once again this suggests that such producers are given scope to invigorate peripheral areas of the repertoire but are not asked to do the same for the nineteenth century core where, apart from the works being box office sound, 'star' singers still perhaps hold sway. As with Sellars, Brook and Stein, the same small, tight-knit 'floating opera company' is maintained so that, for example when *La Calisto* was revived (or to be more accurate developed) in 1989, seven of the nine singers had appeared when the production was new, five years earlier. Few British theatre companies have remained so constant, or so controversial. *Calisto* was in modern dress, opening with Miss Nature, Miss Eternity, and Miss Destiny as competitors in a beauty contest which Calisto herself, when not distracted by her yo-yo, aims to win. Jove was

a greasy businessman, Juno his wife in silver-fox furs, the woodland creatures ruggerbuggers, Jove's magic spring a bottle of Coke and so on.

17. Sellars returned to Glyndebourne for Handel's *Theodora* in 1996. As I mentioned in Chapter 4 there is a distinct feeling in which even the most conservative of houses requires the whiff of production scandal to fetishise opera as 'new', 'live', 'exciting', but only to a degree.

18. Sellars (Clements 1995: 1263) claims that *Tannhäuser* 'has the awful tabloid quality of making Wagner's own affairs the subject of his opera'.

19. It was with Verdi's grander and more demanding works, indeed with Verdi himself following his experience of the French methods of mounting his works such as *Les vêpres Sicilienne*, he insisted on comparable production books. That from Paris for *Les vêpres* was translated into Italian, and all subsequent works had their own *disposizione scena* prepared and printed by Ricordi.

20. John Copley, as this reference suggests, is a producer with conservative leanings.

21. On the increasing use of choreography and dance in opera see Macaulay (1991).

7 'Operatic' commodities

You'll hear the world's greatest opera stars[1] singing arias and choruses so beautiful they've been cherished for centuries. These are timeless masterpieces of enduring beauty—some so popular you frequently hear them as the irresistible themes to Academy Award winning movies, Broadway plays, and even today's TV commercials. Each of the 50 electrifying selections you'll receive has been chosen because it is considered to be the greatest and most memorable performance of that particular aria (Advertisement for *50 Great Moments in Opera*, 3 CD set from The Beautiful Music Company of New York State USA).

Introduction

'A music's social function may diverge from the social meaning it embodies' (Adorno 1976: 61-2), and nowhere is this more clearly demonstrated than with the popularisation and commodification of opera which owes much to the bite-sized aria and its commercial exposure by 'stars'. EMI Angel Studio in North America have successfully marketed compilation albums such as: *Opera Goes to War, Opera Goes to Hell, Opera Goes to the Movies, Son of Opera Goes to the Movies, Opera Goes Nuts* and *Madison Avenue Goes to the Opera,* in which contemporary commercial culture plunders and fragments the original.

Opera developed in a culture where the development of emotion or mood spun out in real time created tension and deepened

347

feeling. In our media culture time is never real and is always formulated. In sitcom form we have one-minute teaser, one-minute credits, two minute commercial, eleven minute first act (four scenes), three minute commercial, nine-minute second act (three scenes), two-minute commercial, one minute end credits. Movies are written much the same way with subliminal rather than actual commercials (Innaurato 1993: 14).

The Beautiful Music Company of New York State USA present their *50 Great Moments in Opera* on three cassettes, four record albums or three CDs which retailed in early 1995 at $19.98, $19.98 and $29.98 respectively, and were 'sold' through TV and radio stations, specialist and not so specialist magazines. The company declared itself 'proud' to be able to bring this 'giant collection' of 'the world's most exciting and romantic music' to its customers. *The Readers Digest* marketed their *Magical World of Opera* as 'A Once in a Lifetime Collection of Unforgettable Melodies that You'll Enjoy Forever' (*The Sunday Times* 27 February 1994).

Imagine the power of Pavarotti, the depth of Domingo, and the colour of Callas in one collection ... add the resounding talents of the enchanting Kiri Te Kanawa, the legendary Joan Sutherland, the one and only José Carreras ... Thrill to their vivid interpretations of truly rousing favourites like the BBC theme to the last World Cup, perhaps the best loved melody of all time *Nessun dorma*. Delight in the romance of marvellous tunes like ... the Flower Duet from Delibes *Lakmé* (better known as the emotive backing to the Kleenex and British Airways commercials).[2]

One principal route by which opera can enter into, and remain in, the popular consciousness in a consumerist economy is via advertising:

The psychology of music is still a fairly primitive science, but we do know that a fair measure of the quality of an aria is its memorability. This has been true throughout the history of opera. In the late seventeenth century, Venetian theatres offered a popularized form of the fledgling art. *Da capo* arias in A-B-A form were introduced in contrast to the classic Florentine models of continuous recitative. A gondolier attending a performance one night, whistled a Vivaldi tune at work the next day. Through the eighteenth century tunes were written to be remembered, though the operas they came from might mostly be forgotten ... (Ivry 1989: 20).

As nowadays the products which they market are unlikely to be.

A cry of 'Suicidio!' rends the air ... the TV scene either an elegant hotel lobby or department store, a Callas look alike appears, is this an avant-garde La Giaconda from some European theater? No, it's a commercial for Coco perfume (Fitzgerald 1989b: 4).

Plotkin (1991) claims that 'Opera in advertising is hotter right now than the flames that consume Valhalla', listing more than 50 US TV ads. using opera to sell their wares. Women brush their teeth to the 'Anvil Chorus' from Il traviatore or 'Dance of the Hours' (La Giaconda), a monkey listens to 'Mi chiamano Mimi' (La Bohème) on a Sony Walkman, British Airways flies to Lakmé or Nabucco, Michael J. Fox drinks Diet Pepsi to an Aida chorus. 'Ebben, ne andro lontana' from La Wally backs up the snowy efficiency of a laundry detergent used to wash only the very best clothes ...

... after decades of opera trying to take on a democratic image, here comes that old up-scale image again. Opera News advertising survey falls in line, showing this magazine's readership regularly purchases wine, perfume, theater tickets, travel, hi-fi equipment and expensive automobiles ... Opera these ads imply, is part of the good life—something opera lovers have known all along (Fitzgerald 1989b: 4).

Opera is used in advertising in three ways. First it is used to create mood to sell the product, there being almost universal agreement in the advertising industry that opera lends sophistication, warmth, elegance and emotional immediacy to a product. Second, opera is sometimes used as a target of ridicule—most frequently as the object of humour, such as a fat soprano in Wagnerian helmet and full cry:

The screaming soprano appears ... in a spot for Chanel's Coco perfume in which a coltish, chicly late woman struggles to her seat under the disapproving gaze of the singer. But there is no question who smells better (ibid.: 14).

Third, there are also ads which use opera straight as its subject:

> These are rare because they are expensive and advertisers think the effort will be lost on most viewers ... You have to strike the right balance between amusement and persuasion, making certain the subject of the amusement is a dramatic issue about the product. If the amusement does not flow from the product, then it is irrelevant (Nancy Bachrach, Grey Advertising quoted in ibid.: 14).

It helps that standard repertory opera is in the public domain in both cultural and legal/economic senses: arias and, in generalised stereotypical ways, the works they come from and the 'lifestyle' associated with them constitute a cultural stockpile of recognisable readily remobilised references to 'quality' music, 'quality' life, whether alien or aspirational for viewers exposed to them. Bite-sized arias, already of ideal length for commercial usage, require only a few bars, or even a chord, to signal their presence and activate their 'tracing' (Foucault 1985/86: 8).[3] Just as importantly, these arias from the fossilised standard repertoire are largely out of copyright. As we have seen, the use of opera in other media is nothing new. From the cinema's earliest days, opera plots and 'stars' played a prominent role and opera music continues to be used extensively in soundtracks as recent examples such as *Fatal Attraction, Pretty Woman, Raging Bull, Apocalypse Now, Hannah and her Sisters, A Room With a View,* and *Diva* demonstrate. Cartoons too have used opera for 50 years or more, so from this one cinematographic source alone—the 'culture industry's' technological equivalent to that lonesome gondolier— opera 'hits' become familiar to people who have never seen an opera. And this is increasingly the trend worldwide, advertisers recognising all too well that classical music in general, but opera especially, has secured a place in popular, generalised cultures as a concentrated shorthand signifier of 'high art', high status and wealth. British Airways uses opera in its advertisements because it has this 'universal equity'—an 'equity' being that which makes a product distinct across cultural frontiers.

Music on its own is clearly freed from the potential textual limitations of cross-cultural marketing and understanding, but opera's problematic relationship between texts from different languages performed to audiences who are not always expected to hear or understand them—the very problems which currently beset opera in the opera house—serve the generalised international 'equity' requirements of advertising well. Opera is the most universal of all possible means for establishing product distinctiveness and value: 'These advertisements play equally well wherever the airline flies' (Cathy Constable of the US agency used by British Airways, quoted in Plotkin 1991: 15). As the extracts from the marketing of popular opera record compilations above demonstrate, the familiar use of certain arias from commercials is then ironically or cannibalistically deployed to feed back into the sale of aria as once more an aria, not as part of the opera from which it comes, but as part of the detergent it sells. 'Aura' in this consumerist world circulates so that, at points in the cycle, it is Kleenex which confers 'quality' on a duet from *Lakmé*, which even the most fanatical of opera lovers will have great difficulty in seeing 'live' and complete. All the consumer need know is that they can experience a 'quality moment' by listening to what they are assured, almost commanded, is 'a beautiful melody' which induces an 'unforgettable moment'.[6]

These compilations sell well everywhere. In the December 1994 *Sunday Times* Classical Chart, *Classic Commercials* was at no.10, and, in the US, the CD *Madison Square Goes to the Opera* sold especially well. It included *'La donna è mobile'* (from *Rigoletto* used to advertise Little Caesar's Pizza) and *'Largo al factotum'* (sung by the Barber himself in *The Barber of Seville*, used for Braun cordless shavers), but the promoter of the CD talked of everyone liking opera in *hors d'oeuvres* form—and that new opera audiences in the opera house are unlikely to result. Does such a use of opera trivialise it? 'That's the price you pay. To expand an audience, you in many instances trivialize' (Ray Johnson, Vice President of agency McCann-Erickson). According to Young and Rubicon:

> Most opera lovers feel that the use of opera in advertising will broaden opera's appeal, since it is almost always presented as elegant, upscale, and desirable. On the other hand rock and roll fans think that the use of their music in commercials belittles it.

For singers the use of opera in advertising certainly broadens earnings. In Japan, Domingo and Battle sing as alcoholic beverages are being served, Bartoli as the Fuji Bank is promoted, Pavarotti is one amongst many who won't leave home without their Amex cards, Kiri Te Kanawa and Domingo advertise their Rolex watches, but none of this is, in the US at least, new: Met tenor and non-smoker Jan Peerce truthfully testified from the 1940s through to the mid-60s that Lucky Strikes never irritated his throat! If opera arias provide advertisers with a 'universal equity' so too, clearly, do those singers who have achieved a star status beyond the opera house—those who are 'stars' before they are opera stars. They sell themselves as commodities which enshrine all the qualities along the 'high art'/ wealth and status axis and as they sell whatever it is they sell, opera becomes a mere subtext which consumers don't even have to listen to. Kiri Te Kanawa probably came to worldwide popular prominence as the soprano soloist wearing what some fashion critics called a 'striking' hat at the wedding of Prince Charles and Lady Diana Spencer. From then on, her 'star' status was assured, especially once elevated at a relatively young age, to a Damehood:

'Time I value above all things. It just gets more and more precious'. Without question, her career has been triumphantly consistent over the years. Yet Dame Kiri Te Kanawa readily admits that one thing has changed: her attitude to time. 'It is so beautifully expressed in *Der Rosenkavalier*', she says, translating the part of the The Marschallin from memory; 'I go through the house in the middle of the night and I hear the ticking of the clocks. I cannot stop them; I cannot turn them back. It is like the snow falling.' Dame Kiri may well feel, as she says, that time has speeded up year by year until January to January now flies. Her punishing schedule completely fills her diary five years in advance. Yet Dame Kiri remains her usual straightforward and uncompromising self. 'To arrive early is unfortunate, but to be late is the rudest thing imaginable', she insists. Then, relenting, she smiles, and she adds that sometimes she does not know 'whether I organise time, or whether time organises me'. One thing however remains clear. As a family woman, she finds time is the most precious to her 'when I'm leaving, when I have to say goodbye; that's the hardest part of all'. For seventeen years Dame Kiri has worn a Rolex and insists that she would never be without it. Of her gold Lady Datejust Chronometer with its diamond bezel she says: 'it is very beautiful, very elegant, quite wonderful'. It is gratifying indeed to hear that in an ever accelerating world, certain things at least remain constant.

The Three Tenors

Carreras, Pavarotti, Domingo, alternatively known as 'The Blessed Trinity' (Pitman 1994: 8) also have 'universal equity, as evidenced by their high selling 'arena' concerts, together or separately, and their classical albums, many of which, as with Te Kanawa, are of the 'crossover' variety—mixtures of opera, popular songs and so on—or eschew opera altogether. Decca's *The Essential Pavarotti* was the first classical album to enter the pop charts (1972) and to reach no.1. Domingo's *Be my Love ...* album was advertised as 'An Intimate Musical Seduction by the World's Most Romantic Tenor' and included, as well as the title track: *La Vie En Rose, Spanish Eyes,* and *Somewhere Over The Rainbow.* All their individual 'miked', mass audience 'aircraft hangar' affairs with the technical paraphernalia of the sporting events which they simulate—large screens either side of stage to show close-ups, expensive, glossy programmes, stalls selling CDs and other memorabilia—popularise 'opera' as general entertainment, promote the singers as personalities, cash in on their 'equity' more than that of the arias, but by all criteria (opera house box office takings and complete opera recording sales) do not seem to create greater popularity for the original source of this equity. Opera:

> You can't sing Tosti ballads, Zarzuela numbers and pseudo-Hispanicisms like *Granada* in the same mixed bag as real opera without everything being touched with a sense of vulgar display, and any real refinement gets lost in the amplification system. This sort of circus is not really good for opera, in spite of the proud reports of recordings in the charts (Monelle on a Glasgow Carreras concert at the Scottish Exhibition Centre 1992: 243).

It was also clear at this concert that the natives became restless if unknown Tosti and Zarzuela were not frequently punctuated by known *Carmen* and the like. Hilary Finch noted similar characteristics in Carreras' come-back concert after treatment for leukaemia, in the more conventionally auratic surroundings of the Royal Opera House, Covent Garden on 18 April 1989:

It was a night for the promoters too. A colour supplement of a programme (undated, multipurpose, frequently misprinted) spared nothing, verbally or pictorially, in its apparent attempts to portray illness as yet another romantic ingredient in the soft-focus, tenor-hero image of this 'slim Catalan with the interesting streak of silver in his black hair'. A paying-in slip for the International José Carreras Leukaemia Foundation was tucked between its lurid pages (1989: 748).

Pavarotti, Domingo and Carreras 'Three Tenors' concerts include a great deal of non-operatic music—for example from *West Side Story, Cats, 'O Sole Mio'*. On his own, Pavarotti is the most likely to team up with Michael Bolton, Meat Loaf or whoever for charity events, at which, as with his solo concerts, audience celebrities outnumber those on stage. Milnes described the latter's, famous, immensely profitable, 'star-studded' (Charles and Di, John Major and Michael Heseltine all drenched in the operatic downpour), 'Pavarotti in the Park' concert in Hyde Park London on 3 July 1991, and in the process illustrated yet again the discursive hierarchy which competes for control of opera or, in this instance, 'opera':

The build up to this amiable event was truly extraordinary: front page news in daily papers of every shape and size, endless 'stories' on wireless and TV. Then there was the converse. *Opera*'s switchboard approached meltdown with reporters from papers and TV trying to find someone to badmouth either Harvey Goldsmith [promoter] or Pavarotti, preferably both. No takers at this address. Pavarotti is a very good singer, and Goldsmith is doing a lovely job ... it is ... difficult to keep a sense of proportion when writing about this event. Pavarotti was in fine voice, and a crowd of over 100,000 stood in Hyde Park under steady rain to hear him sing popular and not so popular arias and songs. And they loved it. The sound system worked well [though] ... from a position far back in the crowd I would hate to have to swear which language *O Paradis* was sung in ... What it all meant I should hate to have to say, though I'd welcome any serious explanation for Pavarotti's undeniable and genuine mass popular appeal, given the fact that he has neither the advantage of Mick Jagger's pelvis, nor Arnold Schwarzenegger's pectorals. Are niceness and musicianship enough? ... One might have to go back to the castratos—star tenors' immediate predecessors—and wax nervously lyrico-psychological about the effort required to sing high notes as analogue to the Big O. Is Pavarotti the greatest known ambassador for opera, bringing untold thousands to its heady delights, or is he just a slightly unconventional but decidedly cuddly pop star? I'm not sure, but one of our readers at least has no doubts (Milnes 1991c: 1228-9).

I had the misfortune to attend Pavarotti's concert in Hyde Park ... I went because I like Pavarotti and think he is a thrilling singer of particular operas. But my interest in him turned out to be a minority one. I moved to various different spots searching for a place from which he could be heard to best advantage. In every place the majority reaction of the audience was the same they talked, joked and laughed and occasionally jumped up and down to see if they could see Pavarotti on the stage, pausing only to produce thunderous applause at the end of each aria. It became clear from all this that a Pavarotti event has very little to do with opera as such, but everything to do with Pavarotti as a phenomenon. Through continuous hype, he has now become so famous that it is imperative to see him when he appears, much as one visits Madame Tussaud's on coming to London, or goes to see the three handed man at the fairground. That he happens to sing opera is relatively tangential. The argument that Pavarotti is a man of the people bringing opera to the masses is a load of tosh, since the masses at Hyde Park showed little interest in listening. At the end he was vociferously applauded. Clearly the audience loved him; whether they like opera is something else again (letter to *Opera* October 1991:1138).

It is as two of 'The Three Tenors' however that Pavarotti and Carreras demonstrate the extent to which 'opera' can make money. With rumours of a world tour commencing in the autumn of 1995, *The Sunday Times* commented:

Their concerts have created a huge money spinning venture. A total of 1.3 billion people watched their 1994 concert and, if their next album sells just half as much as their first they can expect to earn £2m each from royalties (13 August 1995).

Elliott (1991) gives a detailed account of the first of their concerts at the Caracalla Baths Rome, on the eve of the 1990 World Cup soccer final. By the time he wrote the article the recording had sold 5,000,000 CDs and cassettes for Decca worldwide, climbing to the top of the UK, Dutch and Spanish pop charts. In the UK the video edged Madonna off the no. 1 spot for a while. In March 1991 it was at no. 43 in the US Billboard pop charts, the highest reached by a classical recording since the beginning of rock in the mid-1960s.

> 'We created a hit', understates David Weyner, president of PolyGram Classics and Jazz, Decca/London's parent company. With money, a little bit of class and some very good planning, we created a hit'. In the US domestic sales for a classical recording range when new from 5-10,000 in a similar time frame. Its success is attributable to a combination of sheer celebrity draw, exquisite timing, a marketing plan with lofty goals and, most important, the money to make that plan work. 'We have funded the promotion of this project very much the way the pop business would because we believed from the outset we had a property that could reach millions as opposed to our natural target audience' (quoted in Elliott 1991: 34).

The idea for the concert allegedly originated with Carreras who wanted his friends and football fans to be together for the play-offs. Zubin Mehta who, by the second Three Tenors concert in Los Angeles for the following World Cup was also being given 'star' promotion by Decca, conducted the 210 instrumentalists, the concert being broadcast live throughout Europe. Meanwhile the BBC decided to use Pavarotti's recording of 'Nessun dorma' as the signature tune for its coverage of the competition. It went to no.1 in the UK pop charts, and the album from which it came, *The Essential Pavarotti*, went to the same position in the album charts. So the combination of the Roman Baths, a full moon, supposedly 'the three greatest tenor', male stars trading on the tenor's 'macho' image in voice, demeanour and, many suspected, competitiveness, each taking his turn in the spotlight singing a time-honoured crowd-pleaser proved irresistible. As one left the stage and another came on, they shook hands or high-fived each other, their chumminess reaching its peak in a 20 minute medley ranging from *West Side Story* to *Cats*. The audience numbered 6000, the broadcast audience 1.5 billion. The North

American market had no broadcast upon which to launch the recording, nor was soccer a crowd-puller there: 'One of the first questions to come over from Europe was "Shall we call this the World Cup Concert?", And we said, "Don't call it World Cup anything. It dates it, and it means nothing in the market"' (ibid.: 34). Stores were targeted with 'a teaser postcard campaign. The cards went to all the key buyers at the chain stores as well as individual store managers '... to get the market stirred up. Next there was the solicitation video featuring footage from the chummy moments as well as dramatic, held-note tonsil shots' (ibid.: 35). The stores were given a four page stencil sheet outlining its marketing plans including TV news coverage of the concert in news bulletins on CBS, ABC, CNN and A&E, press coverage in *Time, Newsweek, People, The New York Times* and *USA Today*, advertising in *Billboard, Opera News, Vanity Fair, The New York Times Magazine*, television and radio. The record came out on Tuesday 11 September and was 'reported No.1 on the Billboard classical charts in the next cycle' (ibid.: 35). Belief in being able to 'reach' people was part of the battle.

> In Concert has even been advertised on VH-1 a pop-music cable station and on an array of moving targets: trains (Metro North), subways and city buses ... The promotional monies we have spent on this record have been extraordinary from day one' says Weyner who quite understandably won't name a figure' (ibid.: 36).

The recording and marketing 1994 concert rights were bought by Warner International, along with the 'brand name' of the stars: '... This has come to us as manna from heaven ...' (Michael Letchford, Marketing Director at Warner Classics International, noted in Pitman 1994: 10), 'It's a marketing dream. The name has become a generic term. It's just so, so strong. What we will be doing is taking a classical record and marketing it as a pop record without alienating the traditional classical listeners' (Val Azzoli, General Manager of Warner's US pop subsidiary Atlantic Records, quoted in Pitman 1994: 10). Fees per singer were estimated at £750,000 plus, each television channel paying £500,000; Warner Music rumoured to have paid £10.3m for its full recording deal and Atlantic Records spent £645,000 on advertising.

The press at least hyped up the effect of this event on 'every man/woman'. *The Observer* (8 May 1994: 8) was typical. Under the headline: 'Gargled arias of baritones in the bathroom' it described, amongst others, Gerry Walsh who had been sitting on his sofa drinking tea when he heard Pavarotti, Domingo and Carreras being beamed into his home in Runcorn, Cheshire, from the Terme di Caracalla.

Mr Walsh, a roofer, was inspired. He did not know his arias from his elbow, but was filled with a burning desire to sing opera. He is not alone. Others share his dream and are enrolling for the Central Academy of Singing, a school that aims to help armchair opera buffs perform the classics. The project is the idea of Rona Campbell, a former principal singer with the Metropolitan Opera de Caracas, Venezuela, now settled in the Liverpool suburb of Mossley Hill. More than 60 students have auditioned. The biggest problem is the obvious one—not all of them can sing. But Miss Campbell has no intention of turning anyone away. With the tone-deaf in mind, some of the courses are specifically tailored to the musically challenged. Workshops range from intensive study of classical works in the original language, which lead to public performances, to lunchtime singing sessions aimed at relieving office stress and beginners' classes in basic breathing and voice relaxation. 'Everyone's singing can be improved', claimed the former diva. 'We hold auditions so that I can judge what they are capable of, then recommend a suitable course. Some are more interested in musicals and show tunes, we've a class for them too.' Luckily Mr Walsh has a decent tenor voice. Since that fateful night in 1990, he has been nurturing his secret passion with regular practice. 'I went out and bought a record of the concert and started singing along. The best place for me to concentrate on hitting the notes is in the bath.'

Among those auditioned in the presence of the reporter were Stan Partington a taxi driver from Anfield who 'wants to be another Pavarotti'; Tony Carroll, 62, retired insurance salesman 'who has always wanted to sing like Mario Lanza'; Lesley Belinsohn, 47, a Liverpool housewife who 'wants to sing opera and Streisand ballads'. Another would only admit to being Mrs X ('I don't want my friends to know I'm here'). Mr Carroll observed: 'Lanza, had it, Jolson had it. Once I wanted to be a famous tenor, but I stayed in a secure job. Now I practice on the landing at home and dream of what might have been.' Miss Campbell 'puts them through their paces'. Mrs X is told to lie flat on her back with a book on her stomach. She grabs the woman's neck firmly and rolls her head around checking for individual tension points. 'Before you can sing you must relax'. Miss Belinsohn keeps missing a high note [in] *'O mio babbino caro'* ... She is told to bend over and sing. Hanging forward like a rag-doll, she almost gets the note, but is defeated by a coughing fit. 'Phlegm' sniffs the teacher. 'There's a tremendous amount of it in Liverpool ... When Pavarotti sang *'Nessun dorma'* ' he brought a whole new audience to opera'. She turns to a singer giving an horrendous rendition of *'Ave Maria'*. 'Perhaps you could rest your voice for a few months and take a drama course' she suggests. 'No, I want to sing opera. I love to sing opera', he replies. Luciano, what have you done?

Crossover

One of the crucial things that Pavarotti has done, apart from present himself as a fairly close approximation of the stereotypical Italian tenor and through his size and open face be simultaneously ordinary and extraordinary, is to 'crossover'. Te Kanawa, Pavarotti, Carreras, Domingo, are merely the latest in a long line of opera 'stars' who have sought popular star status by doing so, following, as just a sample: Rosa Ponselle, recordings of whom made in the 1920s have been recently marketed by Pearl as 'the first crossover album'; Leontyne Price allegedly as a riposte to Barbra Streisand's *Classical Barbra* album; Eileen Farrell with several to her credit; Cesare Siepi, who appeared on Broadway in the musical *The Crime of Giovanni Venturi* and recorded Cole Porter songs; and Jon Vickers.[5] 'Crossover' is not a new phenomenon. Eileen Farrell began making 'crossover' albums when still singing Wagnerian opera; other Wagnerian *divas* (for example, Rita Hunter) like to include light songs in their concert repertoires.[6] However, it is a risky business for opera singers to market themselves outside the genre which has given them their 'universal equity'. They may be able to 'sell' the the glamorous wealth and sophisticated side of their 'equity', conferring on standard songs a degree of 'high art' respectability in the process, but their vocal training and singing remains inappropriately operatic. Kiri has made several 'crossover' recordings, indeed one is called *Sidetracks*, all promoted via her undoubted good, glossily cosmeticised looks. She has sold records, but not her ambitions, to critics:

> Watching Previn nudging tortuously the great diva through a trifle like *Teach me Tonight* you know that pop music, if it isn't dead, is far too deranged to be released into the community. 'I enjoy making crossover records ... Why should my voice be exclusive to opera?' Well, because that's what it's good at. Her television duet with Tom Jones on *It's Not Unusual* was fun, because Jones is a fairly operatic kind of guy anyway. But otherwise these are small songs with a narrow range that don't call for all this high-C chasing: opera is a lot of emotional generalities; popular song is specific and close up. If Dinah Sheridan and Frank Sinatra had announced that they were doing *Tristan und Isolde*, we'd pelt them with rotten fruit. Yet when the opera cats do show toons, it's somehow seen as ennobling the material. But who in their right minds would want José Carreras singing *As Time Goes By?* The poor dope sings the thing as though addressing a footwear convention: 'Dee worl' weel alwyas welcome loafers/As time coes by ...' But it is true that no matter how you slice it, no one's written a well-loved operatic aria since *'Nessun dorma'* 70 years ago. If you're Placido Domingo or José and you've made your recital albums of the same dozen arias in a different order, what's left? Either you do *'Nessun dorma Bossa Nova'* or you head for the lusher pastures of pop standards (Mark Steyn, *The Daily Telegraph* 5 March 1994: 15).[7]

Lesley Garrett

With such excursions we have the commodification of 'opera' through the opera 'star' commodity. There are other, usually more modest, local 'stars' used, or who themselves seek, to promote opera itself whilst they 'crossover' back and forth not only on recordings but on popular TV, in broadsheets, tabloids and such like, where their attempts at popularisation invariably involve a considerable amount of 'debunking' of opera's status—intellectual as well as economic. In Britain Lesley Garrett is one such, variously described as 'Britain's Favourite Opera Star', 'the people's soprano' (Burt 1995: 26), 'Madonna of the opera world' (Garrett 1990; di Giovanni 1994: 3, 7).

She is nevertheless an accomplished stage artist as her portrayal of the *Cunning Little Vixen* (Janacek) and other roles at the ENO during the *Power House* years and after, have demonstrated. Her albums have been consistent best sellers: *Diva: A Soprano at the Movies* and *Prima Donna*, the first and fourth highest sellers of 1993, outselling similar albums by Carreras and Te Kanawa. What is being 'sold' through Garrett, however, is not the confirmation of sophisticated and ennobling style epitomised by Te Kanawa. On the contrary, Garrett promotes opera as popular entertainment to non-opera buffs not as élite art, and in the process as something that is more overtly 'sexy'.[8] The cover for *Prima Donna* (featuring 'songs' by Handel, Massenet, Puccini, Rossini, Orff, Weill, Flotow, Canteloube, Burgon, Gershwin, Herbert, Johann Strauss) showed the singer reclining, on a modern metal easy chair, her legs raised above the level of her head and revealing her thigh, wearing high shiny patent leather stilettos (part of porn's basic iconography) and what looks like a strapless silk dress, (possibly no more than a loose silk sheet), her head thrown back and mouth open, in a clear intimation of sexual abandon. Few other female singers are so obviously marketed as sexual commodities—a strategy with which she clearly concurs: 'Opera is sexy ... It's an opportunity to do fantastic and outrageous things. It's about love and passion, hate and jealousy' (Garrett quoted in di Giovanni 1994: 7).

> Maria Callas, perhaps the most famous diva of the century, might have talked about love and passion and hatred and jealousy, made controversial films with her friend Pier Paolo Pasolini, or had a passionate affair with Aristotle Onassis, but somehow one cannot see her posing, pregnant in a tight dress, rather like a pale imitation of Demi Moore (ibid.: 7).

Garrett has achieved mass media celebrity status, appearing on TV shows where she has trampled tomatoes in a bucket, posed in a bath, received a 'Gotcha Oscar' on *Noel's House Party*, guested on Channel 4's late-night anarchic *The Word*, had her own *Lesley Garrett Special*, and written magazine columns such as 'My First Job' for American Express's *Expression* (November/December 1994: 82) (not so incidentally it was as an artist's nude model). She is generally required to spread the word that opera is neither highbrow nor élitist:

Opera was in our home. It was only when I came to London I discovered it is something only the intelligentsia were supposed to enjoy. That's a load of bollocks. Opera is full of passion—and passion is part of all our lives (Burt 1995: 26).

This 'bouncy working class girl' (ibid.) asked to describe *My Perfect Weekend* (*The Times*, 5 February 1994) includes as music she would listen to:

Frank Sinatra, Nat King Cole and Ella Fitzgerald. 'I would not listen to classical music, I get enough of that at work'. Which film would she watch? *'Diva* of course'. What three things would she most like to do? 'Sleep, eat and make love'.

She recounts how her future stardom was, even in such an ordinary setting, never in doubt:

I can remember leaping up on the windowsill behind the drawn curtains. Then I would give the signal for my two younger sisters to pull back the drapes ever so slowly—and shine torches on my face as I burst into song. I was noisy precocious and a pain. I think I should apologise to my sisters for being so hideous. But I couldn't help it I was born that way (Garrett 1994: 70).

Her first role was 'in an opera called *Orlando* by Handel and I was Dorinda, the shepherdess who upstaged everybody. She had all the best lines. I expected my career to unfold gradually but it went whoomphh!' (Burt 1995: 26). Her 'whoomphh' is what brought eventual press notoriety and stardom, in Richard Jones, ENO production of *Die Fledermaus* (1988):

It's very difficult to talk about this *Fledermaus* business because people are determined to think it was a calculated thing, that it was all publicity for me and the ENO. But it wasn't like that at all. Actually what I did was born out of the music—you don't have to believe me, but look at the words and they're all about stripping. Besides I didn't do a strip-tease. What I did was a very fleeting moment of artistic nudity which was just part of the show that was full of extraordinary visual moments. You have to take it in its context. It was a crazy, wonderful, visually extravagant evening of which my bottom was the sensation, I completely upstaged the whole thing (ibid.: 26).

Garrett, whose idols are Madonna and Michael Jackson, is for some journalists '... part of today's *diva* package', with 'fellow *divas*... Cecilia Bartoli, Amanda Roocroft and Sally Burgess' there is 'a new breed', cut from a different cloth from Dame Joan Sutherland, Renata Tebaldi or Callas. 'They are young boisterous and marketed more like pop stars than the traditional diva: regal, grand, stately' (di Giovanni 1994: 7), and Garrett understands 'the package':

> I passionately believe that in historical terms opera has just about every element that is relevant to today's market, and to today's vision of entertainment. When I see how pop singers present their work, with a video attached, I think how like a mini opera that is ... (Franks 1995: 24).[9]

Faced with such barefaced populism, 'priests' defend opera's discursive hierarchy in classical social closure style:

> Marketing is a new thing. Garrett is a modestly endowed singer with a good stage presence, and happy to show it off, and good luck to her. She is also for 'true' opera fans rather vulgar ... Garrett is not selling to rock music's fans or Cliff Richard fans [but] to middle-class people who might also have a Pavarotti tape (Rupert Christiansen quoted in di Giovanni 1994: 7).

The Garrett campaign, masterminded by Keith Cooper then director of public affairs at the ENO (now at Covent Garden), was as deliberate as the Haagen Dazs advertisements, designed to have instant appeal. He aimed for younger hipper audiences 'who could identify with Garrett's warmth, open smile, plunging necklines, and familiarity. Last year she made six singles for Classic FM' (di Giovanni 1994). Cooper describes her and other young male and female opera singers as much like the

> ... target market we wanted to appeal to... attractive and sexy, not the image of a heavyweight Italian soprano or tenor. What we were missing as a selling point was that opera singers look like ordinary human beings. They are young people and that is

consistent with the direction record companies are taking (ibid.: 7).

Di Giovanni questions the wisdom of such campaigns, mentioning that, in the flesh, the singers may disappoint, and that the campaign around Garrett may be simply too manufactured (as for Madonna or Kylie). Harriet Smith of *Gramophone* responds that opera singers have learnt a lot from their pop counterparts in order to reach a wider (and more profitable) audience, although critic Edward Greenfield reiterates that those marketed in this way are not the best singers of their generation, but the most marketable for other reasons, Garrett being described as no more than 'a tremendous personality'. Di Giovanni likens her to 'an Ethel Merman type, a blowsy Broadway star more interested in showbiz, glitter, lights than music' but the hype has worked. *Diva,* released in 1991, has sold 60,000 copies; *Prima Donna* (1992) entered the British classical charts at no.2. At Christmas 1993 her single of *'Ave Maria'* reached no.16 in the pop charts. James Jolly, editor of *Gramophone,* believes Garrett to be not far behind the 'Three Tenors phenomenon and the Italia 90 exposure of *"Nessun dorma"* in raising British awareness of opera' (Franks 1995: 24). 'When she does signing sessions in record shops ("and this thrills me more than I can tell you", she claims), they say things like, "We would never have listened to this music if it hadn't been for you"' (Burt 1995: 26). Part of her appeal is her 'ordinary' background:

> When I look back on my childhood it's a real Cinderella contrast, but even then all I ever wanted to be was the centre of attention ... It was such a poor area that you had to make your own entertainment. My Dad's a great busker ... In fact all my relatives sang and played and there wasn't one of them who couldn't get up and do a turn of some sort. The people around me were fantastically resourceful ... Dad was the busker but Mum gave me the discipline. There were no barriers, no great dividing lines which put opera off limits or made it all seem terribly aristocratic, untouchable. It pains me to think that people still separate posh music from common. That was crap as far as we were concerned (Garrett 1994: 70).

At school she lived for 4pm when the choir and orchestra practices started. Doing well at science, she suddenly thought 'There's no such life as a life without music'. She was 17 when she had her first singing lesson (in a class with 15 others).

> It took three different buses and all my pocket money to get to the 20 minute lessons each week. But it was vital. Otherwise I would have stayed an amateur musician having fun with my music ... the idea of earning a living from music seemed totally crazy to my parents. I'd come all this way and now they were telling me not to do it. It was as if a light bulb had been turned on in my head saying 'I can do this' That was the moment that my childhood ended (ibid.: 70).

At one point she had to give up singing. Her first marriage to a teacher had broken up, she became ill with a kidney infection and eventually lost her voice. Through the Alexander Technique she learnt that she had lost it as a result of lost physical self-confidence. 'It was the first time I realised you sing with your whole body. It was a revelation. It's not just this bit of gristle in your neck. You sing with your whole body and mine was very weak' (Burt 1995: 27). After meeting her second husband—'I knew I'd met the father of my children and he knew he'd met the mother of his' (ibid.:27)—there came:

> ... this explosion of creativity—I went creatively berserk ... I'm interested in photography... and in all my photographic work, I try to show my love of fantasy, accessing your own emotions and releasing them. That's why I'm so passionate about music reaching more people. People have said to my record company 'How do you get her to be photographed like that?' But these photos are honest representations of what a listener can expect to hear on an album. So if you pick up one of my albums, and see a photograph showing wild passion, then that's what they'll hear on the record. Or if it's a contemplative picture, then that's what they can expect to hear (ibid.: 27).

Her role of Vixen has a special appeal to her because 'She's had to struggle through her life, she met the man of her dreams and they fell in love and had children right away—all those little cubs—so that's very personal' (ibid.: 27). She does it all 'on adrenalin and some sort of natural energy top up. Please' and she gestures upwards once more 'just keep it going' (ibid.: 27). In some respects, Garrett's earthy persona appears more in touch with the grand tradition of *prima donna* than her promoters realise, like 'Angiolina Bosio, who looked elegant on stage but at dinner took snuff out of a "huge not particularly clean handkerchief"', or E. M. Forster's 'hot lady' (modelled on Tetrazzini), who told the British tourists in the first-class carriage that 'never, never before had she sweated so profusely' (quoted in Rosselli: 182).

Apart from being a key marketing weapon within entertainment, Garrett believes that her role is to convince people that they do not need a PhD to appreciate 'great, and even not so great operas' (Franks 1995: 24), nor will she allow opera to be attacked for being élitist: 'Every opera house in the country has a reasonable pricing policy ... you can get in [most places] for a tenner ... audiences are going up. I don't consider myself a diva at all. It's 'just bloody hard work, quite extraordinarily hard' (ibid.: 24).

Kiri, Pavarotti, Domingo, Carreras and Garrett all affirm that the commercialisation of 'opera', in addition or complementary to, the stockpile of generalised opera representations in popular culture, depends crucially also on the sustained commodification of the 'star' with popular or mass audience appeal. Garrett, however, and to a degree Pavarotti, demonstrate that this process does not inevitably mean the commodification and reification of 'grand-damery' but may involve populist deconstruction. The market is ironically amoral and classless; whilst it exploits opera = Kiri = Rolex = conspicuous consumption, it also counters with opera = Lesley Garrett = CD mass consumption. For impresarios and record companies who are all ultimately uninterested in selling opera, what they sell as opera matters little, whether it be an ersatz élitist Glyndebourne-style picnic plus opera at Garsington or generalised short attention-span 'moments' of 'contemplation, 'passion', 'romance', 'unforgettable' 'timeless masterpieces', in 'once in a life time collections' listened to in one's living room, and which they will ingeniously encourage consumers to replace a short time hence. In truth, of course, the Garsington picnicker, after the picnic interval at least, is as likely to apostrophise the 'experience' in similarly generalised terms.

'Active' consumption

In France the retail outlet Fnac have created opera catalogues promoting opera as a popular art form.

> L'Opéra n'est pas reservé a un public averti. C'est un art rendu populaire par des voix célèbres celles que Luciano Pavarotti, Barbara Hendricks, ou Montserrat Caballé. Pour cadeux que l'art lyrique intéressé— et vous êtes de plus en plus nombreux dans ce cas—il était necessaire de disposer d'un guide, d'un instrument de choix fondé sur une selection rigoreuse et les interpretations les plus brillantes.

All the recordings are available at Fnac stores *naturellement*. The catalogue includes a guide to *'les voix dans l'opéra: un instrument de musique pas comme les autres'*. Different opera cultures employ different terms and categorisations. Here they are *soprano léger, soprano lyrique* and *soprano dramatique, mezzo soprano, contralto, tenore léger, lyrique* and *dramatique, baryton Martic (du nom d'une célèbre chanteur) voix peu puissante mais trés souple: e.g. Pelléas; baryton Verdi* and *baryton grave*, with finally the *'basse'*. The characteristics of these voices are identified through *'L'etendue (Les notes limités qu'une voix peut atteindre) La Tessiture (Le registre dans lequel une voix peut se déployer à l'aise) Le timbre (Le résulte des sons harmoniques émis en même temps, que le son principal. C'est le timbre qui permet de reconnâitre un chanteur (que l'on pense à Maria Callas). C'est lui qui donné à la voix sa couleur expressive, qui est elle-même en grande partie fonction de la technique vocale'* and *'La Puissance (Une grande voix s'opéra depasse 120 decibels. Une voix d'opérette est inférieure à 100)'*, plus diagrams and a Dr Christophe de Seze on *'Les Problèmes Vocaux'*. The catalogue also recommends videos and books on opera.

In Britain at least, opera and/or 'opera' consumers are apparently not merely passive 'buyers' of commodities, many seem to want to get in on the act. Opera karaoke discs have been marketed, but there are also schemes to involve groups in rehearsals and 'events'. *The Times* (6 November 1993) under 'The trill at the opera', reported on a Royal Opera House weekend at Chichester College of Technology in which 'ordinary opera-goers' are coached by professionals over two intense days. The ROH education department subsidises each event:

individuals pay £45 per head, including two meals, to be 'worked like dogs' from 6pm on Friday to a public performance on Sunday afternoon. 'Scores may be bought in advance', 'The chorus I notice has to sing awful things like "A delight-ful sugges-tion/Let's drown all our cares/In a glass filled with spar-kling champagne" but perhaps nobody will notice' (Purves: 23). Director Richard Gregson insists that this is an educational exercise open to all:

> Even the tone deaf, that's absolutely crucial, people must be able to come in from rock bottom. We have choir people of course, and good amateurs: some young professionals got their first confidence on these weekends. But anyone can come.

He did his first weekend on an impulse when invited to lecture for two days on *Carmen* at a festival:

> I thought it would be too boring. So all these people turned up expecting to listen, and I told them they were putting it on. There's no point in concerts of opera. It's a dramatic form.

Some ROH principals help with more difficult bits, otherwise the paying guest has to provide props, basic costumes and so on.

> We limo through the score. Vague understanding stirs. I start to see how the dramatic sinews of opera, the recitatives and asides and links, throw the 'lollipops'; arias and choruses into relief. Singing them, however badly, helps you to understand. I feel better. The principals are chosen next, according to who put their hands up first: three amateur Violettas and three Alfredos will sing in relays. 'Sopranos don't despair. We have ways of making you trill'. They are instructed in the social role of courtesans and that 'Words come first, Words, tempo, weight. The tune a long way after. Words. For God's sake you're at a party in Paris, not a choral society doing a Requiem! Act'. 'I cannot motivate all 70 of you individually. Decide on who you are, and stay in character as you move'. [Purves states] I have always loved opera because of the extremity of it, the effort: the way it goes the extra mile. Sing in harmony, react, move, dance, smile, keep your eye on the conductor ... Look this might seem a period piece but it wasn't at the time. It was shocking. We are talking about a corrupt society:

in some productions what is on offer at Flora's party is girls under 12. I don't put that on stage explicitly but it has to be there. You will find very few operas are just fun and pretty tunes: that sort don't survive. It is the edge of deep bitterness, even in *Don Pasquale*, which makes opera live. It is drama! (Purves: 23).

Purves gets to know others: 'Valerie a primary-school teacher "I only sing things like *Wheels on the Bus* normally". There is draughtsman Big John, and Janet, a gentle pensions administrator with a beautiful soprano.' For the more popular audience, or the more bashful, singalongathons provide the setting for involvement. At the Royal Albert Hall on Sunday 26 June 1995 there was an 'Opera Singalong' as part of The National Music Day Celebration: 'Your chance to sing the great opera choruses including "Chorus of the Hebrew Slaves"... "Humming Chorus" "Easter Hymn" and "Anvil Chorus"'. Interestingly, the opera sources of these choruses were not listed in adverts. There were also arias and duets by 'star soloists' Susan Bullock, Sally Burgess, Bonaventura Bottone and Jason Howard. The hosts were Gloria Hunniford and Matthew Kelly of TV 'fame'. This 'event' was an extension of the 'Classical Gala Nights' which are a common feature of Saturday and Sunday evening concerts in London, such as the following at the Royal Festival Hall 'with fantastic laser display' by the London Concert Orchestra featuring:

Bolero, Finlandia, *'Nessun dorma'*, Skater's Waltz, *Pearl Fishers* Duet, Liberty Bell March, Ride of the Valkyries, Tritsch-Tratsch Polka, Grand March from *Aida*, *William Tell* Overture, Khachaturian Sabre Dance, Chorus of the Hebrew Slaves, *O Fortuna* from *Carmina Burana*, Pomp and Circumstance March No. 1, Intermezzo from *Cavalleria rusticana* [and] a grand finale of the 1812 Overture 'with Cannon and Mortar Effect'.

Opera tourism

The commodification of opera depends on the commodification of its sociocultural as well as musical or theatrical elements. Indeed the latter cannot be separated from the former. As such, opera is incorporated into related forms of consumption in leisure and lifestyle economies, at least for those with sufficient money to spend.

Numerous travel companies now cater for the opera tourist. Tourism draws together processes of cultural commodification, consumerism and citizenship: 'Being able to go on holiday, to be obviously not at work, is presumed to be a characteristic of modern citizenship which has become embedded into people's thinking about health and well-being' (Urry 1990: 24). The conversion of tourist services into a satisfactory holiday involves a great deal of 'work' by both those determined to have a 'good time' and those selling the services provided who, to varying degrees, try to guarantee a particular holiday experience.

> ... part of the social experience involved in many tourist contexts is to be able to consume particular commodities in the company of others. Part of what people buy is in effect a particular social composition of other consumers [which] ... the providers of the services must ensure (Urry 1990: 25).

This is what opera has always provided in the opera house—indeed, in different parts of the opera house:

> No ticket seller at any American movie theater has ever asked me whether I wanted orchestra or balcony, a box or obstructed view; every seat is economy class. Our subway system offers only steerage. What would Tocqueville, Whitman, Sandburg say if they were asked to define themselves as Dress Circle, Grand Tier or Balcony? Your opera ticket takes you back a century in time, transports you ... to nineteenth century Europe, even India (Baker 1991: 26-8).

The travel agent allows you, at cost, to move sideways as well. In general it is difficult for the providers of tourism to ensure the 'social composition' referred to by Urry, but with specific cultural interest group tourism this is not the case. The New York Met's Opera Guild advertises a 'Members Travel Programme' distributed through its *Opera News*. These are 'Deluxe, Escorted Opera and Music Tours' entitled for example, 'Exotic Eastern Europe', 'Best of Britain', 'Italian Opera Festivals'. The first in 1989 advertised a tour between 18 May and 5 June stopping off at Berlin, Dresden, Prague, Budapest and Vienna. Eight operas were included in the itinerary plus ballets and concerts with 'specialised sightseeing, Festive meals ... [and] Fine accommodation'. Perhaps more is promised, for the promotion leaflet by Managing Director, G. Palmer LeRoy begins 'Dear Member of the Metropolitan Guild, A young man's fancy may turn to love come spring, but all of us regardless of our age, fancy foreign travel almost any time of the year ...' In the US Dailey-Thorp Travel offer a wide array of such tours (for example, 'A Musical Festival at Sea On Board the QE2') stopping off at Honolulu, Lahaina, Kona, Los Angeles, Acapulco, Panama Canal, Curacao, St Thomas, Fort Lauderdale, New York: another is less promisingly though perhaps more intriguingly called 'Barging in England'! Great Performance Tours of New York ('The sophisticated traveller's alternative to package tours') employ star singers names and photographs to convey what they have to offer for example, Eva Marton in Vienna *Turandot* and *Forza*, Marilyn Horne in Santa Fe's *Orfeo*: The common commodity, however, is opera:

> ... the tourist is interested in everything as a sign of itself. All over the world the unsung armies of semioticians, the tourists, are fanning out in search of the signs of Frenchness, typical Italian behaviour, exemplary oriental scenes, typical American thruways, traditional English pubs (Culler 1981: 127).

... and French opera, German opera, Italian opera, except that with the universalisation of opera as a commodity the tourist can rest assured that they will see little untoward. There will be no rare contemporary Latvian studio setting of *Margaret Thatcher: The Coup* for them, rather familiar singers, in familiar productions, succoured by 'Festive fare'. 'Major destinations are the most popular: La Scala, Vienna, Bregenz, Verona, London and Munich are offered by most companies, and all would offer Bayreuth, Glyndebourne and Salzburg, if they could get tickets' (Markow 1994: 16). But all this opera is expensive opera, opera as prestige. Sahlins (1976: 169) has noted that an object produced doesn't take on its full meaning until consumed, and there can be little doubt that the full meaning of opera tourism marketed by these companies encompasses the consumption style as well as act—the membership of an 'exclusive' 'community' if only for ten-day breaks at a time. What is consumed is not just opera but opera with degrees of status and difficulty. Individual applications for Bayreuth tickets can take up to eight successive years to be successful, so joining a tour can clearly be an advantage. At Salzburg tour operators are forced to buy tickets for lesser or unpopular events in order to successfully obtain tickets for the major events, and a donation to the Festival's Friends and Patrons is also required. Such contributions are made by many of the larger American tour companies in order to find favour when ticket allocations are made and, for such companies, the tickets have to be the best and most expensive. For top US companies such as Rudolph Travel, Ovations International and Great Performance Tours, accommodation and dining also has to be first-class or de luxe: 'Most customers on these tours are prepared to pay for luxury to realize their dreams. Saving a few dollars on hotels doesn't affect the total cost much anyway' (Markow 1994: 17). Introductory cocktail receptions and farewell parties are also included in with the total 'experience' and cost which, for a two week European tour for North American parties can typically cost between $5000 and $8000 per person and excluding supplements. Within such specialist tours further specialisms exist: Now Voyager Co., for example, offers guided tours which trace Mozart's own lifetime movements. All provide highly qualified guides. '"Free time" can be a bone of contention, some want time to explore on their own; others crave structured activities' (ibid.).

Although the advertising for opera tourism is less high profile Britain, the *Opera Now* 'Guide to Opera Travel Companies' in its International Showcase Edition 1995/96 listed 24 travel companies with opera as a special offering (ibid.: 39). Some 'combined opera and wine tours', some general 'cultural tours', some 'lecturer accompanied', and most offer 'individualised, personalized' arrangements 'for clients wanting to escape being processed in the mass market', providing hotel, restaurant as well as travel and opera bookings. A few merely guarantee tickets, whilst one, HF Holidays Ltd., provides 'music holidays [which] offer coaching in singing, opera and orchestral playing ... If you enjoy singing opera here's a chance to enter a full programme of study and rehearsal'. The regular articles in *Opera News* and *Opera Now* provide as much information as the independent traveller might need and would suffice for all but the more cossetted. *Opera News*, for example, has included a guide to 'European box offices' ('Presented by KLM Royal Dutch Airlines') which warns '... a successful tour requires planning and perseverance' (Zietz 1991: 18). Readers are given key foreign phrases such as: 'sold out' (*'tutto esaurito'*—Italian; *'ausverkauf'*—

German) and 'performances not open to the general public' (*'serata riservata'*— Italian; *'geschlossene Vorstellung'*—German). Potential travellers are told to be adventurous: star performances will be costly and tickets for them will be scarce, so 'try twentieth century operas and local casts. Avoid opening nights and galas, catch new productions a couple of years down the road.' All of this would seem to be unnecessary advice for all but the traveller paralysed by paranoia but the five pages of European opera house box office details which follow, plus odd variations in box office practices are invaluable. For example, it is crucial to know that:

La Scala accepts reservations for all performances of a particular opera for five days only, Tuesday through Saturday, beginning six weeks before the first performance.. Covent Garden accepts reservations on the 10th of the month two months in advance ... Zurich on the other hand accepts reservations for the entire season for all nonsubscription performances etc. (Zietz 1991: 18).

Finding box offices is not as easy as one might suppose. La Scala's is situated:

... through an unmarked door on Via Giuseppe Verdi (bordering the right side of the theatre) and down a flight of stairs. The Hamburg State Opera's box office is over a block away from the main entrance, down 35 Grosse Theaterstrasse ... few of the personnel speak English, and their willingness to be helpful varies For this reason we have included, a Seat Location entry, with translation, in the Ticket Guide (ibid.: 17).

Most theatres have a queue system for standing room on the day of, or day preceding, the performance, but rules of queuing are often dictated by 'regulars' and unclear to visitors. If all formal attempts (box office, hotel concierge and so on) fail to get a particular hard-sought ticket, the tourist should seek a 'scalper' (tout) (who charges two to three times the face value): 'At La Scala "scalpers" put your name on a list, since they don't know ahead of time how many tickets they will get. Have your ticket in hand before you pay.' As for seat or standing locations (see also Appendix B):

Regrettably some of the most beautiful houses offer some of the worst seats... many seats have a great view—of the other boxes, [so the] rule of thumb is avoid side seats in horseshoe houses, especially those closest to the stage. Standing room visibility, location and price vary from house to house... Vienna and Munich have a *Stehparterre* directly behind the orchestra seats, whereas the standing room at La Scala is behind the Gallery seats, only steps from heaven ... (Zietz 1991: 18).

Start times vary too, and some houses don't put start times on the tickets. Likely disconcerting experiences follow from being unable to find one's seat: 'Ushers are not so visible and plentiful as in the US.' Finally because 'hassle-free' is the intention, the Guide lists hotels within 10 minutes' walk of each opera house. Crouch (1991) also provides a guide for the individual (American) traveller in Europe who is steered away from the obvious principal houses and towards more out-of-the-way places where, even so, one might encounter the odd superstar or two. Critics of such popularising guides are quick to establish their superior credentials: 'One cannot have everything, but I confess I regret Mr Crouch has failed to find room for Toulon, Montpelier and Monte Carlo, towns in whose opera houses I have spent many happy hours' (Law 1992: 448). Beat that, oh intrepid traveller! Most of these texts, and the organised tours in particular, are premised on the expenditure of considerable amounts of money, certainly if one is be armed with a wardrobe sufficient to accompany 'Festive fare', but never fear, Baker instructs the penniless on how to cope 'Down and Out in Salzburg and Bayreuth' (8 December 1990: 26-30, 73).

Media 'promo'/'special offer'

In Britain the broadsheets consistently run promotions for opera (and concert and ballet) going. *The Sunday Times,* for example, in association with the commercial Classic FM radio station 'sold' 'The Best of Britain Concert Series' (25 July 1993) a week after *The Times Magazine* (17 July 1993: 27-29), under the heading 'Everyone Needs Opera' sold ENO seats to readers at 40 per cent discount for six autumn productions. 'As well as cheaper tickets, *Times* readers will be given a free programme and a glass of wine. Readers may reserve a parking space at a discount rate and those who book early will be entered for a prize draw, the winners of which will be given dinner at one of London's leading restaurants' (ibid.: 27). To benefit from this offer, readers had to order tickets for at least two of the six productions (*La Bohème, Simon Boccanegra, Street Scene, The Rape of Lucretia, The Barber of Seville* and *Figaro's Wedding*) all given plot summaries and, where necessary, production warnings:

> Alden's 1987 production of this vast masterpiece [*Boccanegra*] by Verdi, the grand man of 19th century Italian opera, was last seen at the Coliseum five years ago. It was a controversial staging then, visually arresting and dominated by a huge pointing hand whose meaning some had difficulty in understanding... (ibid.: 127).

Not too promising that—certainly not on only one free glass of wine! *La Bohème* is more reassuringly 'ever popular ... [and] still has the power to move the hardest souls with its undeniably sentimental brand of pathos. The melodies are heart rending ... the drama is gripping ...' *The Independent on Sunday Magazine* (16 January 1994: 23) carried a similar promotion:

> *The Independent on Sunday* has got together with the ENO to arrange a series of *IoS Nights* at the London Coliseum, giving readers the chance to see top-class opera at about 30% off the usual prices, including *Die Fledermaus* 'Strauss' joyous farce ...; *Xerxes* Nicholas Hytner's popular production of Handel's Baroque comedy; *Falstaff* 's suitably colourful production by David Pountney'; *The Pearl Fishers* 'Bizet's classic opera ... contains much passion and one of the most famous duets of all ...

Both promotions coincided with the 'new' post-*Power House* ENO regime's first season, when ticket sales were suffering something of a nose-dive. The 1980s in Britain was a period of economic growth, but by the end of the decade recession was blamed, at least in part, for the opera boom going into reverse. Attempts by the broadsheets to get their readers to concerts and opera do not, however, seem to be narrowly related to recession-led shortfalls in regular demand. In any case there are many potential and actual audiences for many different forms of opera as demonstrated by *The Sunday Times* (24 April 1994: 8) announcing, prematurely it would seem, the end of the recession under 'Good times roll for city slickers', referring to displays of corporate extravagance:

> Gone is the feeling of austerity. Balance sheets are bulging ... and the chauffeur driven limos are returning to the season's highlights, Wimbledon, Ascot and Covent Garden—all at company expense. The champagne is flowing again reported Siobhan Sweeney, marketing manager of KP Hospitality, the Wembley based corporate entertainment company.

Each event has its target audience ...

> For those preferring something cultural, £280 will buy an evening of opera at Blenheim Palace with Placido Domingo, followed by dinner with the Duke of Marlborough and the great singer himself.

Kiri Te Kanawa was due to sing at Harewood House between Leeds and Harrogate: 'The North's musical event of the summer' proclaimed full page press ads: 'In the beautiful grounds of Harewood House, Kiri, the world's favourite soprano ...' and so on, but too few tickets (£25 to £65 plus £2.50 booking fee) were sold and the concert cancelled. Meanwhile *The Sunday Times* took steps to promote 'hard' 'high' culture with a series on 'Contemporary Composers'. One edition carried potted biographies of the composers Witold Lutoslawski, Gyorgy Ligeti, Iannis Xenakis and Harrison Birtwhistle, followed by recommended recordings available at reduced cost. None of Ligeti's stage works were referred to but Birtwhistle's biography included reference to:

> His biggest statement to date, the bewilderingly complicated opera *The Mask of Orpheus* premiered at the Coliseum in 1986, in which mythical characters appear in triplicate: as singer puppet and mime... Birtwhistle's most recent opera *Gawain* w a s successfully launched at Covent Garden in 1991 ... (*The Sunday Times* 16 January 1994: 9, 28-29).[10]

As we have seen in earlier chapters, opera companies such as the ENO and the Royal Opera employ sometimes shocking and 'vulgar' techniques to advertise their wares, other companies in Britain do likewise. In 1995 Scottish Opera assaulted Scots with 'Get off your arias' posters, and in September 1993 the Welsh National Opera, no doubt to attract the unconfident, advertised its *Lucia di Lammermoor* below a pre-Raphaelite face cut across by a bolt of lightening, with the following ascribed quotes: 'Dynasty in kilts' (Gore Vidal); 'The soprano's Everest' (Dame Joan Sutherland); and 'Combines Romeo and Juliet with Wuthering Heights' (Sir George Bernard Shaw).

Generally it would seem that although classical music is being consumed more than at any stage this century, its consumption in the concert hall and opera house is, if not declining, at least not cast-iron guaranteed. *The Times* (19 January 1994: 33) asked, under the heading 'A classic case for going pop', 'Will a glamorous awards gala devised by Bob Geldof win new fans for classical music?' 'the very concept of which must make the *cognoscenti* shudder.' The gala was held at the Royal Albert Hall by Harvey Goldsmith who staged the *Pavarotti in the Park* concert. The Japanese hi-fi firm Kenwood sponsored the awards to the tune of £500,000. The report by Richard Morrison claimed that, despite Classic FM's high listening figures, those listening were neither buying CDs nor going to concerts. Apart from the odd Gorecki and Three Tenors disc, classical record sales were obstinately static. Box office figures in major classical venues were in decline. The intention was to guarantee a prime time slot on TV worldwide. The programme was hosted by all-purpose TV 'high arts' presenter and writer Melvyn Bragg and percussionist Evelyn Glennie. Goldsmith attacked *afficionados* for sectarian views which had done much damage over the years—the damage presumably having been mainly commercial.

By most accounts one of the most important media promotions of opera, certainly one of the most curious, occurs every two years with the Cardiff Singer of the World competitions. Winners have included Dmitri Hvoroshovsky (Bryn Terfel won the Lieder prize the same year). In 1993 the winner was Inger Dam-Jensen who had her debut concert in London (Barbican, 18 January 1994) sponsored by the competition's sponsors BP ('For All Our Tomorrows'). She was joined by 1993's Lieder winner Paul Whelan. On the TV coverage of the 1991 competition Alan Blyth wrote:

[it] is still too much in the nature of a public relations exercise ... Humphrey Burton ... still tended to praise too indiscriminately. Seckerson and Gomez (commentators) created a double act of bubbling enthusiasm, tending to go to extremes in their

judgements. Once more the singing voices were distant as compared with the speaking ones, which broke in after the singers' offerings as if they were commercials ... (1991: 981).

The 1995 competition, again screened on BBC 1 each evening for a week and in severely truncated form showed a deterioration in the BBC's faith in the event. The greatest emphasis seemed to be on giving the competitors, through basic interviews, a 'personality' or 'face' at the cost of being able to hear them sing a single aria from beginning to end. Bite-sized they may be but arias are mostly too long for 25-minute broadcasts of this kind. Introduced by a gushingly generalised Nathalie Wheen who asked a different 'expert' each night for their opinions, little apart from the 'excitement' of competition seemed to be conveyed to audiences no doubt responding according to the generalised scripting provided by *The Reader's Digest* and The Beautiful Music Company of New York State. To accompany the 1993 broadcast (14-19 June 1993) the BBC included a segment on 'selling' opera, marketing singers, including interviews with record company promoters (from EMI and Sylva Screen, the latter company promoting Garrett), the use of 'pop' promotion techniques, T-shirts, videos, 'singles', for example the duet from *Lakmé*. Roger Lewis ('think MTV') noted that 'glamour is not a new phenomenon' but this missed the point—Garrett sells 'sex'. As a 'saleable commodity' marketing men want 'a pretty face, a dynamic personality, the voice is less important'. The possibility of a marketable tenor with a 'Chippendale' physique proved more difficult to be certain about but, in their different ways, Domingo and Carreras do sell 'sex'. It was acknowledged that audiences and potential audiences have different and varied sensibilities and that to 'sell' classical music, many of these sensibilities have to be eroded.

Recording companies may set out to erode sensibilities but, as we have seen, they are as likely to reinforce them. Garrett may sell 'opera' to some, but Te Kanawa sells the full auratic equity to others. To some extent though, despite their differences, as predicted by Adorno, technology and commodification have changed the ways in which both are seen and heard: with the technological reproduction of music the modern hierarchy of the senses has become superseded, so that now we 'see' more than we 'hear' (Negt and Kluge 1987: 66), and what we 'hear' has to be cut down to size.

Classic FM

As with surtitles in the opera house, the technical reproduction of opera and classical music outside are cut down to a morsel size that eases consumption and digestion but destroys any sense of the meal as a whole. In a *Daily Telegraph* Magazine interview with Michael Bukht, the head of Classic FM it was reported that, after 17 months, a weekly audience of 4.7 million and monthly advertising revenues of over £1 million had enabled it to break even much earlier than forecast. It also has a commercial licence in the Netherlands—its first step into Europe. CD sales took off when classical music was exposed to a mass audience (Torvill and Dean and Ravel's *Bolero:* World Cup and Kiri Te Kanawa), and the queues for 'Pavarotti in the Park', even in a downpour:

> I knew a commercial classical station would work because I wanted to listen to one ... I didn't want to fiddle about with tapes, trying to find the best bits. I wanted a station that would do it all for me. Not the Renaissance nose-flute stuff, right, because my taste is Catholic. I wanted Callas' greatest hits and the Mozart piano concertos (Bukhta quoted in Howell 1993).

Like opera house audiences, with 65 per cent of its audience in socioeconomic groups ABC 1, Classic FM is played in homes, studios, cafes, restaurants, changing rooms, gift shops and delicatessens—in other words, as soundtrack to consumption. Bukhta 'runs Classic FM like a rock station. "Our audiences are not necessarily into three and a half hours of Wagner, I mean, join the club. I'm a founder member".' Early mispronunciations of composers' names and foreign titles had them rolling in the aisles at Radio 3 but these *faux pas* gave the press a lot of fun and the station extra coverage. Listeners picked up on the game, 'aware that music was being demystified ...' Presenters now keep a (phonetic) notebook for hard cases such as Peter Nagy (PETTER NOJ) Darius Milhaud (MEE-YO) and Xua-Wei (SHOO-AY-WAY).

> Classic could do nursery rhymes now and get away with it ... At Radio 3 they tell you that Classic FM hasn't harmed their audience and in a sense they are right when they suggest that by increasing the awareness of classical music, Classic can be said to

have promoted their interests. Indeed Radio 3 has put on 400,000 listeners since the new station's launch. But to dismiss Classic as a sampler station, the *hors d'oeuvre* to Radio 3's main dish, is to miss an important point. Classic's rise has not been matched by an equal rise in concert attendances. The new listeners appear to prefer the best bits of their favourite composers served up at home rather than having to endure the *longueurs* of full-length operas and draughty concert halls. They may stay with Classic forever ...

As part of Classic FM's ambition to get Radio 3's audience, opera plays a prominent role. Radio 3 has its largest weekly audience on Saturday evenings with the Texaco matinee broadcasts from the New York Met. Not having sufficient funds to compete with live broadcasts on this weekly scale, Classic FM nevertheless plays full-length opera recordings in the same slot, and Paul Gambuccini's 'chart show' clashes on Saturday mornings with Radio 3's record review.[11]

The upsurge in interest in activity (particularly business) around opera and 'opera' finds certain broadsheet commentators such as Wheatcroft distinctly dispirited:

> Why so much expenditure of time and money and effort on what, when looked at from one angle, is surely a marginal artistic activity? With opera companies sprouting on all sides (despite the occasional ruthless piece of pruning by the Arts Council) it is now possible for a fanatical follower of the lyric stage to hear performances on most nights of the week, in most weeks of the year in up to a dozen cities ... The deleterious cult of opera has never been more intense. Not a week passes without a new book on opera, not a year without some new magazine stuffed full with uncritical and unreflective articles, by popular novelists or well-known society hostesses, the magazines even glossier, their contents ever drossier. Plainly there is a market, not only for genuinely distinguished evenings of International Opera like the recent Covent Garden *Otello*, but for crummy recordings, tatty videos, or gruesome evenings like last summer's Pavarotti recital on the Isle of Dogs ... All this when the art at the centre of the cult is in dire condition (1990: 288).

This tirade is a response to opera becoming 'opera', in various, 'vulgar', 'fragmented' ways, being promoted and consumed outside the opera house by those who can't afford to, nor would want to, get in, especially at an 'International Night' such as a Domingo/Te Kanawa *Otello* at Covent Garden. 'Fanatical followers of the lyric art' are also suspect, for isn't opera a 'deleterious cult'?

All of this makes opera's audience seem dangerous to know and frightening to be with—a far cry from the image conjured from the harassed Scottish Opera marketing spokesperson, following my request for audience details: 'We don't have any, but whoever you speak to, they'll all say the same thing: opera's audience is made up of ABC 1 females over 45, and they're shrinking!'

Notes

1. The stars include, and the surnames reeled off demand familiarity: Domingo, Price (Leontyne), Tebaldi, de los Angeles, Te Kanawa, Caruso, Pavarotti, Stevens, Bjoerling, Callas, Gedda, Scotto, Lehmann, Corelli, Schwarzkopf, Prey, Pons, Kraus, Hvorostovsky, Sutherland, Tibbett, von Stade, Ludwig, Traubel, Caballé, Flagstad, Milnes, Pinza, Popp, Moffo, and Siepi. The selection of arias is of interest too: *'Un bel di'*, *'E lucevan le stelle'*, *'O souave fanciulla'*, *'Vissi d'arte'*, *'Mi chiamano Mimi'*, *'O mio babbino caro'*, *'Nessun dorma'*, and *'Che gelida manina'* provide the eight Puccini out of 40 items specified. Verdi provides 12, four from *La traviata*, three each from *Aida* and *Rigoletto*, two from *Otello*. Arias from *I Pagliacci*, *Norma*, *Martha*, *Tristan und Isolde*, *Carmen*, *Der Rosenkavalier*, *Faust*, *Lakmé*, *The Magic Flute*, *The Tales of Hoffmann*, *Samson And Dalila* (sic), *Die Walküre*, *I Puritani*, *The Marriage of Figaro*, and *Daughter of the Regiment* are also referred to, using this mixture of original and anglicised (sometimes of both) titles. 'What a remarkable value!'
2. The contents of the six compact discs were then summarised under the headings: World Famous Arias; All-time Favourites; Great Voices, Beautiful Melodies; Unforgettable Moments; The World's Favourite Choruses; Magical Moments from Golden Operas; Favourite Forever; and Timeless Souvenirs.
3. I have the impression that many of the elements that are supposed to provide access to music actually impoverishes our relationship with it. There is a quantitative mechanism working here. A certain rarity of relation to music could preserve an ability to choose what one hears, and thus a flexibility in listening. But the more frequent this relation is (radio, records, cassettes), the more familiarities it creates; habits crystallize; the most frequent becomes the most acceptable, and soon the only thing perceivable. It produces a 'tracing' as neurologists say (Foucault 1985/86: 8).
4. At the time of the New York Met's celebrations marking the 25th anniversaries of Domingo and Pavarotti in September 1993 these two were called the 'Two Megatenors' (see Muir 1993: 15).
5. Tenor Jon Vickers was offered the *Camelot* lead ($750,000) but turned it down. Herbert von Karajan's recording of *Die*

Fledermaus included an extended gala at Orlofsky's ball in which famous 'guests' such as Birgit Nilsson sang 'crossover' numbers.

6. Cleo Laine has crossed over from the other direction, ostensibly a jazz vocalist with considerable success in pop music, she has sung and recorded Schoenberg's *Pierrot Lunaire*, performed in Weill's *Seven Deadly Sins* with the ENO, recorded *On the Town* alongside Frederica von Stade, Thomas Hampson, Samuel Ramey and so on, and sung Walton's *Façade* at the Royal Festival Hall under the composer's baton.

7. Steyn refers to comments heard on the radio that classical music is the popular music of its day: 'As I understand it, if Beethoven were alive today he'd be a gangsta rapper in the South Bronx Somehow I doubt it. More likely ... he'd be cursing the guy who invented the hearing aid.'

8. Several people have called the CD 'sexy' and 'sexy' is how several artists are now packaged and sold. Under the heading 'Image makers give CDs sex appeal', *The Independent on Sunday* (9 June 1990: 10) published the following:

> Whatever the quality of the next recording of Bach's *Air on a G string* one trembles to think what might be pictured on the record sleeve. Seizing on or perhaps provoking a burgeoning of public interest in classical music, record companies are using pop industry marketing tactics to sell virtuosi as sex symbols. The results speak for themselves as do the implications for classical music, which are beginning to cause some alarm. Neil Hoyle, chief executive of the Incorporated Society of Musicians said yesterday: 'We are watching these developments nervously. They may be a necessary evil in bringing classical music to a wider audience but our code of ethics for performers says 'advertising should only relate to services offered ... publicity should be tasteful and honest'.
>
> The report (by David Lister) goes on to refer to Nadja Salerno-Sonnenberg's plunging neckline 'which failed to influence *The Times* which described her Tchaikovsky violin concerto as 'one of the most vulgar and vacuous displays of self-projection at the expense of the music' and then the full leather gear of Cecilia Bartoli 'the soft focus Garboesque picture of Ute Lemper, the singer of Kurt Weill songs'. Also on

the rack is Ofra Harnoy, the Canadian cellist, whom RCA picture with pouting lips, reclining on a sofa while caressing her cello-giving an edge to a recent review which said that while her playing was beautiful she had much to learn about slow movements'. EMI helped start the classics boom by its marketing of the violinist Nigel Kennedy as a punk haired Aston Villa supporter. His first disc—pre haircut and pre Wogan—sold respectably, but far less than his recent Vivaldi and the Mendelssohn and Bruch concertos, which this week figured in the pop charts, a rare event for a classical release. Terri Anderson for EMI said: 'We've to be careful not to throw the baby out with the bath water. We've now proved that classical music can be sold to a wider audience, turn someone into a pop star and lose the classical audience. There is also sometimes a personality problem with women. Anne-Sophie Mutter, the German violinist and former Karajan protegee was once on the verge of being marketed *à la* Kennedy by EMI for her mixture of gifted playing and good looks, spiced by her taste for strapless frocks, until it was discovered in the words of one executive that she 'lacked the common touch'. A spokesman for HMV record shops said: 'Sexy marketing definitely does help. We sold four times more of Harnoy than we expected. Popular high profile advertising does reach an audience who wouldn't otherwise bear about classical music.' But those who fear that CD might be fast living up to its pronunciation were reminded in the latest issue of the magazine *Classic CD* that there is a tradition of emphasising the charms of female players. One reviewer said that Vivaldi—whose works Kennedy and Harnoy have brought to new audiences—was himself in charge of the musical education of young ladies at a charitable institution for foundling girls in Venice. Apparently one visitor wrote: 'There is nothing so diverting as the sight of a pretty young nun in white, with pomegranate over her ear beating time with all the grace and precision imaginable'.

The Independent on Sunday (4 March 1990) presented a very similar piece, 'Musicians have charms to woo the jaded record buyer':

> Posters of Israeli-Canadian Ofra Harnoy decorate the London Underground, in fully clothed but distinctly sultry repose on a *chaise-longue*. In theory she's selling her recording of Vivaldi's concertos—but in practice her cascading curls and imploring smile are selling her image. The campaign is paying off. With old fashioned promotion, Tower Records in London's Piccadilly would sell perhaps 30 compact discs of a new recording of a popular classic in the first month. With Ms Harnoy it has sold 200 ... the manager (said) 'What dismays me is that people are buying it because of the photographs, not because of the music.' Ms Harnoy evidently supports the hard sell: "She likes the idea of reaching out" said ... her marketing manager at RCA Records. She is not alone. Cecilia Bartoli, a 24 year old Italian mezzo-soprano, was marketed by Decca in a black leather biker's jacket and gloves. She features in fashion as well as music magazines. The German virtuoso Anne-Sophie Mutter was dubbed 'The Strapless Violinist' by *Vanity Fair*. Critics, exclusively male, panned a concert poster that revealed a glimpse of Ms Mutter's cleavage. The leader of such techniques however is male says this report, Nigel Kennedy's *The Four Seasons* having sold 200,000. Like Kylie he does not give concerts he plays gigs. "People are coming into store asking for anything by Nigel Kennedy" said the manager of Tower Records. Christopher Pollard of *Gramophone* believes the trend shows classical music catching up with the real world.

9. Di Giovanni (1994) tries to build the modem packaged *diva* as scandal theme none too successfully, by referring to the incident when Roocroft's boyfriend was widely reported to have punched her Covent Garden tenor lead of the time, of whom he was jealous, as well as to the supposed 'cat fight' resulting from Kenny's 'crossover' album being called by the same name as Garrett's. 'These singers are more famous for their off stage antics than their on stage singing', which must be deeply disappointing to Kenny, a Berlin Staatsoper Countess in *Capriccio* and Covent Garden *Alcina*, and to Roocroft who has moved rapidly to a position of international eminence as a

Mozartian of distinction. But commercial and marketing pressures have progressively constructed a media diva increasingly sold (as are female classical instrumentalists such as Harnoy) through images of suggestive sexuality, from which such mundane popularising reportage cannot be held at bay.

10. Parallel developments affect the concert hall and attempts to attract new and younger audiences. *The Sunday Times* (15 May 1994) was one of many newspapers reporting on the RPO and LPOs decision to abandon black tail suits for its male players. 'Soon it may be not only Nigel Kennedy who abandons the starched black-and-white penguin look on the concert stage' (*The Times* 16 May 1994). The former was reported in negotiation with Austin Reed to design a new wardrobe. Chris Lawrence 'managing director of the LPO said the formality of tails puts off inexperienced concert-goers. "If you're going for new audiences, you've got to find ways of making them feel comfortable ... and we want to experiment with a view to extending it if it works"'.

The RPO is considering different coloured shirts for different moods of music.

'It's about being adaptable, and developing a more casual and accessible image', said an Austin Reed spokesman, 'We're looking at blazers shirts and maybe tails with a twist, such as a dinner shirt in fuschia pink' ... Bob Truman, principal cellist with the LPO wants white shirts and smart waistcoats: 'Comfort is everything to a musician, and the suits are so incredibly hot.' The LPO are thinking of Sunday morning 'family' concerts 'hosted by a television celebrity' (*The Times* 16 May 1994).

The suggestion made in the latter's report is that Classic FM and the CD have created millions of new fans who have never been to a concert and that these are the target new audience. The RPO is also thinking of giant screens projecting large images of conductors and soloists, as is done in the arena concerts of the Three Tenors. *The Times* editorial (also 16 May) reports on the shock of these plans to traditionalists—'Many a good tune can be played in an old-fashioned suit'—and reminded readers that Previn used to conduct in a polo neck and Boulez wore day suits:

'What matters is the music'.

11. Gambuccini moved to Radio 3 in October 1995, his weekday morning programme on Classic FM receiving several brickbats from critics. By January 1997 he had departed from Radio 3.

8   Audiences' opera

Opera—dont'cha hate it?

Yes, I do hate opera.

I hate having to organize my life six months in advance.

I hate having to enclose stamped addressed envelopes.

I hate everyone in the audience who knows less than me (they're fools).

I hate everyone in the audience who knows more than me (they're pretentious).

I hate everyone in front of me in the coffee queue.

I hate Callas bores, Jessye Norman groupies, and everyone who insists that the good recordings, are those which are so old that the music is inaudible.

I hate all singers who are rivals to my own favourites.

I hate critics who disagree with me (they're wrong).

I hate opinionated people.

I hate producers.

I hate people who insist that operas I don't know are neglected masterpieces. I hate people who don't realise that *Der ferne Klang* is a masterpiece. I hate *Faust*.

I hate Alden and Fielding (One of these days ENO will get around to doing *Palestrina*. Knowing my luck it will be with these two, in which case I shall ask the box-office for a refund on my life).

I hate boring, old fashioned productions.

I hate people who write stupid letters to *Opera*. I think of myself as a typical opera lover (O. Toller, *Opera* June 1990: 649).

Introduction

This is more like it! Obsessive yet succinct, astringent but amusing, replete with 'in-group' references suggestive of the ingested knowledge of a subculture effectively closed off from a wider world, yet anything but 'shrinking'. Whilst this may appear to be little more than the mantra of one fanatical cult member, it is far from being the brainwashed mindless repetition of a priesthood's teachings. On the contrary here is a member of opera's laity with strong opinions. In Chapter 1 I commented that academic opera discourses largely remain high-mindedly concerned to remove the works from the theatre as though 'opera is always in danger of lapsing into decadence' (Tanner 1994: 1), because culturally untutored (Shepherd 1987: 60) audiences will insist on having their say. For most in audiences, 'having their say' takes the form of box office demand for operas deemed second- or third-rate by the priesthood, but for self-declared opera *lovers, fanatics, operamanes* or *'regulars'*, it can also mean subversive mutterings in the congregation, loud enough to be considered a threat to order and the hierarchy of orthodox knowledge, which is no doubt why musicologists, practitioners (singers, producers and conductors), and their junior clergy (critics and journalists), seek to control the unruly, and maintain their own superior status by means of the kind of language deployed by Wheatcroft (1990).

Audiences are meant to know their place, socially, ritually and (un)knowledgeably. Encouraged to acquire orthodox knowledge via several languages of varying degrees of difficulty, their relationship to this knowledge is properly deferential, possibly not even fully comprehending. Some may follow tutelage as instructed, most cannot for a combination of social, economic and musicological reasons, leaving them, and their instructors firmly in their respective strata. In his *Observer* review of the premiere of *Arianna*, 'a lost opera by Claudio Monteverdi composed again by Alexander Goehr', Andrew Porter preached: 'Covent Garden has published the libretto bilingually. Read it in advance. Arrive in time to read Alison Latham's programme book, rich in information, stimulation, speculation and iconography' (24 September 1995: 12). Again we are reminded that '... art is a series of rhetorical strategies ... used in the production of types of knowledge ... and the formation of power relations' (Tambling 1987: 20), which rely on the congregation remaining docile when 'the priesthood prattles in its jargon' (McClary 1987: 17).

Perhaps comparable tensions exist in other 'live' arts, but it seems that opera audiences, even the most reserved, are more unruly than most: they are inclined to boo, cheer, hiss, throw flowers (or vegetables), shout *bravo* and, where appropriate, to impress those keen of hearing, *brava*, make derogatory comments mid-aria and stamp their feet. Two unruly audience elements are inclined to make critics tense. Both, though in different ways, draw attention to themselves, one for having too little 'knowledge', the other for having too much and of the wrong sort. Critics like meek, quiet audiences. Anyone who makes a noise out of turn is unwelcome, thus those who parade (listening to others in bar and concourse is a fundamental opera pastime and not difficult as voices usually project!) their ignorance, lack of judgement, taste or respect—possibly by extra-curricular snoring, setting off equally distracting elbow-wielding from embarrassed companions—are not 'true' opera lovers and are suspected of being present for non-operatic reasons. Such reluctant operagoers may be found at all levels of the house, the higher they snore the more likely they are deemed simply to be tired, but as critics sit in stalls and dress circles, the image presented is a traditional one of wealthy inebriated boredom and lack of 'proper' appreciation of what is being witnessed, with perhaps now the added gloss of more highly organised corporate Phillistinism. Such audiences are not 'active' enough in their responses. Here is Milnes on the gala first night audience of Covent Garden's then new *Simon Boccanegra* in 1991:

> Kiri Te Kanawa's exquisite singing of one of the trickiest of all Verdi arias was greeted with stony silence, had the audience any idea what they were hearing? How can artists give of their best under such circumstances? (1992: 105).

Critics are spies; they sit with the congregation but are not of them, paid to be there by the church as monitors of order, their shadowy presence only suspected when notes are scribbled mid-service and by a certain detachment from the audience's 'active' participation.

Philistines and 'queens'

This first type of 'lapsed' or 'collapsed' laity has to be tolerated—in the current financial circumstances of retreating state subsidies and increased sponsorship perhaps even encouraged—but they remain not the 'right' kind of 'serious', ruly congregation, properly in awe of 'high art', although they may well recognise their relatively superior status compared with audiences of lower forms of art, barely comprehending the challenge they set the opera critic. However:

> ... which intellectual category an individual belongs to is not decided by his appreciation of the fine arts—all modern geniuses are known to read detective stories and one doubts Einstein's record collection included Schoenberg and the existence of a mass of generic art appreciators is a myth left over from European aristocratic and pseudo-aristocratic meditations on lost peasant cultures and noble savages... this myth serves the purpose not of art nor of the public but of salesmanship or political propaganda—one who speaks on behalf of an art for The Public is trying to recruit a new public out of existing publics (Rosenberg 1970: 64).

Opera critics tend to be much *more* irritated by the second deviant element—those who in several ways challenge critics as disseminators of knowledge in the body of the kirk. These are 'regulars' who attend performances too often for their own good and ours. They are loud and strident in their declared 'knowledge', based more on experience of opera *in situ* and recordings than from reading the theoretical treatises of the clergy. Accordingly this 'knowledge' is for critics and practitioners mere opinion: 'ask any 50 who should sing a role and you'll get 50 answers' (Sinclair 1993b). Their knowledge is 'false' knowledge: trivial, devoted to singers not the song, live *divas* and dead *divas*, referred to by first, pet-names, autographed *divas* with whom they seem to be or have been, personally—in some instances of 'dead'—even supernaturally, acquainted (see Koestenbaum 1993). These 'fanatics' are to be pitied for, and this is where opera critics show their ultimate regard for 'absolute' principles, they are obsessed by an art form that, apart from a handful of 'masterpieces', is deeply flawed, because of their indiscriminate love of bad works, badly performed by singers who are 'outstanding' usually for the wrong reasons: their interest is 'camp' not genuine because in the opinion of many in the predominantly male priesthood, their interest is not 'serious'; they are 'opera queens', 'outsiders' who've somehow got in. It is interesting how these derided 'fans' are, like the critics who deride them, invariably male. At the turn of the century the *prima donna* captured the imagination of teenage girls, screaming 'gerryflappers' idolised and imitated Geraldine Farrar; a young woman in Chicago killed herself for the thwarted love of Mary Garden; and the heroine of the Australian film *My Brilliant Career* committed suicide with a photograph of Dame Nellie Melba pinned over her head. Audience research suggests that more females than males attend and despite the Three Tenors' association with the *machismo* of football, their audiences and consumers are, it is claimed, chiefly female—yet where are the female opera critics? One or two work for the opera press and do journalistic interviews with singers in the broadsheets, but 'serious' critics and criticism is male and masculine, hence no doubt the vituperation levelled against uppity amateurs as 'queens'. As noted in Chapter 5, men involved in opera, in whatever capacity, frequently justify their involvement with this most artificial, reputationally 'camp', art form, in terms which assert their masculinity. All that is properly good and serious about opera is male, including the power of the predominantly male clergy; all that is trivial and poor is effeminate. Christiansen pleads for 'opera foyers for the happy band of normal healthy opera lovers who could show me how to get "opera love" into rational perspective but then opera works better as a forum for emotions than for rational debates' (1985: 1358). This is the problem: rational debate is a masculine quality, emotions are feminine, the male opera fan is less than rational and less than masculine or male. Wheatcroft gives a classic example of such *machismo* where doubts about manhood mingle with similar doubts about opera itself.

Opera has always been overweening and gross—twenty-five masterpieces ... apart ... anyone who goes continually to the opera is listening to much indifferent music. The crucial case is Puccini. Not long ago Rupert Christiansen wrote that in his heart, every opera lover knows that Puccini is his favourite composer. I don't want to break butterflies, and Mr Christiansen is an amusing fellow, but this was a jest speaking a true word. That is just what

393

many opera lovers do think in their hearts. But surely any *music* lover would give all of Puccini for a single Haydn quartet ... To contrast opera lovers with music lovers is unkind but not unfair. Anyone who goes to the opera regularly must often find *his* fellow opera-goers depressing. I am not thinking so much of the 'unmusical aristocracy' ... the undeserving rich have been the mainstay of opera since Mantua centuries ago. They are participants in the cult but comparatively innocent ones. Much worse are the fanatics whom Jonathan Miller has pithily called 'disgusting old opera queens'. It is not their screaming (or booing) that is so dejecting so much as their infantile canary fancying. Opera may be about the primacy of the singing voice, but singing what? High above the bankers in the stalls are people who would cross the country to hear Rusti-Guzzi in *Emilia di Liverpool* but would not recognise a Beethoven piano sonata. Even critics do not live blameless lives in this respect. Compare the amount of time they spend at and space they devote to opera-going rather than healthier music-making (Wheatcroft 1990: 288-90).

As in debates on 'produceritis', such tirades are not infrequently tinged with a xenophobic mistrust of behaviours at odds with both 'natural' manliness and British reserve. Part of the problem and symptom of 'unhealthy foyers' is the regularity with which 'fans' go to opera. They overdose. It seems strange for a journal, *Opera*, to discourage frequent operagoing but, responding to a correspondent's letter on price increases at Covent Garden pricing out regular operagoers who used ' ... to be found, loyally, in the house sometimes twice or three times a week ...', *Opera* asked 'Is it actually healthy to go to the opera that often?':

We all know that man shall not live by bread alone, but there are worse foundations to a healthy diet. Opera could never be described as bread. Rather it is the richest fruit cake (but) fruit-cake for every meal would prove unthinkable. I take care not to hear Beethoven's Choral Symphony, or the Schubert Quintet, or the Jupiter Symphony, or the Verdi Requiem more than once a year ... I very seriously wonder just how wholesome it is to feel compelled to spend one's spare time with the modern equivalents of Tetrazzini and Caruso, or with people like Salome ... Lulu, Turandot ... (Milnes 1990d: 1031).

Tongue in cheek perhaps? Yet note here that the rarified 'greats' referred to include not one opera. Milnes recommends at most a 'twice a year fix, apart from anything else ... [which] would allow others to try it out', yet he reviews for *The Times* as well as *Opera* at least two or three times a week, apparently in robust health. Wheatcroft, above, refers to Rupert Christiansen as an 'amusing fellow' who is not, however, amused by this loudly opinionated element which trades in three kinds of 'false knowledge'. For Christiansen the problem with opera is:

> ... not that people are singing what they could speak, or that I can't decide between Domingo and Pavarotti ... My problem is the audience: it makes me extremely uncomfortable, to the point of wishing I was somewhere else. Now the usual explanation of such a feeling is that any right minded person is disgusted at the parade of rich Philistines, whose motives for attending are entirely material and superficial, and who take up space which would be better occupied by the poor cramped music loving proletariat upstairs—but this seems to me grossly unfair and inaccurate as a stereotype. The few conspicuously rich people I ever notice at the opera have a persecuted look about them ... They say harmless things like 'It's jolly good', 'It did go on a bit', or 'Is that the woman who sang at the Royal Wedding?' They are ready to admire, usually stupefied by alcohol, and quite ignorant and harmless. No, the real problem I have with the opera audience is not a matter of class and money ... What unnerves me is ... a series of aesthetic snobberies (1985: 1355).

These aesthetic snobberies are threefold. First there are the connoisseurs of singing—'*vieille école* these days'—identifiable by their constant expressions of dissatisfaction such as 'You like this Azucena? But of course you are too young to remember Stignani ...' To be impressed by anyone contemporary borders on the comic, and they have their 78s to back them up. They are 'exclusively male' and obsessive about comparison: if Stignani was good, you may be sure that Olczewska was better, at least in the 1930s. It is interesting that Christiansen should object to non-professionals adopting the very discursive model employed by media critics and reviewers. Second, in 'this age of the producer' we find another dread 'knowledge' incarnated in 'fierce young intellectuals' who interpret opera as

395

though it were a play with incidental music and who seek 'the complete theatrical experience' rather than 'concerts in costume', involving a definite set of priorities: first the production, then the design, third the acting. It is no longer music that is the medium of operatic expression, but the layers of significance that can be extracted from the libretto. He names as an example Peter Conrad, in *The Times Literary Supplement* on *Il barbiere di Siviglia*'s 'appetitive rebellion, the gustatory licence which is the energy of Romanticism'; on *Louise*, an opera 'about what Zola called the experimental laboratory of naturalism'; and Gluck's *Alceste* whose mission initiates her 'into the post-mortem condition of chastened resignation which is the ideal of neoclassicism'. Christiansen states: 'This may be very clever but it fails to acknowledge that any good opera carries its meaning through music rather than its relation to an ism' (ibid.: 1356). This 'aesthetic snobbery' reminds us that the critic is beleaguered on all sides in 'opera as drama' debates, his audience potentially lost to sectarian factions. Third, we have the 'coterie of gigglers' for whom opera is fundamentally ridiculous, best appreciated as an expensive show of 'camp', punctuated by embarrassments, miscalculations and disasters—hats falling off, doors getting stuck, wobbling scenery. Here 'we find the shrines of diva-worship, where grown men dredge books of operatic anecdotes for tales of broad in the beam grand-damerie ...'(ibid.:1357).

Akin to all critics who berate the uppity amateur, Christiansen suggests that these types either don't 'really' like opera or attend for reasons of deep inadequacy. '... opera ... heightens emotion ... enlarges human experience, making it grander, louder, more decisive... makes the opera house a place of fevered tension and expectation, quite unlike the legitimate theatre in atmosphere' (ibid.: 1358). It takes a man to cope! The auditorium is full of people 'in desperate need of something and the importance of prolonged applause in the ritual of operatic performance is an indication of their urgent emotional involvement and intensity of participation'. Christiansen then recounts an anecdote that places his contempt for these aesthetic snobberies in an all too self-revealing context:

> I remember once in the Met (NY) standing room queue, being regaled with an enraptured description of how Obraztsova had driven the audience crazy—'demented' is I believe the expression—by singing *'Mon coeur s'ouvre à ta voix'* lying on her

back with her head dangling over the end of a sofa. Not a word about her tone, her phrasing, her sense of the drama; it was simply the fact of her awkward physical position which made it exciting. 'She should try the flying trapeze next time' I replied in my least ironic tones, 'it might stop the vibrato' (ibid.: 1358).

So there! It is clearly a mistake to assume that all you have to do to go to the opera is dress respectably, get there in reasonable time, keep quiet during the performance and at the final curtain applaud the good and ignore the bad and then go home, for the number one rule of successful operagoing is seemingly 'to make as much impact on your neighbours as do the singers on the stage' (Shearer 1960: 812). Given the weight of musical, textual, social and ritual 'knowledge' layered on operagoers' shoulders this is unsurprising and is commented on with degrees of humour. An impact can be made in several ways: call a roll of the characters as they appear, giving the singers' names as well, although you may need a torch to shine on the programme which somehow ruins the effect. Ideally you need a straight man to feed snippets of information who effects no interest whatsoever whilst appearing to discourage you. Treat overtures and *intermezzi* as opportunities to talk about anything you like. A running commentary on the plot and such speculation as 'Are the Norns Brünnhilde's first cousins or just her step sisters?' can have the desired effect. 'If you are hard pushed try remarks like "There are now one hundred and seventeen people on the stage"' (ibid.: 812-13). Under such a bombardment it is a courageous soul who dares mutter a sound if brave enough to be there at all. Some, however, are not just brave and noisy, they are unrepentant. 'Opera queendom' has been triumphantly turned into a positive quality by a self-outing Koestenbaum:

... the very phrase 'opera queen' performs an accusation. Who dares to wear the name? You call someone an opera queen if you want to criticize his affection for opera, or if, yourself a worshipper of the operatic, you want to elevate your own affection into *affectation* The opera queen seemed the victim of a severe, pleasureless affliction seemed to have given up more reasonable pastimes ... Opera queens [go] to the opera on Monday nights ... put on airs ... keep lists ... catalogue their highs; [don't] categorize or explain. The opera queen must choose one diva ...

remain loyal ... ward off the specter of defection ... tries to befriend her, or renounces all claim and realizes that the states to be savored are absence, sacrifice and search ... you are interested in everything your chosen diva has done—even the mistakes ... The opera queen interprets his desires through a vocabulary of addiction. Love of opera seems a sickness that needs to be controlled ... Pornography like eating falls under the rubric of addiction ... I am afraid of the expert, the opera policeman, the connoisseur ... We have too much in common and therefore proximity is painful. I fear the label 'fanatic', it sounds like 'pervert' (1993: 9-47).

Opera obsessiveness has been likened to pornography by others, Baker (1991) claiming that, in both, heightened emotions are achieved by means of a fetishistic focus on ever reducible fragments of the whole: the aria, the phrase, the singer's tone, rather than breast, stiletto or whip. Again decline, decadence and cult are the terms of the debate:

> Opera... is beginning to show its age. Like some senior citizens, opera is moving slower ... shrinking rather than growing, becoming sadly forgetful and repetitive ... like a fading beauty, Lady Opera begins to concentrate on a tiny number of her choice jewels ... her remaining one or two good features which she elevates into a cult. [It is obsessed with] the fetish of detail ... Not necessarily opera as it is written today (in the rare cases where it still gets written), nor opera as it is generally produced, or as it is analyzed by serious critics. I am referring to opera as it is consumed by its most hardcore public. Most of them who are really vocal (in both senses) completely dismiss overall concern with an operatic work, sacrificing everything to their rabid, eccentric cult of detail. This microscopic focus I contend, is what makes their brand of opera so conservative and decadent ... Fans participate in a series of reductions of the art they love ... (Baker 1991: 8-9).

This brings it down to ever smaller 'bites' via the by now familiar, stages. Opera means the nineteenth century: in fact 1815-1915, especially works by Latin composers that show off the voice. Wagner is not loved by the fan because few 'vocal close-ups' are provided, where a single detail involving a single star performer eclipses everything else, where one voice on a single note can 'stop the show'. Richard Strauss is acceptable because of his use of the high soprano; the *longeurs* are tolerated for the ample vocal close-up rewards, 'total and frontal' (ibid.: 1). The next reduction is as follows. Opera means singing. 'Opera is not music, not drama, and for God's sake not music drama, but singing' (ibid.: 11). Baker suggests that the tyranny of this focus on singing contributes to the rise of radical producer's opera as a means of saying 'Look this aria is *about* something', although unfortunately the producer's something is not necessarily the something composer or librettist intended, nor what this kind of audience wants: for them opera is not even about all singing, but the female voice. Although the stage is cluttered with assorted others, the only singer is the *prima donna*. There are rare 'tenor' exceptions, but opera stars, claims Baker, are female to male by a ratio of 10 to 1. The Three Tenors have not made their popular impact in the opera house but in the 'manly' context of bravura sporting competitions. But, hang on ... Baker next claims that opera is not even female voices, it is high female voices, in fact reducible to their high notes, the narrowing of focus to a series of notes within a canonised singer's range at the top end where the greatest risks are to be encountered. 'Difficult to produce, often painful to hear, high notes are the manna of the opera fan' (Baker 1991:11). For the latter, like the orchestra, libretti, music, even staging and other singers, the *diva's* other notes are regarded as little more than distractions. Who said opera was drama? It is, but not in the sense intended, it is a circus of tension akin to the ever present possibility that the trapeze artist might fall—'will she or won't she make it?'—and the more dangerous it is made to look, the more exciting. In fact opera is a single note in a consecrated throat:

> Sutherland's trill, Nilsson's laser beams, Callas' yodel-like shift from chest to head ... the legendary *pianissimi* of Zinka Milanov ... [indeed] not just the Milanov *pianissimo* that causes the coronaries and inspires the dissertations—it is the Milanov B-flat, and not just any B-flat, but the one in the first act of *La Gioconda*—the note that wouldn't stand still (ibid.: 51).

For Baker here is a fetishism as sexual as in any pornography 'Our overemphasis on the vocal detail calls to mind the porn consumer's fixation on a single anatomical detail. Milanov's B-flat thus becomes like Monroe's D-cup' (ibid.: 51), and gives a new perspective to the man who 'pirate' records a performance, with a tape recorder concealed in his coat pocket. These are examples on the fringes of audience control but they highlight a basic argument of this text:

> ... the beliefs that there is an aesthetic hierarchy of musical styles, and that most people who are not really 'musical' have a profound effect on the production and consumption of music in modern societies. It is the widespread acceptance of such assumptions that enables a small number of 'authorities' to define, on behalf of the whole society, what is to count as 'serious' music, and what is not, and to devalue the experiences of others while claiming public resources for their favoured styles. It is these authorities too who claim the right to define the meaning and the value of music, and whose views are disseminated through the mass media (Wright 1975: 432).

> So it comes about that most people in western societies, although they have unprecedented choice in respect of the music they want to hear, must nevertheless exercise their preferences while submitting to an aesthetic inferiority complex (Martin 1995: 69).

The norm

Most operagoers are not 'fans', 'fanatics', 'maniacs' but just 'goers', and not necessarily particularly engaged 'goers' at that. Indeed it may not be specifically opera which interests them, remembering that this 'them' is not a unitary group and comes together for a combination of sociocultural reasons.

> Today everybody is already a member of some intellectually worked-over group, that is, an audience... The member of the soap-show audience may differ from the Museum of Modern Art first nighter in vocabulary and self-estimation, but not necessarily in intellectual background or capacity; each is where she is largely because of chance or social environment (Rosenberg 1970: 63-4).

The British Market Research Bureau reported in 1990[2] that opera audiences had risen by 15 per cent in the previous four years—an increase particularly strong in the 15-24 age group, many of whom are single and studying at colleges or universities. 'Even more encouraging for impresarios is the finding that the biggest increase in this category comes from those spending at least two or three evenings a year at the opera' *(Opera Now* November 1990: 17). Andy Brown, associate director of BMRB stated: 'These young people, mainly up-market, are enthusiastic and involved. If you add in the Italian World Cup effect which happened after our interviews, then the future for opera looks very good indeed' (ibid.: 17). The findings show that ABs ('upper middle class' and 'middle class'—see Chapter 2 for details) constitute 30 per cent of opera audiences: C1s ('lower middle class') 25 per cent: C2s ('skilled working class') 20 per cent: Ds ('working class') 12 per cent and Es (those at lowest levels of subsistence) 13 per cent. Within such a social class schema the 'upper class' or 'Establishment' audience for whom, as we have seen, the ROH has been described as a club and who run and finance opera, is hidden within 'upper middle class'. Even so the Arts Council of Great Britain (1991) reported that whilst 11.7 per cent of the population attend at least one classical concert during a year (only 4.8 per cent attend more than one), only 5.9 per cent attend an opera, so the audience being dissected in these other accounts is a very small one. For example, CACI Ltd. carried out an analysis of the Welsh National Opera's audience on its regular visits to Birmingham employing ACORN residential location/consumption group neighbourhood groups (CACI 1994). The most significant four groups in the WNO Birmingham audience were labelled 'Affluent Urbanites' (at 4.7 per cent): 'Prosperous Professionals, Metropolitan Areas' (4.1 per cent): 'Better off Executives, Inner City Areas (4.7 per cent) and towering above all others 'Wealthy Achievers, Suburbia' (36.0 per cent). Unfortunately this research didn't pursue the importance of opera consumption to these groups but rather sought correlations against other socioeconomic data such as overall income (emphatically correlated with regard to households with over £40,000 pa) and education level (the percentage with degrees also extremely high). One further group was singled out by CACI —'Comfortable Middle Agers, Mature Home-Owning Areas'—high in audience attendance but low in income.

Females constitute 60 per cent of audiences and the over 55s (30 per cent of the population) half and the over 65s 30 per cent. Many commentators and companies believe that their audience is ageing, but the 1995 ENO survey of its Coliseum audience showed 25-34 year-olds constituting the largest age-range presence, higher than the 45-54s who had dominated their 1993 survey (Kimberley 1995: 1273-4). The over 55s are traditionalists with regard to productions, and also prefer well known works and appreciate surtitles. Of those becoming interested in opera between 1985 and 1990 60 per cent are under 35, they 'enjoy dressing up and making a special occasion of going to the opera and are more likely than the over 55s to go to radical productions of new or less familiar works. They are especially receptive to modern dress performances of the classics' (*Opera Now* 1990: 17). Younger people also support state funding but think that it is not always well spent. Overall there was very strong support for state subsidies (74 per cent rejecting the claim that they were a waste of taxpayers' money, rising to 88 per cent among the better off and the regular operagoers), the belief being that they help to maintain standards and the mounting of more adventurous productions, which also (in London) boost the tourist trade. Somewhat perversely, but possibly explained by the 'up market' character of the new young audience, whilst 71 per cent believed that subsidies helped older people, students and others to go to opera by keeping ticket prices down, the least likely group to offer this view were those aged 15-24. But there was much criticism of how current subsidies are distributed and spent, especially outside London and the south-east, and most markedly in Scotland where 40 per cent of those questioned were dissatisfied with the current spread of aid, calling for stronger support for regional companies. In total only 6 per cent favoured priority being given to national institutions such as the ROH and 20 per cent believed there should be more support for fledgling artists. Commercial sponsorship was favoured but as complement not replacement for subsidies. They also, it was believed, made arts administrators more aware of commercial realities than subsidies were inclined to do. Companies supporting the arts were recognised as thereby receiving valuable publicity, but 43 per cent (46 per cent of women, 48 per cent of the better off and 52 per cent of active operagoers) thought that sponsorship was an excuse for well-paid executives to entertain their friends and colleagues at the company's expense (ibid.:17).

However, despite the increase in audiences, getting people into the opera house, as into the concert hall, remains a problem. The most marked increased interest in opera has been through CD and audio cassette sales, radio listening, TV and video viewing, actual attendance coming fourth on the list of respondents' means of enjoying opera, the top two—listening to recordings and to the radio—being shorn of the visual (and possibly also dramatic) component. Attending operas whilst on holiday is fifth, reading books and magazines on the subject, sixth. Cost is crucial, one in three of relatively affluent ABs claimed that ticket prices were too high for them to go to opera performances more frequently, that it was also difficult to buy tickets at short notice and there was too much travel involved. Outside London the principal complaint was the paucity of opera.

This survey was sponsored by *Opera Now*, also born as part of the supposed 1980s 'opera boom' in Britain—a 'boom' linked to an equally dubious 'de-layering' of stable middle and class structure generally. This BMRB survey identifies a new young audience for opera but in describing many of them as 'studying at colleges and universities', suggests that they are merely the next generation of opera's traditional audience:

> Unusually large, happily prosperous, thoroughly contented and mainly conservative, the middle class has symbolised a national history of continuity and stability. It has often aped aristocratic values while providing a role-model for the working classes (Jacques 1994, 10: 9-10).

Opera's rich mixture of musical and textual linguistic elements, requires considerable experience and effort if it is to be understood: 'These dispositions and habits are learned by constant practice in listening and performing, practice which should, and usually does, begin in early childhood' (Meyer 1972: 61). Opera's future audience is thus reproduced through its present audience, unless, as happened in the immediate post-war period, formal measures are taken to socialise the young in home environments where opera is heard and seen. However, one cannot take the social status and privilege out of this equation, unless the hierarchy of the arts in which opera ranks highly and expensively can also be challenged.

The respondents surveyed here had an overwhelming preference for the core repertoire. Verdi and Mozart the two most favoured composers for performances in conventional theatres, although younger respondents liked 'arena' opera. One in four would consider attending a concert featuring Pavarotti or Domingo. As for opera lovers' other leisure and lifestyle pursuits: after opera they are, in order, the theatre, classical music, art galleries, ballet, cinema, jazz, modern dance and pop/rock concerts. To this survey can be added a brief finding from a *Sunday Times*-sponsored survey of the arts (Mills 1995)[3] in which opera was ranked the sixth favourite art form (music, painting, literature, theatre, cinema above and sculpture, classical music, ballet and poetry below), receiving 5.6 per cent of the samples vote, but came last in the vote for 'most important art form' with just 1.8 per cent support. No opera was ranked in the top ten 'favourite pieces of classical music', *The Ring* being the only operatic 'work' listed in the greatest piece of classical music list at no.8.

Unqualified, *the* opera audience merely describes a coherent unity in the most generalised spatial sense: all present in the auditorium. Beyond that, it is physically, socially and economically segregated and ranked, differentiated by the forms and numbers of 'power/knowledge' reasons for being there and a range of component priorities—music, text, drama, entertainment, spectacle, spiritual uplift, singers, composers, national schools, frequency of attendance—depending on level of interest, finances, work, travel and geographical accessibility. Many will be present for social reasons, others for business or corporate reasons. Some will regard opera attendance as a special 'treat' and will dress and dine accordingly; others will be such 'regulars' that no special preparations or concessions will be made, they may be in the cheaper seats adopting no distinct dress, behaviour or dining habits, or in the more expensive seats, treating the experience as one of being at an exclusive club. The one thing that binds this congregation together is the ritual collectively witnessed and engaged in—a ritual of studied conventions which vary between theatres and countries but always provide the core of opera culture. 'The decisive role of the "style of life" in status honor means that status groups are the specific bearers or all "conventions" ... all "stylization" of life either originates in status groups or is at least conserved by them' (Weber 1967: 191). All artistic activities in their 'art worlds' (Becker 1982) consist of collective action governed by conventions ranging from the tonality or atonality of the music to dress.

In these terms a classical music symphony concert is the setting for a ritual comparable, though more ascetic, in its nineteenth century conventions. This ritual takes place in an expensive custom-built hall, sometimes in other 'auratic' venues—country mansions, palaces, churches—perhaps one reason why some critics express a preference for opera in concert. In a concert, rows of seats face a platform to which the audience has no access, and in front of which there is no proscenium. The focus is the conductor and players in sober 'dress' uniforms. These performers enter from side or rear doors in a fixed order, orchestral players, chorus, leader of orchestra, soloists and the conductor who presents to customary applause himself and all others on the platform. Apart from the conductor and soloists, who have permitted but normatively controlled ways of 'correctly' showing 'feeling' or 'emotion', the rest are expected to be emotionless. Singers, if involved, are permitted greater freedom, not least for females, in dress which is, even so, closely monitored. Several commentators have analysed the 'concert-hall as laboratory' as part of the nineteenth century bourgeois 'auratic' construction, when 'manners of behaving towards art' changed, nourished by the bourgeois 'public sphere' of concert-hall and opera house (Habermas 1989), increased literacy and the burgeoning press, as well as concrete developments such as blacked-out auditoria during opera performances, sunken, enlarged orchestra pits and rules of behaviour on both sides of the proscenium (see Rupp 1992), where 'exhibition of the self' (Vieira de Carvalho 1995: 51) became a key element of the civilising process (Elias 1994). This is when 'authoritarian' relations between stage and audience emerged through which the listener becomes increasingly 'passive' (Supicic 1987: 174). Small addresses the concert as an act which dramatizes and 're-enacts the shared mythology of a culture or social group ... which unifies and, for its members, justifies the "sacred history" of the culture—its creation, the coming of the civilizing heroes, their 'demiurgic' activities, and finally their disappearance (1987-88: 19, 7).

These 'temples' are as soundproof as possible and minimise visual distractions, so that full concentration may be given to the ritual. Most are separated from the outside world by distancing spaces, concourses, halls, and ticket offices where legitimacy of audience membership is guaranteed by the exchange of money. The laity do not socialise with each other during performances where strict rules of decorum and appropriate responses (at the end, clapping or the withholding of it, shouts of 'bravo' or, very questionably, booing) pertain. Anterooms, however, enable socialising around relaxation

405

and refreshments. The interval forms an essential part of the experience, permitting discussion and judgements on what is being performed and how. Intervals are for being seen, and for being heard, for establishing status by either financial means (expense and place of seats occupied, of clothes, 'friends' on so on) and/or expressed knowledge about music in interaction with others. Attendance has to be planned, the booking must be made sometimes far in advance, travel arranged and so on.

The concert ritual consists of clearly annotated works by primarily long-dead composers: '... for the overwhelming majority of music lovers new music has nothing whatever to say to them; they remain apparently content with the familiar world of "The Great Classics"' (ibid.: 7), predominantly drawn from the same late eighteenth to early twentieth century period which provides opera's core repertoire. The composers of the great majority of works performed number fewer than 50, the works played over and over again to audiences also able to hear them repeatedly in recorded form at home. Because this repertoire is also that of a 'museum', practitioners other than the composer become 'key' intermediaries to 'interpretations' and 'skills' that may be distinguished, ranked and which may be extra-musical: Anne-Sophie Mutter, Maxim Vengerov, Joanna MacGregor, Ofra Harnoy, are amongst the many concert instrumentalists who have been marketed in ways which might be termed 'sexual'. There is considerable activity in 'finding' lost masterpieces, 'geniuses' and 'authentic' performances. Overall there is an urge towards preservation reinforced by the record industry. In form the typical symphonic work 'suggests the representation of a passage rite, whose tripartite form has been remarked upon by van Gennep ... (1960: 20). The sequence—(1) separation from the outside world; (2) seclusion and (3) celebration—represents as Turner suggests (1974: 34) ... 'the ultimate victory of life over death' (Small 1987-88: 16).

Concert forms may vary between an overture followed by a stressed symphony and/or concerto (planned almost like courses of a meal [ibid.: 23]); the single large work; or the concert of 'lollipops'. In all symphonic music concerns itself with a wide range of generalised experience: joy, pain, happiness in and loss of love, loyalty, heroism and so on; it avoids 'material realism' and normally explicit treatment of sexual love, desire, or political issues ... such gross realities as are experienced by the persecuted' (ibid.: 25). Full participation of the non-middle class in these rituals requires acculturation and incorporation into 'allied premises and conventions, as well as the necessary scripting (Gagnon and Simon 1986) to comprehend, judge and respond to the performances experienced. As part of the opening of the newly built Glasgow Royal International Concert Hall in 1990, after the first of Strauss' *Four Last Songs* Jessye Norman imperiously shushed the audience which had burst into applause.

In general Small's account of the mythologies which ritually contextualise the presentation, reception and organisation of classical music in concert applies to opera: '... every kind of musical ensemble establishes its own set of relationships, both within itself and between itself and its audience' (1987-88: 30). Opera's rituals are, however, on an altogether grander scale, the theatres, bigger and more luxurious, opportunities to parade through *grandes salles* from Covent Garden's Crush Bar to the Paris Opéra's considerably more ostentatious hall of mirrors, as long as one avoids what Baker calls 'the inverted steerage' of the caste system that is the upper reaches of the opera house. The intervals are longer, the audiences are noisier; the rules of usher tipping, coat checking, bell warnings, late entrance and so on are complex to the uninitiated. In a sense opera is distraction. Singers are all too likely to draw attention to themselves and distract attention from the works they are performing in, which brings little suggestion of 'scientific' truth to the proceedings; it is a 'temple' of an altogether more chaotic, noisy and rich pre-Reformation kind. Similar behavioural conventions apply but, once the house lights are dimmed, the conductor and orchestra applauded and the curtain raised, anything may happen and increasingly does, even in the most respectable of establishments, and their most expensive seats.

> I understood the terms of the contract: my cheap seat gave me acoustical access but little else. The plush velvet, the painted walls, stopped a few tiers below. Forget about knee room, or even eye contact with the stage. At choice moments tired of looking at the ceiling or the opposite side of the Family Circle, I would rise from my seat, secure my footing and lean forward to snatch a quick look at the orchestra working away like ants in the pit. Occasionally there were the better Family Circle seats—which meant a bomber pilot's view of the wig worn by Siepi, Peters or Della Casa (Baker 1990: 28).

That was in the old New York Met's Family Circle, but the traditions were passed on to the new. The opera world is filled with traditions. One of these is the notion that real fans, the aficionados, sit at the top of the house, where the sound is pure. This doesn't take into account that the opera house might be acoustically imperfect, and therefore the most beautiful unamplified sounds in the world might not be heard and understood from the seats furthest from the stage. Yet the tradition continues. Of course, for many, the idea of sitting upstairs is simply not chic enough, but the Met's Family Circle:

> ... now seems to have been staked out by people who genuinely love opera 'The music was the first thing that drew me to opera' says one regular, 'but I never thought I could afford it. Then I discovered these cheaper seats way up high, and I realised that even I could go to the opera.' A regular subscriber in the upper regions of both the Met and the NY City Opera explains [that] even if you get a production you don't like, there's always the score. You can close your eyes and listen. I don't agree that the scenery dominates the music. You can always ignore the scenery.' It's impossible to find a common bond among the denizens of the Family Circle except for the overwhelming love of opera. One longtime subscriber put it best: 'It's not the social thing. It's for my soul' (McGovern 1990:19).

'Those who can do. Those who can't boo'

Opera as ritual requires formal applause at set moments: as the conductor enters and presents the orchestra at the beginning of each act, after arias where local culture deems appropriate, in Italy after specific phrases, but always at curtain calls and so on. The applause may be boosted by cheers, whistles, foot stamping, cries of *bravo* and *brava*, or contested with boos. Critics' power rests in press columns, opera house administrative and financial power in the boardroom, stalls and dress circle, but audience power is exercised *in situ*, whether instantaneously or planned, whether by loose collections or factions of 'fans' or organised *claques*. A *claque* is an organised body of operagoers which hires itself out to singers, conductors and administrations in order to prolong applause or to catcall and boo rival artists, or those who refuse to pay them. Opera 'fans' boo and cheer; *claques* do so to order, for money and cheap or free tickets, the intention being to mobilise the main audience to follow suit. In Italy especially, but also infamously in certain German houses—the Berlin Staatsoper and every summer without fail at Bayreuth too—booing is regular although whether by paid *claques* in this strict sense is not easy to ascertain. However Rosselli claims 'Some sort of *claque* is probably endemic in many opera houses' (1992c: 875), and this may include rival *claques* supporting different artists.[4] Dissatisfaction with a performance can be the least likely reason for booing. 'Booing is by fans of rival sopranos (living, decrepit or dead), for tenors for 'not corresponding to the Gallery's unrevisable definition of *tenure verdiano*, and baritones because they were in poor voice the last time they sang'. Shouting may start early in an opera during the music to cause the maximum disruption (Jamieson 1994a: 534). In Britain *claques* are relatively rare but audiences are increasingly likely to boo without their prompting. Booing is not a new issue in British operagoing however:

> I know that there are gallery goers, who contend that if people who like the play applaud it, the people who dislike it should injustice shew... that the approval is not unanimous. They might as well contend that if a gentleman who admires a lady tells her that she has pretty hands, any bystander who does not admire her should immediately ... tell her she has a red nose ... Why is the lust of the rabble to mock, jeer, insult, deride, and yell bestially at their unfortunate fellow-creatures, recognised as sacred in the gallery when it is suppressed by the police everywhere else? (G.B. Shaw quoted Levin 1993: 16).

Opera house manners have been debated in *Opera* for some time. In 1961 after a Sutherland *Lucia* at Covent Garden, a correspondent described the 'mob hysteria' as 'nothing so much as an unruly football match by people who obviously were there to make a noise'. One front row of gallery slips individual is described as using the bar for leverage as he 'bounced up and down in hobnailed boots' (October 1961: 554), to which another respondent reacted 'these letters would seem to come from [those] who view art as they do medicine, to be taken at regular intervals, but *not* to be enjoyed' (*Opera* December 1961: 816). Others observed:

The singers who are victims of hysterical adulation ... (usually reserved for film stars and guitar strumming crooners) must be as embarrassed as responsible members of the audience at these juvenile displays ... I am unable to hear the orchestra's last bars because of premature applause; this is rank bad manners ... spoiling the pleasure of real music-lovers (November 1961: 746).

Others pointed out that 'flower throwing, arguments, disappointments, ovations, booing and queuing' are an integral part of the operagoing experience, and that 'the dozen or so people who always seem to be hanging around the stage-door' can hardly alter the ovation of an audience of 2000 'which is to underestimate the intelligence of the opera-going public' (November 1961: 748). Most of the debates at this time were, however, concerned with riotous applause and cheering. Levin's reference above to Shaw followed a radio broadcast when Pavarotti was booed at the first night of *Don Carlos* at La Scala in Milan for cracking on two high notes. Levin observes that opera singers exist in such an artificial world that they and their fans tend to perceive them as immortal '... and therefore never fail the most trivial ordeal' and reminds us of the famous Callas incident when having cracked, 'the trap for any singer', she marched to the footlights before the booing could get underway, held up her arm and proceeded to tackle the note again, this time perfectly. Levin argues that boos usually set up louder cheers and he notes how at the Bayreuth Festival the curtains would open and close repeatedly as though encouraging the combat in the auditorium. Can't audiences merely clap less those who have earned their displeasure or less than full enthusiasm?

Anyway booing is for milksops. Coming out of the Opera House, after *Moses und Aron*, some years ago, I saw two men in a fight, a real fist fight, starting in the lobby and spilling out onto the pavement, the *cassus belli* being their respective opinions of the work. As for me, I'll boo any man who says that *Pélleas et Mélisande* isn't ghastly twaddle (Levin 1993: 16).

The 'should opera audiences boo?' debate has been pursued in Britain because of more local displays: the organised activities of enemies of certain types of 'new' music, and by an outburst of booing from Britain's most conservative audience, that of the Glyndebourne

410

Festival. 'Those who can, do. Those who can't boo', exclaimed Richard Morrison (*The Times* 16 April 1994: 16) after the 'Hecklers' led by Frederick Stocken, orchestrated their boos after Covent Garden's first night of its revival of *Gawain* by Harrison Birtwhistle. The 'Hecklers' are committed to driving all 'modern' music from stage and concert hall. *The Times* (18 April 1994) opened its review of *Gawain* with the comment:

> The great mystery is why anyone should have thought Birtwhistle's three year old opera the suitable target for a demonstration against nasty modern music. It is the nicest modern music imaginable, almost easy listening by the standards of contemporary composers, and every bar of it totally absorbing. He makes comparison with the Klytemnestra scene in *Elektra* 'is a whole century of music to be written off at the behest of louts?'

Morrison questioned Stocken's view of the contemporary music which, he observes, is characterised by its 'sheer anarchic pluralism. The Performing Right Society lists no fewer than 21,000 professional composers in Britain and Ireland. Hundreds of new pieces are premiered each week. The rule for music lovers hankering to hear a particular style is surely "seek and ye shall find".' He continues:

> So Mr Stocken you want modern music that sounds as if it was written hundreds of years ago? The BBC has just mounted a large John Tavener festival, just for you. You want witty, bright and communicative new music? Judith Weir's opera, to be premiered on Wednesday at the London Coliseum should be just the thing. Thousands of music lovers now flock to premieres by the likes of Philip Glass, Michael Nyman and John Adams, and find tunes and harmonies quite easy to follow. No, Mr Stocken, it really is perverse to attend a Birtwhistle opera—knowing that you will hate it—when there is so much else going on that will be more to your taste (*The Times* 16 April 1994: 16).

Morrison also claims that the battle fought by Stocken was won 20 years earlier when the musical establishment, including the BBC, was in thrall to Boulez and Stockhausen: 'The pervading attitude then was arrogance towards the public.' Many leading composers of that era, cushioned by subsidies or university residencies, undeniably lost the urge to write music that communicated with large numbers of people. Milton Babbitt, the American electronic composer summed it up in a notorious magazine article entitled 'Who cares if you listen?'. So Stocken's claim that there is an establishment conspiracy to promote music which the public hates might have applied then, but not now. Critics hate the Arts Council, opera houses hate critics, the BBC might even hate Classic FM although they don't say so '... And nobody has the money to schedule music that they do not think the public is interested in hearing'.

Milnes *(The Times* 12 July 1994: 33) reported on the first night of the Glyndebourne *Don Giovanni* directed by Deborah Warner (designed by Hildegard Bechtler in plain abstract sets, costumes by Sue Blane) under the heading 'Luddites are the losers'. A storm of boos greeted the production team which he found 'surprising and rather worrying', because while such behaviour is common in Germany where there are semi-official booing *claques,* and it is all part of the evening, it is relatively rare in this country, and almost unheard of at 'dear old Glyndebourne' (although this was in the new theatre in its first season). The only previous occasion had been for Sellars (rather than Mozart's) *Flute.* Milnes simply could not understand why:

> ... do these people never go to the straight theatre, the RSC or the National, and sample current Shakespeare production styles? If any deviation from the doublet and hose opera is to be rejected by Glyndebourne's core audience (the booing came from the more expensive seats) then 'rather worrying' is an understatement when it comes to future prospects in this glorious new theatre. Top Glyndebourne management may I fear have spent a sleepless night. Warner's production is—shock, horror—in modern dress. Wow! The Commendatore is murdered brutally in his dinner jacket (no problems of audience identification there). Zerlina's and Masetto's wedding party ... is pure Basildon (identification perhaps a bit dodgier). To emphasise Giovanni's blasphemy Warner gives him a plaster Madonna which he subjects to assorted indignities (ibid.: 33).

Other critics also found the production less than sensational by present-day standards; indeed some argued that 'The boos ... ironically ... have saved ... Warner's bacon. For they have permitted sympathetic commentators to describe her production as

412

"controversial" and "interesting" whereas it is ultimately drab and boring ...' (Canning 1994b: 10, 20). Letters to *The Times* arrived by the truckload:

> ... Milnes must know what caused the boos ... centre stage was filled all evening by a large unsightly rectangular pit topped with a lid that went up and down on four hawsers, tilting this way and that ... it seemed to have nothing to do with the music or libretto [and] sometimes the action was held up for it to go up and down. It was an ugly, boring and tiresome distraction and must have cost untold thousands. No wonder people booed.
>
> Those ... who expressed their disapproval ... had paid a lot of money to see the Da Ponte and Mozart opera, not a work which Deborah Warner ... had the temerity to think would be an improvement on the original masterpiece (13 July: 15).

Not all were so sure for they blamed the theatre's new policy of selling some cheap seats and standing places on the day 'to the *hoi-polloi'*. There was a general sense of 'aura-catastrophe', for another letter declared that booing was breaking out everywhere and that even a concert in the 'carved and gilded concert room' of Claydon House where the Lindsay Quartet's performance of Tippett's 5th Quartet had recently been booed by a section of the audience. More letters referred to:

> ... the pernicious notion that, while the music is inviolate, the drama is fair game for any producer who comes along with a bag of trendy notions. Clearly the drama and the music of an opera are an indissoluble whole, and to tear them apart is a barbaric act which certainly justifies loud and persistent vocal disapproval, as well as the avoidance of venues which promote such rubbish (*The Times* 18 July: 17).

Another letter reminded Milnes of some of his earlier reviews of ENO first nights during the *Power House* regime when booing was almost *de rigeur*:

> ... indeed in some quarters the production was hardly deemed to have been a success without it. And can one forget those memorable productions of Beethoven and Meyerbeer operas at

the Royal Opera House which received the same treatment? If an audience is expected to applaud what it has enjoyed, it should equally be allowed the right to express its disapproval at the end of the performance without being patronised by those who happen to disagree.[5]

Comparisons were made between the booing at Glyndebourne and that of Stravinsky's *Rite of Spring* at the Théâtre de Champs Elysees in 1913, deliberately organised by Diaghilev to commandeer media attention, reflecting a point made elsewhere in this text that 'museum' opera needs the (occasional) scandal of a new opera and/or a radical production to reaffirm opera as 'live' art ultimately rightly rooted in its mythological tradition.

Amidst the mayhem, Mary Nash-Wortham of Eastbourne was concerned at the *hoi polloi* slur: 'I hardly think my parents sent me to St Paul's School, London, to be classified as *hoi polloi* for buying £10 Glyndebourne standing room tickets' (*The Times* 1991: 12 July), whilst another letter writer believed that booing at Glyndebourne signalled a crucial collapse of class distinctions nationwide:

> Three cheers for those "loud catcalls from the most expensive seats" at Glyndebourne. They indicate a welcome erosion of old-guard class distinctions. Not so long ago it was only the *hoi polloi* who knew how to catcall.

Another thought that it betokened that Glyndebourne's audience had changed and that the culprits were those guests of corporate sponsorship: 'Most were no doubt present thanks to the generosity of their shareholders and as such should show more gratitude.' On 19 July there was more praise for the booers for *Don Giovanni*, in particular, seems to attract 'dire' productions: 'Many will remember the notorious WNO production of a few years ago which was ruined by the pseudo-psychology of the East German director (Berghaus), so that the cast fell about among quivering swords and teapots on a dried out beach. The music fortunately was superb, but could only be appreciated if one closed one's eyes'.

The issue of opera house manners generally could not be avoided; one correspondent was annoyed by people politely applauding poor performances 'because they believe it is the right thing to do' ... 'If one has enjoyed the performance very much one can clap louder or cheer.

Refraining from applauding still seems to allow the alternative of booing if the show really is disastrous'. Two more letters appeared on 23 July, one suggesting that opera houses should adopt the practice employed by the *Guide Michelin* of putting an 'M' beside certain hotels to indicate: 'their modernity. Happily it enables the traveller to avoid what he wants to avoid. Glyndebourne patrons, of whom probably 90 per cent have to make up their minds in January which operas they wish to see but are not always cognizant of the reputation of the director chosen to produce, would be aided, and a great deal of frustration and disappointment avoided, if the advanced programme included a similar 'M' in front of operas which were to be the subject of experimental or very modern staging' (W. Graham). The other letter returned to the *hoi polloi*, claiming that Glyndebourne is now accessible on a student grant: 'Hoi polloi I may be, but I won't wear jeans, and I won't boo. I'm just grateful.' The story just ran and ran. On 17 July Kate Saunders asked:

> When does a gently bred person in evening dress, with a stomach full of quails' eggs and champagne, behave like a tinny-chucking Millwall fan? ... at what highbrow spectator sport is it permissible for the audience to boo, hiss and hurl insults? Why, a night at the opera of course *(The Sunday Times* 1994: 4: 6).

Saunders claimed that the difference between theatre and opera manners, though less marked in Britain, is becoming more pronounced as 'times—and production fashions change'. The common thread behind all recent 'booing' in British opera houses is:

> ... fear of innovation. I have never heard of a production being booed because it is too traditional and safe. In the straight theatre the director is God. Audiences will make an effort to treat his or her 'interpretation' of a classic with respect. At the opera however a strong minority deeply resents any director who dares to do more than keep the singers from crashing into the furniture. They will also object to any set that deviates from the tradition of opera as a handsome spectacle-hence the booing of designers (ibid.: 6).

Saunders quotes Sir Edward Heath's response after the Sellars' *Flute débâcle*. Namely that Glyndebourne exists to provide the very best Mozart in the world and, if it failed in that objective, the institution no longer has any meaning. Yet Glyndebourne also exists for one of the most élitist audiences in the world. So what is the best Mozart? Should Mozart operas be produced to harmonise prettily with evening dress and champagne or as living works attractive to talented directors with new insights? Glyndebourne has been a little slow to confront this dilemma which has been dividing opera audiences and performers for approaching two decades. Saunders reflects that it has thus remained somewhat removed from the '... explosion of popular interest in opera as a haven for traditionalists also ... terrified that innovation will somehow tarnish the glittery snob value of the Glyndebourne experience'. Opera now has several audiences, and the traditional audience interested in opera as a class possession are seeking to effect forms of 'social closure', barriers against further contamination from below—at Covent Garden and especially the ENO (Saunders doesn't refer to Bourdieu's thesis on 'cultural capital' but she might well have done). 'These are the types who threw away their CDs of *Turandot* and complain when they heard the plumber whistling *'Nessun dorma'*.'

> In Italy, the booing-power resides with the *loggionisti*, the rabble in the gallery. Over here it appears to be the most expensive seats that cause the trouble. They can moan about daring directors and designers, but their real grievance, I suspect, is the increasing democratisation of an art form reserved for the rich (Saunders 1994: 4, 6).

Peter Hillmore (1994: 21) gave three cheers for '... the people with the guts to say boo ... [which] is a lively way of participating in live theatre ... It is a form of speech, a means of communication.' He claims that booing is so unusual in British theatre that Basil Dean, the director of Coward's *Sirocco* mistook the boos for cheers and kept ringing the final curtain up and down to the distress of the cast. Hillmore locates the Glyndebourne audience as 'middle-class people in East Sussex' which is some way under the class mark, and puts the British hatred of audience participation down to British respect for authority, restraint, politeness and emotional constipation:

> You cannot imagine, for example, a member of an English audience responding to a dreadful performance of *The Diary of Ann Frank* starring bimbo Pia Zadora. At the very tense moment,

when German soldiers burst into the house looking for Anne, a disgruntled member of the audience shouted out 'She's in the attic' (ibid.: 21).

Picnics and champagne

It is impossible to discuss the opera audience—any opera audience, especially the British—without reflecting upon hierarchies of class. As the debates about booing demonstrate, the shock of recent outbreaks has been that it has occurred in the more expensive parts of the most socially exclusive houses in Britain. The opening of this new, £33 million, larger Glyndebourne theatre (1200 capacity, orchestra pit for 80) in the summer of 1994: '... a big theatre comparable to say, Parma's Teatro Regio, where Verdi staged *Aida*' (Porter 1994: 12), with 'warmer and less constricted acoustics' attracted a lot of media-hype, much of it concerned with the democratisation of this revered institution. Milnes proclaimed: '... it cannot be called an exclusive club any longer ...', with 'standing-room' for 42 available and an upper circle with some seats costing £10-£30 (Milnes *The Times* 25 May 1994: 37). 'A splendid time is guaranteed for all ... as the new more egalitarian Glyndebourne ... awaits curtain up ...' Director of Productions Graham Vick observed '... there'll be a broader audience-spectrum as people realise it's cheaper and generally more possible'. Milnes refers to the opening of the old house, 60 years to the day, making generalisations which frequently smokescreen élite institutions in Britain: 'the British ... Amiable ... and eccentric only in the sense that the English rather like to disguise seriousness of purpose with a patina of detachment and irony'.

Set in the rolling Sussex countryside, accessible with difficulty by train but mainly attended by the driven, Glyndebourne's social meaning is further summed up by the dress code (dinner suit) and extended supper interval enabling picnics in the gardens. Generally audiences are considered conservative, and they are spreading to other stately settings. Widdicombe (*The Independent* 18 July: 19) observed that not only has Glyndebourne moved into its new—and to nearly all who have had the somewhat restricted opportunity to visit it—perfect theatre in Sussex other outdoor, mainly stately home, venues have appeared perhaps because:

Glyndebourne is dead—if by Glyndebourne you mean a Heath Robinson theatre and Mozart sung in silk pants and hose ... while Glyndebourne has progressed to a state-of-the-art theatre and provocative modern productions, the British appetite for cosy, country house opera thrives. There seems to be no end to the number of new BMW and old Jags parking in bumpy fields, their drivers in crumpled black tie with champagne that explodes like a shotgun when freed from the boot.

After a couple of shaky years one of the most successful, 'top of the pile of the contenders for the title of "The New Glyndebourne"', with matchless setting, literary and status associations and 'twee, dotty and charming' gardens laid out by Lady Ottoline Morrell, especially because it is within safe distance of the moneyed class it serves, is Leonard and Rosalind Ingrams 'enchanting' country house, Garsington Manor in Oxfordshire, which holds a three-week, three-opera, alfresco season for those who like their opera Marie-Antoinette style, in Arcadian, idyllic settings with Glyndebourne style picnics and dress code (ibid.: 19). Canning questioned:

> ... the need for another opera festival for snobs in evening gear, performing in the original language to a largely uncomprehending and (at least before the dinner interval) unresponsive audience (of 400), paying high prices—£65-£85 (£75-£95 in 1994)—for a musical standard and theatrical presentation comparable with, perhaps, English Touring Opera, which rarely charges above £18 for its itinerant productions (Canning 1994: 10, 26).

The 'theatre' is an open-air *terrazzo* which demands considerable ingenuity of set designers to transform it for works as varied in 1994 as *Il barbiere di Siviglia*, *L'incontro improvviso* and *Capriccio*. Garsington's first opera performance was a fund-raiser in 1989; by 1994 20 performances of these three works were all sold out.

> The audience sits ... steeply raked, on scaffolding wrapped in canvas like a huge white parcel. On balmy nights birds sing noisily from surrounding trees; after the interval, a large black canopy glides over the stage, improving the acoustics and the intimacy of the performance.
> If one looks at the programme there are 'serious ads. Good

corporate support (led by Morgan Stanley), an élite group of benefactors called the Constellation of Garsington, plus the name of everyone who has given more than 50p listed in the programme. Like Glyndebourne this blatant attempt to make your audience feel appreciated is balanced by some serious musicology: in the case of the Haydn, an inventory of costumes—complete with buttons and bows, spangles and heron feathers—made for Esterhaza and an article by Albi Rosenthal on Haydn's girlfriends (Widdicombe 1994: 19).

Food and champagne are within dinner interval picnics, part of the whole package of such venues:

> If you want to see a convention of picnic hampers, a convocation of hopes over experience, the greatest, smartest collection of groaning wicker and Buchanan-style tartan travelling rugs in the world, then Glyndebourne is the place ... We watched corpulent, puffing men lug boxes and tables to find just the right spot. As nobody will sit in the open, so everybody searches for a defensible space ... Laid over the primeval fears of eating in the open is the thin tulle of civilisation and snobbery .... There's a terrific amount of showing off, silver and crystal are humped into fields, candelabra and ice buckets, collapsable tables with double damask cloths and numerous bottles and inappropriate sloppy courses with numberless screw top sauces, creams and unctions and garnishes. And most bizarrely of all, little pots of cut flowers. Now who on earth thinks of taking a bunch of carnations and a vase on a picnic? (Gill 1995: 27).

Being witness to such ritual did not cause complete dismay; Gill and partner to save time and bother, though not money, ordered their picnic from Letheby and Christopher, Catering Made Special of Lewes Sussex with prices from £32.50 per person 'including accessories but excluding wine'. So too Widdicombe reports: 'Those who picnic with table-cloths and candelabra have colonised Garsington; and the discarded old panelling from Glyndebourne's old theatre has been installed in a barn, along with franchised caterer ...[6]

Conclusion

Picnic and champagne opera, £280 seats at Covent Garden for 'superstars', the use of £50 million National Lottery funds also for Covent Garden as 'a national institution', corporate funding and sponsorship combine as contemporary developments around and within opera as social ritual. All opera companies in Britain face funding crises with the retreat of state subsidies, but to portray opera as an industry in crisis would be to ignore the contemporaneous evidence of social closure around opera as exclusive club and entertainment, as 'lifestyle' accoutrement for those with wealth and power. Such closure tactics would not be necessary, however, were there no pressures from below on existing patterns of operatic ritual and the social and material meanings of opera. Much doubt has been expressed from many sources in this text on the validity of the 1980s 'opera boom' prognosis and, insofar as the latter relates to opera in the opera house the doubts would appear to be justified, but outside the opera house in the commercialised culture industry there can surely be no doubt that 'opera', as I have chosen to distinguish it has, in fragmented forms and by numerous technologically reproduced means, become greatly commodified. Outside the opera house, 'opera's' popularisation (the Three Tenors, Lesley Garrett, CD compilations, TV and film soundtracks, advertising jingles and the like) has undoubtedly undercut the 'value' of the term, and thus contributed to pressures on those committed to the social exclusivity of opera to take defensive 'closure' action, to reassert their social superiority. From the evidence we have encountered it would appear that the 'vulgar' corporate presence in the opera house, the use of surtitles and the challenges laid down by radical producers, have also instigated further pressure of this kind. Meanwhile in the institution of opera it is the last mentioned producers who now seem to have the greatest power because they were responsible for translating museum pieces into dramatised contemporary relevance and/or giving them and the whole institution a semblance of 'newness'. Their power does not go unchallenged of course, for it brings them into direct conflict with not only the 'authentic' musician and conductor as well as the 'star' performer, but with the established power/knowledge of musicology and music theory based on textual rather than theatrical analysis—the power/knowledge with which this text commenced. In the Preface we encountered Adorno's confident prediction that: 'With the anathematizing of the very pleasure it puts on display the phantasmagoria is infected at the outset with the seeds of its own destruction. Inside the illusion dwells disillusionment' (Adorno 1991: 94), but despite rampant 'disillusionment', if this can be taken to embrace the complex dynamics of contested meanings about opera as artefact, institution, commodity and social ritual of distinction, the beast is not yet dead. On the contrary it has shown, and continues to demonstrate, a remarkable facility for reinvention, reinterpretation and recommodification as the disillusioned compete for control.

Notes

1. Christiansen (1985) quotes Thomas Love Peacock's biography of Shelley, written in the 1850s in which Peacock compares the current London audiences with those of Shelley's day. The former 'vociferous assemblies calling and recalling performers to the footlights and showering down bouquets to the accompaniment of their noisy approbation'—the latter 40 years earlier whose civilised restraint and sensitivity had delighted the poet. What had happened in the meantime was the breakdown of the subscription system and the consequent attempt to bring in 'one-off' customers from the suburbs who could, for the first time, get home by railway after a performance. The Jenny Lind 'hype' of 1847, where the impresario Lumley consciously whipped up public curiosity for an untested product, was the first of many such marketing campaigns which depended for their success on generating an aura around a star. The audience as Chorley, Cox and others believed were suckers.
2. BMRB carried out 3,000 telephone interviews with 'adults' (15 years or over) between 24 August and 13 September 1990.
3. 1098 questionnaires collated by A. North and D. Hargreaves, Department of Psychology, University of Leicester.
4. Chris Merritt (*1992: 7) records his first-hand experience of being booed at La Scala in *I vespri Siciliani* along with Cheryl Studer.
5. Not all were of one voice: a T. McLaughlin of Glasgow observed that when toured to Glasgow the Glyndebourne Sellars *Flute* was 'enthusiastically welcomed. It is to be hoped that Deborah Warner will take heart from this precedent. An imaginative treatment of a much loved Mozart masterpiece may find a more sympathetic reception from a different audience. Perhaps Ms Warner should persuade Glyndebourne Touring Opera to take her *Don Giovanni* into its repertoire'.
6. *The Times* of 26 April 1994 covered the battle at Compton Verney over the proper opera house which would dwarf the Mansion House (seating capacity 1150) and destroy the Capability Brown planned parkland. Its building is being opposed by English Heritage. The site is owned by Sir Willoughby de Broke, who does not, however, own the Mansion House which is owned by the Peter Moores Foundation, great sponsors of opera, and who

support English Heritage's opposition to the building of the house. In the summer of 1997 the residents surrounding Garsington with less than a willing eavesdropping ear for opera responded with hedge-trimmers, lawnmowers and low flying aircraft during several performances.

At Broomhill near Tunbridge Wells, opera and Shakespeare are given under similar circumstances. In 1994 Peter Knapp of Travelling Opera staged *The Magic Flute* and *La traviata* at Banks Fee House, another stone manor house, this one with derelict gardens but a rolling view near Moreton-in-the-Marsh, Gloucestershire. The courtyard (seating capacity 200) was replaced by scaffolding, raising capacity to 400. Knapp considers the scaffolding so successful that he is thinking of hiring it himself and 'touring' to various picturesque historical sites: 'The repertoire would probably favour only the top handful of operas, but since performing animals have become unacceptable, funfairs unsafe, and celebrity concerts like Dame Kiri at Blenheim have flopped. Circus opera? Why not' (Widdicombe 1994).

Appendix A

Littlejohn (1993: 19-27) compiled a list of the top 100 works for all 252 companies reported in *Opera* during the calendar years 1988-1989. He introduced this list with an almost required reflection for 'high-minded' critics, that popular works are often of poor quality: 'Admired works that are difficult to cast, such as *Tristan* and *Norma* end up far below the frothy light operas and tired Victorian warhorses *(Faust, Adriana Lecouvreur)* that many critics would be happy to see retired from the lists for all time (ibid.: 20). The 100, with original titles and, where relevant, English equivalents, with composer and year of first performance and including musical theatre works such as *My Fair Lady* is as follows:

1. *Le nozze di Figaro (The Marriage of Figaro)* (Mozart 1786).
2. *Tosca* (Puccini 1900).
3. *Don Giovanni* (Mozart 1787).
4. *Il barbiere di Siviglia (The Barber of Seville)* (Rossini 1816).
5. *La Bohème* (Puccini 1896).
6. *La traviata* (Verdi 1853).
7. *Die Zauberflöte (The Magic Flute)* (Mozart 1791).
8. *Così fan tutte* (Mozart 1790).
9. *Madama Butterfly* (Puccini 1904).
10. *Rigoletto* (Verdi 1851).
11. *Carmen* (Bizet 1875).
12. *Die Fledermaus* (J. Strauss 1874).
13. *Die Entführung aus dem Serail (The Abduction from the Seraglio)* (Mozart 1782).
14. *Fidelio* (Beethoven 1805/ 1814).

15. *Aida* (Verdi 1871).
16. *Der fliegende Hollander (The Flying Dutchman)* (Wagner 1843).
17. *Salome* (R. Strauss 1905).
18. *Un ballo in maschera (A Masked Ball)* (Verdi 1859).
19. *Les Contes d'Hoffmann (The Tales of Hoffmann)* (Offenbach 1881).
20. *Turandot* (Puccini 1926).
21. *Die lustige Witwe (The Merry Widow* (Lehár 1905).
22. *Falstaff* (Verdi 1859).
23. *Der Rosenkavalier* (R. Strauss 1911).
24. *Hänsel und Gretel* (Humperdinck 1893).
25. *L'elisir d'amore* (Donizetti 1832).
26. *Ariadne auf Naxos* (R. Strauss 1912).
27. *Lucia di Lammermoor* (Donizetti 1833).
28. *Eugene Onegin* (Tchaikovsky 1879).
29. *Faust* (Gounod 1859).
30. *Otello* (Verdi 1887).
31. *Il trovatore* (Verdi 1853).
32. *Die Walküre* (Wagner 1870).
33. *Parsifal* (Wagner 1882).
34. *Cavalleria rusticana* (Mascagni 1890).
35. *I Pagliacci* (Leoncavello 1892).
36. *Don Carlos* (Verdi 1867/ 1884).
37. *Don Pasquale* (Donizetti 1843).
38. *Manon* (Massenet 1884).
39. *Lohengrin* (Wagner 1850).
40. *Das Rheingold* (Wagner 1869).
41. *Nabucco* (Verdi 1842).
42. *Der Freischütz* (Weber 1821).
43. *La Cenerentola* (Rossini 1817).
44. *Elektra* (R. Strauss 1909).
45. *La clemenza di Tito* (Mozart 1791).
46. *Orfeo ed Eurudice* (Gluck 1762).
47. *Andrea Chénier* (Giordano 1896).
48. *Die Meistersinger von Nürnberg* (Wagner 1868).
49. *Orpheus in the Underworld* (Offenbach 1858).
50. *The Bartered Bride* (Smetana 1866).
51. *Götterdämmerung* (Wagner 1876).
52. *Boris Godunov* (Mussorgsky 1874).
53. *Adriana Lecouvreur* (Cilea 1904).
54. *Tannhäuser* (Wagner 1845/1861).

55. *Katya Kabanova* (Janacek 1921).
56. *Werther* (Massenet 1892).
57. *La forza del destino* (Verdi 1862/1869).
58. *Simon Boccanegra* (Verdi 1857/1881).
59. *La Fille du régiment* (Donizetti 1840).
60. *Wozzeck* (Berg 1925).
61. *Macbeth* (Verdi 1847).
62. *Siegfried* (Wagner 1876).
63. *La Vie parisienne* (Offenbach 1866).
64. *The Queen of Spades* (Tchaikovsky 1890).
65. *Zar und Zimmermann* (Lortzing 1837).
66. *Jenufa* (Janacek 1904).
67. *Mefistofele* (Boito 18681 1875)
68. *The Mikado* (Sullivan 1885).
69. The *Gypsy Princess* 1915).
70. *The Pearl Fishers* (Bizet 1863).
71. *L'incoronazione di Poppea* (Monteverdi 1642).
72. *Manon Lescaut* (Puccini 1893).
73. *Idomeneo* (Mozart 1781).
74. *L'italiana in Algeri* (Rossini 1813).
75. *Tristan und Isolde* (Wagner 1865).
76. *Die Frau ohne Schatten* (R. Strauss 1919).
77. *Giulio Cesare in Egitto* (Handel 1724).
78. *West Side Story* (Bernstein 1957).
79. *Arabella* (R. Strauss 1933).
80. *La Belle Hélène* (Offenbach 1864).
81. *My Fair Lady* (Lerner 1956).
82. *Gianni Schicchi* (Puccini 1918).
83. *Norma* (Bellini 1831).
84. *Peter Grimes* (Britten 1945).
85. *Bluebeard's Castle* (Bartok 1911).
86. *Die lustigen Weiber von Windsor (The Merry Wives of Windsor)* (Nicolai 1849).
87. *La finta gardiniera* (Mozart 1775).
88. *The Turn of the Screw* (Britten 1954).
89. *La Grande Duchesse de Gérolstein* (Offenbach 1867).
90. *Eine Nacht in Venedig (A Night in Venice)* (J. Strauss 1883).
91. *Albert Herring* (Britten 1947).
92. *Pelléas et Mélisande* (Debussy 1902).
93. *Thaïs* (Massenet 1894).

94. *Das Land des Lachelns (The Land of Smiles)* (Lehar 1929).
95. *Les Dialogues des Carmélites* (Poulenc 1957).
96. *La Gioconda* (Ponchielli 1876).
97. *Il signor Bruschino* (Rossini 1813).
98. *Samson et Dalila* (Saint-Saëns 1877).
99. *Le Comte Ory* (Rossini 1828).
100. *La sonnambula* (Bellini 1831).

Littlejohn acknowledges the shortcomings of this and all such lists, but notes the stability of the top 60-70 per cent, with an additional 20 or so works hovering below the 100 mark. including: *Luisa Miller* (Verdi 1849): *Fra Diavolo* (Auber 1830); *The Love of the Three Oranges* (Prokofiev 1921); *The Fiery Angel* (Prokofiev 1954); *Lady Macbeth of Mtsensk* (Shostakovitch 1934); *Fiddler on the Roof* (Bock); *A Midsummer Night's Dream* (Britten 1960); *The Rakes Progress* (Stravinsky 1951); *Der Bettelstudent* (Millocker 1882); *Il tabarro* (Puccini 1918); *La rondine* (Puccini 1917); *The Makropoulos Case* (Janacek 1926); *The Cunning Little Vixen* (Janacek 1924); *Die schweigsame Frau* (R. Strauss 1935); *Il matrimonio segreto* (Cimarosa 1792); *Oberon* (Weber 1826); *Prince Igor* (Borodin 1890); *Khovanshchina* (Mussorgsky 1866); *Le convenience ed inconvenience teatrali* (Donizetti — better known as *Viva la Mamma!* 1827); *Médée* (Cherubini 1797); *Porgy and Bess* (Gershwin 1935); *Dido and Aeneas* (Purcell 1689/90); *Rusalka* (Dvorak 1901); *Roméo et Juliette* (Gounod 1867) and three Gilbert and Sullivan operettas (ibid.: 24).

There are several shortcomings to such lists. Despite tendencies towards international uniformity, strong national variations are hidden—for example in many middle European and North American theatres 'musicals' are performed in repertoire alongside operas, whereas elsewhere this is very rare. This is therefore a list based on institutional definitions of the terms opera, including all forms of 'lyric theatre' performed by opera companies. Nor is it a Top 100 'works of the lyric theatre' list because only when performed by opera companies are works such as *My Fair Lady* included. Furthermore, it is not a Top 100 list in terms of performances given, but productions mounted. Works in the Top 20 or 30 and especially 10 are normally given more performances reflecting their greater economic (box office) viability, for example, taking the above points into account, during the 1993-94 season at Köln the most performed work was Lortzing's *Der Wildschütz*. Economic viability also depends on the frequency with which productions are revived over several, not just two, seasons. Works in the lower 30 per cent and just outside the 100 tend to be in vogue for a couple of seasons, often receiving several listings through 'shared' productions between several theatres. Only after several seasons can long term trends be traced.

I carried out three comparative exercises to check the viability of the Littlejohn list. In one I drew on the same source and conditions but for the years 1992-93. There was inevitably some movement largely due to economic viability and fashion. Overall, however, the lists were very similar. In my list for example, *Die Fledermaus, Hoffmann, Trovatore* and *Lucia* were considerably more popular than in 1988-89, *Tosca, Fidelio,* and *Don Giovanni* less so.

In a second exercise I used *Opera Now International Showcase Edition 1995/96* which provided the season's plans for 203 companies. This showed a similar consistency and stability overall: 8 of Littlejohn's Top 10 remained as did 15 of the Top 20 and 22 of the Top 30. The biggest changes were the disappearance out of this Top 100 of *Manon, Lohengrin, Orfeo ed Euridice, Der Freischütz, Orpheus in the Underworld* and *Adriana Lecouvreur* all in Littlejohn's Top 50. One work only, outside *his* Top 100, appears in this other Top 50: Puccini's *Il tabarro*.

In the third exercise I compared the entries for particular works in the *Opera* index of 1960 with that of 1994. The magazine has grown in size during this period, includes more 'features' and changed its review format but allowing for these and the vagaries of any one single season's programmes, the resoluteness of the core works remains both close to each other and to Littlejohn. In 1960 426 individual works are referred to compared with 494 in 1994. Of the 426 and 494, no fewer than 268 and 360 respectively received just one mention. The ten most frequently reviewed works were for 1960 (with positions for 1994 in brackets): 1. *Tosca* (3); 2. *La traviata* (2); *La Bohème* (1): 4.*Carmen* (11): 5. *Madama Butterfly* (10): 6. *Il barbiere di Siviglia* (5): 7. *Aida* (12): 8. *Rigoletto* (9): 9. *Un ballo in maschera* (21): 10. *Die Walküre* (30). In 1994 works in the Top Ten which were not in 1960 are: equal 5. *Turandot* (13 in 1960) and *Così fan tute* (17), equal 6. *Eugene Onegin* (45), *Don Giovanni* (12) and *Die Zauberflöte* (27). It is difficult to perceive great changes of fashion except that Mozart has become more frequently performed, Wagner less so. Serious works by Donizetti and Rossini are more common, as are works by Janacek and Britten. More striking in the 400 plus for each year are the works which have been either passing fad 'discoveries' or short-lived 'new' works. The fate of 1994's 'new' works is of course difficult to predict, but in 1960 one could have attended performances of Yamada's *The Black Ships* in Osaka, Sklavos' *Cassiane* in Athens, Leroux *La Chemineau* in Besançon, Ashrafi's *Dilorom* in Uzbekistan, Gorbulski's *Frank Kruk* in Kaunas, Rottger's *Phaeton* in Dessau as well as Openshaw's *Mr Postwhistle* in Bromley.

The value of such lists and data is as tools enabling basic comparative judgements to be made; they should not be reified beyond that.

Appendix B

On the following pages are examples of opera house auditoria. The Vienna State Opera (1869) is an excellent example of a the grand (on 5/6 tiers) mid-nineteenth century standard horseshoe-shaped house, additionally notable for the considerable size and location (behind the stalls) of its 'standing space' (Stehparterre). It is clear how a large number of side seats have restricted views of the stage but perfect views of each other and the stalls below.

The plan of the Munich State Opera (1818, rebuilt after fire 1825, bombed in 1943, rebuilt in 1963) allows us to appreciate the tiers of these grand nineteenth century houses, as well as the 'royal box' centre circle. Here there are fewer boxes. Standing places are indicated by *. Price groups are listed below but these should be read in conjunction with the discussion of the complexities of seat pricing.

The Geneva Grand Théâtre is typical of the smaller European nineteenth century houses and dates from 1962. Following the seat plan there is a profile presenting auditorium in the context of backstage space, flies, and so on.

Twentieth century purpose-built opera houses have taken sight-lines of all parts of often very large theatres (The Met New York, Bastille Opera Paris) into account. The example given here is the Hamburg State Opera (1955).

WIENER STAATSOPER

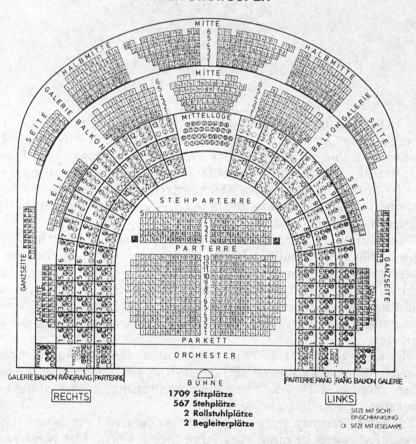

RECHTS

LINKS

1709 Sitzplätze
567 Stehplätze
2 Rollstuhlplätze
2 Begleiterplätze

SITZE MIT SICHT-
EINSCHRÄNKUNG
○ SITZE MIT LESELAMPE

Nationaltheater

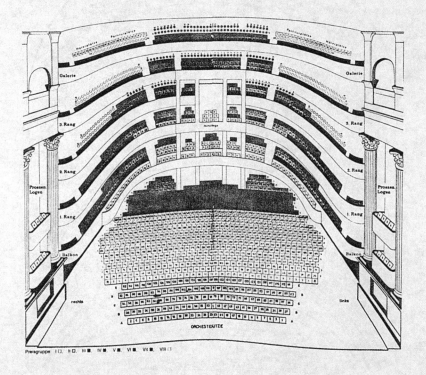

GRAND·THÉATRE DE GENÈVE

Plan de location

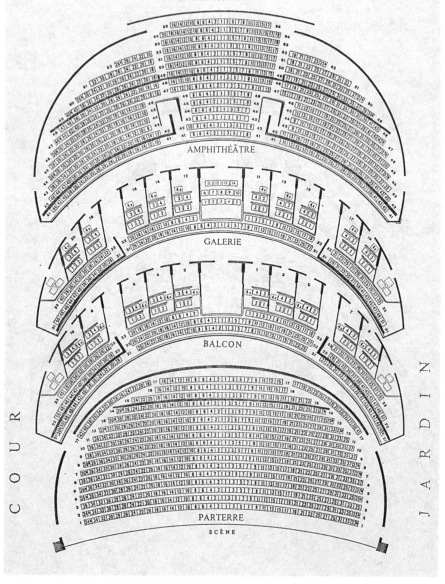

AMPHITHÉÂTRE

GALERIE

BALCON

PARTERRE

SCÈNE

COUR

JARDIN

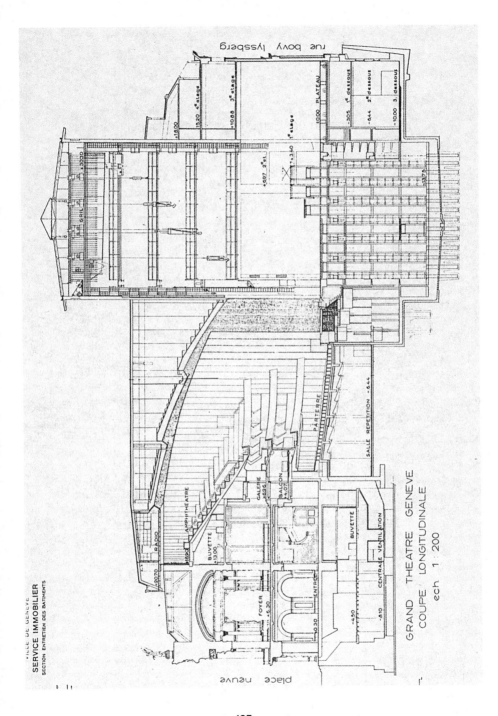

rue bovy lysberg

place neuve

GRAND THEATRE GENEVE
COUPE LONGITUDINALE
ech 1:200

435

Sitzplan der Hamburgischen Staatsoper

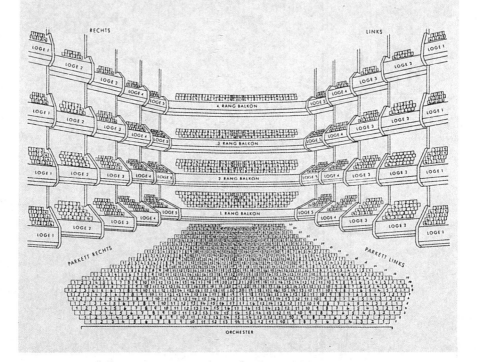

Appendix C

Companies whose documents have been used for Chapters 3 and 4 are (with, where relevant, abbreviations used in the text):

The Royal Opera House Covent Garden, London (ROH).
The English National Opera, London (ENO).
The Welsh National Opera, Cardiff (WNO).
Scottish Opera, Glasgow (SO).
English Opera North, Leeds (EON).
Swedish Royal Opera Stockholm.
Lyric Opera, Chicago.
Vienna State Opera (VSO).
Teatro Communale: Maggio Musicale Fiorentino.
Teatro Communale di Bologna
Los Angeles Music Centre Opera.
Hamburg State Opera.
Zurich Opera.
Bayerische Stadt Oper Munich
San Francisco Opera
Grand Théâtre de Genève
The Australian Opera
Opéra Comique Paris
The New Israeli Opera Tel Aviv.
Teatro la Zarzuela Madrid
Staatsoper Unter den Linden Berlin,
Frankfurt Opera.
The Metropolitan Opera New York (Met).

Deutsche Oper Berlin.
Chatelet Paris.
Kirov Opera St Petersburg.
Gran Teatro del Licieu Barcelona.
Prague National Theatre.

Appendix D

Opera house and company accounting are increasingly complex and present in company reports, year books and even publicity materials. The example given here is for the Metropolitan Opera New York years 1991-92, and is meant to show how such matters are presented for wider readerships and to underline the discursive fact that opera as an artefact addressed in Italian, German, French Czech, English and so on, musical notation and the dramatised 'ideas' of producers, designers, choreographers and so on, is also an industry in which the language of economics and accountancy are of considerable importance.

Appendix E

The constitution of a theatres or companies controlling hierarchies vary enormously as this text indicates. The Grand Théatre Geneva however inclosed in their documentation this summary diagram of the authority network including the presence of representatives of the city of Geneva, the providers of considerable subsidy support.

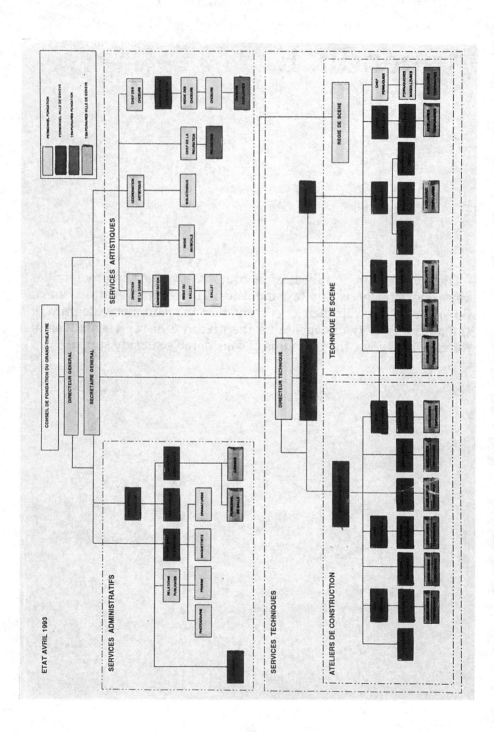

ETAT AVRIL 1993

CONSEIL DE FONDATION DU GRAND-THEATRE

DIRECTEUR GENERAL

SECRETAIRE GENERAL

SERVICES ARTISTIQUES

SERVICES ADMINISTRATIFS

SERVICES TECHNIQUES

DIRECTEUR TECHNIQUE

TECHNIQUE DE SCENE

REGIE DE SCENE

ATELIERS DE CONSTRUCTION

Appendix F

Articles on singers referenced with an asterisk * in the text.

Licia **Albanese,** *Opera News,* W. Price, 3 February 1990, 8-12, 46.
Thomas **Allen,** *Opera,* People 117, M. Loppert, July 1978, 671.
Thomas **Allen,** *Opera Now,* G. Kay, January 1992, 20-24.
June **Anderson,** *Opera Now,* July 1993, 20-22.
Marian **Anderson,** *Opera Now,* March 1992, 26-9.
Francisco **Araiza,** *Opera News,* B. L. Scherer, 2 February 1991, 20-22.
Francisco **Araiza,** *Opera Now,* A. Sinclair, May 1994, 35.
Irina **Archipova,** *Opera* People 208, J. Allison, April 1995, 389-95.
Martina **Arroyo,** *Opera News,* R. M. Story, September 1991, 26-8.
Arleen **Auger,** *Opera Now,* J. Steane, June 1994, 28-30.
Florence **Austral,** *Opera Now,* J. Steane, May 1994, 48-9.
Gabriel **Bacquier,** *Opera* People 130, 1982 June 577-81.
Norman **Bailey,** *Opera,* People 101, E. Forbes, September 1973, 774-80.
Janet **Baker,** *Opera,* People 83, A. Blyth, May 1970, 395-400.
Janet **Baker,** *Opera,* H. Rosenthal, October 1976, 991-7.
Agnes **Baltsa,** *Opera,* People 137, N. Goodwin, May 1985, 483-9.
Rose **Bampton,** *Opera News,* J. W. Freeman, 18 March 1989, 8-13.
Barry **Banks,** *Opera Now,* A. Stewart, September 1994, 34.
Josephine **Barstow,** *Opera,* People 104, E. Forbes, October 1974, 865-74.
Josephine **Barstow,** *Opera Now,* October 1992.
Cecilia **Bartoli,** *Opera Now,* December 1992.
Cecilia **Bartoli,** *Opera News,* W. Price, August 1993, 10-14, 46.

Kathleen **Battle,** *Opera Now*, June 1992.

Hildegard **Behrens,** *Opera*, People 172, A. Blyth, May 1991, 502-8.

Teresa **Berganza,** *Opera*, People 69, M. Harewood, March 1967, 192-6.

Carlo **Bergonzi,** *Opera*, People 116, G. Gualerzi, March 1978, 257-62.

Carlo **Bergonzi,** *Opera Now*, December 1992.

Jussi **Bjoerling,** *Opera Now*, December 1989.

Harolyn **Blackwell,** *Opera News*, S. Flatow, 19 January 1991, 16-17.

Rockwell **Blake,** *Opera Monthly*, S. Horwitz, July 1991, 5-11.

Rockwell **Blake,** *Opera News*, J. T. Kretschmer, 29 February 1992, 20-21.

Barbara **Bonney,** *Opera Now*, A. Sinclair, February 1995, 33.

Olga **Borodina,** *Opera Now*, February 1993.

Bonaventura **Bottone** *Opera Now*, A. Stewart, September 1994, 32.

Sesto **Bruscantini,** *Opera*, People 90, E. Forbes, June 1971, 491-7.

Renato **Bruson,** *Opera*, People 118, G. Gualerzi, March 1979, 214-18.

Grace **Bumbry,** *Opera*, People 84, A. Blyth, June 1970. 506-11.

Grace **Bumbry,** *Opera Now*, A. Stewart, 13 December 1991.

Sally **Burgess,** *Opera*, People 170, E. Forbes, January 1991, 16-21

Montserrat **Caballé,** *Opera*, People 105, F. Glanville-Barker, April 1975, 342-9.

Montserrat **Caballé,** *Opera Now*, A. Stewart, 17 December 1994.

Maria **Callas**, Conversation with ... *Opera*, A. Sievewright, November 1977, 1022-25.

Joan **Carden,** *Opera*, People 199, R. Milnes, April 1994, 410-17.

José **Carreras,** *Opera*, People 149, May 1987, 507-11.

José **Carreras,** *Opera Now*, M. Stoppard, January 1990, 36-9.

José **Carreras,** *Opera Now*, January 1993.

Maria **Cebotari,** *Opera Now*, J. Steane, March 1994, 40-42.

Feodor **Chaliapin,** *Opera News*, P. Horgen, 19 January 1991, 10-14, 52.

Vladimir **Chernov,** *Opera News*, D. McKee, 5 March 1994, 8-11

Boris **Christoff,** *Opera*, November 1974. 963-66, 50-52.

Boris **Christoff,** *Opera Now*, J. Steane, April 1993.

Gina **Cigna,** *Opera*, J. Boraros, January 1970, 23-7.

Graham **Clark,** *Opera*, People 184, S. Blyth, November 1992, 1283-90.

Graham **Clark,** *Opera News*, G. Schmidgall, 22 January 1994, 20-23.

Vinson **Cole,** *Opera News*, H. E. Phillips, 9 December 1989, 26-30.

Marie **Collier,** *Opera*, People 76, A. Blyth, December 1968, 958-65.

Elisabeth **Connell,** *Opera*, People 152, E. Forbes, June 1988, 670-76.

Ileana **Cotrubas**, *Opera*, People 112, A. Blyth, May 1976, 428-33.
Joan **Cross**, *Opera*, Lord Harewood, September 1990, 1032-7.
Regine **Crespin**, *Opera*, A. Tubeuf, April 1963, 227.
Regine **Crespin**, *Opera Now*, January 1993.
Lella **Cuberli**, *Opera News*, C. Battaglia, 21 January 1989, 16-18.
Phyllis **Curtin**, *Opera News*, R. Dyer, November 1990, 10-14, 63.
Toti **dal Monte**, *Opera Now*, J. Steane, March 1995, 44-45.
Inger **Dam-Jensen**, *Opera Now*, G. Kay, January 1994, 20-22.
Victoria **de los Angeles**, *Opera Now*, M. Cooper, April 1990, 54-56.
Victoria **de los Angeles**, *Opera News*, C. Ellison, 7 January 1995, 12-14.
Lisa **della Casa**, *Opera*, People 73, G. Fitzgerald, March 1968, 185-91.
Lisa **della Casa**, *Opera News*, E. Forbes, 4 March 1995, 14-17.
Mario **del Monaco**, *Opera*, People, F. Nuzzo, June 1962, 372.
Giuseppe **de Luca**, *Opera Now*, J. Steane, September 1994, 28-30.
Helga **Dernesch**, *Opera*, T. Smillie, May 1973, 407-13.
Giuseppe **di Stefano**, *Opera Now*, July 1992, 26-8.
Placido **Domingo**, *Opera*, People 94, H. Rosenthal, January 1972, 18-24.
Placido **Domingo**, *Opera Now*, March 1992, 20-25.
Helen **Donath**, *Opera News*, A. Midgette, 11 December 1993, 26-8.
Ludmila **Dvorakova**, *Opera*, People 95, A. Blyth, September 1971, 768-73.
Jane **Eaglen**, *Opera Now*, A. Green, 12 February 1995.
Anne **Evans**, *Opera Now*, April 1989.
Anne **Evans**, *Opera*, People 140, R. Milnes, March 1986, 256-62.
Anne **Evans**, *Opera Now*, M. Hayes, February 1994, 20-22.
Geraint **Evans**, *Opera Now*, November 1992.
Maria **Ewing**, *Opera Now*, September 1989.
Maria **Ewing**, *Opera News*, D. Perlmutter, 25 December 1993, 18-20, 42.
Geraldine **Farrar**, *Opera Now*, October 1992.
Eileen **Farrell**, *Opera News*, B. Kellow, July 1992, 26-9.
Brigitte **Fassbaender**, *Opera*, People 127, S. Gould, August 1981, 789-95.
Brigitte **Fassbaender**, *Opera Now*, October 1990.
Kathleen **Ferrier**, *Opera Now*, June 1992.
Dietrich **Fischer-Dieskau**, *Opera Now*, J. Steane, 28-30 January 1994.
Kirsten **Flagstad**, *Opera Now*, February 1993.

Renée **Fleming,** *Opera News,* L. T. Guinther, September 1994, 24-6.
Bruce **Ford,** *Opera Now,* A. Sinclair, May 1994, 38.
Maureen **Forrester,** *Opera News* B Kellow, 18 January 1992, 22-4, 42.
Judith **Forst,** *Opera News,* J. H. Kestner, September 1990, 30-32.
Mirella **Freni,** *Opera News,* R. Dyer, September 1990, 18-20, 69.
Mirella **Freni,** *Opera Now,* August/September 1990.
Mirella **Freni,** *Opera Now,* M. Hayes, March 1994, 20-22.
Gottlob **Frick,** *Opera,* People 62, W. Schwinger, March 1966, 188-92.
Ferruccio **Furlanetto,** *Opera Now,* A. Stewart, 17 July 1993.
Vera **Galupe-Borszkh,** *Opera News,* B. Kellow, 28-31 August 1991.
Vera **Galupe-Borszkh,** *Opera Now,* A. Stewart, April 1994, 31-2.
Lesley **Garrett,** *Opera Now,* November 1990.
Cecilia **Gasdia,** *Opera Now,* A. Stewart, July 1994, 32.
Micolai **Gedda,** *Opera,* People 67, G. Storjohann, December 1966, 939-44.
Leyla **Gencer,** *Opera,* People 95, R. Celletti, August 1972, 692-7.
Nicolai **Ghiaurov,** *Opera,* People 114, A. Blyth, October 1977, 941-8.
Beniamino **Gigli,** *Opera Now,* M. Scott, March 1990, 44-7.
Peter **Glossop,** *Opera,* People 79, F. Granville Barker, May 1969, 386-91.
Tito **Gobbi,** *Opera,* H. Rosenthal, April 1983, 476-84.
Tito **Gobbi,** *Opera Now,* November 1991.
Galina **Gorchakova,** *Opera Now,* N. Winter, March 1992, 19-21.
Galina **Gorchakova,** *Opera Now,* H. Waleson, March 1995, 22-4.
Susan **Graham,** *Opera Now,* A. Stewart, February 1994, 16-7.
Andrea **Gruber,** *Opera Now,* A. Peattic, April 1990, 30-32.
Franz **Grundheber,** *Opera Now,* A. Stewart, 17-18 March 1993.
Nancy **Gustafson,** *Opera Now,* A. Stewart, 15-16 October 1993.
Jerry **Hadley,** *Opera,* People 187, N. Goodwin, March 1993, 279-285.
Jerry **Hadley,** *Opera Now,* A. Stewart, 18 March 1993.
Joan **Hammond,** *Opera Now,* A. Stewart, March 1993, 16-17.
Thomas **Hampson,** *Opera News,* D. G. Winer, 4 February 1989, 8-11, 46.
Thomas **Hampson,** *Opera Now,* A. Stewart, October 1993, 20-22.
Derek **Hammond-Stroud,** *Opera,* People 139, A. Blyth, December 1985, 1358-64.
Heather **Harper,** *Opera,* People 91, H. Rosenthal, July 1971, 594-600.
Ben **Heppner,** *Opera News,* J. Williams, 16 March 1991, 24-5.
Jerome **Hines,** *Opera News,* B. L. Scherer, 21 December 1991, 30-32.
Joseph **Hislop,** *Opera Now,* September 1992.

Marilyn **Horne,** *Opera News,* E. Newman, 22 December 1990, 11-14, 43.

Marilyn **Horne,** *Opera News,* M. Sevilla-Gonzaga, October 1994, 24-5.

Hans **Hotter,** *Opera,* July 1976, 606-12.

Judith **Howarth,** *Opera Now,* A. Stewart, January 1995, 31.

Gwynne **Howell,** *Opera,* People 176, A. Blyth, September 1991, 1018-25.

Anne **Howells,** *Opera,* People 156, H. Canning, March 1989, 271-7.

Rita **Hunter,** *Opera,* People 109, January 1976, 14-20.

Maria **Ivogun,** *Opera Now,* J. Steane, January 1992, 228-30.

Gundula **Janowitz,** *Opera Now,* A. Stewart, April 1995, 33.

Siegfried **Jerusalem,** *Opera,* People 182, A. Blyth, August 1992, 904-9

Sumi **Jo,** *Opera Now,* October 1991.

Anthony **Rolfe Johnson,** *Opera News,* J. M. Keller, 24 December 1994, 14-15, 44.

Anthony **Rolfe Johnson,** *Opera,* People 189, June 1993, 637-43.

Della **Jones,** *Opera,* People 168, H. Canning, October 1990, 1159-65.

Della **Jones,** *Opera Now,* A. Stewart, July 1994, 34.

Gwyneth **Jones,** *Opera,* People 81, K. Loveland, February 1970, 100-106.

Gwyneth **Jones,** *Opera News,* H. E. Phillips, 6 January 1990, 10-12.

Gwyneth **Jones,** *Opera Now,* R. Fawkes, October 1994, 22-4.

Sena **Jurinac,***Opera,* People 63, U. Tamussino, April 1966, 265-71.

Simon **Keenlyside,** *Opera Now,* A. Stewart, 30 January 1995.

Yvonne **Kenny,** *Opera,* People 185, H. Canning, December 1992, 1385-93.

Yvonne **Kenny,** *Opera Now,* M. Hayes, February 1995, 22-5.

James **King,** *Opera,* People 143, E. Forbes, July 1986, 758-63.

James **King,** *Opera News,* J. James, 2 March 1991, 16-17.

René **Kollo,** *Opera,* People 162, B. Kayser, December 1989, 1415-22.

Alfredo **Kraus,** *Opera,* People 105, R. Cellini, January 1975, 17-22.

Alfredo **Kraus,** *Opera Now,* June 1991.

Alfredo **Kraus,** *Opera News,* E. Newman, November 1991, 10-14, 42.

Otakar **Kraus,** *Opera,* People 103, A. Blyth, December 1973, 1073-1078.

Michael **Langdon,** *Opera,* People 108, H. Rosenthal, December 1975, 1111-17.

Philip **Langridge,** *Opera,* People 142, C. Pitt, May 1986, 499-506.

John **Lanigan,** *Opera,* People 87, A. Blyth, January 1971, 20-26.

Jennifer **Larmore**, *Opera Now*, J. M. Keller, 18 February 1995, 14-17.

Giacomo **Lauri-Volpi**, *Opera Now*, November 1992.

Lotte **Lehmann**, *Opera*, W. Legge, November 1976, 1002-12.

Sergei **Leiferkus**, *Opera*, People 165, E. Forbes, February 1990, 175-80.

Frida **Leider**, *Opera*, E. Turner, H. Burros and N. Feasey, August 1975, 733-8.

Frida **Leider**, *Opera News*, J. B. Steane, October 1991, 18-22.

Marjana **Lipovsek**, *Opera Now*, A. Stewart, July 1993, 16-7.

Robert **Lloyd**, *Opera*, People 131, R. Milnes, April 1983, 368-74.

Robert **Lloyd**, *Opera Now*, R. Hartford, March 1993, 20-23.

Frank **Lopardo**, *Opera News*, M. Gurewitsch, 19 February 1994, 20-21.

Felicity **Lott**, *Opera*, People 160, E. Forbes, October 1989, 1174-80.

Felicity **Lott**, *Opera Now*, May 1991.

Felicity **Lott**, *Opera Now*, May 1992.

Felicity **Lott**, *Opera Now*, A. Sinclair, February 1995, 31.

Christa **Ludwig**, *Opera*, People 98, C. Osborne, March 1973, 216-22.

Christa **Ludwig**, *Opera Now*, December 1989.

Christa **Ludwig**, *Opera News*, R. Domerasky, 13 March 1993, 22-4.

Christa **Ludwig**, *Opera Now*, J. Steane, December 1993, 28-30.

Christa **Ludwig**, *Opera Now*, H. Tims, December 1994, 10.

James **McCracken**, *Opera*, People 68, A. Williamson, January 1967, 7-14.

Donald **McIntyre**, *Opera*, People 106, A. Blyth, June 1975, 529-35.

Marie **McLaughlin**, *Opera*, People 195, A. Clark, December 1993, 1391-9.

Catherina **Malfitano**, *Opera Now*, January 1993.

Catherine **Malfitano**, *Opera*, People 192, R Milnes, October 1993, 1145-53.

Alessandra **Marc**, *Opera Now*, October 1990.

Margaret **Marshall**, *Opera Now*, A. Stewart, December 1993, 15.

Eva **Marton**, *Opera*, People 166, A. Blyth, March 1990, 276-81.

Fritzi **Massary**, *Opera*, P. O'Connor, May 1982, 467-73.

Valerie **Masterson**, *Opera*, People 119, H. Rosenthal, December 1979, 1128-34.

Donald **Maxwell**, *Opera Now*, A. Stewart, April 1993, 23-4.

Anthony **Mee**, *Opera Now*, A. Stewart, September 1994, 33.

Waltraud **Meier**, *Opera*, People 175, A. Clark, August 1991, 886-92.

Lauritz **Melchior**, *Opera Now*, M. Scott, March 1990, 48-50.

Lauritz **Melchior,** *Opera News,* M. Scott, August 1990, 16-18.

Susanne **Mentzer,** *Opera News,* L. T. Guinther, 5 February 1994, 8-11.

Robert **Merrill,** *Opera Now,* J. Steane, April 1995, 46-8.

Chris **Merritt,** *Opera,* People 183, R. Milnes, Fest October 1992, 6-12.

Kirsten **Meyer,** *Opera,* People 102, J. Amis, October 1973, 879-86.

Alastair **Miles,** *Opera Now,* A. Inglis, February 1995, 13.

Sherrill **Milnes,** *Opera,* People 121, T. P. Lanier, June 1980, 538-44.

Yvonne **Minton,** *Opera,* People 113, H. Rosenthal, September 1977, 834-40.

Zinka **Milanov,** *Opera,* A. Blyth, August 1989, 929-32.

James **Morris,** *Opera,* People 154, H. Canning, October 1988, 1177-83.

James **Morris,** *Opera News,* P. Thomason, 24 December 1994, 20-23.

Ann **Murray,** *Opera,* People 153, H. Finch, August 1988, 914-19.

Ann **Murray,** *Opera Now,* May 1992.

Claudia **Muzio,** *Opera,* G. Guarlerzi, June 1986, 643-7.

Birgit **Nilsson,** *Opera,* People, W. Jeffries, September 1960, 607.

Birgit **Nilsson,** *Opera Now,* J. Steane, August 1993, 44-6.

Jessye **Norman,** *Opera Now,* October 1989.

Jarmila **Novotna,** *Opera News,* J. W. Freeman, 23 December 1989, 8-12.

Magda **Olivero,** *Opera News,* S. Hastings, 19 March 1994, 12-15.

Dennis **O'Neill,** *Opera Now,* R. Fawkes, August 1983, 14.

Dennis **O'Neill,** *Opera,* People 198, E. Forbes, March 1994, 285-292.

Dennis **O'Neill,** *Opera Now,* R. Fawkes, July 1994a, 22-4.

Alan **Opie,** *Opera,* People 171, A. Blyth, February 1991, 150-56.

Felicity **Palmer,** *Opera,* People 203, E. Forbes, September 1994, 1031-7.

Luciano **Pavarotti,** *Opera,* People 124, G. Gualerzi, February 1981, 118-25.

Peter **Pears,** *Opera,* June 1986, 624-30.

Jan **Peerce,** *Opera News,* L. Rubinstein, 29 February 1992, 16-19.

Aureliano **Pertile,** *Opera Now,* J. Steane, October 1993, 28-30.

Ezio **Pinza,** *Opera News,* R. Croan, May 1992, 18-24.

Ezio **Pinza,** *Opera Now,* May 1992.

Paul **Plishka,** *Opera News,* B. Kellow, 30 March 1991, 14-16.

Rosalind **Plowright,** *Opera,* People 180, E. Forbes, April 1992, 416-23.

Francoise **Pollet,** *Opera News,* P. Kennicott, 25 December 1993, 21.

Rosa **Ponselle,** *Opera,* January 1977, 13-25.

Rosa **Ponselle**, *Opera Now*, J. Steane, April 1994, 40-42.
Lucia **Popp**, *Opera*, People 128, A. Blyth, February 1982, 132-9.
Lucia **Popp**, *Opera Now*, J. Steane, October 1994, 28-30.
Margaret **Price**, *Opera*, People 138, A. Blyth, June 1985, 607-14.
Elena **Prokina**, *Opera Now*, A. Stewart, July 1994, 33.
Elena **Prokina**, *Opera Now*, R. Fawkes, January 1995, 24-6.
Susan **Quittmeyer**, *Opera News*, W. Price, 5 January 1991, 22-3.
Ruggero **Raimondi**, *Opera*, People 200, A. Clark, May 1994a, 539-45.
Ruggero **Raimondi**, *Opera Now*, K. Hardy, May 1994b, 11.
Samuel **Ramey**, *Opera News*, J. von Rhein, 14 April 1990, 10-14.
Maria **Reining**, *Opera*, A. Blyth, May 1988, 545-50.
Alberto **Remedios**, *Opera*, People 97, E. Forbes, January 1973, 15-22.
Alberto **Remedios**, *Opera Now*, A. Stewart, March 1995, 32-3.
Regina **Resnik**, *Opera*, People 1, I. Cook, January 1963, 13.
Regina **Resnik**, *Opera News*, D. McKee, 10 December 1994, 22-4.
Elisabeth **Rethberg**, *Opera Now*, J. Steane, January 1995, 44-6.
Katia **Ricciarelli**, *Opera*, People 164, A. Blyth, January 1990, 28-33.
Amanda **Roocroft**, *Opera Now*, R. Fawkes, September 1994, 20-2.
Tito **Ruffo**, *Opera*, A. Farkas, August 1983, 832-9.
Leonie **Rysanek**, *Opera News*, P. Kennicott, 11 April 1992, 34-6, 60.
Leonie **Rysanek**, *Opera Now*, May 1990.
Leonie **Rysanek**, *Opera*, People 196, Alan Blyth, January 1994, 45, 15-23.
Elisabeth **Schumann**, *Opera*, A. Mathis, November 1973, 968-80.
Patricia **Schumann**, *Opera News*, D. McGovern, 2 February 1991, 10-14.
Ernestine **Schumann-Heink**, *Opera Now*, J. Steane, November 1994, 30-32.
Elisabeth **Schwarzkopf**, *Opera*, People 111, W. Legge, 3 April 1976, 16-24.
Renata **Scotto**, *Opera*, People 88, E. Gara, March 1971, 199-206.
Irmgard **Seefried** , *Opera*, People 65, E. Werba, August 1966, 611-16.
Amy **Shuard**, *Opera*, D. Arundell, June 1975, 542.
Amy **Shuard**, *Opera*, H. Rosenthal, April 1960, 257.
Anja **Silja**, *Opera*, People 78, W. Schwinger, March 1969, 193-9.
Anja **Silja**, *Opera Now*, June 1989.
Beverley **Sills**, *Opera*, People 86, H. Weinstock, December 1970, 1094-9.
Giulietta **Simionato**, *Opera*, People, G. Gualerzi, February 1964, 87-92.

Elisabeth **Söderström**, *Opera*, People 77, J. Amis, January 1969, 16-20.
Elisabeth **Söderström**, *Opera Now*, April 1991.
Diana **Soviero**, *Opera News*, L. T. Guinther, 2 January 1993, 12-13, 44.
Eleanor **Steber**, *Opera News*, L. Rubinstein, 1993, 10-14, 66.
Rise **Stevens**, *Opera News*, M. Mayer, 24 December 1988, 12-18.
Teresa **Stratas**, *Opera News*, M. Mayer, 9 December 1989, 14-18.
Teresa **Stratas**, *Opera*, People 204, M. Mayer, October 1994, 1146-50.
Cheryl **Studer**, *Opera News*, D. Seabury, July 1990, 12-16.
Cheryl **Studer**, *Opera News*, D. McGovern, 2 February 1991, 10-14.
Cheryl **Studer**, *Opera*, People 201, A. Blyth, June 1994a, 656-62.
Cheryl **Studer**, *Opera Now*, P. Sommerich, June 1994b, 23-5.
Joan **Sutherland**, *Opera Now*, November 1989.
Joan **Sutherland**, *Opera*, R. Christiansen, November 1990, 1284-8.
Joan **Sutherland**, *Opera Now*, March 1991.
Sharon **Sweet**, *Opera News*, F. P. Driscoll, October 1993, 20-24, 53.
Michael **Sylvester**, *Opera News*, G. Schmidgall, November 1992, 34-6.
Martti **Talvela**, *Opera Now*, J. Steane, February 1995, 48-50.
Renata **Tebaldi** , *Opera News*, W. Price, 1 February 1992, 16-18.
Kiri **Te Kanawa**, *Opera*, People 126, E. Forbes, July 1981, 679-85.
Kiri **Te Kanawa**, *Opera Now*, March 1991.
Kiri **Te Kanawa**, *Opera News*, D. J. Baker, October 1994, 12-14, 65.
Bryn **Terfel**, *Opera Now*, A. Stewart, August 1993, 20-22.
Bryn **Terfel**, *Opera News*, M. Kennedy, September 1994, 28-31.
Luisa **Tetrazzini**, *Opera Now*, S. Trezise, April 1990, 48-9.
Blanche **Thebom**, *Opera News*, S. von Buchau, November 1991, 18-20.
Jess **Thomas**, *Opera*, People 64, B. Fischer-Williams, July 1966, 540-46.
Vivian **Tierney**, *Opera Now*, A. Stewart, June 1993, 24-5.
Pauline **Tinsley**, *Opera*, People 129, E. Forbes, March 1982, 258-67.
Stefania **Toczyska**, *Opera News*, D. McGovern, 7 January 1989, 16-18.
John **Tomlinson**, *Opera*, People 167, H. Finch, July 1990, 72-77.
John **Tomlinson**, *Opera Now*, R. Hartford, October 1994, 18-20.
Anna **Tomowa-Sintow**, *Opera*, People 148, H. Rosenthal, March 1987, 250-54.
Anna **Tomowa-Sintow**, *Opera Now*, T. Higgins, December 1993, 48-9.

Tatiana **Troyanos**, *Opera*, People 136, M. Mayer, March 1985, 268-72.

Richard **Tucker**, *Opera News*, various, 21 January 1995, 18-23, 32-5.

Wayne **Turnage**, *Opera News*, B. Cameron, October 1990.

Claramae **Turner**, *Opera News*, B. Kellow, 24 December 1994, 16.

Eva **Turner**, *Opera Now*, I. Stones, March 1990, 59-61.

Ragnar **Ulfung**, *Opera*, People 107, N. Benvenga, September 1975, 837-42.

Theodor **Uppman**, *Opera News*, K. Schmidgall, March 1992, 28 12-16.

Dawn **Upshaw**, *Opera News*, D McGovern, 2 February 1991, 12-14.

Dawn **Upshaw**, *Opera News*, B. Kellow, 16 January 1993, 20-22, 45.

Viorica **Ursuleac**, *Opera*, I. Cook and A. Frankenstein, January 1986, 22-6.

Leontina **Vaduva**, *Opera Now*, D. Couling, October 1994, 9.

Benite **Valente**, *Opera News*, C. Ellison, June 1993, 16-20.

José **van Dam**, *Opera*, People 193, A. Clark, Festival Edition, 1993, 4-14.

Carol **Vaness**, *Opera*, People 157, E. Forbes, April 1989, 418-24.

Julia **Varady**, *Opera*, People 181, A. Blyth, June 1992, 646-52.

Josephine **Veasey**, *Opera*, People 80, A. Blyth, September 1969, 759-63.

Josephine **Veasey**, *Opera*, M. Loppert, July 1990, 798-803.

Shirley **Verrett**, *Opera*, People 100, S. Jerkins, July 1973, 585-90.

Shirley **Verrett**, *Opera News*, R. Dyer, 17 February 1990, 8-12, 52.

Jon **Vickers**, *Opera*, People, N. Goodwin, April 1962.

Jon **Vickers**, *Opera*, M. Oliver, April 1982, 362-7.

Jon **Vickers**, *Opera News*, C. Halperin, 10 April 1993, 14-18, 48.

Jon **Vickers**, *Opera Now*, J. Steane, December 1994, 32-4.

Deborah **Voigt**, *Opera News*, W. Price, 15 February 1992, 34.

Deborah **Voigt**, *Opera Now*, H. Waleson, April 1995, 22-3.

Anne Sophie **von Otter**, *Opera*, People 173, A. Clark, June 1991, 627-34.

Anne Sophie **von Otter**, *Opera Now*, September 1992.

Anne Sophie **von Otter**, *Opera Now*, February 1995, 32.

Frederica **von Stade**, *Opera*, People 120, G. M. Movshon, January 1980, 31-5.

Frederica **von Stade**, *Opera Now*, D. Couling, April 1993, 28-30.

Ian **Wallace**, *Opera*, October 1975, 940-46; September 1975, 827-35.

David **Ward**, *Opera*, People 74, A. Jefferson, July 1968, 540-45.

Claire **Watson**, *Opera*, People 85, G. Rothon, November 1970, 1004-11.

Willard **White**, *Opera*, People 155, M. Loppert, January 1989a, 18-25.

Willard **White**, *Opera Now*, August 1989b.

Wolfgang **Windgassen**, *Opera*, People, K. Honolka, September 1962, 590-97.

Fritz **Wunderlich**, *Opera*, H. Canning, September 1990, 1048-54.

Dolora **Zajick**, *Opera Now*, A. Stewart, November 1994, 15-16.

Renato **Zanelli**, *Opera Now*, J. Steane, April 1992, 26-8.

Giovanni **Zenatello**, *Opera Now*, J. Steane, July 1994, 28-30.

Dolores **Ziegler**, *Opera News*, B. Kellow, 3 March 1990, 18-21.

Bibliography

Abbate, C. and Parker, R. (1989), *Analyzing Opera: Verdi and Wagner*, University of California Press, Berkeley.

Adair, G. (1994), 'The acceptable face of opera', *The Sunday Times*.

Adams, B. (1980), *La Stupenda—A Biography of Joan Sutherland*. Hutchinson, London.

Adorno, T. W. (1967), Prisms, trans. S. and S. Weber, Neville Spearman, London.

Adorno, T. W. (1969), 'Wissenschafliche Erfahrungen in America', in T. W. Adorno, *Stichworte, Kritische Modelle 2*, Edition Suhrkamp, Frankfurt-am-Main, 347.

Adorno, T. W. (1973), *The Philosophy of Modern Music*, trans. A. G. Mitchell and W. V. Blomster, The Seabury Press, New York.

Adorno, T. W. (1976), *Introduction to the Sociology of Music*, trans. E. B. Ashton, The Seabury Press, New York.

Adorno, T. W. (1978a), 'Bugerliche Oper', in R. Tiedemann (ed.), *Gesammelte Schriften*, Suhrkamp, Frankfurt-am-Main.

Adorno, T. W. (1978b), 'Culture and administration', *Telos*, 37.

Adorno, T. W. (1978c), 'On the social situation of music', *Telos*, 35: 130.

Adorno, T. W. (1981), *In Search of Wagner*, trans. R. Livingstone, *New Left Review*, Editions, London.

Adorno, T. W. (1991), *The Culture Industry: Selected Essays on Mass Culture*, (ed.) and Introduction by J. M. Bernstein, Routledge, London.

Adorno, T. W. and Horkheimer, M. (1972), Seabury Press, New York.

Adorno, T. W. and Horkheimer, M. (1973), *Dialectic of the Enlightenment*, Allen Lane, London.

Albrecht, M. C. (1968), 'The art as an institution', *American Sociological Review*, 33, June: 383-97.

Allen, T. (1993), *Foreign Parts: A Singer's Journal*, Sinclair Stevenson, London.

Ardoin, J. (1988), *Callas at Juillard—the Master Classes*, Robson Books, London.

Arundell, D. (1961), 'At work in opera: 1 the producer', *Opera* October, 631-36.

Arundell, D. (1980), 'The critic at the opera: contemporary comments on opera' in *London over Three Centuries*, Da Capo, New York.

Ashbrook, W. (1994), 'Opera singers' in R. Parker (ed.) *The Oxford IllustratedHistory of Opera.*, Oxford University Press, Oxford, 421-49.

Ashbrook, W. and Powers, H. (1991), *Puccini's Turandot: The End of the Great Tradition*, Princeton University Press, Princeton NJ.

Attali, J. (1985), *Noise: The Political Economy of Music*, trans. B. Massumi, University of Minnesota Press, Minneapolis.

Auden, W. H. (1968), *Metalogue to The Magic Flute Collected Longer Poem*, Faber, London.

Austin, J. L. (1962), *How to Do Things with Words* (ed.) J. O. Urmson and M. Sbisa, Clarendon Press, Oxford.

Averino, O. (1991), *Principles and Art of Singing*, Intention Publishers, Risskow, Den.

Babbitt, M. (1963), 'Mr Babbitt answers', *Perspectives in New Music* 2, Fall/Winter, 127-32.

Babuscio,J. (1977), 'Camp and the gay sensibility', in R. Dyer (ed.) *Gays and the Film*, BFI, London.

Baillie, I. (1982), *Never Sing Louder than Lovely*, Hutchinson, London.

Baker, D. J. (1990), 'Down and out in Salzburg and Bayreuth', *Opera News*, 8 December, 26-8, 73.

Baker, D. J. (1991), 'High notes and pornography', *Opera News*, December, 218-11, 51.

Baker, D. J. (1995), 'Opera Paradiso? ... or Opera Inferno?', *Opera News*, May, 14-18.

Baker, J. (1982), *Full Circle*, Julia MacRae, London.

Bakhtin, M. (1977), 'Le Marxisme et la philosophie du langage', Les Editions de Minuit, Paris.

Balk, W. (1985), *The Complete Singer and Actor*, University of Minnesota Press, Minneapolis.

Balzac, H. (1978-79), *Le Spectacle et lafete au temps du Balzac*, Maison de Balzac, Paris.

Banfield, S. (1986), 'British opera in retrospect', *The Musical Times*, 127, April, 205-6.

Barnett, J. (1970), *The Sociology of Art and Literature*, Praeger Publishing Company, New York.

Barnett, J. (1959), *Sociology Today*, Basic Books, New York.

Barthès, R. (1970), *SI Z*, Paris.

Barthès, R. (1972), 'Le grain de la voix', *Musique en Jeu* 9, November. 51-63.

Barthès, R. (1976), *The Pleasure of the Text*, trans. R. Miller, Hill and Wang, London.

Barthès, R. (1977), *Image, Music, Text*, trans. S. Heath, Fontana, London.

Barthès, R. (1982), 'La musique, la voix, la langue', and 'La chant romantique' in *L'Obvie et l'obtus*, Paris, 247-53.

Barzun, J. (1980), 'The meaning of meaning in music: Berlioz once more', *The Musical Quarterly*, LXVI, January, 6.

Bauman, T. (1994), 'The eighteenth century: serious opera', in Parker R. (ed.) *The Oxford Illustrated History of Opera*, Oxford University Press, Oxford.

Bawtree, M. (1990), *The New Singing Theatre: A Charter for the Music Theatre Movement*, The Bristol Press, New York.

Becker, H. S. (1982), *Art Worlds*, University of California Press, Berkeley, Los Angeles, London.

Bekker, C. P. (1924), *Wagner, Das Leben im Werke*, Marton, New York.

Bellini, V. (ed.) (1943), *Epostilario*, L. Cwnbi, Milan.

Berger, J. (1969), *Art and Revolution: Ernst Neiz-vestny and the Role of the Artist in the USSR*, Penguin, Harmondsworth.

Bernheimer, M. (1985b), 'Review of die tote Stadt', *Opera*, December, 1383

Bernstein, J. M. (ed.), (1991), *T. W. Adorno The Culture Industry*, Routledge, London.

Bertisch, K. (1990), *Ruth Berghaus*, Fischer Taschenbuch Verlag, Frankfurt-am-Main.

Betley, M. (1992), 'Sounding out' *Opera News*, 24-26 August.

Bianconi, L. and Walker, T. (1984), 'Production, consumption and political function of seventeenth century Italian opera', *Early Music History* (4), 234-61.

Billington, J. (1980), *Fire in the Minds of Men: Origins of the Revolutionary Fait*, Basic Books, New York.

Billington, M. (1992), review of *Lear* at ENO, *Opera*, May, 584-86.

Blumenfeld, H. (1984), 'Ad vocem Adorno', *Musical Quarterly*, 70, 515-37.

Blumenfeld, H. (1991), 'Cardiff Singer of the World: BBC2 June 22nd', *Opera*, August, 980-81.

Blumenfeld, H. (1993), 'A moment in time', *Opera*, July, 779.

Blyth, A. (1973), *Janet Baker*, Gollancz, London.

Blyth A. (1981), 'Sponsorship—pros and cons', *Opera*, February, 114-16.

Blyth A. (1985a), Review of *Rigoletto*, Welsh National Opera, *Opera*, July.

Blyth A. (1985b), 'Jussi Bjoerling: 1911-60', *Opera*, September, 994-8.

BMRB (British Market Research Bureau) (1988), *Your Lifestyle*, Borovsky, V. (1988), *Chaliapin: A Critical Biography*, Hamish Hamilton, London.

Boulez, P. (1985/86), 'Contemporary music and the public', in discussion with M. Foucault, *Perspectives on New Music*, 24: 6-12.

Boulez, P. (1986a), *Orientations*, ed. J-J. Nattiez, trans. M. Cooper, Faber and Faber, London.

Boulez, P. (1986b), 'Aesthetics and fetishists' in P. Boulez P. Boulez *Orientations* ed. J-J Nattiez, trans. M. Cooper, Faber and Faber, London.

Boulez, P. (1988), 'Iconoclast', Interview from *Der Spiegel* (1966) in R. Christiansen (ed.) *The Grand Obsession: A Collins Anthology of Opera*, Collins, London, 186-94.

Bourdieu, P. (1977), *Outline of a Theory of Practice*, trans. R. Nice, Cambridge University Press, Cambridge.

Bourdieu, P. (1984), *Distinction. A Social Critique of the Judgement of Taste*, Harvard University Press, Cambridge, Mass.

Bourdieu, P. (1990), *In Other Words*, Polity, Cambridge.

Bowie, A. (1989), 'Music, language and modernity', in A. Benjamin, (ed.) *The Problems of Modernity: Adorno and Benjamin*, Warwick Studies in Philosophy and Literature, Routledge, London.

Braddon, R. (1962), *Joan Sutherland*, Collins, London.

Brecht, B. (1977), *Schriften über Theater*, Henschelverlag, Berlin.

Bredin, H. (1988),, 'ENO's contemporary opera studio', *Opera*, December, 1418-20.

Brook, D. (1947), *A Companion to Opera*, Rockliff, London.

Brustein, R. (1965), *The Theatre of Revolt*, Methuen, London.

Bryden, B. (1990), Profile in *Opera Now*, November, 62.

Budden, J. (1994) Review of F. W. Sternfield *The Birth of Opera*, (Oxford University Press, Oxford), in *Opera*, September, 1129-30.

Burger, C. (1986), 'The disappearance of art: the postmodernism debate in the US', *Telos*, 68, Summer, 93-106.

Burger, P. (1981), *Theorie der Avantgarde*, 3rd edn., Frankfurt-am-Main.

Burt, P. (1995), 'The lady is not for squashing—Lesley Garrett', *The Independent on Sunday* Magazine, 19 February, 26-7.

CACI Ltd. (1994), *Analysis of Welsh National Opera Birmingham Audience and Catchment*, prep. by J. Triandafyllou, CACI, London.

Campion, P. (1993), *Ferrier: A Career Record*, Julia MacRae Books, London.

Canning, H. (1991a), 'Christie meets Rameau', *Opera*, March, 277-81.

Canning, H. (1991b), People 179: Graham Vick', *Opera*, November, 1267-72.

Canning, H. (1992), 'Cheryl Studer in demand', *The Gramophone*. November, 24.

Canning, H. (1993a), 'A moment in time' *Opera*, July, 781-2.

Canning, H. (1993b), 'Maria Callas' *The Sunday Times*, The Culture, 12 December, 26.

Canning, H. (1994a), 'Past masters', *The Sunday Times*, The Culture, 15 May, 17.

Canning, H. (1994b), 'The manor borne' *The Sunday Times*, The Culture, 10 July, 26.

Canning, H. (1994c), 'Saying boo to the muse', *The Sunday Times*, The Culture, 17 July, 1020-21.

Canning, H. (1994d), 'After The Powerhouse' *The Sunday Times*. The Culture, 4 September, 26-7.

Canning, H. (1995a), 'Too many mad scenes' *The Sunday Times*, The Culture, 29 January, 9-10

Canning, H. (1995b), Comment. *The Sunday Times*, The Culture, 26 March, 16.

Canning, H. (1995c), 'A force to be reckoned with', *The Sunday Times*, The Culture, 7 May, 10-11.

Canning, H. (1995d), 'The one tenor', *The Sunday Times*, The Culture, 27 August, 1-2.

Canning, H. (1995e), 'Mixed bag' *The Sunday Times*, The Culture, 22

October, 20.

Cannon, R. (1983), 'Stanislavski and the opera—in production', *Opera*, July, 714-20.

Carner, M. (1958), *Puccini: A Critical Biography*, Duckworth, London.

Carner, M. (1969), *Tosca*, Cambridge University Press, Cambridge.

Carreras, J. (1991), *Singing from the Soul*, Souvenir Press, London.

Casanova, C. (1982), *Renata Tebaldi voced 'angelo'*, Electra Editrice, Milan.

Castle, R. and Tauber, D. N. (1971), *This was Richard Tauber*, W. H. Allen, London.

Celletti, R. (1970), 'The Callas debate', *Opera*, September, 806-19.

Celletti, R. (1994), 'The poetics of the marvellous', *Opera News*, July, 10-14.

Celletti, R. (1991), *The History of Bel Canto*, Oxford University Press, Oxford.

Chambers, A. (1990), *Margaret Sheridan: Prima Donna 1889-1958*, Wolfhound Press, London.

Chambers, I. (1985), *Urban Rhythms*, Macmillan, Basingstoke.

Chapple, S. and Garofalo, R. (1977), *Rock n Roll is Here to Pay*, Nelson Hall, Chicago.

Christiansen, R. (1984), *Prima Donna*, The Bodley Head, London.

Christiansen, R. (1985), 'Reflections on the opera audience', *Opera*, December, 1353-58.

Christiansen, R. (ed.) (1988), *The Grand Obsession: A Collins Anthology of Opera*, Collins, London.

Christiansen, R. (1990), 'Gerard Mortier', *Opera Annual Festival Issue*, 9-15.

Clark, A. (1989), 'The Bastille—"Vision fugitive?"' *Opera*, April, 406-12.

Clark, A. (1991a), 'The decline of the East', *Opera*, July, 766-70.

Clark, A. (1991b), 'A tradition in jeapardy—Part 1', *Opera*, September, 1007-17.

Clark, A. (1991c), 'A tradition in jeopardy—Part 2', *Opera*, October, 1151-517.

Clark, A. (1993), 'People 186: Hugues Gall' *Opera*, February, 144-48.

Clark, S. (1993), 'The publicist's Complaint', *Opera News*, September, 20-27.

Clarke, T. (1990), 'Dumb insolence in surf city', *Opera Now*, July, 51-5.

Clement, C. (1989), *Opera: or the Undoing of Women*, Virago, London.

Clements, A. (1985), 'Thursday's child' *Opera*, September, 988-93.

Clements, A. (1989a), 'Leat', *Opera*, March, 280-84.

Clements, A. (1989b), 'Greening up the garden or venturing into space ...' *Opera* July 801-03.

Clements, A. (1989c), 'Half the story so far' *Opera*, October, 1183-87.

Clements, A. (1989d), 'People 161: David Freeman', *Opera*, November, 1297-1302.

Clements, A. (1991a), 'Peter Sellars: As seen on TV', *Opera*, June, 611-14.

Clements, A. (1991b), '"Gawain"—an opera about people', *Opera*, August, 874-9.

Clements, A. (1995), 'Peter Sellars', *Opera*, November, 1260-68.

Cler, A. (1842), *Physiologie du musicien*, Paris.

Cocteau, J. (1921), *Cock and Harlequin*, trans. R. H. Myers, Egoist Press, London.

Cohen, S. (1991), *Rock Culture in Liverpool. Popular Music in the Making*, Clarendon Press, Oxford.

Cole, N. (1990), 'The state of opera', *Opera Now*, November, 2-6.

Cone, J. F. (1993), *Adelina Patti: Queen of Hearts*, Scolar Press, London.

Conrad, P. (1977), *Romantic Opera and Literary Form*, University of California Press, Berkeley.

Conrad, P. (1989), 'Bardolator—Peter Stein', *Opera News*, 4 February, 18-21.

Conrad, P. (1995), Review of A. Sinclair *Arts and Cultures: The History of the 50 Years of the Arts Council of Great Britain*, (Sinclair Stevenson, London), *The Observer*, 13 August, 13.

Cook, S. (1990), Review of C. Clement, *Opera: or the Undoing of Women*, (Virago, London), *Musical Quarterly*, 445-50.

Cooper, M. (1974), 'Realism in opera', *Opera*, December, 1041-7.

Corse, S. (1987), *Opera and the Uses of Language: Mozart, Verdi and Britten*, Dickinson University Press, Fairleigh.

Couling, D. (1991), 'Miller's crossing', Jonathan Miller in conversation. *Opera Now*, July, 17-20.

Couling, D. (1994), 'Taming the beast of the Bastille', *The Independent*, 17 September, 29.

Craker, C. (1993), *Get Into Opera: A Beginner's Guide*, Bantam, London.

Crichton, R. (1991), 'Golem', *Opera*, December, 1489-90.

Crouch, J. P. (1991), *An Opera Lover's Guide to Europe*, Limelight, NewYork.

Crutchfield, W. (1985), 'Authenticity in Verdi—the recorded legacy', *Opera*, August, 866.

Culler, J. (1981), 'The semiotics of tourism', *American Journal of Semiotics*, 1, 127-40.

Dace, W. (1989), 'Towards a definition of opera', *Opera*, August, 934-36.

Dahlhaus, C. (1978), *Die Idee der absoluten Musik*, Laaber-Verlag, Munich and Kassel.

Dahlhaus, C. and Zimmermann, M. (1984), *Musik zur Sprache gebracht*, Barenreiter, Kassel.

Dallapiccola, L. (1961), 'A composer's problem', *Opera*, January, 8-11.

D'Amico, F. (1970), 'The Callas debate', *Opera*, September, 806-19.

Daschra, F., Blari, A., and Deer, D. (eds) (1989), *The Sociology of Music*, Indiana University Press, Bloomington.

Debussy, C. (1962), Monsieur Croche Antidilettante', in *Three Classics in the Aesthetics of Music*, Dover, London.

De Franceschi B. (1982), *Ebe Stignani, una voce e il suo mondo*, Grafiche Galeati, Imola.

De la Laurence, I. (1970), *La Gout musicale en France*, Slatkin Reprints, Geneva.

Dent, E. J. (1965), *Opera*, Penguin, Harmondsworth.

DeNora, T. (1995), 'The musical composition of social reality: music action and reflexivity', *The Sociological Review*, 43, (2), May, 295-315.

Derrida, J. (1982), 'Signature, event, context', in *Margins of Philosophy*, trans. A. Bass, Harvester Press, Brighton.

DiGaetani, J. L. (1991), *An Invitation to the Opera*, Anchor/Doubleday, London.

DiGiovanni, J. (1994), 'Diva fever', *The Sunday Times*, 25 September, 7.

Di Maggio, P. and Useem M. (1978), 'Social class and arts consumption', *Theory and Society*, 5, 141-61.

Di Maggio, P. and Useem M. (1982), 'The arts in class reproduction', in M.W. Apple, *Cultural and Economic Reproduction: Essays on Class Ideology and the State*, Routledge and Kegan Paul, London.

erica: *A Cultural History*, Yale University Press, New Haven and London.

Donaldson F. (1987), *The Royal Opera House in the Twentieth Century*, Weidenfeld and Nicolson, London.

Donington, R. (1965), *The Interpretation of Early Music*, Faber, London.

Donington, R. (1970), 'The robustness of early opera', *Opera*. January, 16-22.

Donington, R. (1981), *The Rise of Opera*, Faber and Faber, London.

Donington, R. (1990), *Opera and its Symbols: The Unity of Words, Music and Staging*, Yale University Press, New Haven.

Douglas, N. (1992), *Legendary Voices*, Andre Deutsch, London.

Driscoll, F. P. (1993), 'Basic instincts', *Opera News*, May, 26-28.

Driscoll, F. P. (1995), Review of F. Plotkin *Opera 101: A Complete Guide to Learning and Loving Opera* (Hyperion, New York) and M. Walsh, *Who's Afraid of Opera?: Highly Opinionated, Informative and Entertaining Guide*, (Fireside Books), Simon and Schuster, New York.

Dupechez,C. (1985), *Histoire de L'Opéra de Paris 1875-1980*, Librairie Perrin, Paris.

Dusek, P. and Schmidt, P. (1993), *Leonie Rysanek. 40 Jahre Operngeschichte*, Hoffmann und Kampe, Hamburg.

Dyer, R. (1979), *Stars*, British Film Institute, London.

Eco, U. (1979), *The Role of the Reader*, Indiana University Press, Bloomington.

Elder, M. (1980), 'The company commitment', *Opera*, October, 976-84.

Elias, N. (1994), *The Civilizing Process*, Blackwell, Oxford.

Elliott, S. (1991), 'In concert: the making of a hit', *Opera News*, March, 30.

Elliott, S. (1992), 'Orient express', *Opera News*, 15 January, 18-21.

Ellison, C. (1992), 'Poetry and precision', *Opera News*, December, 544-9.

Elsner, W. and Busch, M. W. (1986), *Pilar Lorangar*, Stapp Verlag, Berlin.

Empson, W. (1966), *Some Versions of Pastoral*, Penguin, Harmondsworth.

English National Opera (1991), *Financial Statements Year Ending 31st March*, ENO, London.

English National Opera (1992), *Financial Statements Year Ending 31st March*, ENO, London.

English National Opera (1993), *Financial Statements Year Ending*

31st March, ENO, London.

Evans, G. (1983), *A Knight at the Opera,* (with N. Goodwin), Michael Joseph, London.

Fantel, H. (1992), 'Best buys '92' *Opera News,* November, 42.

Fantel, H. (1993), 'Historic reissues on CD' *Opera News,* August, 34-5.

Faris, A. (1961), 'Opera and the musical', *Opera,* May, 295-300.

Farkas, A. (1983) (ed.), *Tito Ruffo An Anthology,* Greenwood Press, London.

Farkas, A. (1990), *Lawrence Tibbett: Singing Actor,* Amadeus Press, London.

Fawkes, R. (1994), 'Star turns' *Opera Now,* Part I, March, 29-32, II, April, 20-22.

Fay, S. (1994), *The Ring: Anatomy of an Opera,* Secker and Warburg, London.

Featherstone, M. (1983), 'Body and consumer culture', *Theory, Culture and Society,* 18-33.

Felsenstein, W. (1966), 'Towards music theatre', in C. Osbome (ed.) *Opera '66,* 47-55.

Felsenstein, W. (1970), 'The road to improvement', *Opera,* January, 8-15.

Felsenstein, W. (1975), 'The staging of opera' in P. P. Fuchs (ed.) *The Music Theatre of Walter Felsenstein,* Norton, London.

Finch, H. (1989), Review of Jose Carreras at Covent Garden in recital. *Opera,* June, 747-8.

Finch, H. (1990), 'The button moulder', *Opera,* July, 876-7.

Fingleton, D. (1983), *Kiri,* Arrow Books, London.

Fish, S. (1980), *Is There a Text in This Class?,* Harvard University Press, Cambridge, Mass.

Fiske, J. (1992), 'The cultural economy of random', in L. Lewis (ed.) *The Adoring Audience: Fan Culture and Popular Music,* Routledge, London.

Fitzgerald, G. (ed.) (1989a), *Annals of the Metropolitan Opera: The Complete Chronology of Performances and Artists,* 2 vols. G. K. Hall/Metropolitan Opera Guild, Boston.

Fitzgerald, G. (1989b), 'Viewpoint', *Opera News,* 18 March, 4

Fitzlyon, A. (1987), *Maria Malibran,* Souvenir Press, London.

Forbes, E. (1984), Review of Northern Ireland Opera trust production of *Don Giovanni* (producer S. Pimlott), *Opera,* August, 919.

Forbes, E. (1993), 'People 188: lan Judge', *Opera,* April, 402-8.

Foucault, M. (1970), *The Order of Things*, Tavistock, London.

Foucault, M. (1981), *The History of Sexuality: An Introduction*, Vol.1, Penguin, London.

Foucault, M. and Boulez, P. (1985/86), 'Contemporary music and the public', *Perspectives in New Music*, Fall-Winter, 6-12.

Frankl, G. (1974), *The Failure of the Sexual Revolution*, Kahn and Averill, Hove.

Franks, A. (1995), 'Baring-all: Lesley Garrett', *The Times Magazine*, April, 23-4.

Friedrich, G. (1955), 'Walter Felsenstein as a Mozart producer', trans. T. Casey, in H. D. Rosenthal (ed.), *Opera Annual 1955-6*, John Calder, London.

Frith, S. and Horne, H. (1987), *Art Into Pop*, Methuen, London.

Froud, N. and Hanley, J. (1988), *Chaliapin: An Autobiography as Told to Maxim Gorky*, Columbus, Ohio.

Fuchs, P. P. (ed.) (1975), *The Music Theatre of Walter Felsenstein*, Norton, New York.

Fulcher, J. (1987), *The Nation's Image: French Grand Opera as Politics and Politicised Art*, Cambridge University Press, Cambridge.

Gagnon, J. H. and Simon, W. S. (1986), 'Sexual scripts: permanence and change', *Archives of Sexual Behaviour*, April, 97-121.

Gara, E. (1970), 'The Callas debate', *Opera*, September, 806-19.

Garrett, L. (1990), 'There's more to it than singing', *Opera Now*, November, 46-51.

Garrett, L. (1994), 'Lesley Garrett: A Childhood', *The Times Magazine*, 15 October, 70.

Gascoigne, B. (1962), *Twentieth-Century Drama*, Hutchinson University Library, London.

Gerth, H.H. and Mills, C.W. (eds) (1967), *From Max Weber*, Routledge and Kegan Paul, London.

Getzels, J. W. and Czikszentimikalzi, D. (1968), 'On the roles, values and performance of future artists: a conceptual and empirical exploration', *Social Problems*, 9, (4), Autumn, 516-18.

Gill, A. A. (1994), 'Picnics at Glyndebourne', *The Sunday Times*, Style, 4 June, 27.

Gilliam B. (1994), *Music and Performance During the Weimar Republic*, Cambridge University Press, Cambridge.

Gilman, S. L. (1988), 'Strauss the pervert, and avant garde opera of the fin-de-siècle', *New German Critique*, 43, Winter, 35-68.

Glass, P. (1988), *Opera on the Beach: Philip Glass on his World of Music Theatre*, Faber and Faber, London.

Glover, J. (1982), 'Cavalli and L'Eritred', *The Musical Times*, 123.

Gluck, W. (1950), 'Dedication to *Alceste*', in O. Strunk (ed.), *Source Readings in Music History*, Norton, New York.

Gobbi, T. (1980), *Tito Gobbi—My Life*, Futura, London.

Goldovsky, B. and Schoep, A. (1990), *Bringing Soprano Arias to Life*, Scarecrow Press.

Gollancz,V. (1966), *The Ring at Bayreuth: And Some Thoughts on Operatic Production*, Gollancz, London.

Greenfield, E. (1972), *Recordmasters No 1—Joan Sutherland*, Ian Allen, London.

Greenfield, H. S. (1991), *Caruso: An Illustrated Life*, Collins, London.

Greenfield, H. S. and Brown. M. (1952), 'The alienation of the artist' in R. N. Wilson (ed.), *The Arts in Society*, Prentice-Hall, NJ.

Griffiths P (1991), 'Filling *The Jewel Box*', *Opera*, January, 24-7.

Groos, A. and Parker, R. (1986), *Giacommo Puccini: La boheme*, Cambridge Opera Handbooks, Cambridge University Press, Cambridge.

Groos, A. and Parker, R. (1990), *Reading Opera*, Princeton University Press, Princeton.

Gruber, P. (1993), *The Metropolitan Opera House Guide to Recorded Opera*, Thames and Hudson Ltd., London.

Guilini (1977), 'Tribute to Callas', *Opera*, November, 1015-17.

Haberfeld, T. (1991), *Gwyneth Jones*, Atlantis Musikbuch-Verlag, Zurich.

Haggin, B. H. (1984), *Music and Ballet*, Horizon, New York.

Haitink, B. (1988), 'A key to the future: a new era at Covent Garden', *Opera*, April, 402-10.

Hall, S. (1980), 'Encoding/decoding' in S. Hall et al. (eds) *Culture, Media, Language: Working Papers in Cultural Studies 1972-9*. Hutchinson, London.

Hall, S. (1986), 'On postmodernism and articulation: an interview with Stuart Hall', *Journal of Communication Inquiry*, 10(2), 45-60.

Hamilton, D. (1987), *The Metropolildn Opera Encyclopedia: A Comprehensive Guide to the World of Opera*, Thames and Husdon, New York.

Hanslick, E. (1854/1891), *The Beautiful in Music*, Novello, Ewer and Co., London.

Harewood, Lord (1977), 'Tribute to Callas', *Opera*, November, 1013-

17.

Harewood, Lord (1989), *Kobbé's Illustrated Opera Book. Twenty Six of the World's Best—loved Operas*, The Bodley Head, London.

Harewood, Lord (1967), 'Felsenstein's theatre re-opens', *Opera*. February, 109, 113.

Harries, M. and Harries, S. (1986), *Opera Today*, Batsford, London.

Hartford, R. (1979), 'The view from Bayreuth', *Opera Festival Issue*, October, 12-18.

Hatch, D. and Watson, D. R. (1974), 'Hearing the blues: an essay in the sociology of music', *Acta Sociologica*, 17.

Hayes, J. (1989a), 'Mayhem set to music', *Opera*, January, 29.

Hayes, J. (1989b), 'Deconstruction—a continuation', *Opera*, April, 414-16.

Headington, C. (1992), *Peter Pears: A Biography*, Faber and Faber, London.

Heartz, D. (1990), *Mozart's Operas*, T. Bauman (ed.), University of California Press, Berkeley.

Hebdige, D. (1979), *Subculture: The Meaning of Style*, Methuen, London.

Hegel, G. (1964), *Vorlesungen uber die Asthetik*, Dritter Band Jubilaumsausgabe, Stuttgart-Bad Cannstatt.

Henahan, D. (1972), 'When the stage director takes over at the opera', *NewYork Times Magazine*, 12 November, 44.

Henderson, R. E. (1990), Review of Peter Sellars *The Magic Flute* at Glyndebourne, *Daily Telegraph*.

Henderson, R.E. (1983), Review of ENO, *Rusalka, Opera*, 558.

Henstock, M. (1990), *Fernando De Lucia*, Duckworth, London.

Hepokoski, A. (1987), *Otello*, Cambridge Opera Handbooks, Cambridge University Press, Cambridge.

Heriot, A. (1975), *The Castrati in Opera*, Calder and Boyars, London.

Herz, J. (1975), 'On the reality of the singing human being', in P. P. Fuchs (ed.) *The Music Theatre of Walter Felsenstein*, W. W. Norton and Co., New York, 145-53.

Heyman, B. B. (1991), 'The second time around: Barber's *Antony and Cleopatra* gets another chance at the Lyric Opera of Chicago', *Opera News*, 7 December, 56-7.

Heymont, G. (1990), 'Land of plenty', *Opera News*, 20 January, 20-21.

Hillmore, P. (1994), 'Three cheers for the people with the guts to say boo', *The Observer*, 17 July.

Hines, J. (1982), *Great Singers on Great Singing*, Gollancz, London.

Hirschkop, K. (1989), 'The classical and the popular: musical form and social context', in C. Norris (ed.), *Music and the Politics of Culture*, Lawrence and Wishart, London, 283-304.

Hirst, R. (1979), review of Parsifal at Covent Garden, *Opera*, May, 548-9.

Hobsbawm, E. (1981), 'The formal march of labour halted?: or observations on the debate', in M. Jacques and F. MuThem (eds) *Observations on the Debate*, New Left Books, London.

Hobsbawm E. and Ranger, T. (1983), *The Invention of Tradition*, Cambridge University Press, Cambridge.

Holden, A. (1990), Review of J. Rosenberg, *Sing Me a Story, The Metropolitan Opera's Book of Opera Stories for Children*, Thames and Hudson, New York, *Opera*, December, 1512.

Holub, R. C. (1984), *Reception Theory: A Critical Introduction*, Methuen, London.

Honneth, A. (1986), 'The fragmented world of symbolic forms: reflections on Pierre Bourdieu's sociology of culture', *Theory, Culture and Society*, 3 (3).

Horkheimer, M. and Adorno, T. W. (eds) (1969), *Aspects of Sociology*, trans. J. Viertel, Frankfurt Institute for Social Research, Beacon Press, Boston.

Horne, M. (1983), *Marilyn Horne—My Life*, Atheneum, New York.

Hunter R. (1986), *Wait till the Sun Shines, Nellie*, Hamish Hamilton, London.

Inglis, A. (1993), 'Production values', interview with David Alden, *Opera Now*, November, 35-7.

Innaurato, A. (1989), 'What makes great performers?' *Opera News*, 9 December, 20-25, 71.

Innaurato, A. (1992a), 'The gong show', *Opera News*, February, 9-11.

Innaurato, A. (1992b), 'The demon divas', *Opera News*, October, 20-37.

Innaurato, A. (1993), 'A matter of voice', *Opera News*, 12-18, 69.

Isaacs, J. (1994), 'Why opera should be a risky business', *The Sunday Times*, The Culture, 11 September, 20-2 1.

Ivanovich,C. (1681), *Memorie teatralidi Venezi*, in Minervadi Tarolini, Venice.

lvry, B.(1989), 'Too strong for fantasies?', *Opera News*, 21 January, 20-21, 46.

Jacobs, A. (1967), Review of *L'Ortnindo, Opera Festival Edition*, October, 30-33.

Jacobs, A. and Sadie, S. (1964), *The Pan Book of Opera*, Pan Books Ltd., London.

Jacobson, R. (1968), New means for new music', *Sociological Review*, 28, September, 57-9.

Jacobson, R. M. (1985), *Magnificence: On Stage at the Metropolitan: 20 Great Opera Productions*, Thames and Hudson, London.

James, J. (1995), *The Music of the Spheres: Music, Science and the Natural Order of the Universe*, Abacus, London.

Jameson, F. (1985), Foreword to J. Attali, *Noise: The Political Economy of Music:* trans. B. Massumi, University of Minnesota Press, Minneapolis.

Jamieson, N. (1994a), 'Instability and change',*Opera*, May, 530-36.

Jamieson, N. (1994b), 'Circus Maximus', *Opera News*, September, 32-3.

Jauss, H. R. (1982), *Toward an Aesthetic of Reception*, University of Minnesota Press, Minneapolis.

Jefferson,A. (1976), *The Glory of Opera*, Peerage Books, London.

Jefferson,A. (1988), *Lotte Lehmann*, Julia McCrae Books, London.

Jonas P. (1989), Letter, *Opera*, 12 November, 95.

Jones, D. (1955), 'An attempt to formulate general aesthetic principles through music-aesthetics', *The Score and LMA Magazine*, 1 1 March, 52.

Jonas, P., Elder, M., Pountney, D. (1992), *Power House: The ENO Experience*, English National Opera, London.

Judd, W. (1988), 'The Garden Venture', *Opera*, December, 1416-18.

Kaden, C. (1984), *Musik soziologie*, Verlag Neue Musik, Berlin.

Kamerman, J. B. (1983), 'The rationalisation of symphony orchestra conductors' interpretive style', in J. B. Kamerman and R. Martorella (eds), *Performers and Performances; The Social Organisation of Artistic Work*, Norton, New York.

Kant, I. (1977), *Kritik der Urteilskraft*, Werkausgabe Band, Frankfurt-am-Main.

Kant, I. (1983), *The Critic of Practical Reason*, London.

Kauffmann, S. (1990), 'The whole truth', *Opera News*, 3 February, 13-15.

Kellow, B. (1994), 'The singing detective', *Opera News*, July, 16-19.

Kendall, A. (1995), *Gioacchino Rossini: The Reluctant Hero*, Gollancz, London.

Kennedy, M. (1990), Review of *The Magic Flute*, Glyndebourne, *The Sunday Telegraph*, 27 May.

Kennett, P. J. (1989), 'Mayhem set to music', *Opera*, January, 29.

Kennicott, P. (1993), 'A la Françoise: Françoise Pollet', *Opera News*, 25 December, 21.

Kerman, J. (1956), *Opera as Drama*, Vintage, New York.

Kerman, J. (1985), *Musicology*, Fontana, London.

Kerman, J. S. and Gray, T. S. (1989), 'Verdi's groundswells: surveying an operatic convention', in C. Abbate and R. Parker (eds), *Analyzing Opera: Verdi and Wagner*, University of California Press, Berkeley.

Kimbell, D. (1991), *Italian Opera*, Cambridge University Press, Cambridge.

Kimberley, N. (1993), 'ENO-Almeida—a chance to breathe', *Opera*, July, 787-91.

Kimberley, N. (1995), 'Opera—future tense', *Opera*, November 1271-7.

Kivy, P. (1988), *Osmin's Rage: Philosophical Reflections on Opera, Drama and Text*, Princeton University Press, Princeton, NJ.

Klees, J. (1960), 'Organizing an opera audience', *Opera*, October, 671-73.

Knapp, J. M. (1984), *The Magic of Opera*, da Capo, New York.

Knopfinger, E. A. (1975), *Wagner und Beethoven*, Gustav Bosse Verlag, Regensburg.

Koban, L. (ed.) (1990), *Joachim Herz: Interviews*, Max Hesses Verlag, Berlin.

Kobbé, G. (1961), *Kobbé's Complete Opera Book*, edited and revised by Lod Harewood, Putnam, London, New York.

Koestenbaum, W. (1993), *The Queen's Throat: Opera, Homosexuality and the Mystery of Desire*, Gay Men's Press, London.

Kolodin, I.(1954), *The Metropolitan Opera 1883-1966: A Candid History*, A. A. Knopf, New York.

Komick, R. H. (1991), *Recent American Opera: A Production Guide*, University of Columbia Press, Columbia.

Kracauer, S. (1938), *Orpheus in Paris: Offenbach and the Paris of his Time*, A. A. Knopf, New York.

Kramer, L. (1990), *Music as Cultural Practice 1800-1900*, University of California Press, Berkeley.

Kretschmer, J. T. (1990), 'Face the music', *Opera News*, June, 28-32.

Kristeva, J. (1980), *Desire in Language*, Oxford University Press, Oxford.

Kristeva, J. (1984), *Revolution in Poetic Language*, trans. M. Waller,

Columbia University Press, New York.

Kristeva, J. (1985), 'The speaking subject', in M. Blonsky (ed.), *On Signs*, John Hopkins University Press, Baltimore.

Laing, P. (1992), 'Sadness, scorpions and single markets: national and transnational trends in European popular music', *Popular Music*, 11(2), 127/39.

Lang, P. H. (1945), 'Background music for "Main Kampf"', *Saturday Review of Literature*, XXVIII, 35-9.

Langdon, M. (1982), *Notes from a Low Singer*, Julia MacRae, London.

Langer, S. K. (1960), *Philosophy in a New Key*, Harvard University Press, Cambridge Mass.

Langhaus, K. (1992), 'Theatre architecture', in S. Sadie (ed.), *The New Grove Dictionary of Opera*, Vol III, 709-22.

Lannes, S. and Nusacc, S. (1986a), 'The Bastille's "Anti-Star"', *Opera*, March, 251-5.

Lannes, S. and Nusacc, S. (1986b), 'The Bastille's "Anti-Star": part 2', *Opera*, May, 511-14.

Lash, S. (1985), 'Postmodernity and desire', *Theory and Society*, 14, 1-33.

Lash, S. (1990), *The Sociology of Post-modernism*, Routledge, London.

Lash, S. and Urry, J. (1987), *The End of Organised Capitalism*, Polity, Cambridge.

Laurence, D. H. (1981), *Shaw's Music*, Dodd Mead, New York.

Lauri-Volpi, G. (1977), *Voci Parallele*, Bongiovani, Bologna.

Law, R. (1987), 'Sponsorship and subsidy—another view', *Opera*, October, 1136-41.

Law, R. (1988), 'Sponsorship and subsidy', letter, *Opera*, January, 19.

Law, R. (1989), Review of Lord Harewood (ed.), Kobbé's Illustrated Opera Book. Twenty Six of the World's Best Loved Operas, *Opera*, July.

Law, R. (1990), Review of E. O. Perrott, *How to be Tremendously Tuned into Opera*, *Opera*, December, 1511-12.

Law, R. (1992), Review of J. P. Couch, The Opera Lover's Guide to Europe, *Opera*, April, 448.

Leider, F. (1966), *Playing my Part*, trans. C. Osborne, Calder and Boyars, London.

Leonard, M. (1988), *Kathleen: the Life of Kathleen Ferrier 1912-53*, Hutchinson, London.

Leppert, R. (1988), *Music and Image,* Cambridge University Press, Cambridge.

Leppert, R. and McClary, S. (eds) (1987), *Music and Society: The Politics of Composition: Performance and Perception,* Cambridge University Press, Cambridge.

Levi, E. (1994), *Music in the Third Reich,* Macmillan, London.

Levin, B. (1993), 'Take a deep breath and boo', *The Times,* 12 January, 16.

Levine, L. W. (1988), *Highbrow-Lowbrow: The Emergence of Cultural Hierarchy in America,* Harvard University Press, Cambridge Mass.

Levi-Strauss, C. (1968), *Structural Anthropology,* Penguin, Harmondsworth.

Lewin, D. (1992), 'Musical analysis as stage direction', in S. P. Scher (ed.) *Music and Text: Critical Inquiries,* Cambridge University Press, Cambridge, 163-76.

Liebermann, R. (1983), 'In support of "Music Theatre"', *Opera,* February, 134-8.

Lindenberger, H. (1984), *Opera: The Extravagant Art,* Cornell University Press, London and Ithaca.

Littlejohn, D. (1992), *The Ultimate Art: Essays Around and About Opera,* University of California Press, Berkeley.

Lockhart, R. B. (1966), Review of Winsel Anatomy of Voice, *Opera,* August, 644-5.

Loesser, A. (1951), *Men, Women and Pianos,* New York.

Loney, G. (1991), 'Mostly Miller, Some Mozart', *Opera Monthly.* July, 20-25.

Loppert, M. (1988), 'Tat is an operatic issue', *Opera,* 10 September, 39.

Loppert, M. (1990a), 'Glasnost on the Mississippi', *Opera,* February, 149-53.

Loppert, M. (1990b), Review of *The Magic Flute,* Glyndebourne, *The Financial Times.*

Loppert, M. (1992a), 'Christoph Willibald Gluck', in S. Sadie (ed.), *The New Grove Dictionary of Opera,* Vol.,E-Lom, 456-60.

Loppert, M. (1992b), 'Low-interest loans' *Opera,* February, 141.

Loppert, M. (1993), 'A moment in time', *Opera,* July, 780.

Loppert, M. (1995), 'Così in limbo—and clothes by Armani', *Opera,* March, 267-73.

Loveland, K. (1994), Review of *Tosca,* Welsh National Opera, *Opera,*

August, 980-81.

Lowe,D. A. (1988), *Callas as They Saw Her*, Robson Books, London.

Lyric Opera of Chicago (1993), *Lyric Opera of Chicago: An Historic Overview*, Chicago.

Macaulay,A. (1991), 'Dance into opera', *Opera*, January, 37-43.

McClary, S. (1983), 'Pitches, expression, ideology: an exercise in meditation', *Enclitic*, 7, 76-87.

McClary, S. (1987), 'The blasphemy of talking politics during the Bach year', in R. Leppert, and S. McClary, (eds), *Music and Society: The Politics of Composition: Performance and Perception*, Cambridge University Press, Cambridge.

McClary, S. (1991), *Feminine Endings: Music, Gender and Sexuality.* University of Minnesota Press, Minneapolis.

McClary, S. (1992), *Georges Bizet's Carmen*, Cambridge University Press, Cambridge.

McGovern, D. (1990), 'Way up there', *Opera News*, 20 January, 19.

McGovern, D. and Winer, D. G. (1990), *I Remember Too Much: 89 Opera Stars Speak Candidly of their Work, their Lives and their Colleagues*, William Morrow, New York.

MacKay, H. (1991), 'Going Hollywood', *Opera News*, 13 April, 10-13, 50.

Mackerras, C. (1990), 'Here we are now', *Opera*, February, 169-74.

McMurray, J. (1989), 'Die Komische Oper Berlin', *Musical Times*, 130, 452-54.

Maddison, D. and Sullivan, G. (1991), *Kein Angst, Baby—A Singer's Guide to German Operatic Auditions in the 1990s*, Rhinegold, London.

Maderna, B. (1967), *Claudio Monteverdi, Orfeo.*

Major, N. (1987), *Joan Sutherland*, Futura, London.

Malitz, N. (1992), 'Synthesizer', *Opera News*, November, 14-16, 30.

Mann, W. (1964), *Richard Strauss: A Critical Study of the Operas*, Cassell.

Markow R. (1994), 'Moveable feasts', *Opera News*, May, 16-18.

Martin, G. (1983), *The Damrosch Dynasty*, Houghton Mifflin Co., Boston, Mass.

Martin, P. J. (1972), *Sounds and Society: Themes in the sociology of Music*, University of Manchester Press, Manchester.

Martindale, D. and Riedel, J. (1958), 'Weber's sociology of music' Introduction to M. Weber *The Rational and Social Foundations of music*, Routledge and Kegan Paul, London.

Martorella, R. (1977), 'The relationship between box-office and repertoire: a case study of opera', *Sociological Quarterly*, 18, (3), 354-66.

Martorella, R. (1982), *The Sociology of Opera*, A. J. F. Bergin, South Hadley, Mass.

Matheopoulos, H. (1986), *Bravo: Today's Great Tenors, Baritones and Basses Discuss Their Roles*, Weidenfeld and Nicholson, London.

Matheopoulos, H. (1991a), *Diva: Great Sopranos and Mezzos Discuss their Art*, Gollancz, London.

Matheopoulos, H. (1991b), 'From stage to stage', *Opera Now*, April, 24-7.

Mauceri, J. (1985), 'Rigoletto for the twenty-first century', *Opera*, October, 1135-44.

Mauceri, J. (1989), 'Sugaring the pill—Weill on Broadway', *Opera*, May, 536-43.

Mauney, K. (1989), 'Brother, can you spare a grand?', *Opera News*, 15 April, 12.

Mayer, M. (1989), review of the Metropolitan Opera New York *Ring Cycle*, *Opera*, May, 659-60.

Mayer, M. (1990), 'Joseph Volpe: new man at the Met', *Opera* December, 1414-17.

Mayer, M. (1992), 'Corigliano's *Ghosts*', *Opera*, March, 306-9.

Meisel, M. (1963), *Shaw and the Nineteenth Century Theatre*, Princeton University Press, Princeton, NJ.

Meyer, M. (1972), 'The economics of opera recording', *Opera News*, 9 December, 12-15.

Meyer, M. (1986), 'People 141: Samuel Ramey', *Opera*, April, 399.

Meyer, M. (1989), 'The Met Ring: gambled and won', *Opera*, June, 655-59.

Middleton, R. (1985), 'Articulating musical meaning/reconstructing musical history/locating the "popular"', *Popular Music*, 5, 545-80.

Midgette, A. (1993a), 'Reunification Blues Part One', *Opera News*, June, 10-14, 51.

Midgette, A. (1993b), 'Reunification Blues Part Two', *Opera News*, November, 20-25.

Milhaud,D. (1949), *Notes sans musique*, Juillard, Paris.

Millar, M. (1993), 'Scottish opera is for all ...', *Scottish Opera Annual Review 1992/3*, Scottish Opera, Glasgow.

Miller, J. (1991), 'Miller's crossing', Jonathan Miller in conversation with Della Couling, *Opera Now*, July, 17-20.

Miller, J. (1992), 'Mostly Miller, Some Mozart', *Opera Monthly*, July, 20-5 by G. Loney.

Millington, B. (1992a), 'Opera production: 1876-1940; since World War II', in S. Sadie (ed.), *New Grove Dictionary of Opera*, Macmillan, London, 1122-9.

Millington, B. (1992b), in S. Sadie (ed.), 'Ruth Berghaus' *The New Grove Dictionary of Opera*, Vol. I, Macmillan, London, 420.

Millington, B. (1992c), in S. Sadie (ed.), 'Gesamtkunstwerk', *The New Grove Dictionary of Opera*, Vol. II, Macmillan, London, 397.

Mills, D. (1995), 'Masters of the arts', *The Sunday Times*, 24 September, 10, 27-9.

Milnes, R. (1983), 'The Boulez Ring: sight and sound', *Opera*, February, 139-43.

Milnes, R. (1984a), Review of Peter Brook's career on Channel 4, *Opera*, May, 5, 70-71.

Milnes, R. (1984b), Review of *La Calisto* Opera Factory, *Opera*, August, 932.

Milnes, R. (1986a), Editorial, *Opera*, November, 1227.

Milnes, R. (1986b), Preface to L. Orrey, *Opera: A Concise History of Opera*, Thames and Hudson, London.

Milnes, R. (1987a), Review of *Die Zaubeflöte* Covent Garden, *Opera*, January, 98-101.

Milnes, R. (1988a), 'Genoa, Watergate and trauma', *Opera*, November, 1290-301.

Milnes, R. (1988b), 'John Tooley at Covent Garden: "prima la musica"', *Opera*, July, 779-85.

Milnes, R. (1989a), '40 years on', *Opera*, March, 269-70.

Milnes, R. (1989b), 'An imaginary football', Steven Pimlott in conversation, *Opera*, June, 664-9.

Milnes, R. (1989c), 'Wanted: a voice', *Opera*, July, 781.

Milnes, R. (1989d), 'Purchase: the Sellars watershed', *Opera Festival Edition*, October, 11-15.

Milnes, R. (1989e), 'Extremely naff', *Opera*, October, 1165.

Milnes, R. (1989f), 'A ball unmasked', *Opera*, 1290-94.

Milnes, R. (1990a), 'Hearts and flowers' *Opera*, February, 143.

Milnes, R. (1990b), '*Macbeth* for today', *Opera*, June, 645-8.

Milnes, R. (1990c), '*Tornrale* ' ,*Opera*, July, 869-71.

Milnes, R. (1990d), 'Health warning', *Opera*, September, 10, 31.

Milnes, R. (1991a), 'Cappriccioso, troppo', *Opera*, March, 269-75.

Milnes, R. (1991b), 'Pavarotti in the Park', *Opera*, October, 1228-9.

Milnes, R. (1991c), 'Apocalypse next week', *Opera*, September, 1001-5.

Milnes, R. (1992), 'New faces 1: Mathew Epstein', *Opera*, May, 516-22.

Milnes, R. (1993a), 'A moment in time', *Opera*, July, 782-3.

Milnes, R. (1993b), 'Peter Moores: A Mycaenas for today', *Opera*, March, 287-90.

Milnes, R. (1994a), Review of Judith Weir's *Blond Eckbert*, *The Times*, 22 April.

Milnes, R. (1994b), 'The new Glyndebourne', *Opera*, June, 651-5.

Milnes, R. (1995a), 'People 207: William Christie', *Opera*, February, 148-53.

Milnes, R. (1995b), 'People 212: James Levine', *Opera*, August, 890-99.

Mitchell, D. (1955), 'Criticism: a state of emergency', *Tempo*. 37 Autumn, 8-9.

Mitchell, D. (1987), *Death in Venice*, Cambridge Opera Handbooks, Cambridge University Press, Cambridge.

Moir, J. (1993), 'There is nothing like a dame', *The Guardian*, Women: 8.

Monelle, R. (1992), Review of José Carreras at the Scottish Exhibition Centre Glasgow, *Opera*, February, 243.

Mordden, E. (1987), *A Guide to Opera Recordings*, Oxford University Press, New York.

Morin, E. (1960), *The Stars*, Grove Press, New York.

Morin, E. (1969), *New Trends in the Study of Mass Communications*, Centre for Contemporary and Cultural Studies, University of Birmingham, Birmingham.

Morrison,R. (1994a), 'Star-struck on Subsidy', *The Times*, 3 February, 35.

Morrison,R. (1994b), 'How the boo boys could say hurrah!', *The Times*, 16 April, 16.

Moshinsky, E. (1984), 'Tannhäuser and the unity of opposites', *Opera*, September, 963-9.

Moshinsky, E. (1992), 'Verdi: a pox on post modernism', *Opera*, October, 1164-8.

Moshinsky, E. (1995), 'Why the Diva's day may be doomed', *The Observer*, 2 April, 20-21.

Mowitt, J. (1987), 'The sound of music in the era of its electronic reproducibility', in R. Leppert, and S. McClary, (eds) *Music and Society: The Politics of Composition: Performance and Perception*, Cambridge University Press, Cambridge.

Muir, K. (1993), 'An event of such magnitude that opera-goers behaved like football fans ...', *The Times*, 29 September, 15.

Myerscough, J. (1988), *The Economic Importance of the Arts in Britain*, Policy Studies Institute, London.

Nattiez, J-J. (1992), *Music and Discourse*, Princeton University Press, Princeton, NJ.

Negt, O. and Kluge, A. (1987), 'The context of life as object of production of media conglomerates', *Media, Culture and Society*, 5, 65-74.

Negus, K. (1992), *Producing Pop Culture and Conflict in the Popular Music Industry*, Edward Arnold, London.

Negus, K. (1995), 'Where the mystical meets the market: creativity and commerce in the production of popular music', *The Sociological Review*, 43 (2) May, 316-41.

Netzer, D. (1978), *The Subsidized Muse: Public Support for the Arts in the US*, Cambridge University Press, New York.

Neubauer, J. (1993), 'Music and literature: the institutional dimensions', in S. P. Scher (ed.), *Music and Text: Critical Inquiries*, Cambridge University Press, Cambridge.

Newlin, D. (ed.) (1950), *Schoenberg: Style and Idea*, University of Michigan Press, Ann Arbor.

Nice, D. (1994), *The Illustrated Story of Opera*, Little Brown, Boston.

Nicholas, J. (1993), *A Beginner's Guide to Opera*, Ebury/Channel 4, London.

Nietzsche, F. (1955), *Beyond Good and Evil*, trans. M. Cowan, Doubleday, New York.

Nietzsche, F. (1967), *The Birth of Tragedy*, trans. W. Kaufman, Vintage, New York.

Nightingale, B. (1993), 'Engulfed by a stylist's ideal', *The Times*, 18 August.

Noble, J. (1969), Review of R. Lepperd, *The Musical Times*, August, 830-32.

Norris, C. (ed.) (1989), *Music and the Politics of Culture*, Lawrence and Wishart, London.

Norton, R. (1984), *Tonality in Western Culture*, University Park, Pennsylvania.

Noske, F. (1990), *The Signifier and the Signified. Studies in the*

Operas of Mozart and Verdi, Clarendon Press, Oxford.

Nott, M. C. (1992), 'The long road to Versailles', *Opera News,* January, 8-11.

O'Connor, P. (1991), 'Virgil Thompson: The discipline of spontaneity', *Opera,* February, 161-166.

Opera Now (1990), Survey: 'Who are the opera-lovers?', January.

Opera Now (1995), International Showcase Edition, 1995/96, August.

Orrey, L. (1992), *The Concise History of Opera,* Scribner and Sons, New York.

Osborn, M. E. (1992), 'Psychicspace', *Opera News,* 5 December, 12-16.

Osborne, C. (1969), *The Complete Operas of Verdi: A Critical Guide,* Gollancz, London.

Osborne, C. (1983), *The Dictionary of Opera,* Mcdonald and Co., Sydney and London.

Page, T. (1994), 'Interrupted melody', *Opera News,* 2 April, 16-17.

Palisca, C. V. (1954), 'Girolamo Mei: mentor to the Florentine Camerata', *The Musical Quarterly,* 40, 10.

Panofsky, W. (1964), *Wieland Wagner,* Wunderlich, Tubingen.

Panovsky,E. (1959), 'Style and medium in the motion pictures' in D. Talbot (ed.) *Film: An Anthology,* University of Califomia Press, Berkeley.

Panovsky,E. (1970), *Meaning in Visual Arts,* Penguin, Harmondsworth.

Paolucci, B. (1991), 'Private lives: Sonja Frissell', *Opera News,* 7 January, 14-15.

Parker, R. (1994), (ed.) *The Oxford Illustrated History of Opera,* Oxford University Press, Oxford.

Parrott, E. O. (1990), *How to be Tremendously Tuned into Opera,* The Viking Press, London.

Partch, H. (1974), *Genesis of a Music,* 2nd. edn., Da Capo Press, New York.

Pavarotti, L. (1995), *My World,* Chatto and Windus, London.

Pavarotti, L. and Wright, W. (1981), *Luciano Pavarotti—My Story,* Sidgwick and Jackson, London.

Paynter, J., Howell, T. Orton, R. and Seymour, P. (1992), *The Companion to Contemporary Musical Thought,* Vol. 2, Routledge, London.

Peattie, A. (1989), 'Following Felsenstein', *Opera Now,* May, 52-57.

Peattie, A. (1991), 'Keeping up with the Jonas', *Opera Now,* July,

13-14.

Peggie, A. (1993a), What makes a singer?', *Opera Now*, November, 32-4.

Peggie, A. (1993b), 'Finishing school', *Opera Now*, December, 34-5.

Pendle, K. (1971), 'Eugene Scribe and the French Opera in the nineteenth century', *Musical Quarterly*, 57.

Perle, G. (1980), *The Operas of Alban Berg: Vol. 1, Wozzeck*, University of California Press, Berkeley.

Perle, G. (1984), *The Operas of Alban Berg. Vol. 2, Lulu*, University of California Press, Berkeley.

Peters, J. (1989), Review of E. Salaman *Unlocking Your Voice: Freedom to Sing*, (Gollancz, London), *Opera*, October, 1276.

Petrobelli, P. (1979), *Music in the Theater: Essays on Verdi and Other Composers*, trans. R. Parker, Princeton University Press, Princeton, NJ.

Petrobelli, P. (1981), 'Music in the theatre (a propos of *Aida* Act I)', in J. Redmond (ed.), *Themes in Drama 3: Drama, Dance and Music*, Cambridge University Press, Cambridge.

Pettitt, S. (1990), 'New worlds in *New Year*', *Opera*, June, 672-6.

Peyser, J. (1971), *The New Music: The Sense Behind the Sound*, Schirmer, New York.

Pfeil, F. (1988), 'Postmodernism as a "structure of feeling"' in C. Nelson and L. Grossberg (eds), *Marxism and the Interpretation of Culture*, Macmillan, Basingstoke.

Picchi, M. (1982a), *Un trone vicino al sol*, Edizione del Girasole, Ravenna.

Picchi, M. (1982b), *E lucevan le stelle*, Edizione Bongiovanni, Bologna.

Pirrotta, N. (1982), 'Studies in the music of the Rennaissance theatre', Part One in N. Pirrotta and E. Povoledo, *Music and Theatre—from Poliziano to Monteverdi*, trans. K. Eales, Cambridge University Press, Cambridge.

Pirrotta, N. (1984), *Music and Culture in Italy from the Middle Ages to the Baroque*, Harvard University Press, Cambridge, Mass.

Pitman J. (1994), 'The blessed trinity', *The Times* Magazine, 4 June, 8-13.

Pitt, C. (1984a), Review of *Aida*, Palais Omnisports de Bercy Paris, *Opera*, August, 899.

Pitt, C. (1984b), Review of *Boris Godunov*, Paris Opera, *Opera*, August, 900.

Platt, N. (1990), 'Art made tongue-tied by Authority', *Opera,* October, 1168-73.

Plaut, E. A. (1993), *Grand Opera: Mirror of the Western Mind,* Ivan R. Dee, Chicago.

Pleasants, H. (1955), *The Agony of Modern Music,* Gollancz, London.

Pleasants, H. (1982), *Serious Music and All that Jazz,* Gollancz, London.

Pleasants, H. (1983), *The Great Singers: From the Dawn of Opera to Our Own Times,* Macmillan, London.

Pleasants, H. (1989), *Opera in Crisis: Tradition, Present, Future,* Macmillan, London.

Plotkin, F. (1991), 'Opera Hucksters' *Opera News,* October, 12-18.

Plotkin, F. (1995), *Opera 101: A Complete Guide to Learning and Loving Opera,* Hyperion, New York.

Plummer, K. (1975), *Sexual Stigma,* Routledge and Kegan Paul, London.

Poizat, M. (1992), *The Angel's Cry: Beyond the Pleasure Principle in Opera,* trans. A. Denner, Cornell University Press, Ithica.

Poole, J. L. (1989), 'Viewpoint', *Opera News,* 21 November, 3.

Porter, A. (1990), 'A golden age?—In some ways ...', *Opera,* February, 154-8.

Porter, A. (1993a), 'A moment in time', *Opera,* July, 778-9.

Porter, A. (1993b), 'Twenty new operas' *Opera,* August, 899-904.

Porter, A. (1994), 'Glyndebourne at its Greatest', *Observer Review,* 5 June, 12-13.

Porter, S. (1994), *With an Air Debonair. Music Theatre in America 1785-1815,* Smithsonian Institute, Washington DC.

Pountney, D. (1992a), 'Sense, condoms and integrity', *Opera,* April, 404-10.

Pountney, D. (1992b), Reader's letter *Opera,* December, 1394-5.

Pountney, D. (1993), 'A moment in time', *Opera,* July, 775-8.

Powdermaker, H. (1950), *Hollywood. The Dream Factory,* Little John, Boston.

Prey, H. (1986), *First Night Fever,* John Calder, London.

Price, W. (1989), 'Board games' *Opera News,* 15 April, 8-11, 44.

Pugliese. G. (1991), *Gigli,* Matteo Editore, Treviso.

Pugliese. G. (1993), *La Toti,* Matteo Editore, Treviso.

Pullen, R. and Taylor, S. (1995), *Montserrat Caballé: Casta Diva,* Gollancz, London.

Randell,E. J. (1994), 'Counter tenors: then and now', *Opera News.,*

July, 24-7, 3.

Rasponi, L. (1984), *The Last Prima Donnas*, Gollancz, London.

Raynor, H. (1972), *A Social History of Music: From the Middle Ages to Beethoven*, Schocken Books, New York.

Reid, S. (1995), 'All het up at the Met', *The Sunday Times*, Style, 4 June, 12-13.

Reise, J. (1991), 'Doctrine of despair' *Opera News*, September, 18-21.

Remy, P-J. (1978), *Maria Callas: A Tribute*, trans. C. Atthifi Macdonald and Janes, London.

Rex, J. (1961), *Key Problems in Sociological Theory*, Routledge and Kegan Paul, London.

Rice. J. A. (1991), *La clemenza di Tito*, Cambridge University Press, Cambridge.

Rich, M. F. (1989), 'Broadening the base: US opera survey 1988-9', *Opera News*, November, 44-52.

Riley, B. (1990), 'Camera angles', *Opera News*, June, 12-15.

Rizzo, F. (1972), 'Memoirs of an invisible man', *Opera News*, 5 and 19 February.

Roberts, D. (1991), *Art and Enlightenment: Aesthetic Theory after Adorno*, University of Nebraska Press, Lincoln.

Roberts, P. (1982), *Victoria de los Angeles*, Weidenfeld and Nicolson, London.

Robinson, P. (1985), *Opera and Ideas: From Mozart to Strauss*, Harper Row, New York.

Rocco, F. (1994), 'When the ample Catalan sings', *The Independent on Sunday* Magazine, 22 May, 12.

Rocco, F. (1995), 'Power and glory to those on high', The Sunday Review, *The Independent on Sunday*, 18 June, 22-4.

Rorem, N. (1991), 'In search of American opera', *Opera News*, July, 8-17.

Rose, G. (1965), 'Agazzari and the improvising orchestra', *Journal of the American Musicological Society*, xviii (3), 82-93.

Rose, G. (1978), *The Melancholy Science: An Introduction to the Thought of Theodor W. Adorno*, Macmillan, London.

Roselli, J. (1992a), 'The sociology of opera', in S. Sadie (ed.), *The New Grove Dictionary of Opera*, Vol III, Macmillan, London.

Roselli, J. (1992b), *Singers of Italian Opera*, Cambridge University Press, Cambridge.

Rosenberg, H. (1970), *The Trachtion of the New*, Thames and Hudson, London.

Rosenberg, J. (1990), *Sing me a Story: the Metropolitan Opera Book of Opera Stories for Children*, Thames and Hudson, New York.

Rosenthal, H. D. (1965), *Great Singers of Today*, Calder, London.

Rosenthal, H. D. (1976), *Covent Garden*, Fofio Miniature, Michael Joseph, London.

Rosenthal, H. D. (1979), 'Producer's licence', *Opera*, July, 528.

Rosenthal, H. D. and Warrack, J. (1980), *The Concise Oxford Dictionary of Opera*, 2nd edn. Oxford University Press, Oxford.

Rosselli, J. (1984), *The Opera Industry in Italy from Cimarosa to Verdi. The Role of the Impresario*, Cambridge University Press, Cambridge.

Rosselli, J. (1992a), *Singers of Italian Opera: The History of a Profession*, Cambridge University Press, Cambridge.

Rosselli, J. (1992b), 'Prima donna': 'Prima uomo', in S. Sadie (ed.), *The New Grove Dictionary of Opera*,Vol. III, Macmillan, London.

Rosselli, J. (1992c), 'Claque' in S. Sadie (ed.). *The New Grove Dictionary of Opera*, Vol. I, Macmillan, London, 875-6.

Rosselli, J. (1994), 'Opera as a social occasion', Chapter 12 of R. Parker (ed.), *The Oxford Illustrated History of Opera*, Oxford University Press, Oxford.

Roudiez, L. S. (1980), 'Introduction' in J. Kristeva, *Desire in Language*, Oxford University Press, Oxford.

The Royal Opera House (1988), *Annual Report 1987/88*, The Yale Press Ltd., London.

The Royal Opera House (1993a), *Annual General Report 1992/93 Art as Industry*, The Beacon Press, Uckfield.

The Royal Opera House (1993b), *Putting Our House in Order*, The Royal Opera House, London.

as Industry, The Beacon Press, Uckfield.

The Royal Opera House (1993c), *Guide to the 1994-95 Season*, The Royal Opera House, London.

Ruffo, T. (1977), *La Mia Parabala. Memories of Tito Ruffo*, Edition Staderinti, Rome.

Rupp, J. C. C. (1992), 'Civilization and democracy: A note on the Norbert Elias theory of the civilizing process', Paper prepared for the *Theory, Culture and Society* 10th Anniversary Conference, August, Champion, Pennsylvania.

Rushmore, R. (1974), *The Singing Voice*, Dember Books, London.

Sadie, S. (ed.) (1993), *The New Grove Dictionary of Opera, Vols I-IV*, Macmillan, London.

Sahlins, M. (1976), *Culture and Practical Reason*, University of Chicago Press, Chicago.

Salaman, E. (1989), *Unlocking Your Voice: Freedom to Sing*, Gollancz, London.

Samaschon, D. (1989), *Opera*, April: 431.

Samaschon, D. and Samaschon J. (1962), *The Fabulous World of Opera*, Rand McNally and Co., New York.

Samuel, R. (1983a), 'The middle class between the wars: part one', *New Socialist*, January/February, 30-36.

Samuel, R. (1983b), 'The middle class between the wars: Part two', *New Socialist*, March/April, 28-30.

Saunders, K. (1994), 'Opera lovers with attitude call the tune', *The Sunday Times*, 17 July.

Savage, M., Barlow, J., Dickens, P. and Fielding, T. (1993), *Property, Bureaucracy and Culture: Middle Class Formation in Contemporary Britain*, Routledge, London.

Savage, R. (1992), 'Production', in S. Sadie (ed.), *The New Grove Dictionary of Opera*, (i) Italy 17th century; (ii) France and England, the Baroque; (iii) Opera seria; (iv) The Enlightennent; (v) Romantic opera; Macmillan, London.

Schenker, H. (1954), *Harmony*, trans. E. Mann, Borghese, Chicago.

Schenker, H. (1974), *Der Meisterwerk in der Musik*, Hildesheim.

Schickel,R. (1974), *His Picture in the Papers*, Charterhouse, New York.

Schmidgall, J. (1989), 'Sewing down a dream', *Opera News*, 1 April, 30-32.

Schoenberg, A. (1950), *Fundamentals of Musical Composition*, University of Michigan Press, Ann Arbor.

Scholes P. A. (ed.) (1959), *Dr. Burney's Musical Tours in Europe*, 2 vols, Oxford University Press, Oxford.

Scott, D. B. (1990), 'Music and sociology from the 1990s: a critical perspective', *The Musical Quarterly*, 74, 385-410.

Scott, J. (1991), *Who Rules Britain?* Polity Press and Basil Blackwell, London.

Scott, M. (1972), 'Top Cs and high fees', *Opera*, April, 592-7.

Scott, M. (1977), *The Record of Singing I*, Duckworth, London.

Scott, M. (1979), *The Record of Singing II 1914-25*, Duckworth, London.

Scott, M. (1988), *The Great Caruso*, Hamish Hamilton, London.

Scott, M. (1991), *Maria Meneghini Callas*, Simon and Schuster,

London.

Scotto, R. (1984), *Scotto: More than a Diva*, Robson Books, London.

Segalini, S. (1983), *Callas—Portrait of a Diva*, Hutchinson, London.

Serafine, M. L. (1984), 'The development of cognition in music', *Musical Quarterly*, 70, 218-33.

Serres, M. (1975), *Esthetique sur Carpaccio*, Hermann, Paris.

Shearer, T. (1960), 'Bel Strepito', *Opera*, December, 812-14.

Shepherd, J. et al. (1977), *Whose Music? A Sociology of Musical Language*, Latimer, London.

Shepherd, J. et al. (1987), 'Towards a sociology of musical style', in A. L. White (ed.) *Lost in Music: Culture Style and the Musical Event*, Sociological Review Monograph, 34, Routledge and Kegan Paul, London.

Shewan, R. (1991), 'Authentic production: a step behind', *Opera*, July, 770-76.

Siff, I. (1991), Interview with B. Kellnow, *Opera News*, August, 28-31.

Silberman (1963), *The Sociology of Music*, Routledge and Kegan Paul, London.

Sills, B. (1988), *Beverley*, Bantam Press, London.

Simmel, G. (1950), *The Sociology of Georg Simmel*, ed. W. Kurt, Free Press, New York.

Simmel, G. (1959), *Georg Simmel 1858-1918. A Collection of Essays*, The Ohio University Press, Columbus.

Sinclair A. (1995), *Arts and Cultures: The History of the 50 Years of the Arts Council of Great Britain*, Sinclair Stevenson, London.

Sinfield, A. (1985), 'Royal Shakespeare', in J. Dollimore and A. Sinfield (eds) *Political Shakespeare*, University of Manchester Press, Manchester.

Singer, M. (1972), *When a Great Tradition Modernizes*, Pall Mall Press, New York.

Singer, M. (1989), 'A flight of nightingales', *Opera News*, 18 February, 20-23.

Skelton, G. (1965), *Wagner at Bayreuth: Experience and Tradition*, Barrie and Rockliff, London.

Skelton, G. (1987), *Wieland Wagner: The Positive Sceptic*, London.

Small, C. (1979), *Music—Society—Education*, Calder, London.

Small, C. (1987/88), 'The social character of music: performance as ritual sketch for an enquiry into the true nature of a symphony concert', *Sociological Revue Monograph*, 34, 6-32.

Smith, D. (1990), *Texts, Facts and Femininity: Exploring the*

Relations of Ruling, Routledge, London.

Smith, P. J. (1971), *The Tenth Muse: A History of the Opera Libretto,* Gollancz, London.

Smith, P. J. (1977), Review of *Einstein on the Beach, Opera,* January, 48.

Smith, P. J. (1979), Review of *Die fliegende Holländer,* New York Met, *Opera,* 585.

Smith, P. J. (1990a), 'Viewpoint', *Opera News,* June, 4.

Smith, P. J. (1990b), 'Order from disorder', *Opera News,* 6 January, 15,45.

Smith, P. J. (1992a), 'Wired for bel canto', *Opera News,* August, 20-22.

Smith, P. J. (1992b), Editorial, *Opera News,* October, 4.

Smith, P. J. (1994), 'The Met Today and Tomorrow', *Opera News,* September, 12-15.

Smith, P. J. (1995a), 'The unkindest cuts', *Opera News,* 7 January, 4.

Smith, P. J. (1995b), 'Cocteau-Glass', *Opera News,* 18 February, 4.

Snook, L. (1967), 'The myth and the "shadow"', *Opera,* June, 454-9.

Snowman, D. (1985), *The World of Placido Domingo,* The Bodley Head, London.

Sontag, S. (1967), 'Notes on camp' in S. Sontag, *Against Interpretation,* Farrar, Strauss and Giroux, New York.

Spotts, F. (1995), 'And the bands played on: musicians in the Third Reich', *Opera News,* July 22-5.

Stancioff, N. (1987), *Maria Callas Remembered,* Sidgwick and Jackson, London.

Stassinopoulos, A. (1981), *Maria Callas,* Hamlyn, London.

Steane J. B. (1974), *The Grand Tradition,* Duckworth, London.

Steane J. B. (1991), *Voices, Singers and Critics,* Duckworth, London.

Steane J. B. (1995), 'Singers of the century: Franco Corelli', *Opera Now,* August/September, 28-30.

Stearns, D. P. (1994), 'Baroque spins', *Opera News,* July, 34-8.

Steber, E. (1994), *Eleanor Steber,* with M. Sloat, Wordsworth, New York.

Stephens, K. (1990), 'A guide to the guides', *Opera,* January, 35-43.

Sternfeld, F. W. (1994), *The Birth of Opera,* Oxford University Press, Oxford.

Stinchelli, E. (1992), *Stars of the Opera,* Grainese International, Rome.

Stivender D. (1988), *Mascagni,* Pro/Am Music Resources Inc., White Plains, NY.

Story, R. M. (1990), *And So I Sing. Afro-American Divas of Opera and Concert*, Warner Books, New York.

Story, R. M. (1991), 'Positively Martina!', *Opera News*, September, 26-8.

Stratton, J. (1982a), 'Reconciling contradictions: The role of the artist and repertoire person in the British music industry', *Popular Music and Society*, 8(2), 90-100.

Stratton, J. (1982b), 'Between two worlds: art and commercialism in the record industry', *The Sociological Review*, 267-85.

Supicic, I. (1987), *Music in Society: A Guide to the Sociology of Music*, Pendragon Press, New York.

Sutcliffe, J. H. (1984), Review of *L'Ormindo* Hamburg, *Opera*, August, 907.

Sutclilffe, J. H. (1989), Review of *Ring*, Bayreuth, *Opera News*, February, 40-41, 43.

Sutcliffe, T. (1990), Review of *The Magic Flute*, Glyndebourne, *The Guardian*, 23 May.

Swanston, H. F. O. (1978), *In Defence of Opera*, Penguin, Harmondsworth.

Swed, M. (1991), 'Going their own way', *Opera News*. August, 20-21.

Swed, M. (1992), 'Moran, Moran', *Opera News*, February, 112-14.

Tambling, J. (1987), *Opera Ideology and Film*, Manchester University Press, Manchester.

Tanner, M. (1994), Classical Express. Music Discount Centre *Newsletter*, 56, August, 1.

Tear, R. (1990), *Tear Here*, Andre Deutsch, London.

Tedeschi, R. (1978), *Addio fiorito asil*, L Cambi, Milan.

Till, N. (1986), 'Crisis? What crisis?', *Opera*, January, 122-9.

Towse, R. (1993), *Singers in the Marketplace. The Economics of the Singing Profession*, Clarendon Press, Oxford.

Tudor, A. (1974), *Image and Influence*, Allen and Unwin, London.

Turing, P. (1983), *Hans Hotter*, John Calder, London.

Turnbull, M. T. R. B. (1991), *Joseph Hislop: Gran tenore*, Scolar Press, Aldershot.

Turner, V. (1974), *The Ritual Process*, Penguin, Harmondsworth.

Tyrrell, J. (1989), *Czech Opera*, Cambridge University Press, Cambridge.

Urry, I. (1990), 'The consumption of tourism', *Sociology*, 24, (1), 23-35.

van Gennep, A. (1960), *The Rites of Passage*, trans. G. L. Caffee, Routledge and Kegan Paul, London.

van der Merwe, P. (1992), *Origins of the Popular Style: The Antecedents of Twentieth Century Popular Music,* Clarendon, Oxford.

Vercher Grau, F. (1990), *Antonio Cortis—il piccolo Caruso,* Organizacion Bello, Madrid.

Vieira de Carvalho, M. (1993a), *Pensar e morrer'on a Teatro de Sao Carlos na mudanaca de sistemas soctocommunicativos desde fins do seculo XVIII aos nossos dias,* Imprensa Nacional-Casa da Moeda, Lisbon.

Vieira de Carvalho, M. (1993b), 'Belcanto-Kultur und Aufklarung: Blick auf eine Widerspruchliche Beziehung in Lichte der Opernrezeption, in H. W. Heister, K. Grech and O. Scheit (eds), *Zwischen Aufklarung und Kulturindustrie Festschrift für Georg Knepler zum 85 Geburtstag 2: Musik-Theater,* von Bockel Verlag, Hamburg.

Vieira de Carvalho, M. (1995), 'From opera to "soap opera": on civilizing processes, the dialectic of Enlightenment and postmodernity', *Theory, Culture and Society,* 12, 41-61.

Vishnevskaya, G. (1984), *Galina,* Hodder and Stoughton, London.

Vogt, H. (1987), *Kirsten Flagstad,* Secker and Warburg, London.

Voss, E. (1971), 'Richard Wagner und die symphonic', in C. Dahlhaus (ed.), *Richard Wagner: Werk und Wirkung,* Gustav Bosse Verlag, Regensburg.

Voss, E. (1977), *Richard Wagner und &c Instrumentalmusik. Wagner's Symphonische Ehrgeiz,* Williamshaven.

Vulliamy, G. (1977), 'Music and the mass culture debate', in J. Shepherd, P. Virden, G. Vulliamy, and T. Wishart, (eds) *Whose Music? A Sociology of Musical Language,* Latimer, London.

Wagner, A. (1961), *Prima Donna and Other Wild Beasts,* Argonaut Books, New York.

Wagner, R. (1966), 'The Revolution in Prose Works', Vol. 8, trans. W. A. Ellis, Broude Bros., New York.

Wagner, R. (1966), 'Du metier du virtuose' (from the Revue et Gazette Musicale 18 October, 1840), in *Prose Works* Vol. 7, Broude Bros., New York.

Wagner, R. (1849), *Das Kunstwerk dr Zukunft,* Opera und Drama.

Wagner, S. (1981), *A Guide to Corporate Giving in the Arts,* Association Council of the Arts, New York.

Walsh, M. (1995), *Who's Afraid of Opera?: A Highly Opinionated, Informative and Entertaining Guide,* Fireside Books, Simon and

Schuster, New York,.

Warner, D. (1992), 'Deborah Warnr', *Opera News*, June, 12-15.

Warrack, J. (1960a), Review of the Carl Rosa Opera Season at the Princes Theatre London, *Opera*, October, 706.

Warrack, J. (1960b), 'Old Germany and new Bayreuth', *Opera*, November, 729-37.

Warrack, J. (1979), Review of *Parsifal*, Covent Garden, *Opera*, July, 604-8.

Weaver, W. and Puccini, S. (1994), *The Puccini Companion*, Norton, London.

Weber, M. (1949), *The Methodology of the Social Sciences*. Routledge and Kegan Paul, London.

Weber, M. (1967), 'Class, status, party' in H.H. Gerth and C.W. Mills (eds), *From Max Weber*, Routledge and Kegan Paul, London.

Weber, M. (1978), 'Value-judgements in the social sciences' in M. Weber, *Selections in Translation*, ed. W. O. Runcie, Cambridge University Press, Cambridge.

Weber, W. (1975), *Music and the Middle-Classes*, Croom Helm, London.

Weber, W. (1984), 'La musique ancienne in the waning of the Ancien Regime', *Journal of Modern History*, March, 86.

Werba, E. (1985), *Maria Jeritza—Primadonna des Verismo*, Osterreichischer Bundesverlag, Vienna.

Wheatcroft, W. (1990), 'Opera—Don'tcha hate it?', *Opera*, March, 288-90.

White, M. (1993), 'Please, Mr Alden, just listen to the score', *Independent on Sunday*, 5 May, 24.

Wilensky, H. (1964), 'Mass society and mass culture: interdependence or independence?',*American Sociological Review*, April, 412-35.

Willett, J. (1967), *The Theatre of Bertold Brecht*, University Paperbacks, Methuen, London.

Williams, R. (1961), *Culture and Society, 1780-1950*, Penguin, Harmondsworth.

Willis, P. (1978), *Profane Culture*, Routledge and Kegan Paul, London.

Wishart, T. (1977b), 'On radical culture', ibid.

Wolff, J. (1987), 'The ideology of autonomous art', in R. Leppert and S. McClary (eds), *The Politics of Composition: Performance and Reception*, Cambridge University Press, Cambridge.

Wright, D. F. (1975), 'Musical meaning and its social determinants', *Sociology*, 9.

Zabel, G. (1989), 'Adorno on music: a reconsideration', *The Musical Times*, April, 198-9.

Zietz, K. L. (1991), *The Opera Lover's Guide to Europe*, John Muir Publications, London.

Zuckerkandl, V. (1956), *Sound and Symbol. Music and the External World*, Routledge and Kegan Paul, London.